THE WESTERN MYSTERIES

Words of Power and Wisdom

Our first introduction to magick is often in stories involving a wizard or witch who produces wonders by using "magick words." These tales have been told across the centuries, throughout the world, and the scenario of a person stirring great forces by reading aloud an incantation from an ancient tome is as potent today as ever. Why should this be?

The answer is told in *The Western Mysteries*. In this comprehensive yet very accessible work, the magickal basis behind each of the major Western alphabets, number systems, and esoteric symbolisms is laid bare. Inside, you will find the occult keys to:

- Greek
- Coptic
- Runes
- Latin
- Enochian
- Tarot
- English

Also included is a key to two unique New World systems: the Aztec and Mayan day glyphs. Although each section is self-contained and can be read as a separate work, each secret tradition parallels the rest. A historical time line and annotated bibliography round out this essential guide to understanding the real power of magickal language.

About the Author

David Allen Hulse was born in the capital of America's 31st state when Sol was in the Rainbow, at 9:45 P.M. on the 346th day of the Old Year in Anno 44 of the New Year. From an early age, he diligently studied the alphabets of the ancient world. As a child, David possessed a great affinity for the alphabets of Egypt, Phoenicia, and Greece.

In college, a reading of MacGregor Mathers' Kabbalah Unveiled opened up the Hebrew alphabet-number technique of Qabalistic research. After Hebrew, many other ancient languages were decoded and studied, including Sanskrit and Tibetan. In 1979, a discovery led to the need to capture the extent of all prior Qabalistic research into one great reference work. Research is still being carried out to discover new definitions for the number series as well as new magickal systems.

To Write to the Author

If you wish to contact the author or would like more information about this book, please write to the author in care of Llewellyn Worldwide and we will forward your request. Both the author and publisher appreciate hearing from you and learning of your enjoyment of this book and how it has helped you. Llewellyn Worldwide cannot guarantee that every letter written to the author can be answered, but all will be forwarded. Please write to:

David Allen Hulse
c/o Llewellyn Worldwide
P.O. Box 64383, Dept. K429–4
St. Paul, MN 55164-0383, U.S.A.

Please enclose a self-addressed, stamped envelope for reply, or $1.00 to cover costs.
If outside U.S.A., enclose international postal reply coupon.

DAVID ALLEN HULSE

the WESTERN MYSTERIES

AN ENCYCLOPEDIC GUIDE TO THE SACRED
LANGUAGES & MAGICKAL SYSTEMS OF THE
WORLD: THE KEY OF IT ALL, BOOK II

2004
LLEWELLYN PUBLICATIONS
ST. PAUL, MINNESOTA 55164-0383, U.S.A

Second Edition, 2000
Second Printing, 2004
(Previously titled *The Key of It All—Book II: The Western Mysteries*)

Cover design: Anne Marie Garrison
Editing, design, and layout: David Godwin
Editing for second edition: Matthew Segaard
Rider-Waite tarot card illustrations reproduced from the designs by
   Pamela Coleman Smith in the 1922 reprint of the original 1910 edition
   of the *Pictoral Key to the Tarot* by Authur Edward Waite, William Rider
   & Son Ltd., London.

Library of Congress Cataloging-in-Publication Data

Hulse, David Allen, 1948-
   The key of it all: an encyclopedic guide to the sacred languages & magickal systems of
the world / David Allen Hulse. -- 2nd ed.
      p. cm. -- (Llewellyn's sourcebook series)
   Includes bibliographical references and index.
   Contents: -- bk. 2. The western mysteries.
ISBN 1-56718-429-4
   1. Magic 2. Symbolism of numbers. 3. Alphabet--Miscellanea. 4. Language and
languages--Miscellanea. 5. Divination. I. Title. II. Series

BF1623.P9 H85 2000
133.3'3--dc21

99-045182

Llewellyn Publications
A Division of Llewellyn Worldwide, Ltd.
P.O. Box 64383, St. Paul, MN 55164-0383
www.llewellyn.com

Printed in the United States of America

OTHER BOOKS BY DAVID ALLEN HULSE

The Truth About Numerology
The Eastern Mysteries: The Key of It All, Book One

THIS VOLUME IS DEDICATED TO

The Seven Pillars of
Modern Western Occultism

The Two Russian Mystics
Blavatsky and Gurdjieff

The Two Gentlemen of the Golden Dawn
Mathers and Wescott

The Two Tarotologists
Waite and Case

And the One Magician Who
Stood Alone
Crowley

M[80]	t	l	a	G[20]	l	r
a	u	o	m	o	i	d
h	T[62]	o	d	n	n	l
a	t	a	h	i	a	a
n	n	t	z	m	d	n
e	o	r	a	r	o	n
P[12]	i	p	a	d	a	n
M[73]	a	n	o	n	a	p
T[34]	s	c	a	c	r	i
V[32]	c	m	o	a	z	C[61]
O[1]	o	t	c	o	l	r
C[29]	o	u	D[91]	a	i	p
T[60]	C[46]	t	n	h	s	a

The 13 Enochian Angels Which Correspond to the 13 Magickal Languages and Their Provinces in the Angelic World

Key to the Thirteen Enochian Angels Which Correspond to the Thirteen Magickal Languages and Their Provinces in the Angelic Worlds

The previous page is a magick square of 7 x 13 Enochian letters. These 91 letters compose 13 seven-letter names for 13 selected angelic Governors of this world. These 13 Governors rule over the 13 countries described in the 13 keys of this two-volume work.

The angelic names should be read starting with the upper left corner of the rectangle, starting with M^{80}. The successive letters should be read on a diagonal line starting at the left and moving diagonally to the top of the rectangle.

Thus the first angelic name is *Mathula*, generated from the following squares:

M^{80}	t	l
a	u	
h		
a		

Each of the 13 capital letters in this rectangle corresponds with the first letter of one of the 13 angelic names. The number at the upper right corner of the letter refers to the order of the angelic Governor name.

The 13 angelic Governors, their seals, numbers, countries, and corresponding keys in this book are given on the facing page.

Key for the Thirteen Enochian Angels

Divine Name	Sigil	Order	Country Governed	Corresponding Key
				Book One:
Mathula		80	Babylon	1. Cuneiform
Toantom		62	Phenices (Phœnicia)	2. Hebrew
Genadol		20	Arabia	3. Arabic
Pothnir		12	India	4. Sanskrit
Mirzind		73	Serici Populi (Tibet)	5. Tibetan
Tapamal		34	Onigap (China/ Japan)	6. Chinese
				Book Two:
Vsnarda		32	Græcia (Greece)	7. Greek
Occodon		1	Ægyptus (Egypt)	8. Coptic
Comanan		29	Germania (Germany)	9. Runes
Totocan		60	Italia (Italy)	10. Latin
Cucarpt		46	Sauromatica (Poland)	11. Enochian
Dozinal		91	Mauritania (Morocco)	12. Tarot
Chirspa		61	Brytania (Great Britain)	13. English

All of the above attributes are drawn from John Dee's Enochian table, *The Book of Earthly Knowledge, Aid, and Victory.*

ACKNOWLEDGEMENTS

I would like to thank the following people for their help, support, and feedback over the last twenty-five years during the creation of this work: Jonathan Aaron, Ed Arnold, Gene Black, Arthur Butler, Tony Cano, Kenn Capps, Bill Caruthers, Miguel Castillo, Oliver Cox, Greg DiRicco, Ray Gabrielli, Grace, Kevin Hartman, Bill Heidrick, Patricia Hulse, Bari Kennedy, Denise King, Gene Klotz, Leonard Larson, Michael Miller, John Mitchell, Barbara Naiditch, Hans Nintzel, Courtney Page, Lee Page, David Pitman, Thomas Puente, Israel Regardie, Karen Ronning, Karen Rylander, Linda Sandidge, Bill Senecal, Devra Shivaiya, Gene Shusko, Robin Singleton, Carlos Suares, Ray Terribile, Gerald Thomas, Harvey Tsuboi, Luigi Velo, Victor Visaya, Bob Ward, Doug Webber, Tom White, Ryan Wiegel, Bob Wright. Special thanks to my parents David and Bernyce and my brother Thomas; the staff of Beers Book Center; Carl, Nancy, and David of Llewellyn Publications; Chuck, Lee, and Allison of LeVel Press; Joe Metz, Liz Osborne, Lyle Giffin, Nancy Doran, and Christine Pavalasky, my inner core Tarot students; and to all my lovers, friends, students, and teachers who have helped me throughout my life work.

MAGICK

The spelling of the word "magic" as "magick" throughout *The Key of It All*, is in accordance with the variant spelling first adopted in the writings of Aleister Crowley. Crowley used the term *magick* to distinguish the tradition of Western ritual magick from the stage magic of illusion popularized by Harry Houdini.

The term "magick" is used throughout this book to denote the Western magickal tradition, which includes Hermetic, Alchemical, and Qabalistic dogma and ritual. It is also used to denote the parallel tradition of magick found in the East.

GENDER

The alphabet number traditions presented in this book came about in the patriarchal age (magickally referred to as the Aeon of Osiris). Therefore, many cosmological schemes use the gender-specific term "Man" to denote humanity, male and female. No effort has been made to mask or modify this identification. Rather, every attempt has been made to preserve the original meanings of every ancient alphabet symbol set decoded in *The Key of It All*.

Table of Contents

List of Tables

Introduction (cont'd.)

Key 13—English (cont'd.)

Magickal Figures

Magickal Figures (cont'd.)

Magickal Figures (cont'd.)

INTRODUCTION

TO BOOK TWO: THE WESTERN MYSTERIES

MH HBVNH = M. A. B. N.

Nothing but a faint resemblance of the letter G! That is not the Master's word, nor a key to it. I fear the Master's word is forever lost.
—from the Third, or Master Mason's, Degree

Three times the initiate is symbolically struck upon the body. The first blow is on the throat with a gauge held by Jubela at the South. The second blow is on the breast with a square held by Jubelo at the West. The third, and final, mortal blow is on the forehead with a setting maul held by Jubelum at the East. Each time the candidate is violently coerced to reveal the secrets of a Master Mason, and each time in response the candidate refuses to reveal the secret fourfold word of power. These three initiatory blows are given to the candidate to open up his fifth, fourth, and sixth chakras: the throat which pronounces the word, the heart which remembers the word, and the mind which understands the word.

Now wrapped in canvas and shrouded in darkness, blinded to the light of the Lodge by a hoodwink, the initiate is poised upon the very brink of the mysteries which he has so longed to penetrate. He has bravely weathered through two other degrees of initiatory ordeals, and now on this, his third degree, he will transcend the very grip of death, to finally recover the "lost word."

Now lying prone on the floor of the Lodge and wrapped in canvas, a sprig of acacia near his head, the candidate's right hand is grasped three times. The first two graspings of the candidate's hand fail to raise him from his symbolic grave. But on the third try the Worshipful Master of the Lodge firmly grasps the candidate's hand in a strong grip resembling the strength of a lion's paw and raises the candidate into the light.

He is dramatically pulled out from the darkness of the grave into the light of the Lodge to hear for the first time the only word which can revive him from death's door. This is the word which was concealed within the Holy of Holies in King Solomon's Temple. As he is pulled up out of his grave, the word is finally heard in the whispered voice of the Worshipful Master, while the Master holds the candidate on "the five points of fellowship," which are foot to foot, knee to knee, breast to breast, hand to back, and cheek to cheek or mouth to ear. This grand word is "MAH HAH BOH NAY," a word always written threefold in the rubrics of the third degree ritual, but secretly pronounced fourfold. However, the candidate will later discover that this not "the grand Masonic word," but rather "the substitute word," whose correct pronunciation and meaning is lost in the modern craft of Freemasonry.

The quest for the "lost word," a word which when properly pronounced can wield power beyond measure, is of great importance within the Western Magickal Tradition. This lost word of power is the greatest of Masonic secrets, and is first found in Masonry as the "substitute word" at the heart of the third degree ritual contained in the rites of the Blue Lodge (the original three degrees of Freemasonry). In the Royal Arch Degree of the York Rite, this "lost word" is rediscovered in the Tetragrammaton as Jehovah. This word of power is also found throughout much of the magickal and mystical literature of the west, as well as in much folklore, and can be seen in such words as ABRACADABRA and RUMPELSTILTSKIN.

This belief in the inherent magickal efficacy of certain words is intimately connected with the language of number symbolism, which for the West comes from a twofold stream of Pythagorean number lore and Hebraic Qabalistic magick.

This second volume of *The Key of It All* will trace this lore of number symbolism as it passed through the many traditions in the West. The earliest, truly Western, source for this magickal language of numbers can be seen in the teachings of Pythagoras concerning the mathematical mysteries of the Greek alphabet.

Pythagoras was able to develop a symbolic set of meanings for the first ten numbers (referred to as the decad). This mystification of the first ten whole numbers has persisted today in the West in the form of modern numerology based on the English alphabet. Other streams of influence in the West for the deeper meaning behind abstract numbers and their intimate connection to the written word include the Egyptian hieroglyphics, the Coptic language, the runic tradition of the North, the Latin alphabet, the obscure secret angelic language of Enochian, and the pictorial key of the Tarot. All these traditions are thoroughly discussed in this second volume.

But for the West, another unique approach to the hidden meaning of numbers, whose influence could never equal the lore of Pythagoras or of the Qabalah, can be found in the New World.

Although the native peoples of North America never developed the sophistication possessed by the Pythagoreans in analyzing the spiritual nature of the first ten numbers, both the Aztecs and Mayans doubled the range of the Pythagoreans and imbued a magickal and mystical meaning for the first 20 numbers in a unique vigesimal Qabalah of their own making, uninfluenced by any other Western (or Eastern) source.

Esoteric Numerology
of the New World

The source for the Western obsession with the esoteric meaning for the number series first seen in the teachings of Pythagoras can readily be traced back to Sumeria, Egypt, and Israel. Yet another ancient source of number symbolism, which is unaffected by the mysteries of the Middle East, is the number lore of the Native Americans, especially the Aztec and Mayan cultures.

The conquest of the New World by the Spaniards brought into Europe the number lore of both Aztecs and Mayans. Though almost all literature was destroyed by the Catholic Church, certain fragments of Aztec and Mayan numerology were preserved as testimony to their heathen practices.

Though the Native American peoples of North America did not possess a symbolic set of meanings for the number series resembling the Pythagorean tradition, the number four as the four directions was sacred in most tribes. But even in the Hopi teachings (which are the most elaborate native lore in all of North America), the first ten numbers were not given special significance. Morever, there was no written language for any of the North American tribes other than the Hopi and Zuni petroglyphs, and these petroglyphs could not be easily associated with number lore.

However, with the Aztecs and Mayans, such numerical symbolism did occur, possibly dating back to 500 BCE, which would make it concurrent with Pythagorean number philosophy. And unlike the Pythagorean tradition, which focuses only on the first ten numbers (as the ten fingers of the hands), the Aztec-Mayan number tradition extended the symbolism of the decad to the first 20 numbers. This vigesimal number code only occurs elsewhere in the Western Esoteric Tradition in the Celtic Ogham alphabet of 20 letters.

For both the Aztecs and the Mayans, the symbolism for the first 20 numbers was preserved in their calendrical system, which classified time as 20 day signs. Each of these 20 days possessed a hieroglyphic image which contained a wealth of symbolism, all tied into the succession of the first 20 numbers.

For the Aztecs and Mayans, the earliest measure of the year cycle was a cycle of 13 months each divided into 20 days, totaling to a cosmic year of 260 days. Later, with more sophistication, their 13-month cycle was extended to 18 months of 20 days, which generated the solar year approximation of 360 days (20 x 18). This was further refined by the addition of five empty days to capture the 365 days of a true solar year.

This calendrical system was of great sophistication, measuring staggering amounts of time (not unlike the Hindu lore concerning the duration of the four ages which governs the earth). But for our purposes, it is the 20 day signs which hold unique esoteric numerical lore, for these 20 glyphs were embodiments in picture form of the innate esoteric meanings of the first 20 numbers. From these 20 day glyphs, we are able to glimpse what these numbers symbolized in the Ancient Americas, and we will discover such rich numerical symbolism bears no direct relationship to any other ancient lore concerning this number series.

From the scant archaelogical evidence that has survived concerning the symbolism of the 20 numbers, it seems that the Aztec lore preceded the Mayan. Four separate sets of symbols have survived for the 20 numbers: one Aztec and three Mayan variants. These four are as follows:

1. The 20 Aztec day signs found engraved in the circular Aztec stone calendar dedicated to the Sun god

2. The 20 parallel Mayan day signs, which are elaborations and variations on the Aztec symbol set

3. The Mayan head count, which uses 20 distinct God heads to symbolize the esoteric meaning of the first 20 numbers

4. The Mayan numerals which have unique number signs for the first 20 numbers (plus the concept of zero)

Though almost all modern scholars view the Aztec calendrical tradition as an extension of the Mayan, the symbols for the day count themselves suggest that the Aztec system served as a prototype that was elaborated upon and further developed within the Mayan numerological tradition. The animal totems which many of these day signs depend upon seem to be more primitive in the Aztec tradition than in the Mayan: the Mayan glyphs are much more abstract. Also, for the first 20 numerals, the Aztecs used a primitive tally of 1 to 20 dots to count the series. For the Mayans, the first 20 numerals are a more sophisticated combination of dots and bars (taking into consideration the powers of 5), while the 20th number is a glyph in and of itself. Further the Mayans were able to develop the highly sophisticated concept of zero, which was never discovered by the Aztecs.

Our knowledge of the Aztec calendar and the lore of the 20 day glyphs was preserved in 1596 CE in *The Book of the Gods and Rites and the Ancient Calendar* written by Fray Diego Duran, in which the priest attempted to record the heresies of the Aztecs for the Catholic Church.

Thanks to Duran, we know much more about the Aztec day count than the parallel Mayan tradition, because the conquering church destroyed almost all native written records. Yet since the Mayan tradition is a further sophistication of the Aztec numerological system, that which has survived concerning the Aztec tradition can also be applied as a way to understand the Mayan cycle.

Duran's record of the esoteric lore of the 20 Aztec day signs has preserved:

• Number

• Day glyph

• Aztec name

• Hieroglyphic image

• Direction

- Color
- Auspiciousness
- Caste in society
- Powers and qualities

All of these descriptions can be equally applied to the Mayan day count cycle of 20 glyphs.

The 20 Aztec Day Glyphs

Number	Glyph	Aztec Name	Image
1		Ce Cipactli	Head of serpent (water snake, alligator)
2		Ehecatl	Wind (breath)
3		Calli	House (temple)
4		Cuetzpallin	Lizard
5		Coatl	Serpent
6		Miquiztli	Death
7		Mazatl	Deer
8		Tochtli	Rabbit
9		Atl	Water

The 20 Aztec Day Glyphs (cont'd.)

Number	Glyph	Aztec Name	Image
10		Itzcuintli	Dog
11		Ozomatli	Monkey
12		Malinalli	Wild Grass
13		Acatl	Reed
14		Ocelotl	Jaguar
15		Cuauhtli	Eagle
16		Cozcacuauhtli	Buzzard
17		Ollin	Motion (Sun, earthquake)
18		Tecpatl	Flint knife (sacrifice)
19		Quiahuitl	Rain (rainstorm, drizzle)
20		Xochitl	Flower

The 20 Aztec Day Glyphs (cont'd.)

Number	Direction	Color	Luck	Caste
1	East	Red	Good	Merchant
2	North	White	Evil	Rover
3	West	Black	Good	Cloistered (hermit)
4	South	Yellow	Good	Prosperous man
5	East	Red	Evil	Ragged beggars
6	North	White	Evil	Craven cowards
7	West	Black	Good	Woodsman
8	South	Yellow	Neutral	Gambler, gamer
9	East	Red	Evil	Grumblers
10	North	White	Good	Generous
11	West	Black	Neutral	Actors (musicians)
12	South	Yellow	Evil	Sickly
13	East	Red	Neutral	Incompetent
14	North	White	Neutral	Farmer (warrior)
15	West	Black	Neutral	Thief
16	South	Yellow	Good	Wise man
17	East	Red	Neutral	King (royalty)
18	North	White	Evil	Sterile
19	West	Black	Evil	Insane
20	South	Yellow	Neutral	Master craftsman

The 20 Aztec Day Glyphs (cont'd.)

Number	Powers and Qualities
1	Outstanding courage, strength
2	Fickle, inconsistent, lazy
3	Seclusion, peaceful, calm
4	Fortunate, wealthy, never hungry
5	Bare, unclad, without a home, dependent on others
6	Melancholy, lax, forgetful, weak-hearted
7	Travel to strange lands, hiker, hunter
8	Swiftness, wager, drinker
9	Apathetic, ill, short life, dissatisfied, angry, unhappy
10	Bliss, courageous, lavish, compliant
11	Graceful, roguish, happy, clever
12	To dry up and then grow again
13	To be hollow, without a heart, empty at the center
14	Independent, daring, proud, to obtain by force
15	Miserly, addicted to theft, haughty
16	Prudent, wise, authoritative, good counsel
17	Rich, powerful, shine like the Sun
18	Hard, harsh, shameful, evil
19	Maimed, leprous, lunatic, blind
20	Artists, skill of hands, hardworking

The Mayan calendrical tradition paralleled the Aztec system. Like the Aztec, the Mayans also had 20 special images for the 20 day count. Archaeologists believe that the Aztec tradition emanated out of the Mayan. In studying the two side by side, however, it is obvious that the Aztec imagery for those 20 day glyphs are more primitive, concrete, and realistic in their portrayal than their Mayan counterparts. The Mayan glyphs are of a highly symbolic and abstract nature in their execution, and by their unique imagery seem to be a refinement rather than a prototype for the Aztec glyphs.

There is almost a dream-like, visionary quality to the Mayan imagery that is not present in the Aztec glyphs. Yet both represent the same esoteric tradition in giving symbolic import to the first 20 numbers. And both systems represent the supreme development for the Native American tradition in perceiving a set of symbolic correspondences of great beauty and complexity for the number series.

For the Mayans, there are three separate sets of symbolic images for these 20 numbers:

1. The day glyphs

2. The alternate God head count

3. The numerical notation of bars and circles

The first system is the Mayan day glyphs, which parallel the Aztec images. Unfortunately, their divinatory nature has been lost to time. Unlike the Aztec tradition, no surviving text exists that can give the full panorama of divinatory meanings for these glyphs. Luckily the tradition preserved for the Aztec day glyphs can equally be applied to these Mayan glyphs. The following table shows the fragments which have survived of this parallel Mayan number tradition:

• Number

• Day glyph

• Mayan name

• Image

• Symbolic meaning

The 20 Mayan Day Glyphs

Number	Glyph	Mayan Name	Image	Symbolic Meaning
1		Imix	Sea Dragon	Water, wine, flower of water lily, earth monsters, crocodile, great green sea
2		Ik	Life-breath	Wind, air, spirit, life
3		Akbal	Interior of Earth	Night, darkness
4		Kan	Ripe Maize	Corn, bread, lizard
5		Chicchan	Celestial Snake	Serpent, green serpent
6		Cimi	Death	Sudden death, white-red death, owl
7		Manik	Deer	Grasp (hard), cloven deer hoof, swift wind of running deer, sting of scorpion, whistler
8		Lamat	Rabbit	Venus as day star
9		Muluc	Rain	Water, fish, jade, seed
10		Oc	Dog	Faithful companion, hunter, dog of Underworld
11		Chuen	Monkey	Craftsman

The 20 Mayan Day Glyphs (cont'd.)

Number	Glyph	Mayan Name	Image	Symbolic Meaning
12		Eb	Brush	Stiff grass, broom, twisted twigs, mist, drizzle, destructive water
13		Ben	Reed	Cane, green maize, food
14		Ix	Jaguar	Jaguar skin, ear, magician
15		Men	Eagle	Bird, wise one, old Moon Goddess of weaving
16		Cib	Vulture	Owl, wax candle, section of shell, souls as insects
17		Caban	Force	Earth, woodpecker, lock of hair of Earth Goddess
18		Etznab	Flint knife	Drawing of blood, killing, bleeder, tear flesh
19		Cauac	Storm	Rain, celestial dragon
20		Ahau	Sun God	Ruler, master of magick, breath, lord, Sun, flower, blow gun

If we compare the Mayan glyphs for the 20 day count with those of the Aztecs, the Mayan images seem more sophisticated and abstract than those of the Aztecs. However, all of the symbology for the Aztec glyphs is equally applicable to the comparable Mayan glyphs.

However, for the Mayan tradition, a rare variant to the above glyphs was developed out of the pantheon of 13 Mayan Gods of the overworld.

This Mayan God head number system takes the normal day count cycle and displaces it by four. The first four Mayan God heads correspond to the last four normal day glyphs. The fifth God head count equals the first day glyph, while the 13th God head is equal to the ninth normal day glyph.

The main reason for this displacement of the normal day count in the revised Mayan God head count is to renumber the sixth day, which is the Aztec day of death symbolized by the human skull, as the tenth day.

The jawbone of the skull becomes the number value of 10. The Mayan God heads for the numbers 13 through 19 are the God head numbers for 3 through 9 with the addition of the skeletal jawbone as the number 10.

Though the 13th God head posesses a separate meaning as a distinct Mayan God, the 14th through 19th God heads are combinations of two separate gods.

The following table shows these 20 Mayan Head Numerals:

Mayan God Head Variant Numerals

Number	Glyph	Name	Deity	Parallel Day Count
1		Hun	Moon (or Earth Goddess)	17 Caban—Earth
2		Ca	God of Sacrifice	18 Etznab—Flint knife
3		Ox	God of Storms	19 Cajac—Storm
4		Can	Sun God	20 Ahau—Lord
5		Ho	Ancient God of Interior of the Earth	1 Imix—Sea Dragon
6		Vac	God of Wind	2 Ik—Air
7		Uuc	Jaguar God of Underworld	3 Akbal—Night
8		Uaxac	Maize God	4 Kan—Maize

Mayan God Head Variant Numerals (cont'd.)

Number	Glyph	Name	Deity	Parallel Day Count
9		Bolon	Serpent God	5 Chicchan— Serpent
10		Lahun	God of Death	6 Cimi—Death
11		Buluc	God of Hunting	7 Manik—Deer
12		Lahca	God of the Sky (Venus)	8 Lamat—Venus
13		Oxlahun	God of Dragon	9 Muluc—Rain of the Deep
14		Canlahun	God of Sun and Death	
15		Holahun	God of Inner Earth and Death	
16		Uaclahun	God of Wind and Death	
17		Uuclahun	God of Underworld and Death	
18		Uaxaclahun	God of Maize and Death	
19		Bolonlahun	God of Serpent and Death	
20		Mi	New Moon, Completion, Expiration, Empty, Death	

The God head count was rarely used, and when in use was invariably employed to measure a great length of time. There is no parallel in the Aztec number system, indicating again that the Mayan is the more sophisticated of the two, and possibly an evolution from the basic Aztec tradition.

Both the Aztec and Mayan calendar used the 20 day count cycle as a measure of one month.

Initially, the Aztec and Mayan year cycle was measured as 260 days or 13 months, each 20 days long. This was eventually expanded to 360 days or 18 months of 20 days each, which generated a much closer approximation of the solar year. This was finally rectified in both the Mayan and Aztec calendars by the addition of five empty days to obtain a true 365-day year.

Thus the three basic year cycles are:

- 260-day year (13 x 20 days)

- 360-day year (18 x 20 days)

- 365-day year (18 x 20 days + 5 extra days)

All of the above calendars are a measure of the Sun rather than the Moon. However, the starting point of a new year cycle often began on the New Moon. The Aztecs had a grand cycle of 52 years. This was made up of 4 cycles of 13 years, each year being made up of 18 months of 20 days each.

The Mayan dating system became so sophisticated that great spans of time were given their own basic units of measure; nine basic units were used in this Mayan Long Count system. These nine divisions of time are as follows:

Mayan Long Count

Name	Day Count	Year Count
Kin	1 day	of 20 day count
Uinal	20 days	20 day month
Tun	360 days	360 day year
Katun	7,200 days	20 years
Baktun	144,000 days	400 years
Pictun	2,880,000 days	8,000 years
Calabtun	57,600,000 days	160,000 years
Kinchiltun	1,152,000,000 days	3,200,000 years
Alautun	23,040,000,000 days	64,000,000 years

Both the Sumerian cuneiform numerals and the Sanskrit Aryabhata system are other ancient examples of gargantuan dating systems.

Beyond this sophisticated dating system, the Mayans developed a simple numeral notation for the 20 basic numbers. In this notation, the first four numbers were designated by one to four circles, while five was designated by a straight bar. Ten was two bars, while 15 was three bars. Twenty had its own separate glyph, which was an image of the moon. The following table shows these 20 Mayan numerals.

Mayan Numeral Notation

Number	Mayan Hieroglyphs	Number	Mayan Hieroglyphs
1	•	11	•̲ (dot over two bars)
2	• •	12	• • over two bars
3	• • •	13	• • • over two bars
4	• • • •	14	• • • • over two bars
5	—	15	three bars
6	• over one bar	16	• over three bars
7	• • over one bar	17	• • over three bars
8	• • • over one bar	18	• • • over three bars
9	• • • • over one bar	19	• • • • over three bars
10	= (two bars)	20	(moon glyph)
		0	(sea shell glyph)

This numeral system was sophisticated enough to have its own separate symbol for zero, which was the image of a sea shell.

The Aztecs did not receive this information from the Mayans, but numbered the 20-day months as a succession of one to 20 circles. The bar for five was not developed, nor the separate signs for 20 and zero.

Though the Aztec and Mayan sacred number traditions were destroyed by the West when it encroached into the New World, the fragments of this tradition that have survived show a unique approach to the symbolic meaning of the first 20 numbers, which does not resemble in metaphor or meaning either the Hebrew Qabalah or the Pythagorean number tradition, which are the two cornerstones of Western number mysticism.

THE WESTERN COSMOLOGICAL MODEL

For Western Magick, the cosmological model that serves as an underlying principle in many esoteric schools of thought is the division of the Universe into the basic building blocks of ancient astrology, which are the elements, planets, and zodiacal signs. This star lore comes to the West through the ancient traditions of Babylonia, Sumeria, Chaldea, and Egypt. Both the Jewish Qabalistic and Hellenistic traditions of astrological magick have markedly influenced the growth of Western Magick in Europe.

THREE BASIC ELEMENTS

At the heart of the Western Esoteric Tradition is the cosmological division of the Universe into its basic elements, and in this Western measurement of the Cosmos three basic classification systems of three, four, and five elements were developed.

The threefold elemental system is found in both Alchemy and the Tarot, and can be seen as the pattern behind the Christian tradition of the Trinity as the three-in-one personages of God. In this system the Universe is seen as a triangle in which the multiplicity of the Universe is formed from the dynamic interaction of two elemental opposites which are resolved in a third equalizing force. This system uses the three elements of Fire, Water, and Air to classify the Cosmos. Fire and Water are the polar opposites that interact as male and female. In this Western scheme, Fire is male and Water is female. The third stabilizing force which issues out of the interaction of Fire and Water is the element Air, seen both as the child and the hermaphrodite, for the child born of the union of Fire and Water is both male and female.

In Alchemy the Cosmos can be broken down to three root-essence elements: Sulfur, Salt, and Mercury. Sulfur is the fiery, active male that is derived from the element Fire, and Salt is the fluidic, receptive female that is derived from the element Water. The slow interaction of Sulfur and Salt results in the emergence of Mercury, which represents the airy, equalizing force, and is derived from the element Air. Waite's version of Key X—The Wheel of Fortune shows these three elemental symbols on the hub of the wheel.

In the Tarot, the threefold elemental nature of Air, Water, and Fire is used in the pattern determining the order of the 22 Major Arcana cards. This pattern is derived from the Hebrew Qabalah, specifically the *Sepher*

Yetzirah. In the cosmological scale of the 22 letters of the Hebrew alphabet, only three elements are used: Air, Water, and Fire. The letter Aleph is Air, the letter Mem is Water, and the letter Shin is Fire. In this triadic system, Fire and Water are likened to the two pans of a scale, where the tongue of the balance is the element Air. Thus Shin and Mem are the fiery and watery elemental forces whose union produces the lofty element of Air, which forms the endless expanses of the sky.

One of the great secrets of Renaissance magick was the correlation of these 22 Hebrew letters to the 22 keys of the Tarot. In the correct scheme, the Fire of Shin is Key XX—Judgement, the Water of Mem is Key XII—The Hanged Man, and the Air of Aleph is Key 0—The Fool.

The following chart will show these threefold correspondences:

Western Threefold Elements

Element:	Fire	Air	Water
Alchemy:	Sulfur	Mercury	Salt
Hebrew:	Shin	Aleph	Mem
Symbol:	Upward triangle	Hexagram	Downward triangle
Quality:	Motion	Balance	Inertia
Power:	Penetrating	Equalizing	Yielding
Gender:	Male	Androgynous	Female
Family:	Father	Child	Mother
Color:	Red	Yellow	Blue
Metallic:	Golden	Variegated	Silvery
Tarot:	Judgement	The Fool	The Hanged Man
Greek IAO:	Alpha (First)	Iota (Middle)	Omega (Last)
Trinity:	Father	Holy Spirit	Son
Gunas:	To be active	To be wise	To be still
Essence:	Soul	Spirit	Body
Geometry:	Triangle	Circle	Square
Tree of Life:	Chockmah	Kether	Binah

A variation in color arises out of the Golden Dawn tradition in regards to Alchemy. In the symbolism of the Rosicrucian vault, Sulfur is red, Mercury is blue, and Salt is yellow. The reason for switching the color of Salt from blue to yellow is based on the fivefold Eastern Hindu Tattva system, where the square symbol for Earth is yellow. This is also the color for Earth in the Chinese Taoist system of the *I Ching*. But in the symbolism of the Jewish Qabalah, which is the strongest influence from the East for Western magick, the color blue is elemental Water, while the color yellow is the element of Air. In all systems red is consistently Fire.

Fourfold Elements and the Four Letters of God

Out of the trinity of alchemical elements evolved the Western system of four elements. This cycle of four elements adds to the three alchemical elements of Fire, Water, and Air a fourth element of Earth, which represents an admixture or amalgam of the other three elements. Like the threefold system, the esotericism of these four elements can be traced to the Hebrew Qabalah. The highest name of God, which is the Tetragrammaton, rendered in the West as both Jehovah and Yahweh, is the secret pattern behind these four elements.

Essentially there are three ways to order these four elements in the Western magickal tradition. One is the Qabalistic method based on the name Yahweh, another is the alchemical-Platonic tradition which ranks the male above the female elements, and a third is the Enochian directional system based on the four quadrants, or corners, of a square.

The secret order of the Tetragrammaton is the basis for the elemental attributes of the Minor Arcana in the Tarot, which is derived from the four elemental weapons of a magician. This secret order is also the fourfold family of father and mother, whose union produces a son and daughter capable of further generations.

Here the interaction of Fire and Water still symbolizes the father and mother as in the threefold scheme, but the child which is the result of their union is now divided into two sexes: son and daughter. The basic symbolism of the Tetragrammaton order for the four elements is as follows.

Elemental Tetragrammaton

Element	Fire	Water	Air	Earth
Tetragrammaton	Yod	Heh	Vav	Heh (final)
Gender	Male	Female	Male	Female
Family	Father	Mother	Son	Daughter
Direction (Enochian)	South	West	East	North
Tarot Suits	Wands	Cups	Swords	Pentacles
Tarot Court Cards	Knight	Queen	King	Page
Color	Red	Blue	Yellow	Black
Archangel	Michael	Gabriel	Raphael	Auriel
Kerub	Lion	Eagle	Angel	Bull

The magick of this fourfold scheme comes in the innovative order of intertwining male with female elements in the successive order of male, female, male, female. It is the final female which is the most powerful of the four, for in her is the seed which will blossom to generate a new cycle of male, female, male, and female. And her element is Earth, as that which contains the essence of the other three elements. It is the Earth which contains in her bosom the three precious elements of gold (Sulfur), silver (Salt), and mercury, ready to be extracted by the alchemist.

The above elemental attributes are in accord with the Golden Dawn correspondences which combines the Qabalah of the Tetragrammaton with the elemental order of Enochian. These attributes are the foundation of all modern magick. However, the *Zohar* gives an alternate set of directional elemental correspondences based on the Tetragrammaton. This variation is as follows.

Zoharic Element

Tetragrammaton:	Yod	Heh	Vav	Heh (final)
Element:	Air	Water	Earth	Fire
Family:	Father	Mother	Son	Daughter
Direction:	East	South	West	North
Color:	Clear	White	Green	Red
Metal:	Brass	Silver	Iron	Gold
Body:	Head	Right Hand	Body	Left Hand
Archangel:	Raphael	Michael	Uriel	Gabriel
Kerub:	Man	Lion	Eagle	Ox

Again, this Qabalistic order was overlapped with the Enochian working of John Dee and intertwined with the Tarot by S.L. MacGregor Mathers as a foundation for all modern magick.

The second most important order of the four elements can be found throughout the writings of Renaissance magick and Alchemy, as the cycle of Fire, Air, Water, and Earth. This order comes out of the Hellenistic tradition of Plato and Aristotle. It orders the four elements as gradations of ever-refined matter from the densest (which is Earth) to the most ethereal (which is Fire). The ordering of the four elements ranks the passive elements below the active. G.I. Gurdjieff and H.P. Blavatsky used this Western system in their own cosmologies, but the tradition emanating from the Golden Dawn, including the works of Aleister Crowley and Paul Foster Case, is based on the Tetragrammaton order for the elements. It seems that the exoteric order is Fire, Air, Water, and Earth while the esoteric order is Fire, Water, Air, and Earth. The following table details this secondary elemental order and is derived in part from *The Magical Calendar of Tycho Brahe:*

Renaissance-Alchemical Elements

Element	Fire	Air	Water	Earth
Quality	Hot	Moist	Cold	Dry
Attribute	Luminous	Transparent	Mobile	Solid
Humor	Choler	Phelgm	Blood	Melancholy
Direction	East	West	North	South
Color	Red	Yellow	Blue	Green
Nature	Animals	Plants	Metals	Stones
Man	Mind	Spirit	Soul	Body
Soul	Intellect	Reason	Imagination	Perception
Gender	Male	Male	Female	Female
Family	Father	Son	Mother	Daughter
Universe	Sun	Sky	Ocean, Rivers	Land
Animal	Crawling	Flying	Swimming	Creeping
Plant	Seeds	Flowers	Leaves	Roots
Jehovah	Yod	Heh	Vav	Heh (final)
Jove	J	O	V	A
Metal	Gold, Iron	Copper, Tin	Quicksilver	Lead, Silver
Archangel	Raphael	Michael	Gabriel	Uriel
Kerub	Lion	Eagle	Man	Bull
Existence	Be	Live	Know	Understand

Up through Francis Barrett's *The Magus*, this elemental cycle of Fire, Air, Water, and Earth was the standard measure. But with the transitional writings of Eliphas Levi and the secret teachings of the Golden Dawn, the cycle of Fire, Water, Air, and Earth predominated. However, there is one more influential elemental order, and that is the Enochian magickal system of John Dee and the refinements to these elemental correspondences by Mathers.

John Dee, with the help of a skryer by the name of Edward Kelley, received in the late 1500s a series of angelic crystal communications in a language called Enochian (from the Hebrew Enoch, "to initiate"). Three hundred years later, this initiated language would become one of the major symbol sets Mathers would weave into the Golden Dawn teachings. In 1584 Dee received the most powerful of magickal teachings in the form of four watchtowers set at the four directions of the Universe by God as gates to the 30 aethyrs or levels of the Enochian Cosmos.

In Dee's system each of the four Watchtowers is an element, a color, and a direction in space. It is these directional correspondences which the

Golden Dawn used instead of the Qabalistic directions found in the *Zohar*. The following table shows these Enochian elemental directions:

Enochian Elemental Attributes

Element	Air	Water	Earth	Fire
Watchtower	East	West	North	South
Color (Dee)	Red	Green	Black	White
Color (G.D.)	Yellow	Blue	Black	Red
Quadrant	Upper Left	Upper Right	Lower Left	Lower Right
Cosmos	Heavens	Oceans	Land	Central Fire

These four watchtowers were magick squares of 156 squares each, on a matrix of 12 by 13 cells. Each of these directional Watchtowers was divided into four quadrants, each assigned to an element. The placement of these elemental quadrants is used by Waite in placing the elemental Kerubic animals in Key X and Key XXI of his Tarot deck. These correspondences are as follows:

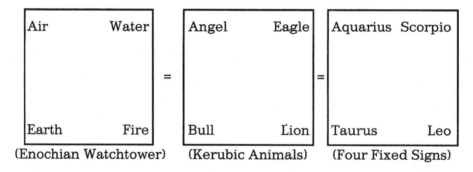

(Enochian Watchtower)   (Kerubic Animals)   (Four Fixed Signs)

The fourfold scheme of the elements developed into one more predominant Western cosmological scheme; that is, the pentagonal cycle of elements symbolized by the five-pointed star, a universal symbol for magick.

THE STAR OF FIVE ELEMENTS

The pentagram is the easiest of all symbols to associate with magick, and its real purpose both in the East and West is to classify a cycle of five elements, in which a sacred fifth crowns a set of four. In the West, this cycle is the four elements crowned by a fifth essential element of Spirit. The oldest use of the elemental pentagram comes from China, and is also the underlying principle for the five Tattvas of India and Tibet.

For the West the fivefold system of elements is first expressed in Plato's five elemental solids, found in his *Timaeus*. The four basic elements are assigned to the four solid shapes of pyramid, cube, octahedron, and icosahedron, while a fifth element, symbolic of the Cosmos and ether, is given the shape of the dodecahedron. These five solid shapes for the five elements have a parallel in the East in the Tattva system, which also attempts to classsify the five elements as solid shapes. The following table will describe these five Platonic solids.

Platonic Elemental Solids

Element	Fire	Air	Earth	Water	Ether (Cosmos)
Solid	Tetra-hedron	Octa-hedron	Cube	Icosa-hedron	Dodeca-hedron
Faces	Four Triangles	Eight Triangles	Six Squares	Twenty Triangles	Twelve Pentagons
Vertices	Four	Six	Eight	Twelve	Twenty
Sides	Six	Twelve	Twelve	Thirty	Thirty

From this fivefold division, Western magick obtained a fivefold system that became intimately connected with the points of the pentagram. The fifth solid that Plato ascribed to the whole as the Cosmos became the apex of this elemental star, and in Western magick became the guiding force of Spirit that rules the four elements of nature.

In the Golden Dawn system of magick, the four lesser points of the pentagram were given their elemental order according to the four quadrants of the Enochian Watchtower. Thus the lower-right point rules Fire, the upper right Water, the upper left Air, and the lower left Earth, while the topmost point is Spirit:

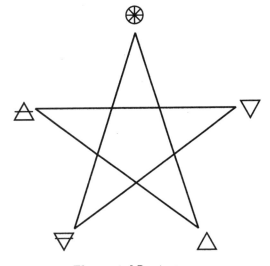

Elemental Pentagram

These five elements were given astrological glyphs derived mainly from the hexagram. If the two triangles composing a hexagram are separated, the four basic elements of Fire, Water, Air, and Earth can be designated.

Fire is the upright triangle, while the complementary Water is the downward triangle. These are the Father and Mother of the elements, and the triangular position of upright and downward denotes male and female. Air is designated by the upright triangle of Fire crossed by a horizontal line, while Earth is the downward triangle of Water also slashed by a horizontal line. These horizontal lines are taken from the parallel arm of the hexagram from which the triangles are derived. The fifth element ultimately became the eight-spoked wheel, symbolizing infinite spirit. Below are these five elemental symbols.

The Glyphs of the Five Elements

	Spirit	Fire	Element — Water	Air	Earth
Symbol	✳	△	▽	⊿	⩡

THE GREAT FIVE-LETTERED NAME OF POWER

With the beginnings of a Christianized Qabalah in the Renaissance, a five-fold word of power directly taken from the Tetragrammaton was discovered by such Christian Qabalists as Johann Reuchlin as a Qabalistic rendition for Jesus. It was first devised in hopes of winning Jewish converts to Christianity by the beauty of this unique Qabalistic name for the Messiah. This name was written in the arms of the pentagram, and later became an integral symbol in Masonry and Rosicrucianism. This name is produced by dividing the elemental Tetragrammaton (IHVH, or יהוה) in half (IH+VH, יה+וה) and letting the spirit of Shin (Sh, ש) descend as the fifth letter, creating the Pentagrammaton (יהשוה). Thus Yahweh becomes Yehoshuah. The Trinity is also suggested in this fivefold name for Jesus, for IH (יה) becomes the Father, VH (וה) the Son, and Sh (ש) the Holy Spirit. The attribution of this name to the elemental pentagram is as follows.

The Pentagrammaton

Element	Fire	Water	Spirit	Air	Earth
Yehoshuah	Yod	Heh	Shin	Vav	Heh (final)
Pentagram	Lower Right	Upper Right	Apex	Upper Left	Lower Left
Color	Red	Blue	White	Yellow	Black
Direction	South	West	Center	East	North
Trinity	Father	Father	Holy Spirit	Son	Son

This ability to classify the Universe as five elements allows the West to be bridged with its predecessor in the East, for the Western elements are parallel to both the Indian Tattvas and the Chinese fivefold elements.

These connections are as follows.

Western and Eastern Elements

West	Spirit	Air	Fire	Water	Earth
India	Akasha	Vayu	Tejas	Apas	Prithivi
China	Earth	Wood	Fire	Water	Metal

From the classification of the Cosmos as a cycle of elements comes the next building block in the Western cosmological model, and that is the ancient cycle of seven planets, the source of the Western obsession with the number seven.

THE SEVEN CELESTIAL SPHERES

Of all the components of astrology, the lore concerning the seven ancient planets has the most direct effect on the Western magickal tradition. The division into seven is the most apparent number in both the Old and New Testaments. The central activity of Alchemy concerns the various treatments of the seven alchemical metals. And the most guarded mystery concerning the occult order of the Tarot depends on an obscure planetary order, which many commentators on the Tarot were unable to penetrate.

The ancient hierarchy of seven planets did not take into account the modern distinction of celestial luminaries, planets, and satellites. To the naked eye, the night sky revealed the five planets of Mercury, Venus, Mars, Jupiter, and Saturn. To these five planets the ancient astrologers added the Sun and Moon, both also visible to the naked eye. These seven celestial bodies became the original hierarchy of seven planets, from a geocentric point of view.

The Universe was perceived as a set of interlocking wheels or spheres, and the Earth was placed directly at the center. The closest sphere to Earth was the Moon, the farthest Saturn. Beyond Saturn was an eighth sphere of fixed stars composing the twelve signs of the zodiac. Beyond this eighth sphere was the divine hierarchy of gods and goddesses, of angels and archangels. And setting into motion and keeeping all spheres in their appointed orbit was the Grand Architect of the Universe, the First Cause, the God beyond all other Gods.

THE MYTHOLOGY OF THE SEVEN PLANETS

The seven ancient planets were interpreted in Renaissance magick as the equivalent Greek and Roman gods and goddesses, because each planetary name in the West is ultimately interpreted through this Graeco-Roman mask. The detailed mythology concerning each of these deities was extensively used in Alchemical texts as a means to discover the true nature of the seven alchemical metals that corresponded directly to these planets.

The following table details the planetary gods and goddesses.

Graeco-Roman Planetary Deities

Planet	Roman Deity	Greek Deity	Symbolic Meaning
Saturn	Saturn	Kronos	Time, number, restriction, death
Jupiter	Jupiter	Zeus	Good fortune, mercy, rulership
Mars	Mars	Ares	Agressiveness, power, war
Sun	Apollo	Helios	Beauty, poise, harmony, music
Venus	Venus	Aphrodite	Love, pleasure, delight, abundance
Mercury	Mercury	Hermes	Magick, art, writing, trickery
Moon	Diana	Artemis	Chaste, the hunt, dreams

The Greek names for the planetary gods and goddess are especially significant when given their original number values in Greek. This is true for the names of the entire Greek pantheon. This rule holds true for the many names found in the Greek New Testament, especially the names of the Messiah, the apostles, and the Antichrist. The original Greek and corresponding number values for the seven planets are as follows:

Greek Qabalah for the Seven Planetary Deities

Planet	Greek Name	Number Value
Saturn	ΚΡΟΝΟΣ	510
Jupiter	ΖΕΥΣ	612
Mars	ΑΡΗΣ	309
Sun	ΗΛΙΟΣ	318
Venus	ΑΦΡΟΔΙΤΗ	993
Mercury	ΕΡΜΗΣ	353
Moon	ΑΡΤΕΜΙΣ	656

Total: 3,751

Based on these mythological planetary correspondences, seven symbols were devised to designate the seven planets. These symbols did not exist in ancient astrology, but were instead a product of Renaissance Alchemy and Hermetism. These symbols and their meanings are as follows:

Astrological Symbols for the Seven Planets

Planet	Symbol	Meaning
Saturn	♄	Scythe or sickle of Kronos
Jupiter	♃	Throne or scepter of Zeus
Mars	♂	Spear and shield of Ares
Sun	☉	Wheels of Helios' celestial chariot
Venus	♀	Mirror of Aphrodite
Mercury	☿	Twin serpents entwining Caduceus
Moon	☽	Horned lunar crown of Artemis

PLATONIC ORDER OF THE SEVEN PLANETS

The order of the seven planets is multiple and varied in the lore of Western magick. The primary order is the Platonic order, which orders the seven planets by the length of their orbit. This order leads with the planet with the greatest orbit, which is Saturn, and ends with the least orbit, which is the Moon. These seven planets correspond directly to the seven Greek vowels, and the order of planetary orbits is set in the heavens by the numerical values of these vowels.

Platonic Planetary Order and the Seven Greek Vowels

Planet	Sphere	Greek Vowel	Number Value
Saturn	Seventh	Ω Omega	800
Jupiter	Sixth	Υ Upsilon	400
Mars	Fifth	O Omicron	70
Sun	Fourth	I Iota	10
Venus	Third	H Eta	8
Mercury	Second	E Epsilon	5
Moon	First	A Alpha	1

In light of this correspondence, the Christian and Gnostic use of Alpha and Omega as the first and last symbolizes the whole range of seven planets, from the first sphere of the Moon (Alpha) to the seventh and last sphere of Saturn (Omega).

Seven Planetary Magick Squares

Out of this planetary lore developed a complex set of numbers associated with each of these seven Platonic planets. Placed upon seven of the ten Sephiroth of the Qabalistic Tree of Life (from Binah, the third emanation, to Yesod, the ninth emanation), each of these seven planets was given a magick square of numbers sacred to that planet. In these magickal configurations of planetary numbers, every line of a planetary square adds up to the same number. Each of the seven planets has its own unique ratio of numbers based on the various squares of numbers associated with that specific planet. These planetary magick squares are the basis for all talismanic magick involving letters or numbers filling a gridded field of squares.

There is much more Qabalistic lore concerning these magick squares, which can be found in such books as Israel Regardie's Golden Dawn compilation. For instance, there is a series of Hebraic angelic names whose number values equal the total number values for each of the planetary squares. There is also a series of sigils drawn upon each square based on the correspondence between the value of the numbers themselves and the alphabet letters composing the angelic names. The most common planetary sigil is drawn from each square by connecting the numbers in successive order from the lowest to highest in value. The following diagrams, however, will show the magick squares according to *The Magical Calendar of Tycho Brahe*, and the corresponding number harmonies.

The Magick Square for Saturn

4	9	2
3	5	7
8	1	6

Number: 3

Number of Squares: 9

Sum of Line: 15

Sum of Square: 45

The Magick Square for Saturn (cont'd.)

Sum of Opposite Pairs: 10

Sum of Four Corners: 20

Sum of Perimeter: 40

Center: 5

Sephirah on Tree of Life: Binah (number 3)

Color of Square: Black

Color of Numbers: White

The Magick Square for Jupiter

4	14	15	1
9	7	6	12
5	11	10	8
16	2	3	13

Number: 4

Number of Squares: 16

Sum of Line: 34

Sum of Square: 136

Sum of Opposite Pairs: 17

Sum of Four Corners: 34

Sum of Perimeter: 102

Center: —

Sephirah on Tree of Life: Chesed (number 4)

Color of Square: Blue

Color of Numbers: Orange

The Magick Square for Mars

11	24	7	20	3
4	12	25	8	16
17	5	13	21	9
10	18	1	14	22
23	6	19	2	15

Number: 5

Number of Squares: 25

Sum of Line: 65

Sum of Square: 325

Sum of Opposite Pairs: 26

Sum of Four Corners: 52

Sum of Perimeter: 208

Center: 13

Sephirah on Tree of Life: Geburah (number 5)

Color of Square: Red

Color of Numbers: Green

The Magick Square for the Sun

6	32	3	34	35	1
7	11	27	28	8	30
19	14	16	15	23	24
18	20	22	21	17	13
25	29	10	9	26	12
36	5	33	4	2	31

Number: 6

Number of Squares: 36

Sum of Line: 111

Sum of Square: 666

Sum of Opposite Pairs: 37

Sum of Four Corners: 74

Sum of Perimeter: 470

Center: —

Sephirah on Tree of Life: Tiphereth (number 6)

Color of Square: Yellow

Color of Numbers: Purple

The Magick Square for Venus

22	47	16	41	10	35	4
5	23	48	17	42	11	29
30	6	24	49	18	36	12
13	31	7	25	43	19	37
38	14	32	1	26	44	20
21	39	8	33	2	27	45
46	15	40	9	34	3	28

Number: 7

Number of Squares: 49

Sum of Line: 175

Sum of Square: 1,225

Sum of Opposite Pairs: 50

Sum of Four Corners: 100

Sum of Perimeter: 600

Center: 25

Sephirah on Tree of Life: Netzach (number 7)

Color of Square: Green

Color of Numbers: Yellow

The Magick Square for Mercury

8	58	59	5	4	62	63	1
49	15	14	52	53	11	10	56
41	23	22	44	45	19	18	48
32	34	35	29	28	38	39	25
40	26	27	37	36	30	31	33
17	47	46	20	21	43	42	24
9	55	54	12	13	51	50	16
64	2	3	61	60	6	7	57

Number: 8

Number of Squares: 64

Sum of Line: 260

Sum of Square: 2,080

Sum of Opposite Pairs: 65

Sum of Four Corners: 130

Sum of Perimeter: 910

Center: —

Sephirah on Tree of Life: Hod (number 8)

Color of Square: Orange

Color of Numbers: Blue

The Magick Square for the Moon

37	78	29	70	21	62	13	54	5
6	38	79	30	71	22	63	14	46
47	7	39	80	31	72	23	55	15
16	48	8	40	81	32	64	24	56
57	17	49	9	41	73	33	65	25
26	58	18	50	1	42	74	34	66
67	27	59	10	51	2	43	75	35
36	68	19	60	11	52	3	44	76
77	28	69	20	61	12	53	4	45

Number: 9

Number of Squares: 81

Sum of Line: 369

Sum of Square: 3,321

Sum of Opposite Pairs: 82

Sum of Four Corners: 164

Sum of Perimeter: 1,312

Center: 41

Sephirah on Tree of Life: Yesod (number 9)

Color of Square: Purple

Color of Numbers: Yellow

Traces of these seven magick squares can be seen throughout the World. The Saturn square of nine cells originated in China, and the alphabets of Sanskrit, Tibetan, Arabic, Persian, Greek, and Hebrew have been traditionally used to number these planetary squares. The square for Saturn can be drawn using the Hebrew alphabet for numerals as follows.

4	9	2
3	5	7
8	1	6

(Number)   (Hebrew)

Most of Western talismanic magick depends on this planetary system of magick squares. The most elaborate form evolved into the Enochian Watchtower system of John Dee, which is fully detailed in the eleventh key of this volume.

PLANETARY SECRETS OF THE TAROT

Beyond the Platonic order which governs the formation of the magick squares, the second most important secret order for the planets in the Western tradition is the secret planetary order for the Hebrew alphabet concealed in the Tarot deck.

The astrological characteristics of the Tarot depends on the nature of the Hebrew alphabet as outlined in the *Sepher Yetzirah*. Out of 22 letters, seven known as the double letters (on account of a double pronunciation) rule the seven planets. Almost all published versions of this Qabalistic text give different planetary orders for these seven letters. Most use the platonic order leading with Saturn and ending with the Moon. Yet the secret order is found in the actual pictures of the Tarot deck, and were rediscovered in the 19th century by S. L. MacGregor Mathers. This secret planetary order, which leads with Mercury and ends with Saturn, is as follows.

Planetary Tarot Order

Planet	Tarot Card	Hebrew Alphabet
Mercury	I—The Magician	Beth (ב) = 2
Moon	II—The High Priestess	Gimel (ג) = 3
Venus	III—The Empress	Daleth (ד) = 4
Jupiter	X—The Wheel of Fortune	Kaph (כ) = 20
Mars	XVI—The Tower	Peh (פ) = 80
Sun	XIX—The Sun	Resh (ר) = 200
Saturn	XXI—The World	Tav (ת) = 400

A full account of this secret planetary system can be found in the addendum to the twelfth key of this book.

ALCHEMICAL PLANETARY METALS

Alchemical symbolism centers on the slow refinement of raw ores into precious metals. One main allegory shows the transmutation of lead to gold, as the goal of the alchemical quest. The correlation of seven metals to the seven planets is another major correspondence in Western talismanic magick. The seven planetary magick squares should be crafted in their corresponding alchemical metals, as should all talismans.

The astrological symbols for the seven planets have their origin in alchemical notation, and designate the metal as well as the planet. This alchemical symbolism for the seven planets is as follows.

Planetary Alchemical Metals

Planet	Metal	Symbol	Meaning
Mercury	Quicksilver	☿	Perfect balance of spirit (circle), soul (crescent) and body (cross)
Sun	Gold	☉	Spiritual illumination, to be at the center of the Universe
Moon	Silver	☽	The soul as the perfect reflector of spirit
Venus	Copper	♀	Spirit in command of body
Mars	Iron	♂	The body dominant over spirit
Jupiter	Tin	♃	The soul emerging from the constraints of the body
Saturn	Lead	♄	The body concealing the light of the soul

All seven metals were combined into an alloy which served as the most powerful metallic conduit of planetary energy when formed into ritual objects and talismans. John Dee, thinking of this magickal electrum of seven sacred metals, devised a unique symbol for the whole range of planets, the *Monas Hieroglyphica*.

DEE'S PLANETARY MONAD

In 1564, John Dee published *The Hieroglyphic Monad*, in which he presents a device that is modeled on the body of the glyph for Mercury and that captures the astrological shapes for all seven planets:

The Hieroglyphic Monad

The seven Platonic planets were extracted by Dee from the various elements making up the *Monas*, notably the crescent, the circle, the dot, the cross, and the stinger (which Dee derived from the Zodiacal sign Aries). The monad itself combines the Zodiacal sign of Taurus (the crescent and circle) with that of Aries (the horns or stinger at the bottom of the cross), containing as well the planetary exaltations for Taurus (being the Moon) and Aries (being the Sun). The following table shows the seven planets as derived from Dee's Monad:

The Seven Planets on the Monad

Planet	Sign	Monad
Saturn	♄	♄
Jupiter	♃	♃
Mars	♂	♂
Sun	☉	☉
Venus	♀	♀
Mercury	☿	☿
Moon	☽	☽

Dee gives many examples in his work of how universal this Monad can be in symbolizing the Universe. Among other things, Dee sees the first four numbers contained in the Monad's cross, whose sum equals all ten numbers. The various alchemical vessels can be suggested by combining the straight lines and curves of the Monad. But his primary analysis of this planetary sigil comes from first dividing the Monad into three parts, the union of the Sun and Moon, the cross of four elements, and the curved horns of Aries the Ram. The following table shows the essence of threefold division of the Monad.

Threefold Monad

Circle and Crescent	The Fourfold Cross	The Horns of the Ram
Taurus	The Four Elements	Aries
Moon	Earth	Sun
The letter Alpha	The Decad of Numbers	The letter Beta
Beginning	Middle	End
Before the Elements	Elements out of Chaos	Ordering of the elements
Birth	Death	Rebirth
Creation	Purification	Transformation
Mortal	Consummation of births	Immortal
Mortifying Self	Cross	Vivifying Self
Power in the Seed	Virtue of Yahweh	Triumph in Glory

Threefold Monad (cont'd.)

Circle and Crescent	The Fourfold Cross	The Horns of the Ram
Earthly Marriage	Martydom on the Cross	Divine Marriage
Born in a Stable	Sacrificed on the Cross	King of All

Dee saw this *Monas* ultimately as a sigil for Mercury. The *Monas* itself is often drawn in the center of an oval egg, and some believe that this oval is the shape of Mercury's orbit around the Sun. Dee created two separate symbols for Mercury out of the *Monas,* and deemed one Solar and the other Lunar. The Solar Mercury is the shape of the *Monas* itself, while the Lunar Mercury is the the *Monas* minus the symbol for the Sun, joining the lunar crescent to the cross and barb. Here are Dee's two symbols for Mercury:

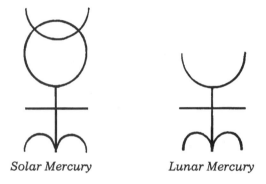

Solar Mercury   *Lunar Mercury*

Dee saw these two Mercuries as celestial and terrestrial, and divided both the planets and the elements by their solar or lunar nature. Dee also assigned three scales of numbers to these two Mercuries: one through four, one through seven, and one through one thousand. These three divisions are the elements, the planets, and the Hebrew/Greek/Arabic alphanumeric range. Here are Dee's correspondences:

Dee's Solar and Lunar Mercuries

Monas	Heaven or Earth	Elements	Planets	Number Ranges (1–4)	(1–7)	(1–1,000)
Solar Mercury	Celestial (Heaven)	Fire	Sun, Mars	4	7	1,000
		Air	Venus, Mercury	3	5, 6	100
Lunar Mercury	Terrestrial (Earth)	Water	Moon, Jupiter	2	3, 4	10
		Earth	Saturn, Earth	1	1, 2	1

Dee's greatest contribution to the Western mysteries is his discovery of the angelic tongue, Enochian, and the magick derived from such language. The eleventh key of this book details this system in its entirety.

There are two more orderings of the planets that we still must consider, and that is the planets as the days of the weeks, and the interior stars of the body known as the chakras.

THE PLANETARY DAYS AND THE SEVEN DAYS OF CREATION

The days of the week are seven in number, and their names in English (among other languages) betray a Scandinavian origin based on the Roman planetary deities. The planetary days of the week are again very important in all acts of ritual and talismanic magick to determine the dominant planet during any given day. Here are the days of the week and their planetary equivalents.

Planetary Days of the Week

Day	Planet	Order	Root Name
Sunday	Sun	First	Sun
Monday	Moon	Second	Moon
Tuesday	Mars	Third	Tiw
Wednesday	Mercury	Fourth	Wodan
Thursday	Jupiter	Fifth	Thor
Friday	Venus	Sixth	Freya
Saturday	Saturn	Seventh	Saturn

This planetary day order is ultimately derived from the Platonic order for the planets. If the seven planets are placed around the seven points of a heptangle in the Platonic order, from Saturn to the Moon, the day order will be generated by following the straight lines of the star from planet to planet.

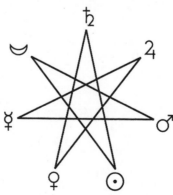

Planetary Day Star

The ultimate application of this planetary week cycle in the West is the cycle of seven cosmic days that God required to create the Cosmos. These seven days of creation when aligned to our own planetary week begin on Sunday and end (and rest) on the following Saturday. The following table shows the planetary correspondences for the Genesis creation cycle.

Seven Days of Creation

Day of Creation	Planet	Manifestation
First Day (Sunday)	Sun	First appearance of light, separation of light from darkness, day from night
Second Day (Monday)	Moon	Separation of waters above from waters below, creating heaven from the expanse
Third Day (Tuesday)	Mars	Collection of water below to reveal dry land, and the blossoming of seeds, herbs, tender sprouts, and fruit trees
Fourth Day (Wednesday)	Mercury	Creation of Sun, Moon, and Stars to serve as rulers of day and night, as a measure of time, and as signs for divination
Fifth Day (Thursday)	Jupiter	Creation and fruitful generation of living souls swarming the waters and flying around the Earth
Sixth Day (Friday)	Venus	Creation of the beasts of the Earth, and the creation of their ruler Adam, male and female, in the likeness of Elohim, and the gift of all life on the Earth in the form of plant, animal, fish, and bird as food for Adam
Seventh Day (Saturday)	Saturn	The completion of all, the resting from work, the blessing and sanctification of that which is created

The mystification of the power of seven is apparent from the first verse of Genesis ("In the beginning Elohim created the Heavens and the Earth"), for in this first verse of creation:

- Seven words appear in the original Hebrew

- The three nouns God, Heavens, and Earth total to 777 in Hebrew: (ALHIM [אלהים] = 86) + (HShMIM [השמים] =395) + (HARTz [הארץ] = 296) =777

- The initial letters of the seven words of this first verse total to 22, which divided by seven approximates the value of Pi:
  B B A A H V H (ה ו ה א א ב ב) = 2 + 2 + 1 + 1 + 5 + 6 + 5 = 22

These seven days of creation were also secretly encoded into the first two words of the Arabic Koran, for the number value of BSM ALLH ("In the name of God") is 168, the exact amount of hours in the seven days of creation (7 x 24 = 168).

The Seven Interior Stars

The ultimate secret concerning the mystification of the number seven in the West has its solution in the East in the tradition of the Chakras, or interior stars of the body. In this Tantrik tradition of India, the lore of Alchemy and the treatment of the seven planetary metals is the language describing spiritual transformation, rather than physical transmutation. The human body is charted along the line of the spine leading to the crown of the head to reveal a network of seven ethereal stars, which in their successive order of development transmit spiritual illumination. These interior stars, known as Chakras, are seen both as the spinning wheel of a potter, and the blossoming petals of a flower.

This tradition was first brought into the West in the literature of Alchemy, but the actual, authentic Indian tradition was not brought into the Western magickal tradition until the last quarter of the 19th century in the writings of Madame Blavatsky. The following table shows the traditonal attributes of the Chakras. Note that the alchemical metals correspond to the same planetary attribution in the East as in the West:

Seven Planetary Chakras

Planet	Metal	Chakra	Order	Position in Body
Saturn	Lead	Muladhara (Foundation)	1st	Between anus and genitals
Mars	Iron	Svadhisthana (Own place)	2nd	Genitals
Jupiter	Tin	Manipura (Pointed Stone)	3rd	Navel, solar plexus
Sun	Gold	Anahata (Soundless Sound)	4th	Heart, breast
Venus	Copper	Visuddha (Pureness)	5th	Throat
Moon	Silver	Ajna (Beyond Knowledge)	6th	Third Eye, forehead
Mercury	Quicksilver	Sahasrara (1,000 petaled)	7th	Crown of head

THE ELEMENTAL PLANTARY STAR

The planets have an elementary nature, especially the five lesser planets. There are many different orders of elemental atttributions for the planets, but the oldest is from the Chinese Taoist cosmology. In this Chinese scheme, each of the planetary names reveals its element. This is known as the Chinese five-star system. These attributions and their direct correlation to the Western planets are as follows

Chinese Pentagonal Planetary Elements

Chinese Name	Western Element	Lesser Planets	Luminaries
Earth Star	Spirit	Saturn	
Fire Star	Fire	Mars	Sun
Water Star	Water	Mercury	Moon
Wood Star	Air	Jupiter	
Metal	Earth	Venus	

These five lesser planets can be arranged around the five points of the pentagram according to the Golden Dawn elemental attributes as follows:

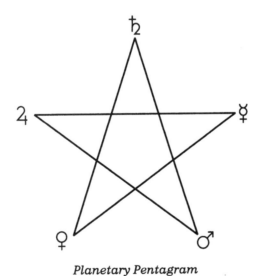

Planetary Pentagram

In addition to this star pattern for the planets, the Platonic cycle of seven planets can also be laid over the shape of a hexagram, the supreme symbol for the macrocosm.

THE HEXAGRAM OF SEVEN PLANETS

In the Golden Dawn system of magick, the shape of the hexagram is used to classify the planetary order of the seven planets from Saturn to the Moon. The six points of the hexagram plus its center are allocated to the seven planets, based on the Tree of Life planetary attributes. This hexagram is laid over the Tree of Life so that the six major points cover the third, fourth, fifth, seventh, eighth, and ninth Sephiroth, while the center is the sixth. This is accomplished by moving the third Sephirah (Binah) to the uppermost point of the hexagram. These are the same seven stations on the Tree of Life used to generate the seven magick squares for the planets.

The following figure shows this hexagonal symbolism for the seven planets.

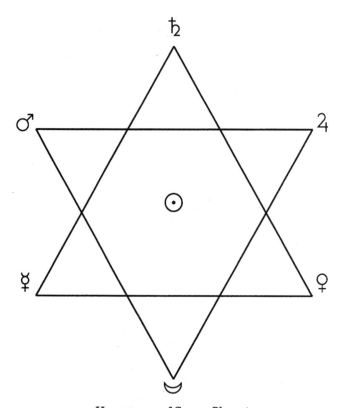

Hexagram of Seven Planets

The power that the seven planets exert in astrology is the rulership of the twelve signs of the Zodiac, because each sign is governed by a specific planet. Each of these twelve signs can also be seen as one of four elements.

THE TWELVE SIGNS OF THE ZODIAC

The third component in the Western cosmological scheme is the twelve signs of the Zodiac. For the West, the astrological traditions of Babylon and Egypt were merged with the Hellenistic astrological teachings to form a body of star lore used in all Renaissance magick. To the ancient star watchers, the seemingly random pattern of stars in the night sky was shaped into fantastic animal and human forms, imbued with the mythology of the time. This zoomorphic quality of the images given to the fixed stars in the night sky in the twelve basic symbolic constellations is the meaning behind the word "Zodiac," for in Greek the Zodiac is **ΖΩΔΙΑΚΟΣ**, meaning circle of animals.

This Zodiacal band of fixed stars was charted by the ancient astrologers as a band 16 degrees wide encircling the Earth and divided into twelve 30-degree segments. Each of these 30-degree segments was attributed to a sign of the Zodiac, based on an animal or human shape.

The Latin names for the twelve basic signs and their symbolic images are as follows.

Twelve Basic Signs of the Zodiac

Order	Name	Image	Order	Name	Image
1	Aries	Ram	7	Libra	Scales
2	Taurus	Bull	8	Scorpio	Scorpion
3	Gemini	Twins	9	Sagittarius	Centaur
4	Cancer	Crab	10	Capricorn	Goat-fish
5	Leo	Lion	11	Aquarius	Water-bearer
6	Virgo	Virgin	12	Pisces	Fish

Manilius in his ancient Latin work *Astronomica,* which is the oldest surviving text on Graeco-Roman astrology (around 90 BCE), divided the twelve signs into those which are bestial, those which are human, and those which are a combination of both, based on their symbolic images. This division is shown on the following page.

Bestial and Human Zodiacal Signs

Bestial	Human	Half Man-Half Beast
Aries	Gemini	Sagittarius
Taurus	Virgo	
Cancer	Libra*	
Leo	Aquarius	
Scorpio		
Capricorn		
Pisces		

(*Libra is implied as human; it is the tool of the scales forged by Vulcan)

Manilius' work also supplied a key to the mythological content of these twelve signs. In an order apart from that of the seven planets, the Gods and Goddesses of the Olympic heavens were allocated to each of the twelve signs as follows.

Mythological Zodiacal

Zodiac	Mythological Image	Agrippa		
		Bird	Beast	Tree
Aries	Pallas	Owl	She-goat	Olive tree
Taurus	Cytherean (Venus)	Dove	He-goat	Myrtle tree
Gemini	Phoebus	Cock	Bull	Laurel
Cancer	Mercury	Ibis	Dog	Hazel
Leo	Jupiter	Eagle	Hart	Aesculus
Virgo	Ceres	Sparrow	Sow	Apple tree
Libra	Vulcan	Goose	Ass	Box tree
Scorpio	Mars	Pie	Wolf	Dog tree
Sagittarius	Diana	Daw	Hind	Palm tree
Capricorn	Vesta	Heron	Lion	Pine tree
Aquarius	Juno	Peacock	Sheep	Ramthorn
Pisces	Neptune	Swan	Horse	Elm tree

The additional mythological symbols of bird, beast, and tree can be found in Agrippa's *Three Books of Occult Philosophy* as well as Barrett's *The Magus*. These correspondences were also used in the Golden Dawn tradition, and can be found in W. Wynn Westcott's *Numbers: Their Occult and Mystic Virtues*.

The Greek astrologers had a series of names for the twelve signs, and each can be numbered in the original Greek. The following table shows the more common appelations for the Zodiac in Greek, and their correpond-ing number values.

The Original Greek Zodiac Names and Their Number Values

Greek Name	Meaning	Zodiac	Number Value
ΚΡΙΟΣ	Ram	Aries	400
ΤΑΥΡΟΣ	Bull	Taurus	1,071
ΔΙΔΥΜΟΙ	Twins	Gemini	538
ΚΑΡΚΙΝΟΣ	Crab	Cancer	471
ΛΕΩΝ	Lion	Leo	885
ΚΟΡΗ	Maiden	Virgo	198
ΖΥΤΟΣ	Balance	Libra	680
ΣΚΟΡΠΙΟΣ	Scorpion	Scorpio	750
ΤΟΞΕΥΤΗΣ	Archer	Sagittarius	1,343
ΑΙΓΟΚΕΡΕΥΣ	Horned Goat	Capricorn	814
ΥΔΡΧΟΟΣ	Water-bearer	Aquarius	1,444
ΙΧΘΥΕΣ	Fishes	Pisces	1,224

Total: 9,818

Each of these twelve signs of the Zodiac has its own graphic symbol, which evolved out of the Hermetic sciences of the Renaissance and took its present shape around 1400 CE. In addition to these graphic shapes, a celes-tial script was devised showing the stars of the Zodiacal constellation as circles connected by lines. Though Agrippa gives a set of these, the follow-ing table shows the variation of Leupoldi from his *Compilcio Leupoldi, Ducis Austriae De Astrorum Scientia* (dating from the 14th century).

Graphic Symbols and Star Sigils for the Zodiac

Sign	Symbol	Meaning	Celestial Character
Aries	♈	The horns of the ram, the two equinoxes	
Taurus	♉	Horns of the bull, the union of the Sun and Moon	

Graphic Symbols and Star Sigils for the Zodiac (cont'd.)

Sign	Symbol	Meaning	Celestial Character
Gemini	♊	Twins embracing each other, Roman numeral II	
Cancer	♋	Crab's claws, sideways movement of a crab	
Leo	♌	Lion's mane or tail **Λ** of **ΛΕΩΝ** (Lion)	
Virgo	♍	Three ears of corn, the hymen, M + V as Maria Virgo, wings of Ishtar, **ΠΑΡ** of **ΠΑΡΘΕΝΟΣ** (virgin)	
Libra	♎	The beam of a balance	
Scorpio	♏	Feet, tail and stinger of scorpion, coils of snake	
Sagittarius	♐	Arrow notched in bow	
Capricorn	♑	Head and horns of goat joined to fish tail **ΤΡ** of **ΤΡΑΓΟΣ** (goat)	
Aquarius	♒	Waves, twin streams from two vases	
Pisces	♓	Twin fishes joined by a chain	

The celestial characters for the Zodiac as circles connected by straight lines resemble the celestial script for Hebrew as well as the 16 shapes of Geomancy.

Basic Classifications of the Zodiac

The lore first recorded by Manilius and later refined in the Middle Ages in Europe divides the twelve signs into various groupings, such as sex, planetary influence, and elemental composition. The first basic division is by sex, giving all odd-numbered signs a masculine character and all even-numbered signs a feminine character. This is based on the Pythagorean tradition for the decad. The signs alternate in sex as shown on the following page.

Zodiacal Gender

Order	Sign	Gender	Order	Sign	Gender
1	Aries	Male	2	Taurus	Female
3	Gemini	Male	4	Cancer	Female
5	Leo	Male	6	Virgo	Female
7	Libra	Male	8	Scorpio	Female
9	Sagittarius	Male	10	Capricorn	Female
11	Aquarius	Male	12	Pisces	Female

The next basic division is into opposite signs, based on dividing the circle into twelve segments and contrasting the six opposite pairs. This division into opposites also classifies the Zodiac into day and night houses, the first six signs being the day and the last six being the night. Here day correponds to the six signs visible in the Northern Hemisphere, and night corresponds to the six signs visible in the Southern Hemisphere:

Day and Night Houses of Opposing Zodiacal Signs

Day Houses	Opposite Signs	Night Houses
Aries	(opposite)	Libra
Taurus		Scorpio
Gemini		Sagittarius
Cancer		Capricorn
Leo		Aquarius
Virgo		Pisces

Both the four elements and the seven planets classify the gradations of the twelve signs of the Zodiac. The simpler of two schemes of classification is the elemental, which we will look at first.

Elemental Triplicities and Quadruplicities

The elemental aspects of the twelve signs are seen as triplicities and quadruplicities. The triplicities, known also as the elemental triplicities, divide the twelve signs of the Zodiac into their basic elemental natures. Three of the twelve signs are classified with each of the four elements by dividing the circle into four separate equilateral triangles, each of 120 degrees. The cycle starts in Aries as Fire and ends in Pisces as Water. By their basic elemental natures, the twelve signs become as a general characteristic either Fiery, Airy, Watery, or Earthy.

Triplicities: The Elemental Division of the Zodiac

Fire	Earth	Air	Water
Aries	Taurus	Gemini	Cancer
Leo	Virgo	Libra	Scorpio
Sagittarius	Capricorn	Aquarius	Pisces

Note that the elemental order is Fire, Earth, Air, and Water, which is yet another unique order for the four elements. This order conceals, however, the secret order of the Tetragrammaton. If the Zodiac begins with Aries but then counts backwards towards Pisces, the elemental order of Fire, Water, Air, and Earth is obtained. This backward order for the Zodiac is known as the precession of the signs and measures the history of the Earth in cosmic proportions, as will be shown further in this section.

Tetragrammaton Elemental Order as the Precession of the Signs

Fire	Water	Air	Earth
Aries	Pisces	Aquarius	Capricorn
Sagittarius	Scorpio	Libra	Virgo
Leo	Cancer	Gemini	Taurus

The second elemental division for the twelve signs is the quadruplicities, or Cross of Seasons. This pattern divides the circle into four unique squares, each of 90 degrees. The grand square in this pattern forms an equilateral cross marking the four seasons. This division of the Zodiac is thus based on the elemental nature of the four seasons and categorizes the twelve signs of the Zodiac as Cardinal, Fixed, or Mutable:

Quadruplicities: The Seasonal Division of the Zodiac

Cardinal	Fixed	Mutable
Aries	Taurus	Gemini
Cancer	Leo	Virgo
Libra	Scorpio	Sagittarius
Capricorn	Aquarius	Pisces

Here the Cardinal signs show the progression of the four seasons. Spring is Aries and Fire, Summer is Cancer and Water, Fall is Libra and Air, and Winter is Capricorn and Earth. Again, the Tetragrammaton order of the elements also orders these four seasons. The first degrees of Aries and Libra herald the Equinoxes, while the first degrees of Cancer and Capricorn herald the Solstices.

The Fixed signs are the four signs which are associated with the Kerubic animals of Ezekiel's celestial vision: Taurus is the bull, Leo is the lion, Scorpio is the eagle, and Aquarius is the angel.

The Mutable signs are the most flexible and changeable of the signs. They represent the signs which precede each Equinox or Solstice, so they represent an element capable of transforming to another element. Gemini is Air transforming into Water, Virgo is Earth transforming into Air, Sagittarius is Fire transforming into Earth, and Pisces is Water transforming into Fire. On account of this symbolism of transformation, the secret Court Cards in the Tarot for these signs are the four Knights mounted on horses.

Planetary Influence of the Zodiac

Beyond the elemental division of the Zodiac, the seven planets also divide the Zodiac into auspicious and inauspicious conjunctions. The seven ancient planets serve as rulers for the twelve signs. The two luminaries of the Sun and Moon each rule one sign, while the other five planets each rule two signs. An alchemical ladder of planets from the lowest (being Saturn as lead) to the highest (being Mercury as quicksilver) is formed by this rulership, crowned by the Sun (being gold) and the Moon (being silver).

Alchemical Ladder of Planetary Rulers for the Zodiac

Sign	Planetary Ruler	Sign
Cancer	Moon/Sun	Leo
Gemini	Mercury	Virgo
Taurus	Venus	Libra
Aries	Mars	Scorpio
Pisces	Jupiter	Sagittarius
Aquarius	Saturn	Capricorn

In this relationship, the signs Leo through Capricorn are solar in nature, while the signs Aquarius through Cancer are lunar in nature. This relationship of sign and planet is also, when combined with 16 counterchanges of the four basic elements, the basis for the Zodiacal attribution to Geomancy.

The influences between the seven planets and the twelve signs are known as the planetary dignities. There are four: Ruler, Detriment, Exaltation, and Fall. The Ruler is the best planet possible to describe that sign. The Detriment represents the worst possible planetary description for a sign, since it is the ruling planet of the corresponding opposite sign of the Zodiac. The Exaltation is the planetary ideal for seven select signs. It is the loftiest possible planetary influence. The Fall is the planetary nightmare for a sign. Like the Exaltations, this planetary influence affects only seven of the twelve signs. It is the lowest of planetary influences, indicating an abberation rather than an ideal.

None of the modern planets (Neptune, Uranus, and Pluto) are included in this discussion since this introduction is concerned with the Renaissance Hermetic magickal model, from which all modern magick is derived.

The following table shows these four planetary dignities.

Planetary Dignities for the Zodiac

Sign	Ruler	Detriment	Exaltation	Fall
Aries	Mars	Venus	Sun	Saturn
Taurus	Venus	Mars	Moon	—
Gemini	Mercury	Jupiter	—	—
Cancer	Moon	Saturn	Jupiter	Mars
Leo	Sun	Saturn	—	—
Virgo	Mercury	Jupiter	Mercury	Venus
Libra	Venus	Mars	Saturn	Sun
Scorpio	Mars	Venus	—	Moon
Sagittarius	Jupiter	Mercury	—	—
Capricorn	Saturn	Moon	Mars	Jupiter
Aquarius	Saturn	Sun	—	—
Pisces	Jupiter	Mercury	Venus	Mercury

DEGREES AND ASPECTS OF THE HOROSCOPE

The joining of a planet to a sign is the heart of astrological prognosis, omen, and interpretation, for the birthchart of an individual shows the position of the seven movable planets in relation to the band of the fixed stars at the time of birth. Horoscope (ΩΡΟΣΚΟΠΙΟ) is a term derived from the Greek roots ΩΡΑ, meaning time, and ΣΚΟΠΟΣ, meaning watcher or observer. As such it designates the observable planets and signs at the time of birth.

When a particular planet appears in the 30-degree band of a specific Zodiac constellation, that conjunction is interpreted first and foremost in light of the above planetary dignities. Those planetary aspects that are Rulerships or Exaltations are beneficent, while the Detriments and Falls are malefic. Each degree of the Zodiac is colored by a further set of elaborate symbols. The basic divisions of the Zodiac sign are as follows.

Degrees of a Sign

Degrees	Name	Division of Circle	Zodiac
30 Degrees	Sign	12	12 x 30° = 360°
10 Degrees	Decan	36	3 x 10° = 30°
5 Degrees	Quince	72	6 x 5° = 30°
1 Degree	Degree	360	30 x 1° = 30°

The images for the above divisions are numerous and would take a book of their own to completely catalog. The 36 decans appear in the Tarot as the pip cards numbered 2 through 10 in the four suits of Wands, Cups, Swords, and Pentacles. The 72 quinces are both the 72 angelic names of the Qabalistic Shem-Hamphoresh (the divided names of God) and the 72 demons of the Lesser Key of Solomon. The actual 360 degrees of the Zodiacal circle have a variety of symbol sets describing them, some quite bizarre. As an example, 18° of Libra, corresponding to the date of October 12th (Crowley's birthday), is given the following three symbols in the systems of Charubel, Sepharial, and Kozminsky:

- Charubel—A man at a desk writing all kinds of hands from the largest hand to the most microscopic

- Sepharial—A well-lighted house with an open door

- Kozminsky—A fireman rescuing a little child from a burning house

With so many varied images available for the images of the decans, quinces, and degrees, the lay of a planet in any degree of any sign can be given special significance.

Beyond these planetary conjunctions and the degrees of the signs are the various patterns known as the *aspects*, which are generated by the seven planets in the birth chart. The are many aspects in astrology, but the basic positions that the planets assume in relation to one another in the twelve signs of the Zodiac are based on the numbers two, three, four, five, six, and eight. As aspects in a chart, the numbers two, four, and eight are unlucky while the numbers three, five, and six are lucky. The basic astrological aspects are as follows.

Planetary Zodiacal Aspects

Divide Circle Into	Aspect	Degrees Between Planets	Planetary Influence
2	Opposition	180°	Worst
4	Square	90°	Bad
8	Semisquare	45°	Bad

Planetary Zodiacal Aspects (cont'd.)

Divide Circle Into	Aspect	Degrees Between Planets	Planetary Influence
3	Trine	120°	Best
5	Quintile	72°	Good
6	Sextile	60°	Good

There are two other basic aspects, the quincunx and biquintile. The quincunx is 150° between two planets and is a negative influence. The biquintile is 144° between two planets, being two quintiles, and is a positive influence. If one or more planets occupies the same position, or is within a few degrees, it is said to be in conjunction. Planets in conjunction combine to influence that particular sign. Whether this blending of planetary influences is harmonious or disruptive depends on the planetary dignities. These combinations of planets and signs must also be interpreted by one other pattern, the twelve houses.

The Twelve Houses of the Zodiac

The twelve houses are the twelve stations of the horoscope, dividing the astrological chart into twelve separate quadrants. The older charts were squares divided into twelve triangles, while the newer charts are circles divided into twelve segments. Each of the twelve divisions of this circle is 30°, and each division corresponds to a Zodiacal sign in its natural order. Thus the first house corresponds to the first sign, Aries, while the twelfth and last house is Pisces. Each of these twelve houses rules certain aspects of the life of the person.

Although the planets fall in specific signs, they must also be interpreted in light of the corresponding house. Only those individuals whose rising sign (that sign which appears to be on the horizon at the time of birth) is in Aries will have an exact correspondence between the order of the Zodiac and that of the twelve houses, since the rising sign always falls in the first house and determines the Zodiacal order of all the other houses.

The names for these twelve astrological houses are not standardized like the names of the signs. Manilius refers to them as "temples" rather than houses and gives two different house allocations in his *Astronomica*. The table on the next page shows the twelve Temples of Manilius as the prototype for the twelve Houses.

The Twelve Temples of the Zodiac

Order	Temple	Influence	Temple Variation	Planet	Sign
1	The Star (Mercury)	Children	Home	Mercury	Aries
2	Typhon's Throne	Fortune, estate	Warfare, foreign travel	—	Taurus
3	Goddess	Brethren	Business	Moon	Gemini
4	Daemonium	Parents	Law	Saturn	Cancer
5	Daemonia (Good fortune)	Children's health	Marriage, friendships	—	Leo
6	Gate of Toil (Bad fortune)	Health	Prosperity	Mars	Virgo
7	Pluto's Portal	Legacies	Dangers	—	Libra
8	Typhon's Throne	Death	Class, rank	—	Scorpio
9	God	Vicissitudes, travels	Children	Sun	Sagittarius
10	Fortune	Marriage, honors	Way of Life, character	Venus	Capricorn
11	Omen of Good Fortune	Friendships	Health and sickness	Jupiter	Aquarius
12	Gate of Toil	Enemies, misfortune	Success	—	Pisces

Out of this temple system developed the twelve houses of modern astrology. Shown below are two house systems, the first from William Lilly's *Christian Astrology* (dating from the 17th century CE) and the second from modern sources:

The Twelve Houses

Order	House of	Modern Variations	Zodiac
1	Life	Personality and appearance	Aries
2	Riches and fortune	Money and possessions	Taurus
3	Brethren, sisters, kindred, short journeys	Knowledge, self expression, mental capabilities	Gemini

The Twelve Houses (cont'd.)

Order	House of	Modern Variations	Zodiac
4	Parents, lands, cities, heredity, treasure	Childhood, family	Cancer
5	Children, messengers	Children, love affairs, pleasures, risks	Leo
6	Sickness, servants	Health, work, service	Virgo
7	Marriage, open enemies, lawsuits, controveries, contracts, wars, thefts	Love, marriage, business	Libra
8	Death, dowry	Death, legacies	Scorpio
9	Religion, pilgrimage, long journeys, dreams	Philosophy, religion, travels, dreams	Sagittarius
10	Government, preferment, office, dignity, command	Career, responsibility, status, reputation	Capricorn
11	Friends, hope, riches of Kings	Friends, social life, hope, desire, ambition	Aquarius
12	Imprisonment, witchery, private enemies, labor, banished men	Enemies, limitations, secrets	Pisces

The signs beyond their mundane use in predictive astrology were categories which could classify both the Microcosm and the Macrocosm. In the Microcosm, the Zodiac divided the human body into twelve zones; in the Macrocosm, the Zodiac divided the ancient world into twelve Zodiacal zones.

Zodiac of the Microcosm

The Zodiac can classify the human body from head to toe. This allocation came to the West through the Greek tradition of astrology.

Indeed, the 24 letters of the Greek alphabet as twelve pairs governed each of these twelve Zodiacal power zones within the human body. As the planets can be seen in the human body as the etheric seven chakras, so too does the Zodiac span the whole body from the head ruled by Aries to the feet ruled by Pisces. In essence, the planets rule the inner spirtual body, while the Zodiac rules the external body.

There is another Zodiacal correspondence for the human body hidden in the Hebrew Qabalah. The Qabalistic text *Sepher Yetzirah*, using the twelve simple letters of the Hebrew alphabet, divides the body into different power zones than the traditional correspondences. Both sets of correspondences are shown below.

The Zodiac of the Human Body

Zodiac	Traditional	Qabalistic
Aries	Head	Right hand
Taurus	Throat, neck	Left hand
Gemini	Shoulders, arms, hands, lungs	Right foot
Cancer	Stomach	Left foot
Leo	Heart, spine, back	Right kidney (testicle)
Virgo	Intestines	Left kidney (testicle)
Libra	Kidneys, buttocks, inner sexual organs	Liver
Scorpio	Genitals	Spleen
Sagittarius	Thighs, hips	Gall
Capricorn	Knees	Stomach, colon
Aquarius	Ankles	Bladder, genitals
Pisces	Feet	Rectum, bowels

The traditional Zodiacal divisions of the body are used in interpreting an astrological chart, in that planets falling to certain signs can indicate the nature of physical strengths and weaknesses. The specific Zodiac sign corresponding to one's sixth house of health or eighth house of death can be interpreted in light of the above bodily correspondences, especially if there are planets apparent in either of the houses.

Many other elements of the little world (known as the Microcosm) were classified according to their astrological signature. One of the most prominent groupings which is connected to Alchemical symbolism is the Greek lore of birthstones known as *Lithica*. The ancient literature of Lithica gave a precious stone for each of the twelve signs, which is the source for our modern lore of birthstones based on the month. The ancient symbolism of stones for the Zodiac is as follows.

Zodiacal Birthstones

Sign	Stone	Sign	Stone
Aries	Hematite	Libra	Agate
Taurus	Emerald	Scorpio	Amethyst
Gemini	Multicolored stones	Sagittarius	Turquoise
Cancer	Adularia	Capricorn	Onyx
Leo	Ruby	Aquarius	Amber
Virgo	Beryl	Pisces	Coral

Beyond this lore of stones, the plant and animal kingdom were also classified by the Zodiac. These classifications can be found in the writings of Agrippa, Barrrett, and Crowley.

Zodiac of the Macrocosm

Just as the human body can be divided into the Zodiac, so can the world. The ancient astrologers were able to give each province of the known world a Zodiacal ruler, based on the characteristics of that country. Modern astrologers also make such correspondences to the world, but most often they will calculcate the nativity of a nation based on the birth of its own constitution or charter.

Manilius, in his *Astronomica,* gives us an account of these Zodiacal governors, based on the Western perception of the world around 90 BCE. Manilius divides the world into the three basic continents of Europe (Europa), Africa (Libya), and Asia. To Europe, he assigns Capricorn, to Asia Taurus, and to Africa Scorpio. The following table shows the major correspondences for the ancient world of Manilius:

The Zodiac in the World

Sign	Countries of the Ancient World	Continent
Aries	Egypt, the Nile, Persia, Syria	Asia
Taurus	Asia, Arabia, Scythia	Asia
Gemini	India, Thrace	Asia, Europe
Cancer	Ethiopia	Africa
Leo	Armenia, Phrygia, Bithynia, Cappadocia, Macedonia	Asia, Europe
Virgo	Greece, Ionia, Rhodes, Caria	Asia, Europe
Libra	Italy, Rome	Europe
Scorpio	Libya, Carthage, Hammonia, Cyrene, Sardinia (and other islands)	Africa, Europe
Sagittarius	Crete, Sicily, Southern Italy	Europe
Capricorn	Spain, Gaul, Germany	Europe
Aquarius	Phoenicia, Tyre, Cilicia, Lycia	Asia
Pisces	Babylon, Ninevah, Asiatic Ethiopia, Euphrates, Tigris, Red Sea, Bactria, Parthia	Asia

John Dee's Enochian workings, which assign angelic governors to 91 divisions of the world, is similar to Manilius' own astrological arrangement.

Yet another measure of the Macrocosm which the Zodiac numbers is the calculation of the Great Solar or Platonic Year. This measure of time is also known as the precession of the Equinoxes.

Each year the Sun begins its journey in Aries on the Spring Equinox, cycles through all twelve signs, and returns to its point of origin in Aries. But each year the Sun falls a little short of where it crossed the year before. It loses one degree (of a 30-degree band of a Zodiac sign) every 72 years. By this Zodiacal measure, the Sun regresses through one sign every 2,160 years (30 x 72 =2,160), and all twelve signs every 25,920 years (12 x 2,160 = 25,920). This grand cycle of 25,920 years is the precession of the Equinoxes, and as a measure is the Great Solar Year or the Platonic Year.

Currently the world is in the Age of Pisces, verging on the Age of Aquarius. If the great Zodiacal year is 2,000 rather than 2,160 years, we are a few years from the Age of Aquarius. But if the measure is 2,160 years, the following measure of 8,640 years emerges (if we assume that the Age of Pisces commenced with the birth of Jesus Christ):

Precession of the Equinoxes

Age	Period of Time	Events	Zodiac
Taurian	4320 BCE–2160 BCE	Origin of number, alphabet	Taurus
Aryan	2160 BCE–0	Qabalah, I Ching	Aries
Piscean	0–2160 CE	Christian Era, Tarot	Pisces
Aquarian	2160 CE–4320 CE	The future of the world	Aquarius

Aleister Crowley felt that this new age for humanity in the appearance of the Aquarian Age had already commenced, beginning in 1904. In 1904 Crowley received in trance *The Book of the Law*, the book promised to the generations of this new Zodiacal age.

Crowley measured the grand Zodiacal year as approximately 2,000 years and developed his own interpretation of the precession of the Equinoxes in light of *The Book of the Law*. His doctrine concerned only three of the ages: the ages of Aries, Pisces, and Aquarius. Each age was presided over by a speaker of one of the three chapters of *The Book of the Law*. And each age had its dominant cult or religion dictated by the Zodiac sign controlling that age.

Crowley's Precession of the Equinoxes

Age	Time	Society	Cult	Family	Egyptian	Liber AL
Aries	2000 BCE–0	Matriarch	Goddess	Mother	Isis	Nu
Pisces	0–1904 CE	Patriarch	Jesus	Father	Osiris	Had
Aquarius	1904 CE–?	Equality	Thelema	Child	Horus	Ra-Hoor-Khu

Crowley, in commenting on the length of this new Age of Aquarius, marked by the Crowned and Conquering Child, hoped that the doctrine of Thelema would last at least 2,000 years. But the excommunicated disciple of Crowley, known as Frater Achad, felt that this new age of the child Horus was aborted as early as 1948 (44 years after its inception) and was supplanted by a fourth Aeon of Maat, marked by the emergence of the Magickal Daughter, fulfilling the fourfold formula of the Tetragrammaton.

BIBLICAL ZODIACAL SYMBOLISM

In addition to the symbolism of the Microcosm and Macrocosm, the mythological groupings of Gods and Goddesses can easily be aligned to Zodiacal symbolism. In the West, this is due in part to the inheritance from the Greeks of the correspondences of both the seven planets and the twelve signs to the Greek Gods and Goddesses.

The Old and New Testaments each contain explicit Zodiacal symbolism, for both the twelve tribes of Israel and the twelve apostles of Jesus are modeled on the twelve signs of the Zodiac. However, the key to either of these Zodiacal dozen is not directly given.

The Tribal Zodiac

There are many systems of allocating the twelve tribes of the Old Testament to the twelve signs of the Zodiac. However, the scheme we will consider here is the Masonic system used by S. L. MacGregor Mathers and taught in the Golden Dawn. The alternate tribes listed are from the Qabalistic astrological research of Rabbi Joel Dobin.

Zodiac of the Twelve Tribes

Zodiac	Twelve Tribes	Value	Banner	Color	Alternate
Aries	GD גד (Gad)	7	Cavalry	White	Benjamin
Taurus	APRAIM אפראים (Ephraim)	332/892	Ox	Green	Reuben
Gemini	MNShH מנשה (Manasseh)	395	Vine and wall	Flesh	Simon
Cancer	IShShKR יששכר (Issachar)	830	Ass	Blue	Levi
Leo	IHVDH יהודה (Judah)	30	Lion	Scarlet	Judah
Virgo	NPThLI נפתלי (Naphtali)	570	Hind	Blue	Zebulun
Libra	AShR אשר (Asher)	501	Cup	Purple	Issachar

Zodiac of the Twelve Tribes (cont'd.)

Zodiac	Twelve Tribes	Value	Banner	Color	Alternate
Scorpio	DN דן (Dan)	54/704	Eagle	Green	Dan
Sagittarius	BNIMIN בנימין (Benjamin)	162/812	Wolf	Green	Gad
Capricorn	ZBVLN זבולן (Zebulon)	95/745	Ship	Purple	Asher
Aquarius	RAVBN ראובן (Reuben)	259/909	Man	Red	Naphtali
Pisces	ShMOVN שמעון (Simeon)	466/1116	Sword	Yellow	Joseph*

Total: 3701/7511

*(through Ephraim and Manasseh)

The Apostolic Zodiac

For the twelve Apostles, the medieval astrological speculations of the Church survive concerning these Zodiacal attributions. The name for Jesus in Greek contains the dimensions of the Zodiac as well, for Jesus Christ in the original Greek is a name of 13 letters. These 13 letters stand for the twelve apostles as the Zodiac encircling the central Sun, which is Jesus.

There is a further Zodiacal mystery in this Messianic name, for "Jesus Christ" in Greek is valued at 2,368, which is also the number value for the phrase "the twelve signs of the Zodiac" in Hebrew. This Hebrew description for the Zodiac is found in the third section of the fifth chapter of the *Sepher Yetzirah* (long version):

$$\text{JESUS CHRIST} = \text{IHΣOΥΣ XPIΣTOΣ} =$$
$$(10 + 8 + 200 + 70 + 200) + (600 + 100 + 10 + 200 + 300 + 70 + 200) =$$
$$888 + 1,480 =$$
$$2,368$$

$$\text{Twelve signs of the Zodiac} = \text{ShThIMf OShRH MZLVTh} =$$
$$\text{שתים עשרה מזלות} =$$
$$(300 + 400 + 10 + 600) + (70 + 300 + 200 + 5) + (40 + 7 + 30 + 6 + 400) =$$
$$483 + 575 + 1,310 =$$
$$2,368$$

Thus by this secret number formula combining Greek and Hebrew Qabalahs, the 13-lettered name of Jesus Christ contains the twelve signs of the Zodiac which encompasses the whole human race, epitomized in the twelve Apostles.

The four evangelists are often associated with the four Kerubic fixed signs of the Zodiac, and are employed in much Church artwork. Their Zodiacal symbolism is shown on the following page.

Four Evangelists as the Zodiac

Evangelist	Symbol	Zodiac Sign	Element
Matthew	Angel	Aquarius	Air
Mark	Lion	Leo	Fire
Luke	Bull	Taurus	Earth
John	Eagle	Scorpio	Water

The complete Zodiac is encoded in the twelve Apostles, and usually substitutes the disciple Matthias for Judas Iscariot. The initiated medieval tradition has survived starting with Simon Peter. Agrippa and Barrett give another magickal order leading with Matthias (and Judas) and this is shown below as a variant order. Within traditional Church masonry there is also a set of symbols or icons, usually displayed on their own shields, corresponding to each Apostle. These are shown below as well. These symbols are often the weapons of the Apostle's martyrdom. The following is the Apostolic Zodiac.

Apostolic Zodiac

Zodiac	Apostle	Greek	Number	Icon	Variant
Aries	Simon Peter	ΣΙΜΩΝΑ ΠΕΤΡΑΝ	1,706	Two crossed keys gold and silver	Matthias (Judas)
Taurus	Andrew	ΑΝΔΡΕΑΝ	211	Saltire cross	Jude of James
Gemini	James the Elder	ΙΑΚΩΒΟΝ	953	Three escallop shells, two above one	Simon
Cancer	John	ΙΩΑΝΗΝ	919	Chalice containing serpent	John
Leo	Thomas	ΘΩΜΑΝ	900	Carpenter square and upright spear	Peter
Virgo	James of Alphaeus	ΙΑΚΩΒΟΝ ΑΛΦΑΙΟΥ	1,965	Vertical saw	Andrew
Libra	Philip	ΦΙΛΙΠΠΟΝ	830	Tall cross and two loaves	Bartholomew
Scorpio	Bartholomew	ΒΑΡΘΟΛΟΜΑΙΟΝ	453	Three flaying knives, one above two	Philip
Sagittarius	Matthew	ΜΑΘΘΑΙΟΝ	190	Three money purses, two above one	James the Elder

Apostolic Zodiac (cont'd.)

Zodiac	Apostle	Greek	Number	Icon	Variant
Capricorn	Simon the Zealot	ΣΙΜΟΝ ΖΗΛΩΤΗΝ	2,304	Fish on an open Bible	Thomas
Aquarius	Jude of James	ΙΟΥΔΑΝ ΙΑΚΩΒΟΥ	1,838	Ship with cross-shaped masts	Matthew
Pisces	Judas Iscariot	ΙΟΥΔΑΝ ΙΣΚΑΡΙΩΘ	1,685	Moneybag with 30 silver coins	James of Alphaeus

Total = 13,954

The last consideration for the twelve signs of the Zodiac is the esoteric correspondence of color.

THE RAINBOW OF THE ZODIAC

Thanks to Mathers again, an esoteric system of color for the Zodiac was developed as the backbone of all Golden Dawn correspondences. This system was inspired in part by the color theories of Goethe and the general occult lore of color, including the teachings of Theosophy. But Mathers' key again was the astrological nature of the Hebrew alphabet filtered through the Tarot and the Tree of Life.

Mathers devised a very logical set of color correspondences for not only the Zodiac but also the planets and elements. All these correspondences were based on dividing the rainbow into twelve basic shades or gradations of color, starting with red for Aries and ending with red violet for Pisces.

The planets and elements were also added to this spectrum of the Zodiac, the planets and elements being aligned to their most sympathetic Zodiacal signs. The twelve tones of the octave were also equated to the Zodiac, Aries being middle C and Pisces being B above middle C. These twelve tones in turn were connected to the corresponding Zodiacal color, allowing any sign of the Zodiac to be invoked by its appropriate color and sound.

These occult correspondences of light and music have their source in Theosophy but reach their ultimate refinement in the Golden Dawn correspondences. Paul Foster Case based much of his Qabalistic magick on the sound harmonies, more so than most descendents of the Golden Dawn tradition.

The table on the following page gives these color (and sound) correspondences for the Zodiac, as well as the planets and signs. Note that the planets have two color correspondences, one based on the ten numbers and one based on the 22 letters of the Hebrew alphabet.

The Powers of Light and Sound in the Zodiac

Sound	Color	Zodiac	Planet (N)	Planet (A)	Element	Alchemy
C	Red	Aries	Mars	Mars	Fire	Sulfur
C#	Red Orange	Taurus				
D	Orange	Gemini	Mercury	Sun		
D#	Yellow Orange	Cancer				
E	Yellow	Leo	Sun	Mercury	Air	Mercury
F	Yellow Green	Virgo				
F#	Green	Libra	Venus	Venus		
G	Blue Green	Scorpio				
G#	Blue	Sagittarius	Jupiter	Moon	Water	Salt
A	Blue Violet	Capricorn	Saturn	Saturn	Earth	
A#	Violet	Aquarius	Moon	Jupiter		
B	Red Violet	Pisces				

In the above correspondences, the planetary colors derived from numbers (Planet N) are taken from the Sephiroth on the Tree of Life numbered 3 through 9; the planetary colors derived from the alphabet (Planet A) are taken from the seven double letters of the Hebrew alphabet as Paths on the Tree of Life.

This color scheme is the key for the both the Tarot and the Qabalistic Tree of Life. It also the basis for the 22 petals of the Rose Cross.

GEOMANCY: WRITINGS IN THE SANDS OF THE DESERT

Geomancy (ΓΕΩΜΑΝΤΕΙΑ) is a general term used to denote any type of divination derived from observing patterns in the Earth. The term comes from the Greek roots ΓΕΩ, meaning Earth, and MANTEIA, meaning system of divination. Geomancy, however, refers to a specific system of magick in the Western tradition that depends on 16 separate symbolic images as the elements used in an Earth-based oracle.

Geomancy is a divinatory system which has its origin in the Middle East and spread into Africa, Madagascar, and Europe. Geomancy is one of the primary modes of divination used in Renaissance magick. It has survived in both the Golden Dawn teachings and the writings of Aleister Crowley.

Geomancy is one of the few divinatory arts permitted by Islamic law, the other major art being the Arabic form of alphabet-number mysticism known as the science of ABJD. Geomancy is referred to in the Quran in the 4th verse of the 46th chapter. Sura 46, Section 1, Verse 4, states:

> Say: Do ye see what it is ye invoke besides Allah? Show me what it is they have created on Earth, or have they a share in the Heavens? Bring me a Book revealed before this, or any remnant of knowledge ye may have, if ye are telling the truth!

This verse is literally a prohibition against idolatrous practices, and bans the knowledge of the ancient mysteries found in the Middle East before Islam. But this verse is read esoterically as a justification for the tradition of Geomancy, and is supported by the title of this Sura, which is AHQAF, or "The Winding Sand-tracts of the Desert." The art of Geomancy is the revealed Book of the secrets of the Earth, as traced in the winding trails of the ever-shifting desert sands. It is the doctrine of signatures as revealed by Allah in the very patterns of His created Earth.

The art of Geomancy is called in Arabic *Khatt Ar Raml*, *Khatt* being the drawing of lines in the sand. The traditional mode for casting a Geomantic reading is the random generation of lines or dots in the sand. Often pebbles were cast in the sand and their pattern and number would determine the four lines which make up a Geomantic image.

Geomancy is the Western equivalent of the Eastern binary divinatory system found in the *I Ching*. Geomancy has 16 basic symbolic images, each made of four lines of either odd or even dots. Like the *I Ching*, each of the 16 Geomantic symbols contain many magickal correspondences to aid in its oracular interpretation. First and foremost, the 16 figures of Geomancy can be classified by the Western elements, planets, and Zodiacal signs. Many different systems of astrological correspondences exist, but the system detailed later in this section is the correspondences used in the Golden Dawn, derived from Dr. Thomas Rudd's Enochian workings.

The 16 basic Geomantic shapes, their Latin titles, and meanings are as follows.

Sixteen Basic Geomantic Shapes

Populus	Via	Conjunctio	Carcer	Fortuna Major	Fortuna Minor	Acquisitio	Amissio
People	Path	Union	Prison	Greater Fortune	Lesser Fortune	Gain	Loss

Sixteen Basic Geomantic Shapes (cont'd.)

Tristia	Laetitia	Rubeus	Albus	Puella	Puer	Caput Draconis	Cauda Draconis
Sadness	Joy	Red	White	Girl	Boy	Head of Dragon	Tail of Dragon

LATIN GEOMANCY

The 16 Latin titles were well established by the Renaissance and remained as the traditional titles in the Golden Dawn system. These 16 titles have a variety of minor meanings which add to the divinatory vocabulary and, since they are in Latin, they can be numbered. The most profound set of numbers comes from using the Simple Qabalah (Cabala Simplex) for Latin, where A = 1 and Z = 22. The following table gives the detailed meanings and numbers for these Latin titles.

Latin Names, Numbers, and Meanings for Geomancy

Geomancy	Name	Number	Meanings
	Populus	106	People, community, congregation, crowd
	Via	29	Way, street, journey, path of initiation
	Conjunctio	111	Union, joining, conjunction, marriage
	Carcer	44	Prison, jail, cell, restrict, bind, delay, confine
	Fortuna Major	135	Great fortune, internal aid, wealth

Latin Names, Numbers, and Meanings for Geomancy (cont'd.)

Geomancy	Name	Number	Meanings
• • • • • •	Fortuna Minor	146	Lesser Fortune, external aid, protection
• • • • • •	Acquisitio	115	Gain, acquisition, receive, add to
• • • • • •	Amissio	77	Loss, lost, that which is taken away
• • • • • • •	Tristitia	119	Sadness, sorrow, melancholy, debauchery
• • • • • • •	Laetitia	75	Joy, delight, pleasure, laughter
• • • • • • •	Rubeus	78	Red, ruddy, reddish, passion, temper
• • • • • • •	Albus	49	White, bright, fair, light, wisdom
• • • • •	Puella	59	Girl, maiden, beauty, daughter
• • • • •	Puer	54	Boy, beardless, rash, yellow, son
• • • • •	Caput Draconis	130	Dragon's Head, entrance, in, upper

Latin Names, Numbers, and Meanings for Geomancy (cont'd.)

Geomancy	Name	Number	Meanings
•			
•	Cauda	103	Dragon's Tail, exit, out, lower
•	Draconis		
• •			

Total: 1,430

Note that the 16 Geomantic shapes in the above order fall naturally into eight pairs. Each is a mirror image of the other. This is also true for the hexagrams of the *I Ching*, for in that system there are 32 symmetrical pairs of hexagrams. The logic that governs the esoteric shapes of the *I Ching* can also shed light on the esoteric structure of Geomancy.

THE ESOTERIC STRUCTURE OF GEOMANCY

Each Geomantic shape is made up of four lines. The basic building blocks for these figures is one central dot or two parallel dots. The two shapes generate odd or even numbers, but unlike the Pythagorean system which makes the Monad positive and the Duad negative, two is positive and one is negative in Geomancy. The prototype for Geomancy gives us this information, for originally the Middle Eastern method of divination using random marks in the desert sands created only one line, instead of the four lines of a modern Geomantic figure.

In this simple method, the diviner drew quickly, without regards to count, a series of lines or marks in the sand. These marks were then removed two at a time until either one or two marks remained. If only one mark remained it was a bad omen and represented disappointment, failure, or bad luck. But if two marks remained, it was a good omen, and represented happiness, success, or good luck.

This method eventually evolved into marking four sets of lines in the sand to generate one Geomantic shape of four lines. The top or first line formed represented the topmost point of the Geomantic figure, while the bottom or fourth line formed represented the foundation point of the Geomantic figure.

Each of the 16 Geomantic shapes is made up of two top lines and two bottom lines. These bigrams are four in number and can be defined by four corresponding Geomantic figures. The top bigram is the starting point, while the bottom bigram is the ending point, for in Geomancy the top line is the beginning point while the bottom (fourth) line is the last line. In this Geomancy differs from the *I Ching*, for the hexagrams begin at the bottom line and end at the top. The table on the following page shows the four bigrams which compose all 16 Geomantic figures.

Four Bigrams of Geomancy

Bigram	Shape	Element	Meaning	Geomancy
• •	Straight line Odd Odd	Air	Access, movement path, way (life)	Via
• • •	Upright triangle Odd Even	Fire	Loss, blockage off balance	Amissio
• • •	Downward triangle Even Odd	Water	Gain, addition in balance	Acquisitio
• • • •	Square, portal Even Even	Earth	To collect, group unite (death)	Populus

The Geomantic shapes listed are composed of the associated bigram as a pair, one above and one below. The elemental attributes above are based on the shape of the bigram (taken from alchemical correspondences).

In light of these elemental associations to the four bigrams, every Geomantic shape can be seen as a unique combination of two elements. These combinations are the 16 counterchanges for the four basic elements. The top bigram is the predominant element, while the bottom bigram is the subordinate element. Thus the Geomantic shape Conjunctio can be seen as Fire of Water, while Carcer is Water of Fire. Below are the 16 elemental combinations for the 16 Geomantic figures. The elements are designated by their initials (F = Fire, W = Water, A = Air, E = Earth).

Elemental Nature of Geomantic Bigrams

E of E	A of A	F of W	W of F	A of E	E of A	W of W	F of F

W of E	E of F	E of W	F of E	A of F	W of A	A of W	F of A

The above arrangement is not traditional; it is a secret order dependent upon the symbolism of the *I Ching*, specifically the concept of each hexagram being interpreted as two elemental trigrams. There are two more traditional elemental schemes for the Geomantic figures that will be shown in this section, based on Arabic and Golden Dawn correpondences.

The Four Elemental Levels of a Geomantic Figure

From the Arabic tradition of Geomancy, the four-lined figures are formed from top to bottom, the top being the first line. Each line is associated with an element as well as an Arabic alphabet letter and number. The top two lines are heaven as the elements Fire and Air, while the bottom two lines are Earth as the elements Water and Earth. Here are the attributes modeled on the ideal elemental Geomantic figure of Via.

Four Levels of an Arabic Geomantic Figure

Figure	Line	Element	Letter	Number
•	1	Fire	B	2
•	2	Air	Z	7
•	3	Water	D	4
•	4	Earth	H	8
Via				

In this elemental system, if any of the four lines of a Geomantic figure are composed of one dot, the corresponding element is present in that particular Geomantic figure. By this method, Via is the only figure with all four elements active, while the complementary figure of Populus has no elements active. Since each element is also assigned a corresponding letter of the alphabet, a number can also be totaled with these letters for each different elemental combination. The following table shows the elemental composition of all 16 figures as well as their number values:

Arabic Elemental Nature of Sixteen Geomantic Figures

—	F A W E	A W	F E	W E	F A	A E	F W
(0)	(21)	(11)	(10)	(12)	(9)	(15)	(6)
E	F	A	W	F W E	F A E	A W E	F A W
(8)	(2)	(7)	(4)	(14)	(17)	(19)	(13)

In the foregoing table, the elements are designated by the first letters of their names, while the numbers below in parentheses are the total values of the corresponding four letters of the Arabic alphabet.

Note that Populus is the only figure without elemental characteristics, and can therefore designate Spirit with no elemental admixture. It is also the figure for death in most African Geomantic systems, because it is devoid of all elements, just as Via is the African symbol for life, since it alone contains all four elements.

THE ASTROLOGY OF GEOMANCY

In the Western magickal tradition, each of the 16 Geomantic figures is given elemental, planetary, and Zodiacal qualities. Many different systems exist, the most popular being that of Agrippa. The one we will use, however, is the Golden Dawn system derived from the Enochian workings of Dr. Rudd. This system with some minor adjustments was also used by Crowley.

Within the scheme of four elements, 16 subelements can be generated. In these 16 counterchanges the four predominant elements of Fire, Water, Air, and Earth, are each classified as containing all four elements. Thus Fire would be subdivided into Fire of Fire, Water of Fire, Air of Fire, and Earth of Fire. The counterchange of Fire of Fire would be Fire in its essential state, while the other three counterchanges would be modifications of the basic element. Thus Water of Fire could be seen as lava, Fire of Air an explosive gas, and Fire of Earth the Earth's fiery core.

In the Golden Dawn system, these 16 elemental counterchanges classify the 16 Geomantic shapes. From these elemental associations the twelve signs of the Zodiac and their planetary rulers are also connected to the Geomantic shapes. They are derived directly from16 selected letters of John Dee's Enochian alphabet. These correpondences are as follows:

Golden Dawn Geomantic Astrological Correspondences

Geomancy	Element	Zodiac	Planet	Enochian
• • • • • • Acquisitio	Fire of Fire	Sagittarius	Jupiter	I (ⵧ) = 60
• • • • • Puer	Water of Fire	Aries	Mars	B (ⵖ) = 5

Golden Dawn Geomantic Astrological Correspondences (cont'd.)

Geomancy	Element	Zodiac	Planet	Enochian
• • • • • • **Fortuna Major**	Air of Fire	Leo	Sun	G (ᗷ) = 9
• • • • • **Cauda Draconis**	Earth of Fire	Tail of Dragon	Saturn (Mars)	F (𝄐) = 300
• • • • • • • **Laetitia**	Fire of Water	Pisces	Jupiter	R (Ɛ) = 100
• • • • • • • • **Populus**	Water of Water	Cancer	Moon	P (Ω) = 8
• • • • • • • **Rubeus**	Air of Water	Scorpio	Mars	N (Ӡ) = 50
• • • • **Via**	Earth of Water	Cancer	Moon	L (Ϲ) = 40
• • • • • • • **Albus**	Fire of Air	Gemini	Mercury	E (ꓸ) = 7
• • • • • **Puella**	Water of Air	Libra	Venus	O (L) = 30

Golden Dawn Geomantic Astrological Correspondences (cont'd.)

Geomancy	Element	Zodiac	Planet	Enochian
• • • • • • • Tristitia	Air of Air	Aquarius	Saturn	M (Ɛ) = 90
• • • • • • Fortuna Minor	Earth of Air	Leo	Sun	Z (P) = 1
• • • • • • Conjunctio	Fire of Earth	Virgo	Mercury	S (ℸ) = 10
• • • • • • Carcer	Water of Earth	Capricorn	Saturn	U (Ω) = 70
• • • • • • Amissio	Air of Earth	Taurus	Venus	A (ℵ) = 6
• • • • • Caput Draconis	Earth of Earth	Head of Dragon	Jupiter (Venus)	T (✓) = 400

In the foregoing attributes, Leo and Cancer appear twice. In this scheme each of the seven planets is allowed two Geomantic figures. Since the Sun and Moon are the only two planets that have but one sign each to rule, both Leo and Cancer appear twice. The remaining two Geomantic figures are given to the constellation Draco as the Head of the Dragon (the Moon's northern node) and the Tail of the Dragon (the Moon's southern node).

The connection between Geomancy and Enochian is from Rudd, as well as the planetary and Zodiacal attributes. The 16 counterchanged elements are Mathers' work, as are the number values for the 16 selected

Enochian alphabet letters. These number values were taken from the Yetziratic number values for Hebrew, based on the astrological values of Rudd. The subelement of each dominant element held the astrological key. The subelements of Fire are the Mutable Zodiac signs, the subelements of Water are the Cardinal Zodiac signs, the subelements of Air are the Fixed signs, and the subelements of Earth are the elements themselves. The primary or dominant element determines the elemental quality of the Zodiac.

Using this pattern Mathers took Rudd's Enochian letters and numbered the twelve Zodiac attributes as the twelve simple letters of the Hebrew alphabet. For the remaining four elemental signs, Mathers used the three Mother letters, plus Tav (ה) as the element Earth.

GEOMANTIC DIVINATION

Divination with Geomancy can be very complex. The Ifá tradition of African Yoruba Geomancy casts two Geomantic figures at each reading. There is a set of 256 meanings for the various possible combinations of 16 pairs. When both figures are the same Geomantic shape, the oracular meaning read is the pure sense of the one figure alone. When two different shapes are cast, one blends with the other to modify its meaning. This is similar to an *I Ching* reading when two hexagrams are cast as a result of changing lines.

A very simple method of casting one Geomantic shape has survived in modern times, using a pencil or pen and a piece of paper. Quickly jot down on paper four sets of marks from right to left or top to bottom. Mark enough marks in each column so that you lose count. Then cross out two marks at a time in each column until you have either one or two marks.

The top or right column is the first line of the figure, while the left or bottom column is the last line. Mark either one or two parallel dots for each column total. The resulting figure is the Geomantic figure you have randomly cast. Instead of paper and pencil, a tray of sand and a pointer can be substituted, this being more in line with the original method of Arabic Geomancy.

In the more complex Arabic and European traditions, four Geomantic shapes are cast by drawing 16 separate sets of lines or marks. From these four Geomantic figures, known as the four mothers, twelve other subordinate figures are generated by combining the lines composing the four mothers in various fashions. This method can be found detailed in various books, such as Israel Regardie's *The Golden Dawn* and Donald Tyson's recent edition of Agrippa's *Three Books of Occult Philosophy*.

GEOMANCY AND THE *I CHING*

Like Geomancy, the *I Ching* of China is a binary divinatory system. The 16 Geomantic figures as eight complementary pairs can be seen as 16 selected hexagrams of the *I Ching* as well. Their similar symbolism can offer insight into the pattern behind the Geomantic figures themselves. The following table lists the parallel Tetragrams and Hexagrams.

Geomantic Tetragram and I Ching Hexagram

Geomancy	I Ching	Comment
Via	1—The Creative	Both are solid pathways to heaven
Populus	2—The Receptive	Both are open channels or gates
Conjunctio	11——Peace	Female above male brings peace
Carcer	12—Standstill	Male above female brings discord
Fortuna Major	42—Increase	Potential in growth
Fortuna Minor	41—Decrease	Opportunities narrowing
Acquisitio	63—After Completion	Odd and Even are in the right place
Amissio	64—Before Completion	Odd and Even are in the wrong place
Laetitia	23—Splitting Apart	Top solid, the rest open
Tristitia	24—Return	Bottom solid, the rest open
Albus	29—Abysmal	White is the Moon
Rubeus	30—Clinging	Red is the Sun
Puella	10—Treading	Opening above (female)
Puer	15—Modesty	Opening below (male)
Caput Draconis	43—Breakthrough	Opening at Top
Cauda Draconis	44—Coming to Meet	Opening at Bottom

The reader should compare the descriptions of the hexagrams found in the sixth key of the first volume with the actual Geomantic figures.

African and Arabic Oracular Geomancy

One final consideration concerning Geomancy is the wealth of oracular meanings outside of the Latin names for the 16 figures. The Arabic tradition is the source for later meanings. Its movement into West Africa in the Geomantic lore of Chad, Dahomey, and Mali extended the meanings for the 16 figures far beyond their European counterparts. The table on the following page gives much of this oracular vocabulary for Geomancy.

For both the Arab and African diviners, Via, not Populus, should lead off the series of figures, Via being life while Populus is death. For the nomadic tribes of both the expansive deserts and deep forests, finding the path (Via) was the difference between life and death.

The order the Geomantic shapes are laid out in the following table is the African Ifá order of the Yoruba tribe that leads with Via, the figure with the fewest marks, and ends with Acquisitio, the most balanced figure, with female in the first and third positions and male in the second and fourth postitions. In this African order, Life and Death lead as Via and Populus, while War and Conquest end the order as Amissio and Acquisitio. This parallels the *I Ching* order that leads with Heaven and Earth and ends with Perfect Harmony and Discord.

In the following African attributes, four selected figures rule the four directions. This system is derived from the original Arabic lore, which assigned the four cardinal directions and the twelve signs of the Zodiac to the 16 figures.

Arabian and African Oracular Vocabulary for Geomancy

Geomancy	Arabic Oracles	African Oracles
Via	Journey, road	Life, east, day, passage, men, children
Populus	People, gang, band	Death, west, night, ancestors, crowd
Conjunctio	Meeting, gathering	Force, south, fierce animals, hunger
Carcer	Bond, tie, arrest	Containment, north, woman, copulation
Fortuna Minor	Outside help	Accident, byways, weapons, peace
Fortuna Major	Hidden help	Illness, highways, young men, prosperity
Laetitia	Joy, head, bearded	Health, liberty, possessions, tribe
Tristitia	Inverted, genitals	Death, misfortune, twins, hut, rope
Cauda Draconis	To go out	Women, large buttocks, sword, erection
Caput Draconis	To go in	Men, magick, beauty, bush, scrub
Rubeus	Red, danger	Red, blood, wound, snake, friendship
Albus	White, wasteland	White, joy, chance, water, pregnant
Puer	Generosity, youth	Earth, death, soul, safe journey
Puella	Pure, clean, girl	Fate, speech, mouth, high place
Amissio	Give away, take out	War, chiefs, misfortune, breaking
Acquisitio	Taking possession	Iron, conqueror, strength, to be caught

Geomancy is the Western equivalent of the Chinese *I Ching*. Its origins lie in the deserts of ancient Arabia, and from there the tradition spread through Africa ultimately to Europe. Both the *I Ching* and Geomancy are oracles arising out of the Earth, interpreting the Universe as a series of complementary pairs, and creating a cosmology out of polar opposites. But the West also holds in common with the East something else of great magickal importance: the power of the Word.

WORDS OF POWER

The power hidden in certain words has fascinated the West for centuries, and survives today in the many magickal traditions of the world. The New Testament opens with "In the beginning was the word (ΛΟΓΟΣ)," and the formation of the Universe by a single magickal word is contained in many mythologies.

Sanskrit holds the Eastern word of power most familar in the West, thanks to Theosophy, and that is the sacred syllable OM. The Universe as we know it was brought into being by the sounding of the syllable AuM, and will remain in existence until the divine sounding of the syllable HUM, when all of existence will cease to exist.

Egyptian and Babylonian creation myths involve the correct pronunciation of God's own name, bringing creation into existence. This tradition continued in the sacred Tetragrammaton of the Hebrew Qabalah. For the pronunciation of this highest name of God is unknown to almost all but the most initiated, and is passed down only on an oral basis.

The power of the Jewish Tetragrammaton was such that its spelling entered into almost every medieval text of magick. To know God's true name is to know God. Thus so much of medieval magick is concerned with intimate knowledge of the hierarchy of God's heavenly kingdom, from cherubs, angels, and archangels to the very names of God.

With the introduction of the Jewish Qabalah into Western magick, a technique was available that allowed the measuring of God, by measuring the numerical dimensions of his name. With both the Jewish Qabalah and the Pythagorean number lore, all divine names in Hebrew and Greek could be numbered. This secret tradition of measuring sacred words and names by their alphabet number values has survived today, and is the basis of much new magickal teaching in many circles of esoteric research.

This ability to number words is intimately connected with the coining of new magickal words of power. Abracadabra, a word of great antiquity, was built on its numerical properties, just as was the famous SATOR AREPO anagram square.

The nine-lettered Hebrew word ABRAKDBRA (אברכדברא) was a magickal formula which could reduce fevers and protect from fires. As such, it is a talismanic formula of protection. The proper way to write this talisman is in an inverted triangle of letters starting with all nine letters, and then reducing the word by one ending letter on each successive line. As the words of the formula are reduced to their final Aleph (א), the fever is diminished and the fires quenched. This formula of Abracadabra is written as follows.

```
A  B  R  A  K  D  B  R  A
 A  B  R  A  K  D  B  R
  A  B  R  A  K  D  B
   A  B  R  A  K  D
    A  B  R  A  K
     A  B  R  A
      A  B  R
       A  B
        A
```

Abracadabra Pyramid

The number value of ABRAKDBRA (1 + 2 + 200 + 1 + 20 + 4 + 2 + 200 +1) is 431. This number added to the final A, which is valued at 1, produces the number 432. And 432 in Hebrew is also the value for:

- ChDVDITh (חדודית) (8 + 4 + 6 + 4 + 10 + 400 = 432)—Pyramid, cone, the shape of the Abracadabra talisman

- KThIB (כתיב) (20 + 400 + 10 + 2 = 432)—Spelling, to letter a word, in this case referring to the reduced lettering in the talisman

Though no real meaning can be given to Abracadabra, the most esoteric interpretation views this word as an anagram of DBRA K ARBA (דברא כ ארבא), loosely defined as the Word of Four or Fourfold Word.

Crowley also adapted this powerful Qabalistic word to his own magickal cosmology by substituting the letter H for the letter C. The resulting word, ABRAHADABRA, had the Egyptian God HAD between two letterings of ABRA (which Crowley saw as "father"). As Hebrew, the eleven lettered formula of ABRAHADABRA (אברהאדאברא) numbered as 418, which Crowley connected with his own personal angel, Aiwass, for Aiwass in Greek also numbered to 418 (ΑΙFΑΣΣ).

TALISMANS AND MAGICK SQUARES

Talismanic magick depends on this number harmony as well. Talismans and amulets are objects engraved with special symbols, alphabet letters, and numbers, designed to attract or repel certain energies. Many talismans are drawn upon the gridded square used in the magick squares for the planets. Sacred words are interwoven on the square appropriate to the astrological influence of the talisman.

The gridding off of the names of power in these magick squares is a means to ground the sacred in the profane. By encasing the names of God in the evenly spaced cells of a magick square, the talisman draws the beneficial influence into these squares by the matrix of number. Hidden in all the lettered talismans are the potential number values of the various sacred alphabets used. Such talismans become subtle circuits of numbers, which in their measure influence cosmic forces. The user of such a talisman is thus brought into this complex web of numbers at the root of all letters employed in the talisman.

One of the most famous of all talismans is the SATOR AREPO square, which is a very early Christian talisman. It also appears in the Greater Key of Solomon, and is seen by some authorities as the source for the word TAROT. It is a five lettered formula which can be read backward and forward as well as up and down. Twenty-five letters are placed on the five-by-five square of Mars. This talisman is therefore especially linked to the number five, the pentagram, the color red, and the planet Mars. This magick square is usually lettered in Latin (but also in Greek, Coptic, and Hebrew) and appears as follows:

S	A	T	O	R
A	R	E	P	O
T	E	N	E	T
O	P	E	R	A
R	O	T	A	S

SATOR AREPO Square

There are many interpretations for the meaning of the words in this five-by-five square. It appears lettered in Hebrew as the second panticle of Saturn in Mathers' version of the Greater Key of Solomon. Mathers' esoteric interpretation based on a mixture of Latin and Greek is "The Father (Sator) slowly moving (AREPO) maintains (TENET) his creation (OPERA) as vortices (ROTAS)." As Greek-Coptic, it can be translated as "The sower Horus binds, toils, and tortures" (according to the research of Miroslav Marcovich).

But the most impressive explanation shows this talisman clearly as Christian, for the 25 letters of the SATOR AREPO square can be rearranged in Latin as a cross to reveal both PATER NOSTER (Our Father) and ALPHA and OMEGA (as the letters A and O) twice each. This Catholic talismanic cross of power is shown on the following page.

```
                    A

                    P

                    A

                    T

                    E

                    R

A   P A T E R N O S T E R   O

                    O

                    S

                    T

                    E

                    R


                    O
```

Pater Noster Cross

The following lettered squares generate each part of this cross. The two appearances of *noster* (of Our Father) share the same letter N, which occupies the central 13th square of this talisman. They fill 11 tangent squares of as follows.

S	–	T	O	–
–	R	–	–	–
–	E	N	E	–
–	–	–	R	–
–	O	T	–	S

NOSTER on Square

Pater (of Our Father) also occurs twice on the SATOR square as two sets of five tangent squares. They occupy the following ten cells.

–	A	–	–	R
–	–	E	P	–
T	–	–	–	T
–	P	E	–	–
R	–	–	A	–

PATER on Square

The final four letters of the square are the letters A and O, twice each, symbolizing Alpha and Omega. They form an oblong square in which each Alpha can be paired with an Omega, as follows.

–	–	–	–	–
A	–	–	–	O
–	–	–	–	–
O	–	–	–	A
–	–	–	–	–

Alpha and Omega on Square

As a variant to the above Pater Noster solution, the SATOR AREPO square can also be rearranged as ORO TE PATER SANAS ORO TE PATER, which translates as "I pray to you, Father. Thou healest. I pray to you, Father."

The medieval manual of Solomonic magick known as the Lemegeton is the best known book containing a system of talismanic magick squares inscribed with divine as well as infernal names of God. The above SATOR AREPO square appears in this work, as well as countless other word squares. Examples of this medieval Latin manuscript in Greek have survived, dating this work much before the Middle Ages. But this one work is extremely important in that two of its five books have survived in the modern lore of magick.

It is the genius of Mathers again that has brought the lore of talismanic magick involving magick squares of sacred letters and numbers into the mainstream of modern magick. Four basic traditions have been passed to us from Mathers:

1. The Greater Key of Solomon

2. The Lesser Key of Solomon

3. The Sacred Magic of Abramelin

4. The Enochian Watchtower system of John Dee

Thanks to Mathers, new magickal workings with these archaic talismanic systems continue today, but a new stream of magickal terminology has only recently entered into modern magick. Crowley, for the 20th century magician, has developed a completely new corpus of magickal words of power, all empowered by their own specific number values. Of great importance to Crowley was the crafting of words of power which could be measured as 93. Other numbers of great importance to Crowley were 156, 333, 418, and 666, 729, and host of other minor numbers. Many of these new words of power come directly from Crowley's inspired writings, such as "ABRAHADABRA," which can be found in *The Book of the Law.*

In the last 20 years, two new magickal grimoires have appeared, the first edited by Simon and the second edited by George Hay, each purporting to be the original version of H. P. Lovecraft's fabled *Necronomicon.* Lovecraft candidly confessed in his own personal letters that this "Book of Dead Names" was invented by him, in name only, solely as a vehicle for his own fiction. The cited author, Abdul Alhazred, the mad Arab, was Lovecraft's own alter ego as a young boy.

Lovecraft had no respect for magick or grasp thereof, though in his personal letters he loved to spell anything ending with a C as CK, in imitation of the style of writing of the 18th century. He was aware of Crowley, but viewed him as a charlatan. Lovecraft preferred astronomy to astrology and pessimistic rationalism to magick. Yet in creating the name of a fabled book of dark dread, a book containing the lore of ancient magick now long forgotten, Lovecraft became the godfather of a new magickal current, only beginning to awaken in the modern magickal community.

Out of these two versions of the *Necronomicon* has evolved a new tradition of magick, replete with new names of power, based on the hierarchy of cosmic forces which preceded the ancient Gods and Goddesses of Babylon and Sumer. Whether or not it is made up, and of course the real *Necronomicon* never existed outside of Lovecraft's imagination, nevertheless, both the lore of the *Necronomicon* and the magickal writings of Crowley are the new groundwork for modern magick. Both traditions will be viewed by future generations of magicians as the real, authentic magickal teachings of the past, just as we now view the magickal writings of Dee, Agrippa, and the like.

As to the power of the word in the West, no tradition contains a more esoteric legend than the Masonic symbolism of the Lost Word.

THE LOST WORD

The Masonic lore of the lost word is found in the rituals and legend of the third degree concerning the assassination and exhumation of King Solomon's chief architect, Hiram Abiff. After the murder of Hiram, his body is found and is only raised from the grave by the utterance of the "Lost Word."

The word uttered is "Mah Hah Bone," but it is not the lost word. It is the "substitute word," which will serve as the password until the true lost word is recovered.

The secret concerning this substitute word is its correct pronunciation. It is always written in Masonic rubrics as the three syllables Mah Hah Bone. Yet it should be pronounced in four syllables as Mah Hah Boh Nay.

As we shall see later in this section, Crowley was aware of the fourfold nature of this secret password and lettered his own version to total his favorite number, 93.

Modern Masonic scholarship considers the word Mah Hah Bone to be of possible French origin, because of the word Bone. But most scholars see it as a nonsense word with no real meaning other than a handy substitute for the real lost word. But the actual origin for this lost word of the third degree is Hebrew, which is the source language for so many other Masonic symbolic words. For Masonic symbolism as we know it was derived from a Renaissance magickal understanding of the Hebrew Qabalah.

As Hebrew, Mah Hah Boh Nay must be translated liberally; but the meaning of this lost word becomes clear in light of Hebrew, and Hebrew alone. Such a literal, liberal translation is needed in analyzing most Masonic esoteric symbolic words, for the grasp of both Hebrew and the Qabalah was not perfect in the founders of the many degrees of Freemasonry.

The correct lettering in Hebrew for Mah Hah Boh Nay is:

$$\text{MH HBVNH} = \textit{Mah? Ha-Boneh?} = \text{(מה הבונה)}$$

which literally translates as the question, "What? (MH) Is this (H) the Builder's (BVNH) (Word)?" where "Word" must be assumed. Therefore Mah Hah Boh Nay becomes the question "What? Is this the Builder's Word?" meaning, "Is this the real word, or the substitute word?" The answer is, of course, that Mah Hah Boh Nay is not the lost word but the substitute. The true lost word is the Tetragrammaton, the word Jehovah as the four lettered name of God in Hebrew, the word which was written on parchment and hidden in the holy of holies of King Solomon's temple as the cornerstone.

MH H BVNH is valued at 113 in Hebrew. This is relevant in that 113 is the value in Latin of *mortuus* meaning death or corpse, as well as the phrase *deus et homo*, God and Man. It is also the value in Sankrit of KaNKaLa, meaning skeleton. All these images support the imagery of the third-degree ritual at the imparting of the lost word.

Crowley, inheriting the rituals of the O.T.O., developed a third-degree password, the word of a Master Magician, to conform with the fourfold Mah Hah Boh Nay. Taking only the initials with a little modification, Crowley was able to develop another Hebrew password which would number to his most favored of all numbers, the number of both Will and Love in Greek, the number 93.

In his published works and diaries he gives a few clues to its true spelling. In his *Equinox of the Gods,* it is shown in a one-page table of Qabalistic correspondences as the formula:

$$III° + + + + = 93$$

In his own personal diaries, the word is shown as M + + + = 93, giving us the first letter of the secret third-degree password.

From these clues, we know the word is four letters, begins with the letter M, and totals to 93. We do not know what language these four letters are written in, but it is safe to assume that it is Hebrew. When it is seen as the equivalent of Mah Hah Boh Nay, using only the initial letters, the following solution occurs:

M + + + = M A B N (מ א ב נ) = 40 + 1 + 2 + 50 = 93 = Mah hAh Boh Nay

Within the III° ritual of the O.T.O., four clues are given for the four letters of the Word of a Master Magician. M.A.B.N. in Hebrew satisfies these clues perfectly. These clues and their solutions are as follows:

Four Letters of the Word of a Master Magician

Clue in Ritual	Letter	Number	Justification
First letter of Silence	M (מ)	40	Mem is the mute mother letter
Second letter of Breath	A (א)	1	Aleph is Air as the life breath
Third letter of Going	B (ב)	2	Beth is Mercury ruling travel
Fourth letter of Generation	N (נ)	50	Nun is Scorpio as the genitals

With these four initials the progressive order of mother, father, and child (son) is generated by combining two letters at a time as three successive pairs, this order being Crowley's own version of the precession of the Equinoxes:

MABN—Mother, Father, Son

Hebrew	Meaning	Book of the Law	Tetragrammaton	Zodiacal Age
MA (מא)	Mother	Nu (Chapter 1)	Heh (ה)	Aries
AB (אב)	Father	Had (Chapter 2)	Yod (י)	Pisces
BN (בנ)	Son	Ra Hoor Khu (Chapter 3)	Vav (ו)	Aquarius

In M.A.B.N., Crowley has the best of both worlds, melding orthodox Freemasonry with the doctrine of Thelema, bringing the old Hebrew substitute word into a new Hebrew format numbering to 93, the current of the New Aeon.

Crowley has also given the Western Mysteries one other extension of magick, and that is the search for a Qabalah for English.

THE ENGLISH QABALAH

The Book of the Law gives this promise in the end of the 54th verse and the 55th verse of the second chapter:

> ... the letters? change them not in style or value! Thou shalt
> obtain the order & value of the English Alphabet; thou shalt
> find new symbols to attribute them unto.

This task of finding a valid code for English is the next stage in the evolution of modern magick. Crowley, in researching this 55th verse, discovered two basic codes. The predominant method Crowley used all his life was to change English letters into Hebrew equivalents, such as numbering M.A.B.N. as Hebrew to get the value 93. Crowley, however, premised another code that ordered the English alphabet to begin with the letters I, L, and C as the values 1, 2 , and 3. This order is set forth in his *Liber Trigrammaton*.

All of the relevent codes for English, including classical numerology, are given in the 13th and final chapter of this book. I am inclined to see the most workable Qabalah for English as the natural serial order of the English alphabet (A=1, Z=26), a code used as well in German Rosicrucian writings dating from the 17th century using the 26 letters of the German alphabet as a cipher.

Whatever numerical code is finally confirmed for English, let its values reinforce, continue and extend into new heights the traditon already firmly established by the magickal languages of the world, East and West. Let English be added to the pages of the secret Rosicrucian Number Dictionary, *Liber Thesaurus*, for establishing a workable Qabalah for the English alphabet is the next step in the evolution of the Western Mysteries.

THE SIX SILVER KEYS OF THE WESTERN TEMPLE

Seventh Key

Greek

Overview

This seventh key of Greek inaugurates the number traditions of the West. It can be argued that my basic division of Eastern and Western traditions is incorrect. For instance, Hebrew, which I have placed in the East, is at the heart of Western magick and mysticism in the form of the Qabalah. Within this text, you will find my constant reference to the Qabalah as part of the Western, not Eastern, magickal tradition. However, I have placed Hebrew in the East because, in the context of Western Magick in the Middle Ages, "the wisdom from the East" means that which is Hebraic (rather than Indian, Tibetan, or Chinese). Possibly a better device would have been to make distinctions between Far Eastern, Eastern, Middle Eastern, and Near Eastern traditions, but I have used the present chapter divisions as a poetic device to present successive interconnecting traditions, in their order of impact on the Western traditions of magick.

Greek, as opposed to Hebrew, is clearly from the West. Many European magickal and Masonic traditions have embraced Greek rather than Hebrew as the ultimate mystery language of the ancient world. But, as I have argued elsewhere, the heart of symbolic correspondences for the West is the Hebrew Qabalah. Without reference to the Qabalah, any Western Magickal Tradition is incomplete in its approach to the higher levels of the magickal universe.

From the Greek tradition, the secret schools of Western magick have utilized:

- The 8 + 8 + 8 division of the Greek alphabet
- The Gnostic concept of 30 Aeons
- The Pythagorean lore concerning the first ten numbers

This chapter begins with a timeline for Greek beginning in 1700 BCE and ending in 450 BCE. In the debate concerning whether Hebrew or Greek was the first language to receive number value, few commentators have brought out the fact that Greek originally read from right to left in imitation of Hebrew. The pattern rather than retrograde was actually *boustrophedon,* or "as the ox turns." The first line would be read right to left, the second from left to right, and the third right to left again. It was reversed to read from left to right by 600 BCE. From my own research it is apparent that the Hebrew tradition of ascribing a symbolic and numerical content to their alphabet preceded the development of Greek into a numbered language by as much as 1,000 years. The numerical code we know for Greek in the range 1 through 800 was not apparent until 500 BCE, while Hebrew may have contained its innate number code as far back as 1500 BCE.

The main body of this chapter begins with a discussion of the proto-Greek alphabet of 16 characters known as "Cadmean" Greek. This alphabet (whose origin may be as old as 1700 BCE) did not possess a number value. However, with the addition of eight "Ionic" letters by 800 BCE, the potential for numbering Greek was established. By 750 BCE, this 24-letter alphabet developed its first set of number values based on serial order. Alpha, the first letter, became 1, while Omega, the last letter, became 24. This cipher was secretly encoded into the 24 chapter headings of Homer's epic poems, the *Iliad* and the *Odyssey.* This code is shown in the table entitled "Homeric Greek Numerals."

By 600 BCE, the Herodianic numeral system (akin to Roman numerals) was devised for a select group of Greek letters. This code had a more practical than esoteric application. This code is shown in the table "Herodianic Greek Numerals." By 400 BCE, the number value we are familiar with for Greek was established. This code is shown in the table "Pythagorean Greek Numerals." My contention is that this code represents the ultimate secret Pythagoras imparted to his third-degree initiates (though no document survives to substantiate my claim).

Like Hebrew, each Greek alphabet letter has a name, which when written in full, can generate a secondary number value. This is shown in the table entitled, "24 Greek Letter Name Number Values." Unlike Hebrew, these letter names have no direct meanings which can be linked to their hieroglyphic names (i.e., A in Hebrew, written in full, is Aleph, defined as "bull," which is also the hieroglyphic shape of the letter A). Therefore, these Greek letter names, when first penned, were in imitation of the Hebrew alphabet.

Next comes a discussion of the Gnostic diagram known as Soma Sophia (The Body of Wisdom). In this scheme, the 24 letters of the Greek alphabet are drawn up as 12 pairs (Alpha and Omega being the first pair) and then spread out upon infinite stars and infinite space, symbolized by the naked body of a beautiful woman. Each of these 12 alphabet pairs is placed on the 12 traditional Zodiacal zones for the body. Almost all surviving records of this diagram blind one set of attributes out of prudishness. This is the Zodiacal zone of Scorpio, which is the genitalia. However, this blind has been rectified in the chart offered in this seventh key.

Following this chart is a discussion of the seven planetary vowels, as well as the three elemental vowels of IAŌ. In combination, the 12 Zodiacal pairs of 24 letters and the seven planetary vowels can form the classic planetary-hour chart (common to medieval texts on ritual magick). The 24-hour division of the day can appropriately fall to the 24 letters of the alphabet (based on their Zodiacal pairing), while the seven-day division of the week can be encompassed by the seven planetary vowels (in their planetary day order). A reconstruction of this chart is shown in the table entitled "The Greek Planetary-Hour Chart." Finally, the rule governing the numbering of the obsolete Greek letter *stau* is described.

Beyond the alphanumeric symbolism discussed above, the Greek cosmology of a universe categorized by 30 successive Aeons is discussed. This Aeonic cosmology is also the source for John Dee's division of his Enochian universe into 30 Aethyrs. Three tables describe this Gnostic concept of 30 Aeons:

- The Primal Ogdoad of Eight Aeons
- The Gnostic Ogdoad that divides the Greek alphabet into three groups of eight letters
- The complete scale of 30 Aeons, showing the correspondence between those Aeons and the Greek alphabet

This is followed by a complete discussion of Christian number symbolism in Greek. Included is a discussion of 666, the nine triple numbers, and the holy names associated with Jesus.

This key to Greek ends with an addendum that fully details the number philosophy of Pythagoras. The addendum first describes the Pythagorean symbol for the decad of numbers known as the Tetractys (plural: Tetractyes). This supreme Pythagorean pyramidal symbol for the first ten numbers is shown as:

- A pyramid of ten dots
- A fourfold division of the universe
- A tenfold division of the universe
- Eleven sets of four levels of symbols
- The Hebrew Tetragrammaton
- The Greek *Theos* (God)
- The first ten letters of Greek (including the obsolete letter Stau)
- The ten stations of the Tree of Life

Next comes a complete discussion of every surviving Pythagorean symbol, or metaphor, for each of the first ten numbers. Most of these symbols have been derived from the translations of the 18th-century Platonist, Thomas Taylor. Unlike the Hebraic or Chinese cosmology of numbers, the Pythagorean system does not premise a set of symbols for the concept of zero, but begins with one (the Monad).

This addendum concludes with an in-depth numerical analysis of the name "Pythagoras" in its original Greek format. This is the first time that these secret numerical appellations, based on the esoteric Pythagorean number of 864, have been openly given in print.

ORIGIN

1700 BCE—The Cretan alphabet serves as a model for development of the sixteen letters of Cadmus, derived also from the Phoenician alphabet

800 BCE—Sixteen-character alphabet evolved to 24 characters, and the direction of writing changed from "right to left" to "left to right"

775 BCE—Development of Homeric serial order code of 1–24 for the Greek alphabet

600 BCE—Development of Herodianic numeral signs using six selected alphabet letters

450 BCE—The establishment of the secret Pythagorean number code of 1–800 for Alpha to Omega

ALPHABET CODE

Greek in its original form possessed 16 alphabet letters: 11 consonants inspired by Palamedes and 5 vowels inspired by the three Fates. This original form was named Cadmaen, in honor of its creator, Cadmus. This Cadmean alphabet evolved into the 24 letter shapes with the addition of 8 Ionic letters: 6 consonants from Simondes and Epicharmus and 2 vowels from Apollo. (In relation to the development of the Germanic-Scandanavian runes, the exact inverse is true. For Greek, the alphabet evolved from 16 to 24 characters, whereas the rune alphabet evolved from 24 to 16 characters.) The following table illustrates both the Cadmean and Ionic alphabets. Both the lower-case and capital forms are shown.

The Greek Alphabets
Cadmaen Greek

| From the Three Fates | | | From Palamedes | | |
Letter	Vowel		Letter	Consonant	
A, α	A	Alpha	B, β	B	Beta
E, ε	E	Epsilon	Γ, γ	G	Gamma
I, ι	I	Iota	Δ, δ	D	Delta
O, o	O	Omicron	K, κ	K	Kappa
Υ, υ	U	Upsilon	Λ, λ	L	Lamda
			M, μ	M	Mu
			N, ν	N	Nu
			Π, π	P	Pi
			P, ρ	R	Rho
			Σ, σ, ς	S	Sigma
			T, τ	T	Tau

Ionic Greek

From Apollo		From Simonedes and Epicharmus	
Letter	Vowel	Letter	Consonant
H, η	H̄ Eta	Z, ζ	Z Zeta
Ω, ω	Ō Omega	Θ, θ	Th Theta
		Ξ, ξ	X Xi
		Φ, φ	Ph Phi
		X, χ	Ch Chi
		Ψ, ψ	Ps Psi

With the evolution of this alphabet, three letters were lost in establishing a 24-character alphabet. These three lost letters are Stau (ς) (or Digamma [ϝ]), Koppa (ϙ), and Sampi (ϡ) (or San [ϻ]). All three are used in an extended 27-numeral cipher system.

The first use of the Greek alphabet as number appears in the time of Homer (750 BCE). In the transcription of Homer's epic poems, the *Iliad* and the *Odyssey*, each book was intentionally composed of 24 chapters. Each of the chapters was headed by one of the 24 Greek letters. This chapter division conceals the following number values for the Greek alphabet.

Homeric Greek Numerals

A	= 1	I	= 9	R	= 17
B	= 2	K	= 10	S	= 18
G	= 3	L	= 11	T	= 19
D	= 4	M	= 12	U	= 20
E	= 5	N	= 13	Ph	= 21
Z	= 6	X	= 14	Ch	= 22
H	= 7	O	= 15	Ps	= 23
Th	= 8	P	= 16	Ō	= 24

In 600 BCE, an alpha-numeral system was devised resembling the Roman numeral system. This method, known as Herodianic numerals, utilized six selected letters to produce the number range 1 through 10,000. The code is shown on the following page.

Herodianic Greek Numerals

Greek Letter	Value	Parallel Roman Numeral
I (I)	1	I
P (Π)	5	V
D (Δ)	10	X
P + D* (Γᵈ)	50	L
H (H)	100	C
P + H* (Γᴴ)	500	D
Ch (X)	1,000	M
P + Ch* (Γˣ)	5,000	V̄
M (M)	10,000	X̄

*These two letters were combined as one character, Pi being the predominant letter with the other letter placed directly within Pi.)

By 400 BCE, a 27-character alphanumeric code for Greek was established, paralleling the Hebrew 27 alphabet model of King Ezra. This code must have been the most esoteric teaching of Pythagoras, although no document survives to substantiate this claim. This code is as follows.

Pythagorean Greek Numerals

Greek Alphabet	Greek Letter Name	Number Value	Homeric Variant	Herodianic Numeral	Parallel Hebrew
A (A, α)	Alpha	1	1	I	Aleph (א)
B (B, β)	Beta	2	2	II	Beth (ב)
G (Γ, γ)	Gamma	3	3	III	Gimel (ג)
D (Δ, δ)	Delta	4	4	IIII	Daleth (ד)
E (E, ε)	Epsilon	5	5	Π	Heh (ה)
St (ς)	Stau	6	—	ΠI	Vav (ו)
Z (Z, ζ)	Zeta	7	6	ΠII	Zain (ז)
H (H, η)	Eta	8	7	ΠIII	Cheth (ח)
Th (Θ, θ)	Theta	9	8	ΠIIII	Teth (ט)
I (I, ι)	Iota	10	9	Δ	Yod (י)
K (K, κ)	Kappa	20	10	ΔΔ	Kaph (כ)
L (Λ, λ)	Lambda	30	11	ΔΔΔ	Lamed (ל)
M (M, μ)	Mu	40	12	ΔΔΔΔ	Mem (מ)
N (N, ν)	Nu	50	13	Γᵈ	Nun (נ)

Pythagorean Greek Numerals (cont'd.)

Greek Alphabet	Greek Letter Name	Number Value	Homeric Variant	Herodianic Numeral	Parallel Hebrew
X (Ξ, ξ)	Xi	60	14	ΓΔ	Samekh (ס)
O (O, o)	Omicron	70	15	ΓΔΔ	Ayin (ע)
P (Π, π)	Pi	80	16	ΓΔΔΔ	Peh (פ)
Q (ϙ)	Koppa	90	—	ΓΔΔΔΔ	Tzaddi (צ)
R (P, ρ)	Rho	100	17	H	Qoph (ק)
S (Σ, σ, ς)	Sigma	200	18	HH	Resh (ר)
T (T, τ)	Tau	300	19	HHH	Shin (ש)
U (Υ, υ)	Upsilon	400	20	HHHH	Tav (ת)
Ph (Φ, φ)	Phi	500	21	Γʰ	Kaph Final (ך)
Ch (X, χ)	Chi	600	22	ΓʰH	Mem Final (ם)
Ps (Ψ, ψ)	Psi	700	23	ΓʰHH	Nun Final (ן)
Ō (Ω, ω)	Omega	800	24	ΓʰHHH	Peh Final (ף)
S (ϡ)	Sampi	900	—	ΓʰHHHH	Tzaddi Final (ץ)

One other code for Greek exists, and that is the number value for each of the alphabetical letter names. These names are based on the Hebrew letter names. For the most part, unlike their Hebrew counterparts, they have no meaning in the Greek language. The letter-name code is as follows.

Twenty-Four Greek Letter-Name Number Values

Greek Letter	Letter Name	Number Value
A (A, α)	ALPhA (αλφα)	532
B (B, β)	BHTA (βητα)	311
G (Γ, γ)	GAMMA (γαμμα)	85
D (Δ, δ)	DELTA (δελτα)	340
E (E, ε)	E PsILON (ε ψιλον)	865
Z (Z, ζ)	ZHTA (ζητα)	316
H (H, η)	HTA (ητα)	309
Th (Θ, θ)	ThHTA (θητα)	18

Twenty-Four Greek Letter-Name Number Values (cont'd.)

Greek Letter	Letter Name	Number Value
I (I, ι)	IŌ TA (ιωτα)	1,111
K (K, κ)	KAPPA (καππα)	182
L (Λ, λ)	LAMBDA (λαμβδα)	78
M (M, μ)	MU (μυ)	440
N (N, ν)	NU (νν)	450
X (Ξ, ξ)	XI (ξι)	70
O (O, o)	O MIKRON (ο μικρον)	360
P (Π, π)	PI (πι)	90
R (P, ρ)	RŌ (ρω)	900
S (Σ, σ, ς)	SIGMA (σιγμα)	254
T (T, τ)	TAU (ταυ)	701
U (Υ, υ)	U PsILON (υ ψιλον)	1,260
Ph (Φ, φ)	PhI (φι)	510
Ch (X, χ)	XI (ξι)	610
Ps (Ψ, ψ)	PsI (ψι)	710
Ō (Ω, ω)	Ō MEGA (ω μεγα)	849

Like Hebrew, both the Homeric and Pythagorean codes are additional in nature. Each letter of a word is first converted to its number value and then these numbers are totaled together to produce the specific number value of that word.

The technical Greek term for reckoning the number value of a word is ISOPsHPhOS (ισόψηφος), which literally means two equal piles of stones. Isopsephos refers to the use of counting stones as an aid in reckoning the number value of any given word. It specifically refers to the instance when two words equal the same number (i.e., two equal piles of stones). This Greek term is the root for the linguistic classification of "isopsephic," a language whose alphabet serves both as phonemes and numbers.

The Church Fathers, especially Irenaeus in his polemic *Against Heresies*, have also documented a Gnostic astrological code for the 24-character Greek alphabet. The Zodiac in the night sky is seen as stars studding the infinite naked body of a celestial woman (reminiscent of the Egyptian Nuit, or Nut) whose name is SŌMA SOPhIA (Σῶμα Σοφία), the Body of Wisdom. She is pictured as floating above the earth in the night sky, and the Greek alphabet is assigned in 12 pairs to the 12 Zodiacal zones of her body. The following table delineates this Zodiacal attribution.

Soma Sophia—The Body of Wisdom

Greek Alphabet		Zodiac Sign	Zone of Body
Right Side of Body	**Left Side of Body**		
A (A)	Ō (Ω)	Aries	Head
B (B)	Ps (Ψ)	Taurus	Throat
G (Γ)	Ch (X)	Gemini	Shoulders (Hands)
D (Δ)	Ph (Φ)	Cancer	Chest
E (E)	U (Υ)	Leo	Heart
Z (Z)	T (T)	Virgo	Stomach
H (H)	S (Σ)	Libra	Intestines
Th (Θ)	R (P)	Scorpio*	Genitalia
I (I)	P (Π)	Sagittarius	Thighs
K (K)	O (O)	Capricorn	Knees
L (Λ)	X (Ξ)	Aquarius	Ankles
M (M)	N (N)	Pisces	Feet

*This attribute is blinded in many versions of Soma Sophia, thighs being substituted for genitalia.

The seven Platonic planets are also given alphabetical attributes. Two traditions survive: one based on the Orphic ladder that descends from heaven to earth (spirit to matter), the other based on seven concentric planetary orbits centered around the Earth.

The Orphic ladder assigns the planet Saturn and the letter Alpha, denoting spirit and heaven, to the top or first rung. The bottom or seventh rung is the Moon and the letter Omega, denoting matter and the center of the earth (or Hades).

The seven planetary spheres reverse the above symbolism and assign the least orbit from Earth to both Alpha and the Moon, since Alpha is valued at 1, while Saturn, the seventh and greatest orbit from Earth, is assigned to Omega, since Omega is the vowel with the greatest numerical value, 800. Note that the seven planets from the Moon to Saturn have orbital ratios of 1:5:8:10:70:400:800.

The Seven Planetary Vowels

	Greek Alphabet/Number	
Planet	**Orphic Ladder**	**Planetary Orbit**
Saturn	A = 1	Ō = 800
Jupiter	E = 5	U = 400
Mars	H = 8	O = 70
Sun	I = 10	I = 10
Venus	O = 70	H = 8
Mercury	U = 400	E = 5
Moon	Ō = 800	A = 1

Lastly, the triliteral Gnostic mantra of Iota Alpha Omega—IAŌ (ΙΑΩ)—conceals the elemental structure of Air, Water, and Fire (paralleling the three Hebrew Mother Letters). By the Orphic and planetary attributions of the vowels, two sets of elemental attributes are produced. Note that Iota is the Sun in both systems.

Iota, Alpha, Omega

		The Three Elemental Vowels		
Planet	**Element**	**Orphic**	**Planetary**	**Hebrew Model**
Sun	Fire	I	I	Shin
Moon	Water	Ō	A	Mem
Saturn	Air	A	Ō	Aleph

The seven planetary days of the week as two twelve-hour Zodiacal cycles, totaling to 168 hours, can easily be charted by the astrological attributions of the Greek alphabet.

The table on the opposite page allocates the twelve pairs and seven vowels of the Greek alphabet as the 168 stations of the week. The planetary ruler for each of the 168 hours of the week is shown, in light of traditional medieval magick. These planetary hours determine the auspiciousness or inauspiciousness of any given hour of the week. Planetary hours corresponding to their planetary days are especially appropriate for any magickal working whose aim is to tap the energy of a specific planet.

Note that the planet for the first hour of each day (midnight to 1:00 AM) is the same as the planet ruling the entire day.

The seven planetary days are assigned to the seven vowels by their planetary orbit attributions, while the double twelve-hour stations of the day are assigned to the twelve pairs of Greek letters that rule the Zodiac. Any hour in the week can therefore be symbolized by two Greek letters, one for the day and one for the hour. Thus Saturday at 12:30 PM is Omega of Omega (Omega = both the day Saturday and the hour 12 noon–1:00 PM).

The Greek Planetary-Hour Chart

24 Zodiac Hours of Day	Zodiacal Letter	Seven Planetary Days of the Week/Planetary Vowel						
		Sunday Sun (I)	Monday Moon (A)	Tuesday Mars (O)	Wednesday Mercury (E)	Thursday Jupiter (U)	Friday Venus (H)	Saturday Saturn (O)
Midnight–1 AM	Aries (A)	Sun	Moon	Mars	Mercury	Jupiter	Venus	Saturn
1–2 AM	Taurus (B)	Venus	Saturn	Sun	Moon	Mars	Mercury	Jupiter
2–3 AM	Gemini (G)	Mercury	Jupiter	Venus	Saturn	Sun	Moon	Mars
3–4 AM	Cancer (D)	Moon	Mars	Mercury	Jupiter	Venus	Saturn	Sun
4–5 AM	Leo (E)	Saturn	Sun	Moon	Mars	Mercury	Jupiter	Venus
5–6 AM	Virgo (Z)	Jupiter	Venus	Saturn	Sun	Moon	Mars	Mercury
6–7 AM	Libra (H)	Mars	Mercury	Jupiter	Venus	Saturn	Sun	Moon
7–8 AM	Scorpio (Th)	Sun	Moon	Mars	Mercury	Jupiter	Venus	Saturn
8–9 AM	Sagittarius (I)	Venus	Saturn	Sun	Moon	Mars	Mercury	Jupiter
9–10 AM	Capricorn (K)	Mercury	Jupiter	Venus	Saturn	Sun	Moon	Mars
10–11 AM	Aquarius (L)	Moon	Mars	Mercury	Jupiter	Venus	Saturn	Sun
11 AM–Noon	Pisces (M)	Saturn	Sun	Moon	Mars	Mercury	Jupiter	Venus
Noon–1 PM	Aries (O)	Jupiter	Venus	Saturn	Sun	Moon	Mars	Mercury
1–2 PM	Taurus (Ps)	Mars	Mercury	Jupiter	Venus	Saturn	Sun	Moon
2–3 PM	Gemini (Ch)	Sun	Moon	Mars	Mercury	Jupiter	Venus	Saturn
3–4 PM	Cancer (Ph)	Venus	Saturn	Sun	Moon	Mars	Mercury	Jupiter
4–5 PM	Leo (U)	Mercury	Jupiter	Venus	Saturn	Sun	Moon	Mars
5–6 PM	Virgo (T)	Moon	Mars	Mercury	Jupiter	Venus	Saturn	Sun
6–7 PM	Libra (S)	Saturn	Sun	Moon	Mars	Mercury	Jupiter	Venus
7–8 PM	Scorpio (R)	Jupiter	Venus	Saturn	Sun	Moon	Mars	Mercury
8–9 PM	Sagittarius (P)	Mars	Mercury	Jupiter	Venus	Saturn	Sun	Moon
9–10 PM	Capricorn (O)	Sun	Moon	Mars	Mercury	Jupiter	Venus	Saturn
10–11 PM	Aquarius (X)	Venus	Saturn	Sun	Moon	Mars	Mercury	Jupiter
11 PM–Midnight	Pisces (N)	Mercury	Jupiter	Venus	Saturn	Sun	Moon	Mars

Two last remarks concerning the numbering system of Greek should be made. Although there are no final letter forms as in Hebrew, there is a method to indicate 1,000 times the value of a letter. In Hebrew, the alphabet letter is enlarged, but in Greek a dot is placed above the letter to designate this thousandfold value.

Finally, the obsolete letter Stau (ϛ), the missing value of 6 in the Pythagorean system, has a peculiar rule in Greek numbering. If the letters Sigma and Tau, S and T (σ and τ), appear together in a word, their normal combined value of 500 can be replaced by 6 (the value of Stau [St]). As an example, the word for cross, STAUROS (σταυρός), has two number values, since S and T appear together:

1. S and T as normal values:

    (S = 200) + (T = 300) + (A = 1) + (U = 400) + (R = 100) + (O = 70) + (S = 200) = 1271

2. S and T as their substitute value of 6:

    (ST = 6) + (A = 1) + (U = 400) + (R = 100) + (O = 70) + (S = 200) = 777

Beyond the alphanumeric symbolism of the Greek alphabet, a cosmology was developed within the Gnostic tradition to describe the universe as 30 successive Aeons (or Worlds).

THE THIRTY AEONS

The basic Gnostic magickal classification of the Universe is the system known as the Aeons. The Greek Gnostic term Aeon can be defined as age, duration, time, cycle, division, level, or emanation. The basic number of Aeons was the scale of eight, known as the ogdoad. This is the source for Greek mysticism concerning the musical scale. As eight divisions, this Aeonic scale can also classify the Greek alphabet of 24 characters.

The primal or first ogdoad emanated out of the Abyss. From the Abyss came Silence to produce the Mind, which could conceive Truth. These four heavenly concerns of Abyss, Silence, Mind, and Truth produced the four complementary earthly concepts of the Word, Life, Man, and Church. Thus the primal ogdoad is:

1. Bythos—forefather, beginnings

2. Ennoia—thought, silence

3. Nous—mind

4. Aletheia—truth

5. Logos—word

6. Zoe—life

7. Anthopos—man

8. Ecclessia—church

These eight produced a planetary grouping of eight, as well as eight degrees of the passion of Sophia (the Goddess of Wisdom). The following table shows the Greek alphabet, octave, primal ogdoad, planetary ogdoad, and Sophia ogdoad.

The Gnostic Ogdoad

Scale of 8	Greek Alphabet	Musical Octave	Primal Ogdoad	Planetary Ogdoad	Ogdoad of Sophia	Sex	Element
1	A I R (A Ι Ρ)	do	Abyss	Demiurge (Zodiac)	Achamoth (Goddess of Wisdom)	Male	Fire
2	B K S (Β Κ Σ)	ti	Silence	Saturn	Desire	Female	Water
3	G L T (Γ Λ Τ)	la	Mind	Jupiter	Grief	Male	Air
4	D M U (Δ Μ Υ)	sol	Truth	Mars	Fear	Female	Earth
5	E N Ph (Ε Ν Φ)	fa	Word	Sun	Bewilderment	Male	Fire
6	Z X Ch (Ζ Ξ Χ)	mi	Life	Venus	Ignorance	Female	Water
7	H O Ps (Η Ο Ψ)	re	Man	Mercury	Turning	Male	Air
8	Th P Ō (Θ Π Ω)	do	Church	Moon	Matter	Female	Earth

An elaborate cosmology of 30 divisions, or Aeons, developed out of this primal group of eight. Eight produced ten, which in turn produced twelve. The following tables show the variants of this 30-fold universe.

The Thirty Aeons

Aeon	English	Greek	Numerical Value
Ogdoad:			
1. Bythos	Deep (n.)	BUThOS (Βυθός)	681
2. Ennoia	Idea	ENNOIA (Έννοια)	186
3. Nous	Mind	NOUS (νοῦς)	720
4. Aletheia	Truth	ALHThEIA (Ἀλήθεια)	64
5. Logos	Word	LOGOS (Λόγος)	373
6. Zoe	Life	ZŌH (Ζωή)	815
7. Anthropos	Humanity	ANThRŌPOS (Ἄνθρωπος)	1310
8. Ecclesia	Church	EKKLHSIA (Ἐκκλησία)	294
Decad:			
1. Bythios	Deep (adj.)	BUThIOS (Βύθιος)	691
2. Mixis	Mixing	MIXIS (Μίξις)	320
3. Ageratos	Unaging	AGHRATOS (Ἀγήρᾰτος)	683
4. Henosis	Union	ENŌSIS (Ἕνωσις)	1265
5. Autophyes	Self-Existent	AUTOPhUHS (Αὐτοφῠής)	1879
6. Hedone	Pleasure	HDONH (Ἡδονή)	140
7. Akinetos	Immovable	AKINHTOS (Ἀκίνητος)	659
8. Syncrasis	Blending	SUNKRASIS (Συνκρᾶσις)	1181
9. Monogenes	Only-begotten	MONOGENHS (Μονογενής)	496
10. Makaria	Happiness	MAKARIA (Μᾰκᾰρία)	173
Dodecad:			
1. Parakletos	Advocate	PARAKLHTOS (Πᾰράκλητος)	810
2. Pistis	Faith	PISTIS (Πίστις)	800
3. Patrikos	Fatherly	PATRIKOS (Πατρῐκός)	781
4. Elpis	Hope	ELPIS (Ἐλπίς)	325
5. Metrikos	Motherly	MHTRIKOS (Μητρικός)	748
6. Agape	Love	AGAPH (Ἀγάπη)	93
7. Aeinous	Ever-thinking	AEINOUS (Ἀείνοῦς)	736
8. Synesis	Understanding	SYNESIS (Σύνεσις)	1065
9. Ecclesiastikos	Church-like	EKKLHSIASTIKOS (Ἐκκλησίαστικος)	1094
10. Makariotes	Felicity	MAKARIOTHS (Μᾰκᾰριοτης)	650
11. Theletos	Desired	ThELHTOS (Θέλητός)	622
12. Sophia	Wisdom	SOPhIA (Σοφία)	781

The first Aeon of the Ogdoad is sometimes given as Proarche (PROARChH, Προαρχή, 959), "before the beginning," or Propater (PROPATHR, Προπᾰτήρ, 739), "before-father." Probably due to a misreading, the latter is sometimes given as Propator (PROPATŌR, Προπάτωρ, 1531), "pre-possessor." The second Aeon of the Ogdoad is sometimes cited as Charis (ChARIS, Χάρις, 911), "grace," or Sige (SIGH, Σίγή, 221), "silence."

The third Aeon of the Ogdoad is sometimes called Monogenes, but that name more properly belongs to the ninth Aeon of the Decad.

Probably due to an error, one annotator of Irenaeus gives the meaning "metrical" for Metrikos. The Greek spelling would in that case be METRIKOS (Μετρικός), with an epsilon (E) substituted for the eta (H). The same authority translates Theletos (the 11th Aeon of the Dodecad) as "desiderated, volition" rather than the related meaning of "wished for" or "desired."

Aeinous, the seventh Aeon of the Dodecad, is sometimes given as Ainos (AINOS, Αἶνος, 331), "praise," but Aeinous is more probable.

The Thirty Aeons (cont'd.)

The Angels Who Guard the Thirty Aeons (Scale of Thirty)	Greek Alphabet	Aeons	
		Valentinus	Hippolytus
The First Group of Eight			
1. Ampsiu	A	Depth	Depth
2. Ouraan	B	Silence	Idea
3. Bucua	G	Mind	Mind
4. Thartun	D	Truth	Truth
5. Ubucua	E	Reason	Word
6. Thardedia	Z	Life	Life
7. Metaxas	H	Man	Man
8. Artababa	Th	Church	Church
The Second Group of Ten			
9. Udua	I	Comforter	Depthlike
10. Casten	K	Faith	Commingling
11. Amphian	L	Fatherly	Unaging
12. Essumen	M	Hope	Union
13. Vannanin	N	Motherly	Self-Productive
14. Lamer	X	Charity	Bliss
15. Tarde	O	Eternal	Immovable
16. Athames	P	Intelligence	Blending
17. Susua	R	Light	Alone-Begotten
18. Allora	S	Beatitude	Happiness
The Third Group of Twelve			
19. Bucidia	T	Eucharistic	Comforter
20. Damadarah	U	Wisdom	Faith
21. Alora	Ph	Profundity	Father-like
22. Dammo	Ch	Mixture	Hope
23. Oren	Ps	Unfading	Mother-like
24. Lamaspechs	Ō	Union	Love
25. Amphiphuls	I	Self-born	Everlasting
26. Emphsboshbaud	H	Temperance	Understanding
27. Assiouache	S	Only-Begotten	Church-like
28. Belin	O	Unity	Happiness
29. Dexariche	U	Immovable	Limit (Time)
30. Massemo	S	Pleasure	Wisdom

These 30 Aeons are seen as a ladder of 30 rungs which spans from earth to the heavens. The top rung of this cosmic ladder is the First Aeon, the source of all, God, while the bottom rung is the Thirtieth Aeon, the material world. On each rung of this ladder was an angelic guardian whose name and nature had to be known in order to progress to the next rung of the Aeonic ladder. The second Aeonic model was a series of 30 concentric circles, each circle being one rung of the cosmic ladder. Ultimately, this Gnostic division of 30 categories became the basis for the Enochian system of magic of Elizabethan magician John Dee.

CHRISTIAN NUMBER MYSTICISM

Out of this Gnostic cosmology, which unites letter with number, emerged a secret Christian mystical tradition of allocating number value to word. Though the Ante-Nicene and Post-Nicene Church Fathers labeled the Gnostic teachings as heretical, the Greek version of the New Testament was crafted with an eye to the letter-number mysticism of the Greek alphabet. The name Jesus in Greek, for example, was intentionally spelled with six letters that when totaled would equal 888, to bring the sacred name into line with the planetary current of Mercury symbolized in the triple 8.

It seems that the triple numbers 111 through 999 were very important in this Christian system of number symbolism, and were derived from the Gnostic veneration of the great number 9,999. The only concrete example of the use of the alphabet as numbers that can be found in the Bible is in the New Testament disclosing the power of the sacred triple number 666:

> Here is wisdom. Let him that hath understanding count the number of the beast: for it is the number of a man; and his number is Six hundred threescore and six. (Revelation 13:18)

In this verse the process of measuring a name by substituting number values for letters of the alphabet is seen as a secret tradition of wisdom, that only the initiated (i.e., the one "who hath understanding") can decipher. And in this decipherment the number 666 will be the value of both the beast and the man. The solution to this numerical puzzle can be found in Greek in two numerical equations:

1. The number of the beast as 666 is found in Greek in the phrase:

TO ΜΕΓΑ ΘΗΡΙΟΝ—The Great Wild Beast

However, this phrase cannot be found directly in the New Testament, but rather in the Qabalistic investigations of Aleister Crowley.

Modern scholarship sees the solution to this puzzle in the Hebrew lettering of the name Caesar Neron, which is also valued at 666 (QSR NRVN, or קסר נרון). Crowley, in his own research as to the Hebrew origin of this number, discovered that *Therion*, which is Greek for "Beast," is also 666 when written with Hebrew characters:

ThRIVN (תריון) = 400 + 200 + 10 + 6 + 50 = 666

In Greek, the allocation of 666 to Caesar Nero is supported by the following two numbers:

- One half of 666 is 333; in Greek, 333 is the value of Caesar as ΚΑΙΣΑΡΑ.

- Twice 666 is 1332; in Greek, Caesar Neron is 1332 as ΝΕΡΩΝ ΚΑΕΣΑΡ.

This second number, 1332, sheds much light on the meaning of 666, for twice 666 as 1332 is the value of the following in Greek:

The Double 666 Current as 1332

Greek	Meaning
ΑΛΦΑ Ω	Alpha O(mega) (Rev. 22:13)
ΒΑΣΙΛΕΙΑΣ ΟΙΚΟΥΜΕΝΗΣ	The Kings of the Inhabited Earth (Rev. 16:4)
ΓΗΣ ΚΑΤΩ	The earth below (Acts 2:19)
ΘΕΟ ΨΟΡΗΤΟΣ	Inspired by a God or Goddess
ΙΔΟΥ ΒΑΣΙΛΕΥΣ	Behold the King (John 2:15)

Other phrases and words valued at 666 will be shown later in this section.

2. The numbering of 666 to equal the name of man is shown secretly in the verse itself, for the number 2,368 is the value of the following phrase:

KAI O˜ ΑΡΙΘΜΟΣ ΑΥΤΟΥ ΧΞ𝑭 =
(31 + 70 + 430 + 1171 + 666) =
2,368—"and his number is 666"

This number 2,368 is a key number in the Christian Qabalah, for 2,368 is the value in Greek of Jesus Christ as:

ΙΗΣΟΥΣ ΧΡΙΣΤΟΣ = (888 + 1480 = 2368) = Jesus Christ

Thus secretly encoded into this triple number of 666 is the following equation:

666 = The Beast = Man = Jesus Christ

Therefore the lowest is redeemed by the highest, and Man (created on the sixth day) is the intermediary link between the worst and the best, between Satan and God. In this secret equation each of the three can be linked to a power of 6 as:

$$𝑭 = 6 = \text{The Beast}$$
$$Ξ = 60 = \text{Man}$$
$$X = \underline{600} = \text{Jesus Christ}$$
$$666$$

In this three-lettered formula, the letter Stau as 6 is the mark of the beast, the letter Xi as 60 is the normal lifespan of Man, and the letter Chi as 600 is in the shape of the Cross of Jesus.

As pointed out above, the triple numbers from 111 to 999 held great significance in the Christian number mysteries. The following table shows the key words in Greek for these nine sacred triple numbers.

The Christian Mysteries Concerning the Triple Numbers 111 to 999

Number	Original Greek	Meaning
111 (3 x 37)	ΚΛΑΞ ΕΝΝΕΑ ΟΙΚΙΑ	Key Nine House, dwelling
222 (6 x 37)	ΝΑΖΑΡΗΝΕ ΙΒΙΣ ΓΑΙΗΣ	Nazarene, a title of Jesus (Luke 4:34) Ibis, bird sacred to Thoth (Mercury) Earth
333 (9 x 37)	ΚΑΙΣΑΡΑ ΑΚΡΑΣΙΑ ΑΚΟΛΑΣΙΑ	Caesar (John 19:15) (2 x 333 = 666) Excess Licentious, intemperance
444 (12 x 37)	ΣΑΡΞ ΚΑΙ ΑΙΜΑ ΣΠΕΙΡΗΜΑ	Flesh and blood Spiral, coils of snake, folds of a wreath
555 (15 x 37)	ΔΡΑΚΟΝΤΙ ΕΠΙΘΥΜΙΑ	The Celestial Dragon (Satan) (Rev. 13:4) Lust (1 John 2:16)
666 (18x37)	Η ΦΡΗΝ	The heart, breast, seat of life, the mind, reason, understanding
	Η ΗΛΙΟΣ ΚΑΙ Η ΣΕΛΗΝΗ ΗΛΙΟΣ ΚΑΙ ΑΣΤΕΡΕΣ ΘΕΟΣ ΕΙΜΙ ΕΠΙ ΓΑΙΗΣ ΛΟΓΟΣ ΑΓΑΠΗΣ Ο ΑΓΓΕΛΟΣ ΘΕΟΣ ΟΙ ΕΜΠΟΡΟΙ ΓΗΣ ΠΕΝΤΑΚΙΣ	The Sun and the Moon Sun and stars I am the God upon Earth The word of love The angel of God The merchants of earth (Rev. 18:3) Five times—the number of Christ's wounds
	ΠΛΕΥΡΑΝ	Side (John 19:35) (the spear wound of Christ on the cross)
	ΠΗΜΟΝ ΕΠΟΙΗΣΕΝ ΤΕΡΑΣΙΝ	Made of clay (John 19:14) Wonders (2 Thess. 2:19)
777 (21 x 37)	ΣΤΑΥΡΟΣ ΑΝΕΧΟΜΑΙ ΤΑ ΕΝΟΝΤΑ ΟΙ ΚΛΗΤΟΙ ΒΑΣΙΛΕΙΑ ΑΓΑΠΗΣ ΘΕΟΥ	Cross (ΣΤ = 6) Suffer, endure, bear with, forebear The inward being of man Those called to the Kingdom Love of God (Rom. 8:39)

The Christian Mysteries Concerning
the Triple Numbers 111 to 999 (cont'd.)

Number	Original Greek	Meaning
888 (24 x 37)	ΙΗΣΟΥΣ	Six-lettered formula for the name Jesus
	Ο ΘΩΘ	The Thoth, the Egyptian Mercury whose sacred number is 8
	ΛΟΓΟΣ ΕΣΤΙ	He is the Word
	Η ΖΩΗ ΕΙΜΙ	I am the Life
999 (27 x 37)	Ο ΑΠΟΡΡΗΤΟΣ	The ineffable
	ΘΕΟΣ ΑΝΕΚΛΑΛΤΟΣ	The ineffable God
	ΤΟ ΑΡΡΗΤΟΝ	The ineffable place, the locus of the unseen God
	ΑΝΑΒΛΕΨΙΣ	Recovery of sight

The nine triple numbers 111 through 999 are all multiples of 37. These multiples of 37 are obtained by adding together the three digits composing each number, as follows:

Harmony of 37 in the Nine Triple Numbers

$111 = 1 + 1 + 1 = 3 \ (3 \times 37 = 111)$ $222 = 2 + 2 + 2 = 6 \ (6 \times 37 = 222)$

$333 = 3 + 3 + 3 = 9 \ (9 \times 37 = 333)$ $444 = 4 + 4 + 4 = 12 \ (12 \times 37 = 444)$

$555 = 5 + 5 + 5 = 15 \ (15 \times 37 = 555)$ $666 = 6 + 6 + 6 = 18 \ (18 \times 37 = 666)$

$777 = 7 + 7 + 7 = 21 \ (21 \times 37 = 777)$ $888 = 8 + 8 + 8 = 24 \ (24 \times 37 = 888)$

$999 = 9 + 9 + 9 = 27 \ (27 \times 37 = 999)$

The secret key to the meaning of 37 in the above is found in Hebrew rather than Greek, for 37 is the value of IChIDH (יחידה), a name for the essential self as the unique point, a title of Kether on the Tree of Life, and a symbol of the point of light or flame of spirit which dwells in every living soul.

THE POWER OF 9,999

As stated above, this veneration of the nine triple numbers was inspired by the Gnostic veneration of the number 9,999, which was the number symbolic of the Universe in its ultimate stage of evolution and completion (symbolized as four sets of 9), spanning the entire 30 Aeons (symbolized as 30 letters). This number was secretly written in Gnostic talismans as a formula of 30 Greek letters, one for each of the 30 Aeons, written as six levels and valued at 9,999.

This Gnostic formula is as follows:

$$ΧΑΒΡΑΧ = 1,304$$
$$ΦΝΕΣΧΗΡ = 1,463$$
$$ΦΙΧΡΟ = 1,280$$
$$ΦΝΥΡΩ = 1,850$$
$$ΦΩΧΩ = 2,700$$
$$ΒΩΧ = \underline{1,402}$$
Total: 9,999

Thirty-Lettered Gnostic Magickal Formula of 9,999

The 30 letters in six groups do not form any words, but were rather a formula constructed on two numbers, the 30 Aeons and the upper limit of counting as 9,999. The number 9,999 can also be represented in Greek by the ninth letter, Iota, for the letter name for I as Iota (ΙΩΤΑ) is valued at 1111. Thus 9 x 1111= 9,999.

This mysticism of 9,999 can be seen as two 99's, and indeed the number value for 99 is at the heart of the Christian number mysteries, for 99 is the value of the following in Greek:

The Power of 99 in Greek

Greek	Meaning
ΑΚΟΝ	The ear, sense of hearing
ΑΜΗΝ	Amen, so be it, verily, of a truth, certainty
ΒΗΘΛΕΕΜ	Bethelehem (Matt. 2:1)
ΚΛΗΜΑ	Branch, limb, shoot
ΜΑΘΗΜΑ	That which is learned, a lesson
ΜΕΓΑΝ	Great (Rev. 12:12)
ΠΗΓΗ	The source, fountain, well

Note that 99 held a special significance in counting to the ancient Greek shepherds, for the first 99 numbers were always counted on the fingers of the left hand, the number 100 being the first number to be counted with the fingers of the right hand. From this counting system arose the Christian number metaphor, that out of 100 sheep 99 would be saved but one would be lost.

There are many more numbers used in the Christian Greek Qabalah, too many to cover adequately in this chapter. It would take a complete book to trace the many numbers relevent to Christian number symbolism, but we will analyze a few more relevent numbers here before turning to other matters.

THE MAGICKAL INITIALS ALPHA OMEGA AND IOTA THETA

Two usages of alphabet initials as numbers are prominent in Christian iconography: the pair of letters Alpha and Omega and the pair Iota and Theta.

The letters Alpha and Omega serve as a talisman signifying beginning and end. Their value is 801. Iranaeus informs us that the Gnostic veneration for this number is based on another word valued at 801, which is the Greek word for dove. Thus the symbolic dove descending upon the head of Jesus at the time of his baptism is symbolic of Alpha and Omega. The following key words will illustrate this Gnostic number of 801.

Alpha and Omega as 801

Greek	Meaning
Α Ω	The initials of Alpha and Omega, the pair of letters which rule the astrological zone of Aries and the head
ΠΕΡΙΣΤΕΡΑ	The dove
ΟΝΟΜΑΤΟΣ	Name (Rev. 13:17)
ΠΡΟΣΝΤΑ	Pre-living
ΦΟΒΕΙΣΗΕ	Be ye fearful, reverential (Mark 6:50)

The second most common alphabet pair in Christian iconography is formed of the letters Iota and Theta. These two letters are the intials of Jesus (Iota) and God (Theta). Their combined value is 19, which in Hebrew is the value of both the proper names Eve (ChVH, חוה) and Job (AIVB, איוב), two Biblical personages greatly tested by God. In Greek 19 is the value of the following:

Iota and Theta as 19

Greek	Meaning
Ι Θ	The initials of ΙΗΣΟΥΣ and ΘΕΟΣ, Jesus and God
ΑΓΙΕ	Holy (John 17:11)
Η ΓΗ	The Earth
ΘΕΕ	O God! (Wis. of Sol. 9:1)
ΙΔΕ	Lo, behold, see

THE GNOSTIC FORMULA IAO

There is one other very prominent Gnostic alphabet talisman and that is the use of the three-vowel formula IAO. This formula is a combination of the letter Iota with the alphabet pair Alpha Omega. As Alpha is beginning and Omega is end, Iota becomes the middle. This is brought out in the planetary symbolism of the seven Greek vowels, where IAO becomes the following correspondences:

I	A	Ω
Middle	First	Last
Sun	Moon	Saturn
Gold	Frankincense	Myrrh
4th orbit	1st orbit	7th orbit
(10)	(1)	(800)

The total number value for this formula is 811, which is 10 more than Alpha and Omega as 801. The key phrases for 811 in Greek are as follows:

The Formula of IAO as 811

Greek	Meaning
IAΩ	The letters Iota Alpha Omega as beginning (first), middle (fourth), and end (seventh) planetary orbits
AIΩ	To perceive, become aware, to breathe
ΑΣΤΕΡΕΣ	Stars (Jude 1:13)
ΤΕΣΣΕΡΑ	The four (Rev. 5:14), the four-sided sacred figure

THE HOLY NAMES FOR JESUS

Beyond the use of alphabet symbolism, every sacred name in the New Testament can be analyzed by number. This is true as well for the pantheon of ancient Greek Gods and Goddesses. Prominent numbers for Jesus are 808, 888, 1,480, and 2,368, for these four numbers are the values of Rabbi Jesus, Jesus, Christ, and Jesus Christ. As our final analysis of Christian number symbolism, we will look at these four number names for Jesus in depth.

808 as Rabbi Jesus

Greek	Meaning
ΙΗΣΟΥ ΡΑΒΒΙ	Rabbi Jesus (Mark 9:5) (808 is Mercurial and is related to 88, 818, and 888)
ΑΖΩ	To be awestruck, to stand in awe or dread of the Gods
ΕΓΩ	I (root of Ego)
ΖΩΑ	Living creatures (Rev. 5:14)
ΩΗ	The now, the present moment

888 as Jesus

Greek	Meaning
ΙΗΣΟΥΣ	The six-lettered name of Jesus
ΕΚΒΑΛΛΩ	I expel, cast out (demons) (Luke 11:19)
Η ΕΠΤΑ ΕΚΚΛΗΣΙΑΣ	The seven churches
ΗΛΩΝ	Nails (of crucifixion) (John 20:25)
Ο ΠΑΡΑΚΛΗΤΟΣ	The comforter, the Paraclete (a title of Christ)

1,480 as Christ

Greek	Meaning
ΧΡΙΣΤΟΣ	The seven-lettered name of Christ, the annointed one, the cosmic awakening; as Jesus is six and terrestrial, Christ is seven and celestial
ΑΛΦΑ ΩΜΕΓΑ ΑΜΗΝ	Alpha, Omega, Amen: the first, the last, the end
ΑΓΑΘΩΣΥΝΗ	The hero, the good one
Η ΑΓΙΩΣΥΝΗ	The holy sanctuary
Η ΑΛΗΘΕΙΑ ΣΩΤΗΡ	The truth (is) our salvation
Η ΑΝΑΣΤΑΣΙΣ ΕΚ ΘΕΟΥ	The awakening through God, the resurrection out of God
ΚΤΙΣΙΣ ΕΚ ΠΑΡΘΕΝΟΥ	Creation out of a virgin, the virginal womb
Ο ΠΑΝΔΟΧΕΥΣ	The host (Luke 10:25)
ΥΙΟΣ ΚΥΡΙΟΣ	Son (and) Lord

2,368 as Jesus Christ

Greek	Meaning
ΙΗΣΟΥΣ ΧΡΙΣΤΟΣ	The 13-lettered name of Jesus Christ (the first letter, Iota, being the Sun and the remaining 12 letters from Eta to Sigma being the 12 signs of the Zodiac)
Η ΠΟΛΙΣ ΧΡΥΣΟΥΣ	The Golden City
ΙΗΣΟΥΣ Ο ΠΑΙΣ ΤΟΥ ΙΣΡΑΗΑ	Jesus, the Son of Israel
ΙΗΣΟΥΣ Ο ΠΑΙΣ ΤΟΥ ΔΑΥΙΔ	Jesus, Son of David
ΙΗΣΟΥΣ ΥΙΟΣ ΚΥΡΙΟΣ	Jesus, Son, Lord
Ο ΑΓΙΟΣ ΤΩΝ ΑΓΙΩΝ	The Holy of Holies
Ο ΘΕΟΣ ΤΩΝ ΘΕΩΝ	The God of Gods
Ο ΑΡΤΟΣ ΣΤΑΥΡΟΤΥΠΟΣ	The wafer marked with a cross (ΣΤ = 6)

Many more numbers could be analyzed in terms of their sacred nature in Christian symbolism, but such an in-depth analysis will have to wait until another volume. However, we will examine one more aspect of Greek number symbolism, and that is the number lore of Pythagoras.

Addendum

Pythagorean Number Symbolism

The Pythagorean school of number symbolism developed a series of metaphors for the first ten whole integers, which in their imagery described the secret symbolism behind this number series.

One main symbol, known as the Tetractys, summarized in its pyramidal shape the complete series of ten numbers. This symbol, upon which all oaths were administered, was most sacred to the Pythagoreans.

The shape of the Tetractys is a four-leveled pyramid demonstrating the mathematical formula $1 + 2 + 3 + 4 = 10$.

The Tetractys

Each of the four levels represented one of the first four numbers, as follows:

```
        1——————————1
      1   2——————————2
    1   2   3 ——————3
  1   2   3   4 ———4
```

The Fourfold Tetractys

Ultimately all ten numbers were applied to the ten points, as follows:

```
          1
        2   3
      4   5   6
    7   8   9   10
```

The Tenfold Tetractys

With the placement of the ten numbers upon the Tetractys, a similarity to the nine-cell magick square for Saturn is established, for both number diagrams allocate 5 to the center (or heart) of the diagram.

The Tetractys is a cosmological diagram in the form of a pyramid of ten numbers which in essence categorizes everything in the universe. This is secretly concealed in the original Greek, for Tetractys in Greek is TETRAKTUS (τετρακτύς), which is valued at 1626, the same number value as the Greek phrase PANTI EN KOSMO (πάντι ἐν κόσμῳ), which means "Everything in the Universe." Thus the equation generated is the Tetractys = 1626 = Everything in the Universe.

The connection between the Tetractys and the pyramid is seen in the two numbers 55 and 831, because the sum of the ten numbers which compose the Tetractys is 55, the same value in Greek for EN (ἐν), the numeral name for "One." Thus the ten numbers of the Tetractys emanate out of the number 1. Further, the Coptic term for the capstone of the pyramid (KLGhE, ⲕⲗⲁϫⲉ) is valued at 55, connecting 1 with the concept of the top of the pyramid just as 1 occupies the capstone position of the ten numbers arranged as the Tetractys.

This first number of the letter is equated to the element Fire (pyr, PUR, πῦρ), and therefore a connection arises between the capstone of the pyramid, the number one, and the element Fire. This is supported in the Greek word for pyramid, which is pyramis (PURAMIS, πῦράμίς); i.e., vessel (AMIS, ἀμίς) for Fire (PUR, πῦρ), which has been construed as a reference to the pyramids as light-towers.

Pyramis in Greek is valued at 831, the value for the letter-name Aleph (ALP, אלף, 1 + 30 + 800) in the corresponding Hebrew Qabalah. Thus the pyramid is equated to "A," which is 1 in both Greek and Hebrew, bringing us back to the value of 55 for one (ἐν) in Greek.

Since 1 is 55 by Greek, the ratio 1:55 can be construed, which is the ratio of the capstone to the body of the Great Pyramid at Giza. Thus the Tetractys clearly represents by its shape the number value of the Egyptian pyramid.

The Tetractys as a four-layered pyramid possesses eleven classifications of the universe. These eleven sets of Tetractyes (recorded in Theon of Smyrna's *Mathematacal Treatise on Plato*) measure the universe from abstract number to the ages of Man. The 11 Tetractyes are shown in the table on the following page.

The Cosmology of Eleven Tetractyes

Sets	Number (Layer of Tetractys Pyramid)			
	1	2	3	4
1st—Composition of Numbers	1	2	3	4
2nd—Multiplication of Numbers	1 (even), 1 (odd)	2 (even), 3 (odd)	4 (even), 9 (odd)	8 (even), 27 (odd)
3rd—Magnitude	Point	Line	Superficies	Solid
4th—Simple Bodies	Fire	Air	Water	Earth
5th—Figures	Pyramid	Octahedron	Icosahedron	Cube
6th—Vegetative Life	Seed	Increase in length	Increase in breadth	Increase in thickness
7th—Communities	Man	House	Street	City
8th—Judicial Powers	Intellect	Science	Opinion	Sense
9th—Parts of Living Beings	Rational soul	Irascible soul	Epithymetic soul	The body in which the soul subsists
10th—Seasons of the Year	Spring	Summer	Autumn	Winter
11th—Ages of Man	Infant	Lad	Man	Old man

This veneration of four within the Tetractys is the basis for the Jewish Qabalistic veneration of the highest name of God, the Tetragrammaton (IHVH, יהוה). In fact, this Hebraic god name was worked into a Tetractys by Hebrew Qabalists as follows.

$$
\begin{array}{cccc}
\text{I} & & & \\
\text{I} & \text{H} & & \\
\text{I} & \text{H} & \text{V} & \\
\text{I} & \text{H} & \text{V} & \text{H}
\end{array}
\quad = \quad
\begin{array}{cccc}
 & & & \text{י} \\
 & & \text{ה} & \text{י} \\
 & \text{ו} & \text{ה} & \text{י} \\
\text{ה} & \text{ו} & \text{ה} & \text{י}
\end{array}
$$

This model can be applied as well to the four-lettered Greek word for God (ThEOS, θεός), as follows.

$$
\begin{array}{cccc}
\text{Th} & & & \\
\text{Th} & \text{E} & & \\
\text{Th} & \text{E} & \text{O} & \\
\text{Th} & \text{E} & \text{O} & \text{S}
\end{array}
\quad = \quad
\begin{array}{cccc}
\theta & & & \\
\theta & \epsilon & & \\
\theta & \epsilon & o & \\
\theta & \epsilon & o & \varsigma
\end{array}
$$

The ten numbers of the Tetractys can also be the first ten alphanumeric letters (with Stau) of the ancient Greek alphabet.

$$
\begin{array}{cccc}
\text{A} & & & \\
\text{B} & \text{G} & & \\
\text{D} & \text{E} & \text{St} & \\
\text{Z} & \text{H} & \text{Th} & \text{I}
\end{array}
\quad = \quad
\begin{array}{cccc}
\text{A} & & & \\
\text{B} & \Gamma & & \\
\Delta & \text{E} & \varsigma & \\
\text{Z} & \text{H} & \Theta & \text{I}
\end{array}
$$

In this layout of letters and numbers, the vowel "A" becomes the capstone of the pyramid of letter-numbers and the beginning of the Tetractys, while the ancient cryptic two-vowel inscription EI (EI) found over the entrance to the Oracle of Delphi becomes the center and end of the Tetractys. Therefore, the three Greek vowels AEI (AEI) become the beginning, middle, and end of the Pythagorean Tetractys. These three vowels combined as AEI became the root word for *Aeon*, and can be defined in Greek as ever, always, perpetual, eternity, an apt definition for the span of the ten numbers composing the Tetractys.

The Tetractys can also be artificially coupled to the Qabalistic Tree of Life. Utilizing the Golden Dawn Rainbow (Queen) color scale as well as planetary attributes for the ten Sephiroth of the Tree of Life, the four levels of the Pythagorean Tetractys can take on a new avenue of symbolism.

Tree of Life Tetractys

Level of Tetractys	Number in Tetractys	Pythagorean Decad	Tree of Life Sephirah	Color (World of Briah)	Planetary Attribute (Platonic order)
First (top)	1	Monad	Kether—Crown	White	The Primum Mobile
Second	2	Duad	Chokmah—Wisdom	Gray	The Fixed Stars (8th sphere)
	3	Triad	Binah—Understanding	Black	Saturn
Third	4	Tetrad	Chesed—Mercy	Blue	Jupiter
	5	Pentad	Geburah—Severity	Red	Mars
	6	Hexad	Tiphereth—Beauty	Yellow	Sun
Fourth (bottom)	7	Heptad	Netzach—Victory	Green	Venus
	8	Ogdoad	Hod—Splendor	Orange	Mercury
	9	Ennead	Yesod—Foundation	Violet	Moon
	10	Decad	Malkuth—Kingdom	Russet, Citrine, Olive, Black	Fire, Air, Water, Earth (Pythagorean order)

The ten numbers which form these ten points of the Tetractys were each given a title and a plethora of symbols by both Pythagoreans and the school of the Neo-Pythagoreans.

The ten Pythagorean titles for the number series and the corresponding geometric shapes are as follows.

Ten Pythagorean Number Titles

Number	Title	Geometric Shape
1	Monad	Point
2	Duad	Line
3	Triad	Triangle
4	Tetrad	Square
5	Pentad	Pentalpha
6	Hexad	Hexagram
7	Heptad	Triangle and Square
8	Ogdoad	Two Squares
9	Ennead	Three Triangles
10	Decad	The Tetractys

A variety of symbolic images has been developed for each of these numbers by the evolution of Pythagorean number philosophy. These images can be categorized into 15 different sets of imagery:

1. Number
2. Geometry
3. Measure
4. Gender
5. Time
6. Music
7. Cosmos
8. Positive (Superior) Attributes
9. Negative (Inferior) Attributes
10. Abstract Ideas
11. Man
12. Mind of Man
13. Symbols
14. Appelations of God
15. Gods and Goddesses

The following ten tables give the varied attributes for each of the ten Pythagorean numbers. Note that each number may not partake of all 15 categories.

The Ten Pythagorean Numbers

Monad (A - 1)

Number—One, the root of all numbers, unity, principle of all things, indivisible, immutable, the number in which reality mingled all things, that which makes an odd number even and an even number odd

Geometry—Point, point within circle, right angle, figures of equality, sameness and similitude, scalene triangles, oblong figures

Measure—The middle, the equal, the moderate, form (which circumscribes and bounds everything), source of all colors, void of mixture (on account of its simplicity)

Gender—Male and female (containing the odd and even), void of mixture

Time—The present now

Music—The order of the symphony

Cosmos—The first cause, Fire (the first element), Saturn (the highest rung of the Orphic ladder), Moon (the smallest planetary orbit), matter (standing alone by a negation of all things), the Sun

Positive (Superior) Attributes—Essence, subterranean profundity (beyond all knowledge)

Negative (Inferior) Attributes—Chaos (which resembles the infinite), confusion, commixtion, obscurity, darkness (to be one without differentiation), a chasm (between the bound and the infinite), horror (the ineffable being unknown), ambiguous

Abstract Ideas—The simple paradigm, the cause of truth

Man—Friend, life, felicity, the prophet, a rigid virgin (from its purity)

Mind of Man—Intellect (source of all ideas), spermatic reason

Symbols—Axis, ship, chariot, tower (of Jupiter), altars, beams of timber

Appellations of God—Adytum of God, nourished silence, the ineffable (as the cause of all multitude)

Gods and Goddesses—Androgynos (containing odd and even); Apollo; Atlas (the ineffable supporting, connecting and separating of all things); Jupiter (the God of Gods); Lethe (oblivion of God); Mnemosyne (mother of the Muses, source of the multitude); Morpho; Prometheus (nothing is beyond the ineffable); Proteus (comprehends everything in itself); Pyralios; Styx (immutable sameness of essence); Tartarus (extremity of the universe); Vesta (fire at the center of the earth, the middle of the four elements)

Duad (Β - 2)

Number—Two, first even, first increase, first change from unity, indefinite, infinite, principle and cause of the even; not evenly even, unevenly even, nor evenly-odd; first prime number (only divisible by itself and 1)

Geometry—Line, unfigured (between point and triangle), acute and obtuse angles; figures of inequality, difference and dissimilitude; sphere, circle, isosceles triangle

Measure—Unequal, interval between monad and multiple (unity and number), cause of dissimilitude, difference, cause of multitude

Gender—First female

Time—Night and day as a twofold aspect

Harmony—Fountain of all symphony; the duple, measure of 16 to 8 for Venus, of 36 to 18 for the eighth sphere, of 18 to 9 for the Sun, and 24 to 12 for Jupiter

Cosmos—Matter (as cause of bulk and division), Jupiter (as second Orphic rung from top), Mercury (as second planetary orbit from Earth), Air (as second element of four); the two luminaries (the Sun and Moon)

Positive (Superior) Attributes—Power, summit, patience, harmony, root

Negative (Inferior) Attributes—Strife, dissension, indistinction, falsehood, ignobility, ignorance, defeat

Abstract Ideas—Fountain of distribution

Symbols—Feet of Mount Ida abounding with fountains (root of region of ideas); nature; justice

Appellations of God—Fate, death, Phanes (intelligible intellect, occult power itself)

Gods and Goddesses—Aeria; Asteria; Ceres; Cupid; Cytherea; Diana (as the Moon); Dictynna; Dindymene; Dione; Disamos; Eleusinia; Erato; Esto; Isis; Lydia; Mychaea; Phyrgia; Rhea (mother of Jupiter, feminine, and therefore even); Venus (all as the energy found in the feminine Duad)

TRIAD (Γ - 3)

Number—Three, first odd, first number to be called multitude, first of numbers bound to the infinity of numbers, cause of plurality of numbers, most principal of numbers, allows power of monad to proceed into energy and extension; second prime number

Geometry—The triangle, the most perfect of shapes, the Mistress of Geometry (being the equilateral triangle); the icosahedron (the element Water) whose 20 faces are each equilateral triangles

Measure—Middle, analogy, similar and same, homologous and definite, triple cross of dimensions and all solid objects (as height, width, and depth), three interlinking monads as first-middle-last

Gender—The first male number

Time—Past-present-future as a threefold measure of time

Music—The triple measure of 24 to 8 ascribed to Jupiter

Cosmos—Mars (as the third rung of Orphic ladder from top), Venus as third orbit from Earth, Water as third element, Saturn as a three-by-three magick square. From this number the authority in astronomy and the nature of the heavenly bodies is divided in the form of triplicities of four elements to the twelve zodiac signs and the three divisions of decans to each of the twelve signs, as well as the aspect of a trine in the horoscope.

Positive (Superior) Attributes—Every virtue is suspended from this number; harmony, good counsel

Mind of Man—Intellect, intelligence, knowledge

Symbols—Horn of Amalthea; the bear (in the night sky)

Appellations of God—The Ineffable who was, is, and shall be

Gods and Goddesses—Achelous, Agyiopeza, Charitia, Craetaeide, Curetide, Damatrame, Dioscoria, Erana, Gorgonia, Hecate, Helice, Latona, Loxia, Lydios, Metis, Muse Polymnia, Naetis, Ophion, Phorcia, Pluto, Saturn, Symbenia, Thetis, Trigemina, Trisamos, Tritogeneia, Triton

Tetrad (Δ - 4)

Number—Four, first square number among even (2^2); equally even (2 x 2); every number as $\Sigma(1-4) = 10$; second even number

Geometry—The square as the constitution and permanency of the mathematical disciplines; the crossing of two lines; the first depth (forming all solids); the face of the cube; the tetrahedron

Measure—Capacity; the four directions

Gender—Female in first extension; to open and shut the recesses of generation

Time—The four seasons

Music—The quadruple measure of 36 to 9 ascribed to the eighth sphere, and of 32 to 8 ascribed to Saturn

Cosmos—The Sun as the center and fourth of both the Orphic ladder and planetary orbit; the fourth element Earth as well as the four elements as a whole; Fire as the Platonic solid the tetrahedron, Jupiter (as the four-by-four magick square)

Positive (Superior) Attributes—Fountain of natural effects; the key-bearer of nature

Negative (Inferior) Attributes—Excites Bacchic fury

Abstract Ideas—

The Four Aristolean Causes

Four Causes	Four Effects	Greek and Number
Divinity	by which	UP OU (ὑπ οὐ, 950)
Matter	from which	EX OU (ἐξ οὐ, 535)
Form	through which	DI OU (δί οὐ, 484)
Effect	to which	PROS OU (πρός οὐ, 920)

Man—The cause of arousal of virility; the dead who exchange the three blessings of this world for the fourth blessing of the next world

Mind of Man—The fourfold division of Man in terms of soul, body, and desire:

Fourfold Man

Division	1	2	3	4
Soul	Prudence	Temperance	Fortitude	Justice
Body	Acuteness of sensation	Health	Strength	Beauty
Object of Desire	Prosperity	Renown	Power	Friendship (Love)

Symbol—The Tetractys (consisting of four levels)

Appellations of God—Every Divinity; the greatest miracle (the extremity of the intelligible triad), a God after another manner (comprehending all mundane natures)

Gods and Goddesses—Aeolus, Bacchus, Bassareus, Bimater, Dioscorus, Eriunius, Harmonia, Hercules, Jupiter, Mercury, Muse Urania, Soccus, Son of Maia (Maia Deus) (tetrad son of duad mother), Soritas

PENTAD (E - 5)

Number—Five, first number to combine odd and even; the mean number of any two numbers totaling to the decad; second odd number; privation of strife (as a number uniting 3 + 2); unconquered (since $5^2 = 3^2 + 4^2$); third prime number

Geometry—The hypotenuse of a right triangle; the pentalpha (formed of five interlaced alphas as 5 x 1); the twelve faces of the dodecahedron (being the fifth element of Ether, as well as cosmos and deity); circular (the sphere)

Measure—Alliation, or change of quality; the five senses; equilibrium

Gender—Male (as odd); male and female (as 3 + 2); unmarried (as 3 + 2 as separate and distinct)

Time—The quince or 5° of the 360° Zodiacal circle

Music—The five notes of the ancient pentatonic scale; the fifth, the first interval capable of sound; the sesquialter measure (ratio of 3:2) which measures Mercury and Jupiter as 12 to 8, the Sun and Jupiter as 18 to 12, and the eighth sphere as 36 to 24

Cosmos—Venus (as fifth rung from top of Orphic ladder), Mars (as the fifth orbit from Earth and the five-by-five magick square), Ether (as the fifth element), the five greater planets (Saturn, Jupiter, Mars, Venus, and Mercury); the cosmos in its entirety (as both the fifth element and fifth Platonic solid); five descending and ascending meteors:

Five Meteors

Number	Descending	Ascending
1	Snow	Vapor
2	Dew	Smoke
3	Hail	Clouds
4	Rain	Mist
5	Frost	Whirlwind

Positive (Superior) Attribute—Justice

Negative (Inferior) Attribute—Vengeance

Abstract Idea—Smallest extremity of vitality

Man—The leader of the five species of Earth as (1) men, (2) quadrupeds, (3) reptiles, (4) flying animals, and (5) swimming animals

Symbol—Tower (of Jupiter); stable axis; heart (five as the heart or middle of both the Tetractys and the magick square of nine cells); the ancient rainbow of five colors (white, red, green, blue, and black), the tongue of the scale; the beam of a balance; light as three dimensions, transformed to a sphere, transformed to circular light

Appellations of God—Demigoddess (five as half of the decad); immortal (containing the quintessence)

Gods and Goddesses—Acreotis, Androgynia, Bubastia, Cardiatis, Cythereia, Didymaea, Gamelia, Muse Melpomene, Nemesis, Orthiatis, Pallas, Venus, Zonaea

HEXAD (ς - 6)

Number—Six, first perfect number (equal to the sum of its aliquot part as $\Sigma(1–3) = 6$); unequally equal (2×3); third even number, form of form (as the first perfect number), far-darting (as one triad joined to another)

Geometry—The six faces of the cube (which can unfold into a cross); the intersecting of two triangles to form a hexagram; six triangles joined as a hexad (symbolized in Acmon); triformed (as $\Sigma(1–3) = 6$)

Measure—Half of the whole; union of the parts of the universe; the six directions of space

Gender—Female (as even), nuptial, marriage as the first even times the first odd

Time—Regeneration (which occurs after $6 \times 6 \times 6$ years)

Music—six semitones as half of the octave (of 12 semitones)

Cosmos—One half of the Zodiac (six signs above the Earth, six signs below the Earth); the universe (as six directions); Mercury (as the sixth rung from the top of the Orphic ladder); Jupiter (as the sixth orbit from Earth); the element Earth (as the Platonic solid, the cube); the Sun (as the magick square of six-by-six cells)

Positive (Superior) Attributes—Harmony, perfection of parts, benevolence, peace, principle

Abstract Idea—The cause of vital habit

Man—Friendship, panacea, health, beauty of proportion (symmetry of the body)

Mind of Man—Truth, only number adapted to the soul of Man

Symbol—The marriage ritual (as the wedding of 3×2)

Appellations of God—Fabricator of the soul

Gods and Goddesses—Anchidice, Androgynaea, Amphitrite, Lachesis of the Fates, Muse Thalia, Persea, Trivia, Venus, Zygia, and Zygitis

Heptad (Z - 7)

Number—Seven, only number in decad that did not arise from any union and does not unite with anything; the fourth prime number; the third odd number

Geometry—The heptagon, the seven-pointed star (which can only be approximated); the triangle within the square (3 + 4); the center of the hexagram (1 + 6); the four-sided pyramid (whose sides are a triangle and base of a square); the two lesser sides of the right triangle (the $3^2 + 4^2$) whose angle of junction is the right angle of 90°

Measure—The three dimensions of length, breadth, and depth plus the four boundaries of point, line, superficies, and solid; the seven directions of the cube as East, West, North, South, Above, Below, and Center; integrity of parts (as seven measurable dimensions as above)

Gender—Male (as odd); motherless and virgin (as the fourth prime)

Time—The lunar cycle as four sets of seven days (and $\Sigma[1–7] = 28$ days)

Music—Voice and sound (seven elementary sounds to the scale; the measure of sesquiterian (the ratio of 3:4), which measures Mercury as 12 to 9, Venus as 16 to 12, Jupiter as 24 to 18, Saturn as 32 to 24, and the eighth sphere as 24 to 18

Cosmos—The Moon (as the seventh and lowest rung of the Orphic ladder); Saturn (as the seventh and highest orbit from the Earth); Venus (as the magick square of seven-by-seven cells); the seven planets as a whole headed by Saturn; the seven stars of the Great Bear

Positive (Superior) Attributes—Veneration

Man—Fortune and opportunity (governing mortal affairs)

Mind of Man—Dream (vision)

Appellations of God—Victory (motherless and virgin); judgment; much-implored

Gods and Goddesses—Acreotis, Adrastia, Aegis, Agelia (seven archangels and angels), Alalcomenia, Amalthea (the horn of, emanating from the monad), Atrytone, Ergane (the artificer), Glaucopis, Mars, Minerva, Muse Clio, Obrimopatra, Osiris, Panteuchia (Minerva's every type of armor), Phylacitis (seven guardian stars of the universe), Polyarete, Telesphoros (perfector), Tritogenia

Ogdoad (H = 8)

Number—Eight, first cube number among even, first cube of energy, fourth even number, evenly even (4 x 2); combination of the monad and the heptad (one and the fourth prime)

Geometry—Three-dimensions (since the first cube); the sphere; the eight faces of the octahedron; two squares interlaced to form an eight-pointed star

Measure—All things are eight (all things are comprehended in the eighth celestial sphere); the eight compass points

Gender—Producing cause of females (as 2 x 2 x 2); female (as fourth even number), immature; conception

Time—One third of day, the day divided into 8 + 8 + 8 hours; the eighth day as rejuvenation or regeneration of the cycle of seven days

Music—Universal harmony, the eight notes of the octave

Cosmos—The eighth sphere (being the fixed stars), the twelve signs of the Zodiac, between God and the seven planets, the element Air (as the octahedron), Mercury (as the magick square of eight-by-eight cells)

Man—Love and friendship

Symbols—Law (as [2 + 2] x 2) and Justice (as both 2 x 2 x 2 and 2 x 4), a possible source for the Tarot key, Justice, numbered VIII in the old decks

Appellations of God—The tutelar goddess (divine inspiration of artists and mystics); the Grand Matriarch; Mother

Gods and Goddesses—Cadmeia, Cybebe, Cybele, Dindymene, Metis, Muse Euterpe, Oreia, and Themis

ENNEAD (Θ – 9)

Number—Nine, first square number among odd numbers; second square number; equally equal (as 3 x 3); fourth odd number; the appellation similitude (as the first odd square); the number which flows round the other numbers within the decad like the ocean round the earth; the first triangular number (3 x 3)

Geometry—The enneagram (the nine-pointed star) composed of three interlacing equilateral triangles; the nine numbers of the magick square attributed to Saturn

Gender—Doubly masculine (as odd and as the first odd square)

Time—The nine months of gestation

Music—The ninth note which begins the new octave; the ratio of 9:8 (known as sesquioctave) which is assigned to the Moon

Cosmos—The Moon (as the magick square of nine-by-nine cells), Saturn (as the magick square of nine cells)

Positive (Superior) Attributes—Concord, freedom from strife

Man—Persuasion

Symbol—The horizon (for no single-digit number is beyond nine)

Appellation of God—The Ineffable (as that which is beyond the eighth sphere)

Gods and Goddesses—Agelia, Agyica, Curetis, Enyalius (Mars), Helios (to collect all numbers into one), Hyperion (limit of all numbers); Juno (conjunction with monad), muse Terpsichore (causing all numbers to spiral into a dance), the nine muses as a whole, Nysseis (piercing all other numbers), Paean, Perseia, Prometheus (no number can be behind nine), Proserpine (three triads), Telesphorus (bringing to an end), Tritogenia (three triads), Vulcan (Fire as the summit of the four elements)

Decad (1 - 10)

Number—Ten, which contains in itself both even and odd, the fourfold number (as $\Sigma[1-4] = 10$); that which contains every number in itself in extension; the fifth even number

Geometry—The pyramid of ten numbers as the Tetractys

Measure—The ten basic numbers that measure the dimensions of the Universe

Gender—Containing both male and female

Music—The measure of double sesquiterian (the ratio 7:3), which measures Mars

Cosmos—The Sun, the world (since all things are ordered 10), heaven (the most perfect boundary of the numbers), the sum of the four elements (as $\Sigma[1-4] = 10$)

Positive (Superior) Attributes—Strength (ruling over all other numbers), faith, necessity

Man—The ten fingers of man, the source of counting

Mind of Man—Memory (as mental calculation)

Symbols—Recipient; receptacle of all things; ten points of the Tetractys; key-bearer; branch-bearer

Appellations of God—Fate (containing all numbers); Eternity (extending to infinity), Unwearied; God of Gods

Gods and Goddesses—Atlas (which supports all), Mnemosyne, Phanes, Urania

One final comment concerning the Pythagorean school should be made in this section in regards to the name Pythagoras. The name Pythagoras in Greek (PUThAGORAS, Πυθαγόρας) is valued at 864, which immediately can be recognized as a veneration for the ogdoad as both 8 and 8^2 (as 64). The ogdoad is the eighth sphere of the Pythagorean cosmos and is above and beyond the influence of the seven planets, while the connection of 8 to 64 immediately brings to mind the magick square of 64 squares, which is assigned to Thoth-Hermes-Mercury, the mythic source of number, letter, sound, and color.

In addition, 864 is the value of the following words and phrases in Greek, which may be the real intention behind the nine Greek letters composing the name of Pythagoras, which begin with a letter valued at 80, while all nine letters form the numbers 800 and 8^2:

- AGIŌN (ἀγιών)—The holy of holies within the center of the temple; the secret adytum of the temple

- GŌNIA (γωνία)—AGIŌN rearranged becomes GŌNIA, the cornerstone, the capstone (which is also concealed in the Tetractys), corner, quarter, angle

- ThEŌN (θεών) —The Temple of the Gods

- ThRONOS ABRAXAS (θρόνος Αβραξας)—The Throne of Abraxas, which is the Sun in its 365 day journey through the sky of Earth in a given year

- ThUSIASTHRION (θὐσίαστήριον)—Altar, the center of the Temple

- IEROUSALHM (Ιερουσαλήμ)—Jerusalem, the center of the Universe

- O ThEOS MOU (ο θεός μου)—My God

- POLU-ThEOS (πολυ-θεος)—Of many Gods, dedicated to many Gods, consisting of many Gods

Tradition avers that the disciples of Pythagoras, out of reverance to the numerical formula found in his name, addressed him not as Pythagoras, but rather by the title, "The Master." This may be an allusion not only to the above numerical equations, but to the Hebrew phrase which is also valued at 864: the appellation "The Master" as RB BNIMf (Hebrew רב בנים)—Chief Architect, Master Builder, Grand Master of the Lodge of Heaven.

EIGHTH KEY

COPTIC

OVERVIEW

This eighth key is one of the shortest of the 13 keys. As Arabic is to Hebrew, Coptic is to Greek. Therefore, Coptic (though emanating out of Egypt) is included among the Western rather than the Eastern keys. Coptic is the last form of ancient Egyptian, a reduction of the hieroglyphic language. The alphabet is composed of 32 (sometimes 33) letters. Twenty-seven of these letters are derived directly from the Greek alphabet, while six additional letters are based on the Egyptian hieratic alphabet. These additional six letters receive no number value, while the remaining 27 letters retain the number value of their parallel Greek model.

This chapter first gives the 27 Coptic letters which receive number value followed by the six letters possessing no number value. Next the astrological attributes of Greek are brought into agreement with their Coptic counterparts. This is followed by a table clearly delineating the Coptic connection to the 32 paths of the Tree of Life, in accordance with the Qabalistic harmonies propagated by the Order of the Golden Dawn.

Included as well is the use of number symbolism found in ancient Egyptian hieroglyphs. Egyptian hieroglyphic writings (like Mayan hieroglyphs) cannot be numbered in their entirety.

At the beginning of my own research I had hoped to uncover a numerical basis for the construction of Egyptian hieroglyphs. Unfortunately, such a canon does not exist. Since the Egyptian language in its original format was hieroglyphic rather than alphabetic, the rules which govern most alphanumeric languages cannot apply here. However, since we have discovered in the sixth key that each Chinese character possesses a numerical value, based on the number of strokes required to execute such a character, this esoteric rule of numbering may have also been applicable for Egyptian hieroglyphic writing.

Possibly, each hieroglyph was associated to the specific number of strokes required to correctly execute that symbol. However, this is only a tentative conjecture on my part; no text has survived that details the number of strokes required for each hieroglyph, let alone a text that identifies this technique as the correct method for numbering Egyptian. Most likely, both Egyptian and Mayan written languages were obtained by humanity at a time when the brain had not yet fully developed to the point of being able to successfully mesh the concept of number and word. If this is true, then the supposed sacred language of Atlantis, which would predate Egyptian, would also have no number basis for its alphabet.

There are four basic tables of alphabetical correspondences detailed in this chapter, as follows:

1. The eight Egyptian hieroglyphs used as numbers

2. The six divisions of the Egyptian Eye of Horus (the Udjat) used as fractions

3. The Egyptian year cycle of 12 30-day months plus five additional year-end days

4. The Egyptian hieroglyphic model used to create the numerical languages of Phoenician, Hebrew, and Greek.

In terms of the last table listed above, it should be noted that the correspondences in this table are not those of standard academic equivalents, but rather are rectified in light of the esoteric symbolism of the Hebrew alphabet.

My own theory on this subject is that the 22-letter Phoenician alphabet (the shared source for both Hebrew and Greek) was modeled upon 22 selected Egyptian hieroglyphics for the exact shape of the alphabet letters, but was also modeled upon Cuneiform for their phonetic equivalents.

As an addendum to this key, the ancient research by Horapollo concerning the esoteric meanings of the Egyptian hieroglyphics is included. This work dates back to at least 400 CE, and was a Greek copy of a supposed Egyptian text. Listed in two separate parts are the secret meanings for around 200 Egyptian hieroglyphics.

This is the oldest surviving record which lists the initiated meanings for the Egyptian language. Rather than addressing the phonetic structure of the hieroglyphic writing system (which was only discovered 200 years ago), the symbolic imagery of this system was analyzed as a language of its own.

This text was the primary source in Europe during the Renaissance. It was only abandoned in the 19th century after the archaeological research of Jean Champollion radically changed the way the West viewed this most ancient language.

ORIGIN

200 BCE–400 CE—The last remnant of the Egyptian language is Coptic, superseded by Islamic Arabic around 700 CE. Coptic represents the last evolution of the Egyptian hieratic alphabet—and the first time the Egyptian alphabet possessed a complete range of number values. In the hieroglyphic system, seven selected hieroglyphs represented the number values 1 through 1,000,000 (1 was a vertical stroke, 10 a rounded arch), while the six composite parts of the Eye of Horus represented the fractions from 1/2 to 1/64. However, with the creation of the Coptic alphabet, a complete alphanumeric code based upon the Greek alphabet was developed.

ALPHABET CODE

Coptic reads from left to right.

The number values for the Coptic alphabet are modeled on the Greek alphabet. The Coptic alphabet is composed of 32 (sometimes 33) letters: 27 letters based on the Greek alphabet plus six additional letters based on the hieratic alphabet of the Egyptian language. These six additional letters receive no number value, while the remaining 27 letters retain the number value of their parallel Greek model. The alphabet code is shown on the following page.

Coptic Alphabet

Letter	Transliteration	Name	Number	Letter	Transliteration	Name	Number	Letter	Transliteration	Name	Number
ⲁ	A	Alfa	1	ⲓ	I	Joda	10	ⲣ	R	Rou	100
ⲃ	B	Veda	2	ⲕ	K	Kabba	20	ⲥ	S	Samma	200
ⲅ	G	Gamma	3	ⲗ	L	Lola	30	ⲧ	T	Dav	300
ⲇ	D	Dalda	4	ⲙ	M	Mej	40	ⲩ	U	He	400
ⲉ	E	Eje	5	ⲛ	N	Ni	50	ⲫ	Ph	Fij	500
ⲋ	So	Sou	6	ⲝ	Ks	Eksi	60	ⲭ	Ch	Kij	600
ⲍ	Z	Zada	7	ⲟ	O	Ou	70	ⲯ	Ps	Ebsi	700
ⲏ	Ē	Hada	8	ⲡ	P	Bej	80	ⲱ	Ō	Omega	800
ⲑ	Th	Tutte	9	ⲧ	F	Faj	90	ⲣ	Ṣ	(Sampi)*	900

*The 33rd letter, often not included in the alphabet order.

Six Coptic Letters with No Value

Letter	Transliteration	Name
ⲱ	X	Saj
ⳋ	Ḥ	Haj
ⳍ	H	Hori
ⳉ	Gh	Ganga
ⳝ	C	Sima
ϯ	Ti	Dij

The number code, like Hebrew, is additional. Every letter of a word is added together to form the number value of a word. The word EN (ⲈⲚ), meaning One, is therefore valued at E + N, 5 + 50, which adds to 55.

If one of the six additional hieratic-Coptic letters appears in a word, no number value is given to that specific letter. Thus in the word KLGhE (ⲔⲀⳉⲈ), meaning capstone of a pyramid, the letter Gh (ⳉ) receives no number value. Therefore KLGhE would be numbered as 20 + 30 + 0 + 5, which adds to 55.

An astrological code also exists for Coptic. This is based on the Greek Soma Sophia (cf. Seventh Key). The astrological alphabet equivalents are as follows.

Astrology and the Coptic Alphabet

Letter	Astrological Equivalent	Letter	Astrological Equivalent
A	Aries, Moon, Water	N	Pisces
B	Taurus	Ks	Aquarius
G	Gemini	O	Capricorn, Mars
D	Cancer	P	Sagittarius
E	Leo, Mercury	F	(no equivalent)
So	(no equivalent)	R	Scorpio
Z	Virgo	S	Libra
Ē	Libra, Venus	T	Virgo
Th	Scorpio	U	Leo, Jupiter
I	Sagittarius, Sun, Fire	Ph	Cancer
K	Capricorn	Ch	Gemini
L	Aquarius	Ps	Taurus
M	Pisces	Ō	Aries, Saturn, Air

Ṣ, X, Ḥ, H, Gh, C, and Ti have no astrological equivalents.

In addition to the traditional astrological attributes, both MacGregor Mathers and Aleister Crowley detailed an allocation of the 32 Coptic letters to the 32 Paths of the Tree of Life.

Coptic Tree of Life Correspondences According to Golden Dawn Ring and Disk and Crowley's Liber 777 (Column LI)

Path on Tree of Life	Coptic	Number Value	Astrological Attribution
1	So	6	Primum Mobile
2	C	—	Zodiac
3	Ti	—	Saturn
4	Ė	8	Jupiter
5	Ph	500	Mars
6	Ō	800	Sun
7	E	5	Venus
8	F	90	Mercury
9	Gh	—	Moon
10	S	200	Four Elements
11	A	1	Air (Spirit)
12	B	2	Mercury
13	G	3	Moon
14	D	4	Venus
15	H	—	Aries
16	U	400	Taurus
17	Z	7	Gemini
18	Ḥ	—	Cancer
19	T	300	Leo
20	I	10	Virgo
21	K	20	Jupiter
22	L	30	Libra
23	M	40	Water
24	N	50	Scorpio
25	Ks	60	Sagittarius
26	O	70	Capricorn
27	P	80	Mars
28	Ps	700	Aquarius
29	Ch	600	Pisces
30	R	100	Sun
31	X	—	Fire
32	Th	9	Saturn (Earth)

EGYPTIAN NUMBER SYMBOLISM

For the West, Egypt rather than India or China has been viewed as the source of all magickal traditions. The Western Renaissance revival of Hermeticism centered around the Greek and Coptic preservation of Gnostic and Egyptian magick.

In just the last 100 years of magickal development, Egypt has played a pivotal role. For example:

- The Egyptian imagery found in the Golden Dawn Qabalistic-Masonic rituals and symbolism

- The early psychic training gained by Madame Blavatsky, founder of the Theosophical Society, during her stay in Egypt

- The later use of Egyptian imagery in all of Blavatsky's writings, including her continual reference to the Secret Brotherhood of Luxor (in Egypt) as well as her first monumental work, *Isis Unveiled*

- The references within Gurdjieff's writings to a secret group, the Seekers of Truth, whose occult research included a deep penetration of the mysteries of Egypt and its pyramids

- Crowley's reception of *The Book of the Law* while residing in Cairo, dictated through the masks of the three Egyptian god-forms: Nu, Hadit, and Ra-Hoor-Khuit

- Crowley's revival of Etteilla's identification of the Tarot and Egypt with Crowley's 1944 issuance of his own *Book of Thoth*

However, though Coptic (the last Egyptian language) is alphanumeric in basis, allowing a number assignment to any given word, the ancient Egyptian hieroglyphic and hieratic alphabets did not possess a number basis. The Egyptian mysteries that both the Jewish and Hellenistic magickal traditions absorbed were embroidered into the mythic legends rather than the language itself.

Like the Mayan language, a select group of Egyptian hieroglyphics described the number range in their symbolism. However, neither the Egyptian nor Mayan language can be reduced to number.

EGYPTIAN NUMERALS

In Egyptian hieroglyphic writing, eight basic ideograms were developed for the number range of 1 to 1,000,000, while six related shapes, derived directly from the Egyptian Udjat (Horus Eye), were developed for the fractional number range of 1/2 to 1/64.

The eight basic numbers expressed the decimal system in the series: 1, 10, 100, 1,000, 10,000, 100,000, 1,000,000, 10,000,000. The first four numbers of 1, 10, 100, and 1,000 are the building blocks for the number range of both the Hellenistic and Semitic alphabets. The following table shows the eight hieroglyphic numerals, their symbolic meaning, and the parallel Hebrew and Greek letters of like number.

Eight Egyptian Hieroglyphic Numerals

Hieroglyph	Phonetic Value	Number Value	Parallel		Symbolic Meaning of Hieroglyph
			Hebrew	Greek	
—	UA	1	A	A	Upright post or wooden dowel; the penis; one finger; one tally; bottom edge of a stele; axis, pole, that which connects above to below
∪	MET	10	I	I	Shrine; the arch of a stele; the arched body of Nuit as the sky above the Earth; thicket, grove; vagina
☙	SAA	100	Q	R	Coil (spiral) of rope, cord; string of counting beads; string of 100 beads; the tail, the hair tied to the back of the head, the beard
⚘	KHA	1,000	Ȧ	Ả	Lotus flower, growing abundantly in the waters, and therefore counted as 1,000; the Egyptian parallel to the Indian Crown Chakra, known as the 1,000-petaled Lotus
⌐	TAB	10,000	i	i	Finger of the hand, the limit to which the hand can calculate, counting by the hand
🐸	HE-FENNU	100,000	Q̇	Ṙ	Tadpole, hence proliferation that is beyond reckoning by hand and therefore 100,000

Eight Egyptian Hieroglyphic Numerals (cont'd.)

Hieroglyph	Phonetic Value	Number Value	Parallel		Symbolic Meaning of Hieroglyph
			Hebrew	Greek	
	HEH	1,000,000	ThMf	U'C'h	An exclamation of joy and exuberance in being alive, the soul, the number of souls in the Universe and therefore a number only the Gods can reckon
	SEN	10,000,000	No symbol (the Aleph beyond reckoning)	No symbol	This numeral is used only to designate time; the sun rising above the horizon; the number beyond the number of souls, the number for eternity and therefore infinity; the ankh is a combination of 10,000,000 and 1 (SEN + UA), being one soul descending from the eternal-infinite

EGYPTIAN FRACTIONS

As to the expression of fractions, the Egyptian hieroglyphic for the Eye of Horus (Udjat) was divided into its component parts to express the fractions from 1/2 to 1/64.

According to legend, the God Set tore the eye of the hawk-headed Horus into fragments, into the fractions of 32/64, 16/64, 8/64, 4/64, 2/64, and 1/64. Later the ibis-headed Thoth restored the torn eye, joining the fractions together to form the value 63/64. Thoth was able to magickally replace the missing 1/64 from his own affinity to this one fraction (64 being the number of squares associated with Thoth as Mercury), restoring the eye as the Udjat (or Sound Eye).

The six fractions formed from the torn eye are as follows.

Egyptian Udjat Fractions

Part of Udjat	Fraction	Symbol
	1/2 (32/64)	The right side of the right eye (left side of left eye)
	1/4 (16/64)	The iris of the eye, the Sun (in the right eye), the Moon (in the left eye)
	1/8 (8/64)	The right (or left) eyebrow
	1/16 (4/64)	The left side of the right eye, the right side of the left eye
	1/32 (2/64)	Hieroglyph resembling coil of rope (valued at 100); possibly the nostril (right for right eye, left for left eye)
	1/64	Hieroglyph resembling inverted feather; possibly the ear (right for right eye, left for left eye)

Fractions whose numerator were always one were also identified in Egyptian by the conjunction of the ideogram "R" (part) ⬭ and the Egyptian number for the denominator below the "R" sign.

Thus Nu's sacred fraction 1/72 is represented as:

—the number 72 below the sign for fraction and one as the numerator.

EGYPTIAN CALENDAR

The mythological use of 1/72 in regards to Nu is recorded in the legend concerning the origin of the 365-day calendar. In this myth, Thoth wins a game of draughts with the Moon and gains 1/72 of the Moon's light. From this lunar light, Thoth created five extra days (five being sacred to Thoth, and assigned to the Greek letter E as 5 in astrological-letter symbolism) which did not belong to the 360 days of the Sun God, Ra. Nu conceived five children to reign as Gods and Goddesses over the five extra days of the year in the order of: Osiris, Horus, Set, Isis, and Nephthys.

Thus with the aid of Thoth's magick, Nu transformed the 360 days of the Old World year to 365 days of the New World year.

The 365-day Egyptian year began with the month of the God Thoth, corresponding to our current date of August 29. From August 29th, 12 cycles of 30-day months progressed.

Thus April 8th, the first of the three days that Aleister Crowley received *The Book of the Law* in Cairo, would correspond to the 13th day of the 8th Egyptian month of Pharmuthi.

The Egyptian 12-month cycle and its correspondence to our current calendrical system, as well as the epagomenic cycle of five extra days in the Egyptian calendar is as follows.

Conversion Tables for Egyptian Year Cycle
Ra's 360-Day Cycle

Twelve Egyptian Months	Days of Year	Twelve God-Forms for the Months	Twelve Thirty-Day Cycles
1st of Winter (Akhet)	1–30	1. Thoth	August 29–September 27
2nd of Winter	31–60	2. Paopi	September 28–October 27
3rd of Winter	61–90	3. Hathor	October 28–November 26
4th of Winter	91-120	4. Khoiak	November 27–December 26

Conversion Tables for Egyptian Year Cycle (cont'd.)

Twelve Egyptian Months	Days of Year	Twelve God-Forms for the Months	Twelve Thirty-Day Cycles
1st of Spring (Pert)	121-150	5. Tobi	December 27–January 25
2nd of Spring	151-180	6. Mekhir	January 26–February 24
3rd of Spring	181-210	7. Phamenoth	February 25–March 26
4th of Spring	211-240	8. Pharmuthi	March 27–April 25
1st of Summer (Semut)	241-270	9. Pakhon	April 26–May 25
2nd of Summer	271-300	10. Paoini	May 26–June 24
3rd of Summer	301-330	11. Epep	June 25–July 24
4th of Summer	331-360	12. Mesore	July 25–August 23

Nu's Five Extra Days of the Year

Epagomenic Day	God-Form	Five Extra Days of the Year
361	Osiris	August 24
362	Horus	August 25
363	Set	August 26
364	Isis	August 27
365	Nephthys	August 28

EGYPTIAN HIEROGLYPHS

Although the Egyptian hieroglyphs cannot be numbered in their entirety, both the alphabets of ancient Rock Hebrew and Greek numbered in their entirety and were modeled in their shape directly from selected Egyptian hieroglyphs. Most studies involving a connection between Egyptian, Hebrew, and Greek via the Phonencian alphabet have made the connection only on a phonetic basis. But the phonetic source for Hebrew and Greek was the Babylonian Sumerian Cuneiform; the real Egyptian influence was the shape of the hieroglyphs rather than their phonetic values.

The following table demonstrates the Egyptian hieroglyphic graphic shapes behind Phoenician, Hebrew, and Greek. This table is set out as follows:

- The proto-Egyptian hieroglyph used as the model for Phoenician

- The translation of the 22 Hebrew letter names which describe the hieroglyphic shapes of the original Hebrew alphabet. This is the basis for selecting the matching Egyptian hieroglyphs.

- The 22 letters of the Phoenician script (around 1100 BCE) paired to the hieroglyphic models

- Proto-Hebrew in the form of Rock Hebrew (which was engraved into rock) from 1000 BCE

- Archaic Greek from around 800 BCE when Greek was written from right to left, betraying its Semitic origin. This selection of Greek tables out only the 22 letters which are directly derived from the Phoenician-Hebrew alphabet order

- The phonetic equivalents for Hebrew and Greek,

- The number values for Hebrew and Greek

The Egyptian Hieroglyphic Model for Proto-Hebrew and Proto-Greek

Egyptian Hieroglyph	Hieroglyph Model Meaning	Hieroglyph from Hebrew Letter Name	Archaic Phoenician	Rock Hebrew Derived from Phoenician	Ancient Greek Script	Phonetic Value Heb.	Grk.	Number Value Heb.	Grk.
	The Bull	Ox	✗	✗ Aleph	Alpha	A	A	1	1
	Plow								
	Pyramid								
	House	House	ᓇ	Beth	Beta	B	B	2	2
	Temple								
	The throwing stick, return (reincarnation)	Camel	⟨	Gimel	Gamma	G	G	3	3
	The Moon								
	Walking								

The Egyptian Hieroglyphic Model for Proto-Hebrew and Proto-Greek (cont'd.)

Egyptian Hieroglyph	Hieroglyph Model Meaning	Hieroglyph from Hebrew Letter Name	Archaic Phoenician	Rock Hebrew Derived from Phoenician	Ancient Greek Script	Phonetic Value Heb.	Phonetic Value Grk.	Number Value Heb.	Number Value Grk.
	Vagina	Door	◁	△ Daleth	△ Delta	D	D	4	4
	Door (half of Door)								
	Door (as entrance to temple)								
	Soul (Ka), Vitality	Window	E	Є Heh	E	H	E	5	5
	Lo, joy				Epsilon				

The Egyptian Hieroglyphic Model for Proto-Hebrew and Proto-Greek (cont'd.)

Egyptian Hieroglyph	Hieroglyph Model Meaning	Hieroglyph from Hebrew Letter Name	Archaic Phoenician	Rock Hebrew Derived from Phoenician	Ancient Greek Script	Phonetic Value Heb.	Phonetic Value Grk.	Number Value Heb.	Number Value Grk.
(finger)	Finger	Peg, nail	Y (Vav)	Y (Vav)	(Stau)	V	St	6	6
(phallus)	Phallus								
Y	Support								
X	Headrest								
(scepter)	Scepter	Sword, Weapon	I (Zain)	‡ (Zain)	Z (Zeta)	Z	Z	7	7
(sword)	Sword								
Ⱄ	Road, Path, Canal								

The Egyptian Hieroglyphic Model for Proto-Hebrew and Proto-Greek (cont'd.)

Egyptian Hieroglyph	Hieroglyph Model Meaning	Hieroglyph from Hebrew Letter Name	Archaic Phoenician	Rock Hebrew Derived from Phoenician	Ancient Greek Script	Phonetic Value Heb.	Phonetic Value Grk.	Number Value Heb.	Number Value Grk.
(fence)	Fence	Fence, Enclosure	(symbol)	(symbol) Cheth	(symbol) Eta	Ch	H	8	8
(ladder)	Ladder which soul ascends to Heaven								
(coil)	A coil of Rope, Twist, Spiral								
(crossed circle)	City, Crossing of Roads	Serpent	(symbol)	(symbol) Teth	(symbol) Theta	T	Th	9	9
(ouroboros)	Oroborous, a Sign for Infinity								

The Egyptian Hieroglyphic Model for Proto-Hebrew and Proto-Greek (cont'd.)

Egyptian Hieroglyph	Hieroglyph Model Meaning	Hieroglyph from Hebrew Letter Name	Archaic Phoenician	Rock Hebrew Derived from Phoenician	Ancient Greek Script	Phonetic Value Heb.	Phonetic Value Grk.	Number Value Heb.	Number Value Grk.
	Hand	Hand, Fist		Yod	Iota	I	I	10	10
	Forearm								
	Fist								
	The Hollow of the Hand, to hold in the Palm of the Hand	Palm of Hand, Cupped Hand		Kaph	Kappa	K	K	20	20
	Cobra	Ox-goad		Lamed	Lambda	L	L	30	30
	Water, current, to flow	Water		Mem	Mu	M	M	40	40

The Egyptian Hieroglyphic Model for Proto-Hebrew and Proto-Greek (cont'd.)

Egyptian Hieroglyph	Hieroglyph Model Meaning	Hieroglyph from Hebrew Letter Name	Archaic Phoenician	Rock Hebrew Derived from Phoenician	Ancient Greek Script	Phonetic Value Heb.	Phonetic Value Grk.	Number Value Heb.	Number Value Grk.
	Fish	Fish	ſ	Nun	Nu	N	N	50	50
	Dead fish								
	Djed-column, Spine of Osiris as Ladder to Heaven	Tent Peg, Foundation, Support	‡	Samekh	Xi	S	X	60	60
	Eye	Eye	O	Ayin	Omicron	O	O	70	70
	Eye in Vase as Offering								
	Udjat, or Restored Eye								

The Egyptian Hieroglyphic Model for Proto-Hebrew and Proto-Greek (cont'd.)

Egyptian Hieroglyph	Hieroglyph Model Meaning	Hieroglyph from Hebrew Letter Name	Archaic Phoenician	Rock Hebrew Derived from Phoenician	Ancient Greek Script	Phonetic Value Heb.	Grk.	Number Value Heb.	Grk.
	Mouth	Mouth		Peh	Pi	P	P	80	80
	To Adore, Supplicate, Kneel	Fishing Hook		Tzaddi		Tz	none	90	none
	Locust			none	none				
	Shadow, Mushroom	Back of Head		Qoph	Koppa	Q	Q	100	90
	Head								
	Mirror								

The Egyptian Hieroglyphic Model for Proto-Hebrew and Proto-Greek (cont'd.)

Egyptian Hieroglyph	Hieroglyph Model Meaning	Hieroglyph from Hebrew Letter Name	Archaic Phoenician	Rock Hebrew Derived from Phoenician	Ancient Greek Script	Phonetic Value Heb.	Grk.	Number Value Heb.	Grk.
	One God Flag, Ax	Face Head	(Phoenician)	Resh	Rho	R	R	200	100
	Face, Head								
	Horizon, Sun rising between two mountains	Tooth, Fang	(Phoenician)	Shin	Sigma	Sh	S	300	200
×	To Split	Mark, Token, Cross	(Phoenician)	Tav	Tau	Th	T	400	300
	Cross								
	Ankh, the Symbol of Life								

Within the Western revival of magick in the late 18th and early 19th centuries, the Egyptian hieroglyphics were connected with the 22 pictorial cards of the Tarot, sometimes referred to as the Major Arcana. The Tarot was seen as the lost key of ancient Egyptian magick which would unlock the symbolic meanings of the hieroglyphics. As such, the Tarot became the lost Book of Thoth, and the 22 pictorial-symbolic cards of the Major Arcana became the Atus (or temples) of Thoth. This interest in connecting the Tarot to Egypt has persisted from the copious writings on the Tarot by Etteilla around 1790 to *The Book of Thoth* by Aleister Crowley in 1944.

But the Tarot, rather than unlocking the secrets behind the Egyptian hieroglyphics, is the pictorial key for unlocking the Qabalistic attributes of Hebrew, which are given in a blinded form in the Hebrew text, the *Sepher Yetzirah*.

Addendum

Horapollo's Secret Key for the Egyptian Hieroglyphics

Though the original symbolic meanings of the Egyptian hieroglyphics have been lost to time, a vary rare work has survived which preserves the Greek interpretation for them. Tradition relates that both Plato and Pythagoras were initiated into the Egyptian mysteries, thus linking the ancient traditions of Egypt with Greece. Out of this Hellenistic obsession with the occult tradition of Egypt, a curious work appeared in Europe around the 15th century.

Circulating among the Christian monasteries was a manuscript dating back to 400 CE and known as *The Hieroglyphics of Horapollo*. Originally written in the Egyptian tongue by the author Horapollo Niliacus (also referred to as Horus) and later put into Greek by Philip, this obscure work gives the initiated symbolic meanings to a group of about 200 hieroglyphic emblems.

Many of the hieroglyphics described in Horapollo's work are not of Egyptian origin; yet this work is extremely valuable in that it gives esoteric symbolic meanings to a grouping of Egyptian-like picture images. In essence, though this work purports to give the original symbolic meanings for the Egyptian hieroglyphics, what it really gives is a key to all subsequent Renaissance Hermetic art which uses symbols (or emblems) as a secret symbolic language.

The earliest date of an extant manuscript of this work is 1419 CE. From 1500 to 1600 CE, more than 30 editions of this work appeared in Europe. The first printed edition dates to 1505 CE and served as an addendum to a printing of *Aesop's Fables*. The book is divided into two sections, each written by a different hand. The first section betrays a deeper understanding of the subject than the second section, but both use the same logic in giving symbolic meanings for the various emblems.

As one studies both the description of the hieroglyphic images and their symbolic meanings culled in this emblematic textbook, it becomes obvious that this book is not the lost key to the Egyptian language but rather the true key to the Hermetic language of symbols which blossomed in Europe after 1400 CE in the recondite emblematic mystery texts of Alchemy, magick, Rosicrucianism, and Masonic traditions. Furthermore the symbolic images found in the various versions of the Tarot can be deciphered with Horapollo's Hieroglyphic key. The table on the following page is a collation of all the symbols found in both sections of Horapollo's work in alphabetical order, paired with the secret symbolic meaning.

Secret Key to the Egyptian Hieroglyphics

Emblem	Symbolic Meaning
Anemone flower	Human disease
Ant	Foreknowledge
Aphrodite	Every female who obeys a male
Baboon	Moon, letters of the alphabet, priest, anger, deep sea diver
Baboon seated	The two equinoxes
Baboon crowned, reaching up to the Moon	The moonrise, Moon worship
Baboon with penis	The divisions of time, 24 hours of the day
Basilisk	To be reviled by denunciation and fall sick from it
Bat	To be weak and rash
Bat's wing and ant	To be forced to stay inside
Bat with teeth and breasts	Mother nursing her children
Beaver	To be prevented from suicide
Bee	People obedient to the king
Beetle (one horn)	Sacred to Hermes and Ibis
Beetle (two horns)	Sacred to the Moon and Taurus
Beetle (30 claws)	Thirty stations of the Sun in one month
Beetle (blind)	To be dead from sunstroke
Beetle (catlike)	The progression of the Sun through the three stations of sunrise, noon, and sunset
Bull	Temperance
Bull facing left	Woman who has first borne a female child
Bull facing right	Woman who has first borne a male child
Bull girt with wild figs	To be made temperate by recent misfortune
Bull's ear	Acute hearing
Bull with erect penis	Courage with temperance
Bull with right knee bound	A temperate man easily swayed
Bundle of papyri	Ancient lineage, descent
Burning censer with heart above	Ancient Egypt
Camel	To hesitate to move one's feet
Cicada	To be initiated into the mysteries
Crane in flight	Knowledge of higher things

Secret Key to the Egyptian Hieroglyphics (cont'd.)

Emblem	Symbolic Meaning
Crane on watch	To guard against the plot of enemies
Crocodile	A madman, a lewd man, a fertile man, a plunderer
Crocodile and scorpion	Men at war with one another
Crocodile eyes	Sunrise
Crocodile hunched up	Sunset
Crocodile's blood	Murder
Crocodile's tail	Shadows
Crocodile with ibis feather on head	Rapacious, idle
Crocodile with mouth open	To eat
Crow (dead)	To live a complete life
Crow (one female)	Celibacy
Crows (pair)	Man mating with his wife, marriage
Crows (young)	To be angry and in constant motion, not even resting to eat
Date palm	The year marked by the progression of 13 New Moons
Date palm (branch)	One lunar month
Deer and a flute player	To be deceived by flattery
Deer and viper	To move swiftly, but heedlessly
Dew dropping from heaven	Knowledge only the select few can understand
Dog	Prophet, emblamer, sacred scribe, to look directly at the images of the gods, the spleen
Dog turning back	Escape
Dove	Ingratitude to kindness
Dove (black)	A widow remaining faithful to her death
Eagle	A retired king with no pity for his subjects
Eagle carrying a stone	Living safely within a walled city
Eagle's chick	Bearing of male children, circle, sperm
Eagle with a twisted beak	Old man dying of hunger
Ear	Future work

Secret Key to the Egyptian Hieroglyphics (cont'd.)

Emblem	Symbolic Meaning
Eel	To live in isolation and be hostile to everyone
Electric ray	A man saving many others from drowning
Elephant and pig	A king fleeing from a fool
Elephant and ram	A king fleeing from folly and intemperance
Elephant burying his tusks	To prepare one's own tomb
Elephant with his trunk	To be sensitive to what is expedient, to be master of one's fate
Face of animal with a sword	Impious, undutiful
Feet in water	A fuller of cloth
Feet together and standing	Course of the Sun at the winter's solstice
Feet walking on water	The impossible
Finger	Measurement
Fire and water	Purity, purification
Fish	Abominable, lawless, taboo
Fly	Impudence
Frog	Unformed man, shameless man of keen vision
Goat	Sharp hearing, a fruitful man's penis
Hand	A man fond of building
Hands holding a shield and bow	The jaws of battle
Hare	Alert, to keep one's eyes open
Hawk	God, sublime victory, Sun, sight, blood, heart, soul
Hawk big with young	To abandon one's children because of poverty
Hawk spreading his wings in the air	The wind
Hawks (pair)	Husband and wife, 30 sexual unions of the Sun with the Moon
Headless man walking	That which is impossible
Heads (male looking in, female looking out)	To ward off demons, phylactery, talisman
Heart hanging from gullet	The mouth of a good man
Hippopotamus	An hour

Secret Key to the Egyptian Hieroglyphics (cont'd.)

Emblem	Symbolic Meaning
Hippopotamus claws turned downward	The unjust and the ungrateful
Honey	The center of vital power
Horn (of bull)	Work
Horn (of cow)	Punishment
Horn (of stag)	A long space of time
Horse and bustard	A weak man pursued by a stronger man
Horse (dead)	Many wasps, to swarm
Hyena	To be unstable, changeable, androgynous
Hyena facing left	To be conquered by the enemy
Hyena facing right	To conquer the enemy
Hyena skin	To bear misfortune fearlessly, even to the point of death
Hyena and leopard skin	To be conquered by a weaker opponent
Ibis	Heart, reason, sacred to Hermes
Ink and reed	Scribe, letters of the alphabet
Isis	The star Sothis marking the year
Ladder	A siege
Lamprey	A man who mates with foreigners
Leopard	To live an evil life, but to conceal such evilness
Lion	To inspire fear, spiritedness, sacred to Horus, the rising of the Nile (when Sol is in Leo)
Lion devouring a monkey	To cure oneself of a fever
Lioness	A woman who has conceived only once
Lion (head of)	To be wide awake and on guard
Lion and torches	Anger chastened by fire
Lion's forequarters	Strength
Lion tearing its cubs to pieces	Unmeasurable anger
Lyre	A man who binds together and unites his people
Man eating an hourglass	An astrologer
Man in armor (or shooting an arrow)	A mob

Secret Key to the Egyptian Hieroglyphics (cont'd.)

Emblem	Symbolic Meaning
Man with the head of an ass	To never travel or listen to any stories
Mare kicking a wolf	A woman who has aborted
Marten	A woman acting like a man
Mole	To be blind
Monkey urinating	Concealing one's inferiority
Monkey with a little monkey behind him	A man whose heir is a son whom he hates
Moon	The cycle of a full month
Moon (with downward turned horns)	Fifteen waxings of the Moon
Moon (with upward turned horns)	Fifteen wanings of the Moon
Mouse	Concealment, disappearance, and discrimination
Mouth	Complete taste
Mule	Barren woman
Night owl	Death
Number 5	Fate as five great stars
Number 12	The months of the year
Number 15	The waxing (and waning of the Moon)
Number 16	Pleasure, sexual stirring of adolescence
Number 28	The moon traversing the Zodiac
Number 29	The birth of this world, the union of the Sun and Moon
Number 30	Days of the month
Number 32	Copulation as two 16's (male and female sexual pleasure)
Number 72	Seventy-two ancient countries of the world, number of days for a baboon to die
Number 120	Cycle of preparing for intercourse, for gestation, and for feeding the young for the vulture
Number 500	Years a phoenix lives
Number 1095	Three years of silence
Octopus	To squander badly, to feed lavishly on another's food and later secretly devour one's own food
Origanum (herb)	Absence of ants
Oryx	Impurity

Secret Key to the Egyptian Hieroglyphics (cont'd.)

Emblem	Symbolic Meaning
Ostrich wing	To distribute justice equally
Owl	Foreknowledge (of an abundant harvest of wine)
Owl and maiden hair	To be harmed by an excess of wine and to cure oneself by abstinence
Oyster and crab	To be careless of one's own welfare, but to be provided for
Oysters big with young	Man yoked to a woman
Partridges (pair)	Pederasty
Pelican	Fool, foolishness
Penis pressed by hand	Temperance
Phoenix	The soul delaying on earth a long time, return of the long absent traveler, the Sun who looks down on all things, long enduring restoration
Pig	Pernicious
Pigeon holding a laurel leaf	A man who has been cured by the answer of an oracle
Pigeon with his hind parts erect	A man without bitterness receiving it from another
Pipes of Pan	To lose one's mind, but later recover one's senses
Quail bone	Permanent and steadfast
Roach caught on a hook	A man punished for murder
Royal stole beside a dog	Judge, magistrate
Salamander	Burned by fire
Scarab	Self-begotten, only begotten, not born of a female
Scarab and vulture	Hermaphrodite
Scarus (a fish)	Glutton
Serpent	The strength of the mouth
Serpent (a complete serpent)	The almighty, creator of all
Serpent biting its tail with variegated scales	The cosmos, universe

Secret Key to the Egyptian Hieroglyphics (cont'd.)

Emblem	Symbolic Meaning
Serpent biting its tail with the name of a king written in the middle of its coils	A powerful king who rules the cosmos
Serpent cut in half	A king who rules only part of the empire
Serpent emerging out of shed skin	To be made young again, to be reborn
Serpent in a state of watchfulness	King as guardian
Serpent of gold on the head of the gods and goddesses	Eternity
Serpent's scales	The stars of heaven
Serpent's skin shed	Old age
Serpent upon whose back is a great palace	The king as a cosmic ruler
Seven letters surrounded by two fingers	A muse, the infinite, fate
Shark	To vomit and then again eat one's own fill
She-bear big with cubs	To be deformed, but grow up normal
Sheep and goats grazing on flea-bane	A man who slays sheep and goats
Signed book	The very old
Smoke rising skyward	Fire
Snare	Love
Solar disk cut in two with stars	Pregnant woman
Sparrow and dogfish	To flee one's patron and remain without aid
Sparrow on fire	A fecund man
Spine	Masculinity, the loins, sperm
Spiny lobster and octopus	A man ruling over his fellow citizens
Squid	To yearn for what is right, but fall in with evil
Star	God, twilight, night, time, man's soul, fate, the number five
Stork	Filial affection, gratitude

Secret Key to the Egyptian Hieroglyphics (cont'd.)

Emblem	Symbolic Meaning
Straight line super-imposed on another	The number ten
Sun and Moon	Eternity
Sun and Moon conjoined	Birth of the world, the 29th day
Swallow	Entire wealth of parents left to children
Swan	To love music (in old age)
Thunder	Distant voice
Tongue and bloodshot eye	Speech, command
Tongue between teeth	Incomplete taste
Turtledove	To love dance and music
Two men greeting	Unanimity
Vulture	Sight, foreknowledge, pity, boundaries, the cycle of a year sacred to Athene (as the sky) or to Hera (as the earth)
Vulture upon an Egyptian crown	The mother, all goddesses, the woman as heaven
Viper	A wife who hates her husband, a child who hates its mother
Vulpanser (bird)	Father and mother sacrificing all for the life of their child
Wasp in flight	Murder
Weasel	A weak man unable to take care for himself
Wolf and stone	To be afraid of what may happen from invisible causes
Wolf turning back	Escape
Wolf who has lost the tip of his tail	To be assailed by the enemy, but delivered after small harm
Words and leaves	The very old
Worms (maggots)	A swarm (of gnats)

Ninth Key

Runes

Overview

The runes of Northern Europe represent a pristine Western magickal system independent of Eastern influences. When I first began my research for this chapter, the wealth of new material in English on the rune tradition (especially the elegant analysis of Stephen Flowers) had yet to appear in print. In the absence of these recent runic commentaries, I was forced to turn my attention towards more traditional, scholarly commentaries, which were at best sparse concerning occult information.

As my runic research progressed, I encountered two major obstacles that almost forced me to stop work on this chapter:

- No record of a true number code for the runes has survived

- More importantly, no wealth of original runic words and their meanings have survived

However, as I continued to pursue the number pattern which may govern the runic alphabets, I discovered that most commentators perceived the serial order of the alphabet to be the true number code for the runes. Therefore, I have adapted this numbering method to each variant system of runes. The serial order number code for an alphabet may have been the most readily accessible number pattern for the ancient world. Esoteric languages which possess this serial order code include:

- Tibetan

- Sanskrit (variant)

- Hebrew (variant)

- Homeric Greek

- Latin

Some commentators on number languages have felt that a serial order code is not a valid alphanumeric code, because the resultant number values of any given word would invariably fall to the low end of the range of numbers. The Latin serial order, for instance, numbers most Latin terms in a range spanning 1 to 300. In my own initial research, I felt that, since a specific serial code could not number individual words into the thousands (which languages such as classical Greek are capable of numbering), then that code must somehow be invalid. Yet as my studies progressed to encompass more and more number language codes, I made the fundamental discovery that some codes were devised to flesh out the low range of numbers (such as the serial order for Latin), while other codes were crafted to capture the very high range of number metaphors (such as the Sanskrit ARYaBhaTa code which numbers individual words into the quadrillions). The point I want to emphasize here is that the only way to obtain a complete picture of all the metaphors for the infinite number range is by numbering every existing number language by every conceivable code available. That is the main purpose I have in devising this book, to serve as the necessary reference tool which can unlock all number metaphors through all alphanumeric languages.

The development of the runic tradition in Europe created four distinct runic alphabets (each with its own range of numbers and symbols). These traditions are:

- The Germanic Elder "Futhark" of 24 runes (200 BCE–200 CE)

- The Anglo-Saxon "Futhork" of 33 runes (500–1000 CE)

- The Younger "Futhark" of 16 runes (including Danish, Norwegian, Swedish, and Icelandic variants) (600–1200 CE)

- The modern German Armanen of 18 runes (20th-century variant)

All of the above systems are clearly delineated in this ninth key. Again, since during my initial research I did not have recourse to the wealth of modern runic commentaries, I turned my attention to the surviving runic poems, which delineate the bare skeleton of authentic symbolism for the ancient runes.

The first runic system discussed in this section is the Germanic Elder "Futhark." The name "Futhark" is derived from the first six runes of this system (F, U, Th, A, R, K). This proto-runic alphabet was composed of 24 letters in three groups of eight letters (8 + 8 + 8). This grouping immediately brings to mind the 24-letter Greek alphabet (an alphabet which Julius Caesar found similar to the shapes of the Germanic runes). The table entitled "The Elder Futhark Runes" (the all-Germanic runic staves), attempts to imbue a runic number value based on both the Homeric and Pythagorean Greek alphabet number values. This table is divided into:

- The original name
- Its transliteration
- The German letter name
- The meaning of the letter
- The Greek model for the letter (not based on phonetic equivalent but rather on the 8 + 8 + 8 division of both alphabets)
- The corresponding serial order value (based on Homeric Greek)
- A conjectured number value based on the Pythagorean Greek values (range of 1–800)

This last (Pythagorean) number value is my own innovation; every other text which fixes a number value for these runes utilizes the serial order (shown in [6] above). Using the Greek alphabet correlations I was also able to fix an astrological nature for these 24 runes. This reconstruction is shown in the chart entitled "Astrological Attributes of the Runes."

Next the 33-letter Anglo-Saxon alphabet is analyzed. The table entitled "Anglo-Saxon Futhork Runes" gives the basic attributes as:

- The rune itself
- The letter name
- The transliteration
- The number value based on serial order
- The "Old English Rune Poem" metaphors

After a brief discussion of the Anglo-Saxon runic tradition, the four variants of the "Younger Futhark" are analyzed in light of both the ancient Norwegian and Icelandic rune poems. This Younger Futhark runes table lays out the 16 runic letter attributes as:

- The Danish common letter
- The Norwegian shortened letter
- The transliteration
- The Danish letter name
- The parallel number order from the Elder Futhark
- The Younger Futhark serial order
- The imagery from the Norwegian rune poem
- The imagery from the Icelandic rune poem

Next follows the only surviving historical example of the runic alphabet as calendrical numbers. In the text *Fasti Danci*, first recorded in 1328 CE, the 16 runes of the Younger Futhark were combined with three additional (non-runic) symbols to create a calendrical system whereby each of the 365 days of the year could be equated to one or more runic letters. In this system the runic letter "A" was given its older equivalent of "O" (from Futhork runes). In addition, the 14th and 15th letters were reversed from their normal order of ML to a revised order of LM. This runic calendrical method is fully worked out in this section so that you can convert your own birth date (or any other significant date) to its appropriate runic symbol. For the example given in the text, I have utilized my own birth date of December 11, which by this system encodes the key runic number 13.

This discussion concludes with a brief analysis of the modern German school of 18 Armanen runes. Much has recently been written on the esoteric symbolism of these runes. However, when I first penned this chapter nothing had yet seen print. I therefore followed the clue that this revision of the runes was based on the 18 rune-charms described in the ancient runic poem, the *Havamal*. As such, I reconstructed these attributes based on this Norse poem, as well as a runic chart called The World-Rune Clock devised by Werner von Bulow. After I had typed this chapter, I was exposed to Stephen Flowers' translation of Guido Von List's *Secret of the Runes;* the associations I had premised turned out to be correct.

This ninth key, as sparse as it is, contains an addendum. This addendum details the parallel Celtic alphabets of Ogham and Beth-Luis-Nion to the rune tradition.

The Ogham alphabet is composed of 20 characters. These letters resemble the niche marks of a tally rather than individual letters. Like the runic tradition, very few words in Ogham have survived (since the most common media to inscribe Ogham was perishable wood rather than stone). Most of my research on Ogham concentrated on late 19th-century academic journals specializing in the Celtic tradition. I also depended greatly upon the in-depth research of R.A. McCallister, as well as Robert Graves.

Unlike the runes, a record of a number code for the Ogham alphabet survives in the form of *The Book of Ballymote*. The number values shown in this book are based on the serial order of the alphabet (which also seems to be the true manner for numbering each of the runic variants). Ogham dates back to 300 BCE. Since so few examples have survived, this system may be even older.

The discussion begins with a chart showing the actual Ogham alphabet. There are 20 basic alphabet characters (15 consonants and 5 vowels), as well as five additional characters later developed to capture foreign phonetic sounds. This is followed by the Ogham mudras, or hand postures, which conceal each of the 25 characters. After this hand alphabet, the two basic number values for Ogham are tabled out. The first number value is the serial order as recorded in *The Book of Ballymote*. This code is the established value for Ogham. The second number value is my own innovation, based on the composite strokes required to incise each character (into wood or stone).

Each letter from the Ogham alphabet, like its variant Beth-Luis-Nion, was ultimately linked to a tree. As such, both alphabets were referred to as "Tree" alphabets. The corresponding tree for each Ogham letter is shown in the table entitled "Ogham Tree Alphabet." The letter name for each of these characters is also listed in this table.

Each of the Ogham characters contained a wealth of symbolic poetic imagery. Examples of this poetic vocabulary are shown in the table "Ogham Symbolic Poetic Vocabulary." Each of the 20 basic letters can be symbolized as:

- A color

- A bird

- A saint

- A division of the year

- Categories of family

- Categories of women

- Categories of water

- Categories of dogs

Thus if any of the above imagery was incorporated into a bardic poem, it would secretly connote a letter of the alphabet.

The other Celtic alphabet was the Druidic Beth-Luis-Nion (named after its first three letters of BLN). This alphabet of 13 consonants and 5 vowels resembles both Latin and Greek rather than the runic or Ogham characters. Their symbolic attributes, as well as their secret number values, are shown in the table "Druidic B-L-N Alphabet." This table describes each of the letters as the:

- Original alphabet script

- Transliteration

- Irish letter name

- Latin letter name

- Symbolic tree

- Lunar cycle

- Number value

Surprisingly, the number scheme for Beth-Luis-Nion (which is not linear) encodes the key Qabalistic number of 32. There are no less than six number patterns woven into the order of the BLN alphabet that encode the sacred number 32, the number of divisions to the Qabalistic universe known as the Tree of Life. Since the BLN alphabet is based on the symbolism of trees, and since Irish Celtic artwork, such as *The Book of Kells,* uses the Tree of Life as a recurring motif, there may be a secret Celtic tradition which tapped directly into the Hebraic cosmological model of the 32-tiered Tree of Life.

This addendum ends with phonetic comparison between the BLF Ogham alphabet, the BLN alphabet, the runes alphabet, and their Greek alphabet model. In light of their phonetic equivalents, the corresponding Greek number values are also given.

As pointed out above, there are currently on the market many new texts available to the student describing the esoteric nature of the runic tradition. These should be consulted for a deeper understanding of this tradition. But this overview is free of any modern innovation or interpretation and can be relied upon to present the authentic, historical symbolic meanings for the runic tradition.

ORIGIN

Prior to 200 BCE—Pure symbols (such as the Sun-wheel or swastika) are inscribed on stone and wood; these will serve as a source for the 24 proto-characters of the Elder Futhark rune system.

200 BCE–200 CE—The all-Germanic runic staves, known as the Elder "FUThARK" of 24 characters, are adapted from the religious and magickal symbols inscribed in stone and wood.

500–1000 CE—The Germanic rune alphabet of 24 characters is expanded in England to the Anglo Saxon "FUThORK" of 33 characters. At the end of this period, the "Old English Rune Poem" was devised, which provided metaphorical imagery for the first 29 of 33 runes.

600–1000 CE—The Danish adaption of the Germanic Elder FUThARK, reduces the 24-character alphabet to 16 characters, referred to as the Younger "FUThARK." These Danish runes are referred to as the common or square runes.

1000–1200 CE—The Danish Younger FUThARK is transmitted to Norway and Sweden. The alphabet remains at 16 characters, but the Danish square script is replaced by the Norwegian-Swedish cursive script known as the "Short Twig" Runes.

1200–1300 CE—The "Norwegian Rune Poem" is written, encoding in poetical metaphor the alphabet imagery of the 16-character "Short Twig" Runes.

1328 CE—The Norse calendrical system is created using the 16-character Younger FUThARK plus three additional symbols. This system is eventually published in 1643 CE as *Fasti Danci of the Elder Worm*.

1400 CE—The Icelandic version of the Rune Poem is written based on the 16 square Danish runes of the Younger FUThARK.

1908 CE—The publication of Guido von List's *Secret of the Runes* is the first systematic attempt to record the German revival of the secret meaning behind the runes. The occult symbolism of the modern Armanen Futhark of 18 characters is discussed at length. This modern rune system would find its ultimate application in Adolf Kummer's *Holy Rune Power*, published in 1932.

ALPHABET CODE

Even as the ninth Tarot Key represents light obscured by darkness, so is this ninth key of the runes. In all the esoteric traditions explored in this book, this path and this key are the most recondite.

The word "rune" means whisper, mystery, secret wisdom, that which is communicated orally. As such, the runes have a purely magickal import in their origin. Prior to 200 BCE, certain symbols such as the swastika and cross were engraved in rocks in Northern Europe for ritualist purposes.

These purely magickal symbols were melded with the impact of Italian and Greek alphabets moving northward from the Mediterranean. The resultant alphabet was the proto-German rune alphabet known as the Elder FUThARK (Futhark being the first six letters of the alphabet).

The number of letters was 24, resembling the number of letters in the Greek alphabet (during the period 200 BCE). The Elder Futhark was divided into three families or groups of eight letters each, forming the number pattern of 8 + 8 + 8, the same division into which the Greek alphabet was divided to reveal the numerical value of the Greek "Thoth" as 888 (ὁ θωθ = 888). By this division the runes parallel the Homeric number code for Greek.

Julius Caesar in his *Gallic Wars* commented that the alphabet of the Gauls (the runes) resembled Greek. This indeed seems to be the language which can unlock the number code for the runes, although no surviving code exists for the Elder Futhark.

If the three rune groups of "Fehu," "Hagalaz," and "Teiwaz" parallel the three groups of eight letters found in the Homeric number code, two distinct number values can be assigned to the 24 runes. These two values are the sequential number value of Homer (1–8, 9–16, and 17–24) and the parallel Pythagorean values for these 24 letters (1–9 [excluding 6], 10–80, and 100–800). The alphabet code is shown on the following page.

The Elder Futhark Runes (The All-Germanic Runic Staves)

Runes	Trans-literation	Germanic Letter Name	Meaning of Letter	Greek Model of 24 letters	Number Value: Homeric (serial order)	Number Value: Pythagorean
1st Family of 8				**1st Set of 8**		
ᚠ	F	Fehu	Cattle, possessions	A	1	1
ᚢ	U	Uruz	Strength, wild ox	B	2	2
ᚦ	Th	Thurisaz	Thorn, giant, gate	G	3	3
ᚨ	A	Ansuz	God, mouth, signal	D	4	4
ᚱ	R	Raido	Journey	E	5	5
ᚲ	K	Kaunaz	Torch, opening	Z	6	7
ᚷ	G	Gebo	Gift (from the Gods), partnership	H	7	8
ᚹ	W	Wunjo	Joy	Th	8	9
2nd Family of 8				**2nd Set of 8**		
ᚺ	H	Hagalaz	Hail, sleet, disruption	I	9	10
ᚾ	N	Nauthiz	Need, constraint	K	10	20
ᛁ	I	Isa	Ice, freezing, standstill	L	11	30
ᛃ	J	Jera	Harvest, year	M	12	40
ᛇ	Ei	Eihwaz	Yew tree, rune stave, calendar	N	13	50
ᛈ	P	Perth	Secret, initiation	X	14	60
ᛉ	Z	Algiz	Elk, protection, defense	O	15	70
ᛊ	S	Sowelu	Sun	P	16	80

The Elder Futhark Runes (The All-Germanic Runic Staves) (cont'd.)

Runes 3rd Family of 8	Trans- literation	Germanic Letter Name	Meaning of Letter	Greek Model of 24 letters 3rd Set of 8	Number Value	
					Homeric (serial order)	Pythagorean
	T	Teiwaz	Spear, Mars, warrior, pole-star	R	17	100
	B	Berkana	Birch, tree	S	18	200
	E	Ehwaz	Horse, course of sun, movement	T	19	300
	M	Mannaz	Man, human race, self	U	20	400
	L	Laguz	Water, sea	Ph	21	500
	Ng	Inguz	Hero, fertility	Ch	22	600
	D	Dagaz	Day, light, breakthrough	Ps	23	700
	O	Othila	Home, possessions, retreat	Ō	24	800

The number value of any given word is obtained by adding together the values of each letter. Two codes can be used, either the Homeric, valued between 1 and 24, or the Pythagorean, valued between 1 and 800.

Astrological values can also be assigned to these 24 runes, derived directly from their Greek model (based on *Soma Sophia*, The Body of Wisdom).

Astrological Attributions of the Runes

Rune	Astrological Symbol (Zodiac)
F, O	Aries
U, D	Taurus
Th, Ng	Gemini
A, L	Cancer
R, M	Leo
K, E	Virgo
G, B	Libra
W, T	Scorpio
H, S	Sagittarius
N, Z	Capricorn
I, P	Aquarius
J, Ei	Pisces

	(Planets)
F	Moon, Saturn
R	Mercury, Jupiter
G	Venus, Mars
H	Sun
Z	Mars, Venus
M	Jupiter, Mercury
O	Saturn, Moon

The first revision of the Elder Futhark occured when these runes reached the Anglo-Saxon culture around 500 CE.

From 500 to 900 CE, the Anglo-Saxon rune alphabet expanded the Elder Futhark from 24 characters to 33. The 25th through 29th added letters were all complex vowel intonations to adapt the German phonetic range to Old English.

One of the best surviving records of the symbolic meanings for the runes comes from Anglo-Saxon sources in the form of the Old English Rune Poem (first written around 1000 CE). This poem detailed a poetic meaning for the first 29 of 33 Anglo-Saxon runes. Later this poem was also rewritten in light of both the Norwegian and Icelandic rune traditions.

The table below details the Anglo-Saxon FUThORK runes. The rune, letter name, transliteration, and serial order are given, as well as the symbolic meanings for each rune derived from the Old English Rune Poem.

Anglo-Saxon Futhork Runes

Rune	Letter Name	Trans- literation	Serial Order	Old English Rune Poem Metaphors
ᚠ	feoh	F	1	Wealth as a comfort to man, which must be bestowed freely in order to gain honor
ᚢ	ur	U	2	The great savage aurochs who fight with their horns
ᚦ	thorn	Th	3	The exceedingly sharp thorn which is evil to the touch of a warrior
ᚩ	os	O	4	The mouth as the source of all language and wisdom
ᚱ	rad	R	5	The warrior's journey, which is easy to contemplate but difficult to traverse
ᚳ	cen	K	6	The pale bright flame of the torch which illuminates the king's castle
ᚷ	gyfu	G	7	The gift bestowed on the needy, giving credit, honor, and dignity
ᚹ	wynn	W	8	Joy (bliss) which knows not suffering, sorrow, or anxiety
ᚻ	haegl	H	9	Hail as the whitest grain, which is whirled from the heavens, tossed by the winds, and melted into water
ᚾ	nyd	N	10	Trouble, which at once oppresses the heart, yet serves in its constraint as a source of salvation for those who perceive its true value
ᛁ	is	I	11	Very cold and slippery ice, clear as glass and gem-like
ᛄ	ger	J	12	The harvest, when God suffers the earth to produce fruit and vegetables for rich and poor alike
ᛇ	eoh	E	13	The yew tree, with its rough bark and strong roots, as a guardian of fire

Anglo-Saxon Futhork Runes (cont'd.)

Rune	Letter Name	Trans- literation	Serial Order	Old English Rune Poem Metaphors
	peordh	P	14	The chessmen on a chessboard as a source of recreation and amusement (and initiation) for the warriors
	eolh	Z	15	The elk-sedge, a marsh plant which cuts and draws blood on every warrior who touches it
	sigil	S	16	The Sun, which guides all fishermen back to land from their journey over the ocean
	tir	T	17	The planet Mars (or polestar) as a guiding star that never fails to keep its course over the mists of the night
	beorc	B	18	The birch tree, which bears no fruit, yet is generated without seed from its leaves, whose branches form a heavenly crown
	eh	Eh	19	The warrior's horse, whose pride is in its hoofs, a joy to man
	mann	M	20	Man, who is dear to his kin, but doomed to the grave by the Lord
	lagu	L	21	The unending depths of the ocean, whose waves terrify all who ride them and cannot be bridled
	ing	Ng	22	The hero or leader Yng of the Danish royal family, who moved ever eastward
	ethel	Oe	23	The home, which is the source of all prosperity and happiness for man
	daeg	D	24	God's glorious light of day, which gives hope to all
	ac	Ai	25	The sacred oak, fodder for pigs and noble timber for ships on spear-sharp seas
	aesc	Ae	26	The ash tree, wrought as a shield which protects man from all attacks

Anglo-Saxon Futhork Runes (cont'd.)

Rune	Letter Name	Trans-literation	Serial Order	Old English Rune Poem Metaphors
ᚣ	yr	Ye	27	The axe (or bow and arrow), as reliable weaponry on horseback
ᛡ	ior	Io	28	The beaver, who hunts for food on land and dwells within the waters of the river
ᛠ	ear	Ea	29	The grave, horrible to every warrior, the cool dust of the earth as his bedfellow, marking the decline of all
ᛢ	cweorp	Q	30	The fire-stick whose twirlings kindle the sacred fire
ᛣ	calc	C	31	The cup containing the ritual draught
ᛥ	stan	St	32	The stone which is hewn as an altar
ᚸ	gar	Gh	33	The war spear used by the great warrior God, Odin

(Note: the metaphors for the 30th through 33rd letters are not found in the Old English Rune Poem but are derived from the meaning of their letter names.)

The second revision of the Elder Futhark occurred when the runic tradition was imported into the Danish, Norwegian, and Swedish cultures.

The Danes reduced the Elder Futhark from 24 runes to 16 (in contrast to the Anglo-Saxon expansion of the runes) around 600 CE. These 16 runes were referred to as the Younger Futhark. As the Danish runes, known as common or square runes, moved eastward into Norway and Sweden, the shape of the square Younger Futhark became shortened, developing into a variant simplified script in Norway around 1000 CE. This variant Norwegian rune script was referred to as the "Short Twigs" runes to distinguish it from the Danish "Common" runes.

By 1200 CE, a Norwegian version of the Anglo-Saxon Rune Poem was written to describe the reduced 16 letters of the Younger Futhark. This was followed around 1400 CE with an Icelandic version of the Rune Poem.

The table on the following pages illustrates the Younger Futhark runes as follows.

1. The Danish Common rune form
2. The shortened Norwegian Short Twig rune form
3. The transliteration
4. The Danish letter name
5. The serial order of the Elder Futhark model for each letter of the revised Younger Futhark
6. The number value, recorded in a secret calendrical code of the 14th century
7. The poetic image found in the Norwegian Rune Poem
8. The poetic image found in the Icelandic Rune Poem

The Younger Futhark Runes
(Danish, Norwegian, Swedish, Icelandic)

Rune		3. Trans-literation	4. Danish Letter Name	5. Number Order from Elder Futhark	6. Number Value from Serial Order	7. Norwegian Rune Poem	8. Icelandic Rune Poem
1. Danish	2. Norwegian						
ᚠ	ᚠ	F	Fe	1	1	Wealth as a source of discord among men, a wolf living in a forest	Wealth as a source of discord among kinsmen, a fire on a sea, the path of the serpent
ᚢ	ᚢ	U	Ur	2	2	Dross from bad iron, a reindeer racing over frozen snow	Shower, as tears from a cloud, ruining the harvest and an abomination to the shepherd
ᚦ	ᚦ	Th	Thurs	3	3	A giant who terrifies women, and causes misfortune to men	A cliff-dwelling giant, a husband of a giantess, who tortures women

The Younger Futhark Runes (cont'd.)

| Rune | | 3. Trans-literation | 4. Danish Letter Name | 5. Number Order from Elder Futhark | 6. Number Value from Serial Order | 7. Norwegian Rune Poem | 8. Icelandic Rune Poem |
1. Danish	2. Norwegian						
ᛆ	ᛆ	A	Ass	4	4	Estuary as the way of most journeys, the scabbard as the way of the sword	God as the aged Gawtr, the Prince of Asgard and the Lord of Valhalla
ᚱ	ᚱ	R	Reidh	5	5	Riding a horse, which is the worst thing for a horse, the letter R—the initial of Reginn the forger of the finest swords	Riding a horse, a speedy journey, joy to the horseman, toil to the horse
ᚴ	ᚴ	K	Kaun	6	6	Ulcer, fatal to children, the pale corpse of death	Ulcer, disease fatal to children, a painful spot which is mortifying
ᚼ	ᚼ	H	Hagall	9	7	Hail as the coldest of grain; Christ as the creator of the Old World	Hail as cold grain, a shower of sleet, sickness for serpents
ᚾ	ᚾ	N	Naudhr	10	8	Constraint which does not allow a choice; a naked man chilled by the frost	Constraint which is grief to the bondmaid, a state of oppression and toilsome work

The Younger Futhark Runes (cont'd.)

Rune		3. Trans-literation	4. Danish Letter Name	5. Number Order from Elder Futhark	6. Number Value from Serial Order	7. Norwegian Rune Poem	8. Icelandic Rune Poem
1. Danish	2. Norwegian						
—	—	I	Iss	11	9	The broad bridge of ice; the leading of a blind man	Ice as a bark of rivers, roof of waves and destruction of the doomed
ᛅ	ᛆ	Ā	Ar	12	10	Plenty as a boon to man, symbolized by the generous Danish King Frothi	Plenty as a boon to man, symbolized in good summers and thriving crops
ᛋ	ᛌ	S	Sol	16	11	The Sun as the light of the world, which all bow to in accord with the divine	The Sun as a shield of the clouds and a shining ray which melts ice
↑	ᛏ	T	Tyr	17	12	Mars as the one-handed god of the forge whose one hand strikes the anvil	The God of one hand, the leavings of the wolf, the prince of the temple

The Younger Futhark Runes (cont'd.)

Rune: 1. Danish	Rune: 2. Norwegian	3. Transliteration	4. Danish Letter Name	5. Number Order from Elder Futhark	6. Number Value from Serial Order	7. Norwegian Rune Poem	8. Icelandic Rune Poem
ᛒ	ᛓ	B	Bjarkan	18	13	The birch tree which has the greenest leaves of any tree; Lok—who was lucky in his deceit (of Balder's death)	The birch tree which is a leafy twig, a little tree, and a fresh young shrub
ᛘ	ᛙ	M	Madhr	20	14	Man as an addition to the dust of the earth; the great claw of the hawk	Man as the joyous man, an augmentation of the earth; an adorner of ships
ᛚ	ᛚ	L	Logr	21	15	A waterfall as a river falling from a mountainside; ornaments of gold	Water as an eddying stream, a broad geyser and the land of fish
ᛦ	ᛧ	Y	Yr	13	16	Yew as the greenest tree in winter, which won't crackle when it burns	The Yew tree as a strong bent bow, brittle as iron and possessing a giant arrow

Although for most of the rune alphabets there is no surviving record of an alphabet-number code, there is one substantial record of the Norse runes used as numbers. This record dates from 1328 CE and is found in Elder Worm's *Fasti Danci*, published in 1643 CE. In this work, the 16 runes known as the Younger Futhark and three additional symbols are used to designate calendrical dates. These 19 calendric rune-numbers have five basic shapes. The following table shows these five shapes. The simple rune shape, a mirror-image-like variant of this shape, a tree or cross notched, a stylized version of the tree-cross, and a grouping of dots and crosses.

Norse Calendrical Rune Number Code
Rune Calendrical Golden Number Series, 1–19

Number Value	Rune		Variant Image	Number Crosses	Trees and Hooks	Dots and Crosses
1	F	ᚠ				•
2	U	ᚢ				• •
3	Th	ᚦ				• • •
4	O					• • / •
5	R	ᚱ				∧
6	K					∧
7	H	✳				∧
8	N					∧
9	I					∧
10	A					✝
11	S					✝
12	T	↑				✝

Alphabet of 16 Letters

Norse Calendrical Rune Number Code (cont'd.)

Number Value	Rune		Variant Image	Number Crosses	Trees and Hooks	Dots and Crosses
13	B	ᛒ				
14	L					
15	M					
16	Y					
17	(Three Symbols)					
18						
19						

This runic chronogram system represented a calendar date by two basic methods:

1. As a composite number including month, day, and year

2. As a secret key number between 1 and 364

The first method is similar to our own method of representing a date as numbers. The date October 12th by this rune method would be represented as the numbers 10 (for October) and 12 (for the 12th). Thus by the rune calendric number table, October 12th would be represented as the two letters A and T. For a day-date beyond 19, two letters would be combined. Thus the 31st day of a month would be represented by the letters Th (3) and F (1) conjoined as one: ThF. Since there is no zero symbol in this system, zeros in any date could not be represented. Thus 20 must be symbolized by 2.

This digital-letter method date symbolism extended to year notation as well. Thus the date 1378 could be encoded as follows:

- BHN (13 + 7 + 8), or

- FThHN (1 + 3 + 7 + 8)

The second method for Norse calendrical cryptography concerned itself only with the 365 days of any given year (leap year was not encoded into this system). This method is known as the "key" date and ascribes a number from 1 to 364 for each day of the year. However, this system numbers the days of the year backwards from December 24th (the last date in the Norse year). The number of days between the date intended to be encoded and December 24th inclusive is counted. This tallied number is the secret key number for that specific day. Using the table of 19 rune-numbers, this key number is then reduced to the letters of the alphabet.

As an example of this method, the date December 11th will be numbered as a secret key number:

- December 11th is 13 days from December 24th (24 − 11 = 13).

- Therefore the secret key number for this date is 13.

- By the runes table, 13 can be expressed in two ways, as B or FTh.

- Therefore the secret key for December 11th is 13 as B or FTh.

The following table gives the key number for each of the 365 days of the year:

Rune Key Numbers for the Year

Number	Day of Year	Number	Day of Year	Number	Day of Year
0*	December 24	20	December 4	40	November 14
1	December 23	21	December 3	41	November 13
2	December 22	22	December 2	42	November 12
3	December 21	23	December 1	43	November 11
4	December 20	24	November 30	44	November 10
5	December 19	25	November 29	45	November 9
6	December 18	26	November 28	46	November 8
7	December 17	27	November 27	47	November 7
8	December 16	28	November 26	48	November 6
9	December 15	29	November 25	49	November 5
10	December 14	30	November 24	50	November 4
11	December 13	31	November 23	51	November 3
12	December 12	32	November 22	52	November 2
13	December 11	33	November 21	53	November 1
14	December 10	34	November 20	54	October 31
15	December 9	35	November 19	55	October 30
16	December 8	36	November 18	56	October 29
17	December 7	37	November 17	57	October 28
18	December 6	38	November 16	58	October 27
19	December 5	39	November 15	59	October 26

*No key

Rune Key Numbers for the Year (cont'd)

Number	Day of Year	Number	Day of Year	Number	Day of Year
60	October 25	97	September 18	134	August 12
61	October 24	98	September 17	135	August 11
62	October 23	99	September 16	136	August 10
63	October 22	100	September 15	137	August 9
64	October 21	101	September 14	138	August 8
65	October 20	102	September 13	139	August 7
66	October 19	103	September 12	140	August 6
67	October 18	104	September 11	141	August 5
68	October 17	105	September 10	142	August 4
69	October 16	106	September 9	143	August 3
70	October 15	107	September 8	144	August 2
71	October 14	108	September 7	145	August 1
72	October 13	109	September 6	146	July 31
73	October 12	110	September 5	147	July 30
74	October 11	111	September 4	148	July 29
75	October 10	112	September 3	149	July 28
76	October 9	113	September 2	150	July 27
77	October 8	114	September 1	151	July 26
78	October 7	115	August 31	152	July 25
79	October 6	116	August 30	153	July 24
80	October 5	117	August 29	154	July 23
81	October 4	118	August 28	155	July 22
82	October 3	119	August 27	156	July 21
83	October 2	120	August 26	157	July 20
84	October 1	121	August 25	158	July 19
85	September 30	122	August 24	159	July 18
86	September 29	123	August 23	160	July 17
87	September 28	124	August 22	161	July 16
88	September 27	125	August 21	162	July 15
89	September 26	126	August 20	163	July 14
90	September 25	127	August 19	164	July 13
91	September 24	128	August 18	165	July 12
92	September 23	129	August 17	166	July 11
93	September 22	130	August 16	167	July 10
94	September 21	131	August 15	168	July 9
95	September 20	132	August 14	169	July 8
96	September 19	133	August 13	170	July 7

Rune Key Numbers for the Year (cont'd)

Number	Day of Year	Number	Day of Year	Number	Day of Year
171	July 6	208	May 30	245	April 23
172	July 5	209	May 29	246	April 22
173	July 4	210	May 28	247	April 21
174	July 3	211	May 27	248	April 20
175	July 2	212	May 26	249	April 19
176	July 1	213	May 25	250	April 18
177	June 30	214	May 24	251	April 17
178	June 29	215	May 23	252	April 16
179	June 28	216	May 22	253	April 15
180	June 27	217	May 21	254	April 14
181	June 26	218	May 20	255	April 13
182	June 25	219	May 19	256	April 12
183	June 24	220	May 18	257	April 11
184	June 23	221	May 17	258	April 10
185	June 22	222	May 16	259	April 9
186	June 21	223	May 15	260	April 8
187	June 20	224	May 14	261	April 7
188	June 19	225	May 13	262	April 6
189	June 18	226	May 12	263	April 5
190	June 17	227	May 11	264	April 4
191	June 16	228	May 10	265	April 3
192	June 15	229	May 9	266	April 2
193	June 14	230	May 8	267	April 1
194	June 13	231	May 7	268	March 31
195	June 12	232	May 6	269	March 30
196	June 11	233	May 5	270	March 29
197	June 10	234	May 4	271	March 28
198	June 9	235	May 3	272	March 27
199	June 8	236	May 2	273	March 26
200	June 7	237	May 1	274	March 25
201	June 6	238	April 30	275	March 24
202	June 5	239	April 29	276	March 23
203	June 4	240	April 28	277	March 22
204	June 3	241	April 27	278	March 21
205	June 2	242	April 26	279	March 20
206	June 1	243	April 25	280	March 19
207	May 31	244	April 24	281	March 18

Rune Key Numbers for the Year (cont'd)

Number	Day of Year	Number	Day of Year	Number	Day of Year
282	March 17	310	February 17	338	January 20
283	March 16	311	February 16	339	January 19
284	March 15	312	February 15	340	January 18
285	March 14	313	February 14	341	January 17
286	March 13	314	February 13	342	January 16
287	March 12	315	February 12	343	January 15
288	March 11	316	February 11	344	January 14
289	March 10	317	February 10	345	January 13
290	March 9	318	February 9	346	January 12
291	March 8	319	February 8	347	January 11
292	March 7	320	February 7	348	January 10
293	March 6	321	February 6	349	January 9
294	March 5	322	February 5	350	January 8
295	March 4	323	February 4	351	January 7
296	March 3	324	February 3	352	January 6
297	March 2	325	February 2	353	January 5
298	March 1	326	February 1	354	January 4
299	February 28	327	January 31	355	January 3
300	February 27	328	January 30	356	January 2
301	February 26	329	January 29	357	January 1
302	February 25	330	January 28	358	December 31
303	February 24	331	January 27	359	December 30
304	February 23	332	January 26	360	December 29
305	February 22	333	January 25	361	December 28
306	February 21	334	January 24	362	December 27
307	February 20	335	January 23	363	December 26
308	February 19	336	January 22	364	December 25
309	February 18	337	January 21		

The final revision of the rune order appeared early in the 20th century in Germany. Guido von List, the prime mover in the German revival of early folk history, had a deep fascination with the symbolism of both the ancient runes and the surviving Masonic symbols which concealed these runes.

In 1902 von List was blinded for 11 months after recovering from a cataract operation. In this period of blindness, he had a magickal vision which reduced the 24 Elder German runes to a special order of 18 runes. This 18-rune order would be known as the Armanen runes, and they were ordered in such a way that each rune corresponded to one of the 18 rune-charms recorded in the ancient Norse poem, the *Havamal*.

When von List recovered his eyesight, he published his researches in 1903 in the German Theosophical periodical, *Die Gnosis*. He subsequently developed his thesis in *The Secret of the Runes* (1908). His runic insight was avidly developed by other occult writers, reaching its ultimate expression in Adolf Kummer's *Holy Rune Power* (1932), which went so far as to assign a psuedo-yoga posture to each of the 18 Armanen runes.

As reality often parallels mythic content, von List's recovery of the lost rune order while blinded reminds one of Odin's runic initiation, in which after being hung upside down from the World Tree for nine days in darkness, the Elder Futhark rune order was revealed to him.

The table on the following pages lists the skeleton symbolic meanings for the modern German Armanen runes as follows:

1. The rune itself

2. The letter name

3. Transliteration of the rune

4. The number order and value of the revised 18 runes

5. The number order of the model for each rune from the Elder Futhark

6. The rune-charm (or power) for each rune from the *Havamal*

7. The Norse god-form for each rune

8. The division of the Armanen runes into three families of six runes (as 6 + 6 + 6), just as the Elder Futhark was divided into three families of 8 + 8 + 8.

9. The fourfold family that categorizes three sets of four runes out of the total of 18 runes

10. The order of the Zodiac that corresponds to the first 12 runes, from Aries to Pisces

Modern German Armanen Runes

1. Armanen Runes	2. Letter Name	3. Transliteration	4. Number Value	5. Number Order Elder Futhark	6. Rune Charm Havamal
ᚠ	Fa	F	1	1	Help in hours of anguish and trials
ᚢ	Ur	U	2	2	Aid healing (with leeches)
ᚦ	Thorn	Th	3	3	Blunt the weapons of enemies
ᚨ	Os	O	4	4	Break fetters and shackles
ᚱ	Rit	R	5	5	Stop the flight of arrows, spears, stones
ᚲ	Ka	K	6	6	To reverse a spell and turn it on its sender
ᚺ	Hagal	H	7	9	Stop hot flames
ᚾ	Not	N	8	10	Calm hate in the warrior's heart
ᛁ	Is	I	9	11	Calm the winds and seas
ᚨ	Ar	A	10	12	Exorcise spirits from home

Modern German Armanen Runes (cont'd.)

1. Armanen Runes	2. Letter Name	3. Transliteration	4. Number Value	5. Number Order Elder Futhark	6. Rune Charm Havamal
ϟ	Sig	S	11	16	Lead in battle and return unscathed
↑	Tyr	T	12	17	Empower the dead to speak to the living
⍒	Bar	B	13	18	Protect a warrior by casting water
↾	Laf	L	14	21	Name all the Old Ones; Gods and Elves
Y	Man	M	15	20	Odin's gift and power of foresight
⅄	Yr	Y	16	13	Charm and bind the heart of the young
⋎	Eh	E	17	19	To make a young girl not hate you
X	Gibor	G	18	7	To bind your lover in your arms

Modern German Armanen Runes (cont'd.)

1. Armanen Runes	2. Letter Name	Meaning	7. God-Forms	8. Hierarchy of 6 + 6 + 6	9. Fourfold Family	10. Zodiac
ᚠ	Fa	Transitoriness	Alf-heim	God	Father	Aries
ᚢ	Ur	Primordial	Uller	God	Mother	Taurus
ᚦ	Thorn	Thunderbolt	Thorr	God	Engendering	Gemini
ᚩ	Os	The Mouth	Odin	God	Child	Cancer
ᚱ	Rit	Wheel	Ragnarok	God		Leo
ᚲ	Ka	Maiden	Skadi	God		Virgo
ᚺ	Hagal	Introspection	Balder	Man	Father	Libra
ᚾ	Not	Need	Heimdalr	Man	Mother	Scorpio
ᛁ	Is	Will	Freyja	Man	Engendering	Sagittarius
ᛡ	Ar	Solar Light	Forseti	Man	Child	Capricorn
ᛋ	Sig	Victory	Njodhr	Man		Aquarius

Modern German Armanen Runes (cont'd.)

1. Armanen Runes	2. Letter Name	Meaning	7. God-Forms	8. Hierarchy of 6 + 6 + 6	9. Fourfold Family	10. Zodiac
↑	Tyr	Sword	Vidarr	Man		Pisces
ᛒ	Bar	Song	Skirnir	Spirit, Mind	Father	
↑	Laf	Law	Lodhurr	Spirit, Mind	Mother	
Y	Man	Mothering	Midgaardsormr	Spirit, Mind	Engendering	
⅄	Yr	Rainbow	Ymir	Spirit, Mind	Child	
⅄	Eh	Marriage	Loki	Spirit, Mind		
X	Gibor	Gift	Ginnungagap	Spirit, Mind		

ADDENDUM

THE OGHAM ALPHABET

The Celtic magickal tradition of England and Ireland developed an alphabet tradition distinct from the Celtic runes found on the European continent. This alphabet is known as Ogham. The oldest surviving example, found etched in stone, dates back to 300 CE. The name "Ogham" is derived from the mythic inventor of this alphabet, Ogma. Ogma was the son of Elathan and brother of Breas. His full name was Oghaim Ghuaim (Ghuaim meaning wisdom, Ogma meaning sun-faced). Ogma created this alphabet of 20 characters around 200 BCE. Tradition relates that, while Ogma was the father of Ogham, its mother was the hand and knife.

This mother alludes to the two materials required to write this Celtic alphabet, the hand and the knife. As the hand, the alphabet is a secret hand cipher, in which covert hand signals between two individuals could communicate the letters of the Ogham alphabet. As the knife, the alphabet is a secret niche cipher, in which the alphabet is niched into pieces of wood.

The Ogham alphabet is composed of 20 characters divided into four groups of five basic strokes. With the refinement of the alphabet, five additional strokes were added. The basis for all Ogham characters is a horizontal stemline. Upon this line, groups of one to five strokes are laid to indicate the 20 basic characters. The following table delineates these 20 basic Ogham characters and the five additional characters.

Ogham

Letter					
Transliteration	B	L	F	S	N

Letter					
Transliteration	H	D	T	C	Q

Letter					
Transliteration	M	G	Ng	Z	R

Ogham (cont'd.)

Letter					

| Transliteration | A | O | U | E | I |

Five Additional Characters:

Letter						

Transliteration	Ch	Th	P	Ph	X	Punctuation
	(Ea)	(Oi)	(Ui)	(Io)	(Ae)	stop, end of sentence paragraph

Note that the five additional letters have two phonetic values: consonants and conjoined vowels.

As an alphabet carved by a knife, the Ogham alphabet can for the most part be easily niched into the edge of any piece of wood. Ogham rods, used especially for open communication rather than concealment, were planed into square-edged rods, to allow four surfaces to carve the Ogham script. The stemline of the script represents the edge of the wood; the upper side of the markings is the left, the lower side is the right.

As an alphabet signaled by the hand, the stemline of the alphabet became the ridgeline of the nose, arm, leg, or any object available. One to five fingers were laid upon this ridgeline to designate the various Ogham characters. The upper side of the script was signaled by the left hand, while the lower side was signaled by the right hand.

Special hand signs were evolved to represent the five additional characters. The following table shows this hand alphabet.

Ogham Hand Alphabet

Letter	Hand Sign
B	1 finger of the right hand below ridgeline (of nose, arm, or leg)
L	2 fingers of the right hand below ridgeline (of nose, arm, or leg)
F	3 fingers of the right hand below ridgeline (of nose, arm, or leg)
S	4 fingers of the right hand below ridgeline (of nose, arm, or leg)
N	5 fingers of the right hand below ridgeline (of nose, arm, or leg)

Ogham Hand Alphabet (cont'd.)

Letter   **Hand Sign**

H   1 finger of the left hand above ridgeline

D   2 fingers of the left hand above ridgeline

T   3 fingers of the left hand above ridgeline

C   4 fingers of the left hand above ridgeline

Q   5 fingers of the left hand above ridgeline

M   1 finger of right (or left) hand crossing ridgeline at a slant

G   2 fingers of right (or left) hand crossing ridgeline at a slant

Ng   3 fingers of right (or left) hand crossing ridgeline at a slant

Z   4 fingers of right (or left) hand crossing ridgeline at a slant

R   5 fingers of right (or left) hand crossing ridgeline at a slant

A   1 finger of left (or right) hand crossing ridgeline perpendicularly

O   2 fingers of left (or right) hand crossing ridgeline perpendicularly

U   3 fingers of left (or right) hand crossing ridgeline perpendicularly

E   4 fingers of left (or right) hand crossing ridgeline perpendicularly

I   5 fingers of left (or right) hand crossing ridgeline perpendicularly

Ch   Crossed index fingers of left and right hands at ridgeline

Th   Index and middle fingers of left and right hands touching at ridgeline

P   Index and middle fingers of left and right hands interlaced below ridgeline

Ph   Thumb or index finger spiraled below ridgeline

X   Four fingers of left and right hands interlaced above ridgeline

Like the other magickal alphabets encountered, Ogham also possesses a number value. This code is recorded in the *Book of Ballymote* as a series of pin pricks between 1 and 20 for the Ogham alphabet. The number code is shown in the table on the following page.

Ogham Number Code

Letter	Number Value	Composite Strokes of Alphabet Character
(The B Family)		
B	1	1
L	2	2
F	3	3
S	4	4
N	5	5
(The H Family)		
H	6	1
D	7	2
T	8	3
C	9	4
Q	10	5
(The M Family)		
M	11	1
G	12	2
Ng	13	3
Z	14	4
R	15	5
(The A Family)		
A	16	1
O	17	2
U	18	3
E	19	4
I	20	5
(5 Additional Characters)		
Ch	21	4
Th	22	4
P	23	4
Ph	24	1
X	25	8

Two number values have been given to the Ogham alphabet in the above table: the sequential number values given in the *Book of Ballymote* and the number of strokes required to carve the individual letters (as well as the number of fingers used when formed as sign language).

Both codes are additional in nature when analyzing a word as a number value. The basis of this additional nature is the Greek alphabet when considering the number value, and the rune alphabets of three families of eight when considering the composite strokes which divide the alphabet naturally into four families of five, with five additional characters.

Thus the name "SOIM," the first magickal word Ogma ever carved (upon a piece of birch), can be numbered in two ways.

- As the serial order number value:

SOIM = 4 + 17 + 20 + 11 = 52

- As the composite strokes formed:

SOIM = 4 + 2 + 5 + 1 = 12

The beauty of the Ogham script is its model, for each letter of this script representes a tree. Thus the type of wood used to carve the Ogham script could connote a special meaning to the message it bore. Note that Ogma in carving the first word, SOIM, chose the birch tree, and this tree is the first letter of Ogham, "B." The following table shows the correspondences between the letter names for each of the Ogham characters and the trees that these names designate.

Ogham Tree Alphabet

Letter	Name	Tree
B	Beth	Birch
L	Luis	Elm, Quicken Tree, Mountain Ash
F	Fern	Alder
S	Sail	Willow
N	Nin	Nettle, Ash
H	Huath	Hawthorn, Whitethorn
D	Dair	Oak
T	Tinne	Cypress, Elder
C	Coll	Hazel
Q	Queirt	Apple, Holly, Aspen
M	Muin	Vine (fine branching)
G	Gort	Mistletoe, Ivy
Ng	Getal	Reed, Broom
Z	Straif	Blackthorn
R	Ruis	Elder
A	Ailm	Fir, Apple
O	Orn	Broom, Furze
U	Uir	Heath, Ash

Ogham Tree Alphabet (cont'd.)

Letter	Name	Tree
E	Edad	Ivy, Aspen
I	Idad	Yew
Ch	Ebad	Aspen
Th	Oir	Spindle Tree
P	Uillenn	Honeysuckle
Ph	Iphin	Gooseberry
X	Emhan Coll	Witchhazel, Pine

To the eye of the poet sensitive to this Celtic tree alphabet, Nature herself could spell out in her natural growth of plants and trees a secret alphabet of God. By this code, mistletoe nestled in the branching limbs of an oak tree is transformed into the letters G-D, suggesting the very name of God.

Beyond this tree alphabet, the Celtic Ogham tradition numbered 150 cipher substitutes for the 20 basic letters of Ogham. A color, day of the year, bird, river, family, and saint, to name just a few, were attributed to each of the 20 characters of the Ogham. All 150 codes were required to be memorized before any poetic proficiency could occur in this bardic tree language of Ogham.

The following table will delineate the color, bird, saint, time of year, family, women, water, and dog associated with each of the 20 basic characters of Ogham:

Ogham Symbolic Poetic Vocabulary

Letter	Color	Bird	Saint	Time
B	White	Pheasant	St. Brenaid	Dec. 24–Jan. 21 (Capricorn)
L	Gray	Duck	St. Laisreann	Jan. 22–Feb. 18 (Aquarius)
F	Crimson	Gull	St. Finden	Mar. 19–Apr. 15 (Aries)
S	Heather	Hawk	St. Sinchell	Apr. 16–May 13 (Aries–Taurus)
N	Clear	Snipe	St. Neasan	Feb. 19–Mar. 18 (Pisces)
H	Terrible	Night Crow	St. Hadamnan	May 14–Jun. 10 (Taurus–Gemini)
D	Black	Wren	St. Donnan	Jun. 11–Jul. 8 (Gemini–Cancer)
T	Dark Gray	Starling	St. Tigheanach	Jul. 9–Aug. 5 (Cancer–Leo)
C	Brown	Crane	St. Cronan	Aug. 6–Sept. 2 (Leo–Virgo)
Q	Mouse-colored	Hen	St. Qeran	Aug. 6–Sept. 2 (Leo–Virgo)
M	Variegated	Titmouse	St. Manchan	Sept. 3–Sept. 30 (Virgo–Leo)
G	Blue	Mute Swan	St. Guirgo	Oct. 1–Oct. 29 (Libra–Scorpio)
Ng	Glass-Green	Goose	St. Ngeman	Oct. 30–Nov. 25 (Scorpio–Sagittarius)
Z	Bright-colored	Thrush	St. Crannan	Apr. 16–May 13 (Aries–Taurus)
R	Blood-Red	Rook	St. Ruadhanachd	Nov. 26–Dec. 22 (Sagittarius)
A	Piebald	Lapwing	St. An	Winter Solstice
O	Dun	Cormorant	St. Oena	Spring Equinox
U	Resin-colored	Lark	St. Ultan	Summer Solstice
E	Red-Russet	Whistling Swan	St. Ervan	Fall Equinox
I	White	Eaglet	St. Ite	Winter Solstice

Ogham Symbolic Poetic Vocabulary (cont'd.)

Letter	Family	Women	Water	Dogs
(B Family)				
B	1 man	1 woman	1 rill	1 war dog
L	2 men	2 women	2 rills	2 war dogs
F	3 men	3 women	3 rills	3 war dogs
S	4 men	4 women	4 rills	4 war dogs
N	5 men	5 women	5 rills	5 war dogs
(H Family)				
H	1 woman	1 hag	1 weir	1 greyhound
D	2 women	2 hags	2 weirs	2 greyhounds
T	3 women	3 hags	3 weirs	3 greyhounds
C	4 women	4 hags	4 weirs	4 greyhounds
Q	5 women	5 hags	5 weirs	5 greyhounds
(M Family)				
M	1 warrior	1 maiden	1 river	1 shepherd dog
G	2 warriors	2 maidens	2 rivers	2 shepherd dogs
Ng	3 warriors	3 maidens	3 rivers	3 shepherd dogs
Z	4 warriors	4 maidens	4 rivers	4 shepherd dogs
R	5 warriors	5 maidens	5 rivers	5 shepherd dogs
(A Family)				
A	1 child	1 small girl	1 spring	1 lapdog
O	2 children	2 small girls	2 springs	2 lapdogs
U	3 children	3 small girls	3 springs	3 lapdogs
E	4 children	4 small girls	4 springs	4 lapdogs
I	5 children	5 small girls	5 springs	5 lapdogs

In the foregoing tables, two major forms of poetic symbology are employed. One set of correspondences is based on the initial letter of certain words (such as colors, trees, birds, and saints) while the other set is based on four groups of one to five (family, women, rivers, dogs). The time sequence, which is the one variant to the above rules, allocates the five vowels to the four points of the equinox and solstices and the 15 consonants to 13 lunar cycles, roughly approximating the 12 signs of the Zodiac.

This reduction of 15 Ogham consonants to 13 is the ancient form of Ogham. Ogham, whose alphabet order is BLF, was once BLN. This alphabet of 13 consonants and 5 vowels, known as the Beth-Luis-Nion or BLN alphabet is the prototype for Ogham. However, rather than niches made in wood, this alphabet utilized stylized Roman and Grecian alphabet characters.

The alphabet name Beth-Luis-Nion refers to the letter names of the first three letters. An earlier form in the order B-L-F (as in Ogham) rather than B-L-N was called Bobileth, after its first two letters (Boibel and Loth).

Each letter of the Beth-Luis-Nion alphabet is named after a tree (as in Ogham) and is often referred to poetically as "twigs" or "branch-letters." The letters were written either on tree bark or smoothed birchwood tablets called the Poet's Tablet (Taible Fileadh).

As to the origin for the Beth-Luis-Nion alphabet, the date may have been around 200 BCE, the date the Germanic runes were being adapted from Greek and Italian alphabets. However, as to the origin of Ogham, this alphabet bears no direct relationship to any existing alphabet and may therefore be far older than the Beth-Luis-Nion alphabet.

The table on the following page shows the BLN alphabet, the transliteration, the letter names, corresponding Latin names, the trees (which are the translations of these names), the lunar equinoctial and solstice cycles, and the corresponding number values:

Druidic BLN Alphabet

13 Consonants	Transliteration	Irish Name	Latin Name	Tree	Lunar Cycle	Number Value
b	B	Beith	Betulla	Birch	1st lunar cycle	5
l	L	Luis	Ornus	Rowan	2nd lunar cycle	14
N	N	Nion	Fraxinus	Wild Ash	3rd lunar cycle	13
F	F	Fearn	Alnus	Alder	4th lunar cycle	8
S	S	Saille	Salix	Willow	5th lunar cycle	16
h	H	Huath	Oxiacanthus	Whitethorn	6th lunar cycle	0
d	D	Duir	Ilex	Oak	7th lunar cycle	12
t	T	Tinne	Genista-Spina	Furze (Holly)	8th lunar cycle	11
c	C	Coll	Corylus	Hazel	9th lunar cycle	9
m	M	Muin	Vitis	Vine	10th lunar cycle	6
g	G	Gort	Hedera	Ivy	11th lunar cycle	10
p	P	Peth-bog	Beite	Dwarf Elder	12th lunar cycle	7
R	R	Ruis	Sambucus	Elder	13th lunar cycle	15
Five Vowels						
a	A	Ailm	Ahies	Silver Fir Tree	Winter Solstice	1
o	O	Onn	Genista	Broom (Furze)	Spring Equinox	4
u	U	Ur	Erica	Heather	Summer Solstice	0
e	E	Eghadh	Tremula	Aspen (White Poplar)	Autumnal Equinox	2
i	I	Iodha	Taxus	Yew	Winter Solstice	3

By this system, the letters of any word could be represented as a string of leaves, each leaf corresponding to the particular tree of any given letter of the alphabet.

Note that in the preceding table, the 13 lunar cycles divide the year into 13 groups of 28 days, the first day of the first lunar cycle being December 24. Thirteen times 28 days = 364 days, one day short of 365 days for the year. The missing 365th day is December 23, the Winter Solstice, which is represented by both A and I of the five vowels.

The number pattern assigned to the 13 consonants and 5 vowels is not sequential. However, in their peculiar order, the number 32 can be seen in no less than six groupings of the alphabet:

THE 32 PATTERN IN THE BLN ALPHABET

- First three consonants:

  B   L   N
  (5 + 14 + 13) = 32

- First, middle, and last consonant (1st, 7th, and 13th)

  B   D   R
  (5 + 12 + 15) = 32

- Last three consonants (11th, 12th, and 13th)

  G   P   R
  (10 + 7 + 15) = 32

- Sixth, seventh, eighth, and ninth consonants

  H   D   T   C
  (0 + 12 + 11 + 9) = 32

- Ninth, tenth, eleventh, and twelfth consonants

  C   M   G   P
  (9 + 6 + 10 + 7) = 32

- Last two consonants (12th and 13th) plus the five vowels

  P   R   A O U E I
  (7 + 15) + (1 + 4 + 0 + 2 + 3) = 32

This Celtic use of 32 suggests the Jewish Qabalistic cosmology, which divides the Universe into 32 divisions by the diagram known as the Tree of Life.

Finally, it should be noted that the older BLN order as well as the BLF order of Ogham are both phonetically based on Greek. The table on the following page shows the parallels between the BLF Ogham alphabet, the BLN alphabet, the Scandanavian runes, and the phonetic source of Greek, as well as the number value of the Greek phonetic model.

Celtic-Greek Phonetic Model

BLF Ogham	BLN	Runes	Greek	Greek Number Value
B	B	B	B	2
L	L	L	L	30
F	F	F, W	St	6
S	S	S	S	200
N	N	N	N	50
H	H	H	H	8
D	D	D	D	4
T	T	T	T	300
C	C	K	K	20
Q	—	—	Q	90
M	M	M	M	40
G	—	G, J	G	3
Ng	Ng	Ng	O	70
Z	—	Z	Z	7
R	R	R	R	100
A	A	A	A	1
O	O	O	O	70
U	U	U	U	400
E	E	E	E	5
I	I	I	I	10
Ch (Ea)	—	(Ei)	Ch	600
Th (Oi)	—	Th	Th	9
P (Ui)	P	P	P	80
Ph (Io)	—	—	Ph	500
X (Ae)	—	—	X	60

TENTH KEY

LATIN

OVERVIEW

L atin, the standard language of classical Western knowledge (both exoteric and esoteric), possesses its own distinct numerical Qabalah. Surprisingly, next to nothing has been written about this code in the 20th century. In the copious writings of Blavatsky, Mathers, and Crowley, we find no mention of such a code. Only the Qabalistic work of the American Tarotologist, Paul Foster Case, touches briefly upon this system.

The esoteric evolution of Latin as a magickal language has three basic points of development:

- The initial use of six select alphabet characters (dating back to 300 BCE)

- The creation of a "Latin Cabala" for a group of select Latin letters (to parallel the Hebraic and Arabic Qabalahs) by Raymond Lull (around 1300 CE)

- A complete set of number values for the entire Latin alphabet (emanating from both Italy and Germany around 1500 CE)

All three stages are fully covered in this chapter.

The first code for Latin is the Roman numeral system. This alphanumeric code does not apply to the whole alphabet, but rather a select few characters. The original six letters of C, D, I, L, V, and X are shown, along with three additional refinements of G, H, and M. This system dates back to 300 BCE and is the earliest attempt to view the Latin alphabet as number. But Latin would not reach its full flower as a number language until the Middle Ages.

119

The first real attempt to view Latin as a sacred language, capable of its own Qabalistic symbolism, was accomplished by Raymond Lull around 1300 CE. Lull wanted to create a Qabalah for Latin equal in beauty to the Arabic and Hebraic versions. He conjectured that if such a Qabalistic system could be fully realized for Latin (from a Christian viewpoint), both the Islamic and Jewish religions could be converted to Christianity by the beauty of these Latin Qabalistic proofs.

Lull selected nine basic Latin letters, B, C, D, E, F, G, H, I, and K. Using these nine basic lettered-divisions, Lull was able to erect a grand cosmology of correspondences which united the three worlds of God, Angels, and Man. His ultimate application of the Latin Qabalah was the development of a philosophical machine composed of three interlocking wheels, which could answer any philosophical question posed to it. The imagery of a wondrous "philosophical machine" would permeate the Rosicrucian literature of Europe 200 years after Lull's invention.

The core correspondences for this Latin Qabalah, sometimes referred to as the Lullian Art, are clearly presented at the beginning of this chapter as eight separate systems:

- The nine basic alphabet letters of the system (B-K)

- Lull's digital number system, where A is used for 0 as a place value (my own conjecture)

- The two basic Qabalistic correspondences for Latin: the "A" and "T" tables of the Lullian alphabet

- The 36 possible pairs of the ninefold Lullian alphabet

- The 729 revolutions of the Lullian triple wheel (known also as "the philosophical machine")

- Lull's enneagram of four sets of symbols (the basis of Gurdjieff and Charkovsky's 1916 research on Lull's philosophical machine)

- The 16-letter variant (B-R) to the Lullian alphabet

- Lull's ABCD astrological system, which divides the elements, planets, and Zodiac among the four letters A, B, C, and D

The Lullian triple wheel described above can be used to solve any philosophical question. It can also be used for divination. To use this machine you will first need to construct a basic model. Two methods can be used:

1. Cut out of cardboard or posterboard three concentric circles measuring approximately 3, 4, and 5 inches in diameter. These will eventually be joined in the center. Divide each of the exposed interlocking rims of the circles into nine sections (use a protractor and mark nine 40° angles upon the edge of each circle). Now you must enter nine Lullian Qabalistic correspondences on each of the three wheels, a total of 27 correspondences (3 x 9). Two different sets of symbols can be used here. Either mark the nine letters B, C, D, E,

F, G, H, I, J, K on each of the circles (in three symbolic colors of your choice, such as red, yellow, and blue) or use three distinct sets of nine Lullian correspondences found in the tables of your choosing and write each of the names in full upon the wheel.

After marking the three wheels with the appropriate symbols, join them together at the center with a hasp, pin, or other fastener. (Fastening the three wheels to a heavy backboard will prove to be useful.) You now have a Lullian Philosophical Machine.

2. A simpler method would be to cut out three decks of nine cards and mark upon each set the letters B through K, each set in an appropriate symbolic color (such as red, yellow, and blue).

Now this Hermetic computer of the Middle Ages can be put to use. If you have devised a wheel, the machine can be worked in the following way. As a meditational device, purposely combine the wheel into each of the 729 possible combinations and meditate upon the three separate attributes, blending each of the three symbols into one concrete symbol or meaning. Then, in a journal, record the letter, number, and meaning of that particular combination. Start with the combination BBB by setting these three letters at the top of your wheel (in each of the three circles) and end with KKK. If you have marked the symbolic attributes in full on the wheel, you do not need to revert to any tables to discover the correct attributes of any given triple rotation of the wheels. However, if you have marked just the bare letters B through K, ascertain beforehand which set of nine attributes is designated by each of the three wheels.

You can also construct a philosophical machine to encode the three Lullian worlds shown in the addendum to this key and create a cosmological set of correspondences. In that way you can meditate upon each interaction of the Supercelestial with the Celestial and Terrestrial kingdoms. If you have reverted to the simpler method of 27 cards, the cards themselves can be selected as the three appropriate letters for each of the 729 revolutions of the machine.

This philosophical machine can also be used for divination. A question is first posed and the machine is then consulted. If you have devised the interlocking wheels, spin each of the three wheels and determine which three-letter combination appears at the topmost part of the machine. If you have devised the deck of cards, shuffle the decks and draw one card from each to determine the three-letter combination. Now try to interpret the answer to the question you have posed in light of the symbolism for each of the three wheels.

These two methods of meditation and divination described above were the same basic exercises that were used in the Russian Theosophical circle of Gurdjieff, Ouspensky, Charkovsky, and Butkovsky in 1916. Gurdjieff's Lullian Wheel was a variant to the traditional triple ninefold wheel. In his variant, the three circles each possessed 36 divisions, allowing four sets of nine Lullian attributes for each wheel. This expanded set would require no less than 46,656 revolutions before every possible combination was worked out.

The Lullian section is followed by the Latin ciphers of Italy and Germany, which number every letter of the alphabet. The first table shows three sets of values for the Latin alphabet based on reducing the alphabet to 22 letters in imitation of the 22 sacred letters of the Hebrew Qabalistic alphabet.

Of the three codes listed in this table, the most promising is the "Cabala Simplex," or Simple Cabala. This set of correspondences is based on the serial order of the alphabet (A=1, Z=22). I first came upon this code through the writings of Paul Foster Case, then through the chapter headings of Eliphas Levi's *Dogma and Rituals of High Magic*, next through an in-depth study of Walter Begley, and finally as the secret number cipher Trithemius used for Latin in his 49th table of *Steganographia*.

My initial research into numbering alchemical Latin and Hermetic terminology occurred after I first devised my Hebrew number dictionary. To my surprise, when the Latin Cabala Simplex was applied to a handful of esoteric Latin terms, the following agreement between Latin and Hebrew immediately emerged:

Latin-Hebrew Qabalistic Equivalents

Word	Language	Meaning	Number Value
COR	Latin	Heart	32
LB (לב)	Hebrew	Heart	32
CEREBRA	Latin	Brain	48
MCh (מח)	Hebrew	Brain	48
NIHILO	Latin	Nothing	61
AIN (אין)	Hebrew	Nothing (Void)	61
TAROT	Latin	Anagram of Wheel (ROTA)	66
GLGL (גלגל)	Hebrew	Wheel	66

Using this simple code for Latin, you should explore a few basic alchemical texts, overviews, or dictionaries that contain Latin terminology. In alchemical writings, this terminology is invariably in italics, which will aid in identifying the select terms in the text. Note that original alchemical texts in languages other than English (such as German, French, or Italian) still preserve the select Latin terms in their original in order to preserve the correct hidden numerical correspondence. Add these numbered Latin terms to your existing number dictionary. You should also number a select group of entries by every other code given in this key as reference points for verification at a later date in your number research.

The Italian Qabalah for Latin (based on 22 letters) is followed by the German Latin ciphers (based on 24 letters). Four additional sets of number values are given for Latin, and each is used to number the word LVX (light) as examples of the codes in action. Make sure to explore these values for Latin in your research. Don't be put off by the variety of number values for any given language, but rather realize that every code given in this book adds to the imagery possible for the infinite number range. Possibly a code you would least suspect will give you the correct meaning for a number which you could not clearly define up to that point.

Two more codes for Latin, emanating out of the 18th- and 19th-century French magickal tradition, are given at the end of this chapter.

The addendum to this key details the Western equivalent to the Arabic cosmological model of the universe. This model is the dividing of the universe into three worlds. This basic threefold division creates three rulers for the three worlds: God, Angel, and Man. Lull utilized this threefold division in his own Qabalah. This symbolism should be integrated with the Lullian tables shown in the main body of the chapter.

Three separate sets of Lullian correspondences are given:

- The basic division of the universe into Supercelestial, Celestial, and Terrestrial kingdoms

- A Ladder of Ascent and Descent (resembling the gradations of the Hebraic Tree of Life)

- The 27 rulers of the three worlds of nine kingdoms each

Again, these attributes are well suited for the symbolic meanings to affix upon the three wheels of the Lullian philosophical machine.

Three more Renaissance systems embracing this threefold universe end this addendum. These three cosmology schemes are:

- Francesco Giorgi's threefold Celestial-Numerical Worlds (of 30 categories) utilizing the alphabets of Hebrew, Greek, Coptic, and Arabic

- John Dee's 30 worlds (of 3 x 10 correspondences) utilizing the Greek alphabet of 30 Aeons in light of Giorgi's own threefold system

- Robert Fludd's division of the universe into 22 + 1 categories, utilizing the Hebrew alphabet

ORIGIN

The numbering of Latin has three distinct periods of development:

3rd century BCE—The use of six selected Latin alphabet letters as numbers known as "Roman numerals"

14th century CE—The use of nine selected Latin alphabet letters known as the "Lullian Art" or the "Art of Raymond Lull"

16th century CE—The complete numbering of the Latin alphabet based on both Hebrew and Greek models, known as the "Latin Cabala"

Alphabet Code

The earliest use of the Latin alphabet as numbers occurs in the form of Roman numerals. In its earliest form, the Roman numerals utilized only six selected letters:

$$
\begin{aligned}
D &= 500 \\
C &= 100 \\
L &= \ \ 50 \\
X &= \ \ 10 \\
V &= \ \ \ \ 5 \\
I &= \underline{\ \ \ \ 1} \\
&\ \ \ 666
\end{aligned}
$$

Note that these six letters total to the apocalyptic number of 666. Further refinements in the Middle Ages numbered three additional letters:

$$
\begin{aligned}
M &= 1,000 \\
G &= \ \ \ 400 \\
H &= \ \ \ 200
\end{aligned}
$$

The last two seldom-mentioned letters facilitated the writing of the number range 200–400 as well as 600–800. One other sophistication developed for the range beyond 1,000. If a letter is overscored with a line, its value is one thousandfold. This resembles both the dotted Greek letter and the enlarged Hebrew letter. Thus X is 10 while $\bar{X}$ is 10,000.

In the 14th century CE, the Qabalist Raymond Lull, in an attempt to convert both Jews and Moslems to Christianity, invented a "Latin Cabala" reminiscent of both Jewish and Islamic number mysteries concerning the sacred alphabets of Hebrew and Arabic. In this system, or "Art" as Lull named this discipline, the letter "A" was assigned to the Godhead and as such was unnumbered, while the letters B through K were given the value of one through nine and assigned to nine choirs of angels. The remaining letters of the alphabet were not used.

The Art of Raymond Lull

A = unnumbered	F = 5
B = 1	G = 6
C = 2	H = 7
D = 3	I = 8
E = 4	K = 9

Though not explicity stated in the writings of Lull, these nine Latin letters as numbers can replace the awkwardness of the Roman numerals by numbering digitally, not unlike the Arabic numerals that replaced the Roman numerals. This can be accomplished only if "A," as the unnumbered Godhead, is conjectured to be zero. This Lullian numbering system would be as follows.

Lullian Numbering System

Arabic Numeral	Roman Numeral	Lullian Numeral	Arabic Letter-Number (Eastern Method)
1	I	B	A
2	II	C	B
3	III	D	J
4	IV	E	D
5	V	F	H
6	VI	G	W
7	VII	H	Z
8	VIII	I	Ḥ
9	IX	K	T
10	X	BA	Y
20	XX	CA	K
30	XXX	DA	L
40	XL	EA	M
50	L	FA	N
60	LX	GA	S
70	LXX	HA	O
80	LXXX	IA	F
90	XC	KA	Ṣ
100	C	BAA	Q
200	CC (H)	CAA	R
300	CCC (HC)	DAA	Sh
400	CD (G)	EAA	T
500	D	FAA	Th
600	DC	GAA	Kh
700	DCC (DH)	HAA	Dh
800	DCCC (GG)	IAA	Ḍ
900	DCCCC (CM/DG)	KAA	Tz
1000	DD (M)	BAAA	Gh

This ninefold classification system was expanded by Lull as a universal index, just as Aleister Crowley in *Liber 777* categorized every symbolic doctrine of every great religion by the 32 divisions of the Tree of Life. This ninefold system is the prototype for Gurdjieff's Enneagram. Lull's system was summarized in his treatise *Ars Brevi*. Lull was able to synopsize his entire Qabalistic system with the use of two basic tables (referred to as the "A" or circular table and the "T" or triangular table). The following chart classifies these two basic Lullian attributions.

Lullian Qabalism

Alphabet	"A" Table	"T" Table	Number Value
B	Good (Bonum)	Difference (Differentia)	1
C	Great (Magnum)	Agreement (Concorda)	2
D	Lasting (Durans)	Opposites (Contrariet)	3
E	Powerful (Potens)	Beginning (Principiu)	4
F	Wise (Sapiens)	Middle (Medium)	5
G	Willful (Volens)	End (Finis)	6
H	Virtuous (Virtuosu)	Greater (Majoritas)	7
I	True (Verum)	Equal (Aqualitas)	8
K	Glorious (Glorioso)	Lesser (Minoritas)	9

This system was also utilized as a classification system for the stratification of the celestial hierarchies of the cosmos. Refer to the end of this section for a detailing of this cosmology.

These nine basic categories can be combined with one another to represent every idea man can conceive. Lull worked out two basic combination tables to show these permutations. These two tables were a triangular table demonstrating the 36 possible pairings of 9 letters and a set of three interlocking wheels to demonstrate the 729 possible triads of nine letters.

The Thirty-Six Lullian Pairs

BC	CD	DE	EF	FG	GH	HI	IK
BD	CE	DF	EG	FH	GI	HK	
BE	CF	DG	EH	FI	GK		
BF	CG	DH	EI	FK			
BG	CH	DI	EK				
BH	CI	DK					
BI	CK						
BK							

The 729 Revolutions of the Lullian Triple Wheel

BBB

1. BBB	2. BBC	3. BBD	4. BBE	5. BBF	6. BBG	7. BBH	8. BBI	9. BBK
10. BCB	11. BCC	12. BCD	13. BCE	14. BCF	15. BCG	16. BCH	17. BCI	18. BCK
19. BDB	20. BDC	21. BDD	22. BDE	23. BDF	24. BDG	25. BDH	26. BDI	27. BDK
28. BEB	29. BEC	30. BED	31. BEE	32. BEF	33. BEG	34. BEH	35. BEI	36. BEK
37. BFB	38. BFC	39. BFD	40. BFE	41. BFF	42. BFG	43. BFH	44. BFI	45. BFK
46. BGB	47. BGC	48. BGD	49. BGE	50. BGF	51. BGG	52. BGH	53. BGI	54. BGK
55. BHB	56. BHC	57. BHD	58. BHE	59. BHF	60. BHG	61. BHH	62. BHI	63. BHK
64. BIB	65. BIC	66. BID	67. BIE	68. BIF	69. BIG	70. BIH	71. BII	72. BIK
73. BKB	74. BKC	75. BKD	76. BKE	77. BKF	78. BKG	79. BKH	80. BKI	81. BKK

The 729 Revolutions of the Lullian Triple Wheel (cont'd.)

CCC

82. CBB	83. CBC	84. CBD	85. CBE	86. CBF	87. CBG	88. CBH	89. CBI	90. CBK
91. CCB	92. CCC	93. CCD	94. CCE	95. CCF	96. CCG	97. CCH	98. CCI	99. CCK
100. CDB	101. CDC	102. CDD	103. CDE	104. CDF	105. CDG	106. CDH	107. CDI	108. CDK
109. CEB	110. CEC	111. CED	112. CEE	113. CEF	114. CEG	115. CEH	116. CEI	117. CEK
118. CFB	119. CFC	120. CFD	121. CFE	122. CFF	123. CFG	124. CFH	125. CFI	126. CFK
127. CGB	128. CGC	129. CGD	130. CGE	131. CGF	132. CGG	133. CGH	134. CGI	135. CGK
136. CHB	137. CHC	138. CHD	139. CHE	140. CHF	141. CHG	142. CHH	143. CHI	144. CHK
145. CIB	146. CIC	147. CID	148. CIE	149. CIF	150. CIG	151. CIH	152. CII	153. CIK
154. CKB	155. CKC	156. CKD	157. CKE	158. CKF	159. CKG	160. CKH	161. CKI	162. CKK

DDD

163. DBB	164. DBC	165. DBD	166. DBE	167. DBF	168. DBG	169. DBH	170. DBI	171. DBK
172. DCB	173. DCC	174. DCD	175. DCE	176. DCF	177. DCG	178. DCH	179. DCI	180. DCK
181. DDB	182. DDC	183. DDD	184. DDE	185. DDF	186. DDG	187. DDH	188. DDI	189. DDK
190. DEB	191. DEC	192. DED	193. DEE	194. DEF	195. DEG	196. DEH	197. DEI	198. DEK
199. DFB	200. DFC	201. DFD	202. DFE	203. DFF	204. DFG	205. DFH	206. DFI	207. DFK
208. DGB	209. DGC	210. DGD	211. DGE	212. DGF	213. DGG	214. DGH	215. DGI	216. DGK
217. DHB	218. DHC	219. DHD	220. DHE	221. DHF	222. DHG	223. DHH	224. DHI	225. DHK
226. DIB	227. DIC	228. DID	229. DIE	230. DIF	231. DIG	232. DIH	233. DII	234. DIK
235. DKB	236. DKC	237. DKD	238. DKE	239. DKF	240. DKG	241. DKH	242. DKI	243. DKK

The 729 Revolutions of the Lullian Triple Wheel (cont'd.)

EEE

244. EBB	245. EBC	246. EBD	247. EBE	248. EBF	249. EBG
253. ECB	254. ECC	255. ECD	256. ECE	257. ECF	258. ECG
262. EDB	263. EDC	264. EDD	265. EDE	266. EDF	267. EDG
271. EEB	272. EEC	273. EED	274. EEE	275. EEF	276. EEG
280. EFB	281. EFC	282. EFD	283. EFE	284. EFF	285. EFG
289. EGB	290. EGC	291. EGD	292. EGE	293. EGF	294. EGG
298. EHB	299. EHC	300. EHD	301. EHE	302. EHF	303. EHG
307. EIB	308. EIC	309. EID	310. EIE	311. EIF	312. EIG
316. EKB	317. EKC	318. EKD	319. EKE	320. EKF	321. EKG

250. EBH	251. EBI	252. EBK
259. ECH	260. ECI	261. ECK
268. EDH	269. EDI	270. EDK
277. EEH	278. EEI	279. EEK
286. EFH	287. EFI	288. EFK
295. EGH	296. EGI	297. EGK
304. EHH	305. EHI	306. EHK
313. EIH	314. EII	315. EIK
322. EKH	323. EKI	324. EKK

FFF

325. FBB	326. FBC	327. FBD	328. FBE	329. FBF	330. FBG
334. FCB	335. FCC	336. FCD	337. FCE	338. FCF	339. FCG
343. FDB	344. FDC	345. FDD	346. FDE	347. FDF	348. FDG
352. FEB	353. FEC	354. FED	355. FEE	356. FEF	357. FEG
361. FFB	362. FFC	363. FFD	364. FFE	365. FFF	366. FFG
370. FGB	371. FGC	372. FGD	373. FGE	374. FGF	375. FGG
379. FHB	380. FHC	381. FHD	382. FHE	383. FHF	384. FHG
388. FIB	389. FIC	390. FID	391. FIE	392. FIF	393. FIG
397. FKB	398. FKC	399. FKD	400. FKE	401. FKF	402. FKG

331. FBH	332. FBI	333. FBK
340. FCH	341. FCI	342. FCK
349. FDH	350. FDI	351. FDK
358. FEH	359. FEI	360. FEK
367. FFH	368. FFI	369. FFK
376. FGH	377. FGI	378. FGK
385. FHH	386. FHI	387. FHK
394. FIH	395. FII	396. FIK
403. FKH	404. FKI	405. FKK

The 729 Revolutions of the Lullian Triple Wheel (cont'd.)

GGG

406. GBB	407. GBC	408. GBD	409. GBE	410. GBF	411. GBG	412. GBH	413. GBI	414. GBK
415. GCB	416. GCC	417. GCD	418. GCE	419. GCF	420. GCG	421. GCH	422. GCI	423. GCK
424. GDB	425. GDC	426. GDD	427. GDE	428. GDF	429. GDG	430. GDH	431. GDI	432. GDK
433. GEB	434. GEC	435. GED	436. GEE	437. GEF	438. GEG	439. GEH	440. GEI	441. GEK
442. GFB	443. GFC	444. GFD	445. GFE	446. GFF	447. GFG	448. GFH	449. GFI	450. GFK
451. GGB	452. GGC	453. GGD	454. GGE	455. GGF	456. GGG	457. GGH	458. GGI	459. GGK
460. GHB	461. GHC	462. GHD	463. GHE	464. GHF	465. GHG	466. GHH	467. GHI	468. GHK
469. GIB	470. GIC	471. GID	472. GIE	473. GIF	474. GIG	475. GIH	476. GII	477. GIK
478. GKB	479. GKC	480. GKD	481. GKE	482. GKF	483. GKG	484. GKH	485. GKI	486. GKK

HHH

487. HBB	488. HBC	489. HBD	490. HBE	491. HBF	492. HBG	493. HBH	494. HBI	495. HBK
496. HCB	497. HCC	498. HCD	499. HCE	500. HCF	501. HCG	502. HCH	503. HCI	504. HCK
505. HDB	506. HDC	507. HDD	508. HDE	509. HDF	510. HDG	511. HDH	512. HDI	513. HDK
514. HEB	515. HEC	516. HED	517. HEE	518. HEF	519. HEG	520. HEH	521. HEI	522. HEK
523. HFB	524. HFC	525. HFD	526. HFE	527. HFF	528. HFG	529. HFH	530. HFI	531. HFK
532. HGB	533. HGC	534. HGD	535. HGE	536. HGF	537. HGG	538. HGH	539. HGI	540. HGK
541. HHB	542. HHC	543. HHD	544. HHE	545. HHF	546. HHG	547. HHH	548. HHI	549. HHK
550. HIB	551. HIC	552. HID	553. HIE	554. HIF	555. HIG	556. HIH	557. HII	558. HIK
559. HKB	560. HKC	561. HKD	562. HKE	563. HKF	564. HKG	565. HKH	566. HKI	567. HKK

The 729 Revolutions of the Lullian Triple Wheel (cont'd.)

III

568. IBB	569. IBC	570. IBD	571. IBE	572. IBF	573. IBG	574. IBH	575. IBI	576. IBK
577. ICB	578. ICC	579. ICD	580. ICE	581. ICF	582. ICG	583. ICH	584. ICI	585. ICK
586. IDB	587. IDC	588. IDD	589. IDE	590. IDF	591. IDG	592. IDH	593. IDI	594. IDK
595. IEB	596. IEC	597. IED	598. IEE	599. IEF	600. IEG	601. IEH	602. IEI	603. IEK
604. IFB	605. IFC	606. IFD	607. IFE	608. IFF	609. IFG	610. IFH	611. IFI	612. IFK
613. IGB	614. IGC	615. IGD	616. IGE	617. IGF	618. IGG	619. IGH	620. IGI	621. IGK
622. IHB	623. IHC	624. IHD	625. IHE	626. IHF	627. IHG	628. IHH	629. IHI	630. IHK
631. IIB	632. IIC	633. IID	634. IIE	635. IIF	636. IIG	637. IIH	638. III	639. IIK
640. IKB	641. IKC	642. IKD	643. IKE	644. IKF	645. IKG	646. IKH	647. IKI	648. IKK

KKK

649. KBB	650. KBC	651. KBD	652. KBE	653. KBF	654. KBG	655. KBH	656. KBI	657. KBK
658. KCB	659. KCC	660. KCD	661. KCE	662. KCF	663. KCG	664. KCH	665. KCI	666. KCK
667. KDB	668. KDC	669. KDD	670. KDE	671. KDF	672. KDG	673. KDH	674. KDI	675. KDK
676. KEB	677. KEC	678. KED	679. KEE	680. KEF	681. KEG	682. KEH	683. KEI	684. KEK
685. KFB	686. KFC	687. KFD	688. KFE	689. KFF	690. KFG	691. KFH	692. KFI	693. KFK
694. KGB	695. KGC	696. KGD	697. KGE	698. KGF	699. KGG	700. KGH	701. KGI	702. KGK
703. KHB	704. KHC	705. KHD	706. KHE	707. KHF	708. KHG	709. KHH	710. KHI	711. KHK
712. KIB	713. KIC	714. KID	715. KIE	716. KIF	717. KIG	718. KIH	719. KII	720. KIK
721. KKB	722. KKC	723. KKD	724. KKE	725. KKF	726. KKG	727. KKH	728. KKI	729. KKK

Though these nine Latin letters of B through K were given a numerical basis, the real intent of Lull's system was a universal calculation which could encompass all things. By this basic division of nine, Lull believed that he was indeed able to classify the entire cosmos. This is the basic vision behind every magical number system man has yet invented. The Lullian Art, beyond the "A" and "T" table classification possesses four basic modes of describing the enneagram in action. These four tables are detailed below.

Lull's Enneagram

Letters	Virtues	Vices	Questions	Categories
B	Justice (Justitia)	Avarice (Avaritia)	Whether? (Utrum)	Quantity (Quanitas)
C	Prudence (Prudentia)	Gluttony (Gula)	What? (Quid)	Quality (Qualitas)
D	Strength (Fortitudo)	Excess (Luxuria)	From where? (De Quo)	Relation (Relatio)
E	Temperance (Temperantia)	Arrogance (Superbia)	Why? (Quare)	Active (Actio)
F	Faith (Fides)	Sharpness, Bitterness (Acidia)	How much? (Quantum)	Passive (Passio)
G	Hope (Spes)	Envy (Inuidia)	What kind? (Quale)	Nature (Character) (Habitus)
H	Charity (Charitas)	Anger (Ira)	When? (Quando)	Position (Situs)
I	Patience (Patientia)	Falsehood (Mendacium)	Where? (Ubi)	Time (Tempus)
K	Devotion (Pietas)	Inconsistency (Inconstantia)	In what way, and with what? (Quo modo et cum quo)	Place/Period (Locus)

Lull employed two other basic alphabet classifications. He first added seven more letters to the alphabet, expanding B through K to B through R. Lull's intention for this expansion from 9 to 16 letters may have been to establish an alternate 16-fold elemental system which would allow the classification of four elements counterchanged 16 times. The following table shows the 16 Latin letters B through R, their number values, their Lullian virtues, and a tentative reconstruction of the 16 elements based on the Lullian order of Fire, Air, Water, and Earth.

Lull's Elements

Letter	Virtue	Elemental Counterchange	Number Value
B	Goodness (Bonitas)	Fire of Fire	1
C	Greatness (Magnitudo)	Air of Fire	2
D	Eternal (Eternitas)	Water of Fire	3
E	Power (Potestas)	Earth of Fire	4
F	Wisdom (Sapientia)	Fire of Air	5
G	Will (Voluntas)	Air of Air	6
H	Virtue (Virtus)	Water of Air	7
I	Truth (Veritas)	Earth of Air	8
K	Glory (Gloria)	Fire of Water	9
L	Completion (Perfectio)	Air of Water	10
M	Equity (Justitia)	Water of Water	11
N	Liberality (Largitas)	Earth of Water	12
O	Mercy (Misericordia)	Fire of Earth	13
P	Humility (Humilitas)	Air of Earth	14
Q	Rulership (Dominium)	Water of Earth	15
R	Evident (Patentia)	Earth of Earth	16

The second additional system involved only four letters: A, B, C, and D. With these four letters, Lull was able to summarize all of astrology. In terms of a tool for a horoscope, a chart would be reduced to its component letters. The resultant letters would be analyzed in light of repetitious, as well as opposite or contrasting pairs of letters. The predominant letter of the chart would determine the general astrological characteristics. The basis of this table is the four elements placed by Lull in a special order. Lull's normal elemental order was Fire, Air, Water, and Earth. However, for this elemental system, the order was permutated to Air, Fire, Earth, and Water. The table on the following page delineates this Lullian astrology.

The Fourfold Astrological System of ABCD

Letter	Element	Signs	Planets
A	Air	Gemini, Libra, Aquarius	Jupiter
B	Fire	Aries, Leo, Sagittarius	Mars, Sun
C	Earth	Taurus, Virgo, Capricorn	Saturn
D	Water	Cancer, Scorpio, Pisces	Venus, Moon
ABCD	Ether	The Zodiac	Mercury

Letter	Humor in Man	Elemental Combination (Proper and Appropriated)	Alchemical Element (Derived from Planet)
A	Sanguine	Moist and hot	Tin
B	Choleric	Hot and dry	Iron, Gold
C	Melancholic	Dry and cold	Lead
D	Phelgmatic	Cold and moist	Copper, Silver
ABCD	Soul	All elemental qualities	Quicksilver

Note that the combination of the letters ABCD as Mercury in the above table is equivalent to A in the nine categories of B through K. Both stand for God as the trinity of Essentia, Unitas, et Perfectio (Essential, Oneness, and Perfection).

It was not until the 16th century that the entire alphabet was given a number value. In Germany and Italy, six basic "Cabalas" for Latin developed: Cabala Simplex, Cabala Ordinis (Italian variant), Cabala Ordinis (German variant), Cabala Trigonalis, Cabala Quadratus, and Cabala Pentagonalis.

In these six methods, three distinct alphabets of 22, 23, and 24 letters are employed. The Italian Cabala Simplex (simple or straightforward Cabala) and the German Cabala Ordinis (ordered or serial Cabala) utilize 22 letters (resembling Hebrew in number). In this alphabet series, both K and W are absent. The Italian Cabala Ordinis varies from this 22-letter model by one letter, bringing into play the letter "K" apart and distinct in number from the letter "C." The most sophisticated of the codes, the German polygonal codes of Triangular, Quadrangular, and Pentagonal numerations, add both the letters "K" and "W" to the 22-letter model, creating a Greek model of 24 alphabet letters. The following table shows the Latin alphabet codes of 22 and 23 letters and their Hebrew model.

Italian Latin Ciphers (Hebrew Order of 22)

Latin Alphabet	Cabala Simplex*	Cabala Ordinis (Italian)	Cabala Ordinis (German)	Hebrew Model
A	1	1	1	A
B	2	2	2	B
C	3	3	3	G
D	4	4	4	D
E	5	5	5	H
F	6	6	6	V
G	7	7	7	Z
H	8	8	8	Ch
I (J)	9	9	9	T
(K)	(3)	10	(3)	—
L	10	20	10	I
M	11	30	20	K
N	12	40	30	L
O	13	50	40	M
P	14	60	50	N
Q	15	70	60	S
R	16	80	70	O
S	17	90	80	P
T	18	100	90	Tz
V (U)	19	200	100	Q
X	20	300	200	R
Y	21	400	300	Sh
Z	22	500	400	Th

*(This cipher appears in the 49th table of Trithemius' *Steganographia*, the ultimate Renaissance textbook on political as well as magickal ciphers for the Latin alphabet)

The above table shows a basic serial order of 1 through 22 for Latin, as well as a Semitic-like range of numbers of 1 through 400 (and a variant ending in 500). These three codes are straightforward variations of pre-existing number codes for magical alphabets. However, in the German system of Latin Cabala, three sophisticated systems of numbering evolved from a Hellenistic model of 24 letters. These Cabalas are referred to as polygonal codes. In the most elaborate of German numbering systems, these polygonal tables were progressed to the level of the decagon. However, the basis of this system was threefold.

To a basic Latin alphabet of 24 letters valued at 1 through 24 (serial order), three mathematical computations were performed to produce three polygonal values:

1. **Triangular**—This value is the summation (or Theosophical extension) of any given number: A = 1, B = 1 + 2, C = 1 + 2 + 3, and so on.

2. **Quadrangular**—This value is the square of any given number: A = 1^2 = 1, B = 2^2 = 4, C = 3^2 = 9, etc.

3. **Pentagonal**—This value is twice the value of the square (Quandrangular) minus the value of the summation (Triangular). The formula is $2(n^2) - \Sigma(0\text{-}n)$. Thus A = $2(1^2) - 1 = 1$, B = $2(2^2) - 3 = 5$, C = $2(3^2) - 6 = 12$, and so on.

The following table will delineate this German numbering system and the Greek alphabet of 24 letters which serves as the model for the 24 Latin letters.

German Latin Ciphers (Greek Order of 24)

Latin Alphabet	Simplex, Serial Order	Triangular Cabala	Quadrangular Cabala	Pentagonal Cabala	Greek Model
A	1	1	1	1	A
B	2	3	4	5	B
C	3	6	9	12	G
D	4	10	16	22	D
E	5	15	25	35	E
F	6	21	36	51	Z
G	7	28	49	70	H
H	8	36	64	92	Th
I, J	9	45	81	117	I
K	10	55	100	145	K
L	11	66	121	176	L
M	12	78	144	210	M
N	13	91	169	247	N

German Latin Ciphers (Greek Order of 24) (cont'd.)

Latin Alphabet	Simplex, Serial Order	Triangular Cabala	Quadrangular Cabala	Pentagonal Cabala	Greek Model
O	14	105	196	287	X
P	15	120	225	330	O
Q	16	136	256	376	P
R	17	153	289	425	R
S	18	171	324	477	S
T	19	190	361	532	T
U, V	20	210	400	590	U
W	21	231	441	651	Ph
X	22	253	484	715	Ch
Y	23	276	529	782	Ps
Z	24	300	576	852	Ō

All six of these codes are additional in nature, resembling Hebrew, Arabic, Greek, Coptic, and Tibetan as well as the Celtic languages. The letters of any given word are substituted with the appropriate number values and then these numbers are added together to obtain the specific number value of that word. With six codes, there are six basic values for any given word. As an example, the Latin word for light, LVX (lux), is numbered below by each of the six basic Italian-German Cabalas:

1. Italian Cabala Simplex: LVX = 49
   (L = 10, V = 19, X = 20, 10 + 19 + 20 = 49)

2. German Cabala Ordinis: LVX = 310
   (L = 10, V = 100, X = 200, 10 + 100 + 200 = 310)

3. Italian Cabala Ordinis: LVX = 520
   (L = 20, V = 200, X = 300, 20 + 200 + 300 = 520)

4. German Cabala Triagonalis: LVX = 529
   (L = 66, V = 210, X = 253, 66 + 210 + 253 = 529)

5. German Cabala Quadratus: LVX = 1005
   (L = 121, V = 400, X = 484, 121 + 400 + 484 = 1005)

6. German Cabala Pentagonal: LVX = 1481
   (L = 176, V = 590, X = 715, 176 + 590 + 715 = 1481)

Six distinct values of 49, 310, 520, 529, 1005, and 1481 can be given to the word LVX. Since this Latin word is composed of three Roman numerals, L

+ V + X, a seventh value can be reckoned. If LVX is permutated to LXV, the numeral 65 is formed, a seventh number value for LVX.

Beyond the work of the Italian and German "Cabalists," the only significant numbering variant for Latin to appear is the French code of J. Soubira known as "Cabalisticon," which appeared in the late 18th century. This code appears to utilize 25 letters of the French alphabet (J being the missing letter of 26) rather than a number code intended strictly for Latin.

In the mid-19th century, Eliphas Levi utilized the Italian Cabala Simplex (probably taken directly from Trithemius) in a blinded format as the 22 chapter headings for his *Dogme de la Haute Magie*. The following table illustrates these two French ciphers for Latin.

French Latin Ciphers

Cabalisticon (J. A. Soubira, 1791)		Dogma of High Magic (Eliphas Levi, 1855)				
		Blinded		Value		Corrected
A =	1	A	=	1	=	A
B =	2	B	=	2	=	B
C =	3	C	=	3	=	C
D =	4	D	=	4	=	D
E =	5	E	=	5	=	E
F =	6	F	=	6	=	F
G =	7	G	=	7	=	G
H =	8	H	=	8	=	H
I =	9	I	=	9	=	I
K =	10	K	=	10	=	L
L =	20	K	=	11	=	M*
M =	30	L	=	12	=	N
N =	40	N	=	13	=	O
O =	50	O	=	14	=	P
P =	60	P	=	15	=	Q
Q =	70	Q	=	16	=	R
R =	80	R	=	17	=	S
S =	90	S	=	18	=	T
T = 100		T	=	19	=	U
U = 110		U	=	20	=	X
V = 120		X	=	21	=	Y*
W = 240		Z	=	22	=	Z
X = 130						
Y = 140						
Z = 150						

*Two Ks are replaced by M and Y.

ADDENDUM

THE THREE WORLDS OF THE ANGELIC ALPHABETS

The work of Raymond Lull is the source for the Renaissance-Hermetic obsession with the categorizing of the universe by letter and number. Lull's 14th-century Qabalah for Latin divided the universe into three major worlds. These three worlds are in turn ruled by a fourth: God. This tripartite cosmos of nine basic Latin letters was elaborated in the Renaissance by the works of Giorgi and Fludd to include the range of the Hebrew, Greek, and Arabic alphabets. This threefold world view ultimately became the groundwork upon which John Dee constructed his Enochian cosmology of 30 worlds.

As shown previously, Lull's Latin Qabalah involved the nine Latin letters B through K. These nine categories were numbered 1 through 9 and had a basic subdivision of three groups of three. These basic nine were ultimately expanded by Lull into three sets of three times three in order to categorize the cosmos as three worlds of nine basic divisions. These three major Lullian worlds were the Supercelestial, the Celestial, and the Terrestrial.

This threefold universe was conceived by Lull as the three geometrical shapes of circle, triangle, and square. The following table shows this Lullian triadic logic.

Lull's Threefold Universe

The Three Worlds	Geometry	The Firmament	Constitution of Man's Soul	Three Rulers
Supercelestial	Circle	Zodiac	Intellect	God
Celestial	Triangle	Planets	Memory	Angels
Terrestrial	Square	Elements	Will	Man

The Three Worlds	Alphabet of Nine	Trinity	Constitution of Man
Supercelestial	BCD	Father	Spirit
Celestial	EFG	Holy Ghost	Soul
Terrestrial	HIK	Son	Body

The Supercelestial world embraced the Dionysian Aerogypite ninefold angelic system. The highest of the nine was accorded to the Seraphim, the lowest to the Angels. The celestial world contained the first cause (or primum mobile) as its highest rung and descended into the stars of the Zodiac, followed by the seven Platonic planets ending in the Moon. The Terrestrial world spanned from Man through nature and the four elements to the actual instruments of all sciences and arts.

The basis for the threefold world is Lull's table known as "The Ladder of Ascent and Descent." This table is comprised of nine categories and expands into three groups of nine. The following two tables detail this expansion of 9 concepts into 27.

The Ladder of Ascent and Descent

Letter	Attribute	Worlds
B	Deus—God	Unnumbered Source
C	Angelus—Angels	First World—Supercelestial
D	Coelum—Stars	Second World—Celestial
E	Homo—Man	Third World—Terrestial
F	Imaginativa—Imagination	Third World—Terrestial
G	Sensitiva—Sensation	Third World—Terrestial
H	Vegetables—Plants	Third World—Terrestial
I	Elementativa—The Four Elements	Third World—Terrestial
K	Instrumentativa—Instruments of Art and Science	Third World—Terrestial

The Three Worlds

Three Worlds	Supercelestial	Celestial	Terrestrial
A	God as the unnumbered source of all three worlds		
B	Seraphim	Primum Mobile	Man
C	Cherubim	Zodiac	Imagination
D	Thrones	Saturn	Animals
E	Dominions	Jupiter	Plants
F	Virtues	Mars	Fire
G	Powers	Sun	Air
H	Principalities	Venus	Water
I	Archangels	Mercury	Earth
K	Angels	Moon	Tools of Arts and Sciences

Though Lull detailed the Terrestrial nine, the Celestial and Supercelestial nine were models pre-existing Lullism, which served as the model for the enneagram categorization of the universe.

Aware of this relationship of three sets of nine, Francesco Giorgi adapted this set of 27 + 1 (1 being the unnumbered "A" of God) in his work *The Celestial Harmony of the World*, to correspond to the 27 + 1 letters of the Hebrew and Greek numerical alphabets. The following table shows this Lullian adaptation of the threefold universe.

The Three Celestial-Numerical Worlds of Francesco Giorgi

Serial Order	Number Value	Divine Attribute	Angelic World	Hebrew	Greek	Coptic	Arabic
1	1 (Simple)	God		A	A	A	A
2	2	Seraphim		B	B	B	B
3	3	Cherubim		G	G	G	J
4	4	Thrones		D	D	D	D
5	5	Dominions		H	E	E	H
6	6	Virtues		V	St	So	W
7	7	Powers		Z	Z	Z	Z
8	8	Principalities		Ch	H	E	Ḥ
9	9	Archangels		T	Th	Th	T

1 + 2 + 3 + 4 = 10

(continued on following page)

The Three Celestial-Numerical Worlds of Francesco Giorgi (cont'd.)

Serial Order	Number Value	Divine Attribute		Hebrew	Greek	Coptic	Arabic
10	10 (Root)	Angels (Celestial Government)		I	I	I	Y
11	20	First Cause		K	K	K	K
12	30	Zodiac		L	L	L	L
13	40	Saturn	Celestial World	M	M	M	M
14	50	Jupiter		N	N	N	N
15	60	Mars		S	X	Ks	S
16	70	Sun		O	O	O	O
17	80	Venus		P	P	P	F
18	90	Mercury		Tz	Q	F	Ṣ
19	100 (Square)	Moon (Man)		Q	R	R	Q
20	200	Animals		R	S	S	R
21	300	Reptiles, Fish, Birds, Insects		Sh	T	T	Sh
22	400	Plants	Corruptible World	Th	U	U	Ṭ
23	500	Metals		Kf	Ph	Ph	Th
24	600	Ether		Mf	Ch	Ch	Kh
25	700	Fire		Nf	Ps	Ps	Dh
26	800	Water		Pf	Ō	Ō	Ḍ
27	900	Air		Tzf	Ṣ.	Ṣ	Tz
28	1000 (Cube)	Earth		Ȧ	Ȧ	Ȧ	Gh

10 + 20 + 30 + 40 = 100

100 + 200 + 300 + 400 = 1000

With Giorgi's expansion of Lull's ninefold world into a categorization of 28 (as 3 times 9 + 1), the magical alphabets of Hebrew, Greek, and Arabic could be paralleled to each of the 28 degrees of the universe. Thus, as the nine Latin letters of B through K were the parameters of the Lullian universe, with Giorgi the Hebrew range of Aleph through Tav, as well as the Greek range of Alpha through Omega, expanded the nine Latin letters.

John Dee, upon discovering this set of 28 in Giorgi's work, used this alphabetical universe as the basis for his own Enochian cosmology. Dee was well versed both in Lull and Giorgi, and for a time Giorgi was a student of Dee in England. Dee combined his deep understanding of Lull and Giorgi with the Gnostic cosmology of 30 Aeons and came up with his own vision of the universe as 30 interlocking Aires. Each Aire corresponded to one of Giorgi's categories as well as one of the 30 Aeons. Dee noticed that Giorgi's division of his universe into three groups of nine headed by one controlling category (God) was actually three groups of nine *each* governed by one controlling category. The three controllers or rulers were God, the Celestial Government, and Man. With the inclusion of these two extra rulers (Celestial Government and Man), Dee expanded 28 categories to 30. The following table shows this expansion.

Dee's Cosmology of Thirty Worlds

Thirty Enochian Aires	Giorgi's Thirty Cosmic Divisions	Thirty Coptic-Gnostic Aeons	Greek Alphabet of the Thirty Aeons
1. LIL	God	Depth (Ampsiu)	A
2. ARN	Seraphim	Silence (Ouraan)	B
3. ZOM	Cherubim	Mind (Bucua)	G
4. PAZ	Thrones	Truth (Thartun)	D
5. LIT	Dominions	Reason (Ubucua)	E
6. MAZ	Virtues	Life (Thardedia)	Z
7. DEO	Powers	Man (Metaxas)	H
8. ZID	Principalities	Church (Artababa)	Th
9. ZIP	Archangels	Comforter (Udua)	I
10. ZAX	Angels	Faith (Casten)	K
11. ICH	Celestial Government	Fatherly (Amphian)	L
12. LOE	First Cause	Hope (Essumen)	M
13. ZIM	Zodiac	Motherly (Vannanin)	N
14. UTA	Saturn	Charity (Lamer)	X
15. OXO	Jupiter	Eternal (Tarde)	O
16. LEA	Mars	Intelligence (Athames)	P
17. TAN	Sun	Light (Susua)	R
18. ZEN	Venus	Beatitude (Allora)	S

Dee's Cosmology of Thirty Worlds (cont'd.)

Thirty Enochian Aires	Giorgi's Thirty Cosmic Divisions	Thirty Coptic-Gnostic Aeons	Greek Alphabet of the Thirty Aeons	
19. POP	Mercury	Eucharistic (Bucidia)	T	
20. KHR	Moon	Wisdom (Damadarah)	U	
21. ASP	Man	Profundity (Allora)	Ph	
22. LIN	Animals	Mixture (Dammo)	Ch	
23. TOR	Reptiles, Birds Fish, Insects	Unfading (Oren)		
24. NIA	Plants	Union (Lamaspechs)	Ō	
25. VTA	Metals	Self-Born (Amphiphuls)	I	⎫
26. DES	Ether	Temperance (Emphsboshbaud)	H	
27. ZAA	Fire	Only Begotten (Assiouache)	S	⎬ IHSOUS— Jesus
28. BAG	Water	Unity (Belin)	O	
29. RII	Air	Immovable (Dexariche)	U	
30. TEX	Earth	Pleasure (Massemo)	S	⎭

The threefold model of the universe met its fullest expression in Dee's 30 Aires. However, one other major alphabetical universe was developed out of this tradition by the occultist Robert Fludd. Fludd reduced Giorgi's 28 categories to 22 in order to obtain a system compatible with the 22 mystical letters of the Hebrew Qabalah. Fludd's universe is shown in the table on the opposite page.

Robert Fludd's Alphabetical Universe
of Twenty-Two Divisions

Number Order	Hebrew Letter	Number Value	Cosmic Divisions
0	No Letter	0	God (Deus)
1	A	1	Mind (Mens)
2	B	2	Seraphim
3	G	3	Cherubim
4	D	4	Dominions
5	H	5	Thrones
6	V	6	Powers
7	Z	7	Principalities
8	Ch	8	Virtues
9	T	9	Archangels
10	I	10	Angels
11	K	20	Heaven of Stars (Zodiac)
12	L	30	Saturn
13	M	40	Jupiter
14	N	50	Mars
15	S	60	Sun
16	O	70	Venus
17	P	80	Mercury
18	Tz	90	Moon
19	Q	100	Fire
20	R	200	Air
21	Sh	300	Water
22	Th	400	Earth

ELEVENTH KEY

ENOCHIAN

OVERVIEW

This 11th key is the most difficult of all for the sensibilities of a beginning student. The purpose of almost every other key has been a clear, precise presentation of the basic symbolic-numerical components which make up each particular magickal language. But the purpose of this key is to set the angelic Enochian record straight in regards to the complex symbolism of the four great Enochian directional Watchtowers. Though this chapter adequately details the three major numerical codes contained within the Enochian alphabet (those of Dee, Mathers, and Crowley), the main purpose is to supply in print, for the first time, the true and faithful version of the Enochian Watchtower system. Before now, this complex Enochian system of squares (composed of 644 letters) has never been correctly constructed (not even in the surviving work found in Dee's own magickal diaries).

Since this Watchtower system is the most complicated of all the Golden Dawn magickal systems, it is obviously not food for thought for the beginning student. In fact, in Regardie's own introduction to his classic work on the Golden Dawn, the beginning student is warned not to study the Enochian section prematurely.

Regardie felt that the heart of the Golden Dawn magickal system was Enochian (more about this later). On account of both its complexity and ambiguity, Regardie felt that great harm could befall the student who prematurely tapped into the energy contained within the tension of the intersecting lines and letters of the Enochian Watchtower system. Another important 20th-century Golden Dawn practitioner, Paul Foster Case, shared Regardie's viewpoint. In Case's own Masonic-magickal order,

B.O.T.A., (whose roots are in both the Golden Dawn and Masonic Blue Lodge systems) every reference to the Enochian system has been deleted, although every other Golden Dawn technique, including the Tattva visions, is given as instruction.

Case, by the sheer weight of his membership in the Chicago GD Temple Thoth-Hermes (around 1920), was exposed early on to the Enochian system of magick. Though he never publicly published his views on Enochian, we can deduce his own approach to this subject:

- When first confronted with the Watchtower magickal squares, which many times contain multiple letters in each of their 644 composite squares, Case would not be able to detect the purpose or pattern behind each lettered square.

- Case, in his Qabalistic research, would always letter an unknown word in Hebrew, change it to the Tarot card/Hebrew letter number equivalents, and weigh its magickal significance in light of number and/or astrological symbolism.

- Therefore, Case undoubtedly first changed these Watchtower squares to Hebrew letters and worked out an analysis based on his own deep Qabalistic insights.

- However, at some point in his research, Case would reach an impasse because this Hebraic analysis is not the correct method by which to rectify these squares.

- Case, out of his own confusion over these jumbled squares, or possibly because of having access to a copy of Dee's diary (such as Meric. Casaubon's version) and being shocked by the contents of the angelic records, ultimately deemed the Enochian material to be demonic rather than angelic.

- If Case had access to Dee's own skrying records, he would have found that the Enochian letters, when first dictated as English letters, were so powerful that any word had to be written backwards so as not to set the magickal force in motion prematurely. This may have been another reason why Case became soured with Enochian.

- Still another reason could simply be that Case, who used Crowley's research (such as *Liber 777* and *Sepher Sephiroth*) in the beginning stages of his own Qabalistic research on the Tarot and gematria, ultimately became disillusioned with Crowley. Case, in his later writings, is at pains not to make reference to Crowley. Since Crowley's Enochian workings are found throughout *The Equinox*, Case may have found further reason in this to divorce himself from the Enochian workings.

I myself had an experience similar to that of Case's own revulsion towards Enochian. As a beginning student, I came across Regardie's *Golden Dawn* around 1969. Of all the systems presented, the Enochian seemed the most complicated and therefore the most powerful of all the systems presented. Though the Enochian work appeared last in this gigantic tome, I was immediately attracted to it like a neophyte moth to a candle flame. And like a moth, I was severely singed by my premature dipping into these esoteric waters, for after trying to make sense out of the jumble of letters appearing in the Watchtowers, let alone understand the GD method of extracting Enochian God names from these tablets, I found myself beset with confusion, despondency, and fear.

After being overwhelmed by this gigantic alien system, which was incorrectly lettered to begin with, what little groundwork I had already gained concerning the basic concepts of Qabalistic magick was put into jeopardy. I began to doubt that I had a clear understanding of even the most basic fundamentals. This Enochian system both obsessed and confused me with its tantalizing array of unexplainable letters. My only recourse, at that point in my magickal career, was to stop all studies and recuperate for a few months until I could clearly re-enter the path.

This method of alternating work and hibernation is utilized in my studies to this day. In some ways, it is the only way in which unknown, inaccessible information can be tapped into: by first making new inroads into uncharted territory and then withdrawing and regrouping for a short period in order to allow true assimilation of this new information. It is as if one must first forget something in order to clearly remember it at a future date.

The only point I am trying to make here is to warn the beginning student from rashly undertaking Enochian research. Even though there are many texts on the market today to serve as Enochian guidebooks for the beginner, not one of these books contains the Watchtowers correctly lettered, nor has any one of these new self-help Enochian books penetrated the real pattern behind the 644 lettered squares.

But this one chapter on Enochian solves this Enochian mystery once and for all. This chapter not only gives the Watchtowers in their correct format, but also reveals the true reason for each letter appearing in each square. And though every other version of this system shows more than one square containing multiple letters, the true Enochian Watchtower system as shown in this key displays only one transliterated English letter in each of the 644 squares, with eight of the squares displaying this English transliteration backwards.

To the beginning student, the above discussion may seem beyond his or her abilities to fully understand. But, as I have pointed out, even my own beginning magickal studies were hampered by the temptation to understand the blinded Enochian Watchtowers. So if you want a firm foundation to pursue the Enochian material presented in abundance in other works (such as the fourth volume of Regardie's *Golden Dawn),* you should base all your research on the letters and logic of the Watchtower squares as clearly outlined in this key. In light of this, the 11th key contains some basic, introductory material before proceeding to the heart of the matter. However, I have always intended this chapter to rectify the Watchtower system rather than to serve as a primer or overview of Enochian magick.

This 11th key begins with a discussion of the traditional number values assigned to Enochian by John Dee. This system, shown in the table entitled "The Enochian Alphabet of John Dee," assigns two separate sets of numbers to the alphabet: digital and additional. Both these codes are of my own "invention," first deciphered and reconstructed in the late 1970s. I first detected the use of the Enochian alphabet as numbers in a series of meditational, invocational poems known as the "48 Calls of the Thirty Aires." These poems give 18 Calls and an additional 19th Call as a key to explore the 30 Aires or Aethyrs of the Enochian universe. As I tabled out each alphabet combination and its corresponding number value, I discovered to my chagrin that the majority of these alphanumeric codes were blinded, giving many variant number values to one letter. As an example, the Enochian letter Un, transliterated as A, possesses at least five different number values:

Enochian A and Its Number Variables

Number Letter Code in Calls	Value of A in Example
AF	1
GA	1
ERAN	3
FAXS	3
PEOAL	3
QUAR	3
CLA	6
DAOX	6
ACAM	7
DARG	7
CIAL	9

After much study, my number-letter tables revealed the use of letters as numbers occurring 64 times within the Enochian Calls of the Aires (see Regardie's *Golden Dawn* for the complete text of these Calls). The alphabet was used as a digital number code 32 times, while the alphabet formed words describing number concepts 32 other times. From these 64 examples, 12 uses of the Enochian alphabet as numbers concealed the number pattern behind Dee's Enochian alphabet. And these 12 clues revealed that the Greek alphabet, modeled upon the order of the Hebrew alphabet, generated the digital alphanumeric code found within Dee's original Enochian records. Thus the concealed code within these Calls assigns (as beginning and end) 1 to A and 4(00) to U, modeled upon the Greek Alpha and Upsilon as the Hebraic Aleph and Tav. The 32 alphanumeric digital codes, the 19 basic Calls in which they appear, and their number values as contained in the original text and as their corrected values appear in the table below.

As can be seen from this table, the correct number values were in almost all cases communicated by the Enochian angels to John Dee in a blinded form (possibly to prevent easy decipherment). However, eight clues were extracted from these 32 examples that led to my paralleling

Thirty-Two Digital Numbers Within the Calls

		Number Value	
Letter Code	**Nineteen Calls**	**Blinded**	**Corrected**
L	4,5,10,19 (twice)	1	3
OS	3 (twice)	12	72
CLA	3, 4	456	231
PD	4	33	84
MAPM	5	9639	4184
AF	5	19	16
PEOAL	5	69636	85713
ACAM	6	7699	1214
NI	7	28	51
OX	8	26	76
P	9	8	8
CIAL	9	9996	2113
OP	10	22	78
DAOX	10	5618	4176
O	11	5	7
GA	11	31	31
OB	12	28	72
MIAN	12	3663	4115
UX	13	42	46
OL	10,14	24	73
QUAR	14	1636	9411
DARG	15	6739	4113
EMOD	16	8763	5474
TAXS	17	7336	3162
ERAN	18	6332	5115

Enochian to a Hellenistic-Semitic hybrid alphabet. These eight alphanumeric examples and their clues are as follows:

- A̲F = 19. **AF** is numbered at 19 in Call 5. **A** as 1 is the clue which establishes the identity of the Enochian **A,** with both Alpha and Aleph each valued at 1. It should be noted that the letter name for the Enochian A is *Un*, which is modeled on the Latin root for "one" (as in UNUS, UNA, UNUM). This further reinforces the identity of **A** with 1. **F** as 9 is a blind, for **F** is in reality 6 (modeled on the Greek Stau and the Hebrew Vav). But **F** as 9 in conjunction with the Enochian word name **AFFA,** meaning "empty," is a clue which will be shown below.

- G̲A̲ = 31. **GA** as 31 in Call 11 is the only correct pair of letters numbered openly in the 19 Calls. We have already ascertained **A** to be valued at 1, but by this additional example, **G** can be justified as 3, the value of both the Greek Gamma and the Hebrew Gimel. If Enochian were modeled upon Latin or English, then **G** should be 7. But by this example, the Greek/Hebrew model for Enochian is fully justified.

- O̲S̲ = 12. **OS** as 12 in Call 3 assigns **O** incorrectly as 1 but establishes **S** as 2. This numbering of **S** as 2 equates **S** to the Greek Sigma (valued at 2[00]) rather than the Hebrew Shin, 3(00) or Samekh 6(0).

- O̲X̲ = 26. **OX** as 26 in Call 8 assigns **O** incorrectly as 2 but establishes **X** as 6. Here again, the Greek Xi (valued at 6[0]) is the model rather than the Hebrew Samekh (also valued at 6[0]).

- DA̲O̲X̲ = 5678. **DAOX** as 5678 in Call 10 assigns **D, A,** and **X** to incorrect values, but resolves the numbering for **O,** which was 1 in **OS** and 2 in **OX**. Here the Enochian **O** is derived from both the Hebrew Ayin (valued as 7[0]) and the Greek Omicron (also valued at 7[0]). Enochian, unlike Greek, possesses only one **O**. The last letter of the Greek alphabet, long **Ō** of Omega (valued at 8[00]), is not used as the model for the last Enochian letter. Rather, the last Hebrew alphabet letter Tav will mark the end of Enochian.

- U̲X̲ = 42. **UX** as 42 in Call 13 fixes the last letter of the Enochian alphabet. **X** as 2 is incorrect (for **OX** correctly numbered **X** as 6), but the Enochian **U** as 4 utilizes both Hebrew and Greek to terminate the Enochian alphabet. For, as pointed out above, the position of Tav in the Hebrew alphabet, which marks the last letter as the number 400, is also used for the Enochian letter **U,** which is the secret last letter of Enochian. The phonetic value of **U** is equal to the Greek Upsilon (valued at 400), but the actual letter name for the Enochian U, Vau, brings to mind the Hebrew Tav, conjoined to **U** as **V**.

- P̲=8. **P** as 8 in Call 9 is the only correct instance of one letter used as a number. The Enochian **P** as 8 is further substantiation of a Hellenistic/Semitic model, for both the Greek Pi and the Hebrew Peh number as 8 (as 8[0]).

- OP=22. **OP** as 22 in Call 10 is blinded. From the clue DAOX, **O** is correctly valued at 7; from the clue **P, P** is correctly valued at 8. **OP** is therefore 78 rather than 22. Yet the division of the Tarot is brought to mind at once when associating 22 to 78, for out of 78 total Tarot cards, 22 are numbered from 0 to 21, bearing the Hebrew alphabet. This is a clue to the esoteric construction of Enochian for:

—Enochian numbers 21 letters, just as the Tarot bears the Roman Numerals I through XXI.

—As the Tarot contains an unnumbered card (The Fool), so does the 21-letter Enochian alphabet contain an unwritten character.

—This unwritten 22nd Enochian character is in the position of Theta in the Greek alphabet, Theta being the initial of both **ThEOS** = God and **ThHRION** = Beast. This is paralleled by the obsolete Greek letter Stau, the sixth Greek letter, which is both the mark of Qain and the beast.

—This 22nd unwritten Enochian character possesses the same number value as the Tarot numeral for The Fool, zero. As zero, this unknown Enochian letter (which may resemble the Greek Theta) is used only in digital Enochian notation that possesses a zero. In all the examples of digital Enochian, zero is never rendered as an alphanumeric but only a word name (such as MATB as 1,000).

Beyond these eight clues, four additional hints to support this numbering system can be found in the 32 references of numeral words within the 19 Calls, as shown below:

Thirty-Two Enochian Numeral Names

Numeral Name	Enochian	Call
Empty	AFFA	19
No One	AG L	19
Half	OBZA	9
One	SAGA	19
First	L	2 (twice), 5, 15
First	LA	5
First	LI	3
First	LO	4, 8
First	EL	6
Two	OLANI	9
Second	VIU	2, 4, 5, 6, 16
Third	D	5, 6, 7, 17
Third	PI	8
The ends	ULS	5

Thirty-Two Enochian Numeral Names (cont'd.)

Numeral Name	Enochian	Call
Fourth	S	6
Fourth	ES	7
Sixth	NORZ	3
Nine	EM	6
Hundred	EORS	10
Thousand	MATB	10 (twice)

The four major clues from these numeral names are:

- ULS = the ends. **ULS** as the ends further supports **U** as Upsilon. For as pointed out above (under clue **UX**), the Enochian U is modeled upon the Greek Upsilon (valued at 4[00]) in the position of the parallel Hebrew Tav (also valued at 4[00]).

- AFFA = empty. **AFFA** appears in Call 13, denoting "empty," which can also be construed as zero or nothing. This clue further supports my own premise of a missing, unwritten 22nd Enochian letter. This 22nd letter corresponds in shape and sound to the Greek letter Theta, but bears the number value of zero from the Tarot card, *The Fool*. As a number, this letter is the positional value of zero (not unlike the Sanskrit code KaTaPaYa).

  AF alone in Enochian is 19. Though **F** is in reality 6 (corresponding to the empty, or missing, Greek letter Stau), by its blinded value of 9, **AFFA** can be seen as:
  A = the fool, zero, the empty position
  F = 9 as Theta in Greek, the missing Enochian zero (θ).

- EM = nine. **EM** as the number name nine in Call 6 may be an allusion to the digital values of **E** and **M**. The Enochian **E** = 5 while **M** = 4 (0). 5(E) + 4(M) = 9. This again supports the Hebrew/Greek theory for Enochian.

- D = third. **D** as "third" in Calls 5 ,6, 7 and 17 supports a Tarot parallel model for Enochian. In this model, the Enochian letter A = 0, The Fool, while the Enochian letter **U** = XXI, The World. In this model the Enochian letter **D** corresponds with the third Tarot key, The Empress. Thus **D** = third = The Empress.

Now the above clues premise two number codes, one digital and the other additional. The digital code for Enochian takes the corresponding number value from the Hebrew/Greek model and ignores all zeros. Thus the Enochian letters D, M, and U, derived from Delta (4), Mu (40), and Upsilon (400), are all valued at 4. This code, laboriously demonstrated above, is taken directly from Dee's writings. By this code, every letter of a word becomes the digit of a number, and the composite number formed is its intrinsic number value. A secondary code for Enochian can be premised, which is based upon adding the sum of the number values of each letter, like Hebrew and Greek. A value assigned to Enochian in this additional code is the value of the corresponding Hebrew/Greek model, preserving the zeros. Both of these codes and their astrological correspondences derived from their Hebrew (and Tarot) equivalents are fully detailed in the first major table of this text.

The alphabet table is followed by a discussion debunking the premise that Enochian possesses a logical grammar and syntax, thereby proving that Enochian is a natural, rather than an artificial, language. In reality, Enochian is an artificial magickal language, but such a premise does not diminish its magickal efficacy one iota. Enochian, from my own investigations, is not:

- The mother tongue behind Sanskrit

- The original language of Atlantis

- In existence before 1580 CE.

This does not discredit its integrity, but rather places Enochian in its proper position among the other sacred languages of the magickal tradition.

The real origin of Enochian can only be understood if we have recourse to the original diaries of John Dee, which record the trance crystal skrying sessions of Edward Kelley's angelic conversations. I have compressed the essence of these heavenly communications into a listing called the "Enochian Timeline." By studying this timeline, the true origin of Enochian emerges, as well as the real pattern behind the construction of the four Enochian Watchtowers. From this timeline we can deduce:

- That the Enochian language and angelic messages were not faked by Kelley.

- That Dee was never quite aware of their pattern, nor was Kelley.

- That a consistent pattern for the number value of Enochian was concealed within the angelic communications.

- That the clues to the real pattern for the paramount Enochian system of the four Watchtowers were dictated by the angels before the communication of the actual letters of the Watchtowers.

All of this, and more, is fully worked out within the commentary of this 11th key.

The true pattern for these Watchtowers, which can be seen in the angelic messages, is 91 seven-lettered names for the Governors, or angelic rulers, of 91 separate divisions of the terrestrial world. Each of these 91 names is derived from the Enochian letters appearing on seven tangent squares of the Watchtowers. There are 22 of these names to be generated from each of the four Watchtowers, and an additional three names to be found upon the fifth tablet known as the Tablet of Union. Also, there exists a secret 92nd name generated by two letters each from three of the Watchtowers and one letter from a fourth (all in reverse, or adverse lettering). Each of these Governor names has its own unique sigil. It is these letters, and these letters alone, which should be upon the Watchtowers.

The lead letter of each of the 91 Governor names should be in capital (or upper case) transliterated English. All the other letters of the Watchtowers should be in small (or lower case) transliterated English. The exception is the eight additional capital letters, all of which are written in reverse, seven of which form the secret 92nd Governor, plus one extra which serves as the lead additional letter for the Tablet of Union.

Every variant to these letters, found within certain squares of the Watchtowers in the many translations and commentaries available today on Enochian, are scribal errors which should be eliminated. Their source is Dee's own diary record of the Watchtowers where, in certain squares, Dee crossed an English Enochian letter out and replaced it with a smaller letter in the upper corner, in hopes of rectifying Kelley's original transcription.

Dee never corrected the system, nor discovered its key, yet his initial attempt at rectifying the system has led to misunderstandings over the construction of the Watchtowers since the Golden Dawn Enochian system was first developed. A good example of this transcription error is the reverse letter N found in the 455th square of the Governors' names (in the upper right corner of the Water Watchtower). This N, because it is written backwards in the original, has been misconstrued as the letters "y plus 1" as well as "h." Therefore, in the Golden Dawn version of this square, all four characters—N, y, 1, and h—can be found. In reality, only the backward N is proper, while the other three are the result of misunderstanding this system rather than refining it through astral visions.

The corrected Watchtowers are fully worked out in three tables:

- First, each square of the Watchtower system is assigned a number equal to the specific corresponding letter of a Governor's name. These sequential numbers are the true matrix to the Watchtowers and are the order of the tracing of the 91+1 sigils upon the Watchtowers.

- Next, the name of each Governor, the sequential order of the corresponding squares, and their location upon the Watchtowers are clearly tabulated.

- Finally, the Watchtowers themselves are re-lettered to conform to their true pattern.

This rectification forms the only authentic set of Enochian Watchtowers in print. Even Dee was incapable of making these corrections.

A deep study of these three tables should convince any reader of the accuracy of this system, especially if the reader has had contact with any other version.

A final note should be made upon the original shape of the actual Enochian alphabet. The letters composing the Watchtowers found in Dee's original diaries are in all cases transliterated English, written:

- In a printed rather than a longhand form

- With both upper case and lower case

- With the peculiarity of eight select upper-case letters written backwards

Dee did receive the original Enochian script in one of the Enochian trance session held by Kelley. Supposedly they first appeared as faint yellow outlines upon parchment, which were later inked in by Dee. This received script was used by Dee in the decoration of all ritual implements for skrying (such as the skrying table and wax talismans the table was placed upon). But the source for this Enochian script was one of Dee's most treasured alchemical tracts, Pantheus' *Voarchadumia,* which Dee had had in his library since 1560 CE (predating the Enochian sessions by 20 years).

By borrowing Pantheus' own version of an angelic alphabet for Enochian, Dee secured an ancient-looking alphabet which would add credibility to his Enochian system. But the real Enochian script is English, and not the imitation of the Voarchadumian alphabet. Further, the Enochian Watchtowers require an upper- and lower-case alphabet, which the original Enochian script does not possess. Crowley got around this in his own Watchtowers by drawing these original characters twice as large to denote capitals.

Again, my contention is that the real Enochian script is the English alphabet, ordered upon a Greek/Hebrew model. This special ritual script is only a secondary script that was borrowed from other sources rather than received in trance directly from the angels.

After the Watchtowers are given in full, the Golden Dawn method of analyzing the structure of the Watchtowers is discussed. In this method seven basic divine names can be extracted from each of the four major Watchtowers. These linear names of God were received in a dream by Edward Kelley (on June 20, 1584), before the actual trance session which dictated the squares of the Watchtowers took place. To these seven basic names, an additional four were received by Kelley. Two were excluded from the general Golden Dawn scheme, since they dealt with demonic names. But two other names (that of the Trumpeter and Servants) were not included, since no instructions to their formation have survived in print. But from my own Enochian workings I have been able to offer a tentative reconstruction of these lost names.

As to the names of the Enochian demons, they have also been included, since my own Watchtowers can permit the only correct spellings of these names. When dealing with demonic forces, the correct naming of the demon is often the sole point of authority the beginning magician can wield. This is embodied in many myths and fairy tales, such as that of Rumpelstiltskin. Since my Enochian work can rectify all that has been undone by scribal error, the demonic names have been included.

For each of the four Watchtowers, I have tabled out 11 types of divine names. All are based upon Kelley's dream of June 20, 1584, in which the occupants of four great directional towers were laid out before their castles, like four embroidered carpets rolled out to meet in a common center.

This connection of carpet with the Watchtower symbolism by Kelley is highly significant, since the original Watchtowers described in the Bible were carpets laid out on the sand at the four corners of a desert encampment (see Isaiah 21:5, where TzPH HTzPITh is translated as "watch in the watchtower" but is literally "spread the carpets"). Possibly the most magickally charged medium for creating the Watchtowers would be embroidered ritual rugs, set at the four directional corners of the temple, with the fifth Tablet of Union as a central white carpet upon which the altar is erected.

As for the tables displaying the divine Enochian linear names, the 11 basic types of names are tabled out twice. First each of these names is recorded for every Watchtower in its correct format, obeying the upper and lower case of the Governor names as well as retaining the reversed (adverse) letters. Next, the Air Watchtower is dissected in full to show how each of the 11 types of divine names is generated. These 11 Enochian divine names and the inhabitants of each of the four great castles are as follows:

- Great King
- Trumpeter*
- Servants*
- Ensign Bearers
- Seniors
- Kerubic God Names
- Kerubic Angels
- Servient God Names
- Servient Angels
- Cacodemon God Names*
- Cacodemons*

Again, as I have pointed out earlier, my intention is not to provide a primer in Enochian magick but rather to rectify the errors in Enochian spelling. As such, all of the God names which you will encounter in Golden Dawn Enochian magick, are written correctly here for the first time. However, the beginning student will have to turn to other sources for practical instructions on how to utilize these god names, since space prohibits such an inclusion in this work.

Next is a discussion of the peculiar Enochian order for the elements of Air, Water, Earth, and Fire. By the Golden Dawn allocation of the elements to the four directions, this Enochian elemental hierarchy translates to the directional order of East (Air), West (Water), North (Earth), and South (Fire). East, West, North, and South is an order for the directions peculiar to Western magick, which measures the Earth first by the motion of the

---

*Not included in the Golden Dawn Enochian system.

Sun and then by the extremes of the magnetic poles. This elemental discussion is followed by the powers and potencies latent in each of the four corners of any Watchtower, which is taken directly from Dee's own diaries.

Next the last complete analysis of the Watchtowers is given. Dee received on April 18, 1587, while traveling through Trebone, a cipher number system which would allow any number in the range of 1–624 to conceal an Enochian letter. First the four Watchtowers are set as four tangent squares forming one large square, as:

AIR	WATER
EARTH	FIRE

Then each linear horizontal row of 24 squares is counted in serial order from left to right, forming the number series 1 through 624. The Enochian letter that occupies any given square in this system determines the number-letter cipher substitute. Thus the first letter in the upper left-hand corner of the Air Watchtower is the number 1, while the last letter in the lower-right corner of the Fire Watchtower is number 624.

This logic can encompass the Tablet of Union's 20 additional letters, extending the number range to 644. In this case, the letter "e" in the upper left corner of the Tablet of Union would be 625, while the letter "m" in the lower-right corner would be 644. This cipher-number system is shown in two tables:

- First, the four Watchtowers (and Tablet of Union) are drawn with the corresponding cipher-number substitutes in place of the Enochian letters normally occupying each of the 644 squares.

- Then the number and its equivalent letter (in correct upper, lower, or reverse style) are tabled side by side. With these tables, any number from 1 to 644 encountered in any Enochian material can be converted to a specific letter and quadrant of the Watchtowers.

This Enochian chapter ends with an addendum discussing an alternate method of giving number value found in both the Golden Dawn system and Crowley's *Vision and The Voice*. Although both of these sources show an alternate set of numbers for Enochian, neither source discloses how this peculiar set of numbers was obtained for Enochian. Again, the answer resides in the stacks of the British Museum in which Mathers labored for so many years in establishing the paradigm which would encompass all Western magickal correspondences.

Mathers, at one point of his research, came across Dr. Thomas Rudd's *Treatise on Angel Magic* (Ms. Harley 6482, first composed after 1600). This pristine study of angelic magic was composed just after Dee's own Enochian workings and contains a table which would allow Mathers to give a number value for 16 of the 21 Enochian letters. In the table entitled "The Characters of the Sixteen Figures of Geomancy Expressed in the Greater and Lesser Squares of Tabula Sancta," Dr. Rudd equates 16 Enochian letters to the 16 geomantic figures, and these in turn to a planetary and zodiacal signature.

Mathers' heart must have surged with joy when he realized upon first reading that he now possessed a key for Enochian. For, from Rudd's table, Mathers now knew the correspondences between Enochian, geomancy, and astrology.

The astrological attributes given to the 16 geomantic figures were peculiar to Rudd. But Mathers, from his decoding of the *Sepher Yetzirah* and its correct linkage to the Tarot, knew what Hebrew letter any astrological signature would possess.

So, armed with this Qabalistic information, Mathers linked Rudd's table to both the Hebrew alphabet and to its corresponding number. The link was through Rudd's astrological attributes. From this link, Mathers was then able to give a Hebraic numerical value (based on the astrological equivalents) to 16 select Enochian letters:

Mathers' Enochian Decipherment

Source   **Relationship**

From Dr. Rudd   Enochian—geomancy—astrology
From *Sepher Yetzirah*   Astrology—Hebrew—number

when combined:

Enochian—geomancy—astrology—Hebrew—number

resulting in:

Enochian—number

Because geomancy is the closest link to Enochian in the above formula, only 16 selected Enochian letters can be numbered by the Golden Dawn system. However, Crowley, in his Enochian workings (found in *The Vision and The Voice*) culled meanings for the excluded five Enochian letters by linking these additional letters to the pentagonal elemental correspondences (as devised by Mathers). The above analysis based on Dr. Rudd was only recently detected by myself and is based upon Adam McLean's publication of this work.

As pointed out in the body of this chapter, Mathers reversed the astrological geomantic equivalents for Fam and Graph in working with this table. Crowley, however restored these attributes back to Rudd's original plan. Thus in the Golden Dawn system, S = 10 and E = 7, while in Crowley's revision S = 7 and E = 10. Possibly Mathers' own use of these correspondences required the transposition that occurs in all Golden Dawn Enochian documents using this table.

Mathers made one other correction to Rudd's table. He assigned Leo to both Fortuna Major and Minor, whereas Rudd assigned Capricorn to Fortuna Major rather than Leo. Mathers' correction, in this case, makes Rudd's geomantic correspondences consistent.

My original decipherment of the Golden Dawn system did not take into account Rudd's work. At that point, I felt Mathers must have divined on his own intuitions the Enochian-geomantic correspondences. A letter which I sent to Israel Regardie on July 13, 1980, summarizes the essence of my decipherment for the Enochian system. Much in the tables sent with this letter were not included in my subsequent article, "The Numerical Structure of the Enochian Alphabet," in *The Complete Golden Dawn System of Magic*. I have therefore excerpted this letter below to show in detail my initial decipherment of the pattern behind the Golden Dawn number system, and Crowley's variant:

> ... However, while recently re-reading *The Vision and The Voice* I noticed a clue in Crowley's comment to the 29th Aethyr which had been ignored in previous readings. Crowley states on page 31 of the 29th Aethyr:
>
>> The *geomantic* correspondences of the Enochian alphabet form a sublime commentary.
>
> The attribution of Enochian to Geomancy is then the clue for deciphering the allocation of both the Zodiac and the Hebrew alphabet to the Enochian alphabet, which Crowley extensively used in annotating the 30 Calls.
>
> But where shall we find the Qabalistic Tables which will justify Enochian aligned to Geomancy? The answer is not in the writings of Aleister Crowley, but rather the instructions of the Golden Dawn.
>
> On page 298 of Volume IV of *The Golden Dawn* is the Enochian Table "Notes to the Book of the Concourse of the Forces." This table offers us a correlation between the 16 geomantic figures and 16 select Hebrew letters of the alphabet. Crowley incorporates material from this table in column XLIX of *777*, as well as in his article on Geomancy in *The Equinox*, Vol. I No. 2, p.141.
>
> This table alone does not clarify Crowley's clue that "Geomancy forms a sublime commentary on Enochian," since the attributions do not directly correlate the Enochian alphabet to Geomancy.
>
> If we look through Crowley's major works (*The Equinox, 777, Magick, Book of Thoth, Magick Without Tears*, etc.) we will not be able to discover the Geomantic attributes of the Enochian alphabet. But if we turn to the Golden Dawn instructions again we will find the required table to link Geomancy with Enochian. The needed table is on page 77, Vol. IV, of *The Golden Dawn*, in the article on "Talismans and Sigils."
>
> With the aid of these two basic tables within the Golden Dawn teachings we can now allocate the Enochian alphabet to Geomancy, Astrology, Hebrew, and ultimately the number value of the Hebrew alphabet. These attributes are the source of Crowley's annotations for the 30 Calls of the Aethyrs.

I have constructed the following tables for your convenience; they will illustrate my solution to the Crowley Enochian-Qabalistic system. The Tables are as follows:

Table I—The Geomantic attributes of Enochian (according to the G.D. system).

Table II—The Complete Qabalistic associations to the Enochian alphabet derived from "The Book of the Concourse of the Forces." Enochian is allocated to Geomancy, the Zodiac and the four elements, the Hebrew alphabet, and ultimately the numerical value of the Hebrew alphabet.

Table III—The Calls of the 30 Aethyrs are tabulated as Astrological symbols according to both the orthodox G.D. attributes and Crowley's own system. Note the similarities between the two justifying my analysis. Crowley's variations are in the main two: the interchange of Leo and Cancer (both ruled by the luminaries), and the interchange of Virgo and Gemini (both ruled by Mercury).

Table IV—The Hebrew alphabet is correlated to both the systems of the G.D. and Aleister Crowley.

Table V—The 5 Enochian and 6 Hebrew alphabet letters which are not allocated in the Golden Dawn system are listed. Crowley's own attributes for the excluded 5 Enochian alphabet letters are shown as well.

Table VI—The Hebrew letters (as well as their numerical values) for the 30 Enochian Calls are tabulated according to the Golden Dawn system.

Table VII—A rectification of the above system of attributes for Enochian is tabulated, allowing a Hebrew letter to be attributed to each of the 21 Enochian letters. This rectification is based on both the systems of the Golden Dawn and Aleister Crowley.

Table I
The Geomantic Attributes of the Enochian Alphabet
(from *The Golden Dawn*, Vol. IV, p. 77)

Enochian Letter	Geomantic Figure
P	Populus
L	Via
G	Fortuna Major
Z	Fortuna Minor
S	Conjunctio
O	Puella
N	Rubeus
I	Acquisitio
U	Carcer
M	Tristitia
R	Laetitia
F	Cauda Draconis
T	Caput Draconis
B	Puer
A	Amissio
E	Albus

Table II
Complete Golden Dawn Qabalistic
Attributes of the Enochian Alphabet

Enochian Letter	Geomancy	Zodiac	Hebrew Letter	Number Value
P	Populus	Cancer (Moon waxing)	Ch	8
L	Via	Cancer/Water (Moon Waning)	Ch/M	8/40
G	Fortuna Major	Leo (Sun in South)	T	9
Z	Fortuna Minor	Leo/Air (Sun in North)	T/A	9/1
S	Conjunctio	Virgo	I	10
O	Puella	Libra	L	30
N	Rubeus	Scorpio	N	50
I	Acquisitio	Sagittarius	S	60
U	Carcer	Capricorn	O	70
M	Tristitia	Aquarius	Tz	90
R	Laetitia	Pisces	Q	100
F	Cauda Draconis	Fire (& Cauda Draconis)	Sh	300
T	Caput Draconis	Earth (& Caput Draconis)	Th	400
B	Puer	Aries	H	5
A	Amissio	Taurus	V	6
E	Albus	Gemini	Z	7

Table III
Astrological Symbols of the
Calls for the Thirty Aethyrs

Aethyr	Call	Golden Dawn	Crowley
30	T	Caput Draconis	Cauda Draconis
	E	Gemini	Virgo
	X	—	Earth
29	R	Pisces	Pisces
	I	Sagittarius	Sagittarius
	I	Sagittarius	Sagittarius
28	B	Aries	Aries
	A	Taurus	Taurus
	G	Leo	Cancer
27	Z	Leo	Leo
	A	Taurus	Taurus
	A	Taurus	Taurus
26	D	—	Spirit
	E	Gemini	Virgo
	S	Virgo	Gemini
25	V	Capricorn	Capricorn
	T	Caput Draconis	Caput Draconis
	I	Sagittarius	Sagittarius
24	N	Scorpio	Scorpio
	I	Sagittarius	Sagittarius
	A	Taurus	Taurus
23	T	Caput Draconis	Leo
	O	Libra	Libra
	R	Pisces	Pisces
22	L	Cancer	Cancer
	I	Sagittarius	Sagittarius
	N	Scorpio	Scorpio
21	A	Taurus	Taurus
	S	Virgo	Virgo
	P	Cancer	Leo
20	K	—	Fire
	H	—	Air
	R	Pisces	Pisces

Aethyr	Call	Golden Dawn	Crowley
19	P	Cancer	Leo
	O	Libra	Libra
	P	Cancer	Leo
18	Z	Leo	Leo
	E	Gemini	Virgo
	N	Scorpio	Scorpio
17	T	Caput Draconis	Caput Draconis
	A	Taurus	Taurus
	N	Scorpio	Scorpio
16	L	Cancer	Cancer
	E	Gemini	Virgo
	A	Taurus	Taurus
15	O	Libra	Libra
	X	—	Earth
	O	Libra	Libra
14	U	Capricorn	Capricorn
	T	Caput Draconis	Caput Draconis
	I	Sagittarius	Sagittarius
13	Z	Leo	Leo
	I	Sagittarius	Sagittarius
	M	Aquarius	Aquarius
12	L	Cancer	Cancer
	O	Libra	Libra
	E	Gemini	Virgo
11	I	Sagittarius	Sagittarius
	K	—	Fire
	H	—	Air
10	Z	Leo	Caput Draconis
	A	Taurus	Taurus
	X	—	Earth
9	Z	Leo	Leo
	I	Sagittarius	Sagittarius
	P	Cancer	Leo
8	Z	Leo	Leo
	I	Sagittarius	Sagittarius
	D	—	Spirit

Aethyr	Call	Golden Dawn	Crowley
7	D	—	Spirit
	E	Gemini	Virgo
	O	Libra	Libra
6	M	Aquarius	Aquarius
	A	Taurus	Taurus
	Z	Leo	Leo
5	L	Cancer	Cancer
	I	Sagittarius	Sagittarius
	T	Caput Draconis	Caput Draconis
4	P	Cancer	Leo
	A	Taurus	Taurus
	Z	Leo	Caput Draconis
3	Z	Leo	Leo
	O	Libra	Libra
	N	Scorpio	Scorpio
2	A	Taurus	Taurus
	R	Pisces	Pisces
	N	Scorpio	Scorpio
1	L	Cancer	Cancer
	I	Sagittarius	Sagittarius
	L	Cancer	Cancer

Table IV
Hebrew Alphabet as Enochian According to the
Systems of the Golden Dawn and Aleister Crowley

| | Enochian | |
Hebrew Letter	Golden Dawn	A.Crowley
A	Z	H
B	—	—
G	—	T
D	—	D*
H	B	B
V	A	A, R
Z	E	S
Ch	P, L	G, L
T	G, Z	P, Z, T
I	S	E, S
K	—	—
L	O	O
M	L	Q
N	N	N
S	I	I
O	U	U
P	—	—
Tz	M	M
Q	R	R
R	—	—
Sh	F	K
Th	T	X

---

*Enochian D is also equivalent to Hebrew AL (31 = 3 + 1 = 4 = D)

Table V
Letters Excluded in the
Golden Dawn System of Enochian-Geomancy

Excluded Enochian Letter	Crowley's Attribution	
	Element	Hebrew Letter Equivalent
C	Fire	Sh
D	Spirit	D or AL
H	Air	A
Q*	Water	M*
X	Earth	Th

Excluded Hebrew Letter	Astrological Attribute
B	Mercury
G	Moon
D	Venus
K	Jupiter
P	Mars
R	Sun

These Hebrew letters are six of the seven double letters which rule the planets. Of the seven doubles, however, the Hebrew Th is used only as the element Earth in the G.D. system. The Enochian letters are not the planets because their model is Geomancy, which rules the twelve signs and four elements.

---

*Note: Crowley did not comment on the Enochian letter Q. However, since the excluded five are based on the Elemental Pentagram, and the corresponding Hebrew letters, the logical attribute for Q would be Water and the Hebrew letter M.

Table VI
Hebrew Equivalents for the
Thirty Calls According to the Golden Dawn

Aethyr	Enochian Call	Hebrew Equivalent	Numerical Value of Hebrew
30	T E X	Th Z —	407
29	R I I	Q S S	220
28	B A G	H V T	20
27	Z A A	A V V	13
26	D E S	— Z I	17
25	V T I	O Th S	530
24	N I A	N S V	116
23	T O R	Th L Q	530
22	L I N	Ch S N	118
21	A S P	V I Ch	24
20	K H R	— — Q	100
19	P O P	Ch L Ch	46
18	Z E N	A Z N	58
17	T A N	Th V N	456
16	L E A	Ch Z V	21
15	O X O	L — L	60
14	U T I	O Th S	530
13	Z I M	A S Tz	151
12	L O E	Ch L Z	45
11	I K H	S — —	60
10	Z A X	A V —	7
9	Z I P	A S Ch	69
8	Z I D	A S —	61
7	D E O	— Z L	37
6	M A Z	Tz V A	97
5	L I T	Ch S Th	468
4	P A Z	Ch V A	15
3	Z O N	A L N	81
2	A R N	V Q N	156
1	L I L	Ch S Ch	76

Table VII
Rectification of the Golden Dawn-Crowley Attributions
of the Enochian Alphabet to the Hebrew Alphabet

Enochian Letter	Hebrew Equivalent	
	Golden Dawn	Crowley Variant
B	H	
C		Sh
G	T	
D		D (or AL)
F	Sh	
A	V	
E	Z	
M	Tz	
I	S	
H		A
L	M	
P	Ch	
Q		M
N	N	
X		Th
O	L	
R	Q	
Z	A	
U	O	
S	I	
T	Th	

So ends my early decipherment of the Golden Dawn
Enochian numbering system.

The analysis of the Golden Dawn system of numbering Enochian is followed by an extended, revised version of "The Book of Concourse of
Forces." This book, or table reduces every major Golden Dawn magickal
symbol set to the appropriate Enochian letters. Using the correct Golden
Dawn Tarot correspondences for the Court Cards, in which the Old Knight
= the New King and the Old King = the New Prince (see Key XII below for
more information), I have rectified and extended the set of correspondences for both the 16 Golden Dawn Geomantic Enochian letters and
Crowley's additional five elemental Enochian letters.

For the Golden Dawn set of correspondences, the 16 geomantic-Enochian letters are classified by 20 sets of magickal attributes:

1. Enochian Letter
2. Letter Name: Dee and GD variants
3. Geomancy
4. Geomantic Planetary Rulers
5. Geomantic Zodiacal Rulers
6. Geomancy on the Tree of Life
7. Elemental Counterchange
8. Tetragrammaton
9. Tattva
10. Quadrant of Watchtower
11. Court Card
12. Court Card Astrology
13. Tetragrammaton on Watchtower (Kerubic and Elemental)
14. Hebrew Model (GD)
15. Greek Model (Dee)
16. Major Arcana
17. Hebrew Astrology
18. Tree of Life Color Scale (Paths/Sephiroth)
19. Color (Major Arcana)
20. Number Value (GD/Dee)

The five additional elemental letters as established by Crowley are classified by 15 sets of magickal attributes:

1. Enochian Alphabet
2. Letter Name
3. Planet
4. Element
5. Tree of Life
6. Elemental Counterchange
7. Tetragrammaton
8. Tattva
9. Tablet of Union

10. Major and Minor Arcana

11. Hebrew Model

12. Greek Model

13. Major Arcana

14. Color

15. Number Value (Crowley/Dee)

It must be pointed out that the numerical/astrological attributes portrayed above are those of the Golden Dawn, while the numerical/astrological correspondences shown in the body of this chapter (below) are drawn from my own research on Dee's original Enochian records.

ORIGIN

1584 CE—The core magical system known as the Watchtowers of Enochian is communicated to John Dee and Edward Kelley in Cracow, Poland, by archangelic messengers. Before this period there is no evidence of this language. However, the *Zohar* relates that the "Book of Enoch" (the source of Enochian), which detailed the Qabalistic system of magick, was first given and then taken away from Adam and later returned to Enoch.

1887 CE—S. L. MacGregor Mathers creates a magick system whose basis is a revision of Dee's Enochian work.

ALPHABET CODE

The Enochian language is an artificial magickal language specifically devised by the work of the great Elizabethean magus John Dee. The extant manuscripts dealing with this language consist of angelic invocations or Calls based on squares of letters.

The alphabet is composed of 21 letters, one less than the 22 letters of Hebrew. The phonetic values of the Enochian language are based upon the Greek alphabet, while the order of the Enochian alphabet is based upon the Hebrew alphabet. From the angelic communications, which were often garbled, a double numbering system for Enochian developed. The primary numbering system is digital, not unlike the Katapayadhi system of Sanskrit, while the secondary numbering system is additional, based on the parallel Greek-Hebrew letters.

The digital system is directly used within the 48 Enochian angelic Calls, while the additional system is inferred from the structure of the alphabet itself.

Since the Enochian alphabet model is ultimately Hebrew, the Zodiacal symbolism of the *Sepher Yetzirah* can be extrapolated for the Enochian alphabet, although such correspondences cannot be found in Dee's writings. The following table delineates the Enochian numbering system of Dee.

The Enochian Alphabet of John Dee

Enochian Letter (Dee)	Enochian Letter (G.D.)	Trans-literation	Letter Name	Number Code (Digital)	Number Code (Additional)	Alphabet Model (Greek)	Alphabet Model (Hebrew)	Astrological Attribute (Sepher Yetzirah)
		A	Un	1	1	Alpha	Aleph	Air
		B	Pe	2	2	Beta	Beth	Mercury
		G	Ged	3	3	Gamma	Gimel	Moon
		D	Gal	4	4	Delta	Daleth	Venus
		E	Graph	5	5	Epsilon	Heh	Aries
		F	Orth	6	6	Stau	Vav	Taurus
		Z	Ceph	7	7	Zeta	Zain	Gemini
		H	Na-Hath	8	8	Eta	Cheth	Cancer
		I, J, Y	Gon	1	10	Iota	Yod	Virgo
		C, K	Veh	2	20	Kappa	Kaph	Jupiter
		L	Ur	3	30	Lambda	Lamed	Libra
		M	Tal	4	40	Mu	Mem	Water
		N	Drun	5	50	Nu	Nun	Scorpio
		X	Pal	6	60	Xi	Samekh	Sagittarius

The Enochian Alphabet of John Dee (cont'd.)

Enochian Letter		Trans-literation	Letter Name	Number Code		Alphabet Model		Astrological Attribute (Sepher Yetzirah)
Dee	G.D.			Digital	Additional	Greek	Hebrew	
↲	↲	O	Med	7	70	Omicron	Ayin	Capricorn
↻	↻	P	Mals	8	80	Pi	Peh	Mars
⊔	⊔	Q	Ger	9	90	Koppa	Tzaddi	Aquarius
ℰ	ℰ	R	Don	1	100	Rho	Qoph	Pisces
⌐	⌐	S	Fam	2	200	Sigma	Resh	Sun
⟍	⟍	T	Gisa	3	300	Tav	Shin	Fire
⋔	⋔	U, V, W	Vau	4	400	Upsilon	Tav	Saturn

In the foregoing table, a letter is missing in the Greek-Hebrew model. This letter is the ninth position of the alphabet occupied by Theta in Greek and Teth in Hebrew. Theta is the initial of *Theos,* God, while Teth is the zodical sign Leo. This missing Enochian letter, the 22nd unwritten letter, is the symbol for God or Spirit, and represents the number value of zero. It is parallel to the 19th unwritten Enochian Call that invokes the unnumbered, unknown spirit.

Note also that the letter names for the Enochian alphabet are in the majority of cases not phonemic. The three exceptions are Ged, Na-Hath and Vau. This is one of the indications that Enochian is an artificial language. However, the most important proof that Enochian is artificial is the lack of a true grammar and syntax. Though many scholars have asserted that Enochian contains a true syntax and grammar, in reality it only feigns or pretends to contain a precise grammatical structure.

The following examples of Enochian taken from the Angelic Calls of John Dee show that grammar and syntax are imitated without any consistency.

ALDI—gather up

ALDON—of gathering

The verb "gather up," when the terminal "I" is replaced with "ON," becomes the possessive, "of gathering."

CORMP—numbered, or hath yet numbered

CORMPT—be numbered

The addition of the letter "T" changes "numbered" to "be numbered." As in all the examples cited here, the addition (or deletion) of one arbitrary letter (not consistent in any example) imitates the grammatical changes to a root word.

FAORGT—dwelling places

FARGT—their dwelling places

The deletion of the letter "O" results in the addition of the possessive "their." The addition of a possessive pronoun should be denoted by, if anything, the addition of a letter rather than the deletion of a letter.

GOHE—saith

GOHIA—we say

GOHOL—saying

Though it never occurs in the Calls, "GOH" must be considered the root verb "say." The addition of "E" results in the third person singular present indicative, "saith." With the addition of "OL," the present participle "saying" is created. Again, arbitrary additions of letters ape a true grammatical structure.

HUBAI—lanterns

HUBAR—ever-burning lamps

HUBARD—living lamps

Though it never occurs in print, we can assume that the root noun "HUBA" must be "lamp." With the addition of an "I," the plural form is created. The addition of the letter "R" adds the extra meaning of "ever-burning," which does not make sense. The addition of "RD" results in the adjective "living." This is a perfect example of arbitrary Enochian grammar.

LONSH—is power exalted

LONSHI—power

LONSHIN—their powers

In this example, the root word power is "LONSHI," where by the logic of the other examples the root word should be "LONSH," which is defined as "is power exalted." Again, the arbitrary addition of a letter to a root word changes the meaning of the word without any consistent logic.

LUSD—feet

LUSDA—their feet

LUSDI—my feet

Here the addition of "A" to the root noun "feet" results in the third person possessive pronoun "their," while the addition of "I" results in the possessive adjective "my."

NOCO—servants

NOCOD—thy servants

Here the addition of "D" denotes the possessive form of "thou."

NONCA—unto you

NONCI—O you

NONCP—for you

Though never written, "NONC" must be "you." The addition of "A" denotes "unto," the addition of "I" denotes "O," and "P" denotes the preposition "for." Again, there is no consistent logic to these additions.

OM—know (understand)

OMA—knowing

OMAX—knowest

In this example, "A" results in the addition of "-ing" while "X" results in the addition of "-est."

PARM—run

PARMG—let it run

The addition of "G" to the verb "run" results in "let it." As in all the examples, an extra letter arbitrarily modifies the root word.

PRG—flames

PRGE—with the fire

PRGEL—of fire

This is a good example of one letter modifying the original root word and then a second letter in addition to the first modifying the word once more. "E" denotes "with" while "L" added to "E" denotes the preposition "of."

SOBAM—whom

SOBHA—whose

SOBRA—in whose

The addition of "AM" to the root "SOB" creates the relative objective pronoun "whom," the addition of "AH" creates the relative possessive pronoun "whose," and the addition of "RA" results in the addition of the preposition "in" to "whose."

TORZU—arise

TORZUL—shall rise

TORZULP—rose up

The addition of "L" denotes the future tense "shall," while the addition of "P" adds "up" to the past tense. Again, this is not logical but arbitrary.

The foregoing 38 examples are by no means exhaustive; however, they do betray the inaccuracy of an Enochian "grammar." The table on the opposite page shows the various meanings for the addition of letters to a root word in Enochian.

Enochian Grammatical Terminative

A—ing, their

D—thy

E—with

G—let it

I—O, my

L—shall, of

N—their

P—up, for

R—ever

T—be

X—est

AM—whom

HA—whose

IA—we

OL—ing

ON—of

RA—in whose

RD—living

The source of this artificial angelic language was through visions received in a crystal rather than from any actual materialization of the angels. John Dee communicated with the angelic kingdom and received almost all extant versions of the Enochian language through skrying in crystal by Edward Kelley.

Preliminary skrying was done in England, but the heart of this angelic system was communicated to Dee and Kelley in Poland in 1584 CE, a time when the Hebrew Qabalah was at its height there.

In all the communications that have survived, there are no more than 1,000 different words. The real power of Enochian is not in the language but in the system known as the Watchtowers. All of Dee's extant writings revolve around this one unifying system. Mathers realized this and incorporated the Watchtowers into the heart of his own magickal system.

The Watchtowers are five magickal squares composed of 644 lettered squares. Four of the squares represent the four directions (and the four elements) and are each made up of 156 squares of 12 x 13. The fifth Watchtower is the Tablet of Union, representing the center (and Spirit), and is made up of 20 squares of 4 x 5.

However, although there are many surviving versions of this system, no correct edition of these Watchtowers has ever been published, even in the works of John Dee. Both Dee and Mathers only partly discerned the true pattern of these Enochian Watchtowers. This pattern or matrix consists of the names of the 91 Angelic Governors of the World.

Since Dee only partly understood this secret pattern, he could not have invented this system of Watchtowers on his own. And, as will be shown below, Kelley did not invent it either.

The following timeline shows the date and order of the Dee-Kelley Enochian visions concerning the four Watchtowers which were received in Cracow, Poland.

Enochian Timeline

April 14, 1584—Received the first Call of the 19 Calls, which invokes all 30 levels (or Aires) of the 644 squares of the Watchtowers. Note: the Calls were communicated before the actual Watchtowers. The Calls are the main body of Enochian literature.

April 15, 1584—Second Call obtained in an incomplete form.

April 25, 1584—Third Call and clarification of second Call.

April 28, 1584—Fourth Call.

May 14, 1584—The 5th through 14th Calls in Enochian only (the English was promised to be communicated at a later date).

May 21, 1584—The 91 Angelic Governors are communicated, the real skeleton of the four Watchtowers. The first 42 Governors are named beginning with OCCODON (the first) and ending with OOANAMB (the 42nd).

May 22, 1584—The remaining 49 Angelic Governors are named, beginning with TAHANDO (the 43rd) and ending with DOZINAL (the 91st)

May 23, 1584—The 91 Provinces in the world ruled by the 91 Angelic Governors are dictated for all 30 Aires. This is the greatest secret of Enochian magic: that the names of the 91 Governors, which compose the 644 squares of the Enochian Watchtowers, rule the 91 divisions of our earthly world. Know the correct Governor's name and sigil for any country in the world, and by angelic invocation you can control the government of that kingdom.

June 20, 1584—Kelley has a dream of four gigantic Watchtowers which rule the world. This is the first mention of these Watchtowers, although the 644 letters which compose these Watchtowers had already been secretly communicated in the 91 seven-lettered names of the Angelic Governors.

Kelley's dream details the four Watchtowers as containing the following occupants:

4 Trumpeters with pyramid-shaped trumpets

12 Banners displaying the Names of God

24 Seniors or Senators, bearded and ancient

 4 Kings

20 Princes holding the train of the four Kings, leading 16 crosses

16 Crosses of 4 angles each with 10 faces

<u>256</u> Elemental angels, servants of the crosses

336 total (84 occupants to each of the four Watchtowers)

These 336 occupants are the linear God names that compose the main bulk of Mathers' Enochian Magic in the Golden Dawn. Note that the actual names were not given to Kelley, only anthropomorphic visions of the names upon the Watchtowers. All these names are linear, and the secondary pattern of the Watchtowers. The primary pattern is the 91 Governors.

June 25, 1584—The four Watchtowers as 12 x 13 gridded squares filled with Enochian letters are finally communicated, along with sigils for each of the four Watchtowers. These Watchtower squares are given in English, not Enochian, and capital letters as well as lower-case letters are communicated. The linear names of God derived from these squares cannot justify the capitalization of certain letters. But the 91 Governor names *can* justify these capitalized letters, for each capital letter is the initial letter of one of the 91 Governor names. The proper order of these four elemental Watchtowers was dictated: first, Air; second, Water; third, Earth; and fourth, Fire.

The method of obtaining the God names envisioned by Kelley in his dream of June 20th is also given. But the angels did not dictate to Kelley and Dee that the real pattern or matrix of these Watchtower squares is the 91 Governor names. The angels did not reveal that the random capital letters appearing in the Watchtowers are in fact the initial letters of the Governors. When asked directly by Dee why there existed diverse lettering in the Watchtowers, the reply was that beginning with the capital letters would make the names of wicked spirits. In reality it will make the names of the 91 Angelic Governors.

June 26, 1584—The knowledge contained in the four Watchtowers is detailed. It consists of:

• All human knowledge

• Physics

• The knowledge of all elemental creatures: those contained in the Air, Water, and Earth and in the secret Fire that animates all

• Knowledge of metals and stones

• The joining and destroying of nature

• Moving from place to place (astral travel via the 91 names of the Governors)

- All mechanical crafts

- Formal alchemical transmutations

- All the secrets of men

For the first time it is pointed out that eight of the capital letters appearing on the four Watchtowers are actually written backwards. The 20 letters of the fifth Watchtower, the Tablet of Union, are given for the first time. The method for uniting the letters of the four Watchtowers with this fifth tablet are given. The minor names of the four Watchtowers are given as well.

June 27, 1584—The eight adverse letters are further detailed. Dee questions the angels concerning the construction of the Watchtowers for the first time (and not the last) and asks for greater clarification of the 644 letters of the Watchtowers. By this date Dee has already made over 20 corrections to the original tables of June 25.

July 2, 1584—The only concrete corrections to these Watchtowers are communicated to Dee, though Dee will try up until 1587 to get a corrected set of Watchtowers from the Enochian angels. The corrections (though sometimes misleading) are as follows:

- Kelley made errors in receiving the names of the Governors, including DOCEPAX and TEDOAND. However, both the spelling of the Governor AYDROPL and ANDROPOL are correct.

- The Calls will clarify the Watchtowers (note: the Governors rather than the Calls will clarify the Watchtowers).

- The Princes and the Trumpeters cannot be detailed.

- The capital letters on the Watchtowers can be corrected (the method being the 91 Governors).

- Of the adverse letters PARAOAN, every letter is living fire, but the letter "N" is a vial of destruction.

The above evidence demonstrates that Edward Kelley received these Watchtower squares in trance without knowing their true construction.

- The angels communicated the Governor names (the true pattern of all the 644 squares) before giving the squares. If Kelley understood the relationship and was faking the trance sessions, the squares should have come first in the trance sessions and then the names of the Governors.

- When the squares were dictated through Kelley's trance, they were received with slight errors, showing an incomplete understanding in the role played by the Governors.

- When Kelley tried to receive the squares of the Watchtowers again in trance in 1587, he was unable to do so. He reverted to breaking off the session and hiding from Dee in order to recopy his original in secret. His revised edition contained many more errors than the original. He did not recognize many of the capital letters or the eight adverse letters, betraying the fact that he did not understand the role played by the names of the Governors.

- If Kelley faked the sessions, the Governor names should match the original squares and he should also have been able to duplicate those squares in secret at any given time.

- But Kelley could not duplicate them in 1587. Therefore the original reception in 1584 of the 91 Governor names and controlling squares was truly received in trance by Kelley, but by 1587 Kelley could not retrieve those squares while in or out of a trance.

Dee, apart from Kelley, attempted to correct the Watchtowers after their original reception on June 25, 1584. In these endeavors, Dee placed more than one letter in each Watchtower square to attempt to find the correct version of these squares. By placing more than one letter in certain squares, Dee created a dilemma which has been repeated by every other commentator on these squares, including Mathers, Crowley, and Regardie. Actually, each square contains only one correct letter, which composes part of the 91 Governor names.

Dee, however, after first receiving the Watchtowers, attempted as best he could to find their original format:

- Dee tabled out the 91 Governor names.

- Taking this list, he compared the 91 names with the letters composing the Watchtowers.

- He then discovered that the capital letters on the Watchtowers were the initial letters of the 91 Governors.

- Upon further observation, Dee discovered that the 91 names of the Governors in capitals and lower-case letters were intricately entwined in a complex order upon the 644 squares of the Watchtowers. No two names had the same pattern. Dee therefore created a sigil for each of the 91 Governor names based on the squares they occupied on the Watchtowers.

- However, upon tracing the Governor names, Dee found a conflict in the actual letters of his tables and these names.

- Dee had already tabled all the God names generated on a linear basis (such as the three names of God on the banners) and now found to his dismay that the actual names of the Governors would corrupt the tables he had already established.

- This created a great dilemma for Dee, causing the creation of the multilettered squares in the Watchtower system. Dee took his original Watchtowers, scratched out certain letters, and added corrected letters in accordance at first with the linear names of God and then with the names of the 91 Governors.

- This conflict demonstrates that Dee was unable to ascertain whether the 91 Governors or the linear names of God were the real pattern for the Watchtowers.

- Dee thus attempted to wed both systems into one. It should be noted that Dee's corrections were never completely carried through. This may imply that Dee gave up trying to perfect the system, unable to resolve the true pattern of the Watchtowers.

- The Enochian angels were of no help. When the issue of a conflict in lettering was raised, the angels explained that both sets were correct. On another occasion, the angels explained that any error that occurred was Kelley's and not theirs.

However, despite Dee's failings, the Watchtowers can be correctly reconstructed if the correct names of the 91 Governors are used as the basis for this rectification. Dee supplies us with all we need in a marvelous table that details these 91 Governors. The table shows the country the Governor rules, the name of the Governor, the sigil created by the squares composing the Governor's name, the Aire or level of the universe the Governor controls, the number of servants of each Governor, and the Enochian archangel, Hebraic tribe, and direction each Governor controls. Twelve of the 91 Divine Names for the Angelic Governors are marked with an asterisk. These 12 names have variant sigils that are listed after the following table.

The countries controlled by the 91 Governors are listed as Dee's original locations, based on the geography of Ptolemy. Their modern counterparts are listed in parentheses, based on the discoveries of Robin Cousins, modified by my own research.

The 12 tribes of Israel are given 12 directions, based on the positions of their encampments. Twelve Enochian angels rule over these 12 tribes, which can be given astrological correspondences as tabled in the introduction to this volume.

This table is set forth on the following pages.

Liber Scientiae Auxilii et Victoriae Terrestris
The Book of Knowledge, Aid, and Earthly Victory

90+1	91 Country	91 Divine Name	91 Sigil	30 Aire	91 Num. Value	91 Num. Total	12 Angel	12 Tribe	4 Direction
1	Aegyptus (Egypt)	Occodon*			1 7209		9 ZARZILG	Naphtali	East Right
2	Syria (S. Syria)	Pascomb		ORDO 1° LIL	2 2360	14,931	11 ZINGGEN	Zebulon	West Right
3	Mesopotamia (N. Iraq, NE Syria)	Valgars			3 5362		7 ALPVDVS	Issachar	West Left
4	Cappadocia (Central Turkey)	Doagnis			1 3636		4 ZARNAAH	Manasseh	North
5	Tuscia (Tuscany)	Pacasna		ORDO 2° ARN	2 2362	15,960	2 ZIRACAH	Reuben	South
6	Parva Asia (Asia Minor)	Dialiva*			3 8962		2 ZIRACAH	Reuben	South

Liber Scientiae Auxilii et Victoriae Terrestris (cont'd.)

90+1	91 Country	91 Divine Name	91 Sigil	30 Aire	91 Num. Value	91 Num. Total	12 Angel	12 Tribe	4 Direction
7	Hyrcania (SE Iran)	Samapha			1 4400		9 ZARZILG	Naphtali	East Right
8	Thracia (E. Greece, Turkey, S. Bulgaria)	Virochi		ORDO 3° ZOM	2 3660	17,296	7 ALPVDVS	Issachar	West Left
9	Gosmam (Artic Pole)	Andispi			3 9236		10 LAVAVOT	Gad	South Right
10	Thebaidi (Thebes)	Thotanf			1 2360		10 LAVAVOT	Gad	South Right
11	Parsadal (Persia)	Axziarg		ORDO 4° PAZ	3000	11,660	10 LAVAVOT	Gad	South Right
12	India (India)	Pothnir			6300		12 ARFAOLG	Ephraim	North Right

Liber Scientiae Auxilii et Victoriae Terrestris (cont'd.)

90+1	91 Country	91 Divine Name	91 Sigil	30 Aire	91 Num. Value	91 Num. Total	12 Angel	12 Tribe	4 Direction
13	Bastriane (Afghanistan)	Lazdixi*			1 / 8630		1 / OLPAGED	Dan	East
14	Cilicia (SE Turkey)	Nocamal		ORDO 5° LIT	2 / 2306	16,738	7 / ALPVDVS	Issachar	West Left
15	Oxiana (Border of Russia and Afghanistan)	Tiarpax			3 / 5802		11 / ZINGGEN	Zebulon	West Right
16	Numidia (E. Algeria)	Saxtomp*			1 / 3620		5 / GEBABAL	Asher	East Left
17	Cyprus (Cyprus)	Vavaamp		ORDO 6° MAZ	2 / 9200	20,040	12 / ARFAOLG	Ephraim	North Right
18	Parthia (NE Iran)	Zirzird			3 / 7200		5 / GEBABAL	Asher	East Left

Liber Scientiae Auxilii et Victoriae Terrestris (cont'd.)

90+1	91 Country	91 Divine Name	91 Sigil	30 Aire	91 Num. Value	91 Num. Total	12 Angel	12 Tribe	4 Direction
19	Getulia (W. Sahara)	Obmacas			1 6363		4 ZARNAAH	Manasseh	North
20	Arabia (Saudi Arabia)	Genadol		ORDO 7° DEO	2 7706	20,389	3 HONONOL	Judah	West
21	Phalagon (Greenland)	Aspiaon			3 6320		11 ZINGGEN	Zebulon	West Right
22	Mantiana (N. Iran)	Zamfres			1 4362		5 GEBABAL	Asher	East Left
23	Soxia (Chinese Turkestan)	Todnaon*		ORDO 8° ZID	2 7236	13,900	1 OLPAGED	Dan	East
24	Gallia (France)	Pristac			3 2302		9 ZARZILG	Naphtali	East Right

Liber Scientiae Auxilii et Victoriae Terrestris (cont'd.)

90+1	91 Country	91 Divine Name	91 Sigil	30 Aire	91 Num. Value	91 Num. Total	12 Angel	12 Tribe	4 Direction
25	Illyria (Austria, Hungary, Yugoslavia.)	Oddiorg			1 9996		3 HONONOL	Judah	West
26	Sogdiana (Oxus River)	Cralpir*		ORDO 9° ZIP	2 3620	17,846	10 LAVAVOT	Gad	South Right
27	Lydia (Coast of W. Turkey)	Doanzin*			3 4230		9 ZARZILG	Naphtali	East Right
28	Caspis (Iran by Caspian Sea)	Lexarph*		ORDO 10° ZAX	1 8880		11 ZINGGEN	Zebulon	West Right
29	Germania (Germany)	Comanan*			2 1230	11,727	7 ALPVDVS	Issachar	West Left
30	Trenam (Ivory Coast).	Tabitom*			3 1617		9 ZARZILG	Naphtali	East Right

Liber Scientiae Auxilii et Victoriae Terrestris (cont'd.)

90+1	91 Country	91 Divine Name	91 Sigil	30 Aire	91 Num. Value	91 Num. Total	12 Angel	12 Tribe	4 Direction
31	Bithynia (Turkey by Black Sea)	Molpand			1 3472		10 LAVAVOT	Gad	South Right
32	Graecia (Greece)	Vsnarda		ORDO 11° ICH	2 7236	15,942	6 ZVRCHOL	Simeon	South Left
33	Licia (S. Turkey)	Ponodol			3 5234		3 HONONOL	Judah	West
34	Onigap (China and Japan)	Tapamal		ORDO 12° LOE	1 2658		6 ZVRCHOL	Simeon	South Left
35	India maior (SE Asia)	Gedoons			2 7772	13,821	8 CADAAMP	Benjamin	North Left
36	Orcheny (Tigris and Euphrates)	Ambriol*			3 3391		2 ZIRACAH	Reuben	South

Liber Scientiae Auxilii et Victoriae Terrestris (cont'd.)

90+1	91 Country	91 Divine Name	91 Sigil	30 Aire	91 Num. Value	91 Num. Total	12 Angel	12 Tribe	4 Direction
37	Achaia (S. Greece)	Gecaond			1 8111		10 LAVAVOT	Gad	South Right
38	Armenia (Armenia)	Laparin		ORDO 13° ZIM	2 3360	15,684	1 OLPAGED	Dan	East
39	Cilicia Nemrodiana (NE Russia)	Docepax			3 4213		7 ALPVDVS	Issachar	West Left
40	Paphlagonia (N. of Turkey)	Tedoand			2 2673		5 GEBABAL	Asher	East Left
41	Phasiana (E. Turkey)	Vivipos		ORDO 14° VTA	2 9236	20,139	7 ALPVDVS	Issachar	West Left
42	Chaldei (Chaldea)	Ooanamb			3 8230		12 ARFAOLG	Ephraim	North Right

Liber Scientiae Auxilii et Victoriae Terrestris (cont'd.)

90+1	91 Country	91 Divine Name	91 Sigil	30 Aire	91 Num. Value	91 Num. Total	12 Angel	12 Tribe	4 Direction
43	Itergi (Mongolia)	Tahando			1 1367		9 ZARZILG	Naphtali	East Right
44	Macedonia (N. Greece)	Nociabi		ORDO 15° OXO	2 1367	4620	10 LAVAVOT	Gad	South Right
45	Garamantica (Central Africa)	Tastoxo			3 1886		12 ARFAOLG	Ephraim	North Right
46	Sauromatica (Poland)	Cucarpt			1 9920		2 ZIRACAH	Reuben	South
47	Aethiopia (Ethiopia)	Lauacon		ORDO 16° LEA	2 9230	28,390	3 HONONOL	Judah	West
48	Fiacim (N. Pole)	Sochial			3 9240		12 ARFAOLG	Ephraim	North Right

Liber Scientiae Auxilii et Victoriae Terrestris (cont'd.)

90+1	91 Country	91 Divine Name	91 Sigil	30 Aire	91 Num. Value	91 Num. Total	12 Angel	12 Tribe	4 Direction
49	Colchica (Russian Georgia)	Sigmorf		ORDO 17° TAN	1 7623		2 ZIRACAH	Reuben	South
50	Cireniaca (E. Libya)	Aydropt			2 7132	17,389	1 OLPAGED	Dan	East
51	Nasamonia (NE Libyan coast)	Tocarzi			3 2634		9 ZARZILG	Naphtali	East Right
52	Carthago (Tunisia)	Nabaomi		ORDO 18° ZEN	1 2346		5 GEBABAL	Asher	East Left
53	Coxlant (Earthly Paradise)	Zafasai			2 7689	19,311	7 ALPVDVS	Issachar	West Left
54	Idumea (Jordan)	Yalpamb			3 9276		12 ARFAOLG	Ephraim	North Right

Liber Scientiae Auxilii et Victoriae Terrestris (cont'd.)

90+1	91 Country	91 Divine Name	91 Sigil	30 Aire	91 Num. Value	91 Num. Total	12 Angel	12 Tribe	4 Direction
55	Parstavia (E. of Romania)	Torzoxi			1 6236		12 ARFAOLG	Ephraim	North Right
				ORDO 19° POP					
56	Celtica (NW France, Belgium)	Abaiond			2 6732	15,356	8 CADAAMP	Benjamin	North Left
57	Vinsan (Kazakhstan of Russia)	Omagrap			3 2388		11 ZINGGEN	Zebulon	West Right
				ORDO 20° CHR					
58	Tolpam (Antarctica and Australia)	Zildron			1 3626		5 GEBABAL	Asher	West Left
59	Carcedonia (Tunisia)	Parziba			2 7629	14,889	3 HONONOL	Judah	West
60	Italia (Italy)	Totocan			3 3634		7 ALPVDVS	Issach	West Left

Liber Scientiae Auxilii et Victoriae Terrestris (cont'd.)

90+1	91 Country	91 Divine Name	91 Sigil	30 Aire	91 Num. Value	91 Num. Total	12 Angel	12 Tribe	4 Direction
61	Brytania (British Isles)	Chirspa			1 5536		12 ARFAOLG	Ephraim	North Right
62	Phenices (Phoenicia)	Toantom		ORDO 21° ASP	2 5635	16,829	8 CADAAMP	Benjamin	North Left
63	Comaginen (S. Turkey)	Vixpalg			3 5658		6 ZVRCHOL	Simeon	South Left
64	Apulia (SE Italy)	Ozidaia		ORDO 22° LIN	1 2232		12 ARFAOLG	Ephraim	North Right
65	Marmarica (N. African coast)	PARAOAN* (Laxdizi)			2 2326	6925	1 OLPAGED	Dan	East
66	Concava Syria (N. Syria)	Calzirg			3 2367		12 ARFAOLG	Ephraim	North Right

Liber Scientiae Auxilii et Victoriae Terrestris (cont'd.)

90+1	91 Country	91 Divine Name	91 Sigil	30 Aire	91 Num. Value	91 Num. Total	12 Angel	12 Tribe	4 Direction
67	Gebal (Beirut)	Ronoamb			1 7320		4 ZARNAAH	Manasseh	North
68	Elam (Iran)	Onizimp		ORDO 23° TOR	2 7262	21,915	10 LAVAVOT	Gad	South Right
69	Idunia (Beyond Greenland)	Zaxanin			3 7333		11 ZINGGEN	Zebulon	West Right
70	Media (NW Iran)	Orcamir			1 8200		4 ZARNAAH	Manasseh	North
71	Arriana (Pakistan)	Chialps		ORDO 24° NIA	2 8360	24,796	10 LAVAVOT	Gad	South Right
72	Chaldea (S. Iraq)	Soageel			3 8236	8236	11 ZINGGEN	Zebulon	West Right

Liber Scientiae Auxilii et Victoriae Terrestris (cont'd.)

90+1	91 Country	91 Divine Name	91 Sigil	30 Aire	91 Num. Value	91 Num. Total	12 Angel	12 Tribe	4 Direction
73	Serici populi (Tibet)	Mirzind			1 5632		4 ZARNAAH	Manasseh	North
74	Persia (Persia)	Obuaors		ORDO 25° VTI	2 6333	18,201	2 ZIRACAH	Reuben	South
75	Gongatha (S. Pole)	Ranglam			3 6236		12 ARFAOLG	Ephraim	North Right
76	Gorsin (N. Israel)	Pophand			1 9232		12 ARFAOLG	Ephraim	North Right
77	Hispania (Spain and Portugal)	Nigrana		ORDO 26° DES	2 3620	18,489	8 CADAAMP	Benjamin	North Left
78	Pamphilia (S. Turkey)	Bazchim			3 5637		12 ARFAOLG	Ephraim	North Right

Liber Scientiae Auxilii et Victoriae Terrestris (cont'd.)

90+1	91 Country	91 Divine Name	91 Sigil	30 Aire	91 Num. Value	91 Num. Total	12 Angel	12 Tribe	4 Direction
79	Oacidi (Oasis W. of Nile)	Saziami			1 / 7220		2 ZIRACAH	Reuben	South
80	Babylon (Babylon)	Mathula		ORDO 27° ZAA	2 / 7560	22,043	4 ZARNAAH	Manasseh	North
81	Median (Sinai)	Orpanib			3 / 7263		5 GEBABAL	Asher	East Left
82	Idumian (Scythian Sea)	Labnixp			1 / 2630		10 LAVAVOT	Gad	South Right
83	Foelix Arabia (Yemen and Red Sea)	Focisni		ORDO 28° BAG	2 / 7236	18,066	9 ZARZILG	Naphtali	East Right
84	Metagonitidini (Tangiers)	Oxlopar			3 / 8200		6 ZVRCHOL	Simeon	South Left

Liber Scientiae Auxilii et Victoriae Terrestris (cont'd.)

90+1	91 Country	91 Divine Name	91 Sigil	30 Aire	91 Num. Value	91 Num. Total	12 Angel	12 Tribe	4 Direction
85	Assyria (Assyria)	Vastrim			1 9632		3 HONONOL	Judah	West
86	Affrica (Africa)	Odraxti		ORDO 29° RII	2 4236	21,503	4 ZARNAAH	Manasseh	North
87	Bastriani (Bactriani)	Gomziam			3 7635		12 ARFAOLG	Ephraim	North Right
88	Afnan (N. Zaire)	Taoagla			1 4632		12 ARFAOLG	Ephraim	North Right
89	Phrygia (Central Turkey)	Gemnimb		ORDO 30° TEX	2 9636	27,532	4 ZARNAAH	Manasseh	North
90	Creta (Crete)	Advorpt			3 7632		3 HONONOL	Judah	West
91	Mauritania (Morocco)	Dozinal			4 5632		6 ZVRCHOL	Simeon	South Left

Grand Total of Servants 522,327

Dee offered an alternate diagram in his diary which showed all 91 sigils of the Governors on the four main Watchtowers. In examining these alternate sigils, 12 distinct variants can be found to the sigils listed in the above table. In all 12 cases, these variants follow the correct spelling of the Governor names. These 12 sigils are as follows.

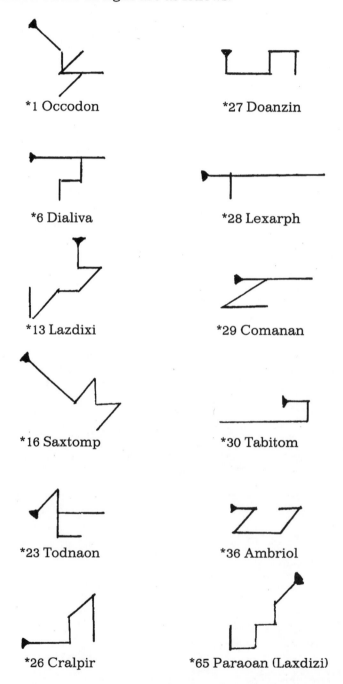

*1 Occodon

*27 Doanzin

*6 Dialiva

*28 Lexarph

*13 Lazdixi

*29 Comanan

*16 Saxtomp

*30 Tabitom

*23 Todnaon

*36 Ambriol

*26 Cralpir

*65 Paraoan (Laxdizi)

Now using the above spellings for the Governors and tracing them on the Watchtowers, we find a sequential order of 1 through 644 created by the 91 names of the Governors. The following Watchtowers show this sequential order.

Sequential Order of Governors
Air Watchtower

355	400	401	402	366	367	344	345	350	374	375	376
354	404	403	365	368	371	346	349	373	323	324	377
353	356	405	406	369	370	347	348	372	326	325	378
351	352	357	309	312	314	315	407	408	327	328	421
337	338	339	310	311	313	299	409	412	410	329	422
343	340	341	391	392	298	295	300	411	413	424	423
303	342	390	389	387	386	297	296	301	425	426	444
304	302	306	307	388	435	436	437	441	427	443	445
453	305	364	308	416	414	438	439	440	442	446	447
454	360	361	363	417	415	429	430	316	317	318	448
358	359	362	418	393	428	432	431	321	320	319	379
331	332	419	420	394	395	396	433	322	381	380	385
330	333	334	335	336	397	398	399	434	382	383	384

Sequential Order of Governors
Water Watchtower

617	618	1	631	632	633	636	637	638	627	628	629
619	623	622	2	4	634	635	639	626	625	630	14
64	620	621	3	6	7	640	641	642	644	624	13
69	65	66	5	36	37	38	39	643	9	12	11
70	68	67	71	72	40	41	15	21	8	10	455
43	44	49	74	73	42	16	20	50	52	53	56
45	47	48	75	76	28	17	18	19	51	54	55
211	46	96	77	98	23	27	26	456	100	102	105
212	213	95	97	22	24	25	457	99	101	103	104
214	215	85	94	93	462	459	458	29	30	31	34
216	217	86	87	92	461	460	218	224	32	33	35
91	89	88	78	79	220	219	223	57	61	62	63
90	84	83	82	81	80	221	222	58	59	60	190

Sequential Order of Governors
Earth Watchtower

520	519	546	484	485	470	534	535	536	537	526	527
521	540	545	544	486	471	533	505	506	538	539	528
522	541	542	543	487	472	473	474	475	507	508	529
523	524	483	482	488	489	490	469	476	509	531	530
514	525	477	478	479	480	481	468	511	510	532	565
513	515	516	517	497	463	466	467	562	561	564	566
512	491	492	518	496	464	465	499	498	563	610	567
451	568	493	494	495	550	551	500	501	504	611	612
452	569	574	573	549	559	560	552	502	503	614	613
603	570	571	572	548	547	558	553	554	616	615.	575
604	589	591	592	582	585	587	557	555	578	577	576
605	590	593	594	583	584	586	588	556	579	580	581
606	607	608	609	595	596	597	598	599	600	601	602

Sequential Order of Governors
Fire Watchtower

229	228	227	234	233	232	241	290	291	113	114	116
230	231	226	235	239	240	242	289	294	292	115	117
127	225	237	236	244	243	288	253	293	259	258	118
132	128	238	245	274	275	276	254	255	256	257	119
133	131	129	164	278	277	279	246	247	252	251	273
281	130	163	165	134	280	260	248	249	250	272	271
286	282	162	166	135	263	261	262	267	268	269	270
285	287	283	167	168	136	264	120	121	122	148	149
106	284	139	138	137	156	265	266	125	123	151	150
171	107	140	109	155	157	158	159	126	124	152	153
170	172	108	110	111	160	161	142	144	146	154	180
169	173	183	112	187	188	141	143	145	147	179	181
174	175	184	185	186	189	449	450	176	177	178	182

Sequential Order of Governors
Tablet of Union

191	192	193	194	195
196	197	198	199	200
201	202	203	204	205
206	207	208	209	210

Location of 91 Governors on the Watchtowers

Governor Name	Sequential Order of Squares	Location on Watchtowers
1. Occodon	1 through 7	Upper Left of Water Watchtower
2. Pascomb	8 through 14	Upper Right of Water Watchtower
3. Valgars	15 through 21	Upper Right of Water Watchtower
4. Doagnis	22 through 28	Lower Left and Right of Water Watchtower
5. Pacasna	29 through 35	Lower Right of Water Watchtower
6. Dialiva	36 through 42	Upper Left and Right of Water Watchtower
7. Samapha	43 through 49	Upper and Lower Left of Water Watchtower
8. Virochi	50 through 56	Upper Right of Water Watchtower
9. Andispi	57 through 63	Lower Right of Water Watchtower
10. Thotanf	64 through 70	Upper Left of Water Watchtower
11. Axziarg	71 through 77	Upper Left of Water Watchtower
12. Pothnir	78 through 84	Lower Left of Water Watchtower
13. Lazdixi	85 through 91	Lower Left of Water Watchtower
14. Nocamal	92 through 98	Lower Left of Water Watchtower
15. Tiarpax	99 through 105	Lower Right of Water Watchtower
16. Saxtomp	106 through 112	Lower Left of Fire Watchtower

Location of 91 Governors on the Watchtowers (cont'd.)

Governor Name	Sequential Order of Squares	Location on Watchtowers
17. Vavaamp	113 through 119	Upper Right of Fire Watchtower
18. Zirzird	120 through 126	Lower Right of Fire Watchtower
19. Obmacas	127 through 133	Upper Left of Fire Watchtower
20. Genadol	134 through 140	Upper and Lower Left of Fire Watchtower
21. Aspiaon	141 through 147	Lower Right of Fire Watchtower
22. Zamfres	148 through 154	Lower Right of Fire Watchtower
23. Todnaon	155 through 161	Lower Left and Right of Fire Watchtower
24. Pristac	162 through 168	Upper and Lower Left of Fire Watchtower
25. Oddiorg	169 through 175	Lower Left of Fire Watchtower
26. Cralpir	176 through 182	Lower Right of Fire Watchtower
27. Doanzin	183 through 189	Lower Left of Fire Watchtower
28. Lexarph	190 through 196	Lower Right Corner of Water Watchtower and Tablet of Union
29. Comanan	197 through 203	Tablet of Union
30. Tabitom	204 through 210	Tablet of Union
31. Molpand	211 through 217	Lower Left of Water Watchtower
32. Vsnarda	218 through 224	Lower Right Water Watchtower
33. Ponodol	225 through 231	Upper Left of Fire Watchtower
34. Tapamal	232 through 238	Upper Left of Fire Watchtower
35. Gedoons	239 through 245	Upper Left of Fire Watchtower
36. Ambriol	246 through 252	Upper Right of Fire Watchtower
37. Gecaond	253 through 259	Upper Right of Fire Watchtower
38. Laparin	260 through 266	Lower Right of Fire Watchtower
39. Docepax	267 through 273	Upper Right of Fire Watchtower
40. Tedoand	274 through 280	Upper Left of Fire Watchtower
41. Vivipos	281 through 287	Upper and Lower Left of Fire Watchtower
42. Ooanamb	288 through 294	Upper Right of Fire Watchtower

Location of 91 Governors on the Watchtowers (cont'd.)

Governor Name	Sequential Order of Squares	Location on Watchtowers
43. Tahando	295 through 301	Upper Right of Air Watchtower
44. Nociabi	302 through 308	Lower Left of Air Watchtower
45. Tastoxo	309 through 315	Upper Left of Air Watchtower
46. Cucarpt	316 through 322	Lower Right of Air Watchtower
47. Lauacon	323 through 329	Upper Right of Air Watchtower
48. Sochial	330 through 336	Lower Left of Air Watchtower
49. Sigmorf	337 through 343	Upper Left of Air Watchtower
50. Aydropt	344 through 350	Upper Right of Air Watchtower
51. Tocarzi	351 through 357	Upper Left of Air Watchtower
52. Nabaomi	358 through 364	Lower Left of Air Watchtower
53. Zafasai	365 through 371	Upper Left of Air Watchtower
54. Yalpamb	372 through 378	Upper Right of Air Watchtower
55. Torzoxi	379 through 385	Lower Right of Air Watchtower
56. Abaiond	386 through 392	Upper and Lower Left of Air Watchtower
57. Omagrap	393 through 399	Lower Left and Right of Air Watchtower
58. Zildron	400 through 406	Upper Left of Air Watchtower
59. Parziba	407 through 413	Upper Right of Air Watchtower
60. Totocan	414 through 420	Lower Left of Air Watchtower
61. Chirspa	421 through 427	Upper Right of Air Watchtower
62. Toantom	428 through 434	Lower Right of Air Watchtower
63. Vixpalg	435 through 441	Lower Right of Air Watchtower
64. Ozidaia	442 through 448	Lower Right of Air Watchtower
65. PARAOAN (Secret name of 92nd Governor)	449 through 455	PA adverse on Fire Watchtower, RA adverse on Earth Watchtower, OA adverse on Air Watchtower, N adverse on Water Watchtower
65a. Laxdizi	456 through 462	Lower Right of Water Watchtower
66. Calzirg	463 through 469	Upper Right of Earth Watchtower
67. Ronoamb	470 through 476	Upper Right of Earth Watchtower
68. Onizimp	477 through 483	Upper Left of Earth Watchtower

Location of 91 Governors on the Watchtowers (cont'd.)

Governor Name	Sequential Order of Squares	Location on Watchtowers
69. Zaxanin	484 throuh 490	Upper Left of Earth Watchtower
70. Orcamir	491 through 497	Lower Left of Earth Watchtower
71. Chialps	498 through 504	Lower Right of Earth Watchtower
72. Soageel	505 through 511	Upper Right of Earth Watchtower
73. Mirzind	512 through 518	Upper Left of Earth Watchtower
74. Obuaors	519 through 525	Upper Left of Earth Watchtower
75. Ranglam	526 through 532	Upper Right of Earth Watchtower
76. Pophand	533 through 539	Upper Right of Earth Watchtower
77. Nigrana	540 through 546	Upper Left of Earth Watchtower
78. Bazchim	547 through 553	Lower Right of Earth Watchtower
79. Saziami	554 through 560	Lower Right of Earth Watchtower
80. Mathula	561 through 567	Upper Right of Earth Watchtower
81. Orpanib	568 through 574	Lower Left of Earth Watchtower
82. Labnixp	575 through 581	Lower Right of Earth Watchtower
83. Focisni	582 through 588	Lower Left and Right of Earth Watchtower
84. Oxlopar	589 through 595	Lower Left of Earth Watchtower
85. Vastrim	596 through 602	Lower Right of Earth Watchtower
86. Odraxti	603 through 609	Lower Left of Earth Watchtower
87. Gomziam	610 through 616	Lower Right of Earth Watchtower
88. Taoagla	617 through 623	Lower Left of Water Watchtower
89. Gemnimb	624 through 630	Upper Right of Water Watchtower
90. Advorpt	631 through 637	Upper Left and Right of Water Watchtower
91. Dozinal	638 through 644	Upper Right of Water Watchtower

Substituting the actual names of the Governors for the above Watchtowers results for the first time in a corrected version of the Watchtowers.

On the following pages are the true Enochian Watchtowers based on the 91 Angelic Goverors.

Air Watchtower
Reconstruction Based on Dee's 91 Angelic Governors

r	Z	i	l	a	f	A	y	t	l	p	a	(e)
a	r	d	Z	a	i	d	p	a	L	a	m	
c	z	o	n	s	a	r	o	Y	a	u	b	(x)
T	o	i	T	t	x	o	P	a	c	o	C	(a)
S	i	g	a	s	o	n	r	b	z	n	h	(r)
f	m	o	n	d	a	T	d	i	a	r	i	(p)
o	r	o	i	b	A	h	a	o	s	p	i	
c	N	a	b	a	V	i	x	g	a	z	d	(h)
O*	i	i	i	t	T	p	a	l	O	a	i	
A*	b	a	m	o	o	o	a	C	u	c	a	(C)
N	a	o	c	O	T	t	n	p	r	a	T	(o)
o	c	a	n	m	a	g	o	t	r	o	i	(m)
S	h	i	a	l	r	a	p	m	z	o	x	(a)

(m) (o) (t) (i) (b)   (a) (T) (n) (a) (n)

*Adverse letter

Water Watchtower
Reconstruction based on Dee's 91 Angelic Governors

(e)	T	a	O	A	d	v	p	t	D	n	i	m
	o	a	l	c	o	o	r	o	m	e	b	b
(x)	T	a	g	c	o	n	z	i	n	l	G	m
(a)	n	h	o	d	D	i	a	l	a	a	o	c
(r)	f	a	t	A	x	i	v	V	s	P	s	N*
(p)	S	a	a	i	z	a	a	r	V	r	o	i
	m	p	h	a	r	s	l	g	a	i	c	h
(h)	M	a	m	g	l	o	i	n	L	i	r	x
	o	l	a	a	D	a	g	a	T	a	p	a
(C)	p	a	L	c	o	i	d	x	P	a	c	n
(o)	n	d	a	z	N	z	i	V	a	a	s	a
(m)	i	i	d	P	o	n	s	d	A	s	p	i
(a)	x	r	i	n	h	t	a	r	n	d	i	L*
	(n)	(a)	(n)	(T)	(a)		(b)	(i)	(t)	(o)	(m)	

*Adverse letter

Earth Watchtower
Reconstruction Based on Dee's 91 Angelic Governors

(m)	(o)	(t)	(i)	(b)			(a)	(T)	(n)	(a)	(n)	
b	O	a	Z	a	R	o	p	h	a	R	a	(a)
u	N	n	a	x	o	P	S	o	n	d	n	
a	i	g	r	a	n	o	a	m	a	g	g	(m)
o	r	p	m	n	i	n	g	b	e	a	l	(o)
r	s	O	n	i	z	i	r	l	e	m	u	(C)
i	z	i	n	r	C	z	i	a	M	h	l	(h)
M	O	r	d	i	a	l	h	C	t	G	a	
R*	O	c	a	m	c	h	i	a	s	o	m	(p)
A*	r	b	i	z	m	i	i	l	p	i	z	
O	p	a	n	a	B	a	m	S	m	a	L	(r)
d	O	l	o	F	i	n	i	a	n	b	a	(a)
r	x	p	a	o	c	s	i	z	i	x	p	(x)
a	x	t	i	r	V	a	s	t	r	i	m	(e)

*Adverse letter

Fire Watchtower
Reconstruction Based on Dee's 91 Angelic Governors

	(n)	(a)	(n)	(T)	(a)			(b)	(i)	(t)	(o)	(m)
(a)	d	o	n	p	a	T	d	a	n	V	a	a
	o	l	o	a	G	e	o	o	b	a	v	a
(m)	O	P	a	m	n	o	O	G	m	d	n	m
(o)	a	b	l	s	T	e	d	e	c	a	o	p
(C)	s	c	m	i	a	o	n	A	m	l	o	x
(h)	V	a	r	s	G	d	L	b	r	i	a	p
	o	i	P	t	e	a	a	p	D	o	c	e
(p)	p	s	v	a	c	n	r	Z	i	r	Z	a
	S	i	o	d	a	o	i	n	r	z	f	m
(r)	d	a	l	t	T	d	n	a	d	i	r	e
(a)	d	i	x	o	m	o	n	s	i	o	s	p
(x)	O	o	D	p	z	i	A	p	a	n	l	i
(e)	r	g	o	a	n	n	P*	A*	C	r	a	r

*Adverse letter

The Tablet of Union
The Fifth Watchtower
Reconstruction Based on Dee's 91 Angelic Governors

(L*)

e	x	a	r	p
h	C	o	m	a
n	a	n	T	a
b	i	t	o	m

*Adverse letter

The role of the eight adverse or backward letters must be described in order to understand the above reconstruction. Each capital letter appearing in the Watchtowers is the initial letter of one of the 91 Governors. However, two letters on each of the four main Watchtowers are written backwards, in the Fire Tablet: PA, in the Earth Tablet: RA, in the Air Tablet: OA, and in the Water Tablet: N and L. The last letter "L" is the initial letter which must be affixed to the Tablet of Union to form the 28th Governor, Lexarph. However the other seven letters PARAOAN form the secret 92nd name of the Governors, the secret ruler of the other 91. Dee shows this name PARAOAN as the 65th Governor. However the real 65th Governor is "Laxdizi," by the letters upon the squares. Thus PARAOAN composed of seven reversed letters is the invisible Governor ruling the visible 91.

As to the 20 letters in parentheses bordering two sides of each of the four Watchtowers, these letters are the 20 letters forming the Tablet of Union. In Dee's original scheme, the four Watchtowers are arranged in a great square separated by an equilateral cross:

Air	Water
Earth	Fire

This grand cross separating the four Watchtowers is formed from duplicate sets of the 20 letters of the Tablet of Union. They are lettered in upper and lower case in accordance with the three Governor's names which make up this fifth Watchtower.

The order which the Watchtowers have been analyzed is the secret order of the 91 + 1 Governors. However, in the Golden Dawn system, only the linear names of God, as originally recorded in Dee's diaries, were utilized in describing the construction of the Watchtowers. In light of the corrected Watchtowers, these Golden Dawn linear names of God can be correctly lettered.

The Enochian hierarchy derived from these linear names of God is twofold. There is first the king with his courtiers and then the angelic populace which the king rules. The king and his attendants are generated from the center of each Watchtower and the Tablet of Union as a great cross. The angelic inhabitants of his kingdom are generated by the squares which compose the four corners or directional quadrants of each Watchtower.

The following two tables detail this Enochian angelic hierarchy. Combined with the 91 + 1 Governors, the total number of god names in the Enochian system is 444.

The Enochian Angelic Hierarchy of Each of the Four Enochian Watchtowers

Number of Names	88 Names of Power	Letters in Names	Watchtower Squares Generating the Names
1	Great King	8	Central 8 squares as a Spiral
1	Trumpeter	2	Central 2 squares
5	Servants (Princes)	2 x 5	10 squares bordering central 8 squares
3	Ensign Bearers	3 + 4 + 5	12 squares of Linea Spiritus
6	Seniors	6 x 7	36 squares of Linea Patris, Filius et Spiritus
8	Kerubic God Names	(4 x 5) + (4)	16 Kerubic squares and 2 Tablet of Union letters and 4 initial letters of Sephirotic Crosses
16	Kerubic Angels	4 x 4 x 4	16 Kerubic squares
8	Servient God Names	4 x (5 + 6)	40 squares of 4 Sephirotic Crosses
16	Servient Angels	4 x 4 x 4	64 Servient (Elemental) squares
8	Cacodemon God Names	4 x (5 + 6)	40 squares of 4 adverse Sephirotic crosses
16	Cacodemons	4 x 4 x 3	32 Servient squares and 8 Tablet of Union letters

444 God Names in the Enochian Watchtower System

4 x 88	Linear Angelic Names of each Watchtower
4 x 22	Governors of each Watchtower
3	Governors of the Tablet of Union
	(+ the lower right corner of the Water Watchtower)
+ 1	Secret name from all four Watchtowers
444	Enochian God Names

Each of the four Elemental Watchtowers contains an angelic hierarchy of 88 god names, excluding the Governors found in each Watchtower.

These 88 god names are the crux of the Golden Dawn Enochian Watchtower system. However, in the transcription of this system, none of the surviving texts and recent editions of Golden Dawn Enochiana obey the correct use of upper- and lower-case transliterations of the Enochian alphabet as appearing in the original Watchtower.

However, in light of the corrected Watchtower letters, these elemental god names for the four Watchtowers can be revised as follows.

Air Watchtower of the East

Great King (Raphael):
Dee: baTaiVA (or) BaTaiVh
Golden Dawn: baTaiVAh (Sun)

One Trumpeter:
Ah

Five Servants:

1st	id	(Spirit)
2nd	on	(Air)
3rd	do	(Water)
4th	xp	(Earth)
5th	Ta	(Fire)

Three Ensign Bearers:

1st	oro
2nd	ibAh
3rd	aospi

Six Seniors:

1st	hAbioro	(Mars)
2nd	Aaoxaif	(Jupiter)
3rd	hTnordA	(Moon)
4th	Ahaospi	(Venus)
5th	hipotga	(Saturn)
6th	AVToTar	(Mercury)

Air Watchtower of the East (cont'd)

	Quadrant of Watchtower			
	Air	Water	Earth	Fire
Kerubic God Names:				
Evoke	erZla	eytpa	hcNba	hxgzd
Command	(rZ)i(la)	(yt)l(pa)	(cN)a(ba)	xg(a)zd
Kerubic Angels:				
Air	rZla	ytpa	cNba	xgzd
Water	Zlar	tpay	Nbac	gzdx
Earth	larZ	payt	bacN	zdxg
Fire	arZl	aytp	acNb	dxgz
Servient God Names:				
Evoke	idoigo	lLacza	aiaoai	aOurrz
Command	ardZa	paLam	O*iiit	alOai
Servient Angels:				
Air	czns	oYub	A*bmo	aCca
Water	ToTt	PaoC	NacO	npaT
Earth	Sias	rbnh	ocnm	otoi
Fire	fmnd	diri	Shal	pmox
Cacodemon God Names:				
Evoke	ogiodi	azcaLl	iaoaia	zrruOa
Command	aZdra	maLap	tiiiO*	iaOla
Cacodemons:				
Air	xcz	xoY	CA*b	CaC
Water	aTo	aPa	oNa	onp
Earth	rSi	rrb	moc	mot
Fire	pfm	pdi	aSh	apm

*Adverse letter

Water Watchtower of the West

Great King (Gabriel):
Dee: raagios (or) raagiol
Golden Dawn: raagiosl (Sun)

One Trumpeter:
sl

Five Servants:
1st	az	(Spirit)
2nd	iv	(Air)
3rd	ra	(Water)
4th	ng	(Earth)
5th	al	(Fire)

Water Watchtower of the West (cont'd.)

Three Ensign Bearers:
1st   mph
2nd   arsl
3rd   gaich

Six Seniors:
1st   lsrahpm   (Mars)
2nd   saiinov   (Jupiter)
3rd   lavazrp   (Moon)
4th   slgaich   (Venus)
5th   ligdisa   (Saturn)
6th   soaiznt   (Mercury)

	Quadrant of Watchtower		
Air	**Water**	**Earth**	**Fire**
Kerubic God Names:			
Evoke	eTaAd	etDim	hMagl	hnLrx
Command	(Ta)O(Ad)	(tD)n(im)	(Ma)m(gl)	(nL)i(rx)
Kerubic Angels:			
Air	TaAd	tDim	Magl	nLrx
Water	aAdT	Dimt	aglM	Lrxn
Earth	AdTa	imtD	glMa	rxnL
Fire	dTaA	mtDi	lMag	xnLr
Servient God Names:			
Evoke	Olgota	nelaPr	maLadi	iaaasd
Command	oalco	omebb	olaaD	aTapa
Servient Angels:			
Air	Taco	inGm	paco	xPcn
Water	nhdD	laoc	ndzN	Vasa
Earth	faAx	VssN*	iiPo	dApi
Fire	Saiz	rVoi	xrnh	rniL*
Cacodemon God Names:			
Evoke	atoglO	rPalen	idaLam	dsaaai
Command	oclao	bbemo	Daalo	apaTa
Cacodemons:			
Air	xTa	xin	Cpa	CxP
Water	anh	ala	ond	oVa
Earth	rfa	rVs	mii	mdA
Fire	pSa	prV	axr	arn

*Adverse letter

Earth Watchtower of the North

Great King (Auriel):
Dee: Czhhca (or) iCzhhcl
Golden Dawn: iCzhhcal (Sun)

One Trumpeter:
al

Five Servants:
1st	dr	(Spirit)
2nd	zi	(Air)
3rd	iC	(Water)
4th	ii	(Earth)
5th	mm	(Fire)

Three Ensign Bearers:
1st	MOr
2nd	dial
3rd	hCtGa

Six Seniors:
1st	laidrOM	(Mars)
2nd	aCzinoR	(Jupiter)
3rd	lzinoPo	(Moon)
4th	alhCtGa	(Venus)
5th	lhiansa	(Saturn)
6th	acmBicV	(Mercury)

	Quadrant of Watchtower			
	Air	**Water**	**Earth**	**Fire**
Kerubic God Names:				
Evoke	abOZa	aphRa	pR*Oam	piaom
Command	(bO)a(Za)	(ph)a(Ra)	(R*O)c(am)	(ia)s(om)
Kerubic Angels:				
Air	bOZa	phRa	R*Oam	iaom
Water	OZab	hRap	OamR*	aomi
Earth	ZabO	Raph	amR*O	omia
Fire	abOZ	aphR	mR*Oa	miao
Servient God Names:				
Evoke	angpOi	anaeeM	cbalpt	spmnir
Command	uNnax	Sondn	A*rbiz	ilpiz
Servient Angels:				
Air	aira	amgg	Opna	mSaL
Water	ormn	gbal	dOof	iaba
Earth	rsni	rlmu	rxao	izxp
Fire	iznr	iahl	axir	stim

Earth Watchtower of the North (cont'd.)

Cacodemon God Names:

Evoke	iOpgna	Meeana	tplabc	rinmps
Command	xanNu	ndnoS	zibrA*	zipli

Cacodemons:

Air	mai	mam	rOp	rms
Water	oor	ogb	adO	aia
Earth	Crs	Crl	xrx	xiz
Fire	hiz	hia	eax	est

*Adverse letter

Fire Watchtower of the South

Great King (Michael):
Dee: edLprna (or) edLprna
Golden Dawn: edLprnaa (Sun)

One Trumpeter:
aa

Five Servants:
1st	tG	(Spirit)
2nd	on	(Air)
3rd	bD	(Water)
4th	Zi	(Earth)
5th	oc	(Fire)

Three Ensign Bearers:
1st	oiP
2nd	teaa
3rd	pDoce

Six Seniors:
1st	aaetPio	(Mars)
2nd	adoeoeT	(Jupiter)
3rd	aLndOod	(Moon)
4th	aapDoce	(Venus)
5th	arinnAP*	(Saturn)
6th	anodoin	(Mercury)

Fire Watchtower of the South (cont'd.)

	Air	Water	Earth	Fire
Quadrant of Watchtower				
Kerubic God Names:				
Evoke	adopa	aanaa	ppsac	pZiZa
Command	(do)n(pa)	(an)V(aa)	(ps)v(ac)	(Zi)r(Za)
Kerubic Angels:				
Air	dopa	anaa	psac	ZiZa
Water	opad	naaa	sacp	iZaZ
Earth	pado	aaan	acps	ZaZi
Fire	adop	aana	cpsa	aZiZ
Servient God Names:				
Evoke	noalmr	Vadali	volxDo	rzionr
Command	oloaG	obava	Sioda	nrzfm
Servient Angels:				
Air	OPmn	Gmnm	datT	adre
Water	absT	ecop	diom	sisp
Earth	scia	Amox	Oopz	pali
Fire	VasG	brap	rgan	A*Car
Cacodemon God Names:				
Evoke	rmlaon	iladaV	oDxlov	rnoizr
Command	Gaolo	avabo	adoiS	mfzrn
Cacodemons:				
Air	mOP	mGm	rda	rad
Water	oab	oec	adi	asi
Earth	csc	cAm	xOo	xpa
Fire	hVa	hbr	erg	eA*C

*Adverse letter

The method for generating the various god names on each Watchtower can be shown by analyzing in detail one Watchtower. The following explanation will show how to extract the eleven types of linear god names using the Watchtower of the East, which is the element Air.

Great King

The Great King is composed of a spiral of eight letters directly at the center of each Watchtower. The first letter of the name appears at the left of the Watchtower, and the name then spirals inward in a clockwise motion. The last two letters of the name are the central two letters of the Watchtower:

Great King: baTaiVAh

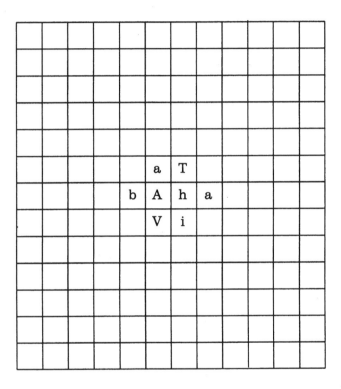

Trumpeter

The Trumpeter is composed of the central two letters of each Watchtower. As such it is also the last two letters of the Great King and therefore heralds the King's presence in Court. This god name does not appear in the Golden Dawn system but was received by Kelley in a dream on June 20, 1584.

Trumpeter: Ah

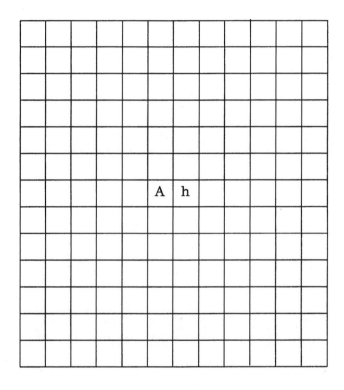

Servants

There are five servants, each composed of two letters. These are not from the Golden Dawn tradition but were received by Kelley in a dream on June 20, 1584. These Servants, or Princes, are found holding the spiral train of the Great King. As such they are the ten tangent squares which surround the central eight spiraling squares of the Great King.

Servants: id, on, do, xp, Ta

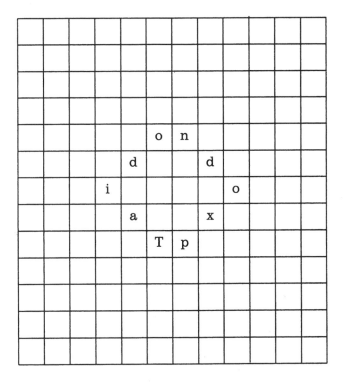

Ensign Bearers

The Ensign Bearers are three in number for each Watchtower and carry three banners composed of three, four, and five letters. These 12 letters are derived from the central (seventh) horizontal line of each Watchtower, referred to as the Linea Spiritus. These three names are read from left to right.

Ensign Bearers: oro, ibAh, aospi

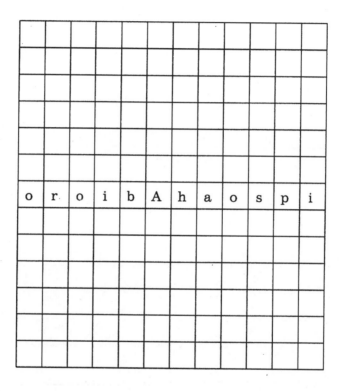

Seniors

There are six Seniors, each composed of seven letters, which are derived from three lines: the central horizontal line, and the two central vertical lines of each Watchtower. The six names begin in the middle of the Watchtower, and end at the edge of the Watchtower. Each of the six Seniors are assigned to six of the seven ancient planets. The Great King represents the seventh omitted planet which is the Sun.

Seniors: hAbioro, Aaoxaif, hTnordA, Ahaospi, hipotga, AVToTar

					f	A					
					i	d					
					a	r					
					x	o					
					o	n					
					a	T					
o	r	o	i	b	A	h	a	o	s	p	i
					V	i					
					T	p					
					o	o					
					T	t					
					a	g					
					r	a					

Kerubic God Names

The Kerubic God Names are two sets of four names. They are formed from the first and eighth horizontal line from the top of each Watchtower. The first five letters and the last five letters of each of the two horizontal lines are counterchanged to the letter parallel to that line standing outside the Watchtower in the Tablet of Union, which forms a great equilateral cross spanning all four Watchtowers.

In the case of the Air Watchtower, the two Tablet of Union letters which parallel the first and eighth horizontal lines are the letters "e" (from exarp) and "h" (from hComa). The letter "e" is prefixed to the first, second, fourth, and fifth letters as well as to the eighth, ninth, eleventh, and twelfth letters of the first (topmost) horizontal line. Likewise, "h" is prefixed to the first, second, fourth, and fifth letters as well as to the eighth, ninth, eleventh, and twelfth letters of the eighth horizontal line. These combinations form the four Kerubic God Names which *evoke*.

The second set of four names is formed by the first five and last five letters of the first and eighth horizontal lines of the Air Watchtower. The third and tenth letters of each line are the power points of these names, just as the Tablet of Union letters prefixed to the earlier four letters are the ruling forces of the names. These four names are used to *command*.

The 22 letters which form these eight Kerubic names are as follows.

Kerubic God Names: erZla, eytpa, hcNba, hxgzd, rZila, ytlpa, cNaba, xgazd

r	Z	i	l	a			y	t	l	p	a	(e)
c	N	a	b	a			x	g	a	z	d	(h)

Kerubic Angels

The 16 names of the Kerubic Angels are derived from the first and eighth horizontal lines from the top of each Watchtower. The first, second, fourth, and fifth as well as the eighth, ninth, eleventh, and twelfth squares of each line form the names of the four basic Kerubic Angels of four letters each. These four letters are in turn permutated three times each to form 16 combinations of Kerubic Angels.

Kerubic Angels: rZla, Zlar, larZ, arZl; ytpa, tpay, payt, aytp; cNba, Nbac, bacN, acNb; xgzd, gzdx, zdxg, dxgz

r	Z		l	a			y	t		p	a
c	N		b	a			x	g		z	d

Servient God Names

The eight Servient God Names are derived from the four Sephirotic Crosses of ten squares each that are situated in the four quadrants of each Watchtower. Each cross is six squares down and five squares across, forming four horizontal god names of five letters each (used to *command*) and four vertical god names of six letters each (used to *evoke*).

Servient God Names: idoigo, lLacza, aiaoai, aOurrz; ardZa, paLam, O*iiit, alOai

		i						l		
a	r	d	Z	a		p	a	L	a	m
		o						a		
		i						c		
		g						z		
		o						a		
		a						a		
O*	i	i	i	t		a	l	O	a	i
		a						u		
		o						r		
		a						r		
		i						z		

Servient Angels

The 16 names forming the Servient Angels are extracted from the eight squares on the lower vertical sides of each Sephirotic Cross. Four sets of four horizontal letters are generated from each cross to form the 16 Servient Angel names.

Servient Angels: czns, ToTt, Sias, fmnd; oYub, PaoC, rbnh, diri; A*bmo, NacO, ocnm, Shal; aCca, npaT, otoi, pmox

c	z		n	s			o	Y	u	b
T	o		T	t			P	a	o	C
S	i		a	s			r	b	n	h
f	m		n	d			d	i	r	i
A*	b		m	o			a	C	c	a
N	a		c	O			n	p	a	T
o	c		n	m			o	t	o	i
S	h		a	l			p	m	o	x

Cacodemon God Names

The eight Cacodemon God Names are derived in the same fashion as the Servient God Names, but they are written backwards. As the Servient God Names are generated from top to bottom and left to right upon the Sephirothic Cross, the Cacodemon God Names are generated from bottom to top and right to left. These names are not part of the Golden Dawn tradition, but are derived from the notebooks of John Dee.

Cacodemon God Names: ogiodi, azcaLl, iaoaia, zrruOa, aZdra, maLap, tiiiO*, iaOla

		i							l		
a	r	d	Z	a			p	a	L	a	m
		o							a		
		i							c		
		g							z		
		o							a		
		a							a		
O*	i	i	i	t			a	l	O	a	i
		a							u		
		o							r		
		a							r		
		i							z		

Cacodemons

The names of the 16 Cacodemons are formed from the first two letters of each Servient Angel name prefixed by the parallel horizontal Tablet of Union square standing outside of the Watchtower. Thus the 16 Cacodemon names are made up of three letters each. These names are not part of the Golden Dawn tradition but originate in the research of John Dee.

Cacodemons : xcz, aTo, rSi, pfm; xoY, aPa, rrb, pdi; CA*b, oNa, moc, aSh; CaC, onp, mot, apm

c	z					o	Y			(x)
T	o					P	a			(a)
S	i					r	b			(r)
f	m					d	i			(p)
A*	b					a	C			(C)
N	a					n	p			(o)
o	c					o	t			(m)
S	h					p	m			(a)

Each Watchtower is divided into four quadrants that contain various powers and potencies. The division of the Watchtower is based on the peculiar Enochian elemental order of Air, Water, Earth, and Fire. The elemental order for each Watchtower is as follows.

Elemental Order of Watchtower

Air	Water
Earth	Fire

This is also the method for laying out the four Watchtowers upon the Great Central Cross (the Tablet of Union). In both Waite's and Case's Tarot deck, this is also the kerubic arrangement found in Key X and Key XXI.

This Enochian elemental order is the basis for the Golden Dawn ritual allocations of the temple. Three sources for the peculiar Enochian order of the elements (as Air, Water, Earth, and Fire) can be traced.

- The Pythagoreans, in describing the formation of the universe, declared that Fire begets Air begets Water begets Earth begets Fire. Excluding the original Fire, this elemental order is the same as the Enochian.

- The *Zohar*, in describing the directional Tree of Life, allocates the four elements to the movement of the Sun. If the four Qabalistic elements are ordered as the cycle from sunrise to midnight, the following Enochian order is obtained: Sunrise (East-Air), Noon (South-Water), Sunset (West-Earth), Midnight (North-Fire). Note that this is not the Golden Dawn *directional* order.

- The four layers of the universe as envisioned by both the Pythagoreans and the Renaissance Hermetists correspond to the Enochian order of the elements as follows: sky above (Air), water descending from heaven covering the earth (Water), the earth below (Earth), and the secret fire at the center of the earth (Fire).

Each of the four quadrants contains three levels of Angelic powers that can be tapped by the Kerubic Angels, Servient Angels, and Cacodemons of each Watchtower.

The table on the following page details these powers and potencies as recorded in Dee's Enochian diaries.

Powers and Potencies

	Quadrant of Watchtower			
	Air (Upper Left)	Water (Upper Right)	Earth (Lower Left)	Fire (Lower Right)
Kerubic Angels	Angel of alchemy, skilled in the mixing and combining of natural substances and other secrets of nature	Angel of astral travel, skilled in transporting oneself from place to place	Angel of all inventions, skilled in the Arts mechanical and all mechanical experiments	Angel of all secrets, skilled in discovering the secrets of any and all men, regardless of their state or condition
Servient Angels	Angel of medicine (elixirs, drugs), skilled in curing all diseases	Angel of metals, jewels and precious stones, skilled in finding hidden treasure	Angel of transformation, skilled in the true knowledge and absolute power of all transformations	Angels of the elementals, skilled in the arcane secrets of the 16 combinations of the four elements and their use by the human race
Cacodemons	To inflict diseases on one's enemy	To conceal wealth from one's enemy	To hide from one's enemy through transformation	To use the power of the elemental kingdom against one's enemy

Dee received the angelic number code on April 18, 1587, giving a cipher substitute value for each of the 624 letters of the Enochian Watchtowers (excluding the 20 letters of the Tablet of Union). The communicating angel explained that if a number between 1 and 624 appears in any angelic communication, the specific Enochian letter appearing in that square should be substituted for the number in question. The Watchtowers in their linear arrangement detail this cipher order, and this order can be extended to the 20 squares of the Tablet of Union. The tables on the following pages show first the Watchtower squares as numbers and secondly the Enochian alphabet substitute for the number range, as derived from the Watchtowers.

As an example of this system, the number 93 is equivalent to the Enochian letter "a," while the number 39 is equivalent to the Enochian letter "l." Thus the number pair of 93 and 39 can be equated to the Enochian letters "al."

Air Watchtower
The Cipher Number Substitution of the Watchtowers
by John Dee (Trebone, April 18, 1587)

1	2	3	4	5	6	7	8	9	10	11	12
25	26	27	28	29	30	31	32	33	34	35	36
49	50	51	52	53	54	55	56	57	58	59	60
73	74	75	76	77	78	79	80	81	82	83	84
97	98	99	100	101	102	103	104	105	106	107	108
121	122	123	124	125	126	127	128	129	130	131	132
145	146	147	148	149	150	151	152	153	154	155	156
169	170	171	172	173	174	175	176	177	178	179	180
193	194	195	196	197	198	199	200	201	202	203	204
217	218	219	220	221	222	223	224	225	226	227	228
241	242	243	244	245	246	247	248	249	250	251	252
265	266	267	268	269	270	271	272	273	274	275	276
289	290	291	292	293	294	295	296	297	298	299	300

Water Watchtower
The Cipher Number Substitution of the Watchtowers
by John Dee (Trebone, April 18, 1587)

13	14	15	16	17	18	19	20	21	22	23	24
37	38	39	40	41	42	43	44	45	46	47	48
61	62	63	64	65	66	67	68	69	70	71	72
85	86	87	88	89	90	91	92	93	94	95	96
109	110	111	112	113	114	115	116	117	118	119	120
133	134	135	136	137	138	139	140	141	142	143	144
157	158	159	160	161	162	163	164	165	166	167	168
181	182	183	184	185	186	187	188	189	190	191	192
205	206	207	208	209	210	211	212	213	214	215	216
229	230	231	232	233	234	235	236	237	238	239	240
253	254	255	256	257	258	259	260	261	262	263	264
277	278	279	280	281	282	283	284	285	286	287	288
301	302	303	304	305	306	307	308	309	310	311	312

Earth Watchtower
The Cipher Number Substitution of the Watchtowers
by John Dee (Trebone, April 18, 1587)

313	314	315	316	317	318	319	320	321	322	323	324
337	338	339	340	341	342	343	344	345	346	347	348
361	362	363	364	365	366	367	368	369	370	371	372
385	386	387	388	389	390	391	392	393	394	395	396
409	410	411	412	413	414	415	416	417	418	419	420
433	434	435	436	437	438	439	440	441	442	443	444
457	458	459	460	461	462	463	464	465	466	467	468
481	482	483	484	485	486	487	488	489	490	491	492
505	506	507	508	509	510	511	512	513	514	515	516
529	530	531	532	533	534	535	536	537	538	539	540
553	554	555	556	557	558	559	560	561	562	563	564
577	578	579	580	581	582	583	584	585	586	587	588
601	602	603	604	605	606	607	608	609	610	611	612

Fire Watchtower
The Cipher Number Substitution of the Watchtowers
by John Dee (Trebone, April 18, 1587)

325	326	327	328	329	330	331	332	333	334	335	336
349	350	351	352	353	354	355	356	357	358	359	360
373	374	375	376	377	378	379	380	381	382	383	384
397	398	399	400	401	402	403	404	405	406	407	408
421	422	423	424	425	426	427	428	429	430	431	432
445	446	447	448	449	450	451	452	453	454	455	456
469	470	471	472	473	474	475	476	477	478	479	480
493	494	495	496	497	498	499	500	501	502	503	504
517	518	519	520	521	522	523	524	525	526	527	528
541	542	543	544	545	546	547	548	549	550	551	552
565	566	567	568	569	570	571	572	573	574	575	576
589	590	591	592	593	594	595	596	597	598	599	600
613	614	615	616	617	618	619	620	621	622	623	624

Tablet of Union
The Cipher Number Substitution of the Watchtowers
by John Dee (Trebone, April 18, 1587)

625	626	627	628	629
630	631	632	633	634
635	636	637	638	639
640	641	642	643	644

Watchtower Number-Letter Cipher

Number	Equivalent Letter	Number	Equivalent Letter	Number	Equivalent Letter
1	r	22	n	43	r
2	Z	23	i	44	o
3	i	24	m	45	m
4	l	25	a	46	e
5	a	26	r	47	b
6	f	27	d	48	b
7	A	28	Z	49	c
8	y	29	a	50	z
9	t	30	i	51	o
10	l	31	d	52	n
11	p	32	p	53	s
12	a	33	a	54	a
13	T	34	L	55	r
14	a	35	a	56	o
15	O	36	m	57	Y
16	A	37	o	58	a
17	d	38	a	59	u
18	v	39	l	60	b
19	p	40	c	61	T
20	t	41	o	62	a
21	D	42	o	63	g

Watchtower Number-Letter Cipher (cont'd.)

Number	Equivalent Letter	Number	Equivalent Letter	Number	Equivalent Letter
64	c	100	a	136	i
65	o	101	s	137	z
66	n	102	o	138	a
67	z	103	n	139	a
68	i	104	r	140	r
69	n	105	b	141	V
70	l	106	z	142	r
71	G	107	n	143	o
72	m	108	h	144	i
73	T	109	f	145	o
74	o	110	a	146	r
75	i	111	t	147	o
76	T	112	A	148	i
77	t	113	x	149	b
78	x	114	i	150	A
79	o	115	v	151	h
80	P	116	V	152	a
81	a	117	s	153	o
82	c	118	P	154	s
83	o	119	s	155	p
84	C	120	N*	156	i
85	n	121	f	157	m
86	h	122	m	158	p
87	o	123	o	159	h
88	d	124	n	160	a
89	D	125	d	161	r
90	i	126	a	162	s
91	a	127	T	163	l
92	l	128	d	164	g
93	a	129	i	165	a
94	a	130	a	166	i
95	o	131	r	167	c
96	c	132	i	168	h
97	S	133	S	169	c
98	i	134	a	170	N
99	g	135	a	171	a

Watchtower Number-Letter Cipher (cont'd.)

Number	Equivalent Letter	Number	Equivalent Letter	Number	Equivalent Letter
172	b	208	a	244	c
173	a	209	D	245	O
174	V	210	a	246	T
175	i	211	g	247	t
176	x	212	a	248	n
177	g	213	T	249	p
178	a	214	a	250	r
179	z	215	p	251	a
180	d	216	a	252	T
181	M	217	A*	253	n
182	a	218	b	254	d
183	m	219	a	255	a
184	g	220	m	256	z
185	l	221	o	257	N
186	o	222	o	258	z
187	i	223	o	259	i
188	n	224	a	260	V
189	L	225	C	261	a
190	i	226	u	262	a
191	r	227	c	263	s
192	x	228	a	264	a
193	O*	229	p	265	o
194	i	230	a	266	c
195	i	231	L	267	a
196	i	232	c	268	n
197	t	233	o	269	m
198	T	234	i	270	a
199	p	235	d	271	g
200	a	236	x	272	o
201	l	237	P	273	t
202	O	238	a	274	r
203	a	239	c	275	o
204	i	240	n	276	i
205	o	241	N	277	i
206	l	242	a	278	i
207	a	243	o	279	d

Watchtower Number-Letter Cipher (cont'd.)

Number	Equivalent Letter	Number	Equivalent Letter	Number	Equivalent Letter
280	P	316	Z	352	a
281	o	317	a	353	G
282	n	318	R	354	e
283	s	319	o	355	o
284	d	320	p	356	o
285	A	321	h	357	b
286	s	322	a	358	a
287	p	323	R	359	v
288	i	324	a	360	a
289	S	325	d	361	a
290	h	326	o	362	i
291	i	327	n	363	g
292	a	328	p	364	r
293	l	329	a	365	a
294	r	330	T	366	n
295	a	331	d	367	o
296	p	332	a	368	a
297	m	333	n	369	m
298	z	334	V	370	a
299	o	335	a	371	g
300	x	336	a	372	g
301	x	337	u	373	O
302	r	338	N	374	P
303	i	339	n	375	a
304	n	340	a	376	m
305	h	341	x	377	n
306	t	342	o	378	o
307	a	343	P	379	O
308	r	344	S	380	G
309	n	345	o	381	m
310	d	346	n	382	d
311	i	347	d	383	n
312	L*	348	n	384	m
313	b	349	o	385	o
314	O	350	l	386	r
315	a	351	o	387	p

Watchtower Number-Letter Cipher (cont'd.)

Number	Equivalent Letter	Number	Equivalent Letter	Number	Equivalent Letter
388	m	424	i	460	d
389	n	425	a	461	i
390	i	426	o	462	a
391	n	427	n	463	l
392	g	428	A	464	h
393	b	429	m	465	C
394	e	430	l	466	t
395	a	431	o	467	G
396	l	432	x	468	a
397	a	433	i	469	o
398	b	434	z	470	i
399	l	435	i	471	P
400	s	436	n	472	t
401	T	437	r	473	e
402	e	438	C	474	a
403	d	439	z	475	a
404	e	440	i	476	p
405	c	441	a	477	D
406	a	442	M	478	o
407	o	443	h	479	c
408	p	444	l	480	e
409	r	445	V	481	R*
410	s	446	a	482	O
411	O	447	r	483	c
412	n	448	s	484	a
413	i	449	G	485	m
414	z	450	d	486	c
415	i	451	L	487	h
416	r	452	b	488	i
417	l	453	r	489	a
418	e	454	i	490	s
419	m	455	a	491	o
420	u	456	p	492	m
421	s	457	M	493	p
422	c	458	O	494	s
423	m	459	r	495	v

Watchtower Number-Letter Cipher (cont'd.)

Number	Equivalent Letter	Number	Equivalent Letter	Number	Equivalent Letter
496	a	532	n	568	o
497	c	533	a	569	m
498	n	534	B	570	o
499	r	535	a	571	n
500	Z	536	m	572	s
501	i	537	S	573	i
502	r	538	m	574	o
503	Z	539	a	575	s
504	a	540	L	576	p
505	A*	541	d	577	r
506	r	542	a	578	x
507	b	543	l	579	p
508	i	544	t	580	a
509	z	545	T	581	o
510	m	546	d	582	c
511	i	547	n	583	s
512	i	548	a	584	i
513	l	549	d	585	z
514	p	550	i	586	i
515	i	551	r	587	x
516	z	552	e	588	p
517	S	553	d	589	O
518	i	554	O	590	o
519	o	555	l	591	D
520	d	556	o	592	p
521	a	557	F	593	z
522	o	558	i	594	i
523	i	559	n	595	A
524	n	560	i	596	p
525	r	561	a	597	a
526	z	562	n	598	n
527	f	563	b	599	l
528	m	564	a	600	i
529	O	565	d	601	a
530	p	566	i	602	x
531	a	567	x	603	t

Watchtower Number-Letter Cipher (cont'd.)

Number	Equivalent Letter	Number	Equivalent Letter	Number	Equivalent Letter
604	i	618	n	632	o
605	r	619	P*	633	m
606	V	620	A*	634	a
607	a	621	C	635	n
608	s	622	r	636	a
609	t	623	a	637	n
610	r	624	r	638	T
611	i	625	e	639	a
612	m	626	x	640	b
613	r	627	a	641	i
614	g	628	r	642	t
615	o	629	p	643	o
616	a	630	h	644	m
617	n	631	C		

Addendum

The Enochian Systems of S. L. MacGregor Mathers and Aleister Crowley

Before ending this section, the Enochian systems of S. L. MacGregor Mathers and Aleister Crowley should be mentioned. Both Mathers and Crowley were unable to rectify the varied letters of the Enochian Watchtowers. However, both were armed with the right key, for both were aware of the 91 Governors and their sigils upon the Watchtowers.

Mathers developed a numbering system for Enochian which differed from the system found in Dee's original Calls, for only 16 select Enochian letters are used. This Golden Dawn numbering system was ultimately derived from a correspondence between geomancy and Enochian as discovered by Mathers. He derived the Enochian-geomantic equivalents directly from Dr. Rudd's *Treatise on Angel Magic,* specifically the chapter entitled "The Characters of the Sixteen Figures of Geomancy Expressed in the Great and Lesser Squares of Tabula Sancta." This chapter gives the following attributes.

Dr. Rudd's Enochian-Geomantic Equivalents

Enochian Alphabet	Geomantic Figure
B	Puer
A	Amissio
S	Albus
P	Populus
L	Via
G	Fortuna Major
Z	Fortuna Minor
E	Conjunctio
O	Puella
N	Rubeus
I (J, Y)	Acquisitio
U (V)	Carcer
M	Tristitia
R	Laetitia
T	Caput Draconis
F	Cauda Draconis

In transcribing these geomantic attributes for Enochian, Mathers switched two letters: Fam (S) with Graph (E). Rudd attributes Fam to Albus and Graph to Conjunctio, which Mathers reversed. Two reasons arise for this reversal.

- Fam (Ⴑ) and Graph (Ⴑ) in their original format are very close in shape and can easily be confused for one another, which Mathers may have done.

- Fam and Graph as geomantic attributes are both ruled by Mercury, which Mathers may have tranced as being corrupted (or blinded) in Rudd's order and which therefore had to be swapped (not unlike Keys VIII and XI of the Tarot) in order to be in the correct esoteric order.

In any event, Crowley restored Fam and Graph to Rudd's order in his own workings with the Golden Dawn Enochian system, as recorded in his annotations to his work, *The Vision and the Voice*.

Crowley, in his investigation of the 30 Aires, expanded this numbering system to include all 21 letters of the Enochian alphabet. The two systems of Mathers and Crowley as well as the double numbering system of Dee are as follows.

The Four Enochian Number Codes

Alphabet	Mathers	Crowley	Dee	
			Digital	**Additional**
A	6	6	1	1
B	5	5	2	2
G	9	9	3	3
D	—	4 or 31	4	4
E	7	10	5	5
F	300	300	6	6
Z	1	1	7	7
H	—	1	8	8
I, J, Y	60	60	1	10
C, K	—	300	2	20
L	40	40	3	30
M	90	90	4	40
N	50	50	5	50
X	—	400	6	60
O	30	30	7	70
P	8	8	8	80
Q	—	40	9	90
R	100	100	1	100
S	10	7	2	200
T	400	400	3	300
U, V, W	70	70	4	400

Using all four numbering systems for Enochian, the Enochian word for number, "COR," can be tabulated as follows.

- Mathers' Number Code
  COR = 130 (C = 0, O = 30, R = 100)

- Crowley's Number Code
  COR = 430 (C = 300, O = 30, R = 100)

- Dee's Original Digital Code
  COR = 271 (C = 2, O = 7, R = 1)

- Dee's Original Additional Code
  COR = 190 (C = 20, O = 70, R = 100)

This Enochian alphabet formed the crux of the Golden Dawn system of magic. The tables on the following pages show the complete Concourse of Forces for the Golden Dawn Enochian alphabet and Crowley's extension of those attributes.

Concourse of Forces for the Golden Dawn Enochian Alphabet with Aleister Crowley's Extensions

Enochian Alphabet	Letter Name Dee (GD Variant)	Geomancy	Geomantic Planetary Rulers	Geomantic Zodiacal Ruler	Geomancy on the Tree of Life
M	Tal	Tristitia (Sadness)	Saturn (Zazel)	Aquarius (Cambriel)	Three Supernals (Kether, Chockmah, Binah)
O	Med	Puella (Girl)	Venus (Kedemel)	Libra (Zuriel)	Netzach
Z	Ceph	Fortuna Minor (Minor Fortune)	Sun (Southern Declination) (Sorath)	Leo (Verchiel)	Tiphereth
E	Graph	Albus (White)	Mercury (Taphthartharath)	Gemini (Ambriel)	Hod

Concourse of Forces for the Golden Dawn Enochian Alphabet with Aleister Crowley's Extensions (cont'd.)

Enochian Alphabet	Letter Name Dee (GD Variant)	Geomancy	Geomantic Planetary Rulers	Geomantic Zodiacal Ruler	Geomancy on the Tree of Life
N	Drux (Drun)	Rubeus (Red)	Mars (Bartzabel)	Scorpio (Barchiel)	Geburah
P	Mals	Populus (Populace)	Moon (Increase) (Chasmodai)	Cancer (Muriel)	Yesod
L	Ur	Via (Way)	Moon (Decrease) (Chasmodai)	Cancer (Muriel)	Yesod
R	Don	Laetitia (Laughter)	Jupiter (Hismael)	Pisces (Amnitzel)	Chesed

Concourse of Forces for the Golden Dawn Enochian Alphabet with Aleister Crowley's Extensions (cont'd.)

Enochian Alphabet	Letter Name Dee (GD Variant)	Geomancy		Geomantic Planetary Rulers	Geomantic Zodiacal Ruler	Geomancy on the Tree of Life
A	Un	Amissio (Loss)		Venus (Kedemel)	Taurus (Asmodel)	Netzach
U	Van(Vau)	Carcer (Prison)		Saturn (Zazel)	Capricorn (Hanael)	Three Supernals
T	Gilg (Gisa)	Caput Draconis (Head of Dragon)		Jupiter and Venus (Hismael, Kedemel)	Caput Draconis (Hismael)	Malkuth
S	Fam	Conjunctio (Union)		Mercury (Taphthartharath)	Virgo (Hamaliel)	Hod

Concourse of Forces for the Golden Dawn Enochian Alphabet with Aleister Crowley's Extensions (cont'd.)

Enochian Alphabet	Letter Name Dee (GD Variant)	Geomancy	Geomantic Planetary Rulers	Geomantic Zodiacal Ruler	Geomancy on the Tree of Life
G	Ged	Fortuna Major (Major Fortune)	Sun (Northern Declination) (Sorath)	Leo (Verchiel)	Tiphereth
B	Pa (Pe)	Puer (Boy)	Mars (Bartzabel)	Aries (Melchidael)	Geburah
F	Or (Orth)	Cauda Draconis (Tail of Dragon)	Saturn and Mars (Zazel, Bartzabel)	Cauda Draconis (Zazel)	Malkuth
I	Gon	Acquisitio (Acquisition)	Jupiter (Hismael)	Sagittarius (Advachiel)	Chesed

Concourse of Forces for the Golden Dawn Enochian Alphabet with Aleister Crowley's Extensions (cont'd.)

Enochian Alphabet	Elemental Counterchange	Tetragrammaton	Tattva	Quadrant of Watchtowers	Court Card	Court Card Astrology
M	Air of Air	VV	Vayu Vayu	Upper Left Air	Prince (King) of Swords	20° Capricorn-20° Aquarius
O	Water of Air	HV	Vayu Apas	Upper Right Air	Queen of Swords	20° Virgo-20° Libra
Z	Earth of Air	H(f)V	Vayu Prithivi	Lower Left Air	Princess (Page) of Swords	Elemental Air
E	Fire of Air	YV	Vayu Agni	Lower Right Air	King (Knight) of Swords	20° Taurus-20° Gemini
N	Air of Water	VH	Apas Vayu	Upper Left Water	Prince (King) of Cups	20° Libra-20° Scorpio
P	Water of Water	HH	Apas Apas	Upper Right Water	Queen of Cups	20° Gemini-20° Cancer
L	Earth of Water	H(f)H	Apas Prithivi	Lower Left Water	Princess (Page) of Cups	Elemental Water
R	Fire of Water	YH	Apas Agni	Lower Right Water	King (Knight) of Cups	20° Aquarius-20° Pisces

Concourse of Forces for the Golden Dawn Enochian Alphabet with Aleister Crowley's Extensions (cont'd.)

Enochian Alphabet	Elemental Counterchange	Tetragrammaton	Tattva	Quadrant of Watchtowers	Court Card	Court Card Astrology
A	Air of Earth	VH(f)	Prithivi Vayu	Upper Left Earth	Prince (King) of Pentacles	20° Aries-20° Taurus
U	Water of Earth	HH(f)	Prithivi Apas	Upper Right Earth	Queen of Pentacles	20° Sagittarius-20° Capricorn
T	Earth of Earth	H(f)H(f)	Prithivi Prithivi	Lower Left Earth	Princess (Page) of Pentacles	Elemental Earth
S	Fire of Earth	YH(f)	Prithivi Agni	Lower Right Earth	King (Knight) of Pentacles	20° Leo-20° Virgo
G	Air of Fire	VY	Agni Vayu	Upper Left Fire	Prince (King) of Wands	20° Cancer-20° Leo
B	Water of Fire	HY	Agni Apas	Upper Right Fire	Queen of Wands	20° Pisces-20° Aries
F	Earth of Fire	H(f)Y	Agni Prithivi	Lower Left Fire	Princess (Page) of Pentacles	Elemental Fire
I	Fire of Fire	YY	Agni Agni	Lower Right Fire	King (Knight) of Wands	20° Scorpio-20° Sagittarius

Concourse of Forces for the Golden Dawn Enochian Alphabet with Aleister Crowley's Extensions (cont'd.)

Enochian Alphabet	Tetragrammaton on Watchtowers Rank (Kerubic)	Column (Elemental)	Hebrew Model (Golden Dawn)	Greek Model (Dee)	Major Arcana	Hebrew Astrology
M	H	V	Tzaddi	Mu	XVII—The Star	Aquarius
O	Y	V	Lamed	Omicron	XI—Justice	Libra
Z	H(f)	V	Aleph	Zeta	0—The Fool	Air
E	V	V	Zain	Epsilon	VI—The Lovers	Gemini
N	H	H	Nun	Nu	XIII—Death	Scorpio
P	Y	H	Cheth	Pi	VII—The Chariot	Cancer
L	H(f)	H	Mem	Lambda	XII—The Hanged Man	Water
R	V	H	Qoph	Rho	XVIII—The Moon	Pisces
A	H	H(f)	Vav	Alpha	V—The Hierophant	Taurus
U	Y	H(f)	Ayin	Upsilon	XV—The Devil	Capricorn
T	H(f)	H(f)	Tav	Tau	XXI—The World	Earth
S	V	H(f)	Yod	Sigma	IX—The Hermit	Virgo
G	H	Y	Teth	Gamma	VIII—Strength	Leo
B	Y	Y	Heh	Beta	IV—The Emperor	Aries
F	H(f)	Y	Shin	Di-Gamma (Stau)	XX—Judgement	Fire
I	V	Y	Samekh	Iota	XIV—Temperance	Sagittarius

Concourse of Forces for the Golden Dawn Enochian Alphabet with Aleister Crowley's Extensions (cont'd.)

Enochian Alphabet	Tree of Life Color Scale (Paths-Sephiroth)	Color (Major Arcana)	Number Value GD/Dee
M	Prince-Prince (Yetzirah-Yetzirah)	Violet	90/4(0)
O	Queen-Prince (Briah-Yetzirah)	Green	30/7(0)
Z	Princess-Prince (Assiah-Yetzirah)	Yellow (Citrine)	1/7
E	King-Prince (Atziloth-Yetzirah)	Orange	7/5
N	Prince-Queen (Yetzirah-Briah)	Blue Green	50/5(0)
P	Queen-Queen (Briah-Briah)	Yellow Orange	8/8(0)
L	Princess-Queen (Assiah-Briah)	Blue (Olive)	40/3(0)
R	King-Queen (Atziloth-Briah)	Red Violet	100/1(00)
A	Prince-Princess (Yetzirah-Assiah)	Red Orange	6/1
U	Queen-Princess (Briah-Assiah)	Blue Violet	70/4(00)
T	Princess-Princess (Assiah-Assiah)	Blue Violet (Black)	400/3(00
S	King-Princess (Atziloth-Assiah)	Yellow Green	10/2(00)
G	Prince-King (Yetzirah-Atziloth)	Yellow	9/3
B	Queen-King (Briah-Atziloth)	Red	5/2
F	Princess-King (Assiah-Atziloth)	Red (Russet)	300/6
I	King-King (Atziloth-Atziloth)	Blue	60/1(0)

Concourse of Forces for the Golden Dawn Enochian Alphabet with Aleister Crowley's Extensions (cont'd.)
The Five Additional Letters according to Aleister Crowley

Enochian Alphabet	Letter Name	Planet	Element	Tree of Life	Elemental Counterchange	Pentagrammaton	Tattva
D	Gal	Venus	Spirit	Kether	Spirit of Spirit	Shin	Akasa Akasa
H	Na-hath	Sun/Moon	Air	Tiphereth and Yesod	Air of Spirit	Vav	Akasa Vayu
Q	Ger	Jupiter/Mercury	Water	Chesed and Hod	Water of Spirit	Heh	Akasa Apas
X	Pal	Saturn	Earth	The Three Supernals and Malkuth	Earth of Spirit	Heh final	Akasa Prithivi
C, K	Veh	Mars/Venus	Fire	Geburah and Netzach	Fire of Spirit	Yod	Akasa Agni

Enochian Alphabet	Major Arcana	Greek Model	Hebrew Model	Major and Minor Arcana	Tablet of Union	Color	Number Value Crowley/Dee	
D	III—The Empress	Delta	Daleth (Aleph Lamed)	0—The Fool	Adverse L	Green (White)	4	4
H	0—The Fool	Eta	Aleph	Ace of Swords	E(XARP)	Yellow (Citrine)	1	8
Q	XII—The Hanged Man	Koppa	Mem	Ace of Cups	H(COMA)	Blue (Olive)	40	9(0)
X	XXI—The World	Xi	Tav	Ace of Pentacles	N(ANTA)	Blue Violet (Black)	400	6(0)
C, K	XX—Judgement	Kappa	Shin	Ace of Wands	B(ITOM)	Red (Russet)	300	2(0)

TWELFTH KEY

TAROT

OVERVIEW

Though the preceding revised "Book of Concourse of Forces" qualifies, by Enochian, every point of Golden Dawn magickal theory and practice, as I have argued elsewhere, the one pristine symbol set from which all Golden Dawn symbolism is derived is the Hebraic-Tarot correspondences, which Mathers rediscovered (as demonstrated in the addendum to Key 12). The supreme magickal formula, upon which is erected the complete Temple of Golden Dawn magick, equates zero with 1 as:

0 = The Fool (Tarot) = Aleph (Hebrew) = 1

so that

0 = 1

It has been argued that the Tarot is not a language, but in reality it serves as the most important esoteric alphabet (and language) in the Western magickal tradition. Arthur Edward Waite, possibly the most influential of all Tarotologists, refers to the Tarot as a "pictorial" language, for truly the Tarot cards in their picture designs encode the mythological symbolism of both the East and West.

Much has been written on the Tarot in the last 25 years, so much that it may seem unnecessary to dedicate a whole chapter of this book to such a well trodden path. However, despite the variety of commentaries available today, the beginning student will be hard pressed to find the esoteric pattern, with all its nuances, in any one text. In the last 15 years, for example, there has appeared a spate of books which in their commentaries on the

Court Cards have confused the basic attributes of the Knight with those of the King. Such basic misunderstandings have been rectified in this key.

Both beginning and advanced practitioners of the Tarot will benefit from this chapter, for it thoroughly analyzes:

- The real divinatory meanings for every modern Tarot deck which has emanated out of the Golden Dawn tradition

- The confusion which has developed over the correct order of the Court Cards

- The connection between the Jewish Qabalah and the Golden Dawn esoteric Tarot system

- The alternate French Qabalistic Tarot system of Levi, Papus, and Wirth

- A reconstruction of how S. L. MacGregor Mathers rediscovered the esoteric Qabalistic order for the Tarot

- A complete analysis of the Qabalistic clues hidden in the 78 cards of the Waite Tarot deck

The Tarot served as my first exposure to the Western magickal tradition. In 1966 I first encountered the term "Tarot." At that time the availability of literature on the Tarot was quite scarce, and Tarot decks such as the Waite-Rider deck, were not easily obtainable. I could find nothing but a written description of the Tarot cards in an encyclopedia article. Armed only with the names, numbers, and a brief written description of each Major Arcana card, I set out to design a 22-card deck intuitively. After six months of effort, I devised my first hand-painted Tarot, which was not influenced by the designs of any established deck. To this date this deck has been a most valuable reference tool for me, allowing me to view my perceptions of the Tarot prior to my exposure to any traditional versions.

If I could stress one thing to any student of the Tarot, it is the need to create your own personal Tarot deck from scratch. You may blanch from such a task, but it does not require, or depend upon, your ability as an artist. Regardless of whether you have drawn anything before, the most valuable Tarot deck you will ever own is the first deck you have wrought by your own hands and ingenuity.

My first hand-drawn Tarot deck was very crude in execution, but it is extremely valuable to me today, serving as a beginning watermark of my understanding of the Tarot. In looking at my first deck years later, I constantly rediscover nuances of color, shape, and symbolism which hold secrets I did not consciously perceive when I first drew the deck. Even if you can only draw stick figures for your Tarot personae, don't hesitate to draw your first deck. No matter how crudely you may execute these cards, you will find that this one hand-painted deck will ultimately become your most valued Tarot.

As to the correct oracular meanings for the 78 cards of the Tarot, no better reference tool has been devised than the tables at the beginning of this chapter which detail the key phrases for each of the cards. The following guideline is written for the beginning student of Tarot divination.

A Guide to Tarot Divination
for the Beginning Student

0. The Tarot properly employed in divination serves as a mirror that can reveal to a divided mind the easiest solution to any dilemma. Once properly understood, the Tarot will never offer muddled or erroneous information.

I. As an oracle it can never be manipulated, distorted, obscured, misunderstood, or misconstrued. Its divination allocations are so precise that the one true meaning of any divination will overwhelm the mind of the diviner, permitting no misinterpretation.

II. The beginning student, aware of the vagueness of his or her own Tarot readings, may ask, "How is this possible?" The answer lies in constant practice with the right formulae. The Hebrew mystical and magickal tradition known as the Qabalah is the basis for the correct meanings of the Tarot cards. If the correct meanings of the 78 cards are memorized and constantly played against each other in various readings, the diviner will eventually realize that only one essential meaning can ever be given to any card. Yet, by virtue of the neighboring cards surrounding any one card in any given reading, the correct meaning of that card is modified; the result is an infinite amount of information available from any one card.

III. It is the blending or modifying of one card with another that is the inspired or trance part of any Tarot reading. By constant work with the tables in this chapter delineating the correct meaning of the cards, a channel of inspiration will open up within the diviner which will spontaneously produce the correct reading for any given spread of cards. When the diviner is able to correctly define a blank deck of cards, marked with only the barest initials for the names of the 78 cards, then the beginning of the inspiration will descend, and a familiarity with the vocabulary of the Tarot will allow an answer to any specified question.

IV. For the beginning student of the Tarot, this one chapter is the most important book available to allow a precise oracular vocabulary. The student should concentrate on the first part of this chapter and commit to memory by constant use the key concepts outlined for each of the 78 cards.

V. The student should obtain two commercially printed decks. The first should be a representation of a traditional Tarot deck, preferably the French Marseilles deck. The second should be one of the following five decks, which are all currently available and encode to one degree or another the Qabalistic symbolism of the Golden Dawn Tarot system:

1. The Golden Dawn Tarot Deck, by Israel Regardie/Robert Wang, U.S. Games Systems

2. Thoth Tarot Deck, by Aleister Crowley/Frieda Harris, Weiser

3. Rider-Waite Tarot Deck, by Arthur Edward Waite/Pamela Colman Smith, U.S. Games Systems

4. Builders of the Adytum Tarot, by Paul Foster Case/Jessie Burns Parke, B.O.T.A.

5. The New Golden Dawn Ritual Tarot Deck, by Chic Cicero/Sandra Tabatha Cicero, Llewellyn Publications

An alternate deck, though more difficult to obtain, is the Hermetic Tarot by Godfrey Dawson, U.S. Games Systems. This deck is also based on the Golden Dawn Tarot system.

VI. The student should then construct two 78-card Tarot decks from scratch. The first deck should be 78 blank cards that should be marked with an abbreviation for the name of each card. Thus for the Ace of Wands, "AW" should be marked on the appropriate card to designate the Ace of Wands. The second deck should include 78 picture images or symbols drawn and colored by the student for each of the Tarot cards. No matter how crude the execution, this deck will be the most potent deck the student can ever possess.

VII. The student will then have four Tarot decks to use in divination.

VIII. The deck in the Golden Dawn tradition will be the primer deck. This deck should be used to initially memorize the divinatory meanings recorded in the first part of this book.

IX. The blank Tarot deck which the student has devised with appropriate abbreviations for each card will serve as the test deck. This deck should be constructed and put to use after the initial vocabulary for the Tarot has been memorized. The interpretations for each card should be recorded and then verified for accurateness.

X. When the blank deck can be used as easily as the Golden Dawn deck, then the student should use the traditional European Tarot deck in divination. At this point, the student will have no difficulty in defining the 40 Minor Arcana cards that are devoid of any symbolism save their pip symbols.

XI. Now, with the oracular language committed to memory, the student should design with any means available a personal deck. This deck will serve as a magickal diary recording the student's perception of the Tarot deck of 78 diverse cards. It will also be the most endearing of the four decks the student will possess, for it will be the most personal of the decks.

XII. To the beginning student, this brings up the first Tarot prohibition. Do not develop a fetish or taboo over the handling of any of your Tarot decks. Although a Tarot deck can be specifically designed so that no one else will ever hold or see such a deck except its creator/owner, the very concept of the Tarot cries out to be handled, shuffled, and seen by all. The true European archetype or personification of all Tarot divination must be seen as the gypsy, openly reading anyone's fortune and allowing all to handle the cards.

XIII. The second Tarot prohibition is a divination secret few diviners ever perceive. There are no evil cards. Every card employed in a divination layout is ultimately a guidepost or directional mark to show the quickest way of resolving any problem. Therefore, cards which outwardly appear as malefic, evil, or negative should be read rather as warnings and indicators of how to overcome obstacles or fears. The oracular vocabulary should ultimately be refined to a language which is wholly supportive and directional in its guidance and insight.

XIV. In light of the above, the Tarot tradition of reversals should be avoided. Each of the 78 cards is perfectly defined as one concept unaltered by its position of being dealt right side up or upside down. The tradition of reversals always gives a negative or malefic meaning to a card falling upside down in a divinatory layout. Therefore, an average of half the cards in any given reading will have a negative connotation assigned. In all honesty, such a process will only bleed the power latent in any given layout and muddle the oracular answer available. Therefore, the student should avoid any such manipulation of the Tarot cards. The actual cards surrounding any given card in any reading will already qualify whether any given card is well disposed or ill disposed.

XV. Since no card is evil, then no suit is evil. This is the greatest misinterpretation by most contemporary commentators on the cards, that the suit of Swords in the Minor Arcana is malefic in nature. The Sword by its elemental nature of Air represents the mind, the intellect, the rational thought process. The discord that this suit can denote is mental, not physical. And such discord is only an indication that the mind must be more flexible than it is in adapting to any given situation. Therefore the diviner should always interpret this suit in divination as an indicator of difficulties which are perceived by the mind (not the body) and guideposts as to their resolution.

XVI. Yet the true nature of another division of the Tarot deck may elude the querent. This division is the 16 cards referred to as the Court Cards, each of which possesses a dual nature in divination. In divination these 16 cards indicate two aspects, one as an individual personality outside of the querent, and the other as a personality the querent will adopt to cope with any given situation. All commentators have been able to perceive the first aspect, or outer face of the Court Cards, yet few have perceived the dual nature or inner face of these 16 cards. Therefore, by its placement in any given reading, a Court Card will denote either a person encountered by the querent or a personality that the querent assumes.

XVII. The Tarot can answer any question. The problem the diviner may encounter is how to address such a question to the Tarot. In divination there are two basic methods for specifying a question. With the intention of an inner silent prayer, the diviner should formulate with as much intensity as possible the question requiring resolution while holding and shuffling the Tarot deck, after the significator has been removed from the deck. Or, if the diviner requires a more concrete means of posing a question to the deck, a select group of cards can be removed before shuffling the cards and laid before the reader as a means of describing the question. Thus if the question posed is, "Should I change my occupation?" two cards can be selected to describe this question adequately: the Two of Pentacles (symbolizing change) and the Six of Pentacles (symbolizing one's occupation).

XVIII. Now armed with a specific means of asking any given question, the diviner may not address the time sequence any given reading may indicate. In reality no accurate time period can be ascertained in any given reading. There is no established formula that can be applied to any given card to determine how long such a card will come into effect. However, any Tarot layout is a flowchart showing an established sequence of events. Therefore, though a specific time period cannot be determined in a reading, the sequence of events can accurately be determined by the position of the card in the reading. Though the near past, present, near future, and far future can be divined in a layout, a specific number of days can never be clearly ascertained with any reliability. Ultimately, the time period delineated by the oracle of the Tarot is always the present moment. The cards are randomly cast, and in their layout they describe the moment in which they were cast. Within this ever-present moment is the seed of the future and the harvest of the past. The present can decipher both the past and the future.

XIX. As to patterns for laying out the cards in divination, the student should be flexible and innovative. Experiment with as many layouts as possible and ultimately tailor down the patterns you work with to a workable format you can be comfortable with in resolving any given problem. My own personal favorite is the Celtic Cross, the spread devised by A. E. Waite, which is detailed in the section, "The Laying of the Cards." Above all, remember to be experimental in the way the cards are arranged in a reading but be inflexible when committing to memory the divinatory meanings outlined in this chapter.

XX. This brings up the question: will 78 cards employed in a reading give more information than a reading involving one card? Surprisingly, experience will show that one card will always give more information than 78 cards, which in their overabundance of divinatory data will tend to muddle a reading. The cumbersome divinatory pattern used in the Golden Dawn has not been included in this book, since this layout gives too much information and therefore tends to obscure rather than clarify any issue. Thus, with practice, the diviner will find that, the more sparse the information, the clearer the answer to any question becomes. The diviner should always avoid over-reading the cards.

XXI. This brief set of guidelines ends with one paramount guideline for any beginning student of divination. Do not believe the Tarot taboo that you cannot read for yourself. Your best possible diviner is yourself. The cards will always serve as the proper intermediary between your problems and their proper solutions. Trust in yourself and the Tarot will always serve as a crystal-clear mirror.

Unlike the *I Ching*, we cannot be sure what the originators of the Tarot intended as oracular meanings for the Tarot. In fact we do not even know who the originators were. We are aware, however, that the Tarot did not exist in print prior to 1300 CE, which makes the Tarot the newest of oracles, rather than a secret, long lost book dating back to ancient Egypt. With the *I Ching*, a book, or canon, has survived which details the real oracular meaning for each of the 64 hexagrams. For the Tarot, however, the meanings for each of its 78 cards can only be derived from the designs themselves, since no written record survives detailing their original meanings.

This chapter begins with a detailed timeline. From this timeline, we find that the real meanings and origins for these divinatory cards were not questioned until the publication of Court de Gebelin's *Primitive World* in 1781.

My research into the real meanings behind the Tarot has led me to the belief that there exists a written text which clearly defines the Tarot. This written text is the Golden Dawn secret instructional manuscript known as, *Book T*. It is allegedly the parchment book found in the hands of founder of the Rosicrucian movement, Christian Rosenkruetz, when his tomb was unearthed 120 years after its initial sealing. But in reality this *Book T* was secretly penned by Mathers as a result of his own intensive Qabalistic research. This premise is fully detailed in the addendum to this key.

Now the Golden Dawn secret document, *Book T*, is easily accessible in print, for it appears in its entirety in Regardie's *Golden Dawn*. Within the few pages of this document, Mathers distilled every Qabalistic insight he possessed concerning the Tarot into a workable oracular language that is still relevant today.

The three most important and influential 20th-century Qabalistic commentaries on the Tarot are:

- *The Pictorial Key to the Tarot* (1910) by Arthur Edward Waite
- *The Book of Thoth* (1944) by Aleister Crowley
- *The Tarot: A Key to the Wisdom of the Ages* (1947) by Paul Foster Case

Each of these commentaries was taken directly from Mathers' *Book T*, for each commentator was a member at one time of the Golden Dawn. Each book contains a wealth of oracular meanings for the Tarot cards, which when critically examined can be directly sourced to Mathers' unique oracular vocabulary for the Tarot.

In light of these similarities, I have constructed a set of tables for each of the three basic divisions of the Tarot deck:

- The 22 cards of the Major Arcana, each corresponding to a letter of the Hebrew alphabet

- The 40 cards of the Minor Arcana, being four suits of 10 numbered cards in each suit

- The 16 Court Cards, being four suits of four cards each

By referring to the tables constructed, the four basic divinatory key terms from Mathers, Waite, Crowley, and Case are tabulated together so that the real meaning for each of these cards can be grasped with the least amount of verbiage. In this sense I have developed a canon, or model, not unlike the preserved text of the *I Ching*, which can clearly give a precise meaning to each of the 78 Tarot cards. Further, these meanings are based on the most precise and pristine Qabalistic interpretations of the cards ever developed.

Even if you have used the Tarot cards for years, these tables should not be ignored, for their very precision may clarify those meanings to the cards which you may have taken for granted in the past. The Tarot tables also contain the various names for each specific card that Mathers, Waite, Crowley and Case have used in their own Tarot textbooks, plus a brief synopsis of the correct astrological and Qabalistic correspondences according to the Golden Dawn.

You will find, after working with these tables for a short period of time, that their value is not in how much is said about each card, but rather how little. By the brevity and sparseness of each oracular definition, the ambiguities that often occur when an oracle offers too much information are guarded against. This permits very precise oracular advice for each of the 78 Tarot cards. These tables also demonstrate, beyond a shadow of a doubt, that the essential oracular insight offered in the writings of Waite, Crowley, and Case (as well as countless lesser commentators) are all based on the secret Tarot instructions contained in *Book T* of the Golden Dawn.

The tables are followed by a short description of the most popular Tarot layout for divination, known as the "Celtic Cross." This pattern was devised by Waite and greatly departs from the elaborate and sometimes awkward Golden Dawn method of Tarot divination. I have included Waite's layout rather than that of the Golden Dawn because from my own experience this simple 10-card layout allows a much clearer oracle than that of the cumbersome Golden Dawn layout. Moreover, it is possibly the most used pattern in contemporary Tarot divination.

The discussion on divination is followed by a detailing of the esoteric pattern which Mathers drew upon for his own divinatory vocabulary. This pattern is the grand Western mandala of the Tree of Life, the Qabalistic blueprint for the cosmos. The composition of the Qabalistic Tree of Life can be broken down into three major components, each of which serves as a model for the Tarot deck. This threefold division is shown below.

This Qabalistic section for the Tarot should be read in conjunction with the Qabalistic knowledge given in the second key (Hebrew), found in Book One. This combination will give you a firm foundation of Qabalistic knowledge for the Tarot, based on the secret information contained in the curriculum of the Golden Dawn.

Threefold Qabalistic Model for the Tarot

Tree of Life	Tarot
The 10 Sephiroth (the first 10 numbered circles) as Four Worlds	The 10 numbered Minor Arcana cards (Ace–10) as Four Suits (Wands, Cups, Swords, Pentacles)
The 22 Paths which connect the 10 Sephiroth as the 22 Hebrew letters	The 22 Major Arcana cards (0, The Fool–XXI, The World)
The 16 invisible Paths on the Tree of Life corresponding to the fourfold counterchange of the four elements	The 16 Court Cards of the Four Suits

Each of these Qabalistic models is thoroughly discussed. The correspondences for the 16 invisible Paths on the Tree of Life are unique to my research. As such, a brief overview may help in grasping the basis for my correspondences.

Since the Supernals, the first three Sephiroth, correspond to the elements Air, Fire, and Water in the Golden Dawn Qabalistic correspondences, I have premised that the 12 invisible Paths which have their source in the elemental Supernals must correspond to their own elements. The four remaining invisible Paths have their source below the Abyss (in Chesed and Geburah) and therefore fall to the fourth element, Earth. These esoteric Court Card correspondences can be summarized as shown in the table on the next page.

As pointed out earlier, the Golden Dawn Qabalistic system is the ultimate model for the Tarot, permitting the deepest possible interpretation for each card of the 78-card deck. However, there is one other major school of esoteric thought for the Tarot, which emanated out of the 19th-century French magickal revival. Specifically the copious writings of Eliphas Levi, Oswald Wirth, and Papus disclose an elaborate set of Qabalistic-Tarot correspondences which are at odds with the insightful discoveries of Mathers. From the available translations of these key writers, I have extracted the core set of Qabalistic correspondences and laid them

Esoteric Qabalistic Pattern for the Court Cards

Source Sephirah	Root Element	Invisible Path Number	Court Card	Basic Element
Kether	Air	41	Knight of Swords	Air
Kether	Air	42	Queen of Swords	Air
Kether	Air	43	King of Swords	Air
Kether	Air	44	Page of Swords	Air
Chockmah	Fire	33	Knight of Wands	Fire
Chockmah	Fire	34	Queen of Wands	Fire
Chockmah	Fire	35	King of Wands	Fire
Chockmah	Fire	36	Page of Wands	Fire
Binah	Water	37	Knight of Cups	Water
Binah	Water	38	Queen of Cups	Water
Binah	Water	39	King of Cups	Water
Binah	Water	40	Page of Cups	Water
Chesed	Below	45	Knight of Pentacles	Earth
Chesed	the	46	Queen of Pentacles	Earth
Geburah	Abyss	47	King of Pentacles	Earth
Geburah	(Earth)	48	Page of Pentacles	Earth

out in a group of tables which form a parallel French Qabalistic dictionary, not unlike *Liber 777*. The basic tables shown are:

- The French Qabalistic Tarot (of Levi, Papus, and Lambert)

- The French astrological variations for the Tarot (of Levi, Kircher, and Wirth)

- The French Qabalistic alphabet (of Levi, Wirth, and Papus)

- Oswald Wirth's Tarot-Sephiroth order

These tables are followed by a new set of astrological alphabet correspondences for the Tarot (derived from my own research). This table correlates the alphabets of Greek, Coptic, Runes, Arabic, Enochian, and Latin for the 22 cards known as the Major Arcana.

The main difference between these two occult schools, that of France (Levi) and that of England (Mathers), is the positioning of the card known as The Fool within the Major Arcana. Levi saw the unnumbered Tarot card, The Fool, appearing between Key XX, Judgement, and Key XXI, The World, making The Magician (or Juggler) the lead card of the deck. Mathers, however, saw The Fool in this lead position of the Tarot, starting the procession of the Major Arcana as the number zero, which precedes all other numbers.

Which system is the correct system? This question can only be resolved by working with both for a long period of time. My experience shows that Mathers' system integrates the Qabalah with the Tarot in a deeper fashion than that of Levi. But I have also discovered that the French exoteric Qabalistic system offers a secondary set of meanings which can sometimes give new insight and meaning to the cards. My advice is to not ignore either system, but to use the French Qabalistic system as a subset of the English system as a means of obtaining supplemental symbolism.

Crowley's communicating angel, Aiwass, may have resolved this question for us in 1904, when dictating the following passage of *The Book of the Law*:

> My prophet is a fool with his one, one, one; are not they the Ox, and none by the Book?
> —(*Liber AL*, I:48)

Here The Fool is equated to:

- One, one, one
- The Ox
- None (by the Book)

These correspondences reveal Mathers' secret order of leading the Tarot with The Fool key and linking it to the Hebrew letter Aleph. The three symbolic correspondences for The Fool all connect to the Hebrew alphabet as:

- 111, the value of Aleph written in full as Hebrew (ALP = 1 + 30 + 80 = 111)
- The ox, the hieroglyphic meaning for the letter name Aleph
- None (by the Book), the number of The Fool in the Tarot (the symbolic picture Book)

How did Mathers come upon this most important Tarot secret? Did he find it contained in a lost secret manuscript? Was he initiated into a secret Masonic lodge that imparted this secret? Or did he come upon this clue by his own diligence? The question is resolved in the addendum to this key.

The official history of the origin of the system of Golden Dawn magick is based on a mysterious manuscript. The Masonic occultist Wynn Westcott discovered in a book stall an old text which contained a set of papers, which became known as the cipher manuscript. These papers contained the observations of a set of Masonic rituals based on the Qabalistic Tree of Life. These observations were written in a skeletal form, utilizing at times, an unknown cipher alphabet. Another version of this story alleges that Westcott discovered this cipher manuscript amid the papers and books of a recently deceased friend (possibly Frederick Hockley). In any event, Westcott, unable to decipher this secret code, enlisted the help of a fellow Freemason, Mathers.

Mathers, on account of many years of self-directed occult study in the British Museum, immediately cracked the code used in this manuscript, recognizing it as a cipher alphabet of the 15th-century occultist Trithemius, found in his work *Polygraphiae*. This cipher alphabet was used by alchemists to conceal their secrets. The manuscript, when deciphered contained all of the information necessary to create what we now know as the Golden Dawn system of magick. It also contained the German address of Anna Sprengel, the contact person for the continental lodge of the Golden Dawn. Westcott secured permission to open a secret lodge in England, and with the help of Mathers and Dr. W. R. Woodman, opened the first English lodge in 1887.

This basic theory has been accepted by most occult writers and has been championed in the writings of Israel Regardie and company. However, in 1972, a book appeared which challenged this theory to its very core. This book, *The Magicians of the Golden Dawn* by Ellic Howe, debunked the mystical origin of the Golden Dawn by proving that the surviving documents showing a true lineage from a pre-existing continental Rosicrucian lodge were in fact forgeries by both Westcott and Mathers.

I would like to believe that these charters of origin were not forgeries, that the Golden Dawn emanated from a European Germanic Rosicrucian Masonic lodge whose roots were in the original Rosicrucian order of the 17th century. Why would I like to believe this? Because the system of magick outlined by the Golden Dawn material is such a workable system, offering the best allocation for the Qabalah to the Tarot and all of Western ritual magick. This is the same reason that urged Regardie to reject Howe's assumptions that:

- The charters for the Golden Dawn were forgeries

- The cipher manuscript itself was concocted by Mathers after the fact

- Because of this spurious origin, the core teachings themselves are corrupt, fabricated, and worthless

I have honestly studied Howe's documentation and thesis in light of other historical research on the origins of the Golden Dawn (such as the writings of Francis King, George Harper, James Webb, and Ithell Colquhoun). The conclusions I was forced to accept were that:

- The Golden Dawn documentation was a forgery by Mathers, directed by Westcott

- Their motivation was to create an aura of historical authenticity for a new synthetic system of Western magick

- By creating this aura, they would be able to persuade more people to accept this system as an accurate system

- The basis for this mythic cipher manuscript was Bulwer-Lytton's novel, *Zanoni*, which begins with a description of a mysterious cipher manuscript written in a strange alphabet, which when correctly translated results in the text of *Zanoni*.

This whole scheme of subterfuge backfired anyway, for one of the members, the poet W. B. Yeats, challenged the authenticity of the founding papers. Upon forming a committee to investigate the true character of these documents, a schism ultimately arose which caused, among other things, the expulsion of Mathers from the magickal order of his own creation. However, the origin of the Golden Dawn was never uncovered by Yeats or his investigative committee.

My premise for the origin of the Golden Dawn material is that Mathers, independently of Westcott, worked for many years in the stacks of the British Museum culling all the information necessary to create the basic material of the Golden Dawn. From his knowledge of Masonic rituals, he invented a new set of rituals which would reenact every Sephirah and Path on the Tree of Life rather than the traditional Masonic themes of King Solomon's Temple or a Templar encampment.

From his knowledge of John Dee's Enochian system, Mathers created his own revision of the system in light of the Hebrew Qabalah and the Tarot. But more important than any other system, Mathers created the most workable system of correspondences for the Tarot from his own rediscovery of the secret order of the Tarot Trumps (the first 22 cards) based on the Jewish Qabalistic text, *The Book of Formation*. These basic Tarot attributes are the pattern upon which all other symbol systems in the Golden Dawn are based, not upon Enochian as some writers have suggested. In fact, Enochian is dependent upon the Tarot-Hebrew alphabet correspondences in order to fit within the Golden Dawn system. Without the Tarot, Enochian cannot fit into the general set of magickal correspondences.

The addendum to this chapter shows in great detail how I feel Mathers must have discovered the true Qabalistic pattern for the Tarot. My premise is that Mathers first worked out these Tarot correspondences, and then built every other system to fit these basic correspondences, which led with equating The Fool with the Hebrew letter Aleph and the element Air (0= 1). Mathers supports this premise in his own introduction to the symbolism of *Book T*, in which he states:

> In all of this I have not only transcribed the symbolism, but
> have tested, studied, compared, and examined it both clair-
> voyantly and in other ways. The result of these has been to
> show me how absolutely correct the symbolism of the *Book
> T* is, and how exactly it represents the Occult Forces of the
> Universe.

In his development of *Book T*, Mathers was faced with three basic mysteries concerning the true order of the Tarot:

- The mystery of what card leads all the other cards

- The mystery of the order of the seven planets within the Trumps

- The mystery of the Zodiacal order of Leo and Libra within the Trumps

How he solved these mysteries is fully worked out in this addendum.

It should be noted that these core correspondences of Mathers were first revealed to the world in print in three basic publications:

- Aleister Crowley's *Liber 777* (1909)—The XIVth table of this text shows Mathers' secret attributes (without acknowledging the source)

- Arthur Edward Waite's *The Pictorial Key to the Tarot* (1910)—Waite does not explicitly reveal Mathers' correspondences, but he used them as a source for all symbols and oracular vocabulary in his book. He does conceal, in symbols, all of the codes necessary to crack the secret symbolism. For instance, Key III, The Empress, contains the correct astrological attribution of Venus on the card itself. This is fully detailed in the addendum to this chapter.

- Paul Case's *Introduction to the Study of the Tarot* (1920)—In this first work of Case, the correct secret order for the Tarot is shown. Case states that these correspondences were a result of his own independent research around 1906. However, a note on page 14 of this text states that "the planetary attributions (for the Major Arcana) are from *Book 777,* London, 1909." This means that he was unsure of the esoteric order of the seven planets within the Tarot until he read 777 in 1909. Crowley's own source for these planetary correspondences was Mathers.

I will end this overview of the 12th key with one alternate set of oracular vocabulary for the Tarot. For each of the 78 Tarot cards, I have developed three basic meanings, each derived from Mathers' *Book T.* These tables were initially created to serve as three alternate meanings (one of which would be randomly selected) for each card, in a computerized Tarot divination system. You may find that this table offers a more flexible Tarot vocabulary, but as I have stressed before, the meanings set out by Mathers for the 78 cards should always be your most important point of reference.

Brief Tripartite Divinatory Meanings for the Tarot

Card   Meanings

0   1. The beginning of anything new
         2. Originality or eccentricity in thought
         3. Folly

1   1. Changing your surroundings to meet your needs
         2. Aiming at one goal
         3. Wisdom and skill

2   1. Penetration into areas previously unknown or obscured
         2. Hidden secrets
         3. Change and fluctuation

Card	Meanings

3
1. Pleasure and happiness
2. Increase, growth, and gain
3. Creative inspiration

4
1. Control
2. Rigidity and inflexibility
3. Reaching a solution

5
1. Intuition
2. Learning from another
3. Union

6
1. Meeting a partner
2. A choice which must be made
3. Attraction and love

7
1. Victory over opposition
2. Health and vigor
3. New direction

8
1. Courage
2. Joy and excitement
3. Exploring the unknown

9
1. Reaching a goal
2. Dependence upon oneself
3. Shedding light or insight

10
1. Good fortune
2. Repetitive cycles
3. Unexpected wealth

11
1. The need for balance and poise
2. A decision
3. A trial or legal affair

12
1. Surrender and acceptance
2. Reversal
3. Sacrifice

13
1. A change not expected
2. Renewal and transformation
3. A new beginning

14
1. A trial, testing, or ordeal
2. Blending or combining
3. The way of escape

Card   Meanings

15   1. Fear
        2. A blind impulse
        3. Illusion

16   1. Collapse of support and security
        2. Illusion shattered
        3. Conflict and competition

17   1. Revelation
        2. Hope and faith
        3. Clarity and insight

18   1. Deception
        2. A slow, toilsome struggle
        3. The brink of an important change

19   1. Pairing or uniting
        2. Innocence or frankness
        3. Gain

20   1. The final decision
        2. Release from restraints
        3. Change of roles

21   1. The outcome, result, or goal
        2. Endurance and perseverance
        3. Dominion or enslavement

AW   1. Strength which is unconquerable
        2. Will or intent
        3. Renewed strength

2W   1. Dominion
        2. Control
        3. Resolution

3W   1. Realization of hope
        2. Established strength
        3. The right decision or path

4W   1. Perfected work
        2. Completion
        3. Conclusions drawn from previous knowledge

5W   1. Strife
        2. Effort
        3. Opposition

Card   Meanings

6W   1. Victory
        2. Mastery
        3. Success

7W   1. Obstacles or difficulties
        2. A small victory
        3. Courage to meet opposition

8W   1. A new perspective or outlook
        2. Swiftness
        3. A surge or rush of energy

9W   1. Inner strength
        2. Tremendous force
        3. Self reliance

10W   1. Depression
        2. Oppression
        3. Losing sight of one's goal

AC   1. A vision of love
        2. Fertility and productiveness
        3. Emotions or feelings

2C   1. Love
        2. Mirror or reflection
        3. Harmony

3C   1. Abundance
        2. Marriage or union
        3. Merriment and hospitality

4C   1. Fulfillment
        2. Luxury and pleasure
        3. Disenchantment with present accomplishments

5C   1. Disappointment
        2. Loss in pleasure
        3. Emotional expectations not met

6C   1. Pleasure in the company of many
        2. Beginning of gain and increase
        3. Presumptuous or defective knowledge

7C   1. Illusionary success
        2. A fantasy fulfilled
        3. Intoxication

Card   Meanings

8C   1. Emotional regret
         2. Abandoned success
         3. Letting go of the past to fully meet the present

9C   1. Happiness
         2. Inner peace
         3. Controlling the emotions

10C   1. Perfected success
         2. Support of family and friends
         3. Emotional satisfaction

AS   1. New direction in thought
         2. An idea, ideal, or truth
         3. A calling upon one's strength

2S   1. Peace restored
         2. An end to a quarrel
         3. Truth and untruth

3S   1. Sorrow
         2. Acceptance rather than resistance
         3. Mental anguish or turmoil

4S   1. A truce
         2. Rest from strife
         3. Ease, rest, and relaxation

5S   1. Defeat
         2. Accepting criticism
         3. Misconceptions

6S   1. Clarity, insight, focus
         2. Study and concentration
         3. Earned success

7S   1. Futility
         2. An unorthodox approach
         3. Giving up a dream

8S   1. Interference
         2. Being afraid of anything new
         3. Giving too much attention to detail

9S   1. Indecision
         2. Despair
         3. Blind obedience

Card **Meanings**

10S
1. Surrender
2. Undisciplined thought
3. Failure of a plan or project

AP
1. Material gain
2. Any plan or project
3. A vision of money

2P
1. Change
2. A need for variety, movement, change
3. A journey or change of residence

3P
1. Creative work
2. Building up, constructing, creating
3. A business or commercial transaction

4P
1. Monetary power
2. A present or offer of money
3. Hiding or concealing a treasure

5P
1. Loss of money or position
2. Worry
3. Carefulness and thrift in money matters

6P
1. Success after much work
2. Power, influence, or recognition
3. Labor, work, or occupation

7P
1. Success unfulfilled
2. Inactivity
3. Loss of promised money

8P
1. Slow, constant effort
2. Prudence
3. Persistence and endurance

9P
1. Material gain
2. Comfort, security, and protection
3. Prosperity and growth

10P
1. Wealth
2. End or result
3. Cleverness in monetary transactions

KnW
1. Seeking after your dreams
2. Person who is active, fierce, and proud
3. Person who is impulsive, unpredictable, and impetuous
   (As significator's birth date: Nov. 13–Dec. 11)

Card   Meanings

QW   1. Being in control of your life
        2. Person who has great attractive power
        3. Person who is domineering and obstinate
           (As significator's birth date: Mar. 11–Apr. 9)

KW   1. Being the center of attention
        2. Person who is strong, generous, and noble
        3. Person who is hasty, opinionated, and rather violent
           (As significator's birth date: Jul. 12–Aug. 12)

PW   1. Being impatient or overenthusiastic
        2. Person who is extremely individualistic, brilliant, and daring
        3. Person who is superficial, theatrical, or unstable

KnC   1. Seeking love or spiritual vision
        2. Person who is grateful, poetic, or artistic
        3. Person who is sensual, indolent, or overly sensitive
           (As significator's birth date: Feb. 11–Mar. 10)

QC   1. Waiting patiently
        2. Person who is imaginative, dreamy, and kind-natured
        3. Person who is very much affected by other influences
           (As significator's birth date: Jun. 11–Jul. 11)

KC   1. Being subtle, secretive, or crafty
        2. Person who has a calm exterior but a fierce, passionate inner nature
        3. Person who is ruthless, intimidating, and powerful
           (As significator's birth date: Oct. 13–Nov. 12)

PC   1. Being receptive, especially to the offer of love
        2. Person who is psychic, receptive, or romantic
        3. Person who lives in a fantasy world

KnS   1. Being single-minded, having one purpose in life
        2. Person who is clever, subtle, skillful, and domineering
        3. Person who is incapable of making a decision
           (As significator's birth date: May 11–Jun. 10)

QS   1. Being in balance during a crisis
        2. Person who is perceptive, a keen observer, and an intense individualist
        3. Person who is unreliable, unbalanced
           (As significator's birth date: Sep. 13–Oct. 12)

KS   1. Being idealistic or overly intellectual
        2. Person who is full of ideas and thoughts and is firm in friendship as well as in enmity

Card	Meanings

KS 3. Person who is a faddist, or overly prejudiced
(As significator's birth date: Jan. 11–Feb. 10)

PS 1. Radically changing your course of action
2. Person who is logical, stern, dexterous, or clever
3. Person who is frivolous, cunning, rebellious, or anxious

KnP 1. Being meticulous, studious, or patient in your work
2. Person who is preoccupied with material things but clever and patient
3. Person who is timid, jealous, or meddling
(As significator's birth date: Aug. 13–Sep. 12)

QP 1. Pushing your talents or ability to the limit
2. Person who is ambitious, practical, greathearted, and truthful
3. Person who is undecided, changeable, moody
(As significator's birth date: Dec. 12–Jan. 10)

KP 1. Toiling, laboring, or working
2. Person who is steady, reliable, practical, and enduring
3. Person who is insensitive, slow to anger, but furious if roused
(As significator's birth date: Apr. 10–May 10)

PP 1. Being passive or silent
2. Person who is benevolent, diligent, and careful
3. Person who is inconsistent or on the brink of a great change

Origin

300 CE—The approximate date for the creation of the *Sepher Yetzirah*, the Jewish Qabalistic manual that details the astrological symbolism of the Hebrew alphabet; the basis for Mathers' Qabalistic Tarot

1367 CE—A prohibition against playing cards appeared in the canon of Bern. The oldest surviving records of the Tarot appear in legal documents banning the Tarot.

If the cards were banned by 1367, then we must date their origin before this date; however, the Tarot does not date from "ancient Egypt." In fact, the Tarot is the "newest" and most current of the arcane systems of oracles developed by man.

Case dates the origin of the Tarot to 1200 CE in Fez, Morocco, but there exists no tangible evidence to support this claim. The best we can assume from present evidence is that the Tarot was in existence in Europe by 1300 CE.

1392 CE—Jacquemin Gringonneur creates three packs of Tarot for the amusement of Charles VI of France. Fragments of these decks form the oldest surviving historical document of the Tarot.

1450 CE—The Visconti-Sforza Tarot series was commissioned in Milan in the mid-15th century. Fragments of a group of decks created for both the families Visconti and Sforza serve as one of our earliest surviving models for the modern Tarot deck of 78 cards.

1500 CE—The earliest list of the Major Arcana as we know it today is given in the Latin manuscript *Sermones de Ludo Cumalis*.

1540 CE—The earliest printed treatise on the Tarot as a divination system appears in Italy in the work *Le Sorti* by Marcolino.

1612 CE—In *The Fame and Confession of the Rosicrucians*, a privately printed and anonymous tract describing the secret Rosicrucian community in Europe, the first reference to the esoteric Tarot appears. It is given the title ROTA and is described as a device or machine which is consulted for information concerning the past, present, and future.

1781 CE—The first association of the Tarot with Egypt is made in Court de Gebelin's encyclopedia entitled *Le Monde Primitif* (The Primitive World). The Hieroglyphic "Book of Thoth" was premised by de Gebelin as the original Tarot deck, which dated back to ancient Egypt. De Gebelin's Egyptian theories were expanded upon in the late 18th century by Etteilla. Their combined efforts have obscured the real history, origin, and structure of the Tarot to this day; so much so that in modern times psuedo-Egyptian Tarot decks have been created in order to justify this supposed Egyptian origin.

1785–1791 CE—The French occultist Etteilla, influenced by Court de Gebelin's theory of an Egyptian origin of the Tarot, writes a series of books establishing an esoteric vocabulary for the Tarot cards. These definitions are not the source for Mathers' own oracular thesaurus. However, Etteilla's constant reference to the Tarot as the Book of Thoth, may be the source for Crowley's own *Book of Thoth* published 160 years later.

1856 CE—The first printed connection between the Qabalah and the Tarot was made by Eliphas Levi in his work *Dogme et Rituel de la Haute Magie* (Dogma and Ritual of Transcendental Magic). This is the pattern which S.L. MacGregor Mathers would elaborate upon to form the Golden Dawn Tarot deck.

1887 CE—With the formation of the secret society the Order of the Golden Dawn, Mathers records the esoteric attributes of the Tarot in his unpublished manuscript, *Book T*.

1889 CE—Papus (Gerald Encausse) publishes *The Tarot of the Bohemians*, which details an erroneous Qabalistic Tarot based on the blinded occult attributes given by Eliphas Levi in *Transcendental Magic*.

1909 CE—Aleister Crowley, in his privately printed *Liber 777*, details the secret order of the Tarot first envisioned by Mathers. Crowley's privately printed occult magazine, *The Equinox*, also discloses this information during 1909–14 (especially *Equinox* I:8). An anonymous author, writing under the initials "V.N.," at this time publically discloses the correct Golden Dawn Tarot attributes in the English magazine, *The Occult Review*, May 1910, by appending tables from Crowley's own 777.

1910 CE—Arthur Edward Waite publishes *The Pictorial Key to the Tarot*, which hints at, but does not detail, the secret Golden Dawn Qabalistic Tarot.

1920 CE—In a series of articles for the magazine *AZOTH*, Paul Foster Case comments upon the Tarot in light of the Golden Dawn school of thought. By 1920, Case claims to have discovered the secret order of the Tarot through veiled hints in the writings of Eliphas Levi.

1937 CE—Israel Regardie publishes the secret instructions of the Golden Dawn, including *Book T*, in his four-volume series of books entitled *The Golden Dawn*.

1944 CE—Crowley's *Book of Thoth* details a new Tarot reconstructed from Mathers' *Book T*, in light of Thelemic magick.

1947 CE—Paul Foster Case's *The Tarot, A Key to the Wisdom of the Ages*, elaborates the Golden Dawn symbolism for the Major Arcana of the Tarot. This edition is the final version of Case's *Introduction to the Tarot*, first published in 1920.

1969 CE–present—A revival of interest in the Tarot results in the reprinting of many older versions of the cards (such as Waite's, Crowley's, and Case's designs) and the creation of new, widely diverse designs (from reconstructed Golden Dawn versions to Salvador Dali's surreal alternative to Aleister Crowley's and Frieda Harris' *Book of Thoth*). *T: The New Tarot*, designed from Ouija trance sessions, appears in 1969, heralding the beginning of many new offshoots and variants of the Tarot.

ALPHABET CODE

The Tarot is the Western equivalent to the Chinese oracular system known as the *I Ching*. As the *I Ching* has 64 basic oracular images, the Tarot has 78.

Divinatory definitions for the 64 combined hexagrams of the *I Ching* were recorded 3,000 years ago and survive to this day. This corpus of oracular symbols known as the *Chou-I* or *I Ching* has preserved the original intentional meanings behind these 64 hexagrams. But for the Tarot, no such definitive text exists.

Although the Tarot's origin is relatively recent (no more than 700 years ago) we do not know the originator of the system, nor the true oracular vocabulary intended for the original 78-card version of the Tarot.

However, at the end of the 19th century, a secret set of instructions for Tarot divination was penned by S.L. MacGregor Mathers under the Rosicrucian title of *Book T*. These secret instructions were an attempt

600 years after the creation of the Tarot to reconstruct the intended Qabalistic oracular vocabulary for the Tarot. Mathers, taking clues from the writings of Eliphas Levi, revised the oracular definitions for the three basic sections of the Tarot in light of the Jewish Qabalah: (1) the Major Arcana was ordered in light of the *Sepher Yetzirah*, (2) the Minor Arcana was ordered in light of the ten sephiroth of the Tree of Life, and (3) the Court Cards were ordered in light of the Tetragrammaton.

Essentially this oracular thesaurus for each of the 78 cards is the canon needed to bring the Tarot to the level of divinatory meanings available in the *I Ching*.

The following table shows the development of Mathers' esoteric Tarot system.

The Development of the Esoteric Tarot

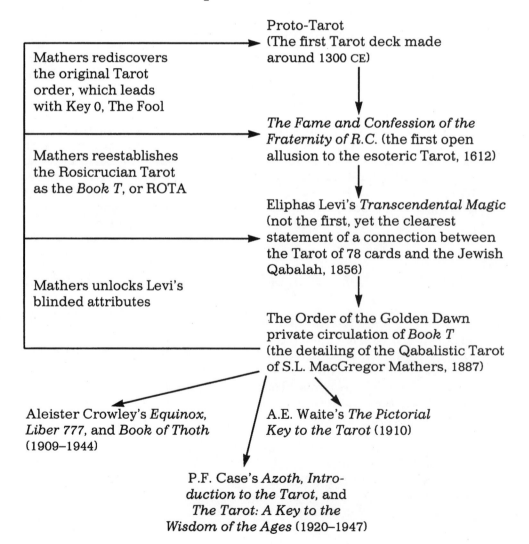

Mathers rediscovers the original Tarot order, which leads with Key 0, The Fool

Proto-Tarot
(The first Tarot deck made around 1300 CE)

Mathers reestablishes the Rosicrucian Tarot as the *Book T*, or ROTA

The Fame and Confession of the Fraternity of R.C. (the first open allusion to the esoteric Tarot, 1612)

Eliphas Levi's *Transcendental Magic* (not the first, yet the clearest statement of a connection between the Tarot of 78 cards and the Jewish Qabalah, 1856)

Mathers unlocks Levi's blinded attributes

The Order of the Golden Dawn private circulation of *Book T* (the detailing of the Qabalistic Tarot of S.L. MacGregor Mathers, 1887)

Aleister Crowley's *Equinox, Liber 777*, and *Book of Thoth* (1909–1944)

A.E. Waite's *The Pictorial Key to the Tarot* (1910)

P.F. Case's *Azoth, Introduction to the Tarot*, and *The Tarot: A Key to the Wisdom of the Ages* (1920–1947)

Though Mathers' work was a secret manuscript for the Order of the Golden Dawn, every modern variant to the Tarot depends upon its symbolism, including such diverse Tarot systems as P.D. Ouspensky's 1912 essay on the Tarot and Salvador Dali's surreal Tarot deck.

Every major commentator on the Tarot, specifically A.E. Waite, A.E. Crowley, and P.F. Case, secretly used Mathers' *Book T* to define and illustrate their own personal Tarot systems.

If the oracular definitions which were penned by Waite, Crowley, and Case are compared to Mathers' original, the oracular canon needed to clearly define each of the 78 cards can be reconstructed.

The following tables are an attempt to reduce each of the 78 cards to its essential oracular vocabulary. These tables are divided into the three major divisions of the Tarot Cards: (1) the 22 picture cards known as the Major Arcana, (2) the 40 pip cards known as the Minor Arcana, and (3) the 16 court personage cards known as the Court Cards.

KEY PHRASES FOR THE MAJOR ARCANA

Division of Topics

Traditional: Number and name of card from traditional European decks. Note that the number system traditionally used is Roman numerals, not Arabic numerals.

Golden Dawn: Golden Dawn title of card (and number variant), from *Book T* by Frater S.R.M.D. (S.L. MacGregor Mathers).

Waite: Arthur Edward Waite's revised title of card (and number variant) from his book, *The Pictorial Key to the Tarot*.

Crowley: Aleister Crowley's revised title of card (and number variant) from *The Book of Thoth* by The Master Therion (Aleister Crowley).

Case: Paul Foster Case's revision of the title of card (and number variant) from his book, *The Tarot*.

Golden Dawn Phrase: Golden Dawn key divinatory phrases, from *Book T*.

Waite Phrase: Arthur Edward Waite's key divinatory phrases from *The Pictorial Key to the Tarot*.

Crowley Phrase: Aleister Crowley's key divinatory phrases, from *The Book of Thoth*.

Case Phrase: Paul Foster Case's key divinatory phrases, from *The Tarot*.

Astrology: The astrological attribute for the card from the Golden Dawn teachings, based on the Hebrew Qabalistic text, the *Sepher Yetzirah* (Book of Formation). The works on the Tarot of both Crowley and Case are based on these attributes. Arthur Edward Waite openly opposed this concept in his writings, but secretly gave voice to it in an introduction to K. Stenring's translation of the *Sepher Yetzirah*. Waite, like Crowley and Case, as a member of the Golden Dawn, was under a magickal oath of obligation not to reveal these attributes. He seems to be the only one with any restraint. These Qabalistic-astrological attributes are the real skeleton for all magickal ritual and philosophy of the 20th century. They are the brainchild of S.L. MacGregor Mathers. Though hinted at, these correspondences never appeared in print until Mathers' secret manuscript *Book T*. The works of Aleister Crowley *(Liber 777* in 1909 and *The Book of Thoth* in 1944), Israel Regardie *(The Golden Dawn* in 1937), and Paul Foster Case *(The Tarot* in 1947) forged from the study and insight of S.L. MacGregor Mathers have preserved this valuable key for future generations.

Qabalah: The secret Hebrew letter, Path on Tree of Life and four colors (corresponding to the four Qabalistic worlds) according to the Golden Dawn system. The colors are given in descending order, the first corresponding to the highest world (Atziloth), the fourth corresponding to the lowest world (Assiah).

The Keys

Traditional: Key 0—The Fool (unnumbered in many traditional decks)

Golden Dawn: The Spirit of Ether (numbered zero and corresponding to the Hebrew letter Aleph)

Waite: The Fool (numbered zero, but appearing in order between Key XX and Key XXI)

Crowley: The Fool (numbered zero and bearing the Hebrew letter Aleph)

Case: The Fool (numbered zero and bearing the Hebrew letter Aleph)

Golden Dawn Phrase: Idea; folly

Waite Phrase: Folly, mania, intoxication

Crowley Phrase: Thought, spirituality; eccentricity, mania

Case Phrase: Originality; folly

Astrology: The element Air, the planet Uranus (god of the sky), Spirit as the fifth apex point of the pentagram; Air as the medium for the articulation of the creative word

Qabalah: 11th Path (connecting Kether to Chockmah); bright pale yellow, sky blue, blue emerald green, and emerald flecked with gold.

Traditional: Key I—The Juggler

Golden Dawn: The Magus of Power

Waite: The Magician

Crowley: The Magus

Case: The Magician

Golden Dawn Phrase: Skill, wisdom

Waite Phrase: Skill, will

Crowley Phrase: Adroitness, elasticity

Case Phrase: Constructive power, initiative

Astrology: Mercury (god of thought and communication)

Qabalah: Beth; 12th Path (connecting Kether to Binah); yellow, purple, gray, and indigo rayed with violet

Traditional: Key II—The High Priestess

Golden Dawn: The Priestess of the Silver Star

Waite: The High Priestess

Crowley: The Priestess

Case: The High Priestess

Golden Dawn Phrase: Change, alteration, increase and decrease

Waite Phrase: Secrets, the future as yet unveiled, silence

Crowley Phrase: Fluctuation, change

Case Phrase: Duality, secrets, unrevealed future

Astrology: The Moon (goddess of the hunt, purity and virginity)

Qabalah: Gimel; 13th Path (connecting Kether to Tiphereth); blue, silver, cold pale blue, and silver rayed with sky blue

Traditional: Key III—The Empress

Golden Dawn: Daughter of the Mighty Ones

Waite: The Empress

Crowley: The Empress

Case: The Empress

Golden Dawn Phrase: Beauty, happiness, pleasure, success

Waite Phrase: Fruitfulness, action, light, truth

Crowley Phrase: Love, luxury, delight

Case Phrase: Fruitfulness, sensuality

Astrology: Venus (goddess of love and emotion)

Qabalah: Daleth; 14th Path (connecting Chockmah to Binah); emerald green, sky blue, early spring green, and bright rose (cerise) rayed with pale green

Traditional: Key IV—The Emperor

Golden Dawn: Son of the Morning

Waite: The Emperor

Crowley: The Emperor (Crowley exchanged this key with Key XVII, The Star, in his later writings in accordance with chapter I, verse 57, of *The Book of The Law*)

Case: The Emperor

Golden Dawn Phrase: War, conquest, victory, strife, ambition

Waite Phrase: Stability, power, reason, will

Crowley Phrase: Energy, vigor, overweening confidence, rashness, stubornness

Case Phrase: Stability, power, reason, control

Astrology: Aries (attribute of sight)

Qabalah: Heh; 15th Path (connecting Chockmah to Tiphereth); scarlet, red, brilliant flame, and glowing red.

Traditional: Key V—The Hierophant

Golden Dawn: Magus of the Eternal Gods

Waite: The Hierophant

Crowley: The Hierophant

Case: The Hierophant

Golden Dawn Phrase: Divine wisdom, manifestation, explanation, teaching

Waite Phrase: Marriage, alliance, concord, inspiration

Crowley Phrase: Stubborn strength, toil, endurance; goodness of heart, help from superiors

Case Phrase: Intuition, inspiration, marriage, alliance

Astrology: Taurus (attribute of hearing)

Qabalah: Vav; 16th Path (connecting Chockmah to Chesed); red-orange, deep indigo, deep warm olive, and rich brown

Traditional: Key VI—The Lovers

Golden Dawn: Children of the Voice Divine

Waite: The Lovers

Crowley: The Lovers

Case: The Lovers

Golden Dawn Phrase: Inspiration, motive, impulse

Waite Phrase: Attraction, love, beauty, trials overcome

Crowley Phrase: Second sight, intelligence; childishness, frivolity, indecision

Case Phrase: Attraction, beauty, love

Astrology: Gemini (attribute of discrimination, as well as smell)

Qabalah: Zain; 17th Path (connecting Binah to Tiphereth); orange, pale mauve, yellow leather, reddish gray to mauve

Traditional: Key VII—The Chariot

Golden Dawn: Lord of the Triumph of Light

Waite: The Chariot

Crowley: The Chariot

Case: The Chariot

Golden Dawn Phrase: Triumph, victory, health, success

Waite Phrase: War, triumph, vengeance, providence

Crowley Phrase: Victory, hope, violence in maintaining traditional ideas, the die-hard

Case Phrase: Triumph, victory

Astrology: Cancer (attribute of speech)

Qabalah: Cheth; 18th Path (connecting Binah to Geburah); amber, maroon, rich bright russet, and dark greenish brown

Traditional: Key XI—Strength (sometimes titled Force)

Golden Dawn: Daughter of the Flaming Sword (numbered VIII, to align with the Zodiacal attribute of Leo)

Waite: Strength or Fortitude (numbered VIII, but no reason given by Waite for the swapping of Key VIII with XI).

Crowley: Lust (numbered traditionally as XI, but given the correct Golden Dawn Hebrew letter of Teth)

Case: Strength (numbered 8 as opposed to 11 and given the Hebrew letter Teth in accordance with the Golden Dawn secret order)

Golden Dawn Phrase: Fortitude, courage, power not arrested

Waite Phrase: Power, energy, action, courage

Crowley Phrase: Courage, energy, action, great passion, resort to magick (i.e., sexual magick)

Case Phrase: Action, courage, power, control of the life force

Astrology: Leo (attribute of taste)

Qabalah: Teth; 19th Path (connecting Chesed to Geburah); yellow, deep purple, gray, and reddish amber

Traditional: IX—The Hermit

Golden Dawn: Magus of the Voice of Light

Waite: The Hermit

Crowley: The Hermit

Case: The Hermit

Golden Dawn Phrase: Wisdom sought for and obtained from above

Waite Phrase: Prudence, circumspection, concealment

Crowley Phrase: Illumination and secret impulse from within; retirement from participation in current events

Case Phrase: Prudence, circumspection

Astrology: Virgo (attribute of coition)

Qabalah: Yod; 20th Path (connecting Chesed to Tiphereth); yellow-green, slate gray, green gray, and plum

Traditional: Key X—The Wheel of Fortune

Golden Dawn: Lord of the Forces of Life

Waite: Wheel of Fortune

Crowley: Fortune

Case: The Wheel of Fortune

Golden Dawn Phrase: Good fortune and happiness, intoxication with success

Waite Phrase: Destiny, fortune, success, luck

Crowley Phrase: Change of fortune

Case Phrase: Destiny, good fortune, turn for the better

Astrology: Jupiter (god of fortune, luck, beneficence)

Qabalah: Kaph; 21st Path (connecting Chesed with Netzach); violet, blue, rich purple, and bright blue rayed yellow

Traditional: Key VIII—Justice

Golden Dawn: Daughter of the Lord of Truth (numbered XI)

Waite: Justice (numbered as XI, in accordance with the Golden Dawn's secret order, but given no justification. Since Waite followed Mathers' rearrangement, most modern decks, being patterned after Waite, contain this switch)

Crowley: Adjustment (traditionally numbered as VIII, but given the secret letter of Lamed)

Case: Justice (numbered 11 and given the Hebrew letter, Lamed, in accordance with the Golden Dawn's Hebrew attritubes for the Tarot)

Golden Dawn Phrase: Eternal justice and balance; strength and force, a court of law, trial, etc.

Waite Phrase: Equity, rightness, law in all its departments

Crowley Phrase: Justice, adjustment, suspension of all action pending decision

Case Phrase: Strength and force; legal affairs

Astrology: Libra (attribute of Action or work); note that the Qabalistic-astrological symbolism of this key, Libra, suggests it should be interchanged with Key XI, Strength (Leo), according to the Qabalistic attributes outlined in the *Sepher Yetzirah*

Qabalah: Lamed; 22nd Path (connecting Geburah to Tiphereth); emerald green, blue, deep blue-green, and pale green

Traditional: Key XII—The Hanged Man

Golden Dawn: Spirit of the Mighty Waters

Waite: The Hanged Man

Crowley: The Hanged Man

Case: The Hanged Man

Golden Dawn Phrase: Enforced sacrifice, punishment, loss

Waite Phrase: Trials, sacrifice, circumspection, discernment, intuition

Crowley Phrase: Suffering, defeat, failure, death

Case Phrase: Surrender to the inevitable; losses, reverses

Astrology: The element Water (the womb of the mother as a symbol of birth), the planet Neptune (god of the sea)

Qabalah: Mem; 23rd Path (connecting Geburah to Hod); deep blue, sea-green, deep olive-green, and white flecked purple

Traditional: Key XIII—Death (in traditional decks often untitled, just as Key 0 is "unnumbered")

Golden Dawn: Child of the Great Transformers

Waite: Death

Crowley: Death

Case: Death

Golden Dawn Phrase: Time, transformation, involuntary change; sometimes, but rarely, death and destruction

Waite Phrase: End, mortality, destruction, corruption

Crowley Phrase: Change, voluntary or involuntary, sudden and unexpected apparent death and destruction, but such interpretation is illusion

Case Phrase: Contrarieties; sudden change; death

Astrology: Scorpio (attribute of walking and motion) traditionally the Zodiacal sign associated with death

Qabalah: Nun; 24th Path (connecting Tiphereth to Netzach); blue-green, dull brown, very dark brown, and livid indigo brown

Traditional: Key XIV—Temperance

Golden Dawn: Daughter of the Reconcilers

Waite: Temperance

Crowley: Art

Case: Temperance

Golden Dawn Phrase: Combination of forces, realization, action

Waite Phrase: Economy, moderation, management, accommodation

Crowley Phrase: Action based on accurate calculation, the way of escape, success after elaborate maneuvers

Case Phrase: Combination, adaption, economy, management

Astrology: Sagittarius (attribute of wrath)

Qabalah: Samekh; 25th Path (connecting Tiphereth to Yesod); blue, yellow, green, and dark vivid blue

Traditional: Key XV—The Devil

Golden Dawn: Lord of the Gates of Matter

Waite: The Devil

Crowley: The Devil

Case: The Devil

Golden Dawn Phrase: Materiality, material force, material temptation; sometimes obsession if associated with Key VI, The Lovers

Waite Phrase: Force, fatality, extraordinary efforts, violence, blindness, weakness

Crowley Phrase: Blind impulse, irresistibly strong and unscrupulous, ambition, temptation, obstinancy, endurance

Case Phrase: Bondage, materiality, necessity, force, fate

Astrology: Capricorn (attribute of mirth, laughter)

Qabalah: Ayin; 26th Path (connecting Tiphereth to Hod); blue-violet, black, blue-black, and cold dark gray nearing black

Traditional: Key XVI—The House of God (alternately titled The Tower)

Golden Dawn: Lord of the Hosts of the Mighty

Waite: The Tower

Crowley: The Tower

Case: The Tower

Golden Dawn Phrase: Ambition, fighting, war, courage; in certain combinations, destruction, danger, fall, ruin

Waite Phrase: Distress, adversity, disgrace, deception, ruin, imprisonment

Crowley Phrase: Quarrel, combat, danger, sudden death, escape from prison

Case Phrase: Conflict, unforeseen catastrophes

Astrology: Mars (god of war)

Qabalah: Peh; 27th Path (connecting Netzach to Hod); scarlet, red, Venetian red, and bright red rayed emerald

Traditional: Key XVII—The Star

Golden Dawn: Daughter of the Firmament

Waite: The Star

Crowley: The Star (in Crowley's final arrangement for the Tarot based on *The Book of the Law,* the position of this key is interchanged with that of Key IV, The Emperor)

Case: The Star

Golden Dawn Phrase: Hope, faith, unexpected help; but also dreaminess, deceived hope

Waite Phrase: Hope, bright prospects; loss, privation, abandonment

Crowley Phrase: Clearness of vision, realization of possibilities, spiritual insight; with bad aspects: error of judgment, disappointment

Case Phrase: Insight, hope, influence over others

Astrology: Aquarius (attribute of meditation and thought)

Qabalah: Tzaddi; 28th Path (connecting Netzach to Yesod); violet, sky blue, bluish mauve, and white tinged purple

Traditional: Key XVIII—The Moon

Golden Dawn: Ruler of Flux and Reflux

Waite: The Moon

Crowley: The Moon

Case: The Moon

Golden Dawn Phrase: Dissatisfaction, voluntary change; error, lying, falsity, deception

Waite Phrase: Deception, darkness, danger, hidden enemies, occult force, inconstancy

Crowley Phrase: Illusion, bewilderment, hysteria, even madness; falsehood, crisis, "the darkest hour before the dawn," the brink of important change

Case Phrase: Deception, hidden enemies

Astrology: Pisces (attribute of sleeping)

Qabalah: Qoph; 29th Path (connecting Netzach to Malkuth); red-violet, buff flecked silver white, translucent pinkish-brown, and stone (mottled gray)

Traditional: Key XIX—The Sun

Golden Dawn: Lord of the Fire of the World

Waite: The Sun

Crowley: The Sun

Case: The Sun

Golden Dawn Phrase: Glory, gain, riches; display

Waite Phrase: Material happiness, fortunate marriage, contentment

Crowley Phrase: Triumph, pleasure, frankness, truth, shamelessness

Case Phrase: Liberation; gain

Astrology: The Sun (god of pleasure and wealth)

Qabalah: Resh; 30th Path (connecting Hod to Yesod); orange, gold yellow, rich amber, and amber rayed red

Traditional: Key XX—Judgement (sometimes The Judgment)

Golden Dawn: The Spirit of the Primal Fire

Waite: Judgement, or The Last Judgement

Crowley: The Aeon

Case: Judgement

Golden Dawn Phrase: Final decision, judgement, sentence, determination of a matter

Waite Phrase: Change of position, renewal, outcome, decision, deliberation

Crowley Phrase: The taking of a definite step, final decision in respect of the past, new current in respect of the future

Case Phrase: Renewable

Astrology: The element of Fire (that which burns away all obstacles), the planet Pluto (god of the inner fire)

Qabalah: Shin; 31st Path (connecting Hod to Malkuth); glowing orange scarlet, vermillion, scarlet flecked gold, and vermillion flecked emerald and crimson

Traditional: Key XXI—The World

Golden Dawn: The Great One of the Night of Time

Waite: The World

Crowley: The Universe

Case: The World

Golden Dawn Phrase: The matter itself; synthesis, world, kingdom

Waite Phrase: Assured success, recompense; change of place; inertia, permanence

Crowley Phrase: The end of the matter; delay, opposition, obstinancy, inertia, patience, perserverance; the crystallization of the whole matter involved

Case Phrase: Synthesis, success, change of place

Astrology: Saturn (the god of restriction, night, and the underworld)

Qabalah: Tav; 32nd Path (connecting Yesod to Malkuth); blue-violet, black, blue-black, and black flecked yellow

KEY PHRASES FOR THE MINOR ARCANA

Division of Topics

Traditional: Number and name of suit

Golden Dawn: Golden Dawn title for card (the title serves as the key divinatory word)

Waite: Key divinatory word or phrase by Arthur Edward Waite

Crowley: Aleister Crowley's revision of title (the title serves as the key divinatory word)

Case: Key divinatory word or phrase by Paul Foster Case

Astrology: Astrological significance from The Golden Dawn tradition

Qabalah: The Sephiroth on the Tree of Life and corresponding Qabalistic World, as well as the Golden Dawn color scale for each Sephirah.

The Keys

Traditional: Ace of Wands

Golden Dawn: The Root of the Powers of Fire

Waite: The starting point of an enterprise

Crowley: The Root of the Powers of Fire

Case: Energy

Astrology: The element Fire

Qabalah: Kether of Atziloth; white brilliance (suit of Wands, red flashing green)

Traditional: Two of Wands

Golden Dawn: Lord of Dominion

Waite: Dominion

Crowley: Dominion

Case: Dominion

Astrology: Mars in Aries (0° to 10° Aries)

Qabalah: Chockmah of Atziloth; soft blue

Traditional: Three of Wands

Golden Dawn: Lord of Established Strength

Waite: Established Strength

Crowley: Virtue

Case: Established Strength

Astrology: Sun in Aries (10° to 20° Aries)

Qabalah: Binah of Atziloth; crimson

Traditional: Four of Wands

Golden Dawn: Lord of Perfected Work

Waite: Perfected Work

Crowley: Completion

Case: Perfected Work

Astrology: Venus in Aries (20° to 30° Aries)

Qabalah: Chesed of Atziloth; deep violet

Traditional: Five of Wands

Golden Dawn: Lord of Strife

Waite: Strenuous competition

Crowley: Strife

Case: Strife

Astrology: Saturn in Leo (0° to 10° Leo)

Qabalah: Geburah of Atziloth; orange

Traditional: Six of Wands

Golden Dawn: Lord of Victory

Waite: A victor triumphing

Crowley: Victory

Case: Victory after Strife (Five of Wands)

Astrology: Jupiter in Leo (10° to 20° Leo)

Qabalah: Tiphereth of Atziloth; clear pink rose

Traditional: Seven of Wands

Golden Dawn: Lord of Valor

Waite: Valor

Crowley: Valor

Case: Valor

Astrology: Mars in Leo (20° to 30° Leo)

Qabalah: Netzach of Atziloth; amber

Traditional: Eight of Wands

Golden Dawn: Lord of Swiftness

Waite: Swiftness

Crowley: Swiftness

Case: Activity

Astrology: Mercury in Sagittarius (0° to 10° Sagittarius)

Qabalah: Hod of Atziloth; violet purple

Traditional: Nine of Wands

Golden Dawn: Lord of Great Strength

Waite: Strength in opposition

Crowley: Strength

Case: Preparedness

Astrology: Moon in Sagittarius (10° to 20° Sagittarius)

Qabalah: Yesod of Atziloth; indigo

Traditional: Ten of Wands

Golden Dawn: Lord of Oppression

Waite: Oppression

Crowley: Oppression

Case: Oppression

Astrology: Saturn in Sagittarius (20° to 30° Sagittarius)

Qabalah: Malkuth of Atziloth; yellow

Traditional: Ace of Cups

Golden Dawn: Root of the Powers of Water

Waite: House of the True Heart

Crowley: Root of the Powers of Water

Case: Fertility

Astrology: The element Water

Qabalah: Kether of Briah; white brilliance (suit of Cups, blue flashing orange)

Traditional: Two of Cups

Golden Dawn: Lord of Love

Waite: Love

Crowley: Love

Case: Reciprocity

Astrology: Venus in Cancer (0° to 10° Cancer)

Qabalah: Chockmah of Briah; gray

Traditional: Three of Cups

Golden Dawn: Lord of Abundance

Waite: Pleasure of the Senses

Crowley: Abundance

Case: Pleasure

Astrology: Mercury in Cancer (10° to 20° Cancer)

Qabalah: Binah of Briah; black

Traditional: Four of Cups

Golden Dawn: Lord of Blended Pleasure

Waite: Blended Pleasures

Crowley: Luxury

Case: Contemplation

Astrology: Moon in Cancer (20° to 30° Cancer)

Qabalah: Chesed of Briah; blue

Traditional: Five of Cups

Golden Dawn: Lord of Loss in Pleasure

Waite: Loss, but something remains over

Crowley: Disappointment

Case: Loss in Pleasure

Astrology: Mars in Scorpio (0° to 10° Scorpio)

Qabalah: Geburah of Briah; scarlet red

Traditional: Six of Cups

Golden Dawn: Lord of Pleasure

Waite: Happiness

Crowley: Pleasure

Case: Beginning of Steady Gain

Astrology: Sun in Scorpio (10° to 20° Scorpio)

Qabalah: Tiphereth of Briah; yellow

Traditional: Seven of Cups

Golden Dawn: Lord of Illusionary Success

Waite: Desire

Crowley: Debauch

Case: Illusionary Success

Astrology: Venus in Scorpio (10° to 20° Scorpio)

Qabalah: Netzach of Briah; emerald

Traditional: Eight of Cups

Golden Dawn: Lord of Abandoned Success

Waite: Deserting an undertaking

Crowley: Indolence

Case: Abandoned Success

Astrology: Saturn in Pisces (0° to 10° Pisces)

Qabalah: Hod of Briah; orange

Traditional: Nine of Cups

Golden Dawn: Lord of Material Happiness

Waite: Success

Crowley: Happiness

Case: Material Success

Astrology: Jupiter in Pisces (10° to 20° Pisces)

Qabalah: Yesod of Briah; violet

Traditional: Ten of Cups

Golden Dawn: Lord of Perfected Success

Waite: Contentment

Crowley: Satiety

Case: Lasting Success

Astrology: Mars in Pisces (20° to 30° Pisces)

Qabalah: Malkuth of Briah; russet, olive, citrine, and black

Traditional: Ace of Swords

Golden Dawn: Root of the Powers of Air

Waite: Triumph of Force

Crowley: Primordial Energy of Air

Case: Invoked Force

Astrology: The element Air

Qabalah: Kether of Yetzirah; white brilliance (suit of Swords, yellow flashing violet)

Traditional: Two of Swords

Golden Dawn: Lord of Peace Restored

Waite: Equipoise

Crowley: Peace

Case: Balanced Force

Astrology: Moon in Libra (0° to 10° Libra)

Qabalah: Chockmah of Yetzirah; gray

Traditional: Three of Swords

Golden Dawn: Lord of Sorrow

Waite: Mental alienation

Crowley: Sorrow

Case: Sorrow

Astrology: Saturn in Libra (10° to 20° Libra)

Qabalah: Binah of Yetzirah; dark brown

Traditional: Four of Swords

Golden Dawn: Lord of Rest from Strife

Waite: Retreat

Crowley: Truce

Case: Rest from Strife

Astrology: Jupiter in Libra (20° to 30° Libra)

Qabalah: Chesed of Yetzirah; deep purple

Traditional: Five of Swords

Golden Dawn: Lord of Defeat

Waite: Loss

Crowley: Defeat

Case: Defeat

Astrology: Venus in Aquarius (0° to 10° Aquarius)

Qabalah: Geburah of Yetzirah; bright scarlet

Traditional: Six of Swords

Golden Dawn: Lord of Earned Success

Waite: Expedient

Crowley: Science

Case: Success after anxiety

Astrology: Mercury in Aquarius (10° to 20° Aquarius)

Qabalah: Tiphereth of Yetzirah; rich salmon

Traditional: Seven of Swords

Golden Dawn: Lord of Unstable Effort

Waite: A plan that may fail

Crowley: Futility

Case: Unstable effort

Astrology: Moon in Aquarius (20° to 30° Aquarius)

Qabalah: Netzach of Yetzirah; bright yellow green

Traditional: Eight of Swords

Golden Dawn: Lord of Shortened Force

Waite: Opposition

Crowley: Interference

Case: Indecision

Astrology: Jupiter in Gemini (0° to 10° Gemini)

Qabalah: Hod of Yetzirah; red russet

Traditional: Nine of Swords

Golden Dawn: Lord of Despair and Cruelty

Waite: Despair

Crowley: Cruelty

Case: Worry

Astrology: Mars in Gemini (10° to 20° Gemini)

Qabalah: Yesod of Yetzirah; very dark purple

Traditional: Ten of Swords

Golden Dawn: Lord of Ruin

Waite: Desolation

Crowley: Ruin

Case: Ruin

Astrology: Sun in Gemini (20° to 30° Gemini)

Qabalah: Malkuth of Yetzirah; russet, olive, citrine, and black (all flecked gold)

Traditional: Ace of Pentacles

Golden Dawn: Root of the Powers of Earth

Waite: Perfect Contentment

Crowley: Root of the Powers of Earth (note: in Crowley's Tarot deck the Pentacle suit is designated as Disks, corresponding to the flat dish upon which the sacrament is laid: a form of the graal)

Case: Material Gain

Astrology: The element Earth

Qabalah: Kether of Assiah; white flecked with gold (suit of Pentacles, russet, olive, citrine, and black all flashing white)

Traditional: Two of Pentacles

Golden Dawn: Lord of Harmonious Change

Waite: Messages in writing

Crowley: Change

Case: Harmony in midst of change

Astrology: Jupiter in Capricorn (0° to 10° Capricorn)

Qabalah: Chockmah in Assiah; white flecked red, yellow, and blue

Traditional: Three of Pentacles

Golden Dawn: Lord of Material World

Waite: Skilled labor

Crowley: Work

Case: Construction

Astrology: Mars in Capricorn (10° to 20° Capricorn)

Qabalah: Binah of Assiah; gray flecked pink

Traditional: Four of Pentacles

Golden Dawn: Lord of Earthly Power

Waite: The surety of possessions

Crowley: Earthly Power

Case: Power

Astrology: Sun in Capricorn (20° to 30° Capricorn)

Qabalah: Chesed of Assiah; deep azure flecked yellow

Traditional: Five of Pentacles

Golden Dawn: Lord of Material Trouble

Waite: Destitution

Crowley: Worry

Case: Concordance

Astrology: Mercury in Taurus (0° to 10° Taurus)

Qabalah: Geburah of Assiah; red flecked black

Traditional: Six of Pentacles

Golden Dawn: Lord of Material Success

Waite: Success in life

Crowley: Success

Case: Material Prosperity

Astrology: Moon in Taurus (10° to 20° Taurus)

Qabalah: Tiphereth of Assiah; gold amber

Traditional: Seven of Pentacles

Golden Dawn: Lord of Success Unfulfilled

Waite: Cause for anxiety regarding money

Crowley: Failure

Case: Success Unfulfilled

Astrology: Saturn in Taurus (20° to 30° Taurus)

Qabalah: Netzach of Assiah; olive flecked gold

Traditional: Eight of Pentacles

Golden Dawn: Lord of Prudence

Waite: Skill in crafted business

Crowley: Prudence

Case: Skill in material affairs

Astrology: Sun in Virgo (0° to 10° Virgo)

Qabalah: Hod of Assiah; yellowish-brown flecked white

Traditional: Nine of Pentacles

Golden Dawn: Lord of Material Gain

Waite: Plenty in all things

Crowley: Gain

Case: Prudence

Astrology: Venus in Virgo (10° to 20° Virgo)

Qabalah: Yesod of Assiah; citrine flecked azure

Traditional: Ten of Pentacles

Golden Dawn: Lord of Wealth

Waite: Gain

Crowley: Wealth

Case: Wealth

Astrology: Mercury in Virgo (20° to 30° Virgo)

Qabalah: Malkuth of Assiah; black rayed yellow

Key Phrases for the Court Cards

Division of Topics

The Golden Dawn allocations for the Court Cards are the most misunderstood symbolic allocations. They have been distorted in almost all recent books dealing with the esoteric Tarot. To correct the errors which have crept into Golden Dawn Tarot symbolism, the true allocations and their justifications are shown in depth in this section.

Traditional: Name of Court Card from traditional European decks. Note that the Court Cards were originally called "Coate Cards," since the figures were portrayed in flowing gowns and robes.

Golden Dawn: Golden Dawn title of card from *Book T*. Mathers revised the titles of the Court Cards from Knight, Queen, King, and Page to King, Queen, Prince, and Princess (where Knight [old] = King [revised] and King [old] = Prince [revised].

Waite: Arthur Edward Waite's revised title of card from *The Pictorial Key to The Tarot*

Crowley: Aleister Crowley's revised title of card from *The Book of Thoth*

Case: Paul Foster Case's revision of the title of card from his book *The Tarot*

Golden Dawn Phrase: Golden Dawn key divinatory phrases from *Book T*

Waite Phrase: Arthur Edward Waite's key divinatory phrases from *The Pictorial Key to the Tarot*

Crowley Phrase: Aleister Crowley's key divinatory phrases from *The Book of Thoth*

Case Phrase: Paul Foster Case's key divinatory phrases from *The Tarot*

Astrology: The astrological attributes of the 16 Court Cards according to the Golden Dawn symbolism of *Book T*. Two basic astrological attributes are given: the allocation of the 12 Zodiacal signs and the four elements, and the counterchange of four elements into 16 combinations.

Twelve of the Court Cards are astrological cusp personalities. Each of these 12 Court Cards represents the last 10 degrees (or third decan) of a preceeding Zodiac sign and the first 20 degrees (or first and second decans) of the succeeding sign. For divinatory purposes, the predominant force of the dual signs can be allocated to each key. Thus the Knight of Wands, which is 20° to 30° Scorpio and 0° to 20° Sagittarius, is predominantly Sagittarius.

This group of 16 Court Cards is the traditional series of cards to draw from to represent the querent (the person whose fortune is being read) in a Tarot divination. Two methods can be employed: either the Court Card which depicts the general physical characteristics of the querent is selected, or the card corresponding to the Sun sign of the querent is selected. When using the latter method, the birth sign of the querent should be calculated to the nearest degree (or decan). The following table approximates the division of the year by the 12 Zodiacal Court Cards. It can be used in lieu of accurate calculation of the birth sign.

The Court Cards and the Division of the Year

Zodiacal Court Card	Zodiacal Rulership	Approximate Period of the Year	Predominant Sun Sign
Knight of Wands	20° Scorpio to 20° Sagittarius	Nov 13–Dec 11	Sagittarius
Queen of Pentacles	20° Sagittarius to 20° Capricorn	Dec 12–Jan 10	Capricorn
King of Swords	20° Capricorn to 20° Aquarius	Jan 11–Feb 8	Aquarius
Knight of Cups	20° to Aquarius to 20° Pisces	Feb 9–Mar 10	Pisces
Queen of Wands	20° Pisces to 20° Aries	Mar 11–Apr 9	Aries
King of Pentacles	20° Aries to 20° Taurus	Apr 10–May 10	Taurus
Knight of Swords	20° Taurus to 20° Gemini	May 11–Jun 10	Gemini
Queen of Cups	20° Gemini to 20° Cancer	Jun 11–Jul 12	Cancer
King of Wands	20° Cancer to 20° Leo	Jul 13–Aug 12	Leo
Knight of Pentacles	20° Leo to 20° Virgo	Aug 13–Sep 12	Virgo
Queen of Swords	20° Virgo to 20° Libra	Sep 13–Oct 13	Libra
King of Cups	20° Libra to 20° Scorpio	Oct 14–Nov 12	Scorpio

The second astrological allocation is that of the 16 combinations of the four elements, corresponding to the 16 Qabalistic combinations of the four-lettered name of God (IHVH). The divinatory meanings derived from these 16 combinations are 16 basic elemental personalities, based on the combination of two basic human characteristics. The following table delineates these elemental personalities.

The Court Cards and the Elemental Personalities

Court Cards	Elemental Counterchange	Divinatory Personality	Divine Name (IHVHf) Combination
Knight of Wands	Fire of Fire	Will reinforcing will	II
Queen of Wands	Water of Fire	Emotion modifying will	IH
King of Wands	Air of Fire	Intellect modifying will	IV
Page of Wands	Earth of Fire	Senses modifying will	IHf
Knight of Cups	Fire of Water	Will modifying emotion	HI
Queen of Cups	Water of Water	Emotion reinforcing emotion	HH
King of Cups	Air of Water	Intellect modifying emotion	HV
Page of Cups	Earth of Water	Senses modifying emotion	HHf
Knight of Swords	Fire of Air	Will modifying intellect	VI
Queen of Swords	Water of Air	Emotion modifying intellect	VH
King of Swords	Air of Air	Intellect reinforcing intellect	VV
Page of Swords	Earth of Air	Senses modifying intellect	VHf
Knight of Pentacles	Fire of Earth	Will modifying senses	HfI
Queen of Pentacles	Water of Earth	Emotion modifying senses	HfH
King of Pentacles	Air of Earth	Intellect modifying senses	HfV
Page of Pentacles	Earth of Earth	Senses reinforcing senses	HfHf

Qabalah: Qabalistic position in the Royal Family for each Court Card and the corresponding card (or throne) among the four suits of the Minor Arcana, the 16 secret invisible Paths of the Tree of Life, and corresponding colors from the Minor Arcana (Tree of Life) and Major Arcana (astrological rainbow).

The association of the family unit to the Court Card division of Knight, Queen, King, and Page is based upon the Qabalistic symbolism of the highest name of God known as the Tetragrammaton (the four-lettered name of God, in Hebrew: IHVH or YHWH [Jehovah or Yahweh—יהוה]). The family unit of Father, Mother, Son, and Daughter corresponds to the four letters of the sacred name Jehovah. These in turn correspond to the four Court Card personages of Knight, Queen, King, and Page. To further this symbolism, each of the four sacred letters corresponds to both the elemental cycle of Fire, Water, Air, and Earth (which are symbolized by the four Minor Arcana suits of Wands, Cups, Swords, and Pentacles) and four select stations on the Tree of Life: the second, third, sixth, and tenth Sephirah (symbolized by the pip cards of 2, 3, 6, and 10 of each suit in the Minor Arcana). Qabalistic tradition concerning the Tree of Life assigns the father to the second station (or Sephirah), the mother to the third, the son to the sixth, and the daughter to the tenth. By this symbolism each Knight is associated with the 2 of its corresponding suit, the Queen to the 3, the King to the 6, and the Page to the 10. This subtlety of symbolism is again the genius of Mathers and seems to have eluded both Waite and Case, although Crowley, in revising the titles of the Court Cards, obeyed this secret symbolism of the Court Cards and the four-lettered name of God. The following table clarifies this symbolism.

The Court Cards and the Four-Lettered Name of God

Court Card	Family Unit	Element	Station on Tree of Life of Pip Card	Minor Arcana Suit	Letter of Tetragrammaton
Knight	Father	Fire	2	Wand	I (Y)
Queen	Mother	Water	3	Cup	H
King	Son	Air	6	Sword	V (W)
Page	Daughter	Earth	10	Pentacle	H

By these Qabalistic allocations it is apparent that the Knight, rather than the King (as assumed by both Waite and Case), is the Father. Further, the Queen is the Mother of the King, which has its symbolic parallel in the Major Arcana relationship of the Empress and the Emperor, that of Mother and Son (epitomized in Mary and Jesus as well as the Greek myth of Jocasta and Oedipus).

There is a Chinese parallel to this fourfold family symbolism found in the eightfold family hierarchy of the eight trigrams. The table on the following page correlates the Tarot Court Cards and the Family of the Trigrams.

Tetragrammaton and Trigram

Tetragrammaton	Court Card	Trigram Family
Father	Knight	Father
Son	King	Youngest Son Middle Son Eldest Son
Daughter	Page	Youngest Daughter Middle Daughter Eldest Daughter
Mother	Queen	Mother

The Keys

Traditional: Knight of Wands

Golden Dawn: Lord of the Flame and the Lightning; King of the Spirits of Fire; King of the Salamanders

Waite: Knight of Wands

Crowley: Knight of Wands—In his revision of Mathers' order for the Court Cards of King, Queen, Prince, and Princess, Crowley kept the old titles of Knight and Queen while adopting Mathers' Prince and Princess for the traditional King and Page.

Undoubtedly this revision was intended to guard against the mistaken identity of the Knight with the King in the traditional design for the Court Cards. This mistake has been made in the research of both Arthur Edward Waite and Paul Foster Case, as well as countless other commentators on Tarot symbolism. The correct Golden Dawn allocations again are as follows:

the old Knight = the new King

the old King = the new Prince

A table of correspondences between Mathers', Crowley's, and the traditional systems will help clarify this allocation (see opposite page).

Case: Knight of Wands

Golden Dawn Phrase: Active, fierce, sudden and impetuous; ill-dignified: cruel

Waite Phrase: A dark young man; journey; discord

Crowley Phrase: Fierceness, impulsiveness, revolutionary

Case Phrase: Dark, friendly young man; departure, change of residence

Astrology: 20° Scorpio to 20° Sagittarius, the Seven of Cups, Eight of Wands, and Nine of Wands in the Minor Arcana; predominantly Sagittarius; the elemental counterchange of Fire of Fire

Qabalah: Father, whose throne is Two of Wands, representing Dominion and Control; 33rd (and first invisible) Path (connecting Chockmah to Geburah); soft blue and deep blue

Allocations of the Court Cards

Traditional (Waite and Case)	Mathers	Crowley	Qabalistic Family via IHVH
Knight	King	Knight	Father
Queen	Queen	Queen	Mother
King	Prince	Prince	Son
Page (Knave)	Princess	Princess	Daughter

Traditional: Queen of Wands

Golden Dawn: Queen of the Thrones of Flames; Queen of the Salamanders

Waite: Queen of Wands

Crowley: Queen of Wands

Case: Queen of Wands

Golden Dawn Phrase: Adaptability, steady rule; great attractive power; ill-dignified: tyrannical

Waite Phrase: Magnetic personality, love of money or success, a dark young woman

Crowley Phrase: Persistent energy, calm authority, easily deceived

Case Phrase: Dark woman, magnetic, friendly; business success

Astrology: 20° Pisces to 20° Aries, the Ten of Cups, Two of Wands, and Three of Wands in the Minor Arcana; predominately Aries; the elemental counterchange of Water of Fire

Qabalah: Mother, whose throne is Three of Wands, representing Established Strength and Virtue; 34th Path (connecting Chockmah to Hod); crimson and red

Traditional: King of Wands

Golden Dawn: Prince of the Chariot of Fire; Prince and Emperor of Salamanders

Waite: King of Wands

Crowley: Prince of Wands

Case: King of Wands

Golden Dawn Phrase: Swift, strong, hasty, rather violent yet just, generous, and noble; ill-dignified: intolerant

Waite Phrase: Noble, ardent, animated, impassioned, honest; good but severe

Crowley Phrase: Intensely noble and generous; courage is fanatically strong, and endurance indefatigable; often violent, especially in the expression of opinion; always fighting against odds, and always winning in the long run

Case Phrase: Dark man, friendly, ardent, honest; possible inheritance

Astrology: 20° Cancer to 20° Leo; the Four of Cups, Five of Wands, and Six of Wands in the Minor Arcana; predominately Leo; the elemental counterchange of Air of Fire

Qabalah: Son, whose throne is Six of Wands, representing Victory and Success; 35th Path (connecting Chockmah to Yesod); pink rose and yellow

Traditional: Page (Knave) of Wands

Golden Dawn: Princess of the Shining Flame; Rose of the Palace of Fire; Princess and Empress of the Salamanders

Waite: Page of Wands

Crowley: Princess of Wands

Case: Page of Wands

Golden Dawn Phrase: Brilliance, courage, beauty, force, sudden in anger or love, desire or power; ill-dignified: unstable,

Waite Phrase: Envoy, faithful, a lover; indecision

Crowley Phrase: Extremely individual; brilliant and daring; sudden, violent and implacable in anger or love; ambitious and aspiring; ill-dignified: shallow and false

Case Phrase: Dark young man (may be young girl); messenger; brilliance, courage

Astrology: The element of Fire, the Ace of Wands in the Minor Arcana and Judgment in the Major Arcana; the elemental combination of Earth of Fire. Note that the four Pages represent the elemental personality devoid of Zodiacal influence; they are four basic temperaments each corresponding to one of the four elements. Thus the Page of Wands is the elemental nature of a fiery personality.

Qabalah: Daughter, whose throne is Ten of Wands, representing Oppression; 36th Path (connecting Chockmah to Malkuth); yellow and red (russet)

Traditional: Knight of Cups

Golden Dawn: Lord of the Waves and the Waters, King of the Hosts of the Sea; King of Undines and Nymphs

Waite: Knight of Cups

Crowley: Knight of Cups

Case: Knight of Cups

Golden Dawn Phrase: Graceful, Venusian, indolent but enthusiastic if roused; ill-dignified: sensual,

Waite Phrase: The higher graces of imagination, arrival, approach, advances, proposition

Crowley Phrase: Graceful, dilettante; amiable in a passive way; exceedingly sensitive to external influence, but with no material depth; ill-dignified the card represents abuse of stimulants and narcotics

Case Phrase: Fair man, Venusian, indolent; arrival, approach

Astrology: 20° Aquarius to 20° Pisces, the Seven of Swords, Eight of Cups, and Nine of Cups in the Minor Arcana; predominately Pisces; the elemental counterchange of Fire of Water

Qabalah: Father, whose throne is Two of Cups, representing Love; 37th Path (connecting Binah to Chesed); gray and red-violet

Traditional: Queen of Cups

Golden Dawn: Queen of the Thrones of the Waters; Queen of Nymphs and Undines

Waite: Queen of Cups

Crowley: Queen of Cups

Case: Queen of Cups

Golden Dawn Phrase: Imaginative; poetic, coquettish, good-natured, underneath a dreamy appearance; ill-dignified: very much affected by other influences

Waite Phrase: The gift of vision; loving intelligence; beautiful, fair, dreamy, happiness, pleasure

Crowley Phrase: Dreaminess, patient, tranquility; the perfect agent, able to receive and transmit everything without herself being affected thereby

Case Phrase: Fair woman; imaginative, poetic; gift of vision

Astrology: 20° Gemini to 20° Cancer, the Ten of Swords, Two of Cups, and Three of Cups in the Minor Arcana; predominately Cancer; the elemental counterchange of Water of Water

Qabalah: Mother, whose throne is Three of Cups, representing Abundance; 38th Path (connecting Binah to Netzach); black and yellow-orange

Traditional: King of Cups

Golden Dawn: Prince of the Chariot of the Waters; Prince and Emperor of Nymphs and Undines

Waite: King of Cups

Crowley: Prince of Cups

Case: King of Cups

Golden Dawn Phrase: Subtle, violent, a fierce nature with calm exterior; powerful for good or evil, but more attracted to evil, if allied with apparent power or wisdom; ill-dignified: merciless

Waite Phrase: Creative intelligence, man of business, law or divinity; science, law, art

Crowley Phrase: Subtlety, secret violence; intensely secret and artistic in all his ways; ruthless

Case Phrase: Fair man; calm exterior; subtle, violent

Astrology: 20° Libra to 20° Scorpio, the Four of Swords, Five of Cups and Six of Cups in the Minor Arcana; predominately Scorpio; the elemental counterchange of Air of Water

Qabalah: Son, whose throne is Six of Cups, representing Pleasure; 39th Path (connecting Binah to Yesod); yellow (gold) and blue-green

Traditional: Page (Knave) of Cups

Golden Dawn: Princess of the Waters; Lotus of the Palace of the Floods; Princess and Empress of the Nymphs and Undines

Waite: Page of Cups

Crowley: Princess of Cups

Case: Page of Cups

Golden Dawn Phrase: Sweetness, poetry, gentleness, kindness; imagination, dreamy; ill-dignified: luxurious

Waite Phrase: The mind taking form, reflection, meditation; studious youth, news, message

Crowley Phrase: Infinitely gracious; all sweetness and voluptuousness; to live in the world of romance, in the perpetual dream of rapture

Case Phrase: Fair, studious youth; reflection; news

Astrology: The element of Water, the Ace of Cups in the Minor Arcana and The Hanged Man in the Major Arcana; the elemental counterchange of Earth of Water

Qabalah: Daughter, whose throne is Ten of Cups, representing Perfected Success and Satiety; 40th Path (connecting Binah to Malkuth); russet, citrine, olive, black, and deep blue (olive)

Traditional: Knight of Swords

Golden Dawn: Lord of the Winds and the Breezes, King of the Spirits of Air; King of the Sylphs and Sylphides

Waite: Knight of Swords

Crowley: Knight of Swords

Case: Knight of Swords

Golden Dawn Phrase: Active, clever, delicate, skillful; courageous but inclined to domineer, also to overvalue small things, unless well-dignified; ill-dignified: deceitful

Waite Phrase: Skill, bravery; defense, war, wrath, destruction, ruin

Crowley Phrase: The idea of attack, activity, skill, cleverness; ill-dignified: incapable of decision

Case Phrase: Active, clever, domineering young man; enmity, wrath, war

Astrology: 20° Taurus to 20° Gemini, the Seven of Pentacles, Eight of Swords, and Nine of Swords in the Minor Arcana; predominately Gemini; the elemental counterchange of Fire of Water

Qabalah: Father, whose throne is Two of Swords, representing Peace Restored; 41st Path (connecting Kether to Chesed); bluish mother of pearl and orange

Traditional: Queen of Swords

Golden Dawn: Queen of the Thrones of Air; Queen of the Sylphs and Sylphides

Waite: Queen of Swords

Crowley: Queen of Swords

Case: Queen of Swords

Golden Dawn Phrase: Intensely perceptive, keen observation, quick, confident, often perseveringly accurate in superficial things, graceful, fond of dancing and balance; ill-dignified: unreliable

Waite Phrase: Familiarity with sorrow, widowhood, female sadness and embarrassment, mourning, privation

Crowley Phrase: Intense individualist, swift and accurate at recording ideas; in action confident, in spirit gracious and just; ill-dignified, these qualities will be turned to unworthy purposes

Case Phrase: Widowhood; mourning. A keen, quick, intensely perceptive, subtle woman, usually fond of dancing

Astrology: 20° Virgo to 20° Libra, the Ten of Pentacles, Two of Swords, and Three of Swords in the Minor Arcana; predominately Libra; the elemental counterchange of Water of Air

Qabalah: Mother, whose throne is Three of Swords, representing Sorrow; 42nd Path (connecting Kether to Geburah); dark brown and green

Traditional: King of Swords

Golden Dawn: Prince of the Chariot of the Winds; Prince and Emperor of Sylphs and Sylphides

Waite: King of Swords

Crowley: Prince of Swords

Case: King of Swords

Golden Dawn Phrase: Full of ideas and thoughts and designs, distrustful, suspicious, firm in friendship and enmity; overcautious; ill-dignified: harsh

Waite Phrase: To sit in judgment, power, command, authority

Crowley Phrase: A person (who) is purely intellectual, a mass of fine ideals unrelated to practical effort; faddists

Case Phrase: Distrustful, suspicious man; full of ideas, thoughts and designs, care, observation, extreme caution

Astrology: 20° Capricorn to 20° Aquarius, the Four of Pentacles, Five of Swords, and Six of Swords in the Minor Arcana; predominately Aquarius; the elemental counterchange of Air of Air

Qabalah: Son, whose throne is Six of Swords, representing Science; 43rd Path (connecting Kether to Netzach); rich salmon and violet

Traditional: Page (Knave) of Swords

Golden Dawn: Princess of the Rushing Winds, Lotus of the Palace of Air; Princess and Empress of the Sylphs and Sylphides

Waite: Page of Swords

Crowley: Princess of Swords

Case: Page of Swords

Golden Dawn Phrase: Wisdom, strength, acuteness, grace and dexterity; ill-dignified: cunning

Waite Phrase: To be alert and lithe, vigilance, examination, spying, over-seeing, what is unforeseen

Crowley Phrase: Stern and revengeful; cleverness and dexterity in the management of practical affairs, especially where they are of a controversial nature; ill-dignified: constant anxiety

Case Phrase: Vigilant, acute, subtle, active youth

Astrology: The element of Air, the Ace of Swords in the Minor Arcana and The Fool in the Major Arcana; the elemental counterchange of Earth of Air

Qabalah: Daughter, whose throne is Ten of Swords, representing Ruin; 44th Path (connecting Kether to Hod); russet, olive, citrine, and black (all flecked gold) and yellow (citrine)

Traditional: Knight of Pentacles

Golden Dawn: Lord of the Wide and Fertile Land; King of the Spirits of Earth; King of Gnomes

Waite: Knight of Pentacles

Crowley: Knight of Disks

Case: Knight of Pentacles

Golden Dawn Phrase: Unless very well-dignified, heavy, dull, and material; laborious, clever and patient in material matters; if ill-dignified: avaricious

Waite Phrase: Slow, enduring, heavy; utility, service, ableness, interest, responsibility

Crowley Phrase: Dull, heavy, and preoccupied with material things; Success due to instinct, to imitation of nature; ill-dignified: slavish

Case Phrase: Laborious, patient, dull young man

Astrology: 20° Leo to 20° Virgo, the Seven of Wands, Eight of Pentacles, and Nine of Pentacles in the Minor Arcana; predominately Virgo; the elemental counterchage of Fire of Earth

Qabalah: Father, whose throne is Two of Pentacles, representing Change; 45th Path (connecting Chesed to Yesod); white (flecked red, blue and yellow) and yellow-green

Traditional: Queen of Pentacles

Golden Dawn: Queen of the Thrones of Earth; Queen of Gnomes

Waite: Queen of Pentacles

Crowley: Queen of Disks

Case: Queen of Pentacles

Golden Dawn Phrase: Impetuous, kind, timid, rather charming, great-hearted, intelligent, melancholy, truthful yet of many moods; ill-dignified: changeable

Waite Phrase: Greatness of soul, serious case of intelligence, opulence, generosity, liberty

Crowley Phrase: The finest of quieter qualities, ambitious, but only in useful directions; immense funds of affection, kindness, and greatness of heart; quiet, hard-working, practical, sensible, domesticated, often (in a reticent and unassuming fashion) lustful and even debauched; inclined to the abuse of alcohol and drugs; ill-dignified: servile

Case Phrase: Generous, intelligent, charming, moody married woman

Astrology: 20° Sagittarius to 20° Capricorn, the Ten of Wands, Two of Pentacles, and Three of Pentacles in the Minor Arcana; predominately Capricorn; the elemental counterchange of Water of Earth

Qabalah: Mother, whose throne is Three of Pentacles, representing Material Work as well as Creative Work; 46th Path (connecting Chesed to Malkuth); gray (flecked pink) and blue-violet

Traditional: King of Pentacles

Golden Dawn: Prince of the Chariot of Earth; Prince and Emperor of Gnomes

Waite: King of Pentacles

Crowley: Prince of Disks

Case: King of Pentacles

Golden Dawn Phrase: Increase of matter, increase of good and evil, practically applies things, steady, reliable; ill-dignified: animal, material, stupid; slow to anger, but furious if roused

Waite Phrase: Valor, realizing intelligence, success; business, intellectual and mathematical aptitudes

Crowley Phrase: Great energy brought to bear upon the most solid of practical matters; persevering, competent, ingenious, imperturbable; lacking almost entirely in emotion, somewhat insensitive; slow to anger, but if driven becomes implacable

Case Phrase: Friendly, steady, reliable married man

Astrology: 20° Aries to 20° Taurus, the Four of Wands, Five of Pentacles, and Six of Pentacles in the Minor Arcana; predominately Taurus; elemental counterchange of Air of Earth

Qabalah: Son, whose throne is Six of Pentacles, representing Material Success; 47th Path (connecting Geburah to Yesod); gold amber and red-orange

Traditional: Page (Knave) of Pentacles

Golden Dawn: Princess of the Echoing Hills, Rose of the Palace of Earth; Princess and Empress of the Gnomes

Waite: Page of Pentacles

Crowley: Princess of Disks

Case: Page of Pentacles

Golden Dawn Phrase: Generous, kind, diligent, benevolent, careful, courageous, perserving, pitiful; ill-dignified: wasteful

Waite Phrase: Application, study, scholarship, reflection; rule, management

Crowley Phrase: All the characteristics of woman, depending entirely upon the influences to which she is subject, but in every case her attributes will be pure in themselves. In one sense her general reputation will be bewildering inconsistency; being on the brink of transfiguration

Case Phrase: Diligent, careful, deliberate youth

Astrology: The element of Earth, the Ace of Pentacles in the Minor Arcana, and The World in the Major Arcana; the elemental counterchange of Earth of Earth; the last of the 16 elemental counterchanges. Note that the four Pages designate four basic types of women defined as elemental personalities, which have their archetypes in the Major Arcana:

Page of Wands: Fiery, active, woman as leader, martial artist, warrior, dancer (Strength in the Major Arcana)

Page of Cups: Watery, receptive, woman as romanticist, lover, occultist, poetess, artist (The High Priestess in the Major Arcana)

Page of Swords: Airy, active woman as idealist, intellectual, philosopher, teacher, scientist (Justice in the Major Arcana)

Page of Pentacles: Earthy, receptive woman as mother, nurturing a family (The Empress in the Major Arcana)

Qabalah: Daughter, whose throne is Ten of Pentacles, representing Wealth; 48th (and last invisible) Path; black rayed yellow and blue-violet. In one sense this is the secret end or last card of the Tarot deck. If the Major Arcana of 0 through XXI is counted as the beginning of the deck, and the Minor Arcana as the end of the deck, then Page of Pentacles would be the 78th card, just as The Fool (Key 0) would be the first card.

THE LAYING OF THE CARDS

The simplest, most direct method of the laying of Tarot cards (which is not Golden Dawn proper but a derivative from the Golden Dawn tradition) is the oracular pattern known as the "Celtic Cross."

This spread is shown on page 305 of A.E. Waite's *Pictorial Key to the Tarot*. The order of this layout is altered slightly below by exchanging the fifth (what is behind) with the sixth (what is before) position. By this exchange, four pillars are created in sequential order of time. Position 5 is the near past; positions 1, 2, 3, and 4 the present; position 6 the near future; and 7, 8, 9, and 10 the future. The layout is as follows.

The Celtic Cross

Near Past	Present	Near Future	Future

Note that positions 5 and 10 are the two extremes of the reading in terms of time; position 5 being the farthest past and position 10 the farthest future. Underneath position 1 is placed a Court Card representing the querent. This card is referred to as the significator and is usually chosen on the basis of the Zodiacal sign of the querent.

The following procedure is used to generate the Celtic Cross:

1. Before shuffling the 78-card deck, choose one card to represent either the querent's personality or the essence of the question being asked.

2. Shuffle the cards (77).

3. Divide into three stacks, and restore into one pile by choosing the middle stack first.

4. Deal out ten cards in the order described in the above ten-card pattern.

5. Read the oracular meanings in sequential order, beginning with the card in position 1 and ending with the card in position 10.

Each of the ten cards of the Celtic Cross is modeled after a station of the Tree of Life. Waite gives a specific title describing the oracular nature for each of these 10 positions. The following table delineates the meanings for this ten-card spread.

Waite's Celtic Cross Tarot Spread

Card Number	Position	Waite Definition	Oracular Meaning	Time	Astrology First Cause	Tree of Life Station
1	Center	What covers him	Present situation, or personality	Present		Kether
2	Center	What crosses him	Obstacles, conflicts	Present	Zodiac	Chockmah
3	Above	What crowns him	Ideals, hopes, and achievements	From Present to Future	Saturn	Binah
4	Below	What is beneath him	That which is hidden from the present; or that which is passing out of influence	From Past to Present	Jupiter	Chesed
5	Left	What is behind him	That which has already transpired	Past	Mars	Geburah
6	Right	What is before him	That which is about to occur	Near Future	Sun	Tiphereth
7	Bottom far right	Himself	Inner future, the future personality or situation	Future	Venus	Netzach
8	Second from Below, far right	His house	Outer future, future home, environment and employment	Future	Mercury	Hod
9	Third from Below, far right	His hopes or fears	Aspirations and concerns of the future	From Near Future to Far Future	Moon	Yesod
10	Top far right	What will come	Solution or outcome of the reading	Far Future	Four elements	Malkuth

The Pattern Behind the Golden Dawn Oracular Thesaurus, the Qabalistic Structure of the Tarot

The skeleton for all oracular meanings for the Tarot is the Jewish Qabalistic diagram known as the Tree of Life. This diagram is a flowchart of the universe unfolding from nothing to physical matter. It is based on the numerical progression of whole integers beginning with zero and can be subdivided into different groupings of numbers, the most common being 10, 16, 22, 32, 40, and 100.

The Tarot groupings of four suits of ten cards (the Minor Arcana), four suits of four cards (the Court Cards), and 22 pictorial images (the Major Arcana) have for their basis the Qabalistic structure of the Tree of Life. The identification of the Tree of Life diagram with the Tarot groupings was first put forth in print in 1856 by the French magician Eliphas Levi in his *Transcendental Magic*. This Qabalistic analysis of the Tarot was further extended by Mathers in his *Book T*. The allocation of the 16 Court Cards to this Tree of Life is incomplete in the research of both Levi and Mathers, but it has been completely developed in this Key. The correct correspondences of the Tarot to the Qabalistic Tree of Life are as follows:

The Minor Arcana

The ten basic circles composing the Tree of Life, numbered 1 through 10, referred to as sephiroth (numbers) correspond to the Minor Arcana. The Ace corresponds to the circle numbered 1, the Two to the circle numbered 2,..., the Ten to the circle numbered 10. (See diagram on next page.) As there are four suits (Wands, Cups, Swords, and Pentacles), numbered 1 through 10, there are also four worlds in the Jewish Cosmology, each composed of 10 circles. The four worlds corresponding to the four suits are as follows:

Four Qabalistic Worlds

Hebrew Name	Qabalistic World	Number	Tarot Suit	Tetragrammaton	Element
Atziloth	Archetype (Impulse)	1st	Wands	I	Fire
Briah	Creative (Actor)	2nd	Cups	H	Water
Yetzirah	Formative (Pattern)	3rd	Swords	V	Air
Assiah	Action (Matter)	4th	Pentacles	Hf	Earth

Just as 1 on the diagram of the Tree of Life is the station for essence, pure energy, and the creative impulse, 10 on the diagram is created matter. Further, as creation descends from station 1 to station 10, energy veers to the right, to the left, and then center, alternating between two extremes and a middle ground. The descent of the number series from 1 to 10 represents a flowchart that shows ten stages, a progression from pure energy to created matter, forming the complete cycle of creation. Note that nine stages precede the present reality that we are now residing in, which is numbered as station 10.

The Minor Arcana as the Ten Sephiroth of the Tree of Life

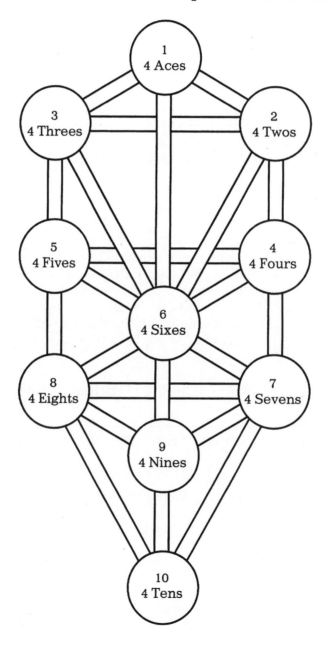

Two measures of balance are used in determining the weakness or strength of these ten stations, which are both the number series 1 through 10 and the Tarot Minor Arcana series of Ace through 10. The first measure is Above, Middle, and Below. Above is epitomized in station 1, Middle in station 6, and Below in station 10. Above is seen as limitless energy; Below is seen as exhausted energy that must be renewed by the inception of a new cycle, while the Middle is seen as a perfect balance between expansion (in 1) and restriction (in 10). Correspondingly, the Minor Arcana of Ace through 10 in any of the four suits can be defined by these parameters. Thus the four Aces are always tokens of the beginning or unrestricted energy, while the four tens imply the end, or exhausted energy. The four sixes are likewise a blend of the two concepts, Above and Below, and are always tokens of balance and harmony because they reside midway between the two extremes of Ace and 10 and occupy the exact center of the Tree of Life.

The second measure of balance which can be applied to the Tree of Life is the division of Right, Left, and Center. As can be seen in the below diagram, there are three basic columns of circles, Right, Left, and Center (or Middle).

The Two Parameters of the Ten Numbers Forming the Tree of Life

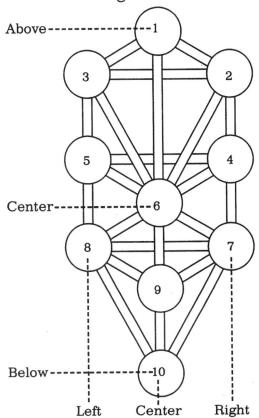

The stations 2, 4, and 7 are of the Right; the stations 3, 5, and 8 are of the Left; and the stations 1, 6, 9, and 10 are of the Middle, or Center. In this measure, the Center is the point of balance, while Right and Left are unbalanced. However, two further gradations qualify these measures. As Right and Left are unbalanced, Right is positive and Left is negative. Further, the first measure of Above and Below is applied to Right and Left, so that a station falling to the Right in the higher portion of the Tree (i.e., station 2) is less out of balance than a station falling to the Right in the lower position of the Tree (i.e., station 7). In applying these two measures to the Minor Arcana series of Ace through 10, we get the following analysis of weaknesses and strengths:

Ace—In balance and the strongest, since it is both Above and Center. It is pure energy without any tendency to veer Right or Left (Kether as One on the Tree of Life).

Two—Strong, but the first tendency to move out of balance to the Right; however, since it is in the higher realm of the Tree, it is not weakened by tending to the Right (Chockmah as Two on the Tree of Life).

Three—Strong, but the first tendency to move out of balance to the Left; like the Two, it is in the higher realm, modifying the fact that it is out of balance. However, since Left is more precarious than Right when out of balance, the Three is weakened to a degree even though it is in the higher quadrant (Binah as Three on the Tree of Life).

Four—As Two marks the first departure to the Right and Three the first departure to the Left, Four, rather than returning to the Center, veers to the Right in an attempt to counter Three's tendency to the Left. As such, it is positive, yet it is the first time Right on the Tree of Life shows any weakness. As Two is also energy at an optimum level, Four implies some depletion of energy, symbolic of compromise. On the Tree of Life, Four esoterically represents the first fall to matter, because the progression of One, Two, and Three (forming a perfect triangle) is seen to be complete in itself. Four's tendency to Right will only be balanced with the inception of Six (Chesed as Four on the Tree of Life).

Five—As One, Two, and Three are complete in themselves, with the establishment of Four, energy descending from Above attempted to center itself but veered instead from the extreme Left of Three to the extreme Right of Four. Now, with the inception of Five, the energy descending the three columns of Middle, Right, and Left has veered to the extreme Left again in hopes of balancing itself. Instead of finding the Center, the extreme Left is reached again, and this is the first real drain of momentum for the descending energy. From Three to Four to Five, energy has been seeking the Center but has failed to find it.

With the Left encountered the second time before centering in the Middle Pillar, the balance and adaptability of the descending energy has been challenged. Five is the most out of balance, and as such dangerous, station on the Tree. In the Qabalah, it is allocated to Mars to show both perseverance of strength and fear of collapse of energy (failure). On account of this symbolism, all four Fives in the Minor Arcana partake of a negative divinatory meaning, for all are concerned with lack of energy and fear (Geburah as Five on the Tree of Life).

Six—The position of Six (i.e., Center) has been aimed for since station One deviated to the Right to form station Two. Stations Three, Four, and Five are all failed attempts to be in balance in the Central or Middle Pillar. However, with the establishment of Six, the energy descending down the Tree is finally in balance again. Six is not only Middle between Right and Left in this diagram, it is also Center between the extremes of Above and Below (personified in stations One and Ten). As such, the four Sixes all partake of harmony, balance, and beauty in divinatory meaning, since Six represents the center of the Tree of Life (Tiphereth as Six on the Tree of Life).

Seven—The position of Seven is the last time energy will veer to the Right. It is in the quadrant of the Tree of Life which is Below, and as such the positive Right combining with the negative Below neutralizes itself in Seven. As such, in divination the four Sevens are restricted energy which, though not negative, are not completely positive in connotation (Netzach as Seven on the Tree of Life).

Eight—As Seven is the last veering to the Right before realization in Ten, Eight is the last veering to the Left. It is also in the quadrant that is Below. However, Eight is established in an attempt to get back on the track (i.e., the Center) and is the last burst of energy to counter the tendency to the Right seen in Seven. Therefore, in divination, the four Eights modify the four Sevens and are portrayed in a restricted though more flexible frame of meaning than the four Sevens (Hod as 8 on the Tree of Life).

Nine—With Nine, the Center that Six and One occupy is firmly established. There will be no more veering to Right or Left, for energy will now descend directly below in the Center column to establish Ten. The four Nines in divination are therefore for the most part positive. However, the Nine of Swords is cast in a negative light to show that, though Nine is centered, it is in the quadrant marked Below, which symbolizes a weakening of energy (Yesod as Nine on the Tree of Life).

Ten—With the inception of Nine, Ten is inevitable. Yet in the descent from One, the momentum of the energy coursing through stations One to Nine has been greatly reduced. Hence the tendency to the Right or Left (which indicates an abundance of force) has been checked. Ten is therefore a pendant to Nine and shows energy that has descended, coming to rest in the physical manifestation of Ten. In divination, therefore, the four Tens represent the need for an inception of a new cycle of energy. Thus they signify the end product, result, or manifestation of the concepts which are portrayed in the four Aces. It should also be pointed out that, in the cosmology of the Tree of Life, the plane of our existence is this station Ten, while stations One through Nine represent forces beyond our normal grasp that have brought our consciousness to birth, and by which we can return and ascend to reach back to the Creator (Malkuth as Ten on the Tree of Life).

In summation, this Tree of Life diagram as ten stations calibrates in divination the meanings given to the four suits of Ace through Ten in the Minor Arcana.

The following table shows the 40 cards of the Minor Arcana as the ten Sephiroth of the Tree of Life, and the positive (well-dignified) or negative (ill-dignified) divinatory meanings derived from their placement on the Tree. In this table, W = Wands, C = Cups, S = Swords, and P = Pentacles.

The Minor Arcana and the Tree of Life

Card and Corresponding Sephirah	Well-Dignified				Ill-Dignified			
1	W	C	S	P				
2	W	C	S	P				
3	W	C		P			S	
4	W	C	S	P				
5					W	C	S	P
6	W	C	S	P				
7					W	C	S	P
8	W			P		C	S	
9	W	C		P			S	
10		C		P	W		S	

The Major Arcana

The 22 cards corresponding to the Major Arcana are the 22 visible Paths which connect the ten Sephiroth (or stations) on the Tree of Life (see diagram on page 330). These 22 channels are the 22 Hebrew letters of the alphabet which connect 1 through 10. The following list delineates the numbers 1 through 10 as they are connected by each of the 22 Paths. The Hebrew letters and Tarot keys corresponding to the Paths are also given.

The 22 Paths of the Tree of Life

Tarot Key	Hebrew Letter	Numbers Connected by Path	Number of Path in the Sepher Yetzirah
0 The Fool	Aleph	1 to 2	11
I The Magician	Beth	1 to 3	12
II The High Priestess	Gimel	1 to 6	13
III The Empress	Daleth	2 to 3	14
IV The Emperor	Heh	2 to 6	15
V The Hierophant	Vav	2 to 4	16
VI The Lovers	Zain	3 to 6	17
VII The Chariot	Cheth	3 to 5	18
VIII Strength	Teth	4 to 5	19
IX The Hermit	Yod	4 to 6	20
X The Wheel of Fortune	Kaph	4 to 7	21
XI Justice	Lamed	5 to 6	22
XII The Hanged Man	Mem	5 to 8	23
XIII Death	Nun	6 to 7	24
XIV Temperance	Samekh	6 to 9	25
XV The Devil	Ayin	6 to 8	26
XVI The Tower	Peh	7 to 8	27
XVII The Star	Tzaddi	7 to 9	28
XVIII The Moon	Qoph	7 to 10	29
XIX The Sun	Resh	8 to 9	30
XX Judgement	Shin	8 to 10	31
XXI The World	Tav	9 to 10	32

Using the parameters outlined above for the stations 1 through 10, the positive or negative divinatory meanings of the Major Arcana card can be determined by analyzing the energy latent in the two stations connected by the corresponding Path.

The 22 Paths of the Major Arcana on the Tree of Life

Major Arcana Number	Title	Connecting Sephiroth	32 Paths	Position	Motion	Astrological Union
0	The Fool	1 to 2	11	Above Center to Above Right	First motion to Right	First Cause-Fixed Stars
I	The Magician	1 to 3	12	Above Center To Above Left	First motion to Left	First Cause-Saturn
II	The High Priestess	1 to 6	13	Above Center to Center	In balance	First Cause-Sun
III	The Empress	2 to 3	14	Above Right to Above Left	First Right to Left	Fixed Stars-Saturn
IV	The Emperor	2 to 6	15	Above Right to Center	Right becoming balanced	Fixed Stars-Sun
V	The Hierophant	2 to 4	16	Above Right to Right Center	Right remaining out of balance	Fixed Stars-Jupiter
VI	The Lovers	3 to 6	17	Above Left to Center	Left becoming balanced	Saturn-Sun
VII	The Chariot	3 to 5	18	Above Left to Left Center	Left remaining out of balance	Saturn-Mars
VIII	Strength	4 to 5	19	Right Center to Left Center	Out of balance	Jupiter-Mars
IX	The Hermit	4 to 6	20	Right Center to Center	Right returning to Center	Jupiter-Sun
X	The Wheel of Fortune	4 to 7	21	Right Center to Lower Right	Right unable to find Center	Jupiter-Venus

The 22 Paths of the Major Arcana on the Tree of Life (cont'd.)

Major Arcana Number	Title	Connecting Sephiroth	32 Paths	Position	Motion	Astrological Union
XI	Justice	5 to 6	22	Left Center to Center	Left returning to Center	Mars-Sun
XII	The Hanged Man	5 to 8	23	Left Center to Lower Left	Left unable to find Center	Mars-Mercury
XIII	Death	6 to 7	24	Center to Lower Right	Center turning out of balance	Sun-Venus
XIV	Temperance	6 to 9	25	Center to Center Below	In balance	Sun-Moon
XV	The Devil	6 to 8	26	Center to Lower Left	Center turning out of balance	Sun-Mercury
XVI	The Tower	7 to 8	27	Lower Right to Lower Left	Out of balance	Venus-Mercury
XVII	The Star	7 to 9	28	Lower Right to Center Below	Out of balance, returning to Center	Venus-Moon
XVIII	The Moon	7 to 10	29	Lower Right to End Below	Centered but exhausted	Venus-Earth
XIX	The Sun	8 to 9	30	Lower Left to Center Below	Out of balance, returning to Center	Mercury-Moon
XV	Judgement	8 to 10	31	Lower Left to End Below	Centered but exhausted	Mercury-Earth
XXI	The World	9 to 10	32	Center Below to End Below	In balance but exhausted	Moon-Earth

The Major Arcana on the Tree of Life

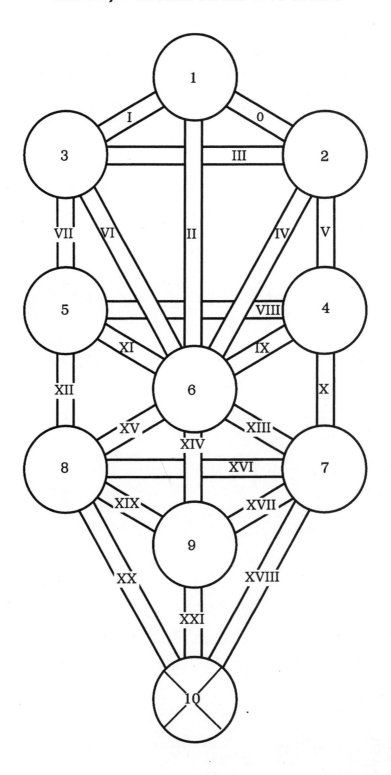

The Court Cards

The Court Cards have two classifications on the Tree of Life. Since the cycle of Knight, Queen, King, and Page corresponds to the Qabalistic name IHVH, this cycle also corresponds to the stations 2, 3, 6, and 10 on the Tree of Life. In addition there are 16 invisible or unconnected Paths on the Tree of Life which also correspond to the 16 Court Cards (see diagram on page 333). The following table will clarify these two sets of attributes for the Court Cards.

The Court Cards and the 16 Invisible Paths of the Tree of Life

Court Card	Numbers Connected by Invisible Path	Astrological Union	Sephirah on Tree	Secret Number of Invisible Path (Sepher Yetzirah)	Enochian Letter
Knight of Wands	2 to 5	Fixed Stars-Mars	2 Fixed Stars	33	I
Queen of Wands	2 to 8	Fixed Stars-Mercury	3 Saturn	34	B
King of Wands	2 to 9	Fixed Stars-Moon	6 Sun	35	G
Page of Wands	2 to 10	Fixed Stars-Earth	10 Earth	36	F
Knight of Cups	3 to 4	Saturn-Jupiter	2 Fixed Stars	37	R
Queen of Cups	3 to 7	Saturn-Venus	3 Saturn	38	P
King of Cups	3 to 9	Saturn-Moon	6 Sun	39	N
Page of Cups	3 to 10	Saturn-Earth	10 Earth	40	L
Knight of Swords	1 to 4	First Cause-Jupiter	2 Fixed Stars	41	E
Queen of Swords	1 to 5	First Cause-Mars	3 Saturn	42	O
King of Swords	1 to 7	First Cause-Venus	6 Sun	43	M
Page of Swords	1 to 8	First Cause-Mercury	10 Earth	44	Z

The Court Cards and the 16 Invisible Paths of the Tree of Life (cont'd.)

Court Card	Numbers Connected by Invisible Path	Astrological Union	Station as 1-10 on Tree	Secret Number of Invisible Path (Sepher Yetzirah)	Enochian Letter
Knight of Pentacles	4 to 9	Jupiter-Moon	2 Fixed Stars	45	S
Queen of Pentacles	4 to 10	Jupiter-Earth	3 Saturn	46	U
King of Pentacles	5 to 9	Mars-Moon	6 Sun	47	A
Page of Pentacles	5 to 10	Mars-Earth	10 Earth	48	T

As in the case of the Major Arcana, the two stations which each Court Card connects determine the divinatory complexion of each Court Card.

Since these 16 invisible Paths correspond to the 16 countercharges of the four elements, they are also the 16 selected Enochian letters of the Golden Dawn system. Thus the visible Paths are governed by Hebrew and the invisible Paths are governed by Enochian.

QABALISTIC ALPHABET OF THE TAROT

Beyond the divinatory use of the Tarot, the heart of the Tarot deck, known as the Major Arcana, is a secret pictorial alphabet corresponding to the Qabalistic alphabet of Hebrew.

The key to unlocking the alphabet-like symbolism of the Tarot is the ancient Hebrew mystical text known as the *Sepher Yetzirah*. Both Mathers and Case discovered this Tarot secret, and with the aid of this text both were independently able to reconstruct the pictorial alphabet key of the Tarot.

The core of the 78-card deck is the Major Arcana, 22 pictorial cards which bear the Roman numerals I through XXI, as well as the cipher symbol "zero." These 22 cards, when properly aligned to the order of the Hebrew alphabet, serve as archetypal images for each of the letters of the Hebrew alphabet, embodying in their symbolism the complex attributions of the Hebrew Qabalah. This alphabet alignment, which both Mathers and Case rediscovered, when correctly applied to the Tarot, allows any word concept in Hebrew to be spelled out in pictorial symbolism.

The table on page 334 will delineate the correct correlation of the Hebrew alphabet to the Tarot.

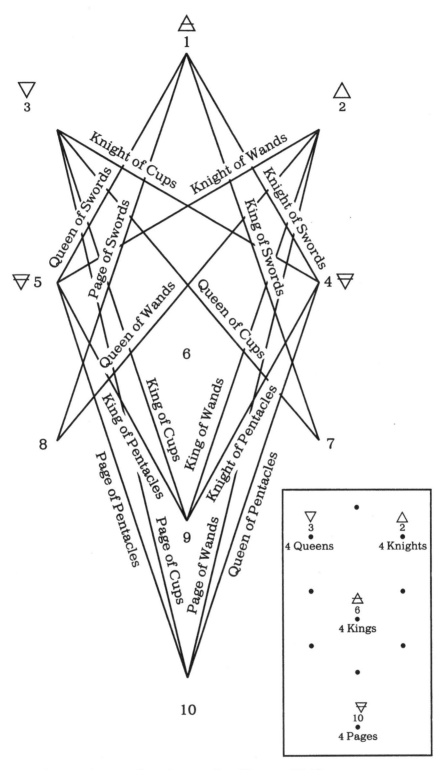

**The Court Cards on the Tree of Life
as 16 Invisible Paths**

The Rectified Hebraic Order of the Tarot

Hebrew Letter	Number Value	Path on the Tree of Life	Tarot Number	Key Name	Astology via Sepher Yetzirah
א (A)	1	11	0	The Fool	Air
ב (B)	2	12	1	The Magician	Mercury
ג (G)	3	13	2	The High Priestess	Moon
ד (D)	4	14	3	The Empress	Venus
ה (H)	5	15	4	The Emperor	Aries
ו (V)	6	16	5	The Hierophant	Taurus
ז (Z)	7	17	6	The Lovers	Gemini
ח (Ch)	8	18	7	The Chariot	Cancer
ט (T)	9	19	8	Strength	Leo
י (I)	10	20	9	The Hermit	Virgo
כ (K)	20	21	10	The Wheel of Fortune	Jupiter
ל (L)	30	22	11	Justice	Libra
מ (M)	40	23	12	The Hanged Man	Water
נ (N)	50	24	13	Death	Scorpio
ס (S)	60	25	14	Temperance	Sagittarius
ע (O)	70	26	15	The Devil	Capricorn
פ (P)	80	27	16	The Tower	Mars
צ (Tz)	90	28	17	The Star	Aquarius
ק (Q)	100	29	18	The Moon	Pisces
ר (R)	200	30	19	The Sun	Sun
ש (Sh)	300	31	20	Judgement	Fire
ת (Th)	400	32	21	The World	Saturn

Eliphas Levi, who must have known these attributes, gave a blinded order in his written works. This blinded order, which assigns The Magician rather than The Fool to Aleph, is known as the exoteric order for the Tarot, while the secret order (and the only workable order) is known as the esoteric order. The exoteric order is the basis for the French Qabalistic-Masonic movement, while the esoteric order is the basis for the English Qabalistic-Masonic movement.

The following table shows both of these systems, as well as the variants to Mathers' Golden Dawn order which Aleister Crowley employed in his own derivation of the esoteric Tarot (found in his works *Liber 777* and *The Book of Thoth*).

Tarot (Major Arcana) Numerals

Hebrew Alphabet	Eliphas Levi (Exoteric)	Golden Dawn (Esoteric)	Aleister Crowley 777	Aleister Crowley Book of Thoth
א (A)	1	0	0	0
ב (B)	2	1	1	1
ג (G)	3	2	2	2
ד (D)	4	3	3	3
ה (H)	5	4	4	17
ו (V)	6	5	5	5
ז (Z)	7	6	6	6
ח (Ch)	8	7	7	7
ט (T)	9	8	11	11
י (I)	10	9	9	9
כ (K)	11	10	10	10
ל (L)	12	11	8	8
מ (M)	13	12	12	12
נ (N)	14	13	13	13
ס (S)	15	14	14	14
ע (O)	16	15	15	15
פ (P)	17	16	16	16
צ (Tz)	18	17	17	4
ק (Q)	19	18	18	18
ר (R)	20	19	19	19
ש (Sh)	0	20	20	20
ת (Th)	21	21	21	21

Eliphas Levi's Tarot order is found in his work *Transcendental Magic* as well as the writings on the Tarot by Papus. The Golden Dawn's order is recorded in Mathers' secret textbook, *Book T*, as well as the writings of Paul Foster Case on the Tarot.

Aleister Crowley's order is recorded in his book *777* and is based on the attributes of *Book T*. However, Crowley restored Key 8 and Key 11 to their older order as Justice and Strength, rather than Mathers' rearrangement to match their esoteric astrological attributes. Crowley's order as recorded in his *Book of Thoth* adds one more variant to Mathers' Tarot system. Key 4 (The Emperor) and Key 17 (The Star) are exchanged in accordance with *The Book of the Law*, I:57.

From the above table a variety of number values can be given to each letter of the Hebrew alphabet. These subset values can be employed as alternate gematric values for Hebrew. As an illustration of this code in action, the Hebrew word for the moon (LBNH, לבנה) will be analyzed by the four separate number codes:

1. LBNH = 12 + 2 + 14 + 5 = 33   Eliphas Levi (Exoteric)

2. LBNH = 11 + 1 +13 + 4 = 29   Mathers & Case (Esoteric)

3. LBNH = 8 + 1 + 13 + 4 = 26   Crowley *(777)*

4. LBNH = 8 + 1 + 13 + 17 = 39   Crowley *(Book of Thoth)*

Beyond the Hebrew alphabet system variants of Levi, Mathers, and Crowley, the four major modern exponents of the Tarot (Mathers, Crowley, Case, and Waite) each place the 78 cards of the Tarot deck in a different serial order. The following table lists these four separate number arrangements for the order of the Tarot. It should be noted that Waite's order parallels the order of Etteilla's Tarot.

The Serial Order of the 78-Card Tarot Deck

Serial Order	Golden Dawn	Crowley	Case	Waite
1	AW	0	0	I
2	AC	I	I	II
3	AS	II	II	III
4	AP	III	III	IV
5	KnW	XVII	IV	V
6	QW	V	V	VI
7	KW	VI	VI	VII
8	PaW	VII	VII	VIII
9	KnC	XI	VIII	IX
10	QC	IX	IX	X
11	KC	X	X	XI
12	PaC	VIII	XI	XII
13	KnS	XII	XII	XIII
14	QS	XIII	XIII	XIV
15	KS	XIV	XIV	XV
16	PaS	XV	XV	XVI
17	KnP	XVI	XVI	XVII
18	QP	IV	XVII	XVIII
19	KP	XVIII	XVIII	XIX
20	PaP	XIX	XIX	XX
21	5W	XX	XX	0
22	6W	XXI	XXI	XXI
23	7W	KnW	AW	KW
24	8P	QW	2W	QW
25	9P	KW	3W	KnW
26	10P	PaW	4W	PaW
27	2S	KnC	5W	10W

The Serial Order of the 78-Card Tarot Deck (cont'd.)

Serial Order	Golden Dawn	Crowley	Case	Waite
28	3S	QC	6W	9W
29	4S	KC	7W	8W
30	5C	PaC	8W	7W
31	6C	KnS	9W	6W
32	7C	QS	10W	5W
33	8W	KS	KW	4W
34	9W	PaS	QW	3W
35	10W	KnP	KnW	2W
36	2P	QP	PaW	AW
37	3P	KP	AC	KC
38	4P	PaP	2C	QC
39	5S	AW	3C	KnC
40	6S	2W	4C	PaC
41	7S	3W	5C	10C
42	8C	4W	6C	9C
43	9C	5W	7C	8C
44	10C	6W	8C	7C
45	2W	7W	9C	6C
46	3W	8W	10C	5C
47	4W	9W	KC	4C
48	5P	10W	QC	3C
49	6P	AC	KnC	2C
50	7P	2C	PaC	AC
51	8S	3C	AS	KS
52	9S	4C	2S	QS
53	10S	5C	3S	KnS
54	2C	6C	4S	PaS
55	3C	7C	5S	10S
56	4C	8C	6S	9S
57	0	9C	7S	8S
58	I	10C	8S	7S
59	II	AS	9S	6S
60	III	2S	10S	5S
61	IV	3S	KS	4S
62	V	4S	QS	3S
63	VI	5S	KnS	2S
64	VII	6S	PaS	AS
65	VIII	7S	AP	KP

The Serial Order of the 78-Card Tarot Deck (cont'd.)

Serial Order	Golden Dawn	Crowley	Case	Waite
66	IX	8S	2P	QP
67	X	9S	3P	KnP
68	XI	10S	4P	PaP
69	XII	AP	5P	10P
70	XIII	2P	6P	9P
71	XIV	3P	7P	8P
72	XV	4P	8P	7P
73	XVI	5P	9P	6P
74	XVII	6P	10P	5P
75	XVIII	7P	KP	4P
76	XIX	8P	QP	3P
77	XX	9P	KnP	2P
78	XXI	10P	PaP	AP

Abbreviations used in table:
Major Arcana: 0–XXI = 22 cards of Major Arcana
Minor Arcana: A = Ace, 2–10 = Two through Ten
Court Cards: Kn = Knight; Q = Queen; K = King; Pa = Page
Minor Suits: W = Wands; C = Cups; S = Swords; P = Pentacles

There exists another Tarot system which developed out of a literal working of Eliphas Levi's Tarot attributes. This system is a product of the French Qabalistic movement of Gérard Encausse (Papus), Stanislas de Guaita, and Oswald Wirth, which developed at the turn of the century.

Although this French Tarot system is considered by Western esoteric standards to be blinded, it does offer a different manner of allocating both the Hebrew alphabet and astrology to the Tarot cards. The basic Tarot attributes of Papus can be found in his *Tarot of the Bohemians*. The allocation of the Hebrew alphabet to the Tarot was taken directly from the writings of Eliphas Levi. Papus took this Hebraic order and added the astrological attributes of the *Sepher Yetzirah* to these Tarot alphabet equivalents, though the planets and Zodiac equivalents were rearranged to fit the Tarot pictures as Papus understood them. Papus did not understand the role of the three elemental Mother Letters, so three of the 22 keys possess no astrological equivalents. Later in his research, however, Papus came across a French translation of the *Sepher Yetzirah* by Meyer Lambert. With this translation, Papus corrected his original attributes (though it should be noted that Lambert did not correctly decipher the Mother Letter Shin). Though both Mathers and Case, using the *Sepher Yetzirah*, were able to correctly decipher the Hebrew allocations of the Tarot (i.e., Aleph = The Fool), Papus, using the same information, was able to justify the order of the Tarot as established by Eliphas Levi (i.e., Aleph = The Magician).

The following table details the *Sepher Yetzirah* equivalents of the Tarot according to Papus.

The French Qabalistic Tarot

Tarot Card	Hebrew Letter	Sepher Yetzirah Papus	Lambert
1. The Juggler	א (A)	No Symbol	Air
2. The High Priestess	ב (B)	Moon	Saturn
3. The Empress	ג (G)	Venus	Jupiter
4. The Emperor	ד (D)	Jupiter	Mars
5. The Pope	ה (H)	Aries	Aries
6. The Lovers	ו (V)	Taurus	Taurus
7. The Chariot	ז (Z)	Gemini	Gemini
8. Justice	ח (Ch)	Cancer	Cancer
9. The Hermit	ט (T)	Leo	Leo
10. The Wheel of Fortune	י (Y)	Virgo	Virgo
11. Strength	כ (K)	Mars	Sun
12. The Hanged Man	ל (L)	Libra	Libra
13. Death	מ (M)	No Symbol	Water
14. Temperance	נ (N)	Scorpio	Scorpio
15. The Devil	ס (S)	Sagittarius	Sagittarius
16. The Lightning-Struck Tower	ע (O	Capricorn	Capricorn
17. The Stars	פ (P)	Mercury	Venus
18. The Moon	צ (Tz)	Aquarius	Aquarius
19. The Sun	ק (Q)	Gemini	Pisces
20. The Judgement	ר (R)	Saturn	Mercury
0. The Foolish Man	ש (Sh)	No Symbol	Earth
21. The Universe	ת (Th)	Sun	Moon

It should be noted that most modern European decks base their pictorial design on Waite (ultimately Mathers) while using the French Hebrew attributes (i.e., Aleph = The Magician).

Beyond this initial astrological system of the *Sepher Yetzirah*, the French Qabalistic school of Papus adapted the cosmological angelic attributes of Athanasius Kircher for the Hebrew alphabet. Oswald Wirth also constructed a set of astrological attributes based on the constellations of the sky. These attributes appear in Papus' *Tarot of the Bohemians*, and may be based on the writings of the Polish Qabalistic Henri Wronski. Again, these attributes have no equivalent in the Golden Dawn Tarot system.

The French Astrological Variations for the Tarot

Tarot Card	Hebrew Letter	Kircher's Astrological Attributes	Wirth's Planisphere Astrological Attributes
1. The Juggler	א (A)	Seraphim (Highest Archangelic order)	Orion—The Bull
2. The High Priestess	ב (B)	Cherubim	Cassiopeia
3. The Empress	ג (G)	Thrones	The Virgin
4. The Emperor	ד (D)	Dominations	Hercules, Lyra, and Boreal Crown
5. The Pope	ה (H)	Powers	The Ram
6. The Lovers	ו (V)	Virtues	Eagle, Antinous, and Sagittarius
7. The Chariot	ז (Z)	Principalities	Great Bear
8. Justice	ח (Ch)	Sons of God	The Balance
9. The Hermit	ט (T)	Angels	The Ox Driver
10. The Wheel of Fortune	י (Y)	God ministering through his Celestial Government	Capricornus (opposed to Sirius)
11. Strength	כ (K)	Primum Mobile and Zodiac	Lion (and Virgin)
12. The Hanged Man	ל (L)	Saturn	Perseus
13. Death	מ (M)	Jupiter and Mars	Dragon of the Pole
14. Temperance	נ (N)	Sun and Venus	Aquarius
15. The Devil	ס (S)	Mercury	Goat and Coachman
16. The Lightning-Struck Tower	ע (O)	Moon	Scorpion, Ophiuchus
17. The Stars	פ (P)	Fire and Air	Andromeda, the Fishes
18. The Moon	צ (Tz)	Water and Earth	Cancer, Sirius, Procyon
19. The Sun	ק (Q)	Mineral	The Twins
20. The Judgement	ר (R)	Animal	The Swans
0. The Foolish Man	ש (Sh)	Vegetable	Cepheus
21. The Universe	ת (Th)	Man	Lesser Bear and Pole Star

The following table delineates the justification for Papus' allocations of the Hebrew alphabet to the Major Arcana (which has no real basis in Hebrew for many of its variations, but rather in the exoteric order of the Tarot).

French Qabalistic Alphabet

Tarot Key	Hebrew Letter	Qabalistic Meaning
I	א (A)	Being, mind, Man or God, chest, breast, unity, mother of numbers, the first substance, center pupil of God's eye as one point
II	ב (B)	Duad, wife, mother, law, gnosis, Qabalah, Man's mouth, house of God and Man, occult church, black disk
III	ג (G)	Triad, the word, nature, the hand taking, plenitude, retribution, triangle
IV	ד (D)	Initiation, power, the breast, table, door, cubic stone or its base, eye within triangle
V	ה (H)	Law, symbolism, philosophy, religion, breath, the one; instruction, demonstration, upright pentagram
VI	ו (V)	Lingam, union, interlacement, the eye-ear, hook, corner, hexagram
VII	ז (Z)	Arrow, weapons, sword, cherubic sword of fire, square surmounted by triangle
VIII (Justice)	ח (Ch)	A field, life, promise and threat, double square
IX	ט (T)	A rooftop, well, good, morality, cross within circle
X	י (Y)	Phallus, virile fecundity, paternal scepter, the index finger, principle, manly honor, counterclockwise swastika
XI (Strength)	כ (K)	The hand grasping and holding, the hand outstretched, conduct, pentagram within hexagram
XII	ל (L)	Example, instruction, public teaching, outstretched arm, discipline, heart, cross surmounting inverted triangle
XIII	מ (M)	Creation and destruction, woman, heaven of Jupiter and Mars, domination and force, crescent appended to cross
XIV	נ (N)	Changes of life, a fruit, heaven of Sun, motion of seasons, double stream of water
XV	ס (S)	Occult science, magick, serpent, heaven of Mercury, mystery, inverted pentagram
XVI	ע (O)	Changes, failures, alterations, materialized link, source, eye, heaven, Moon, spear and shield as arrow and circle
XVII	פ (P)	Immortality, outpourings of thoughts, mouth and tongue, heaven of the soul, eight-pointed star as eight spokes

French Qabalistic Alphabet (cont'd.)

Tarot Key	Hebrew Letter	Qabalistic Meaning
XVIII	צ (Tz)	The elements, visible world, roof, justice, reflected light, symbolism, crescent and triangle
XIX	ק (Q)	Apex, prince of heaven, axe, hatchet, vocation, voice, head, point in center of circle
XX	ר (R)	Generative virtue of the Earth, man's head, eternal life, six-pointed star as six spokes
0	ש (Sh)	The flesh, eternal life, the sensitive principle arrow, teeth, circle
XXI	ת (Th)	Microcosm, the breast, sign, macrocosm, man the sum of all in all, clockwise swastika

In his *Tarot of the Magicians,* Oswald Wirth gives the attribution of the 22 Major Arcana to the ten Sephiroth of the Tree of Life, based on Theosophical reduction of the 22 Tarot numerals:

Oswald Wirth's Tarot-Sephiroth Order

Sephiroth	Tarot Cards
0-Ain Soph Aur	0 The Fool
I-Kether	I The Magician and X Wheel of Fortune
II-Chockmah	II High Priestess and XI Strength
III-Binah	III Empress and XII The Hanged Man
IV-Chesed	IV Emperor and XIII Death
V-Geburah	V Hierophant and XIV Temperance
VI-Tiphereth	VI The Lovers and XV The Devil
VII-Netzach	VII The Chariot and XVI The Tower
VIII-Hod	VIII Justice and XVII The Star
IX-Yesod	IX The Hermit and XVIII The Moon
X-Malkuth	XIX The Sun and XX Judgement, XXI The World

Although the Hebrew alphabet allocations for the Major Arcana of the Tarot have been clearly established both by the Golden Dawn Tarot attributes and the French variation of Papus, the alphabet allocations of other magickal languages are not as clear. Since each Tarot Key possesses a Hebraic astrological attribute (based on the *Sepher Yetzirah),* the most coherent and logical method of allocating other alphabets to this Tarot order is by astrological, rather than numerical, parallels.

The following table, based on the Golden Dawn Tarot astrological order, shows the relationship between the Major Arcana, Hebrew, astrology and other magickal languages (which possess astrological attributes).

Tarot Astrological Alphabetical Correspondences

Tarot (Golden Dawn)	Hebrew Alphabet	Astrology (Sepher Yezirah)	Greek/Coptic		Runes	Arabic	Enochian Dee	Enochian GD	Latin (Cabala Simplex)
0 The Fool	A	Air (Spirit)	AŌ	Ō	O	S	A	Z + H	A
I The Magician	B	Mercury	UE	E	R	T	B	—	B
II The High Priestess	G	Moon	ŌA	A	F	D	G	—	C
III The Empress	D	Venus	OH	Ē	G	R	D	D	D
IV The Emperor	H	Aries	AŌ	AŌ	FO	AHO	E	B	E
V The Hierophant	V	Taurus	BPs	BPs	UD	OHGh	F	A	F
VI The Lovers	Z	Gemini	GCh	GCh	ThNg	KhQK	Z	E	G
VII The Chariot	Ch	Cancer	DPh	DPh	AL	KGSh	H	P	H
VIII Strength	T	Leo	EU	E, Y	RM	ShYḌ	—	G	I
XI The Hermit	I	Virgo	ZT	Z, T	KE	ḌLN	I, J, Y	S	L
X The Wheel of Fortune	K	Jupiter	EU	Y	M	Ḍ	K, C	—	M
XI Justice	L	Libra	HS	Ē, S	GB	RTD	L	O	N
XII The Hanged Man	M	Water	AŌ	A	F	Z	M	L + Q	O
XIII Death	N	Scorpio	ThR	Th, R	WT	DṬZ	N	N	P
XIV Temperence	S	Sagittarius	IP	I, P	HS	ZSṢ	X	I (J, Y)	Q
XV The Devil	O	Capricorn	KO	K, O	NZ	TzThBh	O	U (V, W)	R
XVI The Tower	P	Mars	HO	O	Z	L	P	—	S
XVII The Star	Tz	Aquarius	LX	I, Ks	IP	DhFB	Q	M	T
XVIII The Moon	Q	Pisces	MN	M, N	JEi	BMW	R	R	V
XIX The Sun	R	Sun	I	I	H	N	S	—	X
XX Judgement	Sh	Fire	I	I	H	Ṭ	T	C (K) + F	Y
XXI The World	Th	Saturn (Earth)	AŌ	Ō	O	YṢ	U, V, W	T + K	Z

Addendum

Mathers' Qabalistic Proof of the Tarot

Do you imagine that where such men as Court de Gebelin, Etteilla, Christian and Levi failed in their endeavour to discover the Tarot attributions that I would be able of my own power and intelligence alone to lift the veil which has baffled them?
                    —Letter to Frater Levavi Oculos (Percy Bullock) from
                            S.L. MacGregor Mathers (April 2, 1900)

S.L. MacGregor Mathers undoubtedly solved the secret Qabalistic allocations of the Tarot by force of his own occult scholarship and clairvoyant insight rather than by any clues found within the mysterious "cipher manuscript," which supposedly contained the essence of the Golden Dawn system of magic.

Mathers, in his occult research of the Tarot conducted in the library of the British Museum, had much information already available in open publications:

- In both the writings of Court de Gebelin (1781) and Etteilla (pseudonym of Alliette [1785]), the connection of the Jewish Qabalah with the Tarot was already established in print.

- From the writings of Eliphas Levi, including *Transcendental Magic* in 1856, the Qabalistic theories of Etteilla were elaborated, including the following doctrines which Mathers would incorporate into the Golden Dawn system of magick:

    a. That the 22 Major Arcana cards correspond to the 22 Hebrew letters, where Aleph = The Magician and Shin = The Fool

    b. That the 40 Minor Arcana cards, composed of four suits of ten cards each, correspond directly to the Jewish cosmology of four worlds of ten emanations each

    c. That the 16 court cards of four families, each composed of four members, are the magical permutation of the Tetragrammaton as 4 x 4

    d. That the four suits of Wands, Cups, Swords, and Pentacles correspond to both Fire, Water, Air, and Earth and to Yod, Heh, Vav, and Heh

- From the Latin translations of Rittangelius (1642), Postel (1552), and Pistorius (1587), a valid edition of the Qabalistic text the *Sepher Yetzirah* was available, allowing a tabulation of the astrological attributes of the Hebrew alphabet (although the various translators were at odds as to the correct alignment between the seven planets and the seven Hebrew Double Letters). Indeed, Mathers himself states in his pamphlet *The Tarot*, "The Sepher Yetzirah certainly gives, in my opinion, the Qabalistic key of the Tarot" (p. 33).

Mathers, aided by his own enormous eclectic occult knowledge and armed with the above Qabalistic information, was able to:

• Connect the Tarot of 78 cards with the cosmology of the Jewish Qabalah

• Connect the four suits of ten numbered cards to the ten Sephiroth of the Tree of Life,

• Rearrange the 16 Court Cards to correspond to the secret Qabalistic images of the four-lettered name of God, IHVH, so that Levi's assumption of King, Queen, Knight, and Page would be replaced by Knight (Father), Queen (Mother), King (Son), and Page (Daughter). This deep Qabalistic insight of Mathers' escaped the notice of both Waite and Case, but not Crowley.

• Rearrange the assumed correspondence of the Hebrew alphabet with the order of the Tarot so that The Fool would lead the Tarot series and correspond to the first letter of the Hebrew alphabet, Aleph.

This last discovery of Mathers is the supreme magickal formula of the Golden Dawn system of magick. The teachings concerning geomancy, Tattvas, astrology, Enochian, and the symbolism of the rituals themselves, are all elaborations of the formula Aleph = 0 = The Fool.

It is also restated eloquently in the 48th verse of the first chapter of *The Book of the Law*: "My prophet is a fool with his one, one, one; are not they the Ox, and none by the Book?"

How did Mathers discover this simple yet important Tarot secret, that The Fool and not The Magician is the first card of the Tarot deck? Let us try to reconstruct the logic of Mathers' Qabalistic solution, and we will discover the correct allocation of the Hebrew alphabet to the 22 cards of the Major Arcana:

• First Mathers listed the Tarot order corresponding to the Hebrew alphabet as recorded in the 22nd chapter of Eliphas Levi's *Ritual of Transcendental Magic*, entitled "The Book of Hermes."

Hebrew	Tarot
Aleph	I The Magician
Beth	II The High Priestess
Gimel	III The Empress
Daleth	IV The Emperor
Heh	V The Hierophant
Vav	VI The Lovers
Zain	VII The Chariot

Hebrew	Tarot
Cheth	VIII Justice
Teth	IX The Hermit
Yod	X The Wheel of Fortune
Kaph	XI Strength
Lamed	XII The Hanged Man
Mem	XIII Death
Nun	XIV Temperance
Samekh	XV The Devil
Ayin	XVI The Tower
Peh	XVII The Star
Tzaddi	XVIII The Moon
Qoph	XIX The Sun
Resh	XX Judgement
Shin	0 The Fool
Tav	XXI The World

- Next Mathers tabulated the astrological attributes for the Hebrew alphabet from the *Sepher Yetzirah*.

Hebrew	Astrological Attributes
Aleph	Air/Spirit
Beth	Saturn
Gimel	Jupiter
Daleth	Mars
Heh	Aries
Vav	Taurus
Zain	Gemini
Cheth	Cancer
Teth	Leo
Yod	Virgo
Kaph	Sun
Lamed	Libra
Mem	Water
Nun	Scorpio
Samekh	Sagittarius
Ayin	Capricorn
Peh	Venus
Tzaddi	Aquarius
Qoph	Pisces
Resh	Mercury
Shin	Fire
Tav	Moon

- Next Mathers paralleled the Hebraic astrological attributes to Eliphas Levi's order of the Tarot.

Hebrew	Astrological Attribute	Levi's Tarot Order
Aleph	Air/Spirit	I The Magician
Beth	Saturn	II The High Priestess
Gimel	Jupiter	III The Empress
Daleth	Mars	IV The Emperor
Heh	Aries	V The Hierophant
Vav	Taurus	VI The Lovers
Zain	Gemini	VII The Chariot
Cheth	Cancer	VIII Justice
Teth	Leo	IX The Hermit
Yod	Virgo	X Wheel of Fortune
Kaph	Sun	XI Strength
Lamed	Libra	XII The Hanged Man
Mem	Water	XIII Death
Nun	Scorpio	XIV Temperance
Samekh	Sagittarius	XV The Devil
Ayin	Capricorn	XVI The Tower
Peh	Venus	XVII The Star
Tzaddi	Aquarius	XVIII The Moon
Qoph	Pisces	XIX The Sun
Resh	Mercury	XX Judgement
Shin	Fire	0 The Fool
Tav	Moon	XXI The World

- Then Mathers made the bold decision to adjust this serial order by removing the unnumbered card, The Fool, from the 21st or next to last position and placing it logically at the head of the order. Mathers may have based his decision on the research of Court de Gebelin (*Le Monde Primitif,* 1787), who also placed The Fool at the beginning of the Major Arcana. This radical rearrangement is the key maneuver to recovering the lost esoteric order of the Tarot.

Hebrew	Astrological Attribute	Mathers' Rectification of Levi
Aleph	Air/Spirit	0 The Fool
Beth	Saturn	I The Magician
Gimel	Jupiter	II The High Priestess
Daleth	Mars	III The Empress
Heh	Aries	IV The Emperor
Vav	Taurus	V The Hierophant
Zain	Gemini	VI The Lovers
Cheth	Cancer	VII The Chariot
Teth	Leo	VIII Justice
Yod	Virgo	IX The Hermit
Kaph	Sun	X The Wheel of Fortune
Lamed	Libra	XI Strength
Mem	Water	XII The Hanged Man

Hebrew	Astrological Attribute	Mathers' Rectification of Levi
Nun	Scorpio	XIII Death
Samekh	Sagittarius	XIV Temperance
Ayin	Capricorn	XV The Devil
Peh	Venus	XVI The Tower
Tzaddi	Aquarius	XVII The Star
Qoph	Pisces	XVIII The Moon
Resh	Mercury	XIX The Sun
Shin	Fire	XX Judgement
Tav	Moon	XXI The World

- Next turning his attention to the 12 Tarot keys corresponding to the 12 signs of the Zodiac as well as the 12 Simple Letters of the Hebrew alphabet, Mathers discovered that, if two keys were exchanged in their natural Tarot order, there would be complete agreement between the Tarot picture image, the serial order of the Hebrew alphabet, and the corresponding astrological attribute from the *Sepher Yetzirah*. These two Tarot cards were Key VIII, Justice, and Key XI, Strength. By his newly established order, leading with 0, The Fool, the following astrological equivalents were obtained.

Tarot Order	Tarot Key	Hebrew Alphabet	Astrological Image
Key VIII	Justice	Teth	Leo
Key XI	Strength	Lamed	Libra

With an exchange in serial order, astrological agreement was established.

Rectified Tarot Order	Key	Hebrew	Astrological Attribute
Key VIII	Strength	Teth	Leo
Key XI	Justice	Lamed	Libra

Mathers' logic for this substitution was based on the traditional picture images for these keys. By substituting VIII with XI, the Tarot key involving a symbolic image of the scales would correspond to Libra, while the symbolic image of a Lion would correspond to Leo.

- Lastly Mathers turned his attention to the planetary attributes for seven of the Tarot keys obtained from the *Sepher Yetzirah*. In his new Tarot order, beginning with The Fool, the following seven Tarot keys corresponded to the seven planets.

Seven Tarot Keys, Planets, and Hebrew Double Letters

Tarot Key	Seven Planets Platonic Order	Hebrew Double Letter
I The Magician	Saturn	Beth
II The High Priestess	Jupiter	Gimel
III The Empress	Mars	Daleth
X The Wheel of Fortune	Sun	Kaph
XVI The Tower	Venus	Peh
XIX The Sun	Mercury	Resh
XXI The World	Moon	Tav

Mathers realized, on account of his intensive Qabalistic research, that many translators were in disagreement when it came to the planetary attributes of the Hebrew alphabet in the *Sepher Yetzirah*. By his research, Mathers was able to discover the following disparity in Qabalistic attributes for the seven planets:

Sepher Yetzirah Planetary Order

Hebrew Alphabet	Platonic Order, Mantua Edition	Kircher	Meyer	Kalisch
Beth	Saturn	Sun	Mars	Moon
Gimel	Jupiter	Venus	Jupiter	Mars
Daleth	Mars	Mercury	Saturn	Sun
Kaph	Sun	Moon	Moon	Venus
Peh	Venus	Saturn	Mercury	Mercury
Resh	Mercury	Jupiter	Venus	Saturn
Tav	Moon	Mars	Sun	Jupiter

With the same logic, based on astrological agreement, which motivated the exchange of Justice with Strength, Mathers rearranged the seven planets to correspond unerringly with their seven Tarot picture images. Thus a new secret order for these seven planets was established:

Hebrew	Planet	Tarot Key
Beth	Mercury	Key I. The Magician
Gimel	Moon	Key II. The High Priestess
Daleth	Venus	Key III. The Empress
Kaph	Jupiter	Key X. The Wheel of Fortune
Peh	Mars	Key XVI. The Tower
Resh	Sun	Key XIX. The Sun
Tav	Saturn	Key XXI. The World

Mathers' selection of seven new correlations was conditioned by the pictorial images of these seven cards:

- Beth is associated with Mercury and Key I, The Magician, because the magickal arts are also known as the Hermetic arts, devised by Mercury.

- Gimel is associated with the Moon and Key II, The High Priestess, because the lunar Goddess is symbolized in The High Priestess.

- Daleth is associated with Venus and Key III, The Empress, because the Earth Mother as well as Aphrodite is symbolized in The Empress.

- Kaph is associated with Jupiter and Key X, The Wheel of Fortune, because Jupiter is the guiding God of luck, destiny, and fortune.

- Peh is associated with Mars and Key XVI, The Tower, because the astrological symbol for Mars is the lightning bolt that blasts apart the battlement of the Tower.

- Resh is associated with the Sun and Key XIX, The Sun, because the name and image of this key blatantly correspond to the Hebraic astrological attribute.

- Tav is associated with Saturn and Key XXI, The World, because the secondary Qabalistic attribute of this letter is the element Earth, symbolic of the Tarot title The World, and secondarily because Saturn (which is Binah and the Mother of the Tree of Life) is associated with the element Earth, which is Malkuth and the Daughter on the Tree of Life. Note that the association of Tav with The World is the only attribution which is not a deviation from Eliphas Levi's Qabalistic Tarot order.

The resultant revised order is the esoteric order of the Tarot that is recorded in the Golden Dawn document *Book T*. It should be noted that Paul Foster Case in 1907 independently discovered Mathers' secret order by the same logic of combining the *Sepher Yetzirah* with the Tarot (see Case, *The Tarot: A Key to The Wisdom of the Ages*, pp. 18–19).

This new secret order is not the invention of Mathers, but rather his discovery of the true esoteric order of the 78-card Tarot deck.

The Revised Golden Dawn Tarot Order

Hebrew	Astrology	Tarot
Aleph	Air/Spirit	0 The Fool
Beth	Mercury	I The Magician
Gimel	Moon	II The High Priestess
Daleth	Venus	III The Empress
Heh	Aries	IV The Emperor
Vav	Taurus	V The Hierophant

The Revised Golden Dawn Tarot Order (cont'd.)

Hebrew	Astrology	Tarot
Zain	Gemini	VI The Lovers
Cheth	Cancer	VII The Chariot
Teth	Leo	VIII Strength
Yod	Virgo	IX The Hermit
Kaph	Jupiter	X The Wheel of Fortune
Lamed	Libra	XI Justice
Mem	Water	XII The Hanged Man
Nun	Scorpio	XIII Death
Samekh	Sagittarius	XIV Temperance
Ayin	Capricorn	XV The Devil
Peh	Mars	XVI The Tower
Tzaddi	Aquarius	XVII The Star
Qoph	Pisces	XVIII The Moon
Resh	Sun	XIX The Sun
Shin	Fire	XX Judgement
Tav	Saturn/Earth	XXI The World

In summation Mathers' proof of the Tarot is as follows:

- Parallel Hebrew to Levi

- Parallel Hebrew to Qabalistic astrology via the *Sepher Yetzirah*

- Parallel Hebrew to Levi to Qabalistic astrology

- Permutate Levi to place "0" at the head of the order

- Exchange Key VIII with Key XI

- Qualify the seven Tarot keys (I, II, III, X, XVI, XIX, XXI) to correspond to the seven planets (Mercury, Moon, Venus, Jupiter, Mars, Sun, Saturn) by their Tarot images, thereby establishing a new secret esoteric Tarot order which:

  a. Parallels Hebrew to the Tarot

  b. Starts with Key 0

  c. Has a secret planetary order beginning with Mercury and ending with Saturn

  d. Exchanges the position of Key VIII with XI

ADDENDUM

TAROT ESOTERICA
SECRETS OF THE WAITE DECK

As an erudite Kabalistic book, all combinations of which reveal the harmonies preexisting between signs, letters and numbers, the practical value of the Tarot is truly and above all marvelous.

—Eliphas Levi

A.E. Waite's Tarot deck, illustrated by Pamela Colman Smith and first published in 1910, is the most popular deck of our time. The unique allocation of a picture-scene to each of the pip cards (known as the minor arcana or lesser secrets), which are traditionally barren of any symbolic detail, allows even the beginner an educated guess as to the true meaning of these cards. The title of Waite's deck and his accompanying explanatory text was *The Pictorial Key to the Tarot: Being Fragments of a Secret Tradition Under the Veil of Divination.*

By certain symbols incorporated into the design of his Tarot deck, Waite was able to encode as a "pictorial key" the "secret tradition" of Mathers' Qabalistic allocations for the Tarot, recorded in the unpublished Golden Dawn document *Book T*. That Waite was a member of the Golden Dawn is well known today; however, in 1910 when Waite's *Pictorial Key* was first published, the existence of either the Hermetic Order of the Golden Dawn or a secret Qabalistic Tarot was not well known. Only Crowley's *Equinox* series and his *777* could betray Mathers' secret Tarot, and both of these works were privately printed in limited quantites and available only to the serious collector of occult publications.

By the mere fact that Waite was a member of the Golden Dawn we can conjecture his exposure to Mathers' corrected Tarot order (as shown earlier in this section). Though Waite was extremely long-winded, obtuse, and contradictory in expressing his opinions concerning the Tarot and the Qabalah (as well as any other occult subject, as Crowley would have us believe), if we but excerpt a few of Waite's deep insights published throughout his long writing career we can discover his real convictions concerning the Qabalistic Tarot.

From *The Holy Kabbalah*, first published in 1929, in a chapter entitled "The Kabbalah and the Tarot," Waite acknowledges a connection between the Qabalah and the Tarot:

> I may be permitted to register also my feeling that it [the Tarot] has Kabbalistic connnections, some of which were broadly outlined by Éliphas Lévi. There is, moreover, a Jewish Tarot of great rarity which has never been published; but

it belongs to the worst side of so-called Practical Magic.

This statement is extremely revelatory. First, Waite admits a connection between the Tarot and the Qabalah as first described by Levi (information which Mathers used as a basis for his own Qabalistic Tarot). And second, Waite describes the secret initiatory Golden Dawn Tarot as a Jewish Tarot, which was based upon the ancient Hebraic text *Sepher Yetzirah* and employed in Golden Dawn ritual magick.

Further in the same chapter, Waite details the crux of the problem in wedding the Tarot with the Qabalah, the placement of the trump card known as the Fool in the series of the Major Arcana:

> ... the supposed Hebrew symbolism of the Tarot ... becomes disorganised if there is any doubt as to the attribution of its Trump Cards to the Hebrew Alphabet. Now there is one card which bears no number and is allocated therefore according to the discretion of the interpreter. It has been placed in all cases wrongly, by the uninstructed because they had nothing but their private judgment to guide them, and by some who claimed to know better because they desired to mislead. It happens, however, that they also were at sea. I may go further and say that the true nature of Tarot symbolism is perhaps a secret in the hands of a very few persons, and outside that circle operators and writers may combine the cards as they like and attribute them as they like, but they will never find the right way.

By this statement Waite acknowledges an inner circle of initiates who hold the Qabalistic key to the Tarot; and this key, as paramount proof, places the unnumbered trump the Fool in the Major Arcana series in such a way that there is no doubt in the attribution of the Hebrew alphabet to the Tarot.

This inner circle is of course the Hermetic Order of the Golden Dawn, and the Qabalistic key is the placing of the unnumbered key at the beginning of the series so that the first Hebrew letter, Aleph, is assigned to the Fool, Key 0, while the last Hebrew letter, Tav, is assigned to the World, Key XXI. By the astrological attributions of the Hebrew alphabet assigned in the *Sepher Yetzirah,* the corresponding Tarot keys can be classified and verified. It is this secret symbolism which Waite embellishes throughout his own version of the Major Arcana as clues to the wise, and which will be charted out further in this section.

Waite, in *The Pictorial Key to the Tarot,* comments on his own placement of the Fool in the Tarot series in the chapter entitled "Conclusion as to the Greater Keys":

> ... I have not attempted to rectify the position of the cards in their relation to one another; the Zero therefore appears after No. 20, but I have taken care not to number the World or Universe otherwise than as 21. Wherever it ought to be

put, the Zero is an unnumbered card.

In conclusion as to this part, I will give these further indications regarding the Fool, which is the most speaking of all the symbols. He signifies the journey outward, the state of the first emanation, the graces and passivity of the spirit. ...

By these comments Waite negates his own placement of Key 0 between 20 and 21, which is the exoteric (or French) order he adopts in his commentary to his own Tarot deck. However he gives us as many clues as he can muster in 1910:

- The Zero key is unnumbered.

- It is the most speaking of all the symbols; i.e., it has the most to tell concerning the Tarot order.

- It is the journey outward, hence that which starts or begins.

- It is the state of the first emanation, hence it should lead or begin the series as the first card.

- It is spirit, an alternate value for the Hebrew letter Aleph in the Golden Dawn system of Qabalistic attributions (the primary attribute being Air). And spirit in Latin brings out the correspondence *spiritus* = life breath = Air = Aleph.

One may ask whether Waite ever revealed the esoteric order in print. The answer is found in Waite's introduction to Knut Stenring's translation of the *Sepher Yetzirah*, first published in 1923. On page 11 of his introduction, Waite, apparently debunking a spurious Qabalistic order for the Tarot, in reality reveals the initiated secret he was at such constraint not to reveal in his lifetime:

> The proper placing of the Tarot Fool is the great crux of every attempt—and there are several—to create a correspondence between the Trumps Major and the Hebrew letters. If it be worth while to say so, the correct sequence, which emerges from unexpected considerations, has never appeared in print, and it is not to be confused with a Victorian allocation now well known, but which used to be regarded as important: it referred the cipher-card to Aleph, and therefore to the number one, so that we are confronted by the strange analogy of 0 = 1, the alternative being—as we have seen—that 0 = 300, otherwise 21 in the alphabetical order.

The Victorian allocation is none other than that of Mathers, and in 1923 this allocation was anything but well known. It had appeared four times in limited printings by 1923, the first dating to 1909, the last to 1920. These four publications are:

- 1909—Aleister Crowley's limited, privately published 777, a compendium of Qabalistic tables for the Tree of Life, based on Mathers' Golden Dawn attributes for the Tarot.

- 1910—In the May issue of *The Occult Review* (vol. XI, no. 5), there appears an article entitled "The Truth About the Tarot Trumps" signed only with the initials V.N. (Victor Neuberg?). In this anonymous article, the initiated order of the Tarot is given using clues found in Waite's deck, plus the Hebrew correspondences of the *Sepher Yetzirah.* Appended to this article is a reprint of the first six tables of Crowley's 777. Case dates this article to April (rather than May) and assumes that Crowley wrote it, though the style of the article is definitely not that of Crowley.

- 1912—Aleister Crowley's own journal *The Equinox* gives for the first time in print Mathers secret *Book T,* which gives the entire Tarot system of the Golden Dawn (in volume 1, number 8).

- 1920—Paul Foster Case, in America, publishes his first book on the Tarot, *An Introduction to the Study of the Tarot,* which analyzes Waite's own Tarot deck in light of Crowley's attributes found in his 777. This limited work was published by the occult journal *Azoth,* and was a compilation of articles Case wrote on the Tarot beginning in 1918.

In a style typical of Waite, that which is villified is in reality the secret. The formula 0 = 1, established by the allocation of the Fool, valued at zero, to the Hebrew letter Aleph, valued at one, is the great secret found in the true and correct order for the Tarot, which was first envisioned and reconstructed by Mathers, and Mathers alone.

Waite's final word on the secret order of the Tarot appears in his autobiography, *Shadows of Light and Thought,* published in 1936. In the 20th chapter of this book, entitled "The Great Symbols of the Tarot," Waite admits that there is no extant, historical key for the correct symbolism of the Tarot:

> We have to recognise, in a word, that there is no public
> canon of authority in the interpretation of Tarot symbolism.

Waite's assertion is right; there is no public canon, but there is a secret, unpublished canon, and that canon is the Golden Dawn manuscript *Book T.*

Most of Waite's chapter is concerned with the debunking of the French exoteric Tarot system, as championed by Eliphas Levi, in which the Hebrew letter Aleph is assigned to the Magician rather than the Fool. Yet in his final written commentary on the Tarot, Waite comes closest in print to revealing the true basis for the Golden Dawn Tarot.

After describing Eliphas Levi's connection of the 22 Trumps Major to the 22 letters of the Hebrew alphabet as an arbitrary allocation, Waite reveals the correct method for obtaining the true Qabalistic correspondence between the Tarot and the Hebrew alphabet:

> But he [Levi] was concerned very little with any root anal-
> ogy, or he might have redistributed the Trumps Major,
> seeing that their sequence is, as I have said, subject to
> variations in different sets, and that there seems no par-
> ticular reason to suppose that any arrangement of the
> past has a conscious purpose in view. In this matter he
> might have found some curious points by taking the old
> Yetziratic classification of the Hebrew Letters and placing
> those cards against them which correspond to their con-
> ventional allocation.

This statement is the closest published disclosure of the rationale
behind the Golden Dawn Tarot system that Waite ever made in his lifetime. By this candid disclosure, Waite openly suggests that:

- The 22 letters of the Hebrew alphabet do correspond to the 22
  Trumps Major of the Tarot.

- However, the normal order of the exoteric Tarot, leading with the
  Magician, is not the correct order.

- In order to obtain the correct sequence of the Trumps Major, one
  must first establish the correct astrological attributes of the Hebrew
  alphabet, as found in the *Sepher Yetzirah* (the old Yetziratic classification).

- Having obtained these astrological symbols for the Hebrew alphabet,
  the natural order of the 22 Trumps Major must be rearranged to correspond pictorially to these Yetziratic attributes.

- This results in leading the Tarot sequence with the Fool, rather than
  the Magician, and switching Justice with Strength to correspond with
  the Zodiacal attribute of Leo and Libra.

- With this rearrangement, a perfect harmony can exist between the
  picture images of the Tarot cards and the astrological attributions of
  the Hebrew alphabet.

These six steps are indeed steps Waite took back in 1910 when first
designing his own Tarot deck, a deck the designs of which would influence
almost every subsequent Tarot deck to this day.

If the secret symbolism of the Tarot, detailed in *Book T*, is compared to
the unique symbolism employed by Waite in his own personal Tarot deck,
it will be seen that the secret Qabalistic symbolism of the Tarot is betrayed
by Waite in picture symbol rather than in written word. The following commentary will show the secret symbols and clues Waite concealed in the
construction of his Tarot, which reveal the Golden Dawn Tarot system of
Mathers.

PART ONE—THE MAJOR ARCANA
THE DECIPHERMENT OF THE PICTORIAL KEY

0—The Fool
(Aleph = Air)

The Qabalistic attribution for the Fool is the Hebrew letter Aleph, assigned to the element Air as the breath of life, and the aspect of spirit as the animating principle of all life.

Waite has placed many pictorial clues in this picture, to associate this key to Aleph, the first Hebrew letter:

Dog Aleph Beth

- The most apparent clue is the dog in the foreground. Its body is in the graphic shape of the Hebrew letter Aleph, where its tail is the upper yod of Aleph, its head, body and hind legs the main slanting body of Aleph and its forelegs the actual leg of Aleph. Further its forelegs suggest in their shape the letter Beth, the second letter of the alphabet. Combined Aleph-Beth means source, master, or beginning, as well as alphabet.

- The ten circles emblazoned on the Fool's blouse are suggestive of the ten emanations which form the Jewish Tree of Life, which emanates out of nothing (the Ain Soph Aur). As such, their placement on the Fool's blouse indicates that the Fool is that which precedes the ten emantions of the Qabalistic number series, and as such should lead as zero. Within these ten circles are eight-spoked wheels, the Golden Dawn symbol for Spirit (the alternate attribute for Aleph).

- The Fool's blouse, feather in cap, and hair are being blown by the wind, bringing to mind the associated element of Air. The predominant background color of yellow is also the Golden Dawn scale for Aleph as Air.

- The white Sun with 14 rays, behind the Fool, is a highly esoteric reference to the true position of the Fool on the Tree of Life. The path of the Fool (being Aleph, which is the 11th Path) connects the first Sephirah with the second. And the first Sephirah, titled Kether or Crown, can be represented by this radiant white Sun, the Path of the

Fool by the slanting staff placed over his right shoulder, and the second Sephirah by the yawning abyss below below his feet.

- The direction the Fool is walking is from right to left; this is also a secret key. If the Fool is placed at the head of the Major Arcana series and the 22 cards are arranged successively starting with the Fool from right to left (imitating the Hebrew alphabet), it will be seen that the Fool initiates the cycle of 22 pictures and walks left into the series of cards, while the dancer in the World (Key XXI) is stationed at the end of the series and turns to the right to receive the energy initiated by the Fool. By this order, Death (Key XIII) is the only other card which walks directly into the Fool, Death being the cessation of our present journey on earth as the Fool.

- A complex formula involving gematria, the substitution of numbers for Hebrew letters, is symbolized in the Sun behind the Fool combined with the Moon and star on the Fool's left shoulder. The Sun, Moon, and star are symbolic of the Hebrew letter Aleph by the Qabalistic process of gematria.

  In gematria, two words or phrases which share the same number value also share symbolic meaning. By this process, the Hebrew letter name Aleph, written in full, has the same numerical value as the phrase "the Sun, Moon, and stars," that number being 831:

  1. ALPf (אלף) = 1 + 30 + 800 = 831 = the letter name Aleph written in full, which is the secret Hebrew letter assigned to the Fool

  2. ShMSh LBNH VKVKBIM (שמש לבנה וכוכבים) = (300 + 40 + 300) + (30 + 2 + 50 + 5) + (6 + 20 + 6 + 20 + 2 + 10 + 40) = 640 + 87 +104 = 831 = the phrase "the Sun, Moon, and stars"

- By this same process of gematria, we find that Waite's placement of the Hebrew letter Shin in the yellow eight-spoked circle occupying the lower left hem of the Fool's garment also validates the association of Aleph to Key 0.

  Shin as a letter is valued at 300 (Sh = 300), which is also the value of the phrase "the life breath of the Gods," usually rendered as "the spirit of God," RVCh ALHIM (רוח אלהים) = (200 + 6 + 8) + (1 + 30 + 5 + 10 + 40) = (214) + (86) = 300.

  This "life breath" is the technical phrase in the *Sepher Yetzirah* which is used to describe Aleph as the element Air. Thus Waite is able to secretly allocate Aleph to the life breath (the Fool being in a posture of just inhaling a full breath).

  Further, Shin is the blinded position in which the Fool is placed in the French exoteric Tarot order of Eliphas Levi, falling between Judgment (Key XX) and the World (Key XXI). This is also the position Waite puts the Fool in his own commentary on the Major Arcana.

O

THE FOOL .

Key 0—The Fool

I—The Magician
(Beth = Mercury)

The Qabalistic attribution for the Magician is the Hebrew letter Beth, which is assigned to the planet Mercury. Waite has employed the following symbolism to encode this Mercurial nature of the Hebrew letter Beth:

- The background color of yellow is the correct color for Beth as Mercury in the Golden Dawn correspondences. The actual shape of the garden of flowers above and below suggests the shape of the Hebrew letter Beth.

- The traditional number associated with Mercury is eight (as the planetary magick square for Mercury). Waite encodes this Mercurial number in the figure eight tilted on its side above the Magician's head.

- Waite points out in his own comment to this key that the figure eight used in his Tarot design is the number of Christ. By the process of gematria, the letter Beth, Mercury, Jesus, and the number 8 are all interconnected, and symbolized in the infinity sign hovering over the Magician's head:

1. Eight is the station of the Tree of Life assigned to Mercury as the eighth Sephirah, Hod.

2. 88 is the value of one spelling of Thoth (Mercury) in Greek: $\Theta O \Theta = 9 + 70 + 9 = 88$.

3. 818 is the value of the alternate spelling of Thoth (Mercury) in Greek:

   $\Theta \Omega \Theta = 9 + 800 + 9 = 818$. 818 is also the value in Hebrew for the phrase ATh HBITh (אַת הבּית) ([1+400] + [5+2+10+400] = 818), the letter Beth, the house as the sacred temple.

4. 888 is obtained when the letter omicron precedes Thoth as $O \Theta \Omega \Theta = (70) + (9 + 800 + 9) = 888$. $O \Theta \Omega \Theta$ is the God Mercury, which as 888 is the model for the name Jesus as $IH\Sigma OY\Sigma$ ($10 + 8 + 200 + 70 + 400 + 200 = 888$).

   Therefore in the placing of the figure eight nimbus above the Magician's head, the following Qabalistic formula is encoded:

   8 = Mercury

   88 = Mercury (Thoth)

   818 = Mercury, the Temple (Beth)

   888 = Mercury, Jesus

Key I—The Magician

II—The High Priestess
(Gimel = The Moon)

The Qabalistic attribution for the High Priestess is the Hebrew letter Gimel, which is assigned to the Moon. Waite places the following clues to bring out this lunar association:

- The most obvious key is the crescent Moon cradled in the flowing water-like robe of the priestess. This clearly allocates this key to the Moon. It should be remembered that the esoteric order for the seven planets is the great mystery of the Hebrew alphabet, which no version of the *Sepher Yetzirah* gives in its complete form. This is the order upon which the Tarot depends for its correct Qabalistic attributes. Mathers rediscovered this order by rectifying the initial research of Levi, and Waite in drawing this Tarot deck faithfully adhered to the astrological symbolism established by Mathers.

- The veil behind the High Priestess is emblazoned with pomegranates and palm trees arranged in the shape of the Tree of Life. The actual position which Key II (as Gimel) occupies on the Tree of Life is indicated by the placement of the priestess' crown and head: The top pomegranate on the veil is the position of Kether, the first Sephirah, while the solar cross on the breast of the priestess is the position of Tiphereth, the sixth Sephirah. Therefore the path of Gimel spans the crown, head, and throat of the priestess.

- A further key is found in another of the Major Arcana cards. This card is Key XVIII—The Moon, which is assigned to the sign Pisces, rather than the Moon, in the *Sepher Yetzirah*.

Confusion over whether Key II or Key XVIII should be the astrological attribute of the Moon has tempted many commentators to allocate the Moon to Key XVIII rather than Key II. By placing the crescent Moon in Key II (which traditionally appears instead at the foot of the Empress in Key III), Waite draws to our attention that it is Key II which must be allocated to the Moon.

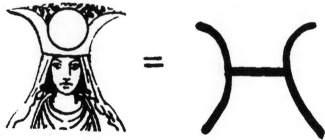

Veiled Crown of Pisces

And as a very subtle symbol, the headdress of the High Priestess in its graphic design suggests the astrological correspondence for Key XVIII The Moon: the headdress as two crescent horns and appended veils

Key II—The High Priestess

graphically encodes the Zodiacal symbol for Pisces, which is two crescent
Moons joined by an horizontal line.

Therefore the Qabalistic-astrological attibutes of the *Sepher Yetzirah*
are reinforced, showing:

Key II = Gimel = The Moon
Key XVIII = Qoph = Pisces

III—The Empress
(Daleth = Venus)

The Qabalistic attribution for the Empress is the Hebrew letter Daleth,
which is assigned to the planet Venus. Waite encodes this Venusian key in
the following ways:

- The most blatant key is the shield of the Empress emblazoned with
  the Zodiacal sign for Venus (a circle surmounting a cross). This symbol is also incorporated in both the designs decorating the robe of the
  Empress and the needlework of her pillows.

  Such apparent use of the well-guarded secrets of the Tarot
  clearly shows us that Waite firmly believed in Mathers' corrected
  secret order, and wished to communicate this order to the general
  public by decorating his revised Tarot deck with hieroglyphic clues.

- The wheat in the foreground, and grain in general, is sacred to Ceres,
  a Greek manifestation of Venus. The grove of trees in the background is also sacred to Venus, as are the pearls around the neck of
  the Empress.

- Though the direct use of an astrological symbol for Venus is enough
  conclusive evidence, Waite further describes the Qabalistic
  attributes of Daleth (the Hebrew letter corresponding to Venus) in a
  very telling passage in his commentary on Key III:

  > In another order of ideas, the card of the Empress signifies
  > the door or gate by which an entrance is obtained into this
  > life, as into the Garden of Venus.

We could not ask for a more explicit Qabalah, for each of the letters of
the Hebrew alphabet is also a name which serves as a hieroglyphic image.
Daleth (whose Greek equivalent is Delta, the triangle) is the letter name
for a door, gate, or tent flap, and is symbolic of the womb or door of the
mother through which life issues.

Key III—The Empress

IV—The Emperor
(Heh = Aries)

The Qabalistic attribution for the Emperor is the Hebrew letter Heh, which is assigned to the first sign of the Zodiac, Aries. Waite encodes this Zodiacal secret in the following ways:

- The traditional image of the Zodiacal sign Aries is the ram. Waite ornaments the throne of the Emperor with four rams' heads to firmly identify this key with Aries.

- The graphic image for Aries is based on the shape of the two horns of the ram. This image is emblazoned on the left shoulder of the Emperor, although only half seen.

- Each sign of the Zodiac rules a part of the human body. Aries rules the head, and Waite crowns the Emperor's head with a helmet whose apex is capped by the graphic symbol for Aries.

- The predominant use of the color red in this key is in conformance with the Golden Dawn color scale for Aries (as well as Mars, the planetary ruler for Aries). The yellow and orange correspond in this case to the Sephirah and Path for the Sun (the planetary exaltation for Aries). Waite is very blatant in his use of Zodiacal symbolism in this key, for he realized that in his revised secret order for the Tarot the key of the Emperor, rather than the key of the Hierophant, would be the first card to correspond to a sign of the Zodiac. Therefore, he loaded this first Zodiacal card so as to guide the reader to the truth of the matter.

Key IV—The Emperor

V—The Hierophant
(Vav = Taurus)

The Qabalistic attribution for the Hierophant is the Hebrew letter Vav, assigned to the Zodiac sign Taurus. Waite incorporates this secret Key as follows:

- Though Waite has been obvious in symbolizing Key IV as Aries, Key V is not as transparent in its Zodiacal symbolism. Waite's intention is to place a few concrete clues and many minor hints scattered among the 22 cards of the Major Arcana so that the student, armed with the astrological alphabet associations found in the *Sepher Yetzirah*, could solve the secret order for the Tarot.

  Each card holds in its design some clue to its true nature; however, some cards are much more explicit than others. If we look back upon the first five keys, we find that Key 0 and Key I contain only indirect representations of these secret astrological clues. However, Keys II, III, and IV are explicit portrayals of these secret clues:
  Key II = The Moon—The crescent Moon at her feet
  Key III = Venus—The Venus symbol set upon her shield
  Key IV = Aries—The rams' heads on the throne

  With Key V we encounter these secret keys only on a secondary level. Four forms of the Hebrew letter Vav, which rules this key, are placed in this design to establish Key V as the letter Vav, and subsequently the Zodiacal sign Taurus. The four forms are as follows:

  1. The ancient rock Hebrew form of the letter Vav is a yoke resembling our letter Y. It is the shape of the yellow albs, or yokes, found on the two priestly ministers in the foreground. It is also seen in the Hierophant's white stole.

  2. The letter Vav has three transliterations in the Golden Dawn system as English. These three letters, U, V, and W, are the other forms of Vav incorporated in Waite's design for Key V:

     U is seen in the capitals of the two pillars flanking the Hierophant.

     V is seen as the Roman numeral assigned to this key, placed above the Hierophant's head.

     W is seen as the ornament marking the top of the Hierophant's crown. It is directly below the Roman numeral V and is superimposed onto the top tiara of the crown.

- Though the incorporation of the four variants of Vav can clearly be delineated, the second major clue in this key is a stylized form of the Zodiacal sign for Taurus (which is a circle crowned by an upturned crescent), which may not be as easy to recognize.

  This clue is incorporated in the arched back of the throne. They are placed on the level of the Hierophant's ears, and are on either side. They are the two dotted circles found centered in the curl of the

Key V—The Hierophant

arch. Attached at an angle to each of these dotted circles is a crescent Moon, and the combination of the crescent and circle is the
graphic shape for Taurus.

- In terms of color symbolism the red-orange of both the Hierophant's
  robe and dais is the correct Golden Dawn attribution for the Hebrew
  letter Vav as Taurus. The planetary ruler for Taurus is Venus, symbolized by the acolyte's green robes embroidered with flowers. The
  planetary exaltation for Taurus is the Moon, symbolized by the Hierophant's blue inner garments.

VI—The Lovers
(Zain = Gemini)

The Qabalistic attribution for the Lovers is the Hebrew letter Zain,
assigned to the Zodiacal sign Gemini. However, if one is conversant in the
magickal tradition of the Golden Dawn, one will be at once struck with the
fact that an archangel has been substituted for cupid, which usually
appears hovering above the lovers in the traditional design for this card.

The archangel portrayed in this key is Raphael, archangel of the East
and the element Air.

This Golden Dawn tradition assigns an archangel to each of the four
directions based on the element that governs each quarter. As Waite has
utilized Raphael for Key VI, three other Tarot keys conceal the other three
archangels. The following table will illustrate these analogies:

Archangels of the Four Quarters

Archangel	Direction	Element	Major Arcana	Symbol of Element
Raphael	East	Air	VI—The Lovers	Clouds below archangel
Michael	South	Fire	XIV—Temperance	Solar orb on brow of archangel
Gabriel	West	Water	XX—Judgement	Ocean below archangel
Auriel	North	Earth	XV—The Devil	Black background and brown body

These Golden Dawn directional-elemental correspondences are
derived from the Enochian system of magick rather than from the
Qabalah. The allocations of specific archangels to the Major Arcana is
Waite's invention, and is also used in the Tarot deck of Paul Foster Case.

In terms of the main figures in the foreground of this card, Waite
reduced the traditional three figures (one male and two females) to a male
and female couple. There are other cards that deal with couples, yet this is
the one key intended to designate the twins of Gemini. Since Waite

Key VI—The Lovers

removed the solar twins in his revision of Key XIX—The Sun (a key which invariably has been confused with Gemini because of the twins in that key), the two lovers in Key VI are the central secret key to allocate this card to its proper Zodiacal sign of Gemini. Waite's revision of Key VI also allows a direct parallel with Key XV—The Devil, his own version being a diabolized version of Key VI.

As to any other direct reference to the Hebrew letter Zain assigned to this key, after much search and contemplation one must admit there is none.

The revision of the Lovers by Waite, which Case retained in his own version of this key, reduces the three central figures in the traditional design by one. The traditional version shows a central male figure at a crossroads, surrounded by two women (one virtue and the other vice) on either side. Above, Cupid shoots his arrow downward, the target of his love arrow varying in each distinct design. By reducing these three lovers to two, as Adam and Eve, we have the one overt clue of this card, the original twins as Gemini.

Case attempted to correct Waite's wanderings from the traditional designs for the Major Arcana. In both Keys XIII and XIX, Case corrected Waite's design format to resemble the more traditional depictions of Death and the Sun. However, Case did not revert Waite's design back to its original image for the Lovers, for he was too enamored with the Qabalistic implications of this revision.

One more bit of information concerning Case's own Tarot deck should be mentioned now, as his designs were based on the designs first established by Waite. Case in redesigning Waite's Major Arcana clearly indicated upon each card the Golden Dawn allocation of the Hebrew alphabet. Case's own designs for the Major Arcana, the Court Cards, and the four Aces were all directly derived from the designs drawn by Pamela Colman Smith for the Waite deck. However, when it came to the Minor Arcana cards from 2 to 10 in each of the four suits, Case imitated the older designs that had no picture image for any of these pip cards. In reading Case's writings on the Tarot, it is apparent that his one aim was to clarify the Qabalistic symbolism which was hinted at, but ultimately obscured, in Waite's designs.

Waite's version of Key VI is his greatest departure from the traditional designs for the Tarot. There is no historical equivalent for Waite's revision, and at first glance it resembles a traditional depiction of the Garden of Eden. Where Waite sacrifices the inherent meanings of the older designs for the Lovers, in his radical revision Waite has also secretly illustrated Qabalistic gematria concerning the nature of Man and Woman. The apparent numbers encoded are 311, 45, 666, and 13, as well as a variety of minor numbers which will not be detailed at this time. The following is a partial analysis of these numbers as symbols within Key VI (which Waite never divulged in his published writings, but which are implicit in his unique design).

- The number 311 is encoded in the triad formed by the angel, man, and woman, for 311 is the value of the following words in Hebrew:
  1. RPAL (רפאל, 200 + 80 + 1 + 30 = 311)—The name Raphael, the

archangel pictured in Key VI, the archangel of Mercury (the planetary ruler of Gemini), and sometimes of the Sun, which is behind the Angel in Waite's design.

2. AISh (אי״ש, 1 + 10 + 300 = 311)—The man, Adam on the right

3. HAShH (האשה, 5 + 1 + 300 + 5 = 311)—The woman, Eve on the left

And 311 is also the value in Hebrew of the word ShIA (שיא, 300 + 10 + 1 = 311), which means to be equal, equivalent, as well as summit, climax, peak. In this aspect, ShIA represents the mountain peak in the background. It is a flow chart depicting the orgasms of the two lovers, which brings the two into one and dissolves into none.

• The number 45 is encoded in the triangle formed by the angel, man, and woman as well as the radiant Sun behind the angel, for 45 is the value of the following Hebrew words:

1. ADM (אדם, 1 + 4 + 40 = 45)—Adam, the name of the first man as well as humanity in general.

2. IHVH + ChVH (חוה + יהוה, [10 + 5 + 6 + 5] + [8 + 6 + 5] = 26 + 19 = 45)— God (Yahweh) and Eve—Here the addition of Yahweh to Eve is equal to Adam as the Qabalistic formula 26 + 19 = 45.

As Adam indicates the male in the lower right of Key VI, Eve is the female in the lower left, while Yahweh is symbolized by the archangel (since the four archangels each symbolize one of the four sacred letters of IHVH in the order of Michael, Gabriel, Raphael, and Auriel). Adam looks into Eve's eyes and beholds God. This tantrik belief is shown mathematically as:

IHVH (יהוה)
(God = 26)

ChVH (חוה)   ADM (אדם)
(Eve = 19)   (Adam = 45)

In support of this secret doctrine Waite has the Sun behind the angel radiating 45 rays to bring attention to this special Qabalistic number.

• The number 666 is shown overtly in three ways in Key VI:

1. As the 12 threefold flames of the Tree of Life behind Adam

2. As the fruits of the Tree of the Knowledge of Good and Evil behind Eve

3. As the Sun above the angel

The 12 flames of the Tree of Life behind Adam are in the shape of the triple flame, which was embroidered upon the Fool's blouse in Key 0. Since these 12 flames are each triple-tongued, there is a total of 36 flames composing this tree. And the sum of 1 through 36 is 666,

(Σ [1-36] = 666). Therefore this fiery Tree of Life conceals in its flames the solar number 666.

The number 666 as the fruits of the Tree (of the Knowledge of Good and Evil) is shown in the original Hebrew description found in the third chapter of Genesis, for 666 is the value of the following two phrases:

AThH HMN HOTz (העץ המן אתה‎, [1 + 400 + 5] + [5 + 40 + 50] + [5 + 70 + 90] = 406 + 95 + 165 = 666) = Hast thou eaten of the tree (Gen. 3:11)

KALHIMf (כאלהים‎, 20 + 1 + 30 + 5 + 10 + 600 = 666) = To be as God (as Elohim) (Gen. 3:5)

The first phrase is God's prohibition to Adam and Eve in partaking of the fruit of the Tree of the Knowledge of Good and Evil, while the second phrase is the results of partaking of this fruit, to become as Gods. Both phrases are implied in the fruit tree behind Eve. These two citations are the first two occurences of the number 666 in the Old Testament.

The Sun above the angel's head is valued at 666 in the original Hebrew, as well as the Sun and the angel (as God). In Hebrew, the following three examples are each valued at 666.

SVRTh (סורת‎, 60 + 6 + 200 + 400 = 666)—The Sun, especially the Sun at noon; also the spirit of the solar magick square (the 36 numbered squares of which total to 666)

IHVH ShMSh (שמש יהוה‎, [10 + 5 + 6 + 5] + [300 + 40 + 300] = 2 + 640 = 666)—God (Yahweh) + The Sun, the Solar God, the Sun as a symbol of one God; rearranged this becomes ShM IHShVH (יהשוה שם‎) (holy name Jesus)

ShMSh KBD (כבד שמש‎, [300 + 40 + 300] + (20 + 2 + 4) = 640 + 26 = 666) —the Sun's glory, the rays radiating from the Sun in Key VI

All the above are encoded in the yellow radiating Sun rising to the zenith above Raphael's head.

There is one more relevant Qabalistic formula for 666 which applies to this card, and it is connected with the Hebrew letter Zain. Zain is the letter name for a sword, and the archetypal sword in the Qabalah is the flaming sword described in Genesis, whose zig-zag pattern forms the Tree of Life. In Genesis 3:24, God places this flaming sword east of Eden to protect the garden. This flaming sword in the original Hebrew is valued at 666:

VATh LHT HChRB (החרב להט ואת‎, [6 + 1 + 400] + [30 + 5 + 9] + [5 + 8 + 200 + 2] = 407 + 44 + 215 = 666 = a flaming sword (Gen. 3:24). This is the third occurence of 666 in the Old Testament.

• The number 13 is secretly encoded in Key VI by Waite in a very subtle way which may be hard to detect. Emeshed in the folds of the violet fabric which clothes Raphael are the faces of a lion and a serpent. The lion is on the right, the serpent on the left. The lion's face is seen

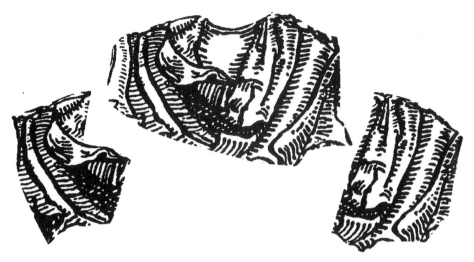

The angel's serpent (left) and lion (right)

in three-quarters perspective, facing left, while the serpent is facing right with an open mouth revealing its fangs. Case faithfully copied this hidden Zodiacal symbol in his own version of this key, but neither Waite nor Case mention this subtle symbolism.

The lion and serpent are Zodiacal symbols which, when combined, total to the number 13. The lion is Leo, the fifth sign of the Zodiac, while the serpent is Scorpio, the eighth sign of the Zodiac. Together their positions within the Zodiacal wheel total to 13 as 5 + 8 = 13. And 13 in Hebrew is the value of the following two key concepts:

AHBH (אהבה, 1 + 5 + 2 + 5 = 13) = Love, lovers (the title of Key VI)

AChD (אחד, 1 + 8 + 4 = 13) = Unity, one, to be as one, unite

Thus 13 represents in relationship to Key VI, the binding power of love, which unites two lovers as one. Further, in the Tarot 13 is the number for Death, which is ruled by Scorpio.

The magickal energy of love can therefore be represented by the lion and the serpent. Waite also shows this energy in his Minor Arcana, in the 2 of Cups (a card traditionally denoting love) as a winged lion's head (combining the wings of an eagle as Scorpio with the head of a lion as Leo).

It should be noted that in Crowley's alchemical symbolism for the sexual force (as used in the workings of the O.T.O.) the union of Leo and Scorpio is used as two separate symbols:

1. The male and female magickal sexual currents are represented by a white lion (Leo as male) and a red eagle (Scorpio as female) as are the genitalia.

2. The secret seed of sexual magick is the lion-headed serpent (combining the lion of Leo and the serpent of Scorpio).

VII—The Chariot
(Cheth = Cancer)

The Qabalistic attribution for the Chariot is the Hebrew letter Cheth, which is assigned to the Zodiacal sign Cancer, ruled by the Moon. Waite works in this lunar Zodiacal symbolism as follows:

- This first bit of lunar symbolism is obscured in many editions of this deck. It is found in the belt buckle of the Charioteer, which is draped across his tunic. This buckle highlights five symbols on this tunic, and two of them are the astrological graphic symbols for Cancer and the Moon.

- The most obvious reference to the sign Cancer, or more appropriately the lunar planetary ruler for Cancer, is the two lunar faces which serve as epaulettes for the Charioteer's armor. They are waxing and waning Moons, representing joy and sorrow. By their isolated appearance they could denote the sign Pisces, or the planetary Moon, as well as Cancer. But, since Waite has already established Key II as the Moon, this card is the Zodiac sign of Cancer, as Key XVIII is the sign of Pisces.

Breastplate of Pisces

- In the collar of the Charioteer's breastplate and the grooves for the arms is concealed the graphic shape for the Zodiac sign of Pisces, resembling the veiled crown of the High Priestess in Key II. This is intentional, and its purpose is to aid the student in the following lunar astrological attributions:

Key II—The High Priestess = The Moon
Key VII—The Chariot = Cancer (ruled by the Moon)
Key XVIII—The Moon = Pisces (though outwardly titled the Moon)

- The Hebrew letter assigned to the Chariot is Cheth, which, as the letter name ChITh (חית), means a fence, wall, or enclosure, as well as the wild beasts of the field. Both images are used in Waite's version of Key VII:

  1. The wall in the background enclosing the city is a direct reference to Cheth as a wall, fence, or enclosure. The chariot, as well as the armor of the charioteer, also serve as symbols of that which encloses.

Key VII—The Chariot

    2. The two sphinxes as the animals which draw the cart of the chariot are direct references to Cheth as the wild beasts, or animals, of the field. The substitution of sphinxes for the more traditional image of horses was first used by Eliphas Levi in his version of this key.

- Cancer as a Zodiacal animal is the crab, whose shell is both a moveable house, symbolized by the wheeled chariot, and protective armor, symbolized by the charioteer's breastplate.

- The star-studded canopy draped over the chariot is an indirect reference to Cancer. Since Cancer is the only Zodiacal sign that is governed by the Moon, which is the ruler of the night sky, the canopy itself suggests the Moon's nocturnal influence.

On a Qabalistic level the Hebrew letter assigned to Key VII, Cheth, is the 18th Path on the Tree of Life. The governing intelligence for this path is "The House of Influence," which is the astrological fate or influence from the stars of the night sky. This is suggested in the starred blue canopy arching over the charioteer as the influence of the night sky.

VIII—Strength
(Teth = Leo)

The Qabalistic attribution for Strength is the Hebrew letter Teth, which is assigned to the Zodiacal sign Leo. The red lion in this key is the obvious Zodiacal symbol for Leo, but Strength is usually the eleventh rather than the eighth key.

Waite places Strength as Key VIII and Justice as Key XI. This switch had never appeared in a printed Tarot deck before Waite's edition of the Tarot, but it seems to have appeared in many subsequent versions. Waite justifies this switch in his evasive commentary concerning this key:

> For reasons which satisfy myself, this card has been interchanged with that of Justice, which is usually numbered eight. As the variation carries nothing with it which will signify to the reader, there is no cause for explanation.

This exchange is solely the inspiration of S. L. MacGregor Mathers. It is made in accordance with the Qabalistic attributions of the Tarot. That Waite adopted Mathers' secret order is tantamount proof that Waite secretly encoded the Qabalistic genius of Mathers in his own Tarot deck.

Mathers premised that, if the Fool is placed before Key I (at the beginning of the deck) and Key VIII and Key XI (traditionally Justice and Strength) are exchanged, then the astrological attributions outlined in the *Sepher Yetzirah* would perfectly match the picture images of the 22 keys of the Major Arcana.

By this order, the Tarot key numbered VIII would be allocated to Leo, while the key numbered XI would be allocated to Libra. The traditional astrological image for Leo is the lion, and for Libra the scales. If we compare

Key VIII—Strength

these images to those used in traditional designs of Keys VIII and XI, we discover that they are counterchanged.

Therefore, in order to get complete harmony between the cards and the Hebrew alphabet, Mathers premised that the old, exoteric order was blinded, and the correct order would exchange Key VIII with Key XI, allowing Strength to be numbered VIII (and aligned to Teth as Leo) and Justice to be numbered XI (and aligned to Lamed as Libra).

That Waite adopted this switch, giving no explanantion for it to the reader, is further proof that Mathers, and not Waite himself, created the design pattern for Waite's deck. As to the secret key Waite encoded in this card, the switch with Justice is itself the key.

As a subtle clue Waite worked into the curls of the lion's mane stylized Zodiacal signs for Leo as further indication of the astrological nature of this key.

IX—The Hermit
(Yod = Virgo)

The Qabalistic attribution for the Hermit is the Hebrew letter Yod, assigned to the Zodiacal sign Virgo. Though this key holds no blatant clue, there are certain hints to this Zodiacal correspondence:

- The star within the lamp is six-sided, bringing to mind the number six. Virgo, the secret astrological sign for this key, is the sixth sign in a series of 12 Zodiacal signs.

- The shape of the corresponding Hebrew letter Yod is suggested by the cap or hood that crowns the Hermit's head. Though this is only implied in Waite's design, Case in his own revision of this key substituted this cap with a clear rendition of the letter Yod.

- The letter Yod is also the initial letter of the word Jehovah. Jehovah is sometimes portrayed as a bearded elder known as the Ancient of Days, which is Waite's model for the hermit himself. Waite points out in his comment to this key that the Hermit is a combination of "The Ancient of Days" with "The Light of the World."

- Yod as a letter name means the hand as a fist (or pointer). Both of the hermit's hands suggest in their shape this letter Yod.

- The solitary, erect posture of the hermit, the upright staff he holds in his left hand, the folds of his robe, and the mountain peaks in the background and foreground all are phallic references, which connect directly with the Qabalistic attributes of Yod. The shape of Yod symbolizes the sperm as well as the seed, while in the *Sepher Yetzirah* Yod is given the attribution of sexual intercourse.

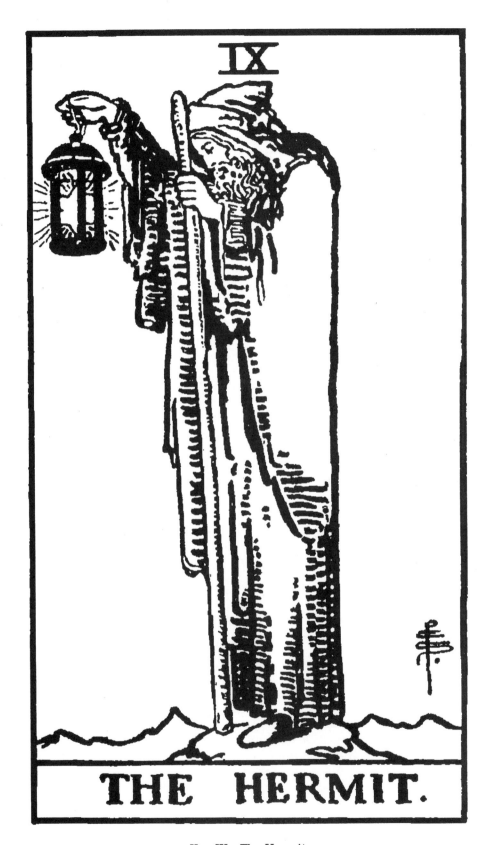

IX

THE HERMIT.

Key IX—The Hermit

X—The Wheel of Fortune
(Kaph = Jupiter)

The Qabalistic attribution for the Wheel of Fortune is the Hebrew letter Kaph, assigned to the planet Jupiter. This is another key which contains no explicit clues. However, with the aid of the *Sepher Yetzirah,* this card must be a planet, because the letter Kaph is one of the seven double letters. The following clues help make this Jupiterian identification:

- Jupiter, the planet assigned to this key, is the God of the sky, thunderbolts, and rainstorms. The inclusion of the billowing clouds in the four corners of this card (a detail not found in traditional decks) is a symbolic reference to Jupiter. The sky blue color as the predominant background of this card is also Jupiterian in nature (being one of two traditional colors for Jupiter, the other being violet).

- The jackal-headed human (the Hermanubis) in its shape suggests the Zodiacal sign for Jupiter as a combination of a crescent and a cross. The arched back of the figure is the crescent, while the crossed legs are the cross.

- The four Kerubic Angels, which drive Ezekiel's heavenly chariot, are placed on the four corners of this key to allude to the number four as Jupiter. As a Sephirah on the Tree of Life, Jupiter is allocated to the fourth number (the magick square of 4 x 4 squares being that of Jupiter). And the summation of the first four numbers totals to ten, the number of this Tarot card (Σ [1-4] =10).

These four Kerubic Angels also encode the four sacred letters of the Tetragrammaton, as follows:

Fourfold Golden Dawn Kerubic Formula

Kerub	Tetragrammaton	Element	Direction	Zodiac	Order
Lion	Yod (10)	Fire	Lower Right	Leo	5th
Eagle	Heh (5)	Water	Upper Right	Scorpio	8th
Man	Vav (6)	Air	Upper Left	Aquarius	11th
Bull	Heh final (5)	Earth	Lower Left	Taurus	2nd

The correlation of element and direction is Enochian in origin, derived from the four quadrants of Dee's Enochian Watchtowers, while the association of the Tetragrammaton and the element/Zodiac is Qabalistic in origin. Note that the specific order of the four Zodiac signs equals the number value for the four letters of the Tetragrammaton: (5 + 8 + 11 + 2) = 26 = (10 + 5 + 6 + 5).

- The design for the wheel in the center of this card is also Jupiterian in nature, in that it is constructed on a fourfold pattern. The pantacle

Key X—The Wheel of Fortune

drawn upon the wheel is not Waite's own design, but rather that of
Eliphas Levi as shown in his work, *The Magical Ritual of the Sanctum
Regnum*. In Levi's original design, four separate sets of four symbols
each were interwoven into the design. These four separate sets of
symbols were the Tetragrammaton, the four Kerubic Angels, the
fourfold Latin word R.O.T.A. (meaning wheel), and four alchemical
symbols (implying the four elements). These four sets came together
on the wheel as follows:

Levi's Fourfold Wheel

ROTA	Kerub	Alchemy	Element	Tetragrammaton
R	Man	Azoth	Water	Yod
O	Bull	Salt	Earth	Heh
T	Eagle	Mercury	Air	Vav
A	Lion	Sulfur	Fire	Heh (final)

These correspondences are not from the Golden Dawn, but rather
from Levi. Azoth is under the sign of Aquarius as a symbol for alchemical
dissolution and represents the agent which can dissolve and recombine
the three alchemical elements.

Levi felt that the formula R.O.T.A. naturally fell to the four letters of the
Tetragrammaton, but secretly regrouped under the formula T.A.R.O. This
is hinted at by placing the letter "T" and the alchemical symbol for Mercury at the top of the wheel.

XI—Justice
(Lamed = Libra)

The Qabalistic attribution for Justice is the Hebrew letter Lamed, assigned
to the Zodiacal sign Libra. This key is of extreme importance in that Waite
renumbered this card 11, although it is traditionally numbered 8.

Waite encodes the secret atttribute of Libra as follows:

- As pointed out under the commentary for Key VIII, Waite, in accordance with Mathers' secret instructions, switched Key VIII and XI.
  The only motivation for this switch is the establishment of astrological agreement between the Tarot and the Qabalistic Hebrew Alphabet. Therefore, the exchange of Strength for Justice serves as a secret
  key.

  It should be noted that, in Crowley's own *Book of Thoth,* this
  secret swap of Leo with Libra was not fully realized. Though Crowley
  exchanged the proper Hebrew letters so that Teth would be aligned
  with Strength and Lamed would be aligned with Justice, he still associated the Roman numeral VIII with Justice and XI with Strength.

Key XI—Justice

Thus he was only able to realize half of Mathers' Qabalistic vision in modeling his own Tarot deck.

- As a result of Waite's exchange of Justice with Strength, the obvious pictorial clue in this key is the scale pans, the traditional symbol for Libra.

- A very subtle symbol used in this card that reinforces the Libra symbolism is the finger extended on the left hand holding the scale pans. The middle finger of the left hand is intentionally pointing downward (reminiscent of the Magician's left hand). By the Golden Dawn system of allocations, the left middle finger is governed by the planet Venus, and Venus is the planetary ruler of Libra, the Zodiacal sign assigned to Justice.

XII—The Hanged Man
(Mem = Water)

The Qabalistic attribution for the Hanged Man is the Hebrew letter Mem, which is assigned to the element Water. Waite is obscure in his clues to this key. However there are four clues intertwined into this design:

- The color assigned to the Hebrew letter Mem as Water is blue. This is the color of the Hanged Man's tunic.

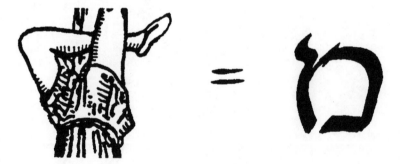

Skirt of Mem

- The actual shape of the Hebrew letter Mem is suggested in the skirt of the blue tunic.

- The Hebrew letter Mem is valued at 40 by the numerical Qabalah. Waite encodes this value as the nimbus or halo around the Hanged Man's head, stylizing this nimbus as 40 rays (though this is intentionally obscured in its rendition).

- The elemental sigil for Water is the downward pointing triangle. Waite has incorporated this graphic image in three ways:

Key XII—The Hanged Man

1. The tree, which is in the shape of a "T," forms an inverted triangle with its branches and trunk.

2. The crossed legs of the Hanged Man are in the shape of a inverted triangle.

3. The two bent elbows and haloed head of the Hanged Man trace an inverted triangle.

XIII—Death
(Nun = Scorpio)

The Qabalistic attribution for Death is the Hebrew letter Nun assigned to the Zodiacal sign Scorpio. This version is Waite's second major departure from all previous traditional designs (his first being the Lovers). His reconstruction of this key, unlike his version of Key VI, contains no extensive Qabalah, and Case's own correction of Waite's design is by far richer in esotericism.

However, this is one of the few Major Arcana keys that in any version immediately becomes verifiable by Mathers' Qabalistic Tarot order, because Death is equivalent to Scorpio in astrology, especially as the house of death in the 12 Zodiacal houses of a horoscope.

Thus Waite's mounted skeleton is the secret clue to the identification of Scorpio with this card. The skull and crossbones ornamenting the harness of death's horse is also a reference to Scorpio.

Unique to Waite's own version of this key are three minor symbols:

• The Hebrew letter assigned to this key, Nun, is the hieroglyphic image of a fish. The river flowing in the background (which is in no traditional design of this key) is an indirect reference to this symbolic fish.

• On the Tree of Life, the letter Nun connects the sixth Sephirah with the seventh. The sixth Sephirah is the station for the Sun, while the seventh Sephirah is the station for Venus. Within this card, the Sun rising between the two pylons refers to the Sun as the sixth Sephirah, while the mystic white rose emblazoned on Death's black banner refers to Venus as the seventh Sephirah.

• In most traditional designs for this key, the skeleton of Death moves a scythe in a field that is littered with severed human hands, feet, and heads. But in Waite's version a mounted Death stands before four figures instead of his harvest of corpses. These four figures can be connected to the fourfold family of the Tetragrammaton as shown on page 390.

Key XIII—Death

Death's Fourfold Family

Figure	Family	Tetragrammaton	Element
Prelate	Father	Yod	Fire
Maiden	Mother	Heh	Water
King	Son	Vav	Air
Child	Daughter	Heh (final)	Earth

In this symbolic relationship, only the fiery Yod remains standing in the face of Death, while the other three letters succumb to his force.

XIV—Temperance
(Samekh = Sagittarius)

The Qabalistic attribution for Temperance is the Hebrew letter Samekh, assigned to the Zodiacal sign Sagittarius. Waite's version of this card incorporates two basic clues to connect Temperance with Samekh and Sagittarius, one dealing with mythology and the other dealing with the Qabalistic pattern of the Tree of Life:

- The flowers to the right of the angel are irises, and the Goddess Iris is the goddess of the rainbow. In Hebrew, the word "rainbow" is the same word used to designate the Zodiacal sign of Sagittarius. This word in Hebrew is QShTh (קשת). Therefore, this iris is a clue for the Hebraic Sagittarius, which governs this key under the auspices of the Hebrew letter Samekh.

- The Path on the Tree of Life occupied by Key XIV connects the ninth Sephirah (the station of the Moon) with the sixth Sephirah (the station of the Sun) on the Middle Pillar of the Tree. Above the sixth Sephirah lies the first Sephirah, the symbol of which is the radiant crown. Waite has illustrated this complex pattern for the Tree of LIfe as follows:

  1. The two chalices held by the angel represent the Sun and Moon as the sixth and ninth Sephiroth of the Tree of Life. The blue vibrating water flowing between the two represents the path of Samekh, which connects the Sun and Moon on the Tree of Life.

  2. The pool of water below the angel symbolizes the ninth lunar Sephirah on the Tree of Life, while the solar disc on the head of the angel symbolizes the sixth solar Sephirah. Connecting the water with the Sun is the robed upright body of the angel, being the path of Temperance bridging the Sun and Moon on the Tree. This angel is the archangel Michael, whose station on the Tree of Life is the sixth Sephirah of the Sun.

XIV

TEMPERANCE.

Key XIV—Temperance

3. The path to left of the angel, which rises from the pool to the distant mountains, symbolizes the path of Temperance. The pool is the ninth Sephirah on the Tree of Life, while the distant mountains towards which the Path rises are symbolic of the sixth Sephirah and that which lies beyond the limits of Sun. The crown vaguely seen above the mountain path in radiant glory is symbolic of the first Sephirah (called the Crown) at which the path of Temperance is ultimately aiming.

XV—The Devil
(Ayin = Capricorn)

The Qabalistic attribution for the Devil is the Hebrew letter Ayin assigned to the Zodiacal sign of Capricorn. Waite shows the Zodiacal correspondence as follows:

- The central figure of the Devil is the obvious key symbol. Waite clearly indicates in his commentary to this key that the Devil is indeed "the horned goat," and this is the traditional image for Capricorn. By Mathers' secret order for the Tarot, many of the main figures in the traditional designs for the Major Arcana can be easily identified with their Zodiacal counterparts. Among the most obvious are:

  1. The lion for Leo in Key VIII

  2. The scales for Libra in Key XI

  3. The skeleton for Scorpio in Key XIII

  4. The goat for Capricorn in Key XV

  5. The twin pitchers for Aquarius in Key XVII

- Capricorn's planetary ruler is Saturn, whose astrological sigil is a cross connected above (or to the side) of a crescent. Waite, as a further clue, has inscribed a stylized form of this sign for Saturn in the raised open right hand of the Devil.

- The tail of Eve terminates in 11 grapes, which represent the intoxicating effects of wine. And by the Hebrew Qabalah, both the word for wine (IIN, ןייֵ) and the letter Ayin (O, עַ) are valued at 70 ([10 + 10 + 50] = 70).

- The shoulders, arms, and knees of the Devil, in combination with the chains that bind Adam and Eve, form the oval shape of the Akasa Tattva. By the Golden Dawn Tattva system, this Tattva governs Saturn, the planetary ruler of Capricorn.

Key XV—The Devil

XVI—The Tower
(Peh = Mars)

The Qabalistic attribution for the Tower is the Hebrew letter Peh, assigned to the planet Mars. Waite shows this Martial attribution as follows:

- The astrological sign for Mars is a circle from which an arrow projects. The projecting arrow is stylized in the lightning bolt that strikes the Tower. This is the most blatant clue indicating Mars for this key. Note that Waite has formed the zigzag of this lightning to resemble the flaming sword of the Qabalah, the twistings and turnings of which mark the ten Sephiroth of the Tree of Life. Connecting these ten Sephiroth are the 22 Paths of the Hebrew alphabet, which Waite shows as the 10 plus 12 yellow flames dancing in the jet-black night sky.

- On the Tree of Life, the Tower connects the seventh Sephirah of Venus with the eighth Sephirah of Mercury. These two Sephiroth are symbolized in the two falling figures; the woman on the right is Venus and the seventh Sephirah, while the man on the left is Mercury and the eighth Sephirah. The tower itself is the Path of Peh, which connects these two Sephiroth.

- Mars is the God of battle and destruction, and the embattled, toppling tower which has just caught on fire suggests the destructive force of war.

XVII—The Star
(Tzaddi = Aquarius)

By the commands of Crowley's *Book of the Law,* Tzaddi is not the Star. But by Mathers' secret order derived from the *Sepher Yetzirah,* Tzaddi is indeed the Star. The Qabalistic attribution for the Star is the Hebrew letter Tzaddi, which is assigned to the Zodiacal sign Aquarius. Waite shows this secret as follows:

- The actual central figure in this card serves as the only open clue. Like many of the cards in the Major Arcana, such as Strength and Justice, the traditional image of a naked woman pouring water from two vessels is the open portrayal of the secret astrological attribute for this key: the traditional symbol for Aquarius is a figure bearing two vessels of water which overflow to show their contents.

  Note that this card can only fall to Tzaddi as Aquarius if Aleph is allocated to the Fool card. In the French exoteric order, Tzaddi and Aquarius fall to the Moon, which we will discover is in reality the card for the Zodiacal sign of Pisces.

- On a more esoteric level, Waite's design shows the position Key XVII occupies as a path on the Tree of Life. The Star connects the seventh Sephirah (ruled by Venus) with the ninth Sephirah (ruled by the Moon). This is shown in two ways in this card:

Key XVI—The Tower

1. The purple mountain in the background is the same color as the ninth Sephirah and thus becomes a symbol of this lunar station on the Tree of Life. The green tree on top of the grass-covered hill is the same color as the seventh Sephirah, being a symbol for this Venusian station on the Tree. The rolling plains of grass spanning between this lunar mountain and Venusian tree become the Path of Tzaddi.

2. The pool reflecting the starlight of the night sky is also a symbol for the lunar ninth Sephirah on the Tree of Life, while a beautiful naked woman is the classic image for the Venusian seventh Sephirah. The water flowing from the vessel in her right hand into the depths of the blue pool before her becomes the actual Path of Tzaddi on the Tree.

- The pattern of the eight stars in the night sky shows the plantary ruler for Aquarius. These stars form a crescent Moon crossed by a straight line, suggesting a handled sickle, which is a symbolic image for Saturn. And in the ancient astrological scheme of planetary rulerships, Saturn is the planet which governs Aquarius.

Planetary Stars

The seven lesser planetary stars are never ordered or named by Waite, but they form a specific pattern that can readily reveal their planetary correspondences. These seven stars are arranged as an inverted horseshoe of six stars with a seventh star outside the arc of the other six. The horseshoe of six stars is arranged as two sets of

Key XVII—The Star

three stars each, three on the right and three on the left. From the position of Adam and Eve in the Lovers, the right is male and the left is female.

Thus the three stars on the left are the female planetary Tarot deities of the Moon, Venus, and Saturn as Keys II, III, and XXI, while the three stars on the right are the male planetary Tarot deities of the Sun, Mars, and Jupiter as Keys XIX, XVI, and X. The seventh star becomes the androgynous planet of Mercury as Key I, combining the male and female forces of the other six planets, especially the Sun and Moon.

The Seven Lesser Stars of Key XVII as Planets

Moon (Key II)	Sun (Key XIX)
Venus (Key III)	Mars (Key XVI)
Saturn (Key XXI)	Jupiter (Key X)
Mercury (Key I)	

These seven planetary Tarot cards will appear again in the Minor Arcana in Waite's unique design for the 7 of Cups, but in a different order.

As to the symbolism of the great central star which occupies the eighth position in the scheme of seven lesser white stars, this eight-pointed yellow luminary represents:

1. Mercury as the King of the Planets

2. The Pole Star around which all other stars revolve

3. The star Sirius

4. The eighth sphere of heaven, as the fixed stars of the Zodiac

5. Spirit as the eight-spoked wheel

Tzaddi Ibis

• The shape of the ibis bird perched in the tree behind Isis in the Star conceals in his body the shape of the Hebrew letter Tzaddi, which is assigned to this card, just as the dog in the Fool card is in the corresponding alphabet letter of Aleph.

• As quoted at the beginning of this key, Crowley's own scheme for the Qabalisitic attributes of the Tarot did not allocate the Hebrew letter Tzaddi to the Star. Instead, Crowley placed this key under the Hebrew letter Heh, which in Mathers' pattern rules the Emperor. This swapping of the letter Tzaddi with that of Heh is concealed in Crowley's own *Book of the Law.*

In the 57th verse of the first chapter, the following command is given: "All these old letters of my Book are aright; but צ is not the Star." "These old letters" refers to the Hebrew alphabet, while "my Book" is a reference to the Tarot. While *The Book of the Law* clearly indicates that Tzaddi should not be allocated to the Star, it does not directly tell us which Hebrew letter should be given to this card.

However, the 73rd verse in the third chapter gives a process that will generate the substitute Hebrew letter for Tzaddi. This 73rd verse reads:

"Paste the sheets from right to left and from top to bottom: then behold!"

The sheets are the 22 individual Tarot keys of the Major Arcana as pages of a book, referred to in the 57th verse of the first chapter as "the old letters of my Book." These 22 sheets are arranged from right to left and from top to bottom, which generates the following pattern for the Tarot:

					Right to Left						
Top to	10	9	8	7	6	5	4	3	2	1	0
Bottom	11	12	13	14	15	16	17	18	19	20	21

Converted to the corresponding Hebrew letters, this arragement, dictated by *The Book of the Law,* becomes the familiar Qabalistic substitution alphabet known as AThBSh (אתבש):

K	I	T	Ch	Z	V	H	D	G	B	A
L	M	N	S	O	P	Tz	Q	R	Sh	Th

or:

כ	י	ט	ח	ז	ו	ה	ד	ג	ב	א
ל	מ	נ	ס	ע	פ	צ	ק	ר	ש	ת

By this code, the top line is substituted for the bottom line as an alphabetical cipher. As such, the substitute letter for Tzaddi is Heh, placing the Star under the rulership of the Hebrew letter Heh, while the Emperor would be governed by Tzaddi. Thus in Crowley's Tarot:

Key XVII—The Star = Heh = Aries
Key IV—The Emperor = Tzaddi = Aquarius

Note also that the word "behold," which ends the 73rd verse of the third chapter, is a literal meaning for the Hebrew letter name Heh.

XVIII—The Moon
(Qoph = Pisces)

The Qabalistic attribution for the Moon is the Hebrew letter Qoph, which is assigned to the Zodiacal sign of Pisces. Waite indicates this Piscean attribution for so obvious a lunar card as follows:

- The central image of the Moon is very misleading in establishing the correct astrological correspondence for this key. The allocation obvious to most commentators is the Moon itself, since this card is followed by the Sun. But where the Sun key is in reality the Sun, the Moon key is not the Moon, but Pisces, the last of the 12 signs.

     Again, if Aleph is given to the Fool as the lead card of 22, then the Moon key would automatically fall to the Hebrew letter Qoph, which is the last of 12 simple letters. The 12 simple letters are the 12 signs of the Zodiac.

     As the last simple letter, Qoph becomes the last of 12 Zodiacal signs, which is Pisces.

     Though Waite gives no concrete Piscean clues in this card, he has given us clues elsewhere in the deck:

    1. In The High Priestess, which is the true key to symbolize the Moon, we have already discovered the secret image of Pisces in the veil and headdress of the priestess. This was placed by Waite to help clarify that Key II is in reality the Moon, while Key XVIII is Pisces. The predominant Moon in Key XVIII thus serves as a link back to Key II.

    2. In the Chariot, we discovered that the breastplate of the charioteer concealed in its shape the sign for Pisces. Since the Chariot is Cancer, ruled by the Moon, the inclusion of Pisces was again intended to clarify that Key XVIII is not the Moon, but Pisces. And the Cancerian crayfish emerging out of the depths in Key XVIII is a link back to Key VII.

- The Hebrew letter Qoph, assigned to Key XVIII, as a hieroglyphic image represents the back of the head, and is assigned to the process of sleep in the *Sepher Yetzirah*. The actual representation of the Moon's face in Key XVIII emphasizes the back of the head. Further, the nighttime image of this card as well as the closed left lunar eye in the face of the Moon are symbols for sleep.

- The two towers through which the path of Key XVIII winds its way are a graphic portrayal of the Tree of Life. This winding yellow path is the Middle Pillar of the Tree (composed of Sephiroth 1, 6, 9, and 10). The tower on the right is the Pillar of Mercy (composed of Sephiroth 2, 4, and 7), while the tower on the left is the Pillar of Severity (composed of Sephiroth 3, 5, and 8).

     By the process of gematria, the Zodiac sign of Pisces is shown in these two towers. The Biblical symbol for the Pillars of Mercy and Severity (which these two towers symbolize) is "the pillars of fire and

THE MOON.

Key XVIII—The Moon

smoke." The number value of this phrase is the same as that of Pisces in Hebrew, which is the number 617:

OMVDI HASh VHONN (עמודי האש והענן, the Pillars of Fire and Smoke) = 617 = DGIMf (דגים, Pisces)

(70 + 40 + 6 + 4 + 10) + (5 + 1 + 300) + (6 + 5 + 70 + 50 + 50) = 617 = (4 + 3 + 10 + 600)

XIX—The Sun
(Resh = The Sun)

The Qabalistic attribution for the Sun is the Hebrew letter Resh, which is also assigned to the Sun. Unlike the Moon key (which is in reality Pisces), the Sun key is directly related to the planet it portrays. This is a deep secret in Mathers' Qabalah for the Tarot.

Waite's version of this key is again at variance with most traditional designs for this key. Where most keys show a naked boy and girl standing arm and arm before a blazing Sun, Waite has substituted the Fool as a naked child astride a horse while holding a flaming solar red banner in his left hand. Waite used as a model for this key certain rare Spanish and Italian Tarots dating from the 18th century, which show an armed mounted warrior on a galloping steed holding in one hand a scarlet banner (which sometimes bears the heraldic device of a white cross).

Two reasons come to mind for Waite's choice of this obscure variation for Key XIX:

- The Sun is often given the erroneous astrological attribution of Gemini, based on the twin children usually drawn in this key. By removing the twins and replacing them with one child upon a horse, the tendency to view this card as Gemini is diminished. And in Waite's design for the Lovers, the true card for Gemini, the traditional three figures of two men and one woman have been reduced to a male and female couple which can serve as a symbolic key for Gemini.

- In ancient Germanic rune lore, one specific rune letter typifies the association of a horse to the Sun itself, the rune Ehwaz (ᛗ). This rune is the 19th rune in the Elder Futhark rune order and is the symbolic image of a horse, whose galloping strength suggests the course of the Sun through the day sky. Waite saw much Celtic influence in the symbolism of the Tarot, and may indeed have been aware of this runic symbolism and its connection to his own design for Key XIX.

The real key to the correct astrological attribution for this key is the radiating Sun itself. For although the Moon is Pisces in the Tarot, the Sun is always the Sun.

Additional clues reinforcing this solar symbolism are:

- The yellow, full human face of the Sun alludes to the Hebrew letter Resh, which is assigned to this key. Resh as a letter-name means

THE SUN .

Key XIX—The Sun

head, face, or aspect. Also, the Sun as a Sephirah on the Tree of Life is the sixth, which is traditionally colored yellow.

- The orange banner held by the child is the hieroglyphic shape for the ancient rock Hebrew form of Resh. The original shape of Resh was a flag, or standard, derived from the Egyptian hieroglyph for "One God." The orange color itself is the Golden Dawn color scale for the path of Resh on the Tree of Life.

- The six flowers wreathed in the yellow hair of the child are also solar symbols. Six is also the number of the sixth Sephirah on the Tree of Life, which corresponds to the Sun. This sixth Sephirah is also the station for the child (or son) of the Qabalistic royal family (corresponding to the four kings in the Court Card series). This is one reason why Waite reduced the usual two children in this card to one male child.

- The four sunflowers on the wall behind the horse and child are obvious tokens of the Sun. They follow the Sun in its orbit, and are solar in shape and color (yellow being the color of the Sephirah and orange the color of the Path for the Sun).

Their original name in Hebrew is ShMShVN (שמשון), which is also the proper name for Samson and is based on the Hebrew root ShMSh (שמש), a word for the Sun.

Resh Mane

- Though less obvious a clue, the mane of the gray horse in Key XIX conceals the graphic shape of the Hebrew letter Resh in its forelock.

Thus Waite clearly establishes that The Sun key is indeed the Sun, just as he deliberately placed the Moon at the feet of the Priestess to establish that The High Priestess is indeed the Moon.

XX—Judgement
(Shin = Fire)

The Qabalistic attribution for Judgement is the Hebrew letter Shin, assigned to the element Fire. In the Golden Dawn Shin is also the alternate attribution of Spirit, when combined with the Tetragrammaton of IHVH (יהוה) to form the Pentagrammaton of IHShVH (יהשוה, the Rosicrucian formula for Jesus in Hebrew).

Waite encodes the Hebrew letter Shin as follows:

- The Hebrew letter Shin is graphically a three-pronged flame. Qabalistically each of the three tongues of flame is one of the family unit Father, Mother, and Child. This is clearly illustrated in the three foreground figures of a child between a man and a woman. The woman is standing in the shape of the Latin letter L, the child in the shape of the Latin letter V, and the man in the shape of the Latin letter X, forming the word LVX, which is "light" in Latin. Here the concept of white light is associated with Fire as Spirit.

Man, woman, and child in Judgement card

- The attitude of the child's upraised hands and head, as well as the three figures in the background, take the shape of the Hebrew letter Shin as three Yods or points radiating from a central base.

- The head and wings of the angel in this key also conceal in their shape the letter Shin, the head being the middle prong of the trident shape while each wing is the extreme left or right prong.

- The scarlet cross on the white banner, the red wings of the angel, and the red and yellow flames of the angel's hair are all symbolic of Shin as the element Fire.

- The white banner with a red cross on the trumpet is patterned on the magick square for Mars, which is composed of 25 squares. The red cross outlines nine of the squares, while the four white corners outline the other 16 squares. Mars as the red planet is the planet assigned to element Fire, the elemental quality of Key XX. And the central point of this red solar cross corresponds to the number 13 at the center of the Mars square, bringing to mind the Death key.

- A great paradox exists in the symbolism of this card, for although it is the element Fire by its Hebrew letter, watery symbolism abounds in this card. Gabriel is in the sky above the clouds, the archangel of Water, rather than Michael, the archangel of Fire. The coffins are floating upon a great expanse of blue water, while a mountain of ice rises in the background.

  This counterchange of Fire and Water is concealed in two words in Hebrew, both starting with the Hebrew letter Shin:

  1. Shin begins the classic word for the fiery Sun, ShMSh (שמש). As the letter Shin is the element Fire, Mem is the element Water. Thus the Sun shows the elemental cycle of Fire, Water, and Fire, showing that at the center of Fire is Water, at the center of Yang is Yin.

  2. Shin is the first letter of the word for sky, or heaven, ShMIMf (שמים). Here the word for heaven is made up of a combination of fire and water as Sh + MIMf (ש + מים) = Sh (ש, the letter Shin as Fire) + MIMf (מים, the letter name for Mem as water). This heaven, or sky, is the great sky-blue expanse behind the archangel in Key XX. This is also reminiscent of the doctrine of the afterlife in the *Zohar,* in which all souls are purified by journeying six months in fire and six months in ice.

XXI—The World
(Tav = Saturn)

The Qabalistic attribution for the World is the Hebrew letter Tav. This correpondence is the only agreement between the Tarot cards and the Hebrew alphabet in both the exoteric French Qabalistic order and the esoteric English Qabalistic order. The French order leads with Aleph as the Magician, while the English order leads with the Fool, yet both end with Tav as the World. The correct astrological attribution for the Hebrew letter Tav is Saturn. Within the Golden Dawn tradition, Tav has the secondary elemental attribute of the fourth element Earth (where Aleph, Mem, and Shin are Air, Water, and Fire).

However, though the French tradition clearly identifies the World with the Hebrew letter Tav, the secret Saturnian nature of this letter was not known. Oswald Wirth, for instance, assigns to Tav the Pole Star, and to the conjunction of the Sun and Jupiter.

Waite shows the double attribution of the planet Saturn and the element Earth for the Hebrew letter Tav as follows:

- The planetary symbol for Saturn is a cross and a crescent. This is graphically shown in the crossed legs of the dancer and the curling

Key XX—Judgement

scarf which spirals around the crossed legs. The curling scarf forms the crescent while the legs form the cross. Note that the scarf is blue-violet, the color assigned to Tav as Saturn in the Golden Dawn tradition.

- The four living creatures at the four corners of this key symbolize the division of the world into four elements, the fourth being the element Earth itself. The title of this card as the World also suggests the earth.

- The wreath in this key is shaped as an oval. In the Golden Dawn Tattva tradition the oval is the shape of the Akasha Tattva, which is assigned to the planet Saturn, and the color blue-violet. The oval wreath that the dancer spirals within is also in the shape of the zero symbol. This alludes to the fact that the beginning of the Tarot journey is Key 0, The Fool, while Key XXI, The World, is the end of the journey. Thus the end is in the beginning and the beginning is in the end.

PART TWO—THE MINOR ARCANA
A PICTORIAL KEY TO MUTE EMBLEMS

As Waite's Major Arcana embodies the concepts of Mathers' esoteric Tarot, the source for Waite's unique picture images for the 56 cards composing the Minor Arcana is also derived from Mathers' Qabalistic revision of the Tarot as recorded in the Golden Dawn document *Book T*. And in the few instances where Waite strays from the orthodox Golden Dawn attributes, his source is still Mathers, using his published pamphlet *The Tarot: Its Occult Signification, Use in Fortune-Telling, and Method of Play*.

Each of Waite's four Aces posesses clues to unlock their unique elemental associations which Mathers developed from Levi (Wands = Fire, Cups = Water, Swords = Air, Pentacles = Earth).

The picture images employed in the 36 cards numbered 2 through 10 for the four suits of Wands, Cups, Swords, and Pentacles are unique to Waite. These images are for the most part taken directly from Mathers' esoteric titles for these cards. They have influenced almost every Tarot deck subsequent to Waite.

Waite's own version of the 16 Court Cards of Knight, Queen, King, and Page in the four suits contains essential clues which reveal the astrological associations for these cards, based on the Tetragrammaton as pioneered by Mathers.

XXI

THE WORLD.

Key XXI—The World

The Four Aces of the Minor Arcana

Ace of Wands
(Root of the Power of Fire)

Waite adopts the order of Mathers' suit division of Wands, Cups, Swords, and Pentacles, but does not specify their elemental nature. However, Waite does acknowledge their elemental nature in his commentary to Key I, for his revision of the Magician has the four tokens of the Minor Arcana clearly on the Magician's table.

The pyramidal castle upon a hill in the background is the only outright clue Waite conceals within the Ace of Wands. This castle resembles the upright triangle which is the elemental sigil for Fire.

Ace of Cups
(Root of the Power of Water)

Where Waite is vague in his elemental portrayal of the Ace of Wands, he is very clear in his elemental depiction of Ace of Cups. The water issuing from the cup to the pool below clearly indicates the elemental nature of the Cup suit as Water. The water lilies which grace the lake below are also Golden Dawn imagery for the Cup suit.

The letter "W" boldly embellished on the cup probably signifies Waite's last name, since many Tarot artists initialed their own name on one of the Aces (usually the Ace of Pentacles). However, it could also stand for Water, the element of the cup suit. It also resembles an inverted "M" more than an upright "W." In this case "M" would be the Hebrew letter Mem, which is assigned to the element Water.

Ace of Swords
(Root of the Power of Air)

The elemental nature of the Ace of Swords, like the Ace of Wands, is not clearly indicated. However the hilt of the sword resembles the elemental sigil for Air as an upright triangle penetrated by a horizontal line.

A second Qabalistic clue is the crown which the point of the sword penetrates. The Crown is the Hebraic name for the first Sephirah, Kether, on the Tree of Life. By the Golden Dawn tradition the first Sephirah is the source for the element Air (as the second is Fire and the third Water). Therefore the crown is a Qabalistic symbol for the element Air, indicating the correct element for the suit of Swords.

Ace of Pentacles
(Root of the Power of Earth)

The elemental nature of the Ace of Pentacles is clearly symbolized in the cultivated enclosed garden occupying the background of this card, which

ACE of WANDS.

ACE of CUPS.

ACE of SWORDS.

ACE of PENTACLES.

The Four Aces of the Minor Arcana

represents the fertile bounty of the earth, for the Pentacle suit is the elemental suit of Earth.

It should also be noted that in each Ace the token of the suit is being held by a radiant hand issuing from a cloud, indicating the hand of God. By Hebrew gematria this hand of God, as Yod, is valued at 14 (ID [יד] = 10 + 4 =14).

Fourteen is also the number of Minor Arcana cards in each of the four suits. Multiplying 14 (the value of hand) by 4 (the number of hands appearing in the four Aces), the resultant number of 56 is equal to the total number of cards composing the Minor Arcana in the Tarot deck.

The 36 Pip Cards of the Minor Arcana

The unique designs Waite came up with for the Minor Arcana, where all Tarot versions before Waite were devoid of such meaningful designs, were drawn directly from the imagination of S.L. Macgregor Mathers. Both Mathers' secret *Book T* and his published pamphlet on the Tarot served as pictorial guides for the creation of the Waite deck.

In the Golden Dawn tradition for the Tarot, the Minor Arcana cards numbered 2 through 10 in each suit correspond to the 36 decans of the Zodiac. The cardinal signs always correspond to the pip cards numbered 2, 3 or 4; the fixed signs always correspond to the pip cards numbered 5, 6, or 7; while the mutable signs correspond to the pip cards numbered 8, 9, or 10. The element of the sign is determined by the pip card: Fire signs are Wands, Water signs are Cups, Air signs are Swords, and Earth signs are Pentacles.

Each of these 36 cards was given a title which for the most part formed Waite's pattern for his designs. It should be noted that Crowley used a modified version of these titles for his own *Book of Thoth*.

Two of Wands
(Mars in Aries)

The Golden Dawn title for this card, representing the first 10 degrees of Aries, which is the beginning point of the Zodiac, is "Lord of Dominion." Mathers in his Qabalistic reconstruction of the Tarot assigned a title to each of the 36 minor pip cards of 2 through 10 in each suit. Each title was prefixed by the honorific "Lord," and in the title's descriptive phrase lay the key meaning to each of these cards. Waite insightfully used these descriptive phrases in developing a picture image, or pictorial key, to each of these 36 cards.

Mathers did not intend these 36 cards to contain a picture image. His own description of these cards involves only the suit emblems held by angelic hands, with the occasionally embellishment of a flower. But with Waite these essential meanings hidden in the titles of the Minor Arcana were given flesh in picture form. And like a gigantic crystal prism Waite's unique pictures for the Minor Arcana have filtered into almost every major modern deck drawn after 1910 (save for Case and Crowley).

Two of Wands

Three of Wands

These 36 Minor Arcana cards also have a unique astrolological character about which Waite is not explicit. Each of the 36 cards is one of the 36 decans of the Zodiacal circle of 12 Zodiac signs. This Zodiacal symbolism will play into the designs in part, but it is the Golden Dawn titles which are the real source for Waite's symbolism. On account of Waite's deck, Mathers unique vision of the Qabalistic meanings for the Minor Arcana has been passed to the modern generation of Tarot practitioners.

The title for Two of Wands as Lord of Dominion is readily worked into Waite's own version of this card. The pictorial key is a robed and crowned ruler looking over his domain while reflecting on a microcosm of his kingdom as a globe of the world in his hand. One hand of this ruler holds a globe while the other holds a wand, reminiscent of Waite's design for Key IV—The Emperor. As Key IV is Aries, ruled by Mars, so also is the Zodiacal influence of 2 of Wands, as the first decan of Aries, ruled by Mars.

Three of Wands
(Sun in Aries)

The Golden Dawn title is "Lord of Established Strength." Waite shows a ruler watching over his fleet of three ships as they leave his kingdom. Waite describes this card as "symbolizing established strength," using Mathers'

Four of Wands

own title as a description of the card's true meaning, and incorporating this principle into his own design by having three firmly planted staves, one of which offers support for the central figure in the card.

The second decan of Aries as the Sun in Aries is the astrological nature of this card. Aries is exalted in the Sun, again linking this card to Key IV—The Emperor. Note that the three ships in this card float upon the same river that is seen behind the Emperor in Key IV.

Four of Wands
(Venus in Aries)

The Golden Dawn title for this card is "Lord of Perfected Work." Waite describes his own version as representing "perfected work," and symbolizes this concept as a trapezoidal arbor before a castle, formed by four upright wands supporting a garland of roses.

The Zodiacal attribution is the third decan of Aries, as Venus in Aries. This Venusian influence is symbolized by the roses intertwined in the arbor's floral canopy, as well as the bouquets held in the hands of the robed couple behind the arbor.

Five of Wands
(Saturn in Leo)

The Golden Dawn title for this card is "Lord of Strife." Waite's pictorial key shows five young men attempting to form a perfect upright pentagram with their five wands. Only the youth on the far left must drop his wand into place and all can be adjusted to form the martial five-pointed star, but in the present state of confusion their efforts seem like a mock battle of crossed staves.

Waite describes this card in his own commentary as representing "strife," and the five contending wands accurately portray this meaning in symbol.

The astrological character is the first decan of Leo, as Saturn in Leo. Saturn represents a restricting force holding back the power of Leo, and can accurately be portrayed as strife or effort in completing a task. Leo is the fifth sign of the Zodiac, and with this number there is a direct connection to the Five of Wands in the Minor Arcana.

Five of Wands

Six of Wands

Six of Wands
(Jupiter in Leo)

The Golden Dawn title is "Lord of Victory." Waite's pictorial key in this card is a laureled horseman returning from battle with a victory wreath surmounting his own upright wand. The king has fought at the side of his subjects in battle and has brought order and victory to the unruly five wands of the previous card. Waite describes this card as the "victor triumphing," echoing Mathers' own title for this card.

The astrological nature of this card is the second decan of Leo, as Jupiter in Leo. As Saturn in the last card held back Leo in strife, Jupiter in this card allows Leo to burst forth in Victory.

Seven of Wands
(Mars in Leo)

The Golden Dawn title for this card is "Lord of Valour." Waite's pictorial key is a warrior courageously holding off with his own staff the advances of six other wands. Waite describes his own version as "a card of valour," clearly revealing the Golden Dawn title as a source for his own version.

The astrological nature is the third decan of Leo, as Mars in Leo. Here Mars portrays the courage of the warrior needed to fight against overwhelming odds. As the Six of Wands is the victory of battle, the Seven of Wands is the fierce determination necessary to turn possible defeat into that victory.

Eight of Wands
(Mercury in Sagittarius)

The Golden Dawn title for this card is "Lord of Swiftness." Waite uses the term "swiftness" as part of his description for this card. His pictorial key of eight wands flying through the air aptly portrays swift motion.

The astrological nature is the first decan of Sagittarius, as Mercury in Sagittarius. Both the number 8 and the concept of swift flight are symbols of Mercury. Further, the image of Sagittarius is an arched bow loosing its arrow into the air, bringing to mind the wands in flight which can be seen as the wooden shafts of arrows.

Nine of Wands
(Moon in Sagittarius)

The Golden Dawn title for this card is "Lord of Great Strength." Waite refers to this card as "strength in oppposition." His pictorial key is an isolated embattled warrior, who standing with the aid of his staff holds off eight other wands. This picture easily connotes great strength.

The astrological nature of this card is the second decan of Sagittarius, as the Moon in Sagittarius. The Moon in the Qabalah governs the ninth Sephirah Yesod on the Tree of Life, which among other correspondences represents the generative organs, especially the male. Waite's eight erect wands are intentionally phallic in this card on account of the Moon, as well as the ninth staff held by the lone figure in this card.

With this card Waite again intentionally uses a card in the Major Arcana as a model: the solitary figure resting on his staff is reminiscent of the mountain-climbing hermit in Key IX, who also supports himself with a phallic staff.

Three traditional astrological symbols terminate in an arrow: the spear head (or lightning bolt) for the planet Mars, the stinger of the scorpion for the Zodiac sign Scorpio, and the arrowhead for the Zodiac sign Sagittarius. In all cases these arrows are phallic in nature.

Ten of Wands
(Saturn in Sagittarius)

The Golden Dawn title for this card is "Lord of Oppression." Waite's pictorial key for this key clearly shows a man burdened by the weight of the ten wands he carries. To further support this symbolism Waite describes the

Seven of Wands

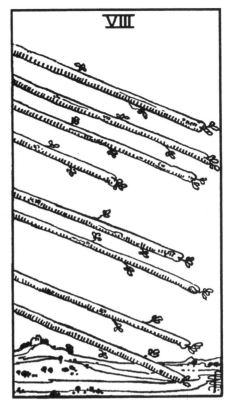

Eight of Wands

Nine of Wands

Ten of Wands

chief meaning of this card as "oppression simply."

The astrological nature of this card is the third decan of Sagittarius, as Saturn in Sagittarius. Here Saturn takes on its malefic characteristic and represents inertia, which results in a lack of Sagittarian will.

This is the first of four cards designating the number 10 in the Minor Arcana. As such, the ten intertwining wands of this card, which crisscross one another, represent the interconnecting paths which join together the 10 Sephiroth of the Tree of Life.

In summation, if we look back at the suit of Wands, we will find that in every case Waite relied upon the secret Golden Dawn titles when illustrating each of these pip cards. In other suits we will find that Waite is not as thorough in using the Golden Dawn as his model. However, when he varies from this canon, he will inevitably still rely on Mathers by copying Mathers' own published booklet on the Tarot.

The Cup suit is the element of Water. The three Water signs govern the following Cups: Cancer is 2, 3, and 4 (of Cups); Scorpio is 5, 6, and 7; Pisces is 8, 9, and 10.

Two of Cups
(Venus in Cancer)

The Golden Dawn title for this card is "Lord of Love." Waite realizes this

Two of Cups

title in his picture of two lovers exchanging cups. His own divinatory meaning for this card as "love" also validates this. The astrological significance of this card is the first decan of Cancer as Venus in Cancer.

The picture of two lovers is the Venus element of this card, while the house on the hill in the background between the lovers is the Zodiac sign of Cancer as the Zodiacal influence which governs the home.

The male and female figures represent the alchemical elements of Fire (the red and yellow of the male on the right) and Water (the blue, white, and green of the female on the left). They are in the same position as Adam and Eve in Key VI—The Lovers. The winged lion arising from their union is the element of Air as the alchemical homunculus or descending soul that hovers over each instance of sexual intercourse in hopes of having a vehicle to enter this world. The caduceus intertwined with two snakes is also a token of the element Air, but in this instance it is the alchemical Mercury which unites the fiery heat of Sulfur with the cooling crystals of Salt.

This winged lion is again the alchemical formula for the male and female genitalia which we have first seen in Key VI, as the serpent and lion secretly woven into the blouse of the angel Raphael. It is again the formula of the lion united with the serpent (or eagle) expressed in the two Zodiacal signs of Leo and Scorpio. In the design of the Two of Cups, this astrological formula is shown as:

Leo = the red lion's face
Scorpio = the red feathered wings (of an eagle), the twin serpents intertwined upon Hermes' caduceus

Three of Cups
(Mercury in Cancer)

Three of Cups

The Golden Dawn title for this key is "Lord of Abundance." The astrological allocation is the second decan of Cancer ruled by Mercury. Here Mercury is seen in its Bacchic incarnation as Pan, God of wine and merriment. Mathers' detailed definition of this key in *Book T* is "plenty, hospitality, eating and drinking, pleasure, dancing, new clothes, merriment." All of these meanings have been artfully woven into Waite's own design of this key.

The three female figures are the three elements of Fire, Water, and Air.

If the Tree of Life is superimposed on this card, the three upraised cups fall naturally to the three supernal Sephiroth of Kether, Chockmah, and Binah.

By their elemental qualities, the three cups are each held by one of the three elements. The figure on the left holds the upmost cup, which is the element Air (as Kether). The middle figure holds up the cup on the right, which is Fire (as Chockmah), while the figure on the right holds up the cup on the left, which is Water (as Binah).

As a subtle reference to Key XV—The Devil, a cluster of grapes is held behind the female figure on the right. This is the same position as the tail of the female figure in Key XV, which also ends with a cluster of grapes. This is a reference to the Goat God Pan whose influence causes the visionary intoxication of sacramental wine.

Four of Cups

Four of Cups
(Moon in Cancer)

The Golden Dawn title for this card is "Lord of Blended Pleasures." This is the third decan of Cancer, as the Moon in Cancer, the Moon being the natural ruler for Cancer.

Waite gives this title as one of the divinatory meanings for his own version, and portrays Mathers' concept of "pleasure, but some slight discomfort and anxieties" as "a man discontent with three cups before him, being offered a fourth from a celestial hand."

The male sitting cross-legged beneath a tree is a perfect image of Buddha meditating under the Bo tree and reaching enlightenment.

If we look at the three cards associated with Cancer, we see three separate ranges of human ecstatic emotions:

Two of Cups = Love (arousal)
Three of Cups = Merriment (intoxication)
Four of Cups = Contemplation (bliss)

Five of Cups
(Mars in Scorpio)

The Golden Dawn title for this key is "Lord of Loss in Pleasure." The astrological significance of this card is the first decan of Scorpio, as Mars in Scorpio. Mars is the natural planetary ruler for Scorpio. Here again, like the Five of Wands, Mars is the ruling planet for a card numbered five, for Mars is the fifth Sephiroth on the Tree of Life, and associated with the planetary magick square composed of 5 x 5 squares. This fivefold martial symbolism is encoded in the five cups surrounding the central figure in the card, which form an inverted pentagram of three cups spilled and two cups upright.
The standing robed figure resembles the lone hermit of Key IX, but here the cloak is black to represent the sorrows of Saturn (and Binah). This brooding, dark figure clearly represents the loss of pleasure as he contemplates his losses before him, oblivious to the bounty behind him.

The river behind this figure appears in many cards, but here it is the river seen in Key XIII—Death, since both Key XIII and the Five of Cups are ruled by Scorpio.

Five of Cups

Six of Cups

Six of Cups
(Sun in Scorpio)

The Golden Dawn title for this card is "Lord of Pleasure." The astrological attribute for this card is the second decan of Scorpio, which is the Sun in Scorpio. This is the only positive card in the Scorpio series denoting emotional pleasure, since the Five of Cups represents emotional disappointment, while the Seven of Cups represents emotional delusion.

Waite's design for this key is the first real deviation from Mathers' definitions for the Minor Arcana. Waite renders this card as "memories of the past" and "looking back on childhood." He portrays two children in a garden before a castle and house, sharing a cup filled with a flower. It is the same exchange of cups as in the Two of Cups, but which has now come to fruition. As the couple in the Two of Cups represents the Father and Mother of the Tetragrammaton, the couple in the Six of Cups represents the Son and Daughter.

As such, Waite may connect Mathers' concept of Scorpionic pleasure with the nostalgic memories of one's past. This is not the meaning given by Mathers in *Book T*, nor does the sixth Sephiroth on the Tree of Life, which this card correponds to, connote the past or looking backwards.

However, Mathers is ultimately Waite's source for this variation. For Waite seems to have relied on Mathers' intentionally misleading pamphlet entitled *The Tarot*, first published in 1888. In this pamphlet, Mathers has recorded the exoteric interpretations of previous writers concerning the Tarot, especially from the French writings of Etteilla. In this pamphlet, under the Six of Cups, Mathers lists as definitions "the past, passed by, dated, vanished, disappeared. R[eversed] The Future, that which is to come, shortly, soon." This is obviously Waite's source for his variance from the esoteric Golden Dawn title. Waite in his own comment to the Six of Cups even lists the reversal definitions from Mathers' pamphlet, to further confirm this pamphlet as Waite's secondary source.

It should be noted that the unique order of the Tarot for both the Major and Minor Arcana appearing in Waite's book on the Tarot, where the Magician leads the order of the Major Arcana, and the Minor Arcana is ordered backwards from 10 to Ace, is the order appearing in Mathers' pamphlet *The Tarot* and not the esoteric order of the Golden Dawn's *Book T*. The ultimate source for Waite's order recorded in Mathers' *The Tarot* is the Tarot research of Etteilla found in *Tarots Egyptiens Grand Jeu de L'Oracle*.

We will discover that Waite had trouble clearly portraying another pip card numbered six: the Six of Swords. Waite again relies on Mathers' pamphlet for his variance in design.

One other unique point of symbolism should be pointed out here. At the foot of the steps below the highest cup is the Rosicrucian coat of arms for Andreas Valentine, a source for the original Rose-Cross, while six five-pointed lilies appear growing from the cups, combining the five of the microcosm with the the six of the macrocosm, an alchemical-Rosicrucian symbol for the Great Work.

Seven of Cups

Seven of Cups
(Venus in Scorpio)

The Golden Dawn title for this card is "Lord of Illusionary Success." Mathers defines this key as a variety of vices and illusions, in line with the astrological attribution of this card as the third decan of Scorpio as Venus in Scorpio. By this astrological conjunction, the seven visions of seven cups beheld by the figure in dark silhouette are of a fantastic, erotic, or lurid nature. Note that the cup in the upper right-hand corner has a serpent whose coils resemble the graphic shape for Scorpio. In both Key X and Key XXI, this is the position in the card for the kerubic Eagle, who also corresponds to Scorpio.

The seven symbols appearing in these cups are tokens of the seven Major Arcana cards which correspond to the seven planets by the secret order of the seven double letters of the Hebrew alphabet. The contents of the seven cups place the seven planets in the following order:

Seven Star-Cups

Venus (III)			Mercury (I)
	Moon (II)		
Mars (XVI)	Jupiter (X)	Saturn (XXI)	Sun (XIX)

The order the seven planets take in the Major Arcana is the most guarded secret of both the Tarot and the Hebrew alphabet, and the greatest discovery made by Mathers in reconstructing the esoteric order for the Tarot. These seven visionary images also correspond directly to Mathers' *Book T* divinatory definitions for this card. The following table shows the seven tokens from the Major Arcana Waite secretly used as the fantastic contents of the seven cups which adorn this card:

Seven Planetary Cups of Vision

Contents of Cup	Major Arcana	Token Image	Seven Planets	Divinatory Meaning
Woman's head	Key III	Head of Empress	Venus	Lust (fornication)
Veiled figure	Key II	Priestess and Veil	Moon	Deception (in love and friendship)
Serpent	Key I	Serpent around Magician's waist	Mercury	Lying (error)
Castle on Sandy Hill	Key XVI	Tower on Mountain	Mars	Promises unfulfilled (wrath)
Jewels (riches)	Key X	Wheel of Fortune	Jupiter	Vanity (success gained but not followed up)
Wreath and Skull	Key XXI	Oval Wreath around Dancer	Saturn	Illusionary Success (victory followed by deception)
Winged Dragon	Key XIX	Horse	Sun	Drunkenness (selfish dissipation)

The sky blue dragon as the Sun is the most obscure association, but as a winged creature which flies through the sky, it parallels the image of a galloping horse rushing throught the sky as the Sun in its daily transit

Eight of Cups

through the heavens. As to the attribution of drunkeness, this is in accord with the vegetable drug under the Sun's rulership, which is alcohol.

Eight of Cups
(Saturn in Pisces)

The Golden Dawn title for this card is "Lord of Abandoned Success." Mathers further qualifies this card in *Book T* as "journeying from place to place." Waite aptly illustrates this as a man journeying away from eight ordered and stacked cups.

The simplicity of this picture and its direct connotation of Mathers' secret meanings for these keys again demonstrate how someone with no understanding of the true meaning for this card can still come directly to the heart of the matter by the picture image alone. It is as if Waite via the imagination can play directly upon one's heart rather than one's brain with these fairy-tale-like designs for the Minor Arcana. Whereas all decks before Waite stand mute in their testimony to the true meaning of the Minor Arcana, with Waite's deck the pip emblems are transformed from rigid implements to fluid, free-flowing picture images, pregnant with meaning.

As to the astrological nature of this card, this is the first of three cards assigned to Pisces. This card is the first decan of Pisces as Saturn in Pisces. This is another key in which Waite introduces the astrological symbolism of the Major Arcana to reinforce the astrological nature of the Minor Arcana. The Pisces nature of this card is clearly established in the Moon in the night sky seen both in crescent and in full face, This symbolism is taken directly from the crescent-faced Moon in Key XVIII—The Moon. And as we have already discovered, the Moon key in the Major Arcana is Piscean rather than lunar in nature.

The Saturnian nature of this key is seen in the caped figure walking with a stick, for this is the Hermit in Key IX, which is a characterization of the Saturnian Father Time. The brooding face of the Moon in the night sky, the figure walking away with only his back showing, and the empty cups abandoned in the foreground all impart a morose nature to this card, which is also Saturnian in nature

Nine of Cups
(Jupiter in Pisces)

Nine of Cups

The Golden Dawn title for this card is "Lord of Material Happiness." Waite again clearly shows this in his picture of a content, jovial man surrounded by nine intoxicating cups of wine that serve as a crescent wall offering shelter from the vicissitudes of life.

As to the astrological nature, this card is the second decan of Pisces, which is Jupiter in Pisces. As the last card denoted the melancholic influence of Saturn, this card shows the beneficience of Jupiter in extending health, wealth, and comfort. Jupiter is also the planetary ruler of Pisces (in a seven-planet system of astrology).

It should be pointed out that Waite, even when portraying the correct esoteric image according to the Golden Dawn title for a Minor Arcana card, will inevitably lapse into quoting from Mathers' exoteric pamphlet *The Tarot*, which has no direct relationship to the esoteric teachings of the Golden Dawn. For the Nine of Cups, Waite's comments include "victory, success, advantage ... (Reversed) mistakes, imperfections." This is taken directly from Mathers' pamphlet concerning the Nine of Cups: "Victory, advantage, success .... (Reversed) mistakes, imperfections."

Waite repeatedly lifts whole passages from Mathers' text and inserts them into his own commentary on the Minor Arcana. Yet Waite is at pains to conceal his plagiarism of Mathers' pamphlet on the Tarot. In Waite's own annotated bibliography, he cites Mathers' pamphlet, *The Tarot*, and his own comment on this pamphlet is very revealing.

Waite describes the divinatory definitions, and the pamphlet as a whole, as "a mere sketch written in a pretentious manner and is negligible in all respects." Yet this pamphlet was anything but negligible to Waite, since it served as his secondary source for the images and divinatory meanings of the Minor Arcana. (His primary source was *Book T.*)

As to Waite acknowledging his own esoteric source as Mathers' work on the Tarot found in *Book T*, Waite may never have known that Mathers really invented the secret order for the Golden Dawn Tarot rather than finding it already written in a secret cipher manuscript. Crowley and Case may also have been unaware of the true author of the Golden Dawn Qabalistic correspondences for the Tarot.

Ten of Cups

Ten of Cups
(Mars in Pisces)

The Golden Dawn title for this key is "Lord of Perfected Success." Waite depicts a happy family whose home is in the background. In a sense this picture symbolizes Mathers' esoteric definitions from *Book T* as success, happiness, and complete good fortune. However, Waite again tends towards Mathers' pamphlet, *The Tarot,* which defines the Ten of Cups as "the town wherein one resides." Waite's own commentary defines this card as "the town, village or country inhabited by the Querent."

The family of four is the Tetragrammaton family of father, mother, son, and daughter. The males are garbed in red for Fire, while the females are garbed in blue for Water.

The arched rainbow of ten cups is another subtle reference to the Tree of Life: the tenth Sephirah (Malkuth), which corresponds to this tenth card, is joined as a pendant to the rest of the Tree of Life by three paths, the letters Tav (ת), Shin (ש), and Qoph (ק). These three paths as Hebrew letters spell the Hebrew word for "rainbow": QShTh (קשׁת). This arched rainbow is a promise pledged to the candidate being ritually initiated into Malkuth as the promise of the illumination afforded by all future initiations.

The astrological attribute for this card is the third, and last, decan for Pisces, as Mars in Pisces. By the Hebrew letters of the Major Arcana, Mars is Peh (פ) while Pisces is Qoph (ק). By their combined number values, these two letters total to 180 as (P = 80) + (Q = 100), and 180 is the arched rainbow as 180 degrees.

The Sword suit is the element of Air. The three Air signs govern the following Swords: Libra is 2, 3, and 4 (of Swords); Aquarius is 5, 6 and 7; Gemini is 8, 9, and 10.

Two of Swords
(Moon in Libra)

The Golden Dawn title for this card is "Lord of Peace Restored." Waite clearly portrays this definition in the form of a female figure blindfolded and holding two swords in perfect balance.

Two of Swords

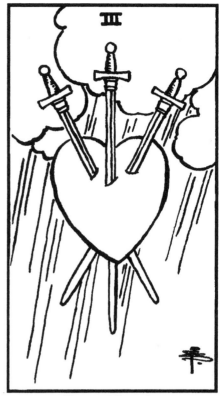

Three of Swords

The astrological nature of this card is the first decan of Libra, as the Moon in Libra. Both these images are the basis for Waite's unique design for this key. The hoodwinked figure holding two swords is reminiscent of the Libra nature of the classic image for Justice as well as Key XI—Justice in the Tarot.

The body of water behind the seated female figure is the ocean that lurks behind of the veil of the High Priestess in Key II, ruled by the Moon. This Moon is seen now no longer at the foot of the seated priestess but high in the night sky.

Thus both the Moon and Libra, as a combination of the eleventh and second Tarot key in the Major Arcana, are interwoven in this key to represent the first decan of Libra as the Moon in Libra.

Three of Swords
(Saturn in Libra)

The Golden Dawn title for this card is "Lord of Sorrow." Waite again is very faithful to Mathers'esoteric title by picturing in the foreground a heart pierced by three swords (sorrow), and in the background the gray clouds and rain of a storm (tears).

Waite's source for this card is ultimately Christian iconography, in the emblem of a winged heart pierced by one single sword, the hilt at the top resembling a cross while the blade at the bottom pierces through the heart. This Christian emblem illustrates the following verse: "Yea, a sword shall pierce through thy own soul." This heart is the sacred heart of Mary, and represents the sorrow of the mother.

This maternal sorrow is also part of the energy associated with the third Sephirah, Binah, on the Tree of Life, and is the station to which the Three of Swords is aligned. As to the heart as Binah, most commentators place the heart at the sixth Sephirah, Tiphereth. However the Qabalisitic schemes of both Athanasius Kircher in the 17th century and the Masonic tradition of the 19th century place the heart at the third Sephirah.

The astrological nature of this key is the second decan of Libra as Saturn in Libra. The Saturnian nature is the sorrow portrayed in the card as the pierced heart and dark raining sky. Saturn is also the planet associated with the third Sephirah, Binah. The Libra nature is only implied by the three swords as the element Air.

Four of Swords
(Jupiter in Libra)

The Golden Dawn title for this card is "Lord of Rest from Strife." Waite readily incorporates this idea as a knight resting on his back in repose or prayer. Case, in commenting on Waite's version of this key, warns his readers that this is not a key of death, for the knight's restful pose can be misconstrued as rigor mortis.

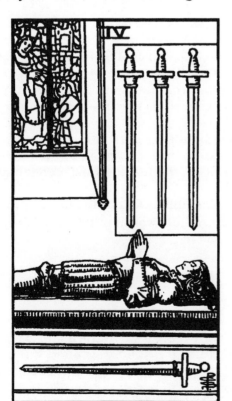

Four of Swords

The astrological nature of this key is the third and last decan of Libra, as Jupiter in Libra. This is not overtly shown in this key. Jupiter is traditionally the number four, and in this sense there is a minor correspondence. Only the first decan of Libra as the Two of Swords is explicit as Libra. Here, other than the presence of a sword, Libra is not strongly suggested.

The stained-glass window holds a clue showing a secondary meaning for this card as Peace. This window shows a haloed Jesus ministering to a kneeling disciple. The halo around the head of Jesus contains the Latin letters PAX, meaning peace.

Note that there is also a Masonic symbol at play here in the positioning of the three upper swords over the prostrate body of the knight. These three sword blades point to the sixth, fifth, and fourth chakras at head, throat, and chest (heart). These are the three areas which were struck to slay Hiram Abiff, the Master Mason of King Solomon's temple. As such, the knight in this card is in the position of the candidate in the third degree of the Master Mason, lying on the lodge floor, ready to be resurrected by the right grip of the Worshipful Master's hand.

Five of Swords

Five of Swords
(Venus in Aquarius)

The Golden Dawn title for this card is "Lord of Defeat." Mathers further defines this card as "Contest finished and decided against the person." Waite clearly incorporates this in his scene depicting the end of a battle in which two losers retreat towards the sea, leaving the remaining winner to pick up five swords from the battlefield. This is similar to Waite's design for the Five of Wands, which shows five young men skirmishing with five wands. As the Five of Wands depicts the actual battle, the Five of Swords depicts the end of a battle resulting in a winner and a loser.

The astrological characteristic of this card is the first decan of Aquarius, as Venus in Aquarius. This symbolism is not readily apparent in this card. As a graphic symbol, Aquarius, which is an Air sign, is a jagged double stream of water. The body of water in the background, as well as the jagged edge to the clouds in the sky, is weak at best in depicting Aquarius. As for Venus, the tunic of the victorious warrior is green, while the undergarments are red, and this flashing conjunction of green and red is symbolic of Venus in the Golden Dawn system of magick.

Six of Swords
(Mercury in Aquarius)

The Golden Dawn title for this card is "Lord of Earned Success." Its essential meaning is success after much labor. This card is the second decan of Aquarius as Mercury in Aquarius.

Crowley refined the title for this key to "Science," denoting hard work, trial and error, and observation. This is in accord with the astrological conjunction of Mercury (as the God of language, word, and number) and Aquarius (as the intellectual mind in deep study).

Six of Swords

Waite's illustration is at odds with the above description, for it depicts two passengers in a boat sitting amidst six swords as they are being poled to the opposite shore by a ferryman.

However, in Mathers' pamphlet *The Tarot*, the definition for the Six of Swords is "Envoy, messenger, voyage, travel." In light of this, Mathers wrote as a postscript to the Six of Swords in *Book T* the divinatory meaning of "journey by water." The astrological justification is that Mercury symbolizes the journey (as the God of roads), and Aquarius symbolizes water (as the symbolic image of two parallel wavy lines of water). Note that Waite placed many parallel wavy lines of water just to the right of the boat to point out the Aquarian nature of this key.

Unfortunately, in Waite's execution of the Six of Swords, only the concept of journeying by water was encoded, a meaning that seems to be a secondary meaning in *Book T*, rather than the essential meaning for the Six of Swords.

Waite, in both this card and the Six of Cups, strays from the Golden Dawn meanings by turning instead to his beloved pamphlet by Mathers. Of all the pip cards, the Six of Swords is the most consistently misread in modern divination. It is often given an additional foreboding interpretation of a forced departure unknown to the querent, when in essence this card represents the mind in its most focused and attentive state, as Tiphereth (Six) of Air (Swords).

Seven of Swords
(Moon in Aquarius)

The Golden Dawn title for this card is "Lord of Unstable Effort." Mathers' comment on this key offers the divinatory meaning of "To detect and spy on another. Inclined to betray confidences." This is the essential meaning of Waite's illustration showing a man (possibly a spy or enemy) stealing away from a pitched camp with five swords in hand, leaving two behind. Perhaps these five swords are the same five swords gathered by the victor in the Five of Swords. Now the opponent has stolen back into the enemy camp to reclaim the five lost swords of his comrades.

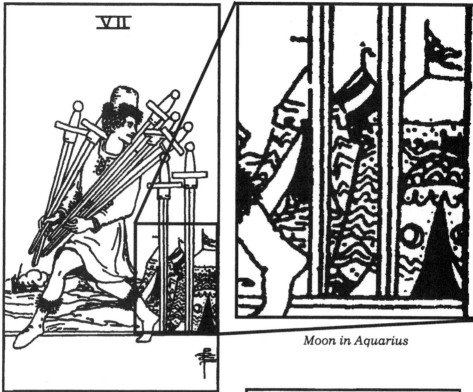

Moon in Aquarius

Seven of Swords

The astrological configuration of this card is the third and last decan of Aquarius, as the Moon in Aquarius. This astrological conjunction is clearly woven into the designs embroidered on the war tents in the background. The Moon is clearly shown on either side of the flap of the tent in the foreground, while the jagged wavy parallel lines of Aquarius are on all of the tents.

Eight of Swords
(Jupiter in Gemini)

The Golden Dawn title for this card is "Lord of Shortened Force." Among Mathers' definitions of this card is the concept Waite incorporated into his own pictorial key: "Narrow, restricted, petty, a prison." Waite's

Eight of Swords

own design is a robed figure, bound and blinded, standing within a surrounding prison of eight swords stuck point downward into the ground. Waite defines this illustration as "a card of temporary durance than of irretrievable bondage." This is in accord with Mathers' title of Shortened Force.

The astrological character of this card is the first decan of Gemini, as Jupiter in Gemini. The color of the main figure's robe is orange, in accordance with Gemini, and the water below this figure (like the water at the foot of the angel in Key XIV) is blue, the color of Jupiter. But again, the explicit symbolism, like the astrological characters found on the Seven of Swords, is not apparent in the Eight of Swords.

There is a Masonic sense to this specific card, just as Four of Swords held Masonic ritual secrets. The figure standing amid eight swords is the candidate for initiation into the Masonic mysteries, while the eight swords are the various officers of the lodge. Entering the initiation, the candidate is hoodwinked with a blindfold and bound around his neck, arm, or waist with a rope known as the cable tow. This cable tow is bound around the candidate in varying lengths, sometimes once, twice, or three times, and allows the blindfolded candidate to be led into the light of the lodge for the first time.

The most appropriate number of loops for this sacred cord is three and a half, since this is the number of coils in which the serpent power Kundalini is bound at the base of the spine in the first chakra. Like all true initiations, the initial ritual opens up the candidate for the first time in order to receive the light, and uncoils the serpent power in the first chakra to slowly raise the energy through all seven chakras within the candidate through successive initiations.

Nine of Swords

Nine of Swords
(Mars in Gemini)

The Golden Dawn title for this card is "Lord of Despair and Cruelty." Waite's own illustration of a woman in lamentation, "who knows no sorrow like unto hers," is an apt picture of Mathers' title.

The astrological configuration of this card is the second decan of Gemini, as Mars in Gemini. Upon two of the blue squares of the bed quilt in this card are inscribed the graphic shapes for Mars and Gemini. However, there are many more symbols than just these two. Waite incorporates into the design of this magickal quilt a six by seven rectangle of 42 squares, 21 emblazoned with the Rosicrucian red rose and 21 studded with the Zodiacal designs of the night sky. The quilt is composed of more than 42 squares; however, only 42 are clearly visible. The 21 astrological symbols form the following rectangular pattern:

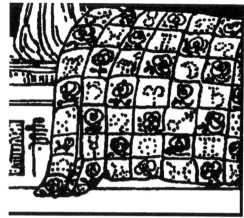

Astro-Quilt

The Astrological Quilt of the Nine of Swords

Mars		Taurus		Cancer		(concealed)
	Pisces		Gemini		Leo	
Virgo		Scorpio		Moon		(concealed)
	Saturn		Aries		Saturn	
Sagittarius		Leo		Mars		(Aquarius)*
	Mercury		Sun		Gemini	
Libra		Jupiter		Pisces		(Taurus)*

*Partially concealed

Aquarius and Taurus are partially seen at the right edge of the quilt, beyond the 21 apparent signs. At the extreme lower left below Libra is a square containing the Rosicrucian rose. Covered by its folds is another obscured blue square which cannot be easily made out. The squares for Mars in Gemini, the influence of this card, can be seen on a diagonal at the lower right of the quilt.

Unfortunately, a deep study of this astrological patttern, such as reducing the symbols to their alphabetical or numerical Qabalistic equivalents, results in very little information. It seems that the order of the Zodiac is haphazardly arranged in sequential order from the top of the rectangle to the bottom. There are many duplications without apparent design, while the Saturnian-ruled Capricorn is absent and the Saturnian-ruled Aquarius only partially hinted at in the hidden folds of the right of the quilt. However, Capricorn may be the square just above the double V of Aquarius hidden at the extreme right of the quilt.

The order in which the planets are interspersed among the signs is of no apparent pattern, and Venus is not directly included in this design. However the planet Venus can be inferred from the shape of the stemmed roses which appear on alternating squares of the quilt. The signs of the Zodiac are sometimes placed in tangent squares to their planetary rulers, such as Sun with Leo, Mars with Aries, Moon with Cancer, Jupiter with Pisces, and Saturn with possibly Aquarius or Capricorn. This may be the only significant order for this astrological pattern.

Essentially, it seems that the artist utilized the Zodiac and the planets haphazardly as a decoration or embellishment, as if one would stud silver in blue to imitate the night sky illuminated by the stars.

The attribution of ornate astrological symbolism specifically to the Nine of Swords does not make Qabalistic sense, other than the fact that both the Suit of Swords and the ninth Sephirah are the element Air, and thus the night sky.

Many modern Tarot diviners see this card as waking from a nightmare, rather than the lamentation engendered from despair and cruelty originally envisioned by Mathers, and the emphasis on dreaming at night may be the real symbolism for a bed quilt made of the stars of the night sky.

The actual astrological rulership as pointed out above is Mars in Gemini, which are tangent squares on the quilt. However, given the general pattern of the design, this may be the result of chance rather than invention. What would have been in keeping with the other pictorial clues in this deck would have been the Yetziratic order for the 22 cards of the Major Arcana woven into the 21 plus 1 astrological squares. Note that, although Waite's astrological quilt contains both the planets and Zodiac, it does not contain the triangular symbols for the elements.

Ten of Swords
(Sun in Gemini)

The Golden Dawn title for this card is "Lord of Ruin." Waite's own divinatory meanings for this card come from Mathers' pamphlet rather than from *Book T*. However, in picture image Waite is again faithful to the secret Golden Dawn title, portraying ruin as a body pierced by ten swords, as the yellow sky behind darkens into blackness (symbolizes a loss of consciousness, a blacking out). Six of the ten swords penetrate the body at the six lower chakras: brow (head), throat, heart, navel, genitals, and perineum, while the spirit as a red stream escapes from the seventh, or crown chakra.

It is a card which contains the Masonic ritualistic view that the body is but a temporary abode for the spirit and must be respected and treated as such. This is also the slain body of Hiram Abiff, Master Mason of King Solomon's temple, who every third-degree Mason experiences on a personal ritualistic level. This is also the heart of Buddhism, the impermanence of this world and the inevitability of death, which only deep work on oneself can conquer.

The ten swords are symbolic of the tenth Sephirah Malkuth on the Tree of Life. Malkuth, which means

Ten of Swords

kingdom, or royalty, is spelt in Hebrew as MLKVTh (מלכות). These five letters can be rearranged to form the phrase KL MVTh (כל מות), which means "everything is subject to death"(literally "all die"). Waite shows this concept admirably as ten swords slaying the physical body (but not the spirit).

As to the astrological nature of this card, this is the third and last decan of Gemini, as the Sun in Gemini. There is no direct correlation to this design. However, Gemini rules the hands, and the one hand shown in this design is in the mudra of the Hierophant's blessing hand, which means "as above so below." This is a bendiction that blesses heaven over earth and points to spirit conquering the travails of the body.

The Pentacle suit is the element of Earth. The three Earth signs govern the following Pentacles: Capricorn is 2, 3, and 4 (of Pentacles); Taurus is 5, 6, and 7; Virgo is 8, 9 and 10.

Two of Pentacles
(Jupiter in Capricorn)

The Golden Dawn title for this card is "Lord of Harmonious Change." Waite intimates this meaning by showing a young man dexterously juggling two pentacles in a a figure-eight pattern. In the background, two

Two of Pentacles

ships gracefully ride the rolling surf to further emphasize harmony and balance in change.

As in many of the other Minor Arcana cards, Waite uses a Major Arcana card as his model. For this card, Key I—The Magician is the basis for the design. The two pentacles being juggled are from the pentacle on the Magician's table. The path they take while rolling through the air is in the figure eight pattern spinning above the Magician's head. In very early Tarot versions, the Magician was titled the Juggler, showing a picture of a juggler standing before his conjuring table covered with the emblems of the Tarot.

The astrological characteristic for this card is the first decan of Capricorn as Jupiter in Capricorn. This is not directly woven into the card, but the Mercurial nature of the Magician does appear, as shown above.

The red conical cap crowning the juggler's head is indeed phallic, resembling the sacred stone linga of India, which could be Capricorn, while the spinning pentacled wheels that are being juggled resemble the whirls of the Jupiterian wheel in Key X.

Capricorn's phallic nature comes from the original Hebrew for Capricorn, which is GDI (גדי), meaning kid goat. Rearranged, this name becomes GID (גיד), which means sinew, thigh, or penis.

Three of Pentacles
(Mars in Capricorn)

The Golden Dawn title for this key is "Lord of Material Works." Mathers further defines this key as "working and constructive force, bulding up, erection, creation." Waite utilizes these concepts in portraying a mason constructing the arch of a temple containing three pentacles arranged in a triangle. Below this triad is the rose cross in a downward-pointing triangle.

This card is rich with Masonic symbolism. There are three figures below the archway. One is a tonsured monk (as a token of Key V—The Hierophant) representing the church for which the building is being crafted; one is the cowled and caped master mason holding the plans of the building (as a token of Key IX—The Hermit) and representing the grand architect; and one is his apprentice with maul in hand (as a token of Key I—The Magician) representing the artisan ready to craft the temple by the guidance of his master. This is Waite's Tarot revision of a traditional Masonic grouping of three men discussing the building of the temple: one is an entered apprentice, another a fellow craft, and the third the master mason.

The grand archway in Masonry is the key symbol for the seventh degree of Royal Arch Masons. This arch is usually made of 13 stones, with the central stone of the arch being the trapezoidal keystone, whose four sides measure by their proportion the four-lettered name of God. This keystone is symbolic of the sacred letter "G," for G is the 13th path as Gimel on the Tree of Life, while G is the seventh letter of both the Latin and English alphabets. Thus the 13 stones and their central seventh are symbolic of this Masonic G. And this "G" stands for God as the Geometer and Grand Architect of the Universe.

Three of Pentacles

The astrological nature of this card is the second decan of Capricorn, as Mars in Capricorn. The delicate archway contains these attributes. Capricorn is seen in the three pentacles, for their points total to 15, the number for Capricorn in the Major Arcana. Further, they are in the same location as the inverted star on the goat's head in Key XV. Mars is seen in the rose cross below the triangle of stars, for the rose is fivefold in its petals and red in color, both signatures of Mars.

If we superimpose the Tree of Life on this card, the triple archway of pentacles becomes the supernal triad of Kether, Chockmah, and Binah, which is the essential self as a radiant crown, which engenders wisdom and understanding. The rose cross becomes the invisible Sephirah Daath, as the Knowledge which leads from the interaction of wisdom and understanding. Within the supernal triad of pentacles is a circle divided by a cross. The upright line in this circle becomes the path of Gimel, while the horizontal line in this circle becomes the path of Daleth (forming the consonants for the word God as G-D). This mark, which is the original symbol for the Tree of Life as a fourfold directional cross, is also symbolic of Daath on the Tree of Life. It is one of the simplified forms of the rose cross, as well as Crowley's mark of the beast (or NOX sign) as found drawn in the 47th verse of the third chapter of *The Book of the Law*.

Four of Pentacles

Four of Pentacles
(Sun in Capricorn)

The Golden Dawn title for this card is "Lord of Earthly Power." Waite aptly illustrates this title as a king upon a throne, crowned by one pentacle and firmly grasping another against his chest, with the remaining two pentacles supporting his feet. Behind the king stretches his empire, which is truly the manifestation of his own earthly power.

Waite's model for this card is again in the Major Arcana, being Key IV—The Emperor, which also shows a crowned ruler seated on a stone throne.

While the Emperor holds his scepter and orb of royalty, the king of the Four of Pentacles holds his own wealth tightly as a shield.

There are four pentacles positioned on the king's body to correspond to the four letters of the Tetragrammaton as allocated in the *Zohar*. The pentacle crowning the head is the letter Yod (ruling the East), the pentacle at the heart is the letter Vav (ruling the West), and the pentacles supporting the right and left legs are the two Heh's, the right being the first Heh (ruling the South) and the left being the second Heh (ruling the North).

The astrological attribution for this card is the third and last decan of Capricorn, being the Sun in Capricorn. Neither attribute is clearly worked into Waite's design. If anything, the current of Aries is more apparent than Capricorn. The acquisition of money and power and the protection it can offer is, however, of a Capricornian nature, and this is the general spirit of this card.

Five of Pentacles
(Mercury in Taurus)

The Golden Dawn title for this card is "Lord of Material Trouble." Waite clearly shows this title in his version of the card as two paupers outside a lighted church window formed by five pentacles, walking destitute in a snowstorm. To further clarify the esoteric meaning of this card, Waite's own comment, incorporating Mathers' title, states that "the card foretells material trouble above all."

The astrological nature of this card is the first decan of Taurus, as Mercury in Taurus. The influence of Taurus is subtly shown in this card as the

Five of Pentacles

Six of Pentacles

bell hanging from the neck of the figure on crutches. This bell is in the shape of the Hierophant's body in Key V, which is also Taurus. It refers to the attribute of hearing as listening to the inner voice of intuition. The yellow light of the stained glass window is the color of Mercury as a path on the Tree of Life.

This card also has an esoteric meaning. The impoverished figures walking in the snow represent the general condition of all humanity. The light coming from within the church is the secret esoteric tradition, which is hidden from the norm. Contact with this light imparts freedom from the travails of life. However, until the teacher accepts the disciple into the sanctuary of the true teaching, the disciple moves in the world unaware of the illumination awaiting within the secret lodge. And this secret teacher is the Taurean card marked V in the Major Arcana, the Hierophant.

Six of Pentacles
(Moon in Taurus)

The Golden Dawn title for this card is "Lord of Material Success." Mathers further defines this key in his esoteric comment as "success in material things, prosperity in business ... power, influence, rank, nobility, rule over people." Waite has shown this to a degree in his own design, but again he combines this definition with the exoteric definition given in Mathers' pamphlet, *The Tarot*. The definition given in this pamphlet is "presents, gifts, gratification." Waite quotes directly from this definition in his own account, and encodes this concept by portraying a rich merchant giving alms to the poor.

It seems Waite had the most trouble in adhering to the Golden Dawn esoteric titles when portraying the Sixes in the Minor Arcana. Although the Six of Wands is faithful to Mathers' esoteric title, the Six of Cups and Six of Swords are both based exclusively on Mathers exoteric pamphlet, and the Six of Pentacles is a blend of both.

A possible justification for this substitution can be found in the pattern of the Tree of Life. The station for Six is the heart or center of the Tree of Life diagram; namely, Tiphereth. Therefore, Waite may have designed three of the four Sixes to protect the integrity of the secret tradition of the Golden Dawn by blinding part of his designs so that the complete picture would not be revealed to the uninitiated. Then again, Waite may have been biased towards the exoteric meanings and may have found fault with the esoteric descriptions of the four Sixes.

The astrological nature of this card is the third and last decan of Taurus, as the Moon in Taurus. The Taurus nature of this card is shown by the model from the Major Arcana used for it, which is again Key V—The Hierophant, also ruled by Taurus. The central robed merchant corresponds to the Hierophant himself, while the two beggars at either side correspond to the two acolytes at the foot of the Hierophant. To further establish the merchant as the Hierophant, Waite places his right hand from which four coins descend in the same Papal blessing as that of the Hierophant, two fingers straight up and two fingers curled. The Moon itself is shown in these four coins being dropped into the hand of the needy, for these four coins are falling in a straight line, which is the Geomantic shape Via, which is ruled by the Moon.

In the Hierophant's left hand is the triple staff of the Tree of Life. Here the merchant holds the scales of Libra. This correpondence is connected to Taurus, because both Libra and Taurus share the same planetary rulership by Venus. However, to the uninitiated, this card may seem by its appearance to be Libran rather than Taurean in nature. The scales in this case represent the proper measure of charity extended equally to all, to assist the needs of a suffering world, which is both Rosicrucian and Buddhistic in its teaching.

Esoterically, as the Five of Pentacles represents the unenlightened mass of humanity passing outside the circle of esoteric knowledge, the Six of Pentacles represents the World Teacher doling out the karmic earned experience of illumination to those ready to receive the light.

Seven of Pentacles
(Saturn in Taurus)

The Golden Dawn title for this key is "Lord of Success Unfulfilled." Mathers further defines this key as "a cultivator of land, and yet is loser thereby ... little gain for much effort." Waite clearly illustrates this as a farmer who

Seven of Pentacles

Misero

has stopped in the midst of his cultivation, as if it is too much effort. Waite's own comment on this key does not explain his own design; however, as usual, his illustration rather than his written comment captures the spirit of Mathers' esoteric title.

The astrological nature of this key is the third and last decan of Taurus, as Saturn in Taurus. Taurus is the work of the abundantly green garden, while the melancholic withdrawal of the laborer is Saturn.

The basis for this design is an ancient variant of the modern 78-card Tarot deck: the Tarocchi of Mantegna (E-Series). This deck, dating back to 1465 CE, is composed of 50 cards consisting of five suits of ten cards. This pattern is based on the Qabalistic division of the universe known as the 50 Gates of Binah. The first card in this deck is titled Misero (Beggar) and shows a beggar leaning on his staff in the exact same position as the farmer in Waite's Seven of Pentacles. Misero corresponds in design to the unnumbered Fool card of the 78 card deck.

Space forbids any real detailing of this alternate Tarot deck, but their titles and numbers are shown on the following page.

Tarocchi of Mantegna

E-Series
(Conditions of Humanity)

1. Misero—Beggar
2. Fameio—Servant
3. Artixan—Artisan
4. Merchadante—Merchant
5. Zintilomo—Gentleman
6. Chavalier—Knight
7. Doxe—Doge
8. Re—King
9. Imperator—Emperor
10. Papa—Pope

D-Series
(Muses)

11. Caliope—Epic poetry
12. Urania—Astronomy
13. Terpsicore—Choral dance
14. Erato—Erotic poetry and mime
15. Polimnia—Hymns
16. Talia—Idyllic poetry and comedy
17. Melpomene—Song
18. Euterpe—Lyric poetry
19. Clio—History
20. Apollo—Patron of the arts

C—Series
(Liberal Arts)

21. Grammatica—Grammar
22. Loica—Logic
23. Rhetorica—Rhetoric
24. Geometria—Geometry
25. Arithmetricha—Arithmetic
26. Musicha—Music
27. Poesia—Poetry
28. Philosofia—Philosophy
29. Astrologia—Astrology
30. Theologia—Theology

B—Series
(Principles and Virtues)

31. Iliaco—Spirit of the Sun
32. Chronico—Spirit of Time
33. Cosmico—Spirit of the World
34. Temperancia—Temperance
35. Prudencia—Prudence
36. Forteza—Fortitude
37. Iustica—Justice
38. Charita—Charity
39. Speranza—Hope
40. Fede—Faith

A—Series
(Firmament)

41. Luna—Moon
42. Mercurio—Mercury
43. Venus—Venus
44. Sol—Sun
45. Marte—Mars
46. Iupiter—Jupiter
47. Saturno—Saturn
48. Octava Spera—Eighth Sphere (Zodiac)
49. Primo Mobile—Prime Mover
50. Prima Causa—First Cause

Eight of Pentacles

Artixan

Compare the foregoing 50 cards to the Qabalistic 50 Gates of Understanding in Key Two, Volume I, of *The Key of It All,* found in the 65th through 69th Sephirotic tables. The first card, Misero, correponds to the first gate of Chaos, while the 50th and last card, Prima Causa, corresponds to the 50th Gate of God.

Two other Pentacle cards in Waite's Minor Arcana are also modeled on the Mantegna Tarot deck, and these two are the Eight and Nine of Pentacles.

Eight of Pentacles
(Sun in Virgo)

The Golden Dawn title for this card is "Lord of Prudence." Mathers' esoteric divinatory definitions include "Industriousness, skill, prudence, cunning." Waite develops this idea in his own portrayal of an apprenticed stonemason, working diligently at engraving eight pentagrams upon eight pentacles.

This design is similar to Waite's Three of Pentacles in that both show work wrought by the hands. As the Three of Pentacles represents art, the Eight of Pentacles represents craft.

As the Sun in Virgo, this card shows the meticulous work of a craftsman who is skilled with hands, which is the general influence of the Zodiac sign Virgo.

Nine of Pentacles

Zintilomo

This card is also loosely based on the Mantegna Tarot series. In this case, the artisan at the bench with his tools of the trade, attentively working at his craft, resembles the third Mantegna card, the Artisan, which shows an artisan busy at work at his workbench with his apprenticed helper behind him.

Nine of Pentacles
(Venus in Virgo)

The Golden Dawn title for this card is "Lord of Material Gain." Waite incorporates this concept in his own illustration of a woman standing in an abundant garden, surrounded and protected by her wealth of nine pentacles.

This card suggests the same type of monetary protection as the design for Four of Pentacles. As the Four of Pentacles denotes power obtained through wealth, this card denotes comfort gained through an inheritance.

This card is also loosely based on the Mantegna Tarot deck. In this case, the lady with her falconed glove resembles the falconer in the fifth card, the Gentleman, which also shows a figure holding a falcon in a raised gloved left hand.

The astrological nature of this card is Venus in Virgo. The gown of the royal lady within the garden is covered with a floral pattern that resembles the astrological sign of Venus, and brings to mind the Venus patterns woven throughout Key III—The Empress. The Virgo quality of this card is the cultivated vineyard of grapes behind the nine pentacles.

Ten of Pentacles
(Mercury in Virgo)

Ten of Pentacles

The Golden Dawn title for this card is "Lord of Wealth." Waite in his own unique execution of this key combines the esoteric meaning outlined in *Book T* of "old age and great wealth" (personified by the old man seated in the foreground of this card) with the exoteric meaning outlined in Mathers' *The Tarot* of "house, dwelling, habitation and family" (personified in the family grouped outside their own house in the background of this card).

The astrological nature of this card is the last decan of Virgo, as Mercury in Virgo. Neither astrological attribute is clearly worked into this card. But above all, this key contains a secret which Waite never openly disclosed in any of his writings on the Tarot: Waite tellingly arranges the ten pentacles of this card in the form of the ten Sephiroth of the Tree of Life, betraying his inner heartfelt conviction that the Tarot secretly encodes the esoteric doctrine of the Jewish Qabalah.

Waite Monogram

There is one more bit of symbolism in this card. The robe of the seated elder is covered with many patterns. There are clusters of grapes in a leaf pattern, and crossbars resembling Templar crosses connected to gridded squares. But at the back of this robe are the letters W-A-I-T-E intertwined in a magickal monogram resembling the sigils for the English alphabet created by Austin Spare.

PART THREE—THE COURT CARDS
THE SECRET ORDER WHICH ELUDES ALMOST ALL

The 16 Court, or Coate, Cards are the most misunderstood division of the Tarot. Mathers established a very unique order for these four-by-four cards, based on the fourfold family division of the Tetragrammaton. This pattern is properly employed by Waite, but it is not apparent. Crowley understood the secret Golden Dawn attributes, which leads with the Knight as the Father (and the letter Yod), but Case faltered in his own understanding. Though Case patently copied the sparse keys Waite placed in his own unique designs for the Court Cards (such as the bull on the throne of the King of Pentacles), Case's own esoteric instructions on the Court Cards reveal that Case confused the Kings with the Knights, as so many other lesser commentators on these cards have done as well.

Though not at all obvious, Waite worked into the pictorial symbols of the 16 Court Cards the true Golden Dawn Zodiacal attributes. As opposed to a card-by-card analysis of these symbols, which has been our method so far in examining Waite's Tarot, we must study the Court Cards in an isolated fashion in order to unravel the true Zodiacal clues. Our first task is to isolate Waite's 16 Court Cards into the four groups of personages (i.e., the four Knights, Queens, Kings, and Pages).

The Four Elemental Pages

Let us first examine the four Pages. They are the least detailed in symbolism of the four groups, and in their lack of detail they symbolize the four basic elements devoid of Zodiacal personality. There are enough apparent clues in these four Pages to clarify the allocation of the four elements to the four suits. This allocation is more distinct than the symbolism found in the four Aces for the four suits.

Page of Wands
(Earth of Fire)

The Page of Wands is the element Fire, as the counterchange Earth of Fire. In the Tetragrammaton, all four Pages represent the feminine power of the daughter, which as a fourfold element is Earth. In each suit, this element is counterchanged by a predominant element, which in the case of the Wand suit is the element Fire. This sixteenfold elemental symbolism is intimately connected with John Dee's Enochian system as well as the 16 Kalas of the Tantrik tradition. The black salamanders which decorate the Page's yellow tunic are the Golden Dawn elemental association for the elemental force of Fire, which is derived from Alchemical symbolism. The landscape itself is the desert, scorched by the heat of the Sun, which is a perfect metaphor for the elemental counterchange of Earth of Fire. The mountains in the background are pyramidal, and the pyramid in its original Greek form of ΠΥΡΑΜΙΣ means "vessel of fire." The pyramid shape is also the shape of the Platonic solid for Fire. The yellow tunic and red tights

are also fiery colors of the Sun and Mars. In addition, the red feather that crowns the cap of the Page resembles a flame in its Yod-like shape, to further indicate the elemental nature of Fire for this key.

Page of Cups
(Earth of Water)

Cap of Mem

The Page of Cups is the element Water, as the elemental counterchange of Earth of Water. The lotus flowers on her tunic are the Golden Dawn elemental symbol associated with the suit of Cups as Water.

The seashore in the foreground is where the ocean meets the earth, and as such the symbol for the counterchange of Earth of Water. The rolling waves in the background, as well as the fish emerging from the cup, are signatures for water as well. The blue and deep orange tunic and blouse of the Page are the traditional colors for the element Water.

Secretly, the blue hat, plume, and scarf of the Page are in the shape of the Hebrew letter Mem, which also corresponds to the element Water.

Page of Swords
(Earth of Air)

The Page of Swords is the element of Air, as the counterchange of Earth of Air. The billowing clouds in the sky and the flight of ten birds, the wind-blown tree in the distance, as well as the flowing hair of the Page all indicate the elemental nature of Air. The tights and tunic of the Page are yellow and mauve, the colors associated with the element Air.

Page of Pentacles
(Earth of Earth)

The Page of Pentacles represents the element Earth as the counterchange of Earth of Earth. In some systems, it is the last card of the Tarot deck, signifying the densest of matter, hence Earth of Earth. In all Tarot decks, it is the last of the 16 Court Cards.

The glen of green trees, the furrowed brown ground, the distant mountain peak, and the vegetation in the foreground all symbolize the element of Earth. The background color of yellow is an association with the Indian Tattva for Earth, which is a yellow square or cube (equivalent in the West to the alchemical element of Salt). The green tunic of the page is the traditional color for Earth in the West, the alternate color being black.

The Twelve Zodiacal Court Cards

With the establishment of the four Pages as personifications of the four basic elements, we can now direct our attention to the remaining 12 Court Cards, which by the sheer weight of their number must correspond to the 12 signs of the Zodiac. We will have to study these remaining 12 cards in a haphazard order, for Waite was not methodical in leaving pictorial clues when dealing with the Zodiacal Court Cards. In many instances, he places the same Zodiacal symbol on more than one card, making it very difficult to know which card is really the appropriate one for that sign of the Zodiac.

This greatly confused Paul Foster Case, and though Case faithfully copied the scant clues left by Waite in his own Tarot deck, Case did not fully understand them. The classic misunderstanding comes in the Knight and King of Pentacles. Though Case retains the bull's head on the throne of the King, he deems this King to be Virgo, while the Knight is Taurus in Case's secret astrological allocations for the Court Cards. This bull-headed throne is only one of two clear-cut clues found in Waite's Tarot deck. It should be noted here that Crowley, copying the same source as Waite's (i.e., *Book T*), came up with the valid Zodiacal correspondences first envisioned by Mathers.

<table>
<tr><td>Queen of Pentacles</td><td>King of Pentacles</td></tr>
<tr><td>(Water of Earth—Capricorn)</td><td>(Air of Earth—Taurus)</td></tr>
</table>

Two concrete clues emerge from the elaborate symbolism incorporated in these remaining 12 Court Cards that are not duplicated among the various design schemes. These two clues are found in the thrones of the Queen and King of Pentacles. If we look closely at the throne of the Queen of Pentacles, we find that the left arm terminates in a goat's head, while engraved on the side of the throne is a crouching Pan playing his panpipe. If we look at the throne of the King of Pentacles, both the arms and headrest are decorated with the head of a bull. Further, the armored foot of the King rests on the stylized effigy of a bull's head. The goat is symbolic of the Earth sign of Capricorn, and is the crest described for the Queen of Pentacles in the Golden Dawn *Book T*. The bull is symbolic of the Earth sign of Taurus, and likewise the Golden Dawn crest designated for the King of Pentacles.

From these two clues we can premise that the Queen of Pentacles is Capricorn and the King of Pentacles is Taurus. This is in agreement with Mathers' own Zodiacal allocation for the Court Cards. These are the only two correct clues Waite permits his uninitiated audience, strewing blinded duplicated Zodiacal clues throughout the remaining Court cards. In this sense Waite was least generous in his pictorial clues for the Court Cards, leaving even someone as astute as Case at a loss to the correct attributes for these cards.

Since Capricorn is one of the four cardinal signs and Taurus is one of the four fixed signs, we can infer from these two basic symbols of goat and

bull that the four Queens correspond to the four cardinal signs of Aries, Cancer, Libra, and Capricorn while the four Kings correspond to the four fixed signs of Taurus, Leo, Scorpio, and Aquarius. This is indeed the logic employed by Mathers in correlating the Court Cards to the constellations of the night sky.

In studying the remaining three Queens and three Kings, other symbols appear which can be deciphered in support of the allocation of the four Kings to the four fixed signs and the four Queens to the four cardinal signs. However, in more than one instance, the Zodiacal clue appears on more than one Court Card, obscuring the correct astrological associations. All of the astrological correlations must be qualified by the concrete clue of the bull for the King of Pentacles and the goat for the Queen of Pentacles.

Queen of Wands
(Water of Fire—Aries)

The Queen of Wands is the cardinal Fire sign of Aries, as the elemental counterchange of Water of Fire. This card contains one of the biggest blinds in the Court Cards, for there are more lions in the Queen's throne, than in the throne of the King, which would lead one to attribute the Queen to the Zodiac sign of Leo. Yet this card is Aries within the Golden Dawn attributions, while Leo is the King.

The abundance of sunflowers in this key is also confusing. This is not dictated by Mathers as an attribute for the Queen, nor does the sunflower denote Aries, but rather a solar influence. Waite uses these sunflowers in another solar card, growing in the enclosed garden in Key XIX—The Sun. In a secondary fashion, these sunflowers can designate Aries, for the planetary exaltation for Aries is the Sun. But with these solar flowers side by side with lions, the image of Leo ruled by the Sun comes directly to mind, rather than Aries.

There are some symbols used by Waite which are taken directly from *Book T*. The brooch of the cape is a leopard's head, which is the crest associated with this card, while the black cat at the Queen's feet is a tame version of the leopard detailed in *Book T*.

King of Wands
(Air of Fire—Leo)

The two lions appearing on the back of the throne of the King of Wands correctly allocate this key to the fixed Fire sign of Leo (whose symbol and name is the lion). Although the lion motif is incorporated to a greater degree in the Queen of Wands (appearing twice in the arms of the throne and twice in the backing of the throne), this is an intentional blind by Waite. The correct Golden Dawn attribution of Leo is to the King rather than the Queen of Wands. The King's robe is covered with salamanders, as

well as his throne, and by his side is a lizard which is also a salamander, the Golden Dawn symbol for elemental Fire. This lizard pattern is also repeated in the cards for the Knight and Page of Wands, but not the Queen.

Queen of Cups
(Water of Water—Cancer)

The throne of the Queen of Cups terminates in a scalloped shell, a signature for the shell of the crab, symbolic of the Zodiacal sign of Cancer.

This shell is also the clasp holding the Queen's flowing cape. The Golden Dawn allocation for the Queen is Cancer, which is a cardinal Water sign. The Queen of Pentacles has already established the identity of the Queen as a cardinal sign, and the Cup suit is the element of Water. This scalloped shell, which denotes Cancer, is an important clue in the Water suit, since it is not duplicated in the other Cup Court Cards.

King of Cups
(Air of Water—Scorpio)

The Zodiacal symbolism of this card is the most obscure of the four Cup Court Cards. However, four clues will help clear up this card:

1. The goat of Capricorn in the Queen of Pentacles

2. The bull of Taurus in the King of Pentacles

3. The lion of Leo in the King of Wands

4. The shell of Cancer in the Queen of Cups

From these clues, the two remaining Kings become the fixed signs of their element, while the two remaining Queens become the cardinal signs of their element.

The King of Cups is therefore the fixed Water sign of Scorpio, though no overt symbol of Scorpio is used, such as the eagle, the serpent, or the scorpion. However, the fish pendant as well as the fish upon the ocean can be seen as Scorpio, in the sense that the Hebrew letter corresponding to Scorpio, which is Nun, is the hieroglyph of a fish. But the fish as a key symbol in this suit qualifies the Knight of Cups as Pisces.

Waite did, however, faithfully reproduce Mathers' own vision of this card, for *Book T* specifies that the King of Cups holds a lotus in one hand, and a cup in the other hand. Waite further uses this lotus symbolism in the actual throne of the King.

Queen of Swords
(Water of Air—Libra)

The Queen of Swords is the cardinal Air sign of Libra, as the elemental counterchange of Water of Air. Again, no symbol clearly indicates the astrological nature of Libra. However the card depicts a throned female figure bearing a sword in her right hand, her left hand raised up as if holding the scales. This resembles Key XI—Justice, which is also Libra.

Waite uses the specifications of *Book T* again in this card for the winged, childlike kerubic head is the crest for Queen of Swords. The butterfly appears in this card in her crown and her throne, but *Book T* assigns the butterfly motif to the King as Aquarius.

King of Swords
(Air of Air—Aquarius)

The King of Swords is the fixed Air sign of Aquarius, as the elemental counterchange of Air of Air. Although most of the imagery in Waite's version of this key is of a general airy nature, such as the billowing clouds in the sky, there are two symbols which denote Aquarius.

The triangle of butterflies at the head of the King's throne denote Aquarius in a minor fashion, for in some variants of Key XVII—The Star, a butterfly rather than a bird rests in the branches of a background tree. Also, Key XVII is assigned to the Hebrew letter Tzaddi, which governs Aquarius.

The problem with this symbol, even if it is Aquarian, is that butterflies abound in the Knight and Queen of this suit as well. The goat and bull of

the pentacle suit must ultimately be our guide in this matter, which means that the King of Swords must correspond to the fixed Air sign Aquarius.

The second clue is the two birds flying parallel to each other in the upper right portion of the sky. These two birds suggest the astrological symbol of two wavy lines, which is the symbol for Aquarius.

The description of this card in *Book T* has the King sitting in a chariot drawn by elemental winged fairies. Though Waite did not follow Mathers' innovation of a chariot for the King, he did embroider these winged fairies into the throne on a level with the head of the King. A butterfly-wing motif is used in describing these arch-fairies, and that is another reason for the butterflies in Waite's own version of the King of Swords. The Golden Dawn crest for the King is a winged angel's head, and Waite works this into the crown of the King as well.

Knight of Wands
(Fire of Fire—Sagittarius)

Now with the establishment of the four fixed signs as the four Kings and the four cardinal signs as the four Queens, we can logically deduce that the four Knights represent the remaining four mutable signs of Sagittarius, Pisces, Gemini, and Virgo. We must logically deduce it, for Waite does not give us the pictorial keys necessary to make such deductions.

KNIGHT of CUPS.

KNIGHT of WANDS.

The Knight of Wands, being the element of Fire, must then be the mutable Fire sign of Sagittarius, and the elemental counterchange of Fire of Fire.

There is nothing peculiar to Sagittarius in this card. The salamanders and the pyramids both denote Fire, but they occur as well in the Page of Wands.

The *Book T* specifications for this key are slightly worked into the card in the red plume of the figure's helmet and the flame-red tongues of his golden-yellow cloak. But the crest for this card is a black horse, as well as the color of the horse itself, which Waite does not use. The helmet should be winged, but Waite ignores this as well, placing these wings instead on the helmet of the Knight of Cups.

Knight of Cups
(Fire of Water—Pisces)

Only one of the four Knights contains any symbolism which can clearly validate this Zodiacal association of the mutable signs to the four Knights, and that is the Knight of Cups. This Knight has many fish emblazoned on his tunic, and in this instance the fish designate the sign of Pisces. Though the fish is incorporated in all four Court cards of the Cup suit, more fish appear in the Knight card than in any of the other three Cup cards, establishing the Knight of Cups as the key for Pisces.

The Golden Dawn specifications for the colors of the horses of the Wand and Cup Knights are the black and white of the pillars of the temple, but Waite instead uses brown and gray for these Hermetic horses.

Knight of Swords
(Fire of Air—Gemini)

Butterflies, seagulls, and hooded falcons abound in Waite's Knight of Swords, but the Gemini nature of this card is not directly indicated in any of these symbols.

Two Golden Dawn symbols from *Book T* are used by Waite in this card: the driving clouds in the sky and the hexagram decorating the helmet, which is the designated crest for the Knight of Swords. The horse, however, should be brown, but Waite again uses gray.

Knight of Pentacles
(Fire of Earth—Virgo)

The final card in our Court Card puzzle is the Knight of Pentacles. This card again has no direct clue to reveal the Zodiacal quality of Virgo. The Knight of Pentacles is the mutable earth sign of Virgo, as the counterchange of Fire of Earth. Though Virgo is not directly implied, Waite used one symbol from

Book T. The crest for the Knight of Pentacles is a stag's head, and Waite places the horns of this stag both on the horse's head and the knight's helmet. The horse should be light brown in a cornfield, but Waite uses neither color nor corn. But the furrowed brown field in Waite's card is symbolic of the harvesting of the field at the time when the sign of Virgo ends.

In looking at all 16 Court Cards, very few pictorial keys are apparent in Waite's unique designs for these cards. It is as though Waite wished to encode the unique Golden Dawn astrological attributes for these cards in the barest amount of symbolism, but intended as well to obscure these clues so that the less persistent researcher would be unable to correctly decipher them.

Conclusion

In summation, our study of Waite's Tarot designs in light of Mathers' *Book T* has disclosed that:

- The Major Arcana conceals in its order and design the Hebrew alphabet Qabalistic attributes rediscovered by Mathers, which assigns the Fool rather than the Magician to the first Hebrew letter, Aleph.

- The picture images illustrating the 36 pip cards of the Minor Arcana peculiar to Waite's version of the Tarot are based on the Golden Dawn esoteric titles and definitions.

- The Court Cards conceal in their symbolism the Golden Dawn astrological attributes for these 16 keys.

All Tarot decks yet to be drawn would be influenced by these unique designs, wrought by the hands of the artist Pamela under the Qabalistic guidance of Arthur. Without these delicate Victorian drawings of an almost faery-like world of magick and wizardry, the shape and destiny of the Tarot would not be of the dimensions it has assumed today. And behind these 78 colored designs is cast the giant shadow of the genius of Mathers, the real creator of the Waite deck.

The One Mercurial Key
Not from the East,
Nor from the West

THIRTEENTH KEY

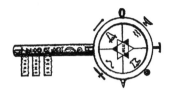

ENGLISH

OVERVIEW

This final chapter is dedicated to a language which is neither East nor West, but because of its Mercurial nature may become the first global language.

English, firmly rooted in the West, does not have an apparent established mystical, numerical, or Qabalistic nature. Beyond the systems of modern numerology and Roman numerals, the association of letter to number does not quickly come to mind for English. However, there are many tentative number codes which can be given to English, some of which have already occurred in print and some of which can be conjectured from the esoteric alphanumeric codes contained in the other chapters of this book. The 13th key does just that, setting out one code after another for English, with a sampling of words numbered to demonstrate the various codes in action.

I have set out the many, varied codes for English in this chapter so that you can first briefly use each one separately in analyzing any English word of your choice, and then use the code (or codes) you feel holds the most promise to change to number a certain group of English magickal terms (such as the Tarot titles, terms in astrology, or a short, sacred poem or text). As always, this number research should be integrated into your number dictionary files and compared to existing entries of the same number value for further verification and validation of your chosen English numerical code.

This key offers the following basic number codes for English from which you can base your own research on the numerical structure of English:

- **Phonetic Cabala.** Rather than a numerical Qabalah, this code equates words which sound alike in different languages, connecting word concepts by sound rather than by number.

- **Serial English Qabalah.** This simple code for English is based on the serial order of the alphabet. In this sense, the alphabet code resembles Homeric Greek, Sanskrit Serial alphabet codes, the Tibetan number code, the Runes, Ogham, Beth-Luis-Nion, and the Latin Cabala Simplex. In this code A = 1, Z = 26.

- **German Alphabet Serial Order.** The same code as above for the German alphabet of 26 letters. In this code A = 1, Z = 26.

- **The English Qabalah of Liber Trigrammaton.** A code for English devised by Crowley based on the trigrams of the *I Ching*. In this code, A = 9, Z = 14.

- **Sanskrit-English Qabalah.** Crowley felt that Sanskrit might hold the true key for numbering the English alphabet. By applying to English the rules for KaTaPaYa, found in the fourth key of this book, Crowley's vision of a Sanskrit key to English can be completed. In this digital code, A = no value or place value, Z = 6.

- **Enochian-English Qabalah.** Crowley felt that Enochian might also be a key to unlocking a numbering system for English. By using the Golden Dawn and Crowley variant number values for Enochian, and pairing them to their corresponding English letters, an Enochian-English code can be developed. In this code A = 6, Z = 1.

- **Phonetic Hebrew-English Qabalah.** Crowley, in his own investigations of the magickal significance of any word, employed a Hebrew phonetic Qabalah to number such English words as his own name. In this code, each English letter can often have more than one number value because of the variety of phonetic transliteration systems available for Hebrew into English. In this code A = 1, 10, or 70; Z = 7, 60, or 90.

- **Phonetic-English Qabalah.** Every letter of the English alphabet has a letter name, based on the phonetic pronunciation of the letter. Thus A would be Ae (or Aye), while Z would be Zee. If these peculiar letter names are numbered according to the serial Qabalah, then another variant Qabalah for English can be established. In this code A= 6 (or 31), Z = 36.

- **German-English Qabalah.** The Latin Qabalah in the German tradition is based on the serial order, which is first added together and then squared to form three separate values for English. In this code, A = 1, 1, 1; Z = 26, 351, 676.

- **Graeco-English Qabalah.** The English alphabet of 26 letters can be paralleled to the 27-letter alphabet of Greek reduced by one letter (Sampi = 900). By this code, the higher range of numbers can be obtained for English, since A = 1 while Z = 800 (as a parallel to Omega).

- **Modern Numerology.** The only established numbering system for English is the reduction of the 26 letters of English to the numbers 1 through 9. In modern numerology A=1 while Z=8.

- **Fadic Numerology.** A variant on modern numerology mates the 26 letters of English to the numbers 1 through 8 based on their phonetic resemblance to Hebrew. In this code A = 1 while Z = 7.

These 12 English number codes are followed by a tabling of the hieroglyphic images for English, based mainly upon the images of ancient alphabets out of which English evolved. These hieroglyphic images transform the letters of the English alphabet into a Tarot-like collage of symbolic images. These symbols can easily be combined into 26 mandalas which you can construct for the English alphabet, as a supplemental deck to your self-made Tarot decks.

Following this table of hieroglyphic images is a listing of the powers and forces of English, if English is paralleled to the Golden Dawn Hebraic-Tarot key. In this parallel of English to Hebrew, the first 22 letters of English are equal to the basic 22 letters of Hebrew.

Thus A → V (English)
(is equal to) Aleph → Tav (Hebrew)

The remaining four English letters become the elemental cycle of Fire, Water, Air, and Earth, as:

W = Fire   X = Water

Y = Air   Z = Earth

This symbol set can be added to your hieroglyphic cards for the English alphabet. The colors tabled out are especially appropriate for such a project.

This English key ends with two major tables that combine every major alphabet given in this text. The first table, "The Magickal Polyglot," sorts every major code by the phonetic order of English. By this polyglot, every possible number value which can be ascribed to the English alphabet can be seen at once. This table also gives a sense of continuity and divergence amid all the number codes of the world's many esoteric languages. The second major table is "The Sieve of Numbers." By this table, every major code in the text is categorized by its intrinsic number values beginning with 0 and progressing to 100,000,000,000,000,000. With this table, you can determine which corresponding magickal alphabet letter to use when a number is employed in ritual or meditation. This table also details the wide range of number values spanned by the many number codes of the world. Thus, with these two major tables, the phonetic and numbering range can be established for every major code appearing in this text.

Origin

800–1200 CE—Old English

1200–1700 CE—Middle English

1700 CE to present—Modern English; serial code of 1 through 26 is a product of Modern English

1904 CE—Reception of the inspired book, *The Book of the Law*, in Cairo by Aleister Crowley, which predicted the correct decipherment of the English Alphabet.

Alphabet Code

English, unlike the other languages analyzed in this book, does not contain a clearly defined set of mystical, magickal, or numerical symbols. English is a phonetic hybrid of many languages, and by its natural association to word groups in other languages, a phonetic cabala for English has developed in the last 200 years, which appears in the writings of, among others, Godfrey Higgins (*Anacalypsis, an Attempt To Draw Aside The Veil of The Saitic Isis*, 1836), H.P. Blavatsky (*Isis Unveiled*, 1877, and *The Secret Doctrine*, 1888), and Fulcanelli (*Le Mystere des Cathedrales*, 1925).

In all the above-mentioned works, words which one is familiar with in any modern European language, including English, can be traced by the more Eastern sources, such as Egyptian, Hebrew, Arabic, and Sanskrit. An example of this phonetic cabala is the English word "man," which can easily be traced to both Sanskrit and Hebrew. As Sanskrit, the English word "man" can be equated to the following term:

MaN—to think, believe, perceive, know, understand, imagine

Further, if "man" is written first backwards and then forwards in Sanskrit, the work NAMaN is produced, meaning "mind," "mark," and "token," as well as "name."

As Hebrew, the English word "man" can be traced to a permutation of AMN, the Hebrew Amen.

This analysis using the logic of the phonetic cabala does not give a numerical equivalent to any one letter of the English alphabet. As a system of symbolic interpretation, it does not address the classical Qabalistic concerns of number and measure but rather seeks to find a common phonetic basis for all languages. However, though the English alphabet does not contain a well-established set of numerical equivalents, a book was received in trance in 1904 CE that predicted the discovery of a correct number value for the English alphabet. This book is Aleister Crowley's *Book of the Law* (also known as *Liber AL*).

This short treatise of 220 verses makes reference in certain passages to a Qabalistic code for English. The 55th verse of the second chapter speaks of an "order & value of the English Alphabet" which Crowley (or possibly someone else) was to obtain and which would include a set of "new symbols to attribute" to the letters of the English alphabet.

English, before 1904, contained a basic numerical set of equivalents as a military cipher as early as the 17th century. This simple code equated the serial order of the 26 letters of the English alphabet as their numerical values. Thus A, the first letter, is valued at 1, while Z, which is the 26th letter, is valued at 26. Modern numerology uses these values and reduces them to a single digit to get their number equivalents. Thus Z, which is 26 in the serial order cipher, is 8 (as 26 = 2 + 6 = 8) in modern numerology.

ENGLISH SERIAL ORDER QABALAH

This military serial cipher for English has been used by many commentators on the secret value of English, including Isidore Kozminsky, Robert Hoffstein, and William Eisen. The following table will delineate the 26 number values for English.

Serial English Qabalah

A = 1	N = 14
B = 2	O = 15
C = 3	P = 16
D = 4	Q = 17
E = 5	R = 18
F = 6	S = 19
G = 7	T = 20
H = 8	U = 21
I = 9	V = 22
J = 10	W = 23
K = 11	X = 24
L = 12	Y = 25
M = 13	Z = 26

If the above code (of A = 1, Z = 26) is applied to the English language at large, the precise set of metaphors produced by other languages which compose the secret tradition of alphabet magick cannot be duplicated. However, two very important Qabalistic equivalents can be produced by this serial number code, one involving the Hebrew Qabalah's highest name for God, and the other involving the key Qabalistic formula found in Crowley's *Book of the Law*.

THE ESOTERIC VALUE OF THE NUMBER 26

The Hebraic secret code that this English Qabalah discloses involves the great name Jehovah (or Yahweh). Both "Jehovah" in Hebrew and "God" in English are equal to the same number value of 26:

Jehovah = IHVH or יהוה (Hebrew) = 10 + 5 + 6 + 5 = 26
God = GOD (English) = 7 + 15 + 4 = 26

Why is this important? Because the most secret number of Qabalistic geometry and word metaphor is 26, which in turn can be equated to the English word "God," which the tradition of Freemasonry initializes as their sacred "G" (although this "G" was originally intended as the initial letter of Geometry).

This letter "G," which is seen at the center of the Masonic square and compass, is equated by Freemasons to the initial letter Yod (I, ') in Hebrew. And by Hebrew gematria and the English serial order these two initials of G and I both contain words equal to each other by number.

G = GOD = 26 (English)
I = IHVH = 26 (Hebrew)

This key number 26 is of extreme importance in Qabalistic symbolism, for 26 is the number which governs the proportions or component parts of:

- The cube

- The golden rectangle

- The squaring of the circle

- The Masonic apron

- The Zodiacal kerubic angels

- The middle pillar

- Dante's cosmology

- Dee's Enochian Sigil Emeth

The Cube. As the proportion of the Cube, 26 is the sum of the component parts which compose the cube, for the cube is made up of six faces, eight corners, and twelve edges, and 6 + 8 + 12 = 26. This key proportion also applies to the octahedron (both are Platonic solids, the cube being Earth and the octahedron being Air), for the octahedron is made up of six corners, eight faces, and twelve edges.

The Golden Rectangle. As the proportion which governs the golden rectangle of ancient, classical, and Renaissance art, 26 is the sum of the borders of such a rectangle. The proportion that governs the construction of the golden rectangle is a rectangle whose sides are 5 by 8 units. In such a rectangle, the perimeter would measure 26 units: 5 + 8+ 5 + 8 = 26.

The Squaring of the Circle. As the Hermetic mathematical puzzle of the squaring of the circle, 26 is the value of the circle and the square combined: the circle is 22 (in light of pi being 22/7) while the square is 4. Thus the circle and square conjoined is 26. This numbering also applies to any symbol combining a circle with a cross (which is also valued at 4).

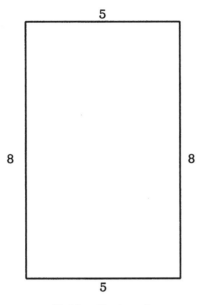

Golden Rectangle

The Masonic Apron. The true proportions of the Masonic apron are the four Hebraic letters of the Tetragrammaton, 10 (׳), 5 (ה), 6 (ו), and 5 (ה), forming the lengths of the four borders of the apron itself.

Thus the borders of the Masonic Apron contain the divine name Jehovah as 10 units + 5 units + 6 units + 5 units. The base of the apron is the lead letter Yod, the top of the apron is Vav, the right side is the first Heh, while the left side is the final Heh. This geometric shape is sometimes referred to as the "Sacred Trapezoid."

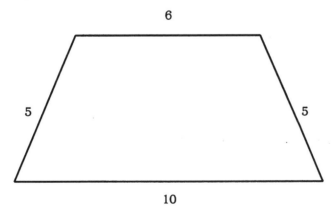

True Proportion of Masonic Apron or Sacred Trapezoid

The Four Kerubic Angels. As the four kerubic angels of Qabalistic angeology, 26 is concealed in the serial order of the four fixed Zodiacal signs of Taurus, Leo, Scorpio, and Aquarius as 2, 5, 8, and 11.

The Four Kerubic Angels as 26

Zodiac Sign	Image in Ezekiel	Element	Zodiacal Order	Number Value
Taurus	Ox (ShVR, שור)	Earth	2nd	2
Leo	Lion (ARIH, אריה)	Fire	5th	5
Scorpio	Eagle (NShR, נשר)	Water	8th	8
Aquarius	Man (ADMf, אדם)	Air	11th	<u>11</u>
				26

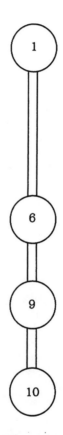

The Middle Pillar of the Tree of Life

The Middle Pillar. As the Middle Pillar of the Tree of Life, 26 is the sum of the Sephiroth (or circles) which compose the central, or middle, pillar of the Tree of Life: 1 (Kether) + 6 (Tiphereth) + 9 (Yesod) + 10 (Malkuth) = 26. These four Sephiroth compose the shamanistic World Tree or Axis, which is a single pole, or shaft, joining Heaven with Earth. It is the path that permits direct communion with God. It is the Tree of Life as a single palm tree (ThMR, תמר in Hebrew).

Dante's Cosmology. As Dante's cosmology, found in his *Divine Comedy*, 26 represents the component division, categories, or stages of the ascent of the soul from hell, through purgatory, to heaven. These three afterlife stations are graded into 26 divisions as 9 + 7 + 10.

Dante's Cosmology

Station	Division	Sum
Inferno	9 rings	9
Purgatorio	7 steps	7
Paradisio	10 levels	<u>10</u>
		26

Dee's Enochian Sigil Emeth. As Dee's grand Sigil Emeth (Hebrew for "truth") that governs all of the Enochian angels, 26 is the sum of the geometric panticles which are enclosed by the grand circle of this sigil. Within the circle of this sigil are four geometric shapes: a pentagram, a heptagon, a heptagram, and another heptagon.

The Panticles of Dee's Sigil Emeth

The sum of these four panticles is 26 (5 + 7 + 7 + 7 = 26). Dee's source for these panticles is the Great Seal of God, found in *The Sworn Book of Honourius, the Magician*. This seal is also composed of a circle containing a heptagon, heptangle, heptagon, and pentagram.

THE ESOTERIC VALUE OF THE NUMBER 93

By this simple serial code for English, the secret word, which is not only in English, can be found within Aleister Crowley's Book of the Law. This early 20th-century trance document declares in the 39th verse of the third chapter, that there exists within its pages, "the word secret & not only in the English." By this serial code, the 39th verse of the first chapter may reveal the "word secret." For this 39th verse reads as a mathematical equation when numbered by both this serial English Qabalah and by the Pythagorean Greek Qabalah. This 39th verse states:

"The word of the Law is θελημα."

By the process of the English serial Qabalah:

"the word" = 93
([20 + 8 + 5] + [23 + 15 + 18 + 4] = 93)

By the process of the Greek Pythagorean Qabalah:

θελημα (*Thelema*, Will) = 93
(9 + 5 + 30 + 8 + 40 + 1) = 93

Therefore:

"the word" = θελημα
93 = 93

Crowley in all his years of Qabalistic research was obsessed with the number 93, yet he never uncovered this simple English/Greek Qabalistic formula, which ties in the 39th verse of the first and third chapters of *The Book of the Law* with a double value of 93.

The connection of the English "the word" to 93 supports the Qabalistic associations for this number that Crowley developed from 1904 to 1947. For example, 93 is the value of "the word" in Greek as:

επη (EPH) = 5 + 80 + 8 = 93,

which when written backwards in Coptic becomes "number":

ⲎⲠⲈ (ĒPE) = 8 + 80 + 5 = 93

And as επη, the words of an epic poem, is 93, so are the three consonants of λογος (LOGOS, the word) when rendered as Hebrew:

לגס (LGS) = 30 + 3 + 60 = 93,

which when written backwards in Arabic becomes "the angel" who bears a message upon a scroll:

سجل (SJL) = 60 + 3 + 30 = 93

And this angel is Crowley's communicator of *The Book of the Law*, Aiwass, as written in Hebrew:

עווז (OIVZ) = 70 + 10 + 6 + 7 = 93

Thus the 93 formulae:

Word (ϵπη) = Number (ΗΠϵ)
Word (לגֹס) = Angel (سجل)
Angel (سجل) = Aiwass (עיוז)
θϵλημα (AL I:39) = "the word" (AL I:39)

THE 93 CURRENT

One more harmony concerning the significance of the Thelemic number 93 should be analyzed. Crowley, in numbering the Flaming Sword (or Lightning Bolt), whose zigzag descent from heaven marks the 10 Sephiroth on the Tree of Life, came up with the number 777. This Qabalistic discovery was used by Crowley as the basis for naming his dictionary classifying the 32 Paths of the Tree as *Liber 777*. This diagram on the Tree of Life is as follows:

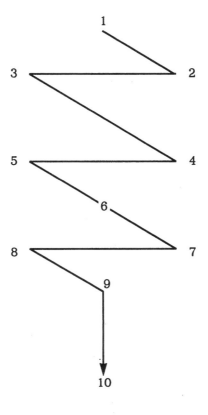

The Flaming Sword on the Tree of Life

By numbering, as Hebrew letters, the corresponding straight Paths that this Flaming Sword follows in its descent from 1 to 10, Crowley obtained the number 777. However, since the Path from 3 to 4 is invisible on the Tree of Life, Crowley substituted the Path connecting 1 to 6 (that of Gimel).

Though Crowley analyzed this Golden Dawn diagram as Hebrew letters, he never considered it in light of the corresponding Tarot cards. If he had done so, he would have discovered that this Flaming Sword is valued at 93, the key Thelemic number. And this sacred value of 93 can be obtained by either Crowley's own order for the Tarot or by the orthodox Golden Dawn order. This numbering is as follows:

The 93 Current on the Tree of Life as the Flaming Sword

Path on Tree as Hebrew	Connecting Sephiroth	Value of Hebrew	Tarot Values Crowley	G.D.
Aleph	1 and 2	1	0	0
Daleth	2 and 3	4	3	3
Gimel	3 and 4 as 1 and 6	3	2	2
Teth	4 and 5	9	11	8
Lamed	5 and 6	30	8	11
Nun	6 and 7	50	13	13
Peh	7 and 8	80	16	16
Resh	8 and 9	200	19	19
Tav	9 and 10	400	21	21
	Total:	777	93	93

Thus the 93 Current, or Current 93, which has come to designate the periodic descent of magickal inspiration, tailored for our present age, can be symbolized as the Lightning Bolt, or Flaming Sword, which turns every which way in forming the 10 Sephiroth on the Tree of Life.

THE GERMAN ALPHABET SERIAL ORDER QABALAH

The earliest magickal use of the German alphabet serial order Qabalah, which is the true esoteric source for the English serial order Qabalah, can be found in the Rosicrucian work, *The Chymical Marriage of Christian Rosenkreutz* (1616 CE). Within this Alchemical-Rosicrucian allegory is a puzzle given by one "Virgo Lucifera," which not only contains the essence of the English Qabalah of A = 1 and Z = 26, but also contains the source for the number-name secret of NU expounded in AL I:24. The riddle reads as follows: "My name contains six and fifty, yet has only eight letters. The third is a third part of the fifth, which added to the sixth will produce a number, the root whereof shall exceed the third by the first precisely, and it is the half of the fourth. The fifth and seventh are equal; so are the last and first. These make with the second as much as the sixth has, and this contains four more than the third tripled."

Note that this Rosicrucian mystery name (a secret name of the Virgin, "Virgo Lucifera") uses the wording "my name contains six and fifty," which is remarkably similar to AL I:24, "my word is six and fifty."

The solution to the above eight-lettered mystery name valued at 56 (six and fifty) requires first that the 26 letters of the German alphabet (and not the Latin alphabet) be numbered in their sequential order (A being 1 and Z being 26). Armed with this serial Qabalah, the eight-lettered name can be obtained, and this mystery name is *alchimia* (Alchemy). By the German serial order *alchimia* is the eight letters totaling 56, because:

$$A = 1 \text{ (1st letter)}$$
$$L = 12 \text{ (2nd letter)}$$
$$C = 3 \text{ (3rd letter)}$$
$$H = 8 \text{ (4th letter)}$$
$$I = 9 \text{ (5th letter)}$$
$$M = 13 \text{ (6th letter)}$$
$$I = 9 \text{ (7th letter)}$$
$$\underline{A = 1 \text{ (8th letter)}}$$
$$\text{ALCHIMIA} = 56 \text{ (eight-letter name)}$$

This eight-letter formula obeys all the number ratios which are found in the riddle. The third letter (C) is valued at 3, which is a third part of 9 (the value of the fifth letter, I). Add this fifth letter to the sixth (I to M) and 22 is produced (9+13), which, when reduced to its root, produces 4 (22 = 2 + 2 = 4). This value of 4 is one more than the third letter (C), one being the value of the first letter (A). Four is also half the value of the fourth letter (H). The fifth and seventh letters are equal (both being I, valued at 9), as well as the first and last letters (both being A, valued at 1). When this first (or last) letter is added to the second letter L (1 added to 12), then the sixth letter M is produced (1 + 12=13). And this sixth letter is 4 more than the third letter C tripled, for (3 x 3) + 4 = 13.

Therefore, since the serial order can be found encoded in this Rosicrucian text, as well as a female mystery name connected with "six and fifty," *The Chymical Marriage* can be seen as an original source for the English serial order Qabalah.

CROWLEY'S ENGLISH QABALAH

Aleister Crowley offered three separate methods of providing a numerical Qabalah for English, while he developed from his Golden Dawn training a fourth phonetic Qabalah. This last method was never tabled by Crowley, but can be derived from the Qabalistic English commentaries which are abundant in his voluminous writings. The first three methods are less detailed in Crowley's writings and are only hinted at in his Cefalu comment to *The Book of the Law*.

> The attribution in *Liber Trigrammaton* is good theoretically; but no Qabalah of merit has arisen therefrom. I am inclined to look further into the question of Sanskrit roots, and into Enochian records, in order to put this matter in more polished shape.
>
> —New Commentary to AL II:55.

The three separate methods Crowley proposes for rectifying the esoteric order of English are:

1. An order for the English alphabet detailed in Crowley's *Liber Trigrammaton*

2. The phonetic structure of Sanskrit

3. The numerical structure of Enochian

Even though Crowley's clues are sparse, all codes can be reconstructed in light of the research presented in the many chapters of *The Key of It All*. The first code Crowley mentions for English is the secret order of the English alphabet utilized in *Liber Trigrammaton*. This secret alphabet order begins with I and ends with U, forming the oldest Egyptian name for God (IU). If these 26 letters are given the serial order of 1 through 26 (in accordance with AL II:55), Crowley's first Qabalah suggested for English can be reconstructed:

The English Qabalah of Liber Trigrammaton

I = 1	Z = 14
L = 2	B = 15
C = 3	F = 16
H = 4	S = 17
X = 5	M = 18
T = 6	N = 19
Y = 7	E = 20
P = 8	R = 21
A = 9	Q = 22
J = 10	V = 23
W = 11	K = 24
O = 12	D = 25
G = 13	U = 26

Although this code resembles an ABC serial order code, no real results as yet have been produced with this Qabalistic order for English. Crowley himself supports this premise in commenting that "no Qabalah of merit has arisen therefrom."

The basis for ordering the English alphabet as I, L, C is the actual graphic shape of each English letter. Crowley broke down each alphabet character to a numerical equivalent according primarily to its shape alone, with Qabalistic considerations as a secondary means of ordering the alphabet. The logic for the first 13 letters is apparent; the remaining 13 appear to be haphazard in their arrangement. It is as if Crowley hit on an interesting device for numbering the English alphabet based on the shape of its letters and then discovered that such attributions would only partially work.

The logic behind the first 13 letters is as follows:

1. I = 1, because this letter is one stroke in the shape of the phallus as well as the Roman numeral for one.

2. L = 2, because L is made of two I's joined at right angles (2 x 1 = 2).

3. C = 3, because C is a crescent or curve which joins two points (1 + 2 = 3).

4. H = 4, because H suggests (and can be contained by) a square. The four extreme points of this letter provide the basis for its numeration of 4 (instead of 5 or 6).

5. X = 5, because X represents 4 extreme points and a 5th point as its center (4 + 1 = 5).

6. T = 6, because T represents the meeting of three straight lines at a common point. Here the straight line receives the value of 2 (because any straight line connects two points) as opposed to the value for "I" as 1 (3 x 2 = 6).

7. Y=7, because three straight lines (each valued at 2) converge at a center point ([2 x 3] + 1 = 7). Note that H is to X as T is to Y. In both cases H and T give no value for a center, while X and Y value the center as 1.

8. P = 8, because P suggests an incomplete figure 8. Here Enochian has also been used as a measure, because P = 8 in Enochian, according to Golden Dawn numerical values.

9. A = 9, because A is composed of three triangles, two at the base and one at the apex (3 x 3 = 9).

10. J = 10, because J is composed of the letter I, valued at 1, and a curving hook, suggestive of zero (1 + 0 = 10).

11. W = 11, because W is double U (or two U's); here duality as 1 + 1 = 11 rather than 2.

12. O = 12, because O suggests in its shape the circular firmament that contains 12 signs of the Zodiac.

13. G = 13, because G is composed of I (valued at 1) conjoined to C (valued at 3) (1 + 3 = 13).

Continuing, the second set of 13 numerical attributes for English weaken in their logic.

14. Z = 14. Z if contained by a square (4) would bisect that square by a diagonal line (1) (1 + 4 = 14).

15. B = 15. Here the construction of the letter suggests 13 more than the allocated number of 15.

16. F = 16, because F is 6 in Greek-Coptic.

17. S = 17, because the Hebrew צ (Tz or S) is Key 17 in the Golden Dawn Tarot.

18. M = 18, because Key 18 in the Tarot begins with "M" (Moon).

19. N = 19 has no apparent correlation, though N follows M in normal alphabetical sequence (note: "nineteen" begins with "N").

20. E = 20, because the 20th path on the Tree of Life is Virgo ruled by Mercury, corresponding to the letter E in Greek.

21. R = 21, has no apparent correlation, though R in shape suggests 1 + 2 conjoined (2 +1 = 21).

22. Q = 22, because Q, like O, is circular. The correlation may be to 22/7.

23. V = 23, because 2 + 3 = 5, and V is both 5 in Roman numerals and as Tarot Hebrew (the 5th Tarot Key = The Hierophant).

24. K = 24 has no apparent correlation, though K is Jupiter in Hebrew, associated with both 20 and 4 (20 + 4 = 24).

25. D = 25, because D in Hebrew has an alternate planetary attribute of Mars, associated with 5, while 25 is 5^2.

26. U = 26 (or last), because U suggests the vagina while "I" suggests the phallus. Thus the phallus leads while the vagina terminates this secret order of the alphabet.

The following are examples of this code in action:

- Aiwaz = 44

- Aiwass = 64

- The Word = 99

- N.O.X. = 36

- Key = 51

- Had = 38

- Nu = 45

Aiwaz as 44 brings out the Horus current associated with the Hebrew word דם (DM, blood), also valued at 44.

Aiwass as 64 brings out the Mercurial nature of this name (8 x 8).

The Word as 99 connects this word with the Greek αμην (AMHN, Amen) also valued at 99. The other four examples are of a lesser level of symbolic correspondence.

Although the application of this "ILC" alphabet order can bring about some interesting results, it cannot equal the concrete solutions that the "ABC" serial order produces.

Crowley's second suggested Qabalah for English involves the use of the phonetic values of Sanskrit as a pattern for English. Crowley did not leave any such correlations in his printed writings. It is extremely doubtful that Crowley was aware of the Vedic numeral code outlined in the Sanskrit chapter found in *Book One: The Eastern Mysteries*. However, had Crowley been exposed to this marvelous numbering system, he would have been equipped with a valid tool which would have enabled him to render the Sanskrit numerical values for the phonetically equivalent English alphabet letters.

If we first parallel the 26 English alphabet letters to their Sanskrit phonetic models, and then substitute the Sanskrit Vedic numbers for the English alphabet numeration, Crowley's envisioned Sanskrit-English Qabalah can be reconstructed.

Crowley's Sanskrit-English Qabalah
Based on Ka-Ta-Pa-Ya-Dhi

English Letter	Sanskrit Model	Number Value	English Letter	Sanskrit Model	Number Value
A	A	no value	N	N	0 (place value)
B	B	3	O	O	no value
C	C	6	P	P	1
D	D	8	Q	Kh	2
E	E	no value	R	R	2
F	Ph	2	S	S	7
G	G	3	T	T	1
H	H	8	U	U	no value
I	I	no value	V	V	4
J	Jh	9	W	V	4
K	K	1	X	Ks	0 (place value)
L	L	3	Y	Y	1
M	M	5	Z	S	6

The rules for numbering English using this code parallel the Vedic code for Sanskrit (Southern Indian Ka-Ta-Pa-Ya-Dhi).

- The code is digital rather than additional.

- Each consonant or conjoined consonant is one digit of the composite number.

- Vowels have no number or place value.

- When two or more consonants appear together without the intervention of a vowel, the last consonant receives the number value.

- The consonant or conjoined consonant farthest to the right is the units place. Each separate consonant from right to left becomes a digit of the composite number.

The following are examples of this code in action:

- Aiwaz = 46

- Aiwass = 47

- The Word = 8 + 48 = 56 (the = 8, word = 48)

- N.O.X. = 0 (zero) + no value + 0 (zero) = 0

- Key = 11

- Had = 88

- Nu = 0 (zero) + no value = 0

This code is far richer in Qabalistic allusions than the previous "ILC" code. "Aiwass" and its variant "Aiwaz" total to our key number of 93. "The Word" is equivalent to Nu's number of 56, and it is Nu who speaks this word in the 39th verse of her chapter. Both N.O.X. and Nu are valued at zero, a wonderful way of equating the infinite expanse of the night sky with the zero, symbolic of the cosmic woman. "Key" is 11, and this number is an important Thelemic number (see AL I:60). "Had" is 88, and further supports the solution for "8, 80 and 418" as a numerical signature for Had (just as "zero" is a perfect number to describe Nu). All in all, the possibilities of this reconstructed Sanskrit-English seem far more detailed than the results obtained from Crowley's "ILC" code.

Crowley's third suggested Qabalistic pattern for English is Enochian. Many commentators have already suggested that the order of the Enochian alphabet should be synonymous with that of English (i.e., from A to Z). Although Crowley was not able to devise a number code for Sanskrit, he was able to do so for Enochian based on the Golden Dawn Enochian attributions. Crowley recorded these number values in his extended notes for his own *The Vision and the Voice*.

Crowley's Enochian-English Qabalah can be reconstructed if an Enochian letter is first allocated to each letter of the English alphabet based on its phonetic similarities, and then the number value for each particular Enochian letter is given to its phonetically equivalent English letter. The following table is a reconstruction of this code.

Enochian-English Qabalah

English Letter	Number Value	English Letter	Number Value
A	6	N	50
B	5	O	30
C	300	P	8
D	4 (or 31)	Q	40
E	7	R	100
F	300	S	10
G	9	T	400
H	1	U	70
I	60	V	70
J	60	W	70
K	300	X	400
L	40	Y	60
M	90	Z	1

The following are examples of this code in action:

- Aiwaz = 143

- Aiwass = 162

- The Word = 612 (or 639)

- N.O.X. = 480

- Key = 367

- Had = 11 (or 38)

- Nu = 120

Though the code itself is novel in its approach to numbering English, the results are by no means as startling as the proposed Sanskrit-English Qabalah of Crowley. Again, the simple "ABC" serial order for English is in many ways the most workable Qabalah.

Beyond these three Qabalahs suggested by Crowley, a fourth cipher value for English was utilized by him throughout his many years of magickal research. This code is a phonetic Hebrew-English Qabalah. Though never directly tabled by Crowley, this Qabalah appears throughout his published and unpublished manuscripts as well as in his many magickal diaries. The crux of this technique was derived from orthodox Golden Dawn teachings. When any strange word was encountered that could not be translated, the word was rendered into Hebrew phonetic equivalents. The letters were in turn given their appropriate number values and then totaled. Thus any word in the world could be numbered by first rendering it into Hebrew and then substituting the Hebrew number value for each letter.

The drawback to such a system is the vagueness of certain transliterations. Crowley's own use (or abuse) of this system would allow up to four alternate transliterations for one letter. The choice of one of four alternatives was not motivated by phonetic values but rather by which number would work best to produce a predetermined final value. Thus the results obtained with this code were much more subjective than any other cipher value and allowed too much leeway for manipulation, distortion, and ultimately abuse of the Qabalistic analysis. The following table delineates this system:

Crowley's English Qabalah Based on Phonetic Hebrew

English	Hebrew Number Value(s)/Letter(s)
A	1 (א, A), 10 (י, I), 70 (ע, O)
B	2 (ב, B), 6 (ו, V)
C	20 (כ, K), 100 (ק, Q), 3 (ג, G)
D	4 (ד, D)
E	5 (ה, H), 1 (א, A), 10 (י, I)
F	6 (ו, V), 80 (פ, P)
G	3 (ג, G)
H	8 (ח, Ch), 5 (ה, H)
I	10 (י, I), 1 (א, A), 6 (ו, V)
J	10 (י, I)
K	8 (ח, Ch), 20 (כ, K), 100 (ק, Q)
L	30 (ל, L)
M	40 (מ, M)
N	50 (נ, N)
O	70 (ע, O), 6 (ו, V), 10 (י, I), 1 (א, A)
P	80 (פ, P), 6 (ו, V)
Q	100 (ק, Q), 20 (כ, K)
R	200 (ר, R)
S	300 (ש, Sh), 60 (ס, S), 7 (ז, Z), 90 (צ, Tz)
T	9 (ט, T), 400 (ת, Th)
U	6 (ו, V), 70 (ע, O)
V	6 (ו, V)
W	6 (ו, V)
X	400 (ת, Th), 60 (ס, S)
Y	10 (י, I)
Z	7 (ז, Z), 90 (צ, Tz), 60 (ס, S)

The inherent problem of this code is the multiple transliterations available for much of the alphabet. This multiplicity of number values permits too much manipulation of the number value of any given word. The magician using such a code tends to anticipate the number value of any questioned word. If a number is produced which is either unknown or contrary to a pet theory, the tendency to ignore that resultant number and substitute an alternate value is great. Thust most research done with such an open-ended system will reinforce already-known numbers and not touch upon unknown numbers. Such a system is a dead-end system and should be used with extreme discretion.

As an example of how open-ended this Hebraic phonetic Qabalah for English can be, the name "Had" is numbered below in light of the available alternate number values. By Crowley's phonetic code, "D" has one value of 4, "H" has two values of 8 and 5, while "A" has three values of 1, 10, and 70.

1. Had = 5 + 1 + 4 = 10
2. Had = 8 + 1 + 4 = 13
3. Had = 5 + 10 + 4 = 19
4. Had = 8 + 10 + 4 = 22
5. Had = 5 + 70 + 4 = 79
6. Had = 8 + 70 + 4 = 82

Another approach to a phonetic English Qabalah outside the Qabalistic work of Crowley can be obtained by using the serial order numerical values of English (the "ABC" cipher) to number the phonetic letter names for the 26 letters of the alphabet. English, like many other magickal languages, provides a letter name for each letter of the alphabet that approximates the phonetic sound of that letter. As "1" can be written as "one," so can "A" be written as "AE." The following table details this theoretical phonetic English cipher:

Phonetic-English Qabalah

Letter	Phonetic Letter Name	Number Value	Letter	Phonetic Letter Name	Number Value
A	Ae (or Aye)	6 (or 31)	N	En	19
B	Bee	12	O	Oe (or Oh)	20 (or 23)
C	Cee	13	P	Pee	26
D	Dee	14	Q	Cue	29
E	Ee	10	R	Ar	19
F	Eff	17	S	Ess	43
G	Gee	17	T	Tee	30
H	Aitch	41	U	You	61
I	Ie (or Eye)	14 (or 35)	V	Vee	32
J	Jay	36	W	Double you	120
K	Kay	37	X	Ex	29
L	Ell	29	Y	Wye	53
M	Em	18	Z	Zee	36

This code is additional in nature. The following are examples of this code as a numbering scheme for English.

- Aiwaz = four values: 182, 203, 232, 253

- Aiwass = four values: 232, 252, 282, 303

- The Word = two values: 254, 257

- N.O.X. = two values: 68, 71

- Key = one value: 100

- Had = two values: 61, 86

- Nu = one value: 80

GERMAN-ENGLISH QABALAHS

From the foregoing examples, it is apparent that this phonetic cipher results in a higher range of number values for English. This was the same motivation that caused German Qabalists to create the "summation" and "square" ciphers for the Latin alphabet. By affixing the serial order of 1 through 26 to the letters from A through Z, both the Germanic serial and square Qabalahs can also be constructed for English. The following table details such alternate English Qabalahs.

German English Qabalahs

Letter	Serial	Summation	Square
A	1	1	1
B	2	3	4
C	3	6	9
D	4	10	16
E	5	15	25
F	6	21	36
G	7	28	49
H	8	36	64
I	9	45	81
J	10	55	100
K	11	66	121
L	12	78	144
M	13	91	169
N	14	105	196
O	15	120	225
P	16	136	256
Q	17	153	289
R	18	171	324
S	19	190	361
T	20	210	400

German English Qabalahs (cont'd.)

Letter	Serial	Summation	Square
U	21	231	441
V	22	253	484
W	23	276	529
X	24	300	576
Y	25	325	625
Z	26	351	676

The following examples show the range of number values available for each word by the serial, sum, and square order.

Word	Serial Value	Summation Value	Square Value
Aiwaz	60	674	1288
Aiwass	72	703	1334
The Word	93	838	1583
N.O.X.	53	525	997
Key	41	406	771
Had	13	47	81
Nu	35	336	637

With this system the number range beyond 1,000 can be defined by certain one-word concepts.

GRAECO-ENGLISH QABALAH

Another known English cipher which permits the encoding of words beyond the higher octave of 1,000 resembles in its construction the Italian-German Latin Ordinis Cabala. This code bases the 26 alphabet numerals on the number range of 1–800 (reminiscent of the Greek range of Alpha to Omega). It has appeared in more than one work on the occult significance of the English alphabet. The table on the next page details this code.

Graeco-English Qabalah

English Letter	Greek Model	Number Value	English Letter	Greek Model	Number Value
A	A	1	N	N	50
B	B	2	O	Ξ	60
C	Γ	3	P	O	70
D	Δ	4	Q	Π	80
E	E	5	R	Ϙ	90
F	ς	6	S	Ρ	100
G	Z	7	T	Σ	200
H	H	8	U	Τ	300
I	Θ	9	V	Υ	400
J	I	10	W	Φ	500
K	K	20	X	Χ	600
L	Λ	30	Y	Ψ	700
M	M	40	Z	Ω	800

The following examples of this code will demonstrate the higher values that this code permits in numbering words.

- Aiwaz = 1311
- Aiwass = 711
- The Word = 867
- N.O.X. = 710
- Key = 725
- Had = 13
- Nu = 350

MODERN NUMEROLOGY

The most popular allocation for English is the modern system commonly referred to as "numerology." This technique was extremely popular between 1880 and 1930 and is still being used today.

We have seen examples of English codes which allow words to be valued at a very high range of numbers, but this numerological code represents the opposite impulse to create a cipher which allows words to be valued at the restricted values of 1 through 9.

This numerology obviously represents the art of gematria at its most degenerate point of development. It evolved out of the more complicated number codes for languages, when such codes were no longer well known and the metaphors for the number range beyond 10 had been forgotten.

The basis of this code is the serial order of ABC. The serial order of 1 through 26 is first tabulated for the alphabet. Then all values beyond 9 are reduced to 1 through 9 by adding together the component digits of that number. Thus 10 would require one reduction as $10 = 1 + 0 = 1$, while 19 would require two reductions as $19 = 1 + 9 = 10 = 1 + 0 = 1$. If two or more words reduce to the same number, they share common symbolic meanings conditioned by that number. The following table delineates this code.

Modern Numerology

A = 1	J $= 10 = 1 + 0 = 1$	S $= 19 = 1 + 9 = 10 + 1 + 0 = 1$
B = 2	K $= 11 = 1 + 1 = 2$	T $= 20 = 2 + 0 = 2$
C = 3	L $= 12 = 1 + 2 = 3$	U $= 21 = 2 + 1 = 3$
D = 4	M $= 13 = 1 + 3 = 4$	V $= 22 = 2 + 2 = 4$
E = 5	N $= 14 = 1 + 4 = 5$	W $= 23 = 2 + 3 = 5$
F = 6	O $= 15 = 1 + 5 = 6$	X $= 24 = 2 + 4 = 6$
G = 7	P $= 16 = 1 + 6 = 7$	Y $= 25 = 2 + 5 = 7$
H = 8	Q $= 17 = 1 + 7 = 8$	Z $= 26 = 2 + 6 = 8$
I = 9	R $= 18 = 1 + 8 = 9$	

The following examples show the mechanics of this cipher.

- Aiwaz $= 1 + 9 + 5 + 1 + 8 = 24 = 2 + 4 = 6$

- Aiwass $= 1 + 9 + 5 + 1 + 1 + 1 = 18 = 1 + 8 = 9$

- The Word $= 2 + 8 + 5 + 5 + 6 + 9 + 4 = 39 = 3 + 9 = 12 = 1 + 2 = 3$

- N.O.X. $= 5 + 6 + 6 = 17 = 1 + 7 = 8$

- Had $= 8 + 1 + 4 = 13 = 1 + 3 = 4$

- Nu $= 5 + 3 = 8$

Of our seven examples, two words share common symbolic meaning: Nu and N.O.X. both reduce to 8. Thus the sign for infinity (∞, or 8) is equated with both the great expanse of the night sky (N.O.X.) and with the great outstretched body of the sky goddess Nu.

Beyond this simplistic equation, an interesting confirmation of the ABC serial order is seen in "The Word," for this phrase first totals to 39 before being reduced to 3. The number 39 is the verse number in which "the word" appears in chapter 1 of *The Book of the Law,* and since 39 is the mirror of 93, both the English serial Qabalistic value of "the word" and the Greek value of Thelema (i.e., θελημα) are engendered.

Fadic Numerology

One further variant to modern numerology is the Fadic numerological system, which, like modern numerology, reduces all number totals beyond 9 to 1 through 9.

Only the first eight numbers are given letters of the alphabet, while all nine numbers are equated to planetary attributes (both ancient and modern).

The Fadic system is as follows.

Fadic Numerology for English

Number Value	English Letters	Nine Modern Planets (excluding Pluto)	Seven Days of Week (Seven Ancient Planets)
1	A, I, J, Q, Y	Sun	Sun
2	B, K, R	Moon	Moon
3	C, G, L, S	Jupiter	Jupiter
4	D, M, T	Uranus	Sun
5	E, H, N, X	Mercury	Mercury
6	U, V, W	Venus	Venus
7	O, Z	Neptune	Moon
8	F, P	Saturn	Saturn
9	No letters	Mars	Mars

The model for the Fadic number values is the Hebrew alphabet, where all number values are reduced by removing their zeroes. The cipher known as Aiq Bekar is also a source, since 1 in the Fadic is AI(J,Y)Q and 2 is BKR.

The Hebrew equivalents for the Fadic attributes are as follows.

Hebrew Key for Fadic System

English Letter	Hebrew Model	Hebrew Number Value	Reduced Fadic Value
A	א (A)	1	1
B	ב (B)	2	2
C	ג (G)	3	3
D	ד (D)	4	4
E	ה (H)	5	5
F	פ (P)	80	8
G	ג (G)	3	3
H	ה (H)	5	5

Hebrew Key for Fadic System (cont'd.)

English Letter	Hebrew Model	Hebrew Number Value	Reduced Fadic Value
I	׳ (I)	10	1
J	׳ (I)	10	1
K	כ (K)	20	2
L	ל (L)	30	3
M	מ (M)	40	4
N	נ (N)	50	5
O	ע (O)	70	7
P	פ (P)	80	8
Q	ק (Q)	100	1
R	ר (R)	200	2
S	ש (Sh)	300	3
T	ת (Th)	400	4
U	ו (V)	6	6
V	ו (V)	6	6
W	ו (V)	6	6
X	ך (Kf)	500	5
Y	׳ (I)	10	1
Z	ז (Z)	7	7

Note that the sequence U, V, W is 666 in the Fadic system. Both C and G are equated to the Hebrew letter Gimel, while X is equated to Kaph final (rather than Tzaddi or Samekh).

There is no 9 in this system, since the English T is equated to the Hebrew letter Tav (valued at 400) rather than Teth (valued at 9). In addition, X, which could have been modeled after Tzaddi (valued at 90) is modeled instead upon Kaph final (valued at 500).

The planetary allocations to number are the invention of the author of the Fadic system. Since Pluto is excluded from the modern planets, this system of astro-numerology must have been devised before 1930 CE.

The Fadic code, when applied to our seven key words, produces the following results.

- Aiwaz = 16 = 7

- Aiwass = 15 = 6

- The Word = 33 = 6

- N.O.X. = 17 = 8

- Key = 8

- Had = 10 = 1

- Nu = 11 = 2

Of the seven examples, the most interesting symbolism concerns the names Aiwaz-Aiwass, because Aiwaz + Aiwass is 31 before being reduced (as 16 + 15 = 31) and 13 after reduction (7 + 6 = 13).

HIEROGLYPHIC ENGLISH

Beyond the various number values available for English, each of the 26 alphabet letters can be interpreted as a symbolic hieroglyphic based both on the graphic shapes of each letter and its ABC serial order number value.

A = 1—The pyramid and its capstone; the eye of the Masonic pyramid; an arrowhead shot at the heavens; the Masonic compass scribing the circle of heaven; a rising to apogee and the corresponding fall; the triangle, delta, vagina; the tripod, incense burner; the ox head and horns; zero and one conjoined (as the Tarot letter "Aleph"); the alchemical element Air (the upward-pointed triangle slashed midway with a horizontal line); the voice as the vowel sound A which originates all words; the initial letter of the mantra A̲UM, which sounds the beginning of creation.

B = 2—The curves of the body (especially a woman's body); the breasts and buttocks (both of which are the upper half of the heart symbol); the joining of the numbers 1 + 3 (as 13); the two halves of a circle forming the upper and lower (hence duality); the fraction 0.12 as generated by dividing the Hebrew ٦ (V) by the Hebrew ﬥ (N); the house or temple of Thoth; the universe of the Grand House of God; the biliteral name Nu.

C = 3—The crescent Moon as a luminous mirror; the curving line and therefore feminine (as opposed to I as a straight, masculine line); the waves of the ocean; a curl (of hair); a hollow, cave; the arcing circumference of a circle; the serpent attempting to bite its own tail; the horns of the bull (portrayed in A); the beginning-middle-end; anything made of three parts.

D = 4—The doorway; the doorway within Venus (the vagina); the halving of a circle; the Tibetan form of the Vayu Tattva; the bow (the arrow already released in flight); the string of a harp; the offering of bread laid on the altar; the brain; the head of a mushroom; the dome of a temple.

E = 5—The three horizontal spaces between the fingers of the left hand; the five fingers of the hand; the five senses; a window of a house (which is the letter B); the pentalpha (formed of five A's); the five A's of AbrAhAdAbrA; the five vowels; note that E equals both 5 A's and (A + I)/2 ([1 + 9]/2); Mars as the pentagram (and ruler of Aries, which is E).

F = 6—The flag (of God); the key (which unlocks the mysteries); the phallus of the bull; the hexagram; the six consonants of aBRaHaDaBRa; the alphabet as ABC = F (1 + 2 + 3 = 6); the hand and the forearm; a peg or post to which lines are tied.

G = 7—The letter C spiraling in upon itself; the coiling of Lunar Light; the crescent Moon and the Tau cross (forming both Saturn and Jupiter); the sevenfold nature as a spiral; the seven sevens of Nu (as [77/7] + 7 + [77/7]); the rose-cross; the Moon rising over the horizon of the earth; the right-angled tool; the boomerang; the Zodiacal sign Gemini; the initial of the ineffable (whose English formula of GO + D is 22 + 4 and as G + OD is 7 + 19); the Masonic letter G at the center of the Eastern Light of Dawn; the half-seven (3 ½) coilings of the serpent Kundalini.

H = 8—A ladder reaching to heaven; the double cube of the altar (as well as the Chariot in Key VII of the Tarot); an archway; a wall, fence, or enclosure; the twisting sign of infinity (as well as the yin-yang as the Zodiacal sign Cancer); the ogdoad; the eightfold nature of Mercury (and Buddha); the left and right pillars of the Masonic temple joined by the veil of Isis.

I = 9—The erect penis (of Had); the upright post; the spine; the world-axis; the Middle Pillar of the Tree of Life; the straight and narrow path; the razor's edge; a pole from heaven to earth; the wand of the magician; the serpent (of Leo) as the wand of Moses; the shaft of the arrow; the numeral one; the hand united with the phallus.

J = 10—The tenfold system of Sephiroth of the Tree of Life as a tenth (Malkuth) hooked onto the first nine (Kether through Yesod); the Sephirah Malkuth as an appendage to the Tree of Life; the fishhook penetrating the ocean; the hooking of a straight path; descent transformed to ascent; matter returning to spirit; a hooking back upon the path.

K = 11—The legs and outstretched arms; the genitals as the center of the body concealed by the Masonic apron; to advance while saluting; to kneel to worship; the secret hand grip of a lodge; to adore; an arrowhead piercing a target; a hexagonal star (formed by two K's joined back to back).

L = 12—The foot joined to the leg; the Masonic 12-inch square marking the four directions of the earth; 90° or the right angle; the arm of the swastika; the plumbline and its shadow; to align a perpendicular plane.

M = 13—The flowing of water; the valley between two mountain ranges; cycles of up and down; radiating or rippling energy; the parallel flow of three forces; the open legs and vagina of Nu; the passing over the mountain range through a secret passageway; the downward pointing triangle; the last letter of the formula AU$\underline{M}$.

N = 14—A gate blocking the path; the joining of two swimming fishes facing opposite directions (yin-yang, Cancer, and Pisces); left joined to the right; the diagonal path; the hypotenuse of a right triangle; the central letter of the magick square SATOR AREPO TE$\underline{N}$ET OPERA ROTAS; the initial of Nu, the sky goddess.

O = 15—The day and image of the Full Moon; the images found in two passages of *The Book of the Law*: "the circumference, is nowhere found" (AL II:3) and "this Circle squared in its failure" (AL III:47); the open eye; the anus; the head of the penis embedded in the vagina; a wheel; the heavens; the cipher zero, nought; the formula 0 = (I + U)/2 (15 = [9 + 21]/2); the formula π = 22/7; the egg; the beginning joined to the end.

P = 16—The flacid penis and testicles (I being the erect penis); the head joined to the spine; the body held upright in meditation; the clean-shaven face of a woman or child (R being the bearded face of a man); the face in profile; the upper heaven of the letter B; the letter D joined to I; the halo of a saint; the pathway of the seven chakras.

Q = 17—The spine meeting the skull; the tail of an animal; the braided hair of a warrior tied to the back of the head; the monkey; the cat; the sperm penetrating the egg; the phallus penetrating the back (or anus); the back of the head; a wheel and its axle; the buttocks or back of the body; the head and shaft of the mushroom; the Egyptian shadow or astral double.

R = 18—The Egyptian profile of the head of a king, bearded and with headdress; rays as arms emanating from the Sun God Ra; to advance grade by grade; the staff of the hermit guiding the hermit (or Senex) in the dark night.

S = 19—The twisting of the snare; the coils of the serpent around the cosmic egg; the two major phases of the Moon (waxing and waning); two Moons (C's) joined together (sign of Pisces); the infinity symbol of Mercury; veil, scarf, ribbon; S joined to T becomes the secret consonants ST, which can be symbolized as a serpent (S) curled around a Tau cross (T), one of the seals for the Theosophical Society derived from Rosicrucian symbolism.

T = 20—The Tree (of Life); the Tau cross; the intersecting of heaven and earth; the intersecting of one plane by another perpendicular to it (a symbol of astral projection); the cross of crucifixion; the Sun as the center of the Tree of Life; the rose-cross.

U = 21—The vessel, offering, urn, container, vase; the three vowels AEO (which total to U as $1 + 5 + 15 = 21$); the central or middle letter of the sacred syllable A_U_M; note that AUM = 35 = NU.

V = 22—The vagina (as the lower half of the heart symbol); the doorway of life (and sunrise in the body of Nu); a valley, the fallen arrow penetrating the earth; full cycle (as 22); a descent and ascent; 5 in Latin, 6 in Hebrew; the five camel tracks across the abyss of the Tree of Life.

W = 23—Sun rising over twin mountain peaks; a mountain range; the crown at the end of the work; completion, attainment; the path winding up the mountain of initiation; the jagged points of the teeth; the serpent fangs; the radiating dance of flames (as opposed to the flowing water of the letter M); the upward-pointing triangle.

X = 24—The cross; the unknown in mathematics; the Ordeal X of *The Book of the Law* (the grand puzzle found in AL II:76); skull and crossbones; two roads crossing demanding a choice; the intersecting of Fire and Water to form the hexagram; the four directions; the square; X which marks the location of buried treasures.

Y = 25—Trinity, triad, triple; a straight path forking right and left (a choice of good and evil); the left- and right-hand paths of magick; the penis (I) penetrating the vagina (V); woman above, man below (the posture of Had and Nu and the 11th hexagram of the *I Ching)*; the chalice or cup containing the elixir of life; the triple formula IAO (since Y = IAO, 25 = 9 + 1 + 15); the pentagram and Mars (as 5^2).

Z = 26—The lightning bolt descending from the heavens; the rain (of Anu) fertilizing the ground (of Adad); above joined to below; the last which is first; as above so below; the last letter of Aiwaz; God as the formula Z = 26 = 7 + 15 + 4 = God; the whole range of the alphabet; the end which is zero; the circle and square as 22 + 4 = 26; to zigzag; a shower of rain descending from the sky.

Concourse of Forces for English

English Letter	Hebrew Model	Greek Model	Tarot	Astrology	Color
A	Aleph	Alpha	0—The Fool	Air (Spirit)	Yellow (White)
B	Beth	Beta	I—The Magician	Mercury	Yellow
C	Gimel	Gamma	II—The High Priestess	Moon	Blue
D	Daleth	Delta	III—The Empress	Venus	Green
E	Heh	Epsilon	IV—The Emperor	Aries	Red
F	Vav	Stau	V—The Hiero-phant	Taurus	Red-Orange
G	Zain	Zeta	VI—The Lovers	Gemini	Orange
H	Cheth	Eta	VII—The Chariot	Cancer	Yellow-Orange
I	Teth	Theta	VIII-Strength	Leo	Yellow
J	Yod	Iota	IX—The Hermit	Virgo	Yellow-Green
K	Kaph	Kappa	X—The Wheel	Jupiter	Violet
L	Lamed	Lambda	XI—Justice	Libra	Green
M	Mem	Mu	XII—The Hanged Man	Water	Blue
N	Nun	Nu	XIII—Death	Scorpio	Blue-Green
O	Samekh	Xi	XIV—Temperance	Sagittarius	Blue
P	Ayin	Omicron	XV—The Devil	Capricorn	Blue-Violet
Q	Peh	Pi	XVI—The Tower	Mars	Red
R	Tzaddi	Koppa	XVII—The Star	Aquarius	Violet
S	Qoph	Rho	XVIII—The Moon	Pisces	Red-Violet
T	Resh	Sigma	XIX—The Sun	Sun	Orange

Concourse of Forces for English (cont'd.)

English Letter	Hebrew Model	Greek Model	Tarot	Astrology	Color
T	Resh	Sigma	XIX—The Sun	Sun	Orange
U	Shin	Tau	XX—Judgment	Fire	Red
V	Tav	Upsilon	XXI—The World	Saturn (Earth)	Blue-Violet
W	Shin (Yod)	Phi	Wands	Fire of Earth	Russet
X	Mem (Heh)	Chi	Cups	Water of Earth	Olive
Y	Aleph (Vav)	Psi	Swords	Air of Earth	Citrine
Z	Tav (Final Heh)	Omega	Pentacles	Earth of Earth	Black

Concourse of Forces for English (cont'd.)

English Letter	English	Number Values Hebrew	Greek	Egyptian God	Perfume	Magickal Weapon	Enochian (G.D.)
A	1	1	1	Nu	Abramelin	Dagger	Z
B	2	2	2	Hadit (Thoth)	Sandalwood	Caduceus	—
C	3	3	3	Isis	Jasmine	Bow	—
D	4	4	4	Hathoor	Rose	Girdle	D
E	5	5	5	Men Thu	Dragon's Blood	Burin	B
F	6	6	6	Osiris	Storax	Effort	A
G	7	7	7	Merti	Wormwood	Tripod	E
H	8	8	8	Hormakhu	Onycha	Furnace	P
I	9	9	9	Ra-Hoor-Khuit	Frankincense	Discipline	G
J	10	10	10	Heru-pa-Kraath	Narcissus	Lamp	S
K	11	20	20	Amoun-Ra	Cedar	Scepter	—
L	12	30	30	Maat	Aloe	Cross of Equilibrium	O
M	13	40	40	Asar	Lotus	Cup	L
N	14	50	50	Typhon	Benzoin	Pain of Obligation	N
O	15	60	60	Nephthys	Lignum Aloes	Arrow	I
P	16	70	70	Set	Musk	Secret Force	U
Q	17	80	80	Horus	Pepper	Sword	—
R	18	90	90	Aroueris	Coconut	Censer	M
S	19	100	100	Khephra	Ambergris	Magic Mirror	R

Concourse of Forces for English (cont'd.)

English Letter	English	Number Values Hebrew	Greek	Egyptian God	Perfume	Magickal Weapon	Enochian (G.D.)
T	20	200	200	Ra	Honey	Lamen	—
U	21	300	300	Mau	Amber	Wand	F
V	22	400	400	Sebek	Myrrh	Sickle	T
W	23	300 (10)	500	Ttoumathph (Jackal)	Cinnamon	Pyramidal Lamp	C
X	24	40 (5)	600	Kabexnuf (Hawk)	Olive	Perfume	Q
Y	25	1	700	Ameshet (Man)	Peppermint	Fan	H
Z	26	400 (5)	800	Ahephi (Ape/Dog)	Patchouli	Pantacle	X

ADDENDUM

THE MAGICKAL POLYGLOT

In light of the various alphabet number values found in the 13 Keys, a Magickal Polyglot can be reconstructed, ordered by the 26 letters of the English alphabet. If these 26 letters are paired to their phonetic equivalents in all 13 Keys, a multitude of ancient number values can be assigned to English. The following is a reconstruction of the Magickal Polyglot based on the serial and phonetic order of English.

Key to Phonetic Alphabet Sort
Found in the Magickal Polyglot

The Phonetic translations found in the 13 Keys are sometimes quite arbitrary in order to be able to discern one letter from another. In devising the alphabetical sort for the Magickal Polyglot, the transliterations found in the text were sorted, by the first letter in the transliteration, to the 26 English alphabet letters. However, in certain circumstances a variant to this linear sort is utilized, as follows.

- Ph is filed under F

- Ch is filed under H

- Ks is filed under X

- Ts, Tz, Ds, and Ps are all filed under Z

Beyond these four variants, there are certain interchangeable English polyglot letters who entries can be combined, as follows.

- C is equal to K

- I is equal to J and Y

- U is equal to V and W

- E is equal to H

- G is equal to C

- P is equal to F

- X is equal to S

- J is equal to G

- F is equal to V

The order for the entries under each major heading is by language in alphabetical order (i.e., from Arabic to Tibetan).

Key to Abbreviations for Both the Magickal Polyglot and the Sieve of Numbers

ARB—Arabic, Egyptian-Eastern number values

ARB-M—Arabic, Moroccan-Western number values

ARB-MN—Arabic letter-names numbered by Moroccan values

ARB-N—Arabic letter-names numbered by Egyptian values

ARB-P—The four variant Persian alphabet letters, valued by their Egyptian Arabic models

ARB-S—The normal sequential order of the Arabic alphabet, the basis for the Moroccan numbering system

BLN—The Irish Beth-Luis-Nion alphabet

CPT—The Coptic alphabet numbered in accordance with its Greek model

CPT-T—The Coptic alphabet as the 32 paths of the Tree of Life (Golden Dawn Tradition)

ENG—English alphabet numbered serially as ABC, the basis of "The English Qabalah"

ENG-F—Modern Fadic numerology for English

ENG-L—The phonetic letter-names numbered by the ABC serial order

ENG-N—The values of modern English numerology

ENG-T—The esoteric order of the English alphabet from Crowley's *Liber Trigrammaton,* the order of ILC

ENO—Dee's Enochian alphabet valued by its Hebrew-Greek model

ENO-C—Crowley's revision of the Golden Dawn Enochian system for five extra Enochian letters

ENO-D—Dee's digital code for Enochian as used in the 48 Calls of the Aethyrs

ENO-G—Golden Dawn numbering system for 16 selected Enochian letters

GEO—The Georgian alphabet numbering system

GK—Greek alphabet as its normal numbering system (Pythagorean)

GK-H—Greek alphabet as serial order of 24 letters (Homeric)

GK-N—Greek letter names valued by their normal value

HEB—Hebrew normal value

HEB-C—Hebrew cube of normal value

HEB-E—Hebrew enlarged letter value; the Hebrew value of 1,000 times the normal value for enlarged alphabet letters

HEB-F—Hebrew final (or major) value; the five letters ranging from 500 to 900 in value

HEB-M—Hebrew minor value; the values given under Hebrew normal value with the zeros removed, as in the cipher Aiq Bekar

HEB-N—Hebrew nominal value; the letter names for the Hebrew alphabet

HEB-P—Hebrew Paths on the Tree of Life; the 22 alphabet paths numbered 11 through 32

HEB-S—Hebrew serial order; the value assigned to the normal order of the alphabet

HEB-SQ—Hebrew square of normal value

LAT—The Italan Latin Cabala Simplex code of Trithemius

LAT-G—The German Lain Cabala Ordinis code

LAT-L—The nine basic letters of Lull's Latin Qabalah

LAT-P—The Latin German Pentagonal code

LAT-Q—The Latin German Quadrangular code

LAT-R—The Latin letters as Roman numerals

LAT-T—The Latin German Triangular code

OG—The Ogham letters as serial order numbers

RUN—The 24-letter alphabet of the Elder Futhark runes

RUN-S—The 33-letter alphabet of the Anglo-Saxon runes

RUN-Y—The 16-letter alphabet of the Younger Futhark runes

SKT—Sanskrit valued by the KaTaPaYaDhi system

SKT-A—Sanskrit valued by the Aryabhata version; vowels are shown as power of place values (V = with Varga consonant; A = with Avarga consonant)

SKT-C—The Sanskrit alphabet as 50 petals of the chakra system

SKT-P—The Sanskrit alphabet as the Pali serial order

TAR—The Golden Dawn secret order of the Hebrew alphabet (based on the *Sepher Yetzirah*) for the Tarot

TAR-C—Crowley's four variant Hebrew values for the Golden Dawn Tarot

TAR-E—The exoteric order of Eliphas Levi for the Tarot as Hebrew letters

TIB—The Tibetan alphabet number values

The Magickal Polyglot

Letter	Language	Number	Letter	Language	Number
A	ARB	1	A	LAT-G	1
A	ARB-M	1	A	LAT-T	1
A	ARB-MN	701	A	LAT-Q	1
A	ARB-N	111	A	LAT-P	1
A	ARB-S	1	A	OG	16
A	BLN	1	A	RUN	4
A	CPT	1	Ae	RUN-S	26
A	CPT-T	11	Ai	RUN-S	25
A	ENG	1	A	RUN-Y	4
A	ENG-F	1	A	RUN-Y	10
A	ENG-L	6	A	SKT	No value
A	ENG-L	31	A	SKT	No value
A	ENG-N	1	Ah	SKT	No value
A	ENG-T	9	Ai	SKT	No value
A	ENO	1	Am	SKT	No value
A	ENO-D	1	Au	SKT	No value
A	ENO-G	6	A	SKT-A (V)	1
A	GEO	1	A	SKT-A (A)	10
A	GK	1	Ai	SKT-A (V)	1,000,000,000,000
A	GK-N	532	Ai	SKT-A (A)	10,000,000,000,000
A	GK-H	1	Au	SKT-A (V)	10,000,000,000,000,000
A	HEB	1	Au	SKT-A (A)	100,000,000,000,000,000
A	HEB-C	1	A	SKT-C	33
A	HEB-E	1,000	Â	SKT-C	34
A	HEB-M	1	Ah	SKT-C	47
A	HEB-N	111	Ai	SKT-C	44
A	HEB-N	831	Am	SKT-C	48
A	HEB-P	11	Au	SKT-C	46
A	HEB-S	1	A	SKT-P	1
A	HEB-SQ	1	A	HEB-SQ	1
A	LAT	1	Â	SKT-P	2

The Magickal Polyglot (cont'd.)

Letter	Language	Number	Letter	Language	Number
Ah	SKT-P	15	B	HEB-M	2
Ai	SKT-P	12	B	HEB-N	412
Am	SKT-P	16	B	HEB-P	12
Au	SKT-P	14	B	HEB-S	2
A	TAR	0	B	HEB-SQ	4
A	TAR-E	1	B	LAT	2
a	TIB	0	B	LAT-G	2
Ah	TIB	30	B	LAT-L	1
B	ARB	2	B	LAT-P	5
B	ARB-M	2	B	LAT-Q	4
B	ARB-MN	3	B	LAT-T	3
B	ARB-N	3	B	OG	1
B	ARB-S	2	B	RUN	18
B	BLN	5	B	RUN-S	18
B	CPT	2	B	RUN-Y	13
B	CPT-T	12	B	SKT	3
B	ENG	2	Bh	SKT	4
B	ENG-F	2	B	SKT-A	23
B	ENG-L	12	Bh	SKT-A	24
B	ENG-N	2	B	SKT-C	5
B	ENG-T	15	Bh	SKT-C	6
B	ENO	2	B	SKT-P	352
B	ENO-D	2	Bh	SKT-P	368
B	ENO-G	5	B	TAR	1
B	GEO	2	B	TAR-E	2
B	GK	2	B	TIB	15
B	GK-H	2	C	BLN	9
B	GK-N	311	C	CPT	0
B	HEB	2	C	CPT-T	2
B	HEB-C	8	C	ENG	3
B	HEB-E	2,000	C	ENG-F	3

The Magickal Polyglot (cont'd.)

Letter	Language	Number	Letter	Language	Number
C	ENG-L	13	D	TAR-E	4
C	ENG-N	3	D	TIB	11
C	ENG-T	3	E	BLN	2
C	ENO	20	E	CPT	5
C	ENO-C	300	Ē	CPT	8
C	ENO-D	2	E	CPT-T	7
C	GEO	2,000	Ē	CPT-T	4
Ç	GEO	4,000	E	ENG	5
Ĉ	GEO	1,000	E	ENG-F	5
Ç̂	GEO	5,000	E	ENG-L	10
C	LAT	3	E	ENG-N	5
C	LAT-G	3	E	ENG-T	20
C	LAT-L	2	E	ENO	5
C	LAT-P	12	E	ENO-C	7
C	LAT-Q	9	E	ENO-D	5
C	LAT-R	100	E	GEO	5
C	LAT-T	6	Ey	GEO	8
C	OG	9	E	GK	5
C	RUN-S	31	E	GK-H	5
C	SKT	6	E	GK-N	865
C	SKT-A	6	E	LAT	5
C	SKT-C	26	E	LAT-G	5
C	SKT-P	80	E	LAT-L	4
C	TIB	6	E	LAT-P	35
Ç	TIB	27	E	LAT-Q	25
D	ARB	4	E	LAT-T	15
Ḍ	ARB	800	E	OG	19
Dh	ARB	700	E	RUN	19
D	ARB-M	8	Ei	RUN	13
Ḍ	ARB-M	60	E	RUN-S	13
D	TAR	3	Ea	RUN-S	29

The Magickal Polyglot (cont'd.)

Letter	Language	Number	Letter	Language	Number
Eh	RUN-S	19	F	LAT-G	6
E	SKT	No value	F	LAT-L	5
E	SKT-A (V)	10,000,000,000	F	LAT-P	51
E	SKT-A (A)	100,000,000,000	F	LAT-Q	36
E	SKT-C	43	F	LAT-T	21
E	SKT-P	11	F	OG	3
E	TIB	90	Ph	OG	24
F	ARB	80	F	RUN	1
F	ARB-M	200	F	RUN-S	1
F	ARB-MN	201	F	RUN-Y	1
F	ARB-N	81	Ph	SKT	2
F	ARB-S	20	Ph	SKT-C	20
F	BLN	8	Ph	SKT-A	22
F	CPT	90	Ph	SKT-P	336
Ph	CPT	500	Ph	TIB	14
F	CPT-T	8	Gh	ARB	1,000
Ph	CPT-T	5	Gh	ARB-M	100
F	ENG	6	Gh	ARB-MN	1,800
F	ENG-F	8	Gh	ARB-N	1,060
F	ENG-L	17	G	ARB-P	20
F	ENG-N	6	Gh	ARB-S	19
F	ENG-T	16	G	BLN	10
F	ENO	6	G	CPT	3
F	ENO-D	6	Gh	CPT	0
F	ENO-G	300	G	CPT-T	13
F	GEO	No value	Gh	CPT-T	9
Ph	GEO	500	G	ENG	7
Ph	GK	500	G	ENG-F	3
Ph	GK-H	21	G	ENG-L	17
Ph	GK-N	510	G	ENG-N	7
F	LAT	6	G	ENG-T	13

The Magickal Polyglot (cont'd.)

Letter	Language	Number	Letter	Language	Number
G	ENO	3	G	SKT-C	23
G	ENO-D	3	Gh	SKT-C	24
G	ENO-G	9	G	SKT-P	32
G	GEO	3	Gh	SKT-P	48
Ĝ	GEO	700	G	TAR	2
G	GK	3	G	TAR-E	3
G	GK-H	3	G	TIB	3
G	GK-N	85	Ḥ	ARB	8
G	HEB	3	H	ARB	5
G	HEB-C	9	Ḥ	ARB-M	6
G	HEB-E	3,000	H	ARB-M	800
G	HEB-M	3	Ḥ	ARB-MN	7
G	HEB-N	73	H	ARB-MN	801
G	HEB-P	13	Ḥ	ARB-N	9
G	HEB-S	3	H	ARB-N	6
G	HEB-SQ	9	Ch	ARB-P	3
G	LAT	7	H	ARB-S	26
G	LAT-G	7	Ḥ	ARB-S	6
G	LAT-L	6	H	BLN	0
G	LAT-P	70	H	CPT	0
G	LAT-Q	49	Ḥ	CPT	0
G	LAT-R	400	Ch	CPT	600
G	LAT-T	28	H	CPT-T	15
G	OG	12	Ḥ	CPT-T	18
G	RUN	7	Ch	CPT-T	29
G	RUN-S	7	H	ENG	8
Gh	RUN-S	33	H	ENG-F	5
G	SKT	3	H	ENG-L	41
Gh	SKT	4	H	ENG-N	8
G	SKT-A	3	H	ENG-T	4
Gh	SKT-A	4	H	ENO	8

The Magickal Polyglot (cont'd.)

Letter	Language	Number	Letter	Language	Number
H	ENO-C	1	H	LAT-Q	64
H	ENO-D	8	H	OG	6
H	GEO	9,000	Ch	OG	21
H	GK	8	H	RUN	9
Ch	GK	600	H	RUN-S	9
H	GK-H	7	H	RUN-Y	7
Ch	GK-H	22	H	SKT	8
H	GK-N	309	Ḣ	SKT	No value
Ch	GK-N	610	Ch	SKT	7
H	HEB	5	H	SKT-A	10
Ch	HEB	8	Ch	SKT-A	7
H	HEB-C	125	H	SKT-C	49
Ch	HEB-C	512	Ch	SKT-C	27
H	HEB-E	5,000	H	SKT-P	512
Ch	HEB-E	8,000	Ch	SKT-P	96
H	HEB-M	5	H	TAR	4
Ch	HEB-M	8	Ch	TAR	7
H	HEB-N	10	H	TAR-C	17
Ch	HEB-N	418	H	TAR-E	5
H	HEB-P	15	Ch	TAR-E	8
Ch	HEB-P	18	H	TIB	29
H	HEB-S	5	Ḥ	TIB	23
Ch	HEB-S	8	Ḥ̇	TIB	0
H	HEB-SQ	25	I	BLN	3
Ch	HEB-SQ	64	I	CPT	10
H	LAT	8	I	CPT-T	20
H	LAT-G	8	I	ENG	9
H	LAT-L	7	I	ENG-F	1
H	LAT-P	92	I	ENG-L	14
H	LAT-R	200	I	ENG-L	35
H	LAT-T	36	I	ENG-N	9

The Magickal Polyglot (cont'd.)

Letter	Language	Number	Letter	Language	Number
I	ENG-T	1	I	SKT-A (A)	1,000
I	ENO	10	I	SKT-C	35
I	ENO-D	1	Î	SKT-C	36
I	ENO-G	60	I	SKT-P	3
I	GEO	10	Î	SKT-P	4
I	GK	10	I	TAR	9
I	GK-H	9	I	TAR-E	10
I	GK-N	1,111	I	TIB	30
I	HEB	10	J	ARB	3
I	HEB-C	1,000	J	ARB-M	5
I	HEB-E	10,000	J	ARB-MN	1,605
I	HEB-M	1	J	ARB-N	53
I	HEB-N	20	J	ARB-S	5
I	HEB-P	20	J	ENG	10
I	HEB-S	10	J	ENG-F	1
I	HEB-SQ	100	J	ENG-L	36
I	LAT	9	J	ENG-N	1
I	LAT-G	9	J	ENG-T	10
I	LAT-L	8	J	GEO	3,000
I	LAT-P	117	Ĵ	GEO	8,000
I	LAT-Q	81	J	RUN	12
I	LAT-R	1	J	RUN-S	12
I	LAT-T	45	J	SKT	8
I	OG	20	Jh	SKT	9
I	RUN	11	J	SKT-A	8
I	RUN-S	11	Jh	SKT-A	9
Io	RUN-S	28	J	SKT-C	28
I	RUN-Y	9	Jh	SKT-C	29
I	SKT	No value	J	SKT-P	112
Î	SKT	No value	Jh	SKT-P	128
I	SKT-A (V)	100	J	TIB	7

The Magickal Polyglot (cont'd.)

Letter	Language	Number	Letter	Language	Number
K	ARB	20	K	HEB-SQ	400
Kh	ARB	600	K	LAT-L	9
K	ARB-M	400	K	LAT-P	145
Kh	ARB-M	7	K	LAT-Q	100
K	ARB-MN	601	K	LAT-T	55
Kh	ARB-MN	8	K	RUN	6
K	ARB-N	101	K	RUN-S	6
Kh	ARB-N	401	K	RUN-Y	6
K	ARB-S	22	K	SKT	1
Kh	ARB-S	7	Kh	SKT	2
K	CPT	20	K	SKT-A	1
K	CPT-T	21	Kh	SKT-A	2
K	ENG	11	K	SKT-C	21
K	ENG-F	2	Kh	SKT-C	22
K	ENG-L	37	K	SKT-P	0
K	ENG-N	2	Kh	SKT-P	16
K	ENG-T	24	K	TAR	10
K	GEO	600	K	TAR-E	11
Ḳ	GEO	20	K	TIB	1
K	GK	20	Kh	TIB	2
K	GK-H	10	L	ARB	30
K	GK-N	182	L	ARB-M	500
K	HEB	20	L	ARB-MN	1,101
K	HEB-C	8,000	L	ARB-N	71
K	HEB-E	20,000	L	ARB-S	23
K	HEB-F	500	L	BLN	14
K	HEB-M	2	Ĺ	CPT	30
K	HEB-N	100	L	CPT-T	22
K	HEB-N	820	L	ENG	12
K	HEB-P	21	L	ENG-F	3
K	HEB-S	11	L	ENG-L	29

The Magickal Polyglot (cont'd.)

Letter	Language	Number	Letter	Language	Number
L	ENG-N	3	Li	SKT-A (V)	100,000,000
L	ENG-T	2	Li	SKT-A (A)	1,000,000,000
L	ENO	30	L	SKT-C	10
L	ENO-D	3	Li	SKT-C	41
L	ENO-G	40	Lî	SKT-C	42
L	GEO	30	L	SKT-P	432
L	GK	30	Ĺ	SKT-P	544
L	GK-H	11	Li	SKT-P	9
L	GK-N	78	Lî	SKT-P	10
L	HEB	30	L	TAR	11
L	HEB-C	27,000	L	TAR-C	8
L	HEB-E	30,000	L	TAR-E	12
L	HEB-M	3	L	TIB	26
L	HEB-N	74	M	ARB	40
L	HEB-P	22	M	ARB-M	600
L	HEB-S	12	M	ARB-MN	2,200
L	HEB-SQ	900	M	ARB-N	90
L	LAT	10	M	ARB-S	24
L	LAT-G	10	M	BLN	6
L	LAT-P	176	M	CPT	40
L	LAT-Q	121	M	CPT-T	23
L	LAT-R	50	M	ENG	13
L	LAT-T	66	M	ENG-F	4
L	OG	2	M	ENG-L	18
L	RUN	21	M	ENG-N	4
L	RUN-S	21	M	ENG-T	18
L	RUN-Y	15	M	ENO	40
L	SKT	3	M	ENO-D	4
Li	SKT	No value	M	ENO-G	90
Lî	SKT	No value	M	GEO	40
L	SKT-A	5	M	GK	40

The Magickal Polyglot (cont'd.)

Letter	Language	Number	Letter	Language	Number
M	GK-H	12	N	ARB	50
M	GK-N	440	N	ARB-M	700
M	HEB	40	N	ARB-MN	2,300
M	HEB-C	64,000	N	ARB-N	106
M	HEB-E	40,000	N	ARB-S	25
M	HEB-F	600	N	BLN	13
M	HEB-M	4	N	CPT	50
M	HEB-N	90	N	CPT-T	24
M	HEB-N	650	N	ENG	14
M	HEB-P	23	N	ENG-F	5
M	HEB-S	13	N	ENG-L	19
M	HEB-SQ	1,600	N	ENG-N	5
M	LAT	11	N	ENG-T	19
M	LAT-G	20	N	ENO	50
M	LAT-R	1,000	N	ENO-D	5
M	LAT-P	210	N	ENO-G	50
M	LAT-Q	144	N	GEO	50
M	LAT-T	78	N	GK	50
M	OG	11	N	GK-H	13
M	RUN	20	N	GK-N	450
M	RUN-S	20	N	HEB	50
M	RUN-Y	14	N	HEB-C	125,000
M	SKT	5	N	HEB-E	50,000
Ṁ	SKT	No value	N	HEB-F	700
M	SKT-A	25	N	HEB-M	5
M	SKT-C	7	N	HEB-N	106
M	SKT-P	384	N	HEB-P	24
M	TAR	12	N	HEB-N	756
M	TAR-E	13	N	HEB-S	14
M	TIB	16	N	HEB-SQ	2,500
Ṁ	TIB	0	N	LAT	12

The Magickal Polyglot (cont'd.)

Letter	Language	Number	Letter	Language	Number
N	LAT-G	30	Ñ	TIB	8
N	LAT-P	247	O	ARB	70
N	LAT-Q	169	O	ARB-M	90
N	LAT-T	91	O	ARB-MN	1,790
N	OG	5	O	ARB-N	130
Ng	OG	13	O	ARB-S	18
N	RUN	10	O	BLN	4
Ng	RUN	22	O	CPT	70
N	RUN-S	10	Ō	CPT	800
Ng	RUN-S	22	O	CPT-T	26
N	RUN-Y	8	Ō	CPT-T	6
N	SKT	0 (place value)	O	ENG	15
Ṇ	SKT	5	O	ENG-F	7
Ṅ	SKT	5	O	ENG-L	20
Ñ	SKT	0 (place value)	O	ENG-L	23
N	SKT-A	20	O	ENG-N	6
Ṇ	SKT-A	15	O	ENG-T	12
Ṅ	SKT-A	5	O	ENO	70
Ñ	SKT-A	10	O	ENO-D	7
N	SKT-C	18	O	ENO-G	30
Ṇ	SKT-C	13	O	GEO	70
Ṅ	SKT-C	25	Oy	GEO	10,000
Ñ	SKT-C	30	O	GK	70
N	SKT-P	304	Ō	GK	800
Ṇ	SKT-P	224	O	GK-H	15
Ṅ	SKT-P	64	Ō	GK-H	24
Ñ	SKT-P	144	O	GK-N	360
N	TAR	13	Ō	GK-N	849
N	TAR-E	14	O	HEB	70
N	TIB	12	O	HEB-C	343,000
Ṅ	TIB	4	O	HEB-E	70,000

The Magickal Polyglot (cont'd.)

Letter	Language	Number	Letter	Language	Number
O	HEB-M	7	P	ENG-T	8
O	HEB-N	130	P	ENO	80
O	HEB-N	780	P	ENO-C	8
O	HEB-P	26	P	ENO-D	8
O	HEB-S	16	P	GEO	80
O	HEB-SQ	4,900	P	GK	80
O	LAT	13	P	GK-H	16
O	LAT-G	40	P	GK-N	90
O	LAT-P	287	P	HEB	80
O	LAT-Q	196	P	HEB-C	512,000
O	LAT-T	105	P	HEB-E	80,000
O	OG	17	P	HEB-F	800
O	RUN	24	P	HEB-M	8
O	RUN-S	4	P	HEB-N	85
Oe	RUN-S	23	P	HEB-P	27
O	SKT	No value	P	HEB-S	17
O	SKT-A (V)	100,000,000,000,000	P	HEB-SQ	6,400
O	SKT-A (A)	1,000,000,000,000,000	P	LAT	14
O	SKT-C	45	P	LAT-G	50
O	SKT-P	13	P	LAT-P	330
O	TAR	15	P	LAT-Q	225
O	TAR-E	16	P	LAT-T	120
O	TIB	120	P	OG	23
P	ARB-P	2	P	RUN	14
P	BLN	7	P	RUN-S	14
P	CPT	80	P	SKT	1
P	CPT-T	27	P	SKT-A	21
P	ENG	16	P	SKT-C	19
P	ENG-F	8	P	SKT-P	320
P	ENG-L	26	P	TAR	16
P	ENG-N	7	P	TAR-E	17

The Magickal Polyglot (cont'd.)

Letter	Language	Number	Letter	Language	Number
P	TIB	13	Q	OG	10
Q	ARB	100	Q	RUN-S	30
Q	ARB-M	300	Q	TAR	18
Q	ARB-MN	501	Q	TAR-E	19
Q	ARB-N	181	R	ARB	200
Q	ARB-S	21	R	ARB-M	10
Q	ENG	17	R	ARB-MN	11
Q	ENG-F	1	R	ARB-N	201
Q	ENG-L	29	R	ARB-S	10
Q	ENG-N	8	R	BLN	15
Q	ENG-T	22	R	CPT	100
Q	ENO	90	R	CPT-T	30
Q	ENO-C	40	R	ENG	18
Q	ENO-D	9	R	ENG-F	2
Q	GEO	7,000	R	ENG-L	19
Q	GEO	800	R	ENG-N	9
Q	GK	90	R	ENG-T	21
Q	GK-N	321	R	ENO	100
Q	HEB	100	R	ENO-D	1
Q	HEB-C	1,000,000	R	ENO-G	100
Q	HEB-E	100,000	R	GEO	100
Q	HEB-M	1	R	GK	100
Q	HEB-N	186	R	GK-H	17
Q	HEB-N	906	R	GK-N	900
Q	HEB-P	29	R	HEB	200
Q	HEB-S	10,000	R	HEB-C	8,000,000
Q	LAT	15	R	HEB-E	200,000
Q	LAT-G	60	R	HEB-M	2
Q	LAT-P	376	R	HEB-N	510
Q	LAT-Q	256	R	HEB-P	30
Q	LAT-T	136	R	HEB-S	20

The Magickal Polyglot (cont'd.)

Letter	Language	Number	Letter	Language	Number
R	HEB-SQ	40,000	S	ARB-MN	1,730
R	LAT	16	Ṣ	ARB-MN	59
R	LAT-G	70	Sh	ARB-MN	1,740
R	LAT-P	425	S	ARB-N	120
R	LAT-Q	289	Ṣ	ARB-N	95
R	LAT-T	153	Sh	ARB-N	360
R	OG	15	S	ARB-S	12
R	RUN	5	Ṣ	ARB-S	14
R	RUN-S	5	Sh	ARB-S	13
R	RUN-Y	5	S	BLN	16
R	SKT	2	S	CPT	200
Ri	SKT	No value	So	CPT	6
Rî	SKT	No value	S	CPT-T	10
R	SKT-A	4	So	CPT-T	1
Ri	SKT-A (V)	1,000,000	S	ENG	19
Ri	SKT-A (A)	10,000,000	S	ENG-F	3
R	SKT-C	9	S	ENG-L	43
Ri	SKT-C	39	S	ENG-N	1
Rî	SKT-C	40	S	ENG-T	17
R	SKT-P	416	S	ENO	200
Ri	SKT-P	7	S	ENO-D	2
Rî	SKT-P	8	S	ENO-G	10
R	TAR	19	S	GEO	200
R	TAR-E	20	Ŝ	GEO	900
R	TIB	25	S	GK	200
S	ARB	60	Ṣ	GK	900
Ṣ	ARB	90	St	GK	6
Sh	ARB	300	S	GK-H	18
S	ARB-M	30	S	GK-N	254
Ṣ	ARB-M	50	Ṣ	GK-N	1,651
Sh	ARB-M	40	St	GK-N	901

The Magickal Polyglot (cont'd.)

Letter	Language	Number	Letter	Language	Number
St	GK-N	407	Sh	SKT	6
S	HEB	60	S	SKT-A	9
Sh	HEB	300	Ṡ	SKT-A	7
S	HEB-C	216,000	Sh	SKT-A	8
Sh	HEB-C	27,000,000	S	SKT-C	4
S	HEB-E	60,000	Ṡ	SKT-C	2
Sh	HEB-E	300,000	Sh	SKT-C	3
S	HEB-M	6	S	SKT-P	496
Sh	HEB-M	3	Ṡ	SKT-P	464
S	HEB-N	120	Sh	SKT-P	480
S	HEB-N	600	S	TAR	14
Sh	HEB-N	360	Sh	TAR	20
Sh	HEB-N	1,010	S	TAR-E	15
S	HEB-P	25	Sh	TAR-E	0
Sh	HEB-P	31	S	TIB	28
S	HEB-S	15	Sh	TIB	21
Sh	HEB-S	21	T	ARB	400
S	HEB-SQ	3,600	Ṭ	ARB	9
Sh	HEB-SQ	90,000	Th	ARB	500
S	LAT	17	T	ARB-M	3
S	LAT-G	80	Ṭ	ARB-M	70
S	LAT-P	477	Th	ARB-M	4
S	LAT-Q	324	T	ARB-MN	4
S	LAT-T	171	Ṭ	ARB-MN	71
S	OG	4	Th	ARB-MN	5
S	RUN	16	T	ARB-N	401
S	RUN-S	16	Ṭ	ARB-N	10
St	RUN-S	32	Th	ARB-N	501
S	RUN-Y	11	T	ARB-S	3
S	SKT	7	Ṭ	ARB-S	16
Ṣ	SKT	5	Th	ARB-S	4

The Magickal Polyglot (cont'd.)

Letter	Language	Number	Letter	Language	Number
T	BLN	11	T	HEB-N	419
T	CPT	300	Th	HEB-N	406
Th	CPT	9	T	HEB-P	19
Ti	CPT	0	Th	HEB-P	32
T	CPT-T	19	T	HEB-S	9
Th	CPT-T	32	Th	HEB-S	22
Ti	CPT-T	3	T	HEB-SQ	81
T	ENG	20	Th	HEB-SQ	160,000
T	ENG-F	4	T	LAT	18
T	ENG-L	30	T	LAT-G	90
T	ENG-N	2	T	LAT-P	532
T	ENG-T	6	T	LAT-Q	361
T	ENO	300	T	LAT-T	190
T	ENO-D	3	T	OG	8
T	ENO-G	400	Th	OG	22
T	GEO	9	T	RUN	17
Ṭ	GEO	300	Th	RUN	3
T	GK	300	T	RUN-S	17
Th	GK	9	Th	RUN-S	3
T	GK-H	19	T	RUN-Y	12
Th	GK-H	8	Th	RUN-Y	3
T	GK-N	701	T	SKT	6
Th	GK-N	318	Ṭ	SKT	1
T	HEB	9	Th	SKT	7
Th	HEB	400	Ṭh	SKT	2
T	HEB-C	729	T	SKT-A	16
Th	HEB-C	64,000,000	Ṭ	SKT-A	11
T	HEB-E	9,000	Th	SKT-A	17
Th	HEB-E	400,000	Ṭh	SKT-A	12
T	HEB-M	9	T	SKT-C	14
Th	HEB-M	4	Ṭ	SKT-C	31

The Magickal Polyglot (cont'd.)

Letter	Language	Number	Letter	Language	Number
Th	SKT-C	15	U	SKT-C	37
Ṭh	SKT-C	32	Û	SKT-C	38
T	SKT-P	240	U	SKT-P	5
Ṭ	SKT-P	160	Û	SKT-P	6
Th	SKT-P	256	U	TIB	60
Ṭh	SKT-P	176	V	ENG	22
T	TAR	8	V	ENG-F	6
Th	TAR	21	V	ENG-L	32
T	TAR-C	11	V	ENG-N	4
T	TAR-E	9	V	ENG-T	23
Th	TAR-E	21	V	ENO	400
T	TIB	9	Ṿ	ENO-D	4
Th	TIB	10	V	ENO-G	70
U	BLN	0	V	GEO	6
U	ENG	21	Vi	GEO	No value
U	ENG-F	6	V	HEB	6
U	ENG-L	61	V	HEB-C	216
U	ENG-N	3	V	HEB-E	6,000
U	ENG-T	26	V	HEB-M	6
U	GEO	400	V	HEB-N	12
U	GK	400	V	HEB-P	16
U	GK-H	20	V	HEB-S	6
U	GK-N	1,260	V	HEB-SQ	36
U	OG	18	V	LAT	19
U	RUN	2	V	LAT-G	100
U	RUN-S	2	V	LAT-P	590
U	RUN-Y	2	V	LAT-Q	400
U	SKT	No value	V	LAT-R	5
Û	SKT	No value	V	LAT-T	210
U	SKT-A (V)	10,000	V	SKT	4
U	SKT-A (A)	100,000	V	SKT-A	6

The Magickal Polyglot (cont'd.)

Letter	Language	Number	Letter	Language	Number
V	SKT-C	1	X	ENO-D	6
V	SKT-P	448	X	GEO	6,000
V	TAR	5	X	GK	60
V	TAR-E	6	X	GK-H	14
W	ARB	6	X	GK-N	70
W	ARB-M	900	X	LAT	20
W	ARB-MN	1,801	X	LAT-G	200
W	ARB-N	13	X	LAT-P	715
W	ARB-S	27	X	LAT-Q	484
W	ENG	23	X	LAT-R	10
W	ENG-L	120	X	LAT-T	253
W	ENG-F	6	X	OG	25
W	ENG-N	5	Kṣ	SKT	0 (place value)
W	ENG-T	11	Kṣ	SKT-C	50
W	LAT-P	651	Kṣ	SKT-P	528
W	LAT-Q	441	Y	ARB	10
W	LAT-T	231	Y	ARB-M	1,000
W	RUN	8	Y	ARB-MN	1,001
W	RUN-S	8	Y	ARB-N	11
W	TIB	20	Y	ARB-S	28
X	CPT	0	Y	CPT	400
Ks	CPT	60	Y	CPT-T	16
X	CPT-T	31	Y	ENG	25
Ks	CPT-T	25	Y	ENG-F	1
X	ENG	24	Y	ENG-L	53
X	ENG-F	5	Y	ENG-N	7
X	ENG-L	29	Y	ENG-T	7
X	ENG-N	6	Y	GEO	60
X	ENG-T	5	Y	LAT	21
X	ENO	60	Y	LAT-G	300
X	ENO-C	400	Y	LAT-P	782

The Magickal Polyglot (cont'd.)

Letter	Language	Number	Letter	Language	Number
Y	LAT-Q	529	Z	ENO-G	1
Y	LAT-T	276	Z	GEO	7
Ye	RUN-S	27	Ẑ	GEO	90
Y	RUN-Y	16	Z	GK	7
Y	SKT	1	Ps	GK	700
Y	SKT-A	3	Z	GK-H	6
Y	SKT-C	8	Ps	GK-H	23
Y	SKT-P	400	Z	GK-N	316
Y	TIB	24	Ps	GK-N	710
Z	ARB	7	Z	HEB	7
Tz	ARB	900	Tz	HEB	90
Z	ARB-M	20	Z	HEB-C	343
Tz	ARB-M	80	Tz	HEB-C	729,000
Z	ARB-MN	21	Z	HEB-E	7,000
Tz	ARB-MN	81	Tz	HEB-E	90,000
Z	ARB-N	8	Tz	HEB-F	900
Tz	ARB-N	901	Z	HEB-M	7
Zh	ARB-P	7	Tz	HEB-M	9
Z	ARB-S	11	Z	HEB-N	67
Tz	ARB-S	17	Z	HEB-N	717
Z	CPT	7	Tz	HEB-N	104
Ps	CPT	700	Z	HEB-P	17
Z	CPT-T	17	Tz	HEB-P	28
Ps	CPT-T	28	Z	HEB-S	7
Z	ENG	26	Tz	HEB-S	18
Z	ENG-L	36	Z	HEB-SQ	49
Z	ENG-F	7	Tz	HEB-SQ	8,100
Z	ENG-N	8	Z	LAT	22
Z	ENG-T	14	Z	LAT-G	400
Z	ENO	7	Z	LAT-P	852
Z	ENO-D	7	Z	LAT-Q	576

The Magickal Polyglot (cont'd.)

Letter	Language	Number
Z	LAT-T	300
Z	OG	14
Z	RUN	15
Z	RUN-S	15
Z	TAR	6
Tz	TAR	17
Tz	TAR-C	4
Z	TAR-E	7
Tz	TAR-E	18
Z	TIB	22
Ts	TIB	17
Tsh	TIB	18
Ds	TIB	19

ADDENDUM

THE SIEVE OF NUMBERS

The Magickal Polyglot can also be reversed by sifting the alphanumeric equivalents through a Sieve of Numbers. By categorizing the different alphanumeric codes by their specific number values, the entire number range spanned by each individual letter can be seen at once. The following table represents the Sieve of Numbers as applied to the 13 Keys.

The Sieve of Numbers

Number	Letter	Language	Number	Letter	Language
0	A	TAR	No value	Ah	SKT
0	a	TIB	No value	Ai	SKT
0	C	CPT	No value	Am	SKT
0	Gh	CPT	No value	Au	SKT
0	H	BLN	No value	E	SKT
0	Ĥ	CPT	No value	F	GEO
0	Ḥ	CPT	No value	Ḣ	SKT
0	H	TIB	No value	I	SKT
0	K̇	SKT-P	No value	Î	SKT
0	Ṁ	TIB	No value	Li	SKT
0	Sh	TAR-E	No value	Lî	SKT
0	Ti	CPT	No value	Ṁ	SKT
0	U	BLN	No value	O	SKT
0	X	CPT	No value	Ri	SKT
0 (place value)	N	SKT	No value	Rî	SKT
			No value	U	SKT
0 (place value)	Ñ	SKT	No value	Û	SKT
			No value	Vi	GEO
0 (place value)	Kṣ	SKT	1	A	ARB
No value	A	SKT	1	A	ARB-M
No value	Â	SKT	1	A	ARB-S

The Sieve of Numbers (cont'd.)

Number	Letter	Language	Number	Letter	Language
1	A	BLN	1	I	ENG-T
1	A	CPT	1	I	ENO-D
1	A	ENG	1	I	HEB-M
1	A	ENG-F	1	I	LAT-R
1	A	ENG-N	1	J	ENG-F
1	A	ENO	1	J	ENG-N
1	A	ENO-D	1	K	SKT
1	A	GEO	1	K	SKT-A
1	A	GK	1	K	TIB
1	A	GK-H	1	P	SKT
1	A	HEB	1	Q	ENG-F
1	A	HEB-C	1	Q	HEB-M
1	A	HEB-M	1	R	ENO-D
1	A	HEB-S	1	So	CPT-T
1	A	HEB-SQ	1	S	ENG-N
1	A	LAT	1	Ṭ	SKT
1	A	LAT-G	1	V	SKT-C
1	A	LAT-T	1	Y	ENG-F
1	A	LAT-Q	1	Y	SKT
1	A	LAT-P	1	Z	ENO-G
1	A	SKT-A (V)	2	Â	SKT-P
1	A	SKT-P	2	B	ARB
1	A	TAR-E	2	B	ARB-M
1	B	LAT-L	2	B	ARB-S
1	B	OG	2	B	CPT
1	B	TAR	2	B	ENG
1	F	RUN	2	B	ENG-F
1	F	RUN-S	2	B	ENG-N
1	F	RUN-Y	2	B	ENO
1	H	ENO-C	2	B	ENO-D
1	I	ENG-F	2	B	GEO

The Sieve of Numbers (cont'd.)

Number	Letter	Language	Number	Letter	Language
2	B	GK	2	U	RUN-S
2	B	GK-H	2	U	RUN-Y
2	B	HEB	3	B	ARB-MN
2	B	HEB-M	3	B	ARB-N
2	B	HEB-S	3	B	LAT-T
2	B	LAT	3	B	SKT
2	B	LAT-G	3	C	ENG
2	B	TAR-E	3	C	ENG-F
2	C	CPT-T	3	C	ENG-N
2	C	ENO-D	3	C	ENG-T
2	C	LAT-L	3	C	LAT
2	E	BLN	3	C	LAT-G
2	Ph	SKT	3	C	LAT-L
2	G	TAR	3	Ḍ	SKT
2	K	ENG-F	3	D	TAR
2	K	ENG-N	3	F	OG
2	K	HEB-M	3	G	CPT
2	Kh	SKT	3	G	ENG-F
2	Kh	SKT-A	3	G	ENO
2	Kh	TIB	3	G	ENO-D
2	L	ENG-T	3	G	GEO
2	L	OG	3	G	GK
2	P	ARB-P	3	G	GK-H
2	R	ENG-F	3	G	HEB
2	R	HEB-M	3	G	HEB-M
2	R	SKT	3	G	HEB-S
2	S	ENO-D	3	G	SKT
2	Ṡ	SKT-C	3	G	SKT-A
2	T	ENG-N	3	G	TAR-E
2	Ṭh	SKT	3	G	TIB
2	U	RUN	3	Ch	ARB-P

The Sieve of Numbers (cont'd.)

Number	Letter	Language	Number	Letter	Language
3	I	BLN	4	D	ENO-C
3	I	SKT-P	4	D	ENO-D
3	J	ARB	4	D	GEO
3	L	ENG-F	4	D	GK
3	L	ENG-N	4	D	GK-H
3	L	ENO-D	4	D	HEB
3	L	HEB-M	4	D	HEB-M
3	L	SKT	4	D	HEB-S
3	S	ENG-F	4	D	LAT
3	Sh	HEB-M	4	D	LAT-G
3	Sh	SKT-C	4	Ḍh	SKT
3	T	ARB-M	4	D	TAR-E
3	T	ARB-S	4	Ē	CPT-T
3	Ti	CPT-T	4	E	LAT-L
3	T	ENO-D	4	Gh	SKT
3	Th	RUN	4	Gh	SKT-A
3	Th	RUN-S	4	H	ENG-T
3	Th	RUN-Y	4	H	TAR
3	U	ENG-N	4	Î	SKT-P
3	Y	SKT-A	4	M	ENG-F
4	A	RUN	4	M	ENG-N
4	A	RUN-Y	4	M	ENO-D
4	B	HEB-SQ	4	M	HEB-M
4	B	LAT-Q	4	Ñ	TIB
4	Bh	SKT	4	O	BLN
4	D	ARB	4	O	RUN-S
4	D	CPT	4	R	SKT-A
4	D	ENG	4	S	OG
4	D	ENG-F	4	S	SKT-C
4	D	ENG-N	4	Th	ARB-M
4	D	ENO	4	T	ARB-MN

The Sieve of Numbers (cont'd.)

Number	Letter	Language	Number	Letter	Language
4	Th	ARB-S	5	J	ARB-S
4	T	ENG-F	5	L	SKT-A
4	Th	HEB-M	5	M	SKT
4	V	ENG-N	5	N	ENG-F
4	V	ENO-D	5	N	ENG-N
4	V	SKT	5	N	ENO-D
4	Tz	TAR-C	5	N	HEB-M
5	B	BLN	5	N	OG
5	B	ENO-G	5	Ṇ	SKT
5	B	LAT-P	5	Ṅ	SKT
5	B	SKT-C	5	Ṅ	SKT-A
5	E	CPT	5	R	RUN
5	E	ENG	5	R	RUN-S
5	E	ENG-F	5	R	RUN-Y
5	E	ENG-N	5	Ṡ	SKT
5	E	ENO	5	Th	ARB-MN
5	E	ENO-D	5	U	SKT-P
5	E	GEO	5	V	LAT-R
5	E	GK	5	V	TAR
5	E	GK-H	5	W	ENG-N
5	E	LAT	5	X	ENG-F
5	E	LAT-G	5	X	ENG-T
5	Ph	CPT-T	6	A	ENG-L
5	F	LAT-L	6	A	ENO-G
5	H	ARB	6	Bh	SKT-C
5	H	ENG-F	6	C	LAT-T
5	H	HEB	6	C	SKT
5	H	HEB-M	6	C	SKT-A
5	H	HEB-S	6	C	TIB
5	H	TAR-E	6	F	ENG
5	J	ARB-M	6	F	ENG-N

The Sieve of Numbers (cont'd.)

Number	Letter	Language	Number	Letter	Language
6	F	ENO	6	W	ENG-F
6	F	ENO-D	6	X	ENG-N
6	F	LAT	6	X	ENO-D
6	F	LAT-G	6	Z	GK-H
6	F	LAT-L	6	Z	TAR
6	Ḥ	ARB-M	7	D	OG
6	H	ARB-N	7	E	CPT-T
6	Ḥ	ARB-S	7	E	ENO-C
6	H	OG	7	G	ENG
6	K	RUN	7	G	ENG-N
6	K	RUN-S	7	G	LAT
6	K	RUN-Y	7	G	LAT-G
6	M	BLN	7	G	RUN
6	Ō	CPT-T	7	G	RUN-S
6	O	ENG-N	7	Ḥ	ARB-MN
6	So	CPT	7	H	GK-H
6	St	GK	7	H	LAT-L
6	S	HEB-M	7	H	RUN-Y
6	Sh	SKT	7	Ch	SKT
6	T	ENG-T	7	Ch	SKT-A
6	T	SKT	7	Ch	TAR
6	U	ENG-F	7	J	TIB
6	Û	SKT-P	7	Kh	ARB-M
6	V	ENG-F	7	Kh	ARB-S
6	V	GEO	7	M	SKT-C
6	V	HEB	7	O	ENG-F
6	V	HEB-M	7	O	ENO-D
6	V	HEB-S	7	O	HEB-M
6	V	SKT-A	7	P	BLN
6	V	TAR-E	7	P	ENG-N
6	W	ARB	7	Ri	SKT-P

The Sieve of Numbers (cont'd.)

Number	Letter	Language	Number	Letter	Language
7	Ṣ	SKT	8	H	GK
7	S	SKT-A	8	Ch	HEB
7	Th	SKT	8	Ch	HEB-M
7	Y	ENG-N	8	Ch	HEB-S
7	Y	ENG-T	8	H	LAT
7	Z	ARB	8	H	LAT-G
7	Zh	ARB-P	8	H	SKT
7	Z	CPT	8	Ch	TAR-E
7	Z	ENG-F	8	I	LAT-L
7	Z	ENO	8	J	SKT
7	Z	ENO-D	8	J	SKT-A
7	Z	GEO	8	Kh	ARB-MN
7	Z	GK	8	L	TAR-C
7	Z	HEB	8	N	RUN-Y
7	Z	HEB-M	8	Ñ	TIB
7	Z	HEB-S	8	P	ENG-F
7	Z	TAR-E	8	P	ENG-T
8	B	HEB-C	8	P	ENO-C
8	D	ARB-M	8	P	ENO-D
8	D	ARB-S	8	P	HEB-M
8	D	SKT	8	Q	ENG-N
8	Ē	CPT	8	Rî	SKT-P
8	Ey	GEO	8	Sh	SKT-A
8	F	BLN	8	Th	GK-H
8	F	CPT-T	8	T	OG
8	F	ENG-F	8	T	TAR
8	Ḥ	ARB	8	W	RUN
8	H	ENG	8	W	RUN-S
8	H	ENG-N	8	Y	SKT-C
8	H	ENO	8	Z	ARB-N
8	H	ENO-D	8	Z	ENG-N

The Sieve of Numbers (cont'd.)

Number	Letter	Language	Number	Letter	Language
9	A	ENG-T	9	T	GEO
9	C	BLN	9	Th	GK
9	C	LAT-Q	9	T	HEB
9	C	OG	9	T	HEB-M
9	Dh	ARB-M	9	T	HEB-S
9	Dh	ARB-S	9	Ṭ	TAR-E
9	Dh	SKT	9	T	TIB
9	Gh	CPT-T	9	Tz	HEB-M
9	G	ENO-G	10	Ā	RUN-Y
9	G	HEB-C	10	A	SKT-A (A)
9	G	HEB-SQ	10	D	LAT-T
9	Ḥ	ARB-N	10	E	ENG-L
9	H	RUN	10	G	BLN
9	H	RUN-S	10	H	HEB-N
9	I	ENG	10	H	SKT-A
9	I	ENG-N	10	I	CPT
9	I	GK-H	10	I	ENO
9	I	LAT	10	I	GEO
9	I	LAT-G	10	I	GK
9	I	RUN-Y	10	I	HEB
9	I	TAR	10	I	HEB-S
9	Jh	SKT	10	I	TAR-E
9	Jh	SKT-A	10	J	ENG
9	K	LAT-L	10	J	ENG-T
9	Li	SKT-P	10	K	GK-H
9	Q	ENO-D	10	K	TAR
9	R	ENG-N	10	L	LAT
9	R	SKT-C	10	L	LAT-G
9	S	SKT-A	10	L	SKT-C
9	Ṭ	ARB	10	Lî	SKT-P
9	Th	CPT	10	N	RUN

The Sieve of Numbers (cont'd.)

Number	Letter	Language	Number	Letter	Language
10	N	RUN-S	11	Y	ARB-N
10	Ñ	SKT-A	11	Z	ARB-S
10	Q	OG	12	Ai	SKT-P
10	R	ARB-M	12	B	CPT-T
10	R	ARB-S	12	B	ENG-L
10	S	CPT-T	12	B	HEB-P
10	S	ENO-G	12	C	LAT-P
10	Ṭ	ARB-N	12	D	BLN
10	Th	TIB	12	Ḍh	SKT-C
10	X	LAT-R	12	G	OG
10	Y	ARB	12	J	RUN
11	A	CPT-T	12	J	RUN-S
11	A	HEB-P	12	L	ENG
11	Ḍ	SKT-C	12	L	HEB-S
11	D	TIB	12	L	TAR-E
11	E	SKT-P	12	M	GK-H
11	I	RUN	12	M	TAR
11	I	RUN-S	12	N	LAT
11	K	ENG	12	N	TIB
11	K	HEB-S	12	O	ENG-T
11	K	TAR-E	12	S	ARB-S
11	L	GK-H	12	T	RUN-Y
11	L	TAR	12	Th	SKT-A
11	M	LAT	12	V	HEB-N
11	M	OG	13	B	RUN-Y
11	R	ARB-MN	13	C	ENG-L
11	S	RUN-Y	13	Ḍ	SKT-A
11	T	BLN	13	Ei	RUN
11	T	TAR-C	13	E	RUN-S
11	Ṭ	SKT-A	13	G	CPT-T
11	W	ENG-T	13	G	ENG-T

The Sieve of Numbers (cont'd.)

Number	Letter	Language	Number	Letter	Language
13	G	HEB-P	14	T	SKT-C
13	M	ENG	14	X	GK-H
13	M	HEB-S	14	Z	ENG-T
13	M	TAR-E	14	Z	OG
13	N	BLN	15	Ah	SKT-P
13	N	GK-H	15	B	ENG-T
13	Ng	OG	15	B	TIB
13	Ṇ	SKT-C	15	Ḍ	ARB-S
13	N	TAR	15	E	LAT-T
13	O	LAT	15	H	CPT-T
13	O	SKT-P	15	H	HEB-P
13	P	TIB	15	L	RUN-Y
13	Sh	ARB-S	15	Ṇ	SKT-A
13	W	ARB-N	15	O	ENG
14	Au	SKT-P	15	O	GK-H
14	D	CPT-T	15	O	TAR
14	D	ENG-L	15	Q	LAT
14	D	HEB-P	15	R	BLN
14	Ḍh	SKT-A	15	R	OG
14	Ph	TIB	15	S	HEB-S
14	I	ENG-L	15	S	TAR-E
14	L	BLN	15	Th	SKT-C
14	M	RUN-Y	15	Z	RUN
14	N	ENG	15	Z	RUN-S
14	N	HEB-S	16	A	OG
14	N	TAR-E	16	Am	SKT-P
14	P	LAT	16	D	HEB-SQ
14	P	RUN	16	D	LAT-Q
14	P	RUN-S	16	D	SKT-C
14	Ṣ	ARB-S	16	F	ENG-T
14	S	TAR	16	Kh	SKT-P

The Sieve of Numbers (cont'd.)

Number	Letter	Language	Number	Letter	Language
16	M	TIB	17	Z	HEB-P
16	O	HEB-S	17	Tz	TAR
16	O	TAR-E	17	Ts	TIB
16	P	ENG	18	B	RUN
16	P	GK-H	18	B	RUN-S
16	P	TAR	18	D	SKT-A
16	R	LAT	18	Ḥ	CPT-T
16	S	BLN	18	Ch	HEB-P
16	S	RUN	18	M	ENG-L
16	S	RUN-S	18	M	ENG-T
16	Ṭ	ARB-S	18	N	SKT-C
16	T	SKT-A	18	O	ARB-S
16	V	HEB-P	18	Q	TAR
16	Y	CPT-T	18	R	ENG
16	Y	RUN-Y	18	S	GK-H
17	Dh	SKT-C	18	T	LAT
17	F	ENG-L	18	U	OG
17	G	ENG-L	18	Tz	HEB-S
17	H	TAR-C	18	Tz	TAR-E
17	O	OG	18	Tsh	TIB
17	P	HEB-S	19	Dh	SKT-A
17	P	TAR-E	19	E	OG
17	Q	ENG	19	E	RUN
17	R	GK-H	19	Eh	RUN-S
17	S	ENG-T	19	Gh	ARB-S
17	S	LAT	19	N	ENG-L
17	T	RUN	19	N	ENG-T
17	T	RUN-S	19	P	SKT-C
17	Th	SKT-A	19	Q	HEB-S
17	Tz	ARB-S	19	Q	TAR-E
17	Z	CPT-T	19	R	ENG-L

The Sieve of Numbers (cont'd.)

Number	Letter	Language	Number	Letter	Language
19	R	TAR	20	W	TIB
19	S	ENG	20	X	LAT
19	T	CPT-T	20	Z	ARB-M
19	T	GK-H	21	Ph	GK-H
19	T	HEB-P	21	F	LAT-T
19	V	LAT	21	Ch	OG
19	Ds	TIB	21	K	CPT-T
20	C	ENO	21	K	HEB-P
20	E	ENG-T	21	K	SKT-C
20	F	ARB-S	21	L	RUN
20	Ph	SKT-C	21	L	RUN-S
20	G	ARB-P	21	P	SKT-A
20	I	CPT-T	21	Q	ARB-S
20	I	HEB-N	21	R	ENG-T
20	I	HEB-P	21	Sh	HEB-S
20	I	OG	21	Sh	TIB
20	K	ARB	21	Th	TAR
20	K	CPT	21	Th	TAR-E
20	Ḳ	GEO	21	U	ENG
20	K	GK	21	Y	LAT
20	K	HEB	21	Z	ARB-MN
20	M	LAT-G	22	D	LAT-P
20	M	RUN	22	Ph	SKT-A
20	M	RUN-S	22	Ch	GK-H
20	N	SKT-A	22	K	ARB-S
20	O	ENG-L	22	Kh	SKT-C
20	R	HEB-S	22	L	CPT-T
20	R	TAR-E	22	L	HEB-P
20	Sh	TAR	22	Ng	RUN
20	T	ENG	22	Ng	RUN-S
20	U	GK-H	22	G	ENG-T

The Sieve of Numbers (cont'd.)

Number	Letter	Language	Number	Letter	Language
22	Th	HEB-S	25	D	ENG-T
22	Th	OG	25	E	LAT-Q
22	V	ENG	25	H	HEB-SQ
22	Z	LAT	25	M	SKT-A
22	Z	TIB	25	N	ARB-S
23	B	SKT-A	25	Ṅ	SKT-C
23	D	RUN	25	R	TIB
23	G	SKT-C	25	S	HEB-P
23	Ḥ	TIB	25	Ks	CPT-T
23	L	ARB-S	25	X	OG
23	M	CPT-T	25	Y	ENG
23	M	HEB-P	26	Ae	RUN-S
23	O	ENG-L	26	C	SKT-C
23	Oe	RUN-S	26	H	ARB-S
23	P	OG	26	L	TIB
23	V	ENG-T	26	O	CPT-T
23	W	ENG	26	O	HEB-P
23	Ps	GK-H	26	P	ENG-L
24	Bh	SKT-A	26	U	ENG-T
24	D	RUN-S	26	Z	ENG
24	Ph	OG	27	Ç	TIB
24	Gh	SKT-C	27	Ch	SKT-C
24	K	ENG-T	27	P	CPT-T
24	M	ARB-S	27	P	HEB-P
24	N	CPT-T	27	W	ARB-S
24	N	HEB-P	27	Ye	RUN-S
24	Ō	GK-H	28	G	LAT-T
24	O	RUN	28	Io	RUN-S
24	X	ENG	28	J	SKT-C
24	Y	TIB	28	S	TIB
25	Ai	RUN-S	28	Y	ARB-S

The Sieve of Numbers (cont'd.)

Number	Letter	Language	Number	Letter	Language
28	Ps	CPT-T	31	X	CPT-T
28	Tz	HEB-P	32	G	SKT-P
29	Ea	RUN-S	32	St	RUN-S
29	Ch	CPT-T	32	Th	CPT-T
29	H	TIB	32	Th	HEB-P
29	Jh	SKT-C	32	Ṭh	SKT-C
29	L	ENG-L	32	V	ENG-L
29	Q	ENG-L	33	A	SKT-C
29	Q	HEB-P	33	Gh	RUN-S
29	X	ENG-L	34	Â	SKT-C
30	Ah	TIB	35	D	ARB-N
30	I	TIB	35	E	LAT-P
30	L	ARB	35	I	ENG-L
30	Ĺ	CPT	35	I	SKT-C
30	L	ENO	36	F	LAT-Q
30	L	GEO	36	H	LAT-T
30	L	GK	36	Î	SKT-C
30	L	HEB	36	J	ENG-L
30	N	LAT-G	36	V	HEB-SQ
30	Ñ	SKT-C	36	Z	ENG-L
30	O	ENO-G	37	K	ENG-L
30	Q	RUN-S	37	U	SKT-C
30	R	CPT-T	38	Û	SKT-C
30	R	HEB-P	39	Ri	SKT-C
30	S	ARB-M	40	L	ENO-G
30	T	ENG-L	40	M	ARB
31	A	ENG-L	40	M	CPT
31	C	RUN-S	40	M	ENO
31	D	ENO-C	40	M	GEO
31	Sh	HEB-P	40	M	GK
31	Ṭ	SKT-C	40	M	HEB

The Sieve of Numbers (cont'd.)

Number	Letter	Language	Number	Letter	Language
40	O	LAT-G	53	J	ARB-N
40	Q	ENO-C	53	Y	ENG-L
40	Rî	SKT-C	55	K	LAT-T
40	Sh	ARB-M	59	Ṣ	ARB-MN
41	H	ENG-L	60	Ḍ	ARB-M
41	Li	SKT-C	60	I	ENO-G
42	Lî	SKT-C	60	Q	LAT-G
43	E	SKT-C	60	S	ARB
43	S	ENG-L	60	S	HEB
44	Ai	SKT-C	60	U	TIB
45	I	LAT-T	60	Ks	CPT
45	O	SKT-C	60	X	ENO
46	Au	SKT-C	60	X	GK
47	Ah	SKT-C	60	Y	GEO
48	Am	SKT-C	61	U	ENG-L
48	Gh	SKT-P	64	D	HEB-C
49	G	LAT-Q	64	Ch	HEB-SQ
49	H	SKT-C	64	H	LAT-Q
49	Z	HEB-SQ	64	Ṅ	SKT-P
50	L	LAT-R	66	L	LAT-T
50	N	ARB	67	Z	HEB-N
50	N	CPT	69	Ḍ	ARB-MN
50	N	ENO	70	G	LAT-P
50	N	ENO-G	70	O	ARB
50	N	GEO	70	O	CPT
50	N	GK	70	O	ENO
50	N	HEB	70	O	GEO
50	P	LAT-G	70	O	GK
50	Ṣ	ARB-M	70	O	HEB
50	Kṣ	SKT-C	70	R	LAT-G
51	F	LAT-P	70	Ṭ	ARB-M

The Sieve of Numbers (cont'd.)

Number	Letter	Language	Number	Letter	Language
70	V	ENO-G	90	Q	GK
70	X	GK-N	90	Ṣ	ARB
71	L	ARB-N	90	T	LAT-G
71	Ṭ	ARB-MN	90	Ẑ	GEO
73	G	HEB-N	90	Tz	HEB
74	L	HEB-N	91	N	LAT-T
78	L	GK-N	92	H	LAT-P
78	M	LAT-T	95	Ṣ	ARB-N
80	C	SKT-P	96	Ch	SKT-P
80	F	ARB	100	C	LAT-R
80	P	CPT	100	Gh	ARB-M
80	P	ENO	100	I	HEB-SQ
80	Ṗ	GEO	100	I	SKT-A (V)
80	P	GK	100	K	HEB-N
80	P	HEB	100	Q	ARB
80	S	LAT-G	100	Q	HEB
80	Tz	ARB-M	100	R	CPT
81	F	ARB-N	100	R	ENO
81	I	LAT-Q	100	R	ENO-G
81	T	HEB-SQ	100	R	GEO
81	Tz	ARB -MN	100	R	GK
85	G	GK-N	100	V	LAT-G
85	P	HEB-N	101	K	ARB-N
90	E	TIB	104	Tz	HEB-N
90	F	CPT	105	O	LAT-T
90	M	ARB-N	106	N	ARB-N
90	M	ENO-G	106	N	HEB-N
90	M	HEB-N	111	A	ARB-N
90	O	ARB-M	111	A	HEB-N
90	P	GK-N	112	J	SKT-P
90	Q	ENO	117	I	LAT-P

The Magickal Polyglot (cont'd.)

Number	Letter	Language	Number	Letter	Language
120	O	TIB	200	S	ENO
120	P	LAT-T	200	S	GEO
120	S	ARB-N	200	S	GK
120	S	HEB-N	200	X	LAT-G
120	W	ENG-L	201	F	ARB-MN
121	L	LAT-Q	201	R	ARB-N
125	H	HEB-C	208	Ḍh	SKT-P
128	Jh	SKT-P	210	M	LAT-P
130	O	ARB-N	210	V	LAT-T
130	O	HEB-N	216	V	HEB-C
136	Q	LAT-T	224	Ṇ	SKT-P
144	M	LAT-Q	225	P	LAT-Q
144	Ñ	SKT-P	231	W	LAT-T
145	K	LAT-P	240	T	SKT-P
153	R	LAT-T	247	N	LAT-P
160	Ṭ	SKT-P	253	X	LAT-T
169	N	LAT-Q	254	S	GK-N
171	S	LAT-T	256	Th	SKT-P
176	L	LAT-P	256	Q	LAT-Q
176	Ṭh	SKT-P	272	D	SKT-P
181	Q	ARB-N	276	Y	LAT-T
182	K	GK-N	287	O	LAT-P
186	Q	HEB-N	288	Dh	SKT-P
190	T	LAT-T	289	R	LAT-Q
192	Ḍ	SKT-P	300	C	ENO-C
196	O	LAT-Q	300	F	ENO-G
200	F	ARB-M	300	Q	ARB-M
200	H	LAT-R	300	Sh	ARB
200	R	ARB	300	Sh	HEB
200	R	HEB	300	T	CPT
200	S	CPT	300	T	ENO

The Sieve of Numbers (cont'd.)

Number	Letter	Language	Number	Letter	Language
300	Ṭ	GEO	400	U	GK
300	T	GK	400	V	ENO
300	Y	LAT-G	400	V	LAT-Q
300	Z	LAT-T	400	X	ENO-C
304	N	SKT-P	400	Y	CPT
309	H	GK-N	400	Y	SKT-P
311	B	GK-N	400	Z	LAT-Q
316	Z	GK-N	401	Kh	ARB-N
318	Th	GK-N	401	T	ARB-N
320	P	SKT-P	406	Th	HEB-N
321	Q	GK-N	407	St	GK-N
324	S	LAT-Q	412	B	HEB-N
330	P	LAT-P	416	R	SKT-P
336	Ph	SKT-P	418	Ch	HEB-N
340	D	GK-N	419	T	HEB-N
343	Z	HEB-C	425	R	LAT-P
352	B	SKT-P	432	L	SKT-P
360	O	GK-N	434	D	HEB-N
360	Sh	ARB-N	440	M	GK-N
360	Sh	HEB-N	441	W	LAT-Q
361	T	LAT-Q	448	V	SKT-P
368	Bh	SKT-P	450	N	GK-N
376	Q	LAT-P	464	Ṡ	SKT-P
384	M	SKT-P	477	S	LAT-P
400	G	LAT-R	480	Sh	SKT-P
400	K	ARB-M	484	X	LAT-Q
400	K	HEB-SQ	496	S	SKT-P
400	T	ARB	500	D	LAT-R
400	T	ENO-G	500	Ph	CPT
400	Th	HEB	500	Ph	GEO
400	U	GEO	500	Ph	GK

The Sieve of Numbers (cont'd.)

Number	Letter	Language	Number	Letter	Language
500	K	HEB-F	700	N	ARB-M
500	L	ARB-M	700	N	HEB-F
500	Th	ARB	700	Ps	CPT
501	Q	ARB-MN	700	Ps	GK
501	Th	ARB-N	701	A	ARB-MN
509	D	ARB-MN	701	T	GK-N
510	Dh	ARB-MN	710	Ps	GK-N
510	Ph	GK-N	715	X	LAT-P
510	R	HEB-N	717	Z	HEB-N
512	Ch	HEB-C	729	T	HEB-C
512	H	SKT-P	731	Dh	ARB-N
528	Kṣ	SKT-P	756	N	HEB-N
529	Y	LAT-Q	780	O	HEB-N
532	A	GK-N	782	Y	LAT-P
532	T	LAT-P	800	Ḍ	ARB
544	Ĺ	SKT-P	800	H	ARB-M
576	Z	LAT-Q	800	Ō	CPT
590	V	LAT-P	800	Ō	GK
600	Ch	CPT	800	P	HEB-F
600	Ch	GK	800	Q̣	GEO
600	Kh	ARB	801	H	ARB-MN
600	K	GEO	805	Ḍ	ARB-N
600	M	ARB-M	820	K	HEB-N
600	M	HEB-F	831	A	HEB-N
600	S	HEB-N	849	Ō	GK-N
601	K	ARB-MN	852	Z	LAT-P
610	Ch	GK-N	865	E	GK-N
650	M	HEB-N	900	L	HEB-SQ
651	W	LAT-P	900	R	GK-N
700	Dh	ARB	900	Ŝ	GEO
700	Ĝ	GEO	900	Ṣ	GK

The Sieve of Numbers (cont'd.)

Number	Letter	Language	Number	Letter	Language
900	W	ARB-M	2,500	N	HEB-SQ
900	Tz	ARB	3,000	G	HEB-E
900	Tz	HEB-F	3,000	J	GEO
901	St	GK-N	3,600	S	HEB-SQ
901	Tz	ARB-N	4,000	Ç	GEO
906	Q	HEB-N	4,000	D	HEB-E
1,000	A	HEB-E	4,900	O	HEB-SQ
1,000	Ĉ	GEO	5,000	Ĉ	GEO
1,000	Gh	ARB	5,000	H	HEB-E
1,000	I	HEB-C	6,000	V	HEB-E
1,000	I	SKT-A (A)	6,000	X	GEO
1,000	M	LAT-R	6,400	P	HEB-SQ
1,000	Y	ARB-M	7,000	Q	GEO
1,001	Y	ARB-MN	7,000	Z	HEB-E
1,010	Sh	HEB-N	8,000	Ch	HEB-E
1,060	Gh	ARB-N	8,000	Ĵ	GEO
1,101	L	ARB-MN	8,000	K	HEB-C
1,111	I	GK-N	8,100	Tz	HEB-SQ
1,260	U	GK-N	9,000	H	GEO
1,600	M	HEB-SQ	9,000	T	HEB-E
1,605	J	ARB-MN	10,000	I	HEB-E
1,651	Ṣ	GK-N	10,000	Oy	GEO
1,730	S	ARB-MN	10,000	Q	HEB-SQ
1,740	Sh	ARB-MN	10,000	U	SKT-A (V)
1,790	O	ARB-MN	20,000	K	HEB-E
1,800	Gh	ARB -MN	27,000	L	HEB-C
1,801	W	ARB-MN	30,000	L	HEB-E
2,000	B	HEB-E	40,000	M	HEB-E
2,000	C	GEO	40,000	R	HEB-SQ
2,200	M	ARB-MN	50,000	N	HEB-E
2,300	N	ARB-MN	60,000	S	HEB-E

Number	Letter	Language
64,000	M	HEB-C
70,000	O	HEB-E
80,000	P	HEB-E
90,000	Sh	HEB-SQ
90,000	Tz	HEB-E
100,000	Q	HEB-E
100,000	U	SKT-A (A)
125,000	N	HEB-C
160,000	Th	HEB-SQ
200,000	R	HEB-E
216,000	S	HEB-C
300,000	Sh	HEB-E
343,000	O	HEB-C
400,000	Th	HEB-E
512,000	P	HEB-C
729,000	Tz	HEB-C
1,000,000	Q	HEB-C
1,000,000	Ri	SKT-A (V)
8,000,000	R	HEB-C
10,000,000	Ri	SKT-A (A)
27,000,000	Sh	HEB-C
64,000,000	Th	HEB-C
100,000,000	Li	SKT-A (V)
1,000,000,000	Li	SKT-A (A)
10,000,000,000	E	SKT-A (V)
100,000,000,000	E	SKT-A (A)
1,000,000,000,000	Ai	SKT-A (V)
10,000,000,000,000	Ai	SKT-A (A)
100,000,000,000,000	O	SKT-A (V)
1,000,000,000,000,000	O	SKT-A (A)
10,000,000,000,000,000	Au	SKT-A (V)
100,000,000,000,000,000	Au	SKT-A (A)

EPILOGOS

This volume must finally come to a close, yet there is so much more to explore, from both the East and West. In these first two books of *The Key of It All* series, I have set out to establish a broad base of information concerning the workings of the major isopsephic languages. It should serve the student, both beginning and advanced, as an essential reference work for discovering the correct numerical value, in the original language, of any mystical or magickal word in the world, both East and West.

Yet these first two books might be only an introduction to the vast storehouse of research which could comprise succeeding volumes in this series. Reminiscent of the Rosicrucian number language dictionary known as *Liber Thesaurus,* the succeeding volumes would form the most comprehensive dictionaries of numerical metaphors for the infinite number range, compiled from 25 years of my own copious research on the 13 traditional magickal languages. The entries for the total dictionary would probably exceed 50,000 entries, each transliterated into its English equivalent as outlined in the 13 keys of the first two volumes.*

The examples will be categorized by each of the 13 languages listed in numerical order, beginning with zero and extending through the number range to the highest number example uncovered by my work.

The first two volumes of *The Key of It All* can always be amended, corrected, and expanded. In light of such potential revision, a sequel to these first two volumes, supplementing my established research, may form a not-yet-planned third volume, prior to the creation of the actual number dictionary.

I am interested in hearing from any reader who discovers any discrepancies in these first two volumes, or may have numerical research which could be included in the forthcoming number dictionary. Those interested can reach me through the publisher of this book.

Editor's note: Inasmuch as any succeeding volumes of The Key of It All *have yet to be written or submitted, Llewellyn Publications naturally cannot commit at this time to publishing them.*

13 Questions Concerning
The Key of It All Series

Q: What is the Magickal Language?

A: The term is Rosicrucian in origin and appears in the first Rosicrucian manifestos published in the early 17th century. The Magickal Language designates those languages in the world whose alphabets contain spiritual dimensions of number value and symbolic attributes. In each case the Magickal Languages have a divine origin in their development, the shapes and attributes of their alphabets being inspired by Spirit.

In all cases the words in these Magickal Languages can be measured by totaling the numerical values assigned to each letter of the alphabet. In this sense word is equated to number, poetry to arithmetic, which results in an intricate set of word concepts symbolically defining the nature of each specific whole integer in the infinite number series. This is the original form of numerology at its most pristine state, allowing abstract number to contain infinite nuances of meaning.

Q: What is the Magickal Language Dictionary?

A: This is a fabled Rosicrucian text. It is referred to cryptically as *Liber Th*, not to be confused with the Golden Dawn *Liber T*. *Liber Th* was the abbreviation for *Liber Thesaurus*, the Magickal Dictionary containing all the world's ancient magickal languages in one book, catalogued by their numerical values. This book was entered into, expanded upon, and read on a daily basis, and served as an oracle to interpret the meaning of numbers encountered in dreams and visions.

In modern occultism Blavatsky first referred to this mysterious book as the lost Chaldean *Book of Numbers*. Crowley used this title for his own reconstruction of the Hebrew portion of this book in his *Sepher Sephiroth*, and currently David Godwin is expanding this work to new heights.

The original Rosicrucian *Liber Th* can be reconstructed by using the 13 major number language codes detailed in *The Key of It All* in numbering each language and then cataloguing the results as a dictionary in numerical order. This is the intention of the third volume of this series.

Every beginning student of the Qabalah can start a personal catalog of their own research into the esoteric meanings of the number series by entering the many number metaphors found within the first two volumes of *The Key of It All*.

Q: How did you become interested in the study of ancient languages?

A: I've always been fascinated by ancient alphabets. As a child of ten, I familiarized myself with the Greek alphabet as well as the alphabets of the ancient Egyptians and Phoenicians. Even at this young age I saw a connection between the shapes of the English alphabets and their ancient precursors. At age 16 two distinct esoteric traditions opened up to me for the first time: the lore of Buddhism and the Tarot. These two traditions from the East and West would consume me for the rest of my life. It was at this time in my life that I first studied Sanskrit in earnest, mostly through Theosophical literature and the Buddhist studies of D. T. Suzuki and Alan Watts.

Then in college I discovered S. L. MacGregor Mathers' *The Kabbalah Unveiled*. This book was a tremendous revelation for me, in that I was first exposed to the number values of the Hebrew alphabet. Because of this work I immediately began numbering and indexing every relevent word I could find in a Hebrew-English dictionary, and in these preliminary notes I rediscovered the hidden meanings for the number series which was now in the 20th century lost knowledge. This was the beginning of my research that would culminate 20 years later in the writing of *The Key of It All* series.

Q: What made you decide to write this encyclopedic guide?

A: This is an interesting question. I have a very well-defined mission to fulfill in the writing of *The Key of It All* series, and that is the extension and continuation of the magickal work first initiated in the late 19th century by both the Theosophical Society of Madame Blavatsky and the Golden Dawn of Mathers and Westcott. *The Key of It All* series has been created to preserve all of the new magickal research I have been able to unearth in my occult archaelogical dig of the last 25 years. And it is an innovative bridge uniting the magickal traditions of the East with those of the West.

Regardie in writing his own account of the Golden Dawn teachings premised that if this system of magick had any real worth a new wave of research would appear at this present time to clarify, continue, and extend the core magickal correspondences found at the heart of the Golden Dawn teachings.

I am one of a handful of independent researchers right now who are recording and releasing into print a new level of knowledge concerning the magickal current which was first initiated in the last 25 years of the 19th century.

Q: What new research can be found in the first two volumes of *The Key of It All*?

A: There are so many new discoveries housed in both of these volumes that I cannot begin to list them all here. But there is a crowning jewel of research found in each of the first two volumes. In *Part One: The Eastern*

Mysteries, there is a deciphering of the actual placement of the Sanskrit letters upon the 50 petals of the 7 chakras. This is a great addition to our current knowledge of the sacred correspondences for the Eastern system of the chakras. No one else in the West has been able to penetrate this recondite Eastern mystery, including Blavatsky and Crowley.

And in *Part Two: The Western Mysteries,* for the first time in more than 400 years the 644 squares that compose John Dee's Enochian Watchtower system have been clearly deciphered and delineated. No one, including John Dee himself, has discovered the true key to this mystery and correctly applied it. In many Enochian books which have recently seen print, not one has correctly given the 644 letters which form the five tablets of the Enochian Watchtower system. And without these correct allocations no Enochian magickal working can be safely or properly performed.

Q: Beyond the secret lore of alphabet magick, is there any other material that can be found in *The Key of It All* ?

A: Both volumes contain elaborate, extensive chapters on the two most important magickal oracles in the world, the I Ching and the Tarot. In the sixth key found in *Part One: The Eastern Mysteries,* there is a detailed explanation of the pattern behind the I Ching which has no equal in any other commentary. In addition, there is an essential reading for the 64 hexagrams which gets to the bottom line in regards to divinatory meanings. In essence, all you need to know about the I Ching, and all the tools necessary to perform a proper divination, are included in this section, as well as an extensive discussion of the connection between the 10 Sephiroth of the Qabalistic Tree of Life and the eight trigrams of the I Ching.

And in Book Two, in the 12th key, more than 200 pages are devoted to every aspect of the Tarot. Both the British and French Qabalistic systems for the Tarot are given, as well as the correct divinatory definitions for the 78 cards of the Tarot. In addition, Mathers' own unique decipherment of the Tarot using the *Sepher Yetzirah* is shown, as well as Waite's own Tarot secrets based on Mathers' own vision of the Tarot, including a card-by-card analysis of the Waite Tarot deck. In short, everything needed for an initiated interpretation of the Tarot is given in *Part Two* of *The Key of It All.*

Q: How did you come up with the title for your series as *The Key of It All?*

A: In the Persian Sufi tradition a mystical work of great importance is often titled so that the numerical value of both the title and the name of the author are of the same number value. This device was also used in many Hebraic Qabalistic texts. As such I wanted to create a numerical correspondence between the title of my series and my own name.

By using the German Rosicrucian alphabet code found in *The Chymical Marriage of Christian Rosenkreutz,* which assigns the numbers 1 through 26 to the letters A through Z, I was able to come up with a title equal to the measure of my name, for both *The Key of It All* and David

Allen Hulse total to the number 149.

And the phrase "the Key of it all" can be found in Aleister Crowley's *Book of the Law* in the 47th verse of the third chapter: "Let him not seek to try: but one cometh after him, whence I say not, who shall discover the Key of it all."

Q: What does your unique cover design for this series symbolize?

A: *The Eastern Mysteries* cover is Divine Man enlightened by Spirit. *The Western Mysteries* cover is Natural Man centered in nature.

The cover design for *The Eastern Mysteries* is representative of the day sky and the sunrise in the East. The figure on the cover is the Buddha, who represents the way of enlightenment open to all through meditation. The body of Buddha is marked by both the seven chakras and the five tattvas, representing the seven inner spiritual centers and the five outer senses. The lotus in the center is the mind illuminated by the bright light of the diamond as the yin/yang, which is the clear mind of superconsciousness. The eight trigrams surround the Budda and are laid out in the Heavenly Sky pattern in which Yang is at the top representing the direction South, while Yin is at the bottom at thedirection North.

The cover design for *The Western Mysteries* is representative of the night sky and the sunset in the West. The figure on the cover is Man extended to the five points of the pentagram centered within the Tree of Life, who represents the way of finding one's place in the cosmos through the secret teachings of the Western Mystery schools. The rose in the center is the heart, raising the sexual force of Eros through the devotion of love. The five lesser planets mark the five points of the star as the five senses, while the luminaries of the sun and moon are at the center of the star. Spread out in the background is the Tree of Life, marking the Western version of the chakras as the ten spiritual centers of the Qabalah.

Q: Who will this series appeal to?

A: First and foremost this series is a must-buy for anyone working the Western magickal traditions, such as the Golden Dawn or O.T.O. systems of magick, or the modern Wiccan or Celtic traditions. Secondly anyone working one of the current Eastern mystical traditions of magick or mysticism, such as Tantric, Buddhist, and Taoist practices, as well as the Theosophical tradition, will benefit greatly from this series.

Beyond these two general groups these books were intended for both the beginning student and the advanced researcher who has a desire to understand the hidden meaning of numbers. Also there is much material to appeal to an astrologer who would like to learn of the ancient alphabetical symbolism associated with the elements, the planets, and the Zodiac. There is also much material for the artist who would like to understand the ancient correspondence between color, shape, word, and number. Finally, students of the Tarot or the I Ching will find new research unavailable in any other printed source.

Q: Do you need to study *Part One: The Eastern Mysteries* before reading *Part Two: The Western Mysteries?*

A: No. The beauty of these two books is that each of the 13 chapters was written as a stand-alone work. Initially these two books were composed as one volume with the intention that the reader could start at the most interesting point of the text and progress from there. Each chapter is cross-referenced to every other relevent chapter, and the two volumes naturally break down these esoteric traditons to the East and the West.

So if the reader was more interested in the Western than the Eastern tradition, the second volume could be read before reading the first.

Q: What future books are you planning in this series?

A: I have always envisioned a third volume in this series. In fact the first two volumes would serve as an introduction to this proposed third volume, for the third volume would be a numerical dictionary defining the number series as the word metaphors derived from the 13 basic traditions outlined in the first two volumes of *The Key of It All*. There is so much research I have gathered in the last 25 years that it may take more than one volume to capture it all.

I would also like to develop at one point an extensive index to the first two volumes. There could also be a slimmer volume of additional research not included in these first two volumes.

Q: What other gems of lost wisdom are hidden in *The Key of It All* that haven't been discussed yet?

A: In Part One, there is a set of 149 tables describing the Hebrew Tree of Life, as well as a complete analysis of the *Sepher Yetzirah*, the oldest extant text showing the secret meanings of the Hebrew alphabet. There is a wonderful discussion of the mysticism of the Arabic alphabet, including a complete numbering of the 99 names of God. In addition there is a unique analysis of the number philosophy of G. I. Gurdjieff, including a decoding of his Enneagram by the Lullian Art. There are also numerous tables showing the attributes of the seven chakras, as well as a complete discussion of the six separate schools for the five elemental Tattvas. For the first time the Sanskrit alphabet is numbered in over eight different secret codes. The remote secret tradition of numbering the Tibetan alphabet is given as well for the first time in print in the West. The complete Chinese Taoist cosmology is not only analyzed but is compared to Western Qabalistic magick as well.

In Part Two, both the secret teachings of Pythagoras concerning the meanings for the first ten numbers and the secret teachings of the Aztecs and Mayans for the first 20 numbers are clearly shown. Greek and Coptic are both fully discussed, as well as an ancient interpretation of the esoteric meaning of the Egyptian Hieroglyphics found in the emblematic work of

Horapollo. The tradition of the Runes is shown in each of its developments from an alphabet of 24, 33, and 16 letters, to 18 letters in modern times. The secret values for the Latin alphabet are also revealed, serving as a Qabalah for Alchemical and Rosicrucian Latin, while the Enochian system of Dee is shown both in its original form and its modern Golden Dawn variation. And a tenative set of number values is shown for the English alphabet, including the work of Aleister Crowley, based on *The Book of the Law*.

Q: Any final comments?

A: *The Key of It All* is the realization of a fabled volume of magick which I desperately searched for in the youth of my occult studies. I have always been a magnet for attracting rare books, and the most recondite texts I have needed to write *The Key of It All* were attracted to me at the right time.

But for years I searched the stacks of rare bookstores and libraries for the lost Rosicrucian text *Book Th*, which would show all the sacred correspondences for the number series found in the ancient languages of the world. But to my chagrin I could never find this one book. So it fell to my path in life to rediscover and recreate this Magickal Dictionary, of which the first two volumes of *The Key of It All* form a tutorial or introduction to the Divine Language of the Gods.

ANNOTATED ESSENTIAL BIBLIOGRAPHY

This listing of reference material is an attempt to capture the essential texts utilized in the formation of *The Key of It All*. Literally hundreds of texts have been read, reread, digested, and internalized to bring about the all-emcompassing scope of this book. However, only the primary sources which were at hand at the time of the actual writing of the *The Key of It All* have been incorporated into this bibliography.

In all subject matters covered in this book, my understanding and insight have stemmed from my own self-taught regime of instruction. My grasp of the myriad of languages employed within this book is dependent upon the many and varied books which are documented in this bibliography. All phonetic renditions of foreign languages have been extracted directly from the source books used in this text, and in the case of such languages as Chinese, many different systems have been combined in the body of the text. Possibly future revisions of this book can correct this unavoidable inconsistency.

Because I have been able to approach this subject from the vantage point of an occult researcher rather than an academic scholar, I have been able to advance the traditional correspondences of esoteric schools beyond the range of any books in print. For, truly, a purely academic approach to the art of gematria would result in disproving that a valid correspondence can exist between word and number. I have therefore tailored my book to every earnest student on the path of Qabalistic knowledge, supplying him or her with the map and compass necessary to explore an otherwise uncharted universe.

This bibliography is arranged topically to correspond to the major trends found in the book itself. Some references can fall under more than one topic.

0. Overview

Numbers and Symbols

Blavatsky, Helena Petrovna. "Occult Systems: Alphabets and Numerals," in *Collected Writings*, vol. XIV. Wheaton, IL: The Theosophical Publishing House, 1985.

A good overview showing the Theosophical viewpoint concerning the mystical use of sacred alphabets as numbers. Much of Blavatsky's writings address the Qabalistic use of alphabet-numbers.

Bond, Bligh, and Thomas Lea. *Gematria: A Preliminary Investigation of the Cabala*. London: R.I.L.K.O., 1977.

One of the most important 20th-century studies on gematria, dealing chiefly with the Greek Qabalah.

Case, Paul Foster. *The Magical Language*. Los Angeles: B.O.T.A., privately printed.

These writings by Paul Foster Case are the highwater mark of Masonic-Qabalistic research concerning gematria. Deals with the Hebrew, Greek, and Latin Qabalahs.

Higgins, Frank C. *Ancient Freemasonry*. New York: Pyramid Book Company, 1923.

Primary source for the Qabalistic research of Paul Foster Case. Appeared first as articles in the magazine *Azoth* during the period when Case was editor for this magazine.

Higgins, Godfrey. *Anacalypsis, an Attempt to Draw Aside the Veil of the Saitic Isis; or, an Inquiry into the Origin of Languages, Nations and Religions*. London: Longman, Rees, et.al., 1836.

An early sourcebook for all subsequent research concerning the occult origins of language and number.

Kozminsky, Isidore. *Numbers, Their Meaning and Magic*. 1912. Reprint. New York: Samuel Weiser, Inc., 1972.

An admixture of real Qabalistic knowledge with pseudo-Qabalistic numerology. Typical of the times.

MacKenzie, Kenneth. *The Royal Masonic Cyclopedia*. 1877. Reprint. Wellingborough, Northamptonshire: The Aquarian Press, 1987.

Contains many articles of Qabalistic-Masonic alphabet ciphers. A sourcebook for the teachings of the Masonic order, the Hermetic Order of the Golden Dawn.

Mathers, S. L. MacGregor. *The Kabbalah Unveiled*. 1926. Reprint. New York: Samuel Weiser, Inc., 1974.

The introduction to this text, by Mathers, is the most lucid and concise article ever written in English on gematria and the Qabalah at large.

Mitchell, John. *City of Revelations*. London: Garnstone Press, 1972.

A modern extension of the primary field work of Bond and Lea.

Sepharial. *The Kabala of Numbers*. Philadelphia: David McKay Company, n.d.

A perfect specimen of pseudo-Qabalistic research.

Skinner, J. Ralston. *Key to the Hebrew-Egyptian Mystery in the Source of Measures Originating the British Inch and the Ancient Cubit*. 1875. Reprint. Savage, MN: Wizards Bookshelf, 1972.

The classic text in which measurements in inches and cubits are equated to the Hebrew and Greek number-letter symbolism.

Stirling, William. *The Canon: An Exposition of the Pagan Mystery Perpetuated in the Cabala as the Rule of All the Arts*. 1897. Reprint. London: Garnstone Press, 1974.

A wonderful study of the symbolic use of alphabets as numbers, greatly influencing the studies of Bond and Lea.

Westcott, W. Wynn. *Numbers: Their Occult Power and Mystic Virtues*. 1890. Reprint. New York: Allied Publication, n.d.

An excellent example of a standard reference available to students of the Golden Dawn regarding the symbolic meaning of certain numbers.

ORIGIN OF ALPHABET NUMERALS FROM A SCIENTIFIC VIEWPOINT

Andrews, W. S. *Magic Squares and Cubes*. New York: Dover Publications, 1960.

Contains a historical overview regarding the development of magic squares.

Bell, E. T. *The Development of Mathematics*. New York: McGraw Hill, 1945.

The standard reference in the field for early number systems. The Greek and Babylonian alphanumeric systems are outlined, as well as the Sanskrit Aryabhata code.

Brunes, Tons. *The Secrets of Ancient Geometry and Its Use*. Copenhagen: International Science Publishers, 1967.

This work would just as easily be entered under the previous section, for it bridges the scholar's and occultist's viewpoints.

Cajori, Florian. *A History of Mathematical Notations*. Chicago: Open Court Publishing Co., 1928.

Discusses the less obscure alphanumeric systems such as Hebrew and Greek.

Diringer, David. *The Alphabet: A Key to the History of Mankind*. New York: Philosophical Library, 1948.

Focuses only on the Hellenistic-Semitic alphanumeric systems.

Ifrah, Georges. *From One to Zero: A Universal History of Numbers*. New York: Viking Penguin, 1985.

The most thorough non-occultist approach to the alphanumeric tradition. Does not address the codes found in the Sanskrit, Tibetan, or Chinese esoteric traditions.

Jensen, Hans. *Sign, Symbol and Script: An Account of Man's Efforts to Write*. London: George Allen & Unwin, 1970.

A far-reaching account of many of the esoteric alphanumeric codes. Discusses both the Runes and Ogham, as well as Hebrew, Greek, Arabic, and Georgian.

Neugebauer, O. *The Exact Sciences in Antiquity*. New York: Dover Publications, 1969.

Much information on Babylonian and Hellenistic astronomy and mathematics.

Van der Waerden, B. L. *Science Awakening*. Groningen, Netherlands: Wolters Noordhoff Publishing, n.d.

A mathematician's discussion of Egyptian, Babylonian, and Hellenistic systems, including an essential overview of Pythagorean mathematics.

The Life of Aleister Crowley

Crowley, Aleister. *The Confessions of Aleister Crowley*. Edited by John Symonds and Kenneth Grant. New York: Hill and Wang, 1969.

The most thorough autobiography, first penned in 1929. Dates may be corrupt.

——————. "The Temple of Solomon the King," in *The Equinox* I:1–10, 1909–1913. Reprint. New York: Samuel Weiser, Inc., 1978.

A serialization of Crowley's life. Contains many important clues concerning both the initial reception of *The Book of the Law* and its subsequent promulgation by Crowley.

——————. "The Magical Diaries from 1906–07," in *The Equinox* V:4. Edited by Marcello Motta. Nashville: Thelema Publishing, 1981.

Serves as a record for the origin of Crowley's *Holy Books*. The value of Motta's pseudo-Equinoctial series is the access it provides to otherwise unknown writings of Aleister Crowley; the handicap is the overediting of the material and the seemingly endless but nearly useless commentaries by the editor.

——————. *The Magical Record of the Beast 666: The Journals of Aleister Crowley.* Edited by John Symonds and Kenneth Grant. Montreal: Next Step Publication, 1972.

A collation of Crowley's magickal diaries from 1914–1920, plus a typesetting of *The Book of the Law* in the least number of pages.

D'Arch Smith, Timothy. *The Books of the Beast.* Great Britain: Crucible, 1987.

Contains the best bibliography describing the original format of Crowley's published writings.

Grant, Kenneth. *The Magical Revival.* New York: Samuel Weiser, Inc., 1972.

The best of Grant's works on Crowley, though at times extremely muddled. Important information concerning Frater Achad's concept of a New Aeon, which cannot be found elsewhere.

King, Francis. *The Magical World of Aleister Crowley.* New York: Coward, McCann and Geoghegan, 1978.

Weak in comparison to King's *Rites of Modern Occult Magic.* Should be relied on as a secondary rather than a primary source on Crowley's life.

——————. *The Rites of Modern Occult Magic.* New York: MacMillan Company, 1970.

This groundbreaking book still serves as the best introduction to a historian's perspective on late 19th- and early 20th-century English and European occultism.

Regardie, Israel. *The Eye in the Triangle: An Interpretation of Aleister Crowley*. St. Paul: Llewellyn Publications, 1974.

Justifies Crowley's early life by a psychological approach to his magickal world view. May well be the source for the Freudian theory that *The Book of the Law* is nothing more than Crowley's suppressed subconscious mind.

Roberts, Susan. *The Magician of the Golden Dawn: The Story of Aleister Crowley*. Chicago: Contemporary Books, Inc., 1978.

Contains some original research from John Symonds' library of Crowley's writings, presented from a journalistic viewpoint.

Symonds, John. *The Great Beast: The Life of Aleister Crowley*. London: Rider and Company, 1955.

Although totally unsympathetic to Crowley, contains much information that does not appear in subsequent studies of Crowley's life. Early editions have a complete bibliography of the published work of Crowley.

THE BOOK OF THE LAW

Achad, Frater (George Stansfield Jones). *The Anatomy of the Body of God*. New York: Samuel Weiser, Inc., 1969.

Includes the Tree of Life as both an ever-expanding and a three-dimensional model. Throws light on some obscure passages of *The Book of the Law*.

——————. *The Egyptian Revival*. New York: Samuel Weiser, Inc., 1973.

Connects the Egyptian deities of *The Book of the Law* with the revived public interest in things Egyptian during the discovery of King Tut's tomb.

——————. *Liber 31 and Other Related Essays*. San Francisco: Level Press, 1974.

The major Qabalistic proofs of *The Book of the Law* by the magickal child, Frater Achad.

——————. *Q.B.L., or The Bride's Reception*. New York: Samuel Weiser, Inc., 1969.

Contains early extracts from Achad's magickal diaries before his revelation as the magickal child. The basis for Achad's reversal of the Tree of Life is also found in this book, which severed him from Crowley for the remainder of his life

——————. *XXXI Hymns to the Star Goddess*. Montreal: 93 Publishing, 1974.

The essence of Achad's vision concerning *The Book of the Law* in a poetical format.

Crowley, Aleister. *The Book of Lies*. New York: Samuel Weiser, Inc., 1978.

A set of cryptic Qabalistic poems, many that interpret passages from *The Book of the Law*. The book which caused Crowley's rapid advancement in the O.T.O.

——————. *The Book of the Law*. New York: Samuel Weiser, Inc., 1976.

This version is the last publication of *The Book of the Law* by Crowley (1938). Contains the original holographic version of the text.

——————. *The Book of the Law*. Quebec: 93 Publishing, 1975.

An attempt to reset the typed version of *The Book of the Law* in light of the original holographic version. Manuscript and typescript are side by side for easy comparison. The puzzle in Chapter II, verse 76, is correct in format only in this published version.

——————. *The Commentaries of AL*. Edited by Marcelo Motta. New York: Samuel Weiser, Inc., 1975.

The most incomplete version of Crowley's commentaries on *The Book of the Law*.

——————. *The Equinox*, I:1-10 and III:1. New York: Samuel Weiser, Inc., 1978 and 1974.

These eleven magazines put out by Crowley on the equinoxes from 1909 to 1919 serve as the best source for understanding the magickal symbolism contained in *The Book of the Law*. This series is indispensible for the study of Crowleyanity.

——————. *The Equinox of the Gods*. Great Britain: privately printed by the O.T.O., 1936.

Crowley's final word on *The Book of the Law*. Contains a facsimile of the original manuscript, hidden in the back cover of the book.

——————. *The Law is for All*. Edited by Israel Regardie. St. Paul: Llewellyn Publications, 1975.

The old and new commentaries by Crowley concerning *The Book of the Law*; more reliable than Motta's version.

——————. *Liber Aleph, or The Book of Wisdom or Folly*. San Francisco: Level Press, 1974.

A series of Qabalistic letters to the magickal child, Frater Achad

—————————. *Magical and Philosophical Commentaries on The Book of the Law*. Edited by John Symonds and Kenneth Grant. Montreal: 93 Publishing, 1974.

The best published collection of Crowley's commentaries; includes *The Commentary called D, by 666*, found nowhere else.

—————————. *Magick*. Edited by John Symonds and Kenneth Grant. New York: Samuel Weiser, Inc., 1974.

Crowley's best dissertation on the subject of magick, including many references to *The Book of the Law*.

—————————. Θελημα: *The Holy Books of Thelema*. Edited by Hymenaeus Alpha and others. New York: Samuel Weiser, Inc., 1983.

A compendium of Crowley's Holy Books. Contains a detailed analysis of the verses found on the Stele of Revealing.

—————————. *The Secret Rituals of the O.T.O.* Edited by Francis King. London: C. W. Daniel Company, 1973.

The complete rituals of the German Masonic group as revised by Aleister Crowley in light of *The Book of the Law*. King's introduction documents the lack of a true lineage to the O.T.O. since the death of Karl Germer in 1962.

Freemasonry, Magick, Rosicrucianism, and Theosophy

Allen, Paul M., ed. *A Christian Rosenkreutz Anthology*. Blauvelt, NY: Rudolf Steiner Publications, 1974.

The most exhaustive anthology to date of Rosicrucian literature and art.

Barrett, Francis. *The Magus: A Complete System of Occult Philosophy*. Secaucus,: The Citadel Press, 1967.

A glimpse of English magick from the beginning of the 19th century.

Blanchard, Charles A. *Revised Knight Templarism Illustrated*. Chicago: Ezra A. Cook, 1947.

A complete detailing of the six Templar degrees found in Freemasonry. Though an exposé of Freemasonry, the information offered is a testament to the beauty of the rituals.

Blavatsky, H. P. *Collected Writings*. 14 volumes. Wheaton: The Theosophical Publishing House, Wheaton, IL: 1977.

The Theosophical equivalent to Crowley's *Equinox* series: the complete writings of Blavatsky.

——————. ed. *Five Years of Theosophy*. Los Angeles: The Theosophy Company, 1980.

Gems collected from the first five years of *The Theosophist*.

——————. *Isis Unveiled*. Wheaton: The Theosophical Publishing House, 1972.

Blavatsky's first attempt to synthesize science with theology, the same aim as Crowley's *Equinox* series.

——————. *The Secret Doctrine*. Wheaton: The Theosophical Publishing House, 1978.

Blavatsky's final word on the origin of both the universe and mankind.

——————. *Theosophical Glossary*. Los Angeles: The Theosophy Company, 1973.

A contributor to this compendium of Theosophical terms was Wynn Westcott, one of the three founders of the Golden Dawn.

Case, Paul Foster. *The True and Invisible Rosicrucian Order*. York Beach, ME: Samuel Weiser, Inc., 1985.

The Masonic grades of the Golden Dawn in light of their Hebraic-Tarot symbolism. Case was the Imperator of the Chicago Thoth-Hermes Golden Dawn Temple in the early 1920s.

Colquhoun, Ithell. *Sword of Wisdom*. New York: G. P. Putnam's Sons, 1975.

A compelling study of the origins of the Golden Dawn, which links the magickal basis of the order to the genius of S.L. MacGregor Mathers.

Crowley, Aleister: *Book 4*. Dallas: Sangreal Foundation, 1972.

The simplest and most straightforward statement concerning the theory and practice of modern Golden Dawn derivative magick.

——————, ed. *The Book of the Goetia, or The Lesser Key of Solomon the King*. Mokelumne Hill, CA: Health Research, 1976.

The classic text on demonic invocation, probably translated by Mathers rather than Crowley.

Duncan, Malcolm C. *Duncan's Masonic Ritual and Monitor*. 3rd ed. New York: David McKay Company, Inc., n.d.

A good illustrated exposition of the first three degrees of the Ancient York Rite comprising the Blue Lodge of Freemasonry.

Hall, Manly P. *Codex Rosae Crucis*. Los Angeles: The Philosophical Research Society, Inc., 1974.

A valuable collection of Rosicrucian manuscripts and commentary.

——————. *An Encyclopedia Outline of Masonic, Hermetic, Qabbalistic and Rosicrucian Symbolical Philosophy*. The Golden Anniversary Edition. Los Angeles: The Philosophical Research Society, Inc., 1977.

This all encompassing work is an important addition to any library. Though brief in his entries, Manly P. Hall's scope of interest in the occult was encyclopedic.

Harper, George Mills. *Yeats's Golden Dawn: The Influence of the Hermetic Order of the Golden Dawn on the Life and Art of W. B. Yeats*. Wellingborough, Northamptonshire: The Aquarian Press, 1987.

Primary source material concerning the Golden Dawn, not found in other published studies. Contains much information about the alleged forgery of the cipher manuscript.

Howe, Ellic. *The Magicians of the Golden Dawn*. New York: Samuel Weiser, Inc., 1978.

A fascinating study of the Golden Dawn, showing its origins to be in the hands of Dr. Wynn Westcott and S. L. MacGregor Mathers. Though not written from an occultist's viewpoint, there is much pertinent magickal information.

King, Francis. *Sexuality, Magic and Perversion*. Secaucus: The Citadel Press, 1974.

A great book, for its title if nothing else. A must for every occultist's bookshelf.

Levi, Eliphas. *Transcendental Magick: Its Doctrine and Ritual*. New York: Samuel Weiser, Inc., 1974.

Eliphas Levi's most thorough exposition on magick. A study of mid-19th-century ritual magick.

Mackenzie, Kenneth. *The Royal Masonic Cyclopædia*. Wellingborough, Northamptonshire: The Aquarian Press, 1987.

The most esoteric of the 19th-century Masonic encyclopedias; a source-book for Golden Dawn teachings.

Mackey, Albert G., and Charles T. McClenachan. *Encyclopædia of Freemasonry*. Revised edition. Chicago: Masonic History Company, 1927.

An extensive Masonic encyclopedia, containing clues to the real password, or lost word, of the third degree.

——————. *Manual of the Lodge*. New York: Clark and Maynard, 1870.

In combination with Duncan's *Ritual of Freemasonry*, a key to understanding the true significance of the first three degrees of Freemasonry.

Mathers, S. L. MacGregor. *The Book of the Sacred Magic of Abra-melin the Mage*. 1897. Reprint. New York: Causeway, 1974.

A Qabalistic ritual for obtaining the knowledge and conversation of one's Holy Guardian Angel. Crowley in working with this material turned all the letters appearing in the magickal squares into Enochian.

——————. *The Key of Solomon the King*. 1888. Reprint. New York: Samuel Weiser, Inc., 1976.

The classic magickal text for invocation and command of the demonic and angelic planes. Contains the magick square of SATOR AREPO TENET OPERA ROTAS as the second pentacle of Saturn.

McIntosh, Christopher. *Eliphas Levi and the French Occult Revival*. London: Rider and Company, 1975.

An adequate biography of Eliphas Levi, dealing with all aspects of his life.

——————. *The Rosy Cross Unveiled*. Wellingborough, Northamptonshire: The Aquarian Press, 1980.

A very thorough investigation of the Rosicrucian phenomenon. The best introductory overview to the subject.

McLean, Adam. *The Magical Calendar*. Edinburgh: Magnum Opus Hermetic Sourceworks, 1980.

All of McLean's *Magnum Opus Hermetic Sourceworks* series are worth having: lucid translations of major hermetic treatises, unavailable elsewhere. This particular work translates the complete magickal calendar attributed to Tycho Brahe.

Regardie, Israel. *The Golden Dawn*. 1940. Reprint. St. Paul: Llewellyn Publications, 1970.

This compendium of Golden Dawn material, largely derived from Crowley's early *Equinox* series, remains the most accurate rendition of the core of Golden Dawn magical techniques.

——————. *The Complete Golden Dawn System of Magic*. Phoenix: Falcon Press, 1984.

This revised anthology of Golden Dawn teachings contains much new information based on earlier material than that used for Regardie's first version of this book. However the essential tables in the main body of the text must be corrected by swapping the attributes of King with Prince (the revised Golden Dawn Court Card titles).

Ryan, Charles J. *H. P. Blavatsky and the Theosophical Movement.* Pasadena: Theosophical University Press, 1975.

A sympathetic and orthodox view of Madame Blavatsky's life. Contains reference to Blavatsky and the Boulak Museum of Cairo.

Symonds, John. *The Lady with the Magic Eyes: Madame Blavatsky— Medium and Magician.* New York: Thomas Yoseloff, 1960.

An unorthodox view of H.P.B. Like Crowley, Blavatsky is dealt with in an unsympathetic manner. However, much material is unique to this book, since Symonds had direct access to original Theosophical material.

Torrens, R. G. *The Secret Rituals of the Golden Dawn.* Wellingborough, Northamptonshire: The Aquarian Press, 1973.

Another rendition of the Golden Dawn rituals, based on manuscript material prior to Regardie's source.

Waite, A. E. *The Brotherhood of the Rosy Cross.* London: Rider and Son, Ltd., 1924.

Waite's best attempt at describing the Rosicrucian movement. Contains a reproduction of one page of the Golden Dawn cipher manuscript, printed upside down in the text.

————. *The Real History of the Rosicrucians.* London: George Redway, 1887.

Waite's first attempt at a history of the Rosicrucians. Includes a contemporary view of the 19th-century Rosicrucian movement in England.

Walker, D. P. *Spiritual and Demonic Magic from Ficino to Campanella.* London: University of Notre Dame Press, 1975.

A historian's viewpoint of Renaissance magick written by a colleague of Francis Yates.

Webb, James. *The Occult Underground.* La Salle, IL: Open Court Publishing Co., 1974.

The best overview of 19th-century magick from a non-magickal viewpoint. Highly recommended.

————. *The Occult Establishment.* La Salle, IL: Open Court Publishing Co.,1976.

Companion to *The Occult Underground,* this volume spans the 20th century.

Miscellaneous

Allen, Richard Hinckley. *Star Names and Their Meanings*. New York: G.E. Stechert, 1899.

Compilation of ancient lore on the constellations, including the original Greek names for the Zodiac, as well as the medieval tradition of the apostolic Zodiac.

Charubel and Sepharial. *The Degrees of the Zodiac Symbolized*. Chicago: Aries Press, 1943.

Two listings of symbolic images for each of the 360 degrees of the Zodiac. The symbols for the 30 degrees of any given sign are surreal, bizarre collages of imagery that almost seem drug-inspired.

Dobin, Rabbi Joel. *To Rule Both Day and Night*. New York: Inner Traditions, 1977.

This work gives an alternate set of Zodiacal correspondences for the 12 tribes of Israel.

Dur'an, Diego. *Book of the Gods and Rites of the Ancient Calendar*. Norman: University of Oklahoma Press, 1971.

The only surviving document penned by the Inquisition that conquered the Aztecs, giving the divinatory nature of the Aztec vigesimal day count.

Manilius. *Astronomica*. Translated by G. Gould. Cambridge: Harvard University Press, 1977.

The oldest extant Latin text on the Hellenistic lore of astrology. The title *Astronomica* may have inspired Lovecraft in his naming of the *Necronomicon*, for Lovecraft was an avid and learned astronomer from his early teens, writing articles on the history of astronomy and debunking the astrology of the 1910s. By substituting "Necro" for "Astro," he changed the "Book of Star Names" to the "Book of Dead Names."

Nuttall, Zelia. *The Book of the Life of Ancient Mexicans*. Berkeley: University of California, 1983.

This book is another ancient Aztec manuscript complementary to Dur'an's work, and gives an alternate series of illustrations of the Aztec day signs. However, it does not contain the extensive divinatory meanings found in Dur'an's work.

Olivastro, Dominic. *Ancient Puzzles*. New York: Bantam Books, 1993.

Much information on the magick squares, including the SATOR AREPO square.

Skinner, Stephen. *Terrestrial Astrology: Divination by Geomancy*. London: Routledge & Kegan Paul Ltd., 1980.

Skinner has contributed to the modern occult scene in all that he writes, but this one work is not only his best, but also the best single work on the history of Geomancy; source for extensive African and Arabic Geomantic lore.

Thompson, John Eric Sidney. *A Catalog of Maya Hieroglyphs*. Norman: University of Oklahoma Press, 1962.

Contains many variations of the same Mayan hieroglyphs and arranges hieroglyphs of similar shape together, consulted for the Mayan day count symbols.

——————. *Maya Hieroglyphic Writing: Introduction*. Norman: University of Oklahoma Press, 1960.

The most extensive commentary on the Mayan day count as well as the esoteric Mayan head count for the 20-day cycle of the Sun, which when combined with our knowledge of the Aztec day count reveals the numerology of the New World, the ancient numerological symbols of the Aztecs and Mayans uninfluenced by Pythagoras or the Jewish Qabalah.

VII. Key Seven

Greek

Berry, George Rocker. *The Classic Greek Dictionary*. Chicago: Follet Publishing Co., 1954.

A workable Greek-English and English-Greek dictionary.

Liddell, Henry George, and Robert Scott. *The Greek Language Dictionary*. Oxford: Clarendon Press, 1940.

The classic Greek-English lexicon, utilized by Crowley in his *Liber Geometria (Liber MCCLXIV)*.

Gnostic and Pythagorean Symbolic Mathematics

Fiedler, David. *Jesus Christ, Sun of God*. Wheaton: Quest Books, 1993.

Extensive work concerning Greek gematria and early Christian symbolism. Fiedler sees the formula ΙΗΣΟΥΣ as a solar number, but in essence as the triple number 888, ΙΗΣΟΥΣ is Mercurial. Fiedler also perceives a progression of 74 in the holy appelations for Jesus, but the real harmony is in the progression of the prime number 37 (74 being twice 37).

Guthrie, Kenneth Sylvan. *The Pythagorean Sourcebook and Library*. Grand Rapids: Phanes Press, 1987.

The most exhaustive compilation to date on the lore of Pythagoras.

Jonas, Hans. *The Gnostic Religion*. Boston: Beacon Press, 1963.

A scholarly overview of Gnosticism.

King, Charles William. *The Gnostics and Their Remains, Ancient and Mediaeval*. Minneapolis: Wizards Bookshelf, 1973.

The classic text on Greek Gnosticism. Contains a complete description of the 30 Aeons.

Lawlor, Robert and Deborah, trans. *Theon of Smyrna's Mathematics Useful for Understanding Plato*. San Diego: Wizards Bookshelf, 1979.

Rare information on the symbolism found in the first decad of numbers as well as the various classification systems of numbers (such as even and odd, prime, composite, square, pyramidal, etc.).

Lea, Simcox, and Bligh Bond. *The Apostolic Gnosis: Part One and Two*. London: R.I.L.K.O., 1979.

A deep study into the realm of Greek alphabet-number symbolism apparent in both the New Testament and Greek Gnosticism. First published in 1919.

Linday, Jack. *The Origins of Alchemy in Graeco-Roman Egypt*. London: Frederick Muller, 1970.

An insightful look into the real hermetic alchemy of Egypt.

McClain, Ernest G. *The Myth of Invariance*. Boulder: Shambhala Publications, 1976.

A linking of Pythagorean and Vedic numerical and musical symbolism without any reference to the Ka-Ta-Pa-Ya-Dhi code for Sanskrit.

Stanley, Thomas. *Pythagoras: His Life and Teachings*. Los Angeles: The Philosophical Research Society, Inc., 1970.

A reprint by Manly P. Hall of the 1687 edition. Contains rare information on the first ten numbers of Pythagorean philosophy.

Taylor, Thomas, trans. *The Cratylus, Phaedo, Parmenides, Timaeus of Plato*. Minneapolis: Wizards Bookshelf, 1975.

The most initiated translation of Plato, exhaustively annotated.

————. *The Theoretic Arithmetic of the Pythagoreans*. York Beach, ME: Samuel Weister, Inc., 1972.

The best overview of the Pythagorean symbolism for the decad of numbers, first published in 1816. This modern version contains an introduction by Manly P. Hall in which Hall describes the Fadic number system for the English alphabet. Although Hall asserts that their number values are arbitrary they are in fact based on the phonetic-number equivalents of Hebrew (i.e., A=1, B=2, G=3).

VIII. KEY EIGHT

COPTIC

Crum, W.E. *A Coptic Dictionary*. Oxford University Press, 1962.

The most exhaustive Coptic-English dictionary in print. Contains the alphanumeric equivalents.

Metzger, Bruce M. *List of Words Occuring Frequently in the Coptic New Testament*. Grand Rapids: Wm. B. Eerdmans Publishing Company, 1961.

A very brief Coptic-English dictionary.

Meyer, Marvin and Richard Smith, Eds. *Ancient Christian Magic*. San Francisco: Harper, 1994.

Contains new information on the Coptic meaning of the SATOR AREPO square. A wonderful compendium of Coptic magickal formulae. These spells and incantations can be numbered by the Coptic number code in Key 8. This is true for all Gnostic talismanic gems lettered in Coptic.

Regardie, Israel. *My Rosicrucian Adventure*. St. Paul: Llewellyn Publications, 1971.

This version contains in its appendix the Golden Dawn Coptic-Tree of Life equivalents, also found in Table LI of Crowley's *Liber 777*.

EGYPTIAN HIEROGLYPHS

Budge, E.A. Wallis. *Amulets and Talismans*. New York: Collier Books, 1970.

This work is a sourcebook for Egyptian magick and more, including essays on Gnostic and Qabalistic talismans as well as Middle Eastern astrological and numerical symbolism.

—————. *Egyptian Magic*. 1899. Reprint. New York: University Books, n.d.

Sir Wallis Budge was the museum curator for the Egyptian Collection of the British Mueseum from 1894 to 1924, rumored to be involved with a lodge of the Golden Dawn, possibly within the Egyptian section of the British Museum. This work provides a good overview of all aspects of Egyptian magic.

—————. *Egyptian Language*. London: Routledge and Kegan Paul, Ltd., 1970.

An excellent introduction to the language of the Egyptian hieroglyphs.

Clarke, John C. *The Origin and Varieties of the Semitic Alphabet*. The American Publication Society of Hebrew, 1884.

A sourcebook for every Semitic alphabet and related scripts. Shows all alphabets evolving out of an Egyptian hieroglyphic prototype.

Farr, Florence. *Egyptian Magic*. Wellingborough, Northamptonshire: The Aquarian Press, 1982.

Represents Egyptian magick from the viewpoint of the Golden Dawn. Originally part of Westcott's 10-volume *Collectanea Hermetica* series published from 1893 to 1896.

Gardiner, Sir Alan. *Egyptian Grammar: Being an Introduction to the Study of Hieroglyphs*. London: Oxford University Press, 1973.

The best grammar and dictionary of the Egyptian language. First published in 1927.

Horapollo. *The Hieroglyphics of Horapollo*. New York: Pantheon Books, 1950.

The only authentic occult text concerning the true esoteric meanings of the Egyptian hieroglyphs, purported to have been written around 400 CE in Greece as a copy of a more ancient Egyptian document, but possibly a compilation from 1400 CE. In any event, this book is the key to unlocking the Alchemical, Hermetic, and Rosicrucian picture symbols.

Mercatante, Anthony S. *Who's Who in Egyptian Mythology*. New York: Clarkson N. Potter, Inc., 1978.

A very readable illustrated dictionary of the Egyptian pantheon.

Piankof, Alexandre. *Mythological Papyri*. Bollingen Series XL, 3. New York: Pantheon Books, 1957.

The beauty of this two-volume work is the portfolio of folding papyri facsimiles contained in the second volume. A must for anyone interested in Egyptian hieroglyphs.

IX. KEY NINE

Runes

Anderson, R.B. *Norse Mythology*. Chicago: S.C. Griggs and Company, 1879.

A systematic overview of the myths of the Eddas, with a very valuable vocabulary of the principal proper names in Norse mythology.

Brodeur, Arthur G. *The Riddle of the Runes*. Berkeley: University of California Press, 1944.

An attempt to source all runic alphabets to the Greek alphabet.

Dickins, Bruce. *Runic and Heroic Poems of the Old Teutonic People*. New York: Kraus Reprint, 1968.

Contains the Icelandic and Scandanavian versions of the rune poem.

Goodrick-Clarke, Nicholas. *The Occult Roots of Nazism*. Wellingborough, Northamptonshire: The Aquarian Press, 1985.

Contains valuable information on Werner von Bulow's "world-rune-clock," which utilized the 18-rune alphabet of Guido von List.

Gordon, Cyrus H. *Riddles in History*. New York: Crown Publishers, Inc., 1974.

Gives copious examples of runes used as chronograms. Conjectures a straight serial order numeration of the runes.

Halsall, Maureen. *The Old English Rune Poem*. Toronto: University of Toronto, 1981.

Contains the Anglo-Saxon version of the rune poem.

List, Guido von. *The Secret of the Runes*. 1908. Reprint. Translated by Stephen Flowers. Rochester, VT: Destiny Books, 1988.

The definitive text on the significance of the Armanen rune system.

Monge, Alf. *Norse Medieval Cryptography in Runic Carvings*. Glendale: Norsemen Press, 1967.

A most valuable work on the numerical significance of the runes. Chapter 5 contains the runic calendar of 19 cryptographic keys.

Osborn, Marijane, and Stella Longland. *Rune Games*. London: Routledge and Kegan Paul, 1982.

The significance of the runes in light of the expanded commentary of the Old English Rune Poem, which details 29 alphabet images.

Thorsson, Edred. *FUTHARK: A Handbbok of Rune Magic*. York Beach, ME: Samuel Weiser, Inc., 1984.

The most authentic new work on rune magic. Contains information on the Armanen rune system.

Ogham and Beth-Luis-Nion

Atkins, G.M. "Ogham Writing." *Journal of the Royal Historical Association of Ireland*. Series IV, vol.4, 1874.

Contains illustrations of the variant Ogham scripts found in the Book of Ballymote.

Bain, George. *Celtic Art: The Methods of Construction*. New York: Dover Publications, 1973.

Contains a chapter on Celtic alphabets and their construction.

Graves, Robert. *The White Goddess*. New York: Farrar, Straus and Giroux, 1966.

The most exhaustive work on the symbolism of the Beth-Luis-Nion tree alphabet. Highly recommended.

MacAlister, R.A. Stewart. *The Archaeology of Ireland*. 1928. Reprint. New York: Benjamin Blom, Inc., 1972.

This study of ancient Ireland contains examples of the Ogham alphabet.

——————. *The Secret Languages of Ireland*. Cambridge: Cambridge University Press, 1937.

The authoritative study on the Ogham alphabet.

O'Brien, Henry. *Atlantis in Ireland & Round Towers of Ireland*. 1834. Reprint. New York: Steiner Books, 1976.

This study attempts to link the Buddhist stupa with the Irish round tower. Contains a rare plate of the Beth-Luis-Nion alphabet.

Sharkey, John. *Celtic Mysteries*. New York: Avon Publishers, 1975.

Contains illustrations of Celtic alphabets.

Spence, Lewis. *The Mysteries of Britain*. 1928. Reprint. Wellingborough, Northamptonshire: The Aquarian Press, 1979.

The second chapter of this work contains illustrations of the Bobileth, Beth-Luis-Nion, and Ogham alphabets.

X. KEY TEN

LATIN

Begley, Rev. Walter. *Biblia Cabalistica, or the Cabalistic Bible*. London: David Nutt, 1903.

The one authentic study of the use of the Latin alphabet as numbers. Contains numerous examples of Qabalistic phrases numbered by each of the Latin Qabalistic codes.

Simpson, D.P. *Cassell's New Compact Latin Dictionary*. New York: Dell, 1971.

A workable dictionary based on classical Latin.

Trithemius, Johannes. *Steganographia*. Frankfurt, 1606.

Contains the Cabala Simplex code in the 49th table of Latin ciphers.

Wheelock, Frederic M. *Latin: An Introductory Course Based on Ancient Authors*. New York: Barnes and Noble, 1968.

A good grammar dealing with classical Latin.

RAMON LULL

Hopper, V.F. *Medieval Number Symbolism: Its Sources, Meaning and Influence on Thought and Symbolism*. New York: Columbia University Press, 1938.

A very scholarly approach to the symbolism of numbers in medieval art and literature. Contains references to Lullism.

Yates, Frances A. *The Art of Memory*. Middlesex: Penguin Books, 1969.

All of Yates's works are worth deep study, though from a scholar's viewpoint much occult material is buried within her books. This treatise establishes the true purpose of all ancient memory systems, including the systems of Raymon Lull.

——————. *Giordano Bruno and the Hermetic Tradition*. Chicago: University of Chicago Press, 1964.

Describes in detail Bruno's Memory Theater of 30 divisions, which parallels both John Dee's and the traditional Gnosticism's world view of 30 levels to the universe.

—————. *Lull and Bruno: Collected Essays*. London: Routledge and Kegan Paul, 1982.

Yates's most extensive analysis of Lull's Latin alphabetical Qabalahs. Contains Lull's astrological Qabalah.

—————. *The Occult Philosophy in the Elizabethan Age*. London: Ark Paperbacks, 1983.

Contains Francesco Giorgi's "Numerological Relationships between the Three Worlds."

ALCHEMY

Burckhardt, Titus. *Alchemy, Science of the Cosmos, Science of the Soul*. Baltimore: Penguin Books, Inc., 1971.

A classic text describing alchemy as an internal, spiritual art. A very readable book covering a most abtruse subject.

Burland, C.A. *The Arts of the Alchemist*. New York: MacMillan Co., 1967.

An objective approach to Alchemy as a physical science, giving much historical information in a readable manner.

Crowley, Aleister. *De Arte Magica*. San Francisco: H.G. White, 1974.

The symbols of alchemy are decoded by Crowley to reveal a technique of sex magick.

Gettings, Fred. *Dictionary of Occult, Hermetic and Alchemical Sigils*. London: Routledge and Kegan Paul, 1981.

A must for every Hermetic library. The most exhaustive compilation of Alchemical sigils, cross-indexed by similar shapes. All of Gettings' works are useful, especially his astrological dictionary.

Grossinger, Richard, and Lindy Hough, eds. *IO Magazine* no. 4: Alchemy Issue. 3rd edition, Plainfield, Vermont, 1973.

Though a poetry journal, much original alchemical material can be found in this issue. The Doctrine of Signatures issue is also worth reading.

Howe, Ellic, ed. *The Alchemist of the Golden Dawn*. Wellingborough, Northhamptonshire: The Aquarian Press, 1985.

This book is a collection of W.A. Ayton's letters, documenting the alchemical outlook of the only alchemist within the original Golden Dawn movement.

Johnson, Kenneth Rayner. *The Fulcanelli Phenomenon*. Jersey: Neville Spearman, 1980.

A very readable study on the most famous alchemist of the 20th century, Fulcanelli.

Jung, C.G. *Alchemical Studies*. Series XX, vol.13. New York: Bollingen Foundation, 1967.

—————. *Mysterium Conjunctionis*. Series XX, vol.14. New York: Bollingen Foundation, 1963.

—————. *Psychology and Alchemy*. Series XX. vol.12. New York: Bollingen Foundation, 1968.

—————. *Symbols of Transformation*. Series XX, vol. 5. New York: Bollingen Foundation, 1956.

These four works are the classic interpretation of Alchemy on a spiritual, rather than a physical plane. Contains many rare Alchemical Hermetic illustrations.

Nintzel, Hans W. "Alchemy." In *The Complete Golden Dawn System of Magic*, by Israel Regardie, vol. 2. Phoenix: Falcon Press,1984.

A highly recommended introductory paper on Alchemy, by a practicing alchemist.

Paracelsus. *The Hermetic and Alchemical Writings*. Edited by A.E. Waite. New York: University Books, Inc., 1967.

The writings of Paracelsus contain Latin alchemical terminology which appears nowhere else (such as *vbera* for "the spine" as a permutation of *verba*, "the word").

Regardie, Israel. *The Philosopher's Stone*. St. Paul: Llewellyn Publications, 1978.

A blending of Golden Dawn symbolism and Jungian psychology as a key to interpret the language of Alchemy.

Rola, Stanislas Klossowski de. *Alchemy: The Secret Art*. New York: Avon Books, 1973.

A sumptuous collection of Alchemical diagrams both in color and in black and white, with a good introductory essay on the meaning of Alchemy.

Ruland, Martin. *A Lexicon of Alchemy*. 1612. Reprint. Translated by A.E. Waite. London: John Watkins, 1964.

A very copious dictionary of alchemical terminology,. A wonderful sourcebook for examples of Latin to be numbered.

Stillman, J.M. *The Story of Alchemy and Early Chemistry*. New York: Dover Publications, 1960.

A scholarly dismissal of any esoteric interpretation of the physical science of Alchemy, first published in 1924. A critical work which can balance out the more extreme interpretations of Alchemy.

Sworder, Mary, trans. *Fulcanelli: Master Alchemist*. London: Neville Spearman, 1971.

Possibly the only authentic Alchemical treatise written in the 20th century, being Fulcanelli's *Le Mystere des Cathedrales*.

Trismosin, Solomon. *Splendor Solis*. 1582. Reprint. Des Plaines: Yogi Publication Society, n.d.

This tract on Alchemy encodes the Alchemical process in 22 hieroglyphic pictures. A work utilized in the teachings of the Golden Dawn.

Westcott, Wynn. *The Science of Alchymy*. 1893. Reprint. London: Neptune Press, n.d.

This treatise on alchemy represents the orthodox Golden Dawn view, as penned by one of the three founders of the Order.

XI. KEY ELEVEN

ENOCHIAN

Causaubon, Meric., ed. *A True and Faithful Relation of What Passed for Many Yeers Between Dr. John Dee and Some Spirits*. London: 1659. Reprint. London: Askin, 1974.

This transcription of Dee's diaries records the period in which the Watchtowers were received and verified.

Crowley, Aleister. "A Brief Abstract of the Symbolic Representation of the Universe Derived by Doctor John Dee through the Skrying of Sir Edward Kelly." *The Equinox* 1.7, 1912. Reprint. New York: Samuel Weiser, Inc., 1978.

Contains Crowley's version of the Watchtowers, as well as the sigils of the Governors upon the Watchtowers, the true key to their construction.

—————. *The Vision and the Voice*. Edited by Israel Regardie. Dallas: Sangreal Foundation,1972.

This version of Crowley's Enochian workings was originally published by Karl Germer. It contains Crowley's annotations, which reveal both

the Golden Dawn Enochian alphabet number values as well as Crowley's own variants.

Dee, John. *The Enochian Evocation of Dr. John Dee*. Edited and translated
by Geoffrey James. Berkeley Heights, NJ: Heptangle Books, 1984.

The most thorough reconstruction of all of Dee's writings to resemble a
medieval magickal grimoire. Contains the Enochian Watchtowers
restored from the original notes of Dr. Dee—which, however, are incorrect.

————. *The Hieroglyphic Monad*. New York: Samuel Weiser, Inc., 1975.

Dee's cryptic published work, which is based on one sigil that combines
the sigils of all seven planets as well as the joining of Aries and Taurus.

————. *The Heptarchia Mystica of John Dee*. Edited and translated by
Robert Turner. Wellingborough, Northamptonshire: Aquarian Press,
1983.

Contains information on the actual magickal Enochian table used during the skrying sessions of Dee and Kelly.

French, Peter J. *John Dee: The World of an Elizabethan Magus*. London:
Routledge & Kegan Paul, 1972.

A good biography of John Dee, though French does not fathom the real
import of the Enochian Watchtowers and assumes they are a political
cipher.

Head, Thomas. "An Introduction to the Enochian Teaching and Praxis." In
The Complete Golden Dawn System of Magic by Israel Regardie. vol.10.
Phoenix: Falcon Press, 1984.

The Enochian number code described in this article did not come from a
Lisp computer program as alleged by the author but rather from a copy
of a page of my own Enochian notebook sent to Head by Regardie in 1979.

Honourius. *The Sworn Book of Honourius the Magician*. 1540. Edited and
translated by Daniel Driscoll. Gillette, NJ: Heptangle Books, 1983.

The Seal of God appearing in Book One of this work is the source for
Dee's own Enochian Sigillum Aemeth. Interestingly, this sigil was also
the basis of Frater Achad's own sigil of the universe that appeared in
The Equinox 3.1.

Hulse, David Allen. "The Numerical Structure of Enochian." In *The Complete Golden Dawn System of Magic*, by Israel Regardie. vol. 10.
Phoenix: Falcon Press, 1984.

Contains material not in *The Key of it All*. Demonstrates Dee's, Mathers', and Crowley's numbering system for Enochian.

Laycock, Donald C. *The Complete Enochian Dictionary*. London: Askin Publishers, 1978.

A very workable Enochian dictionary. Laycock puts forth a test on page 62 of this dictionary to validate any new Enochian material. This test is "what is the Enochian word for seven"; the answer is: the Enochian letters Ceph and Med, Z and O, both valued at 7 by Dee's digital number code.

McLean, Adam, ed. *A Treatise on Angel Magic*. Scotland: Magnum Opus Hermetic Sourceworks, 1982.

This transcription of Harley MS. 6482 in the British Museum is Mathers' source for the Enochian-Geomantic equivalents, which served as the basis for the Golden Dawn Enochian number values.

Regardie, Israel. "An Addendum to the Book of the Concourse of the Forces." In *The Complete Golden Dawn System of Magic* by Israel Regardie. vol.10. Phoenix: Falcon Press, 1984.

If Regardie had completely followed through with the logic of this essay, first written in 1935, he would have been able to correct the Watchtowers and isolate one letter for each of the 644 squares composing the Watchtower system.

Turner, Robert. *Elizabethan Magic*. Dorset: Element Books, 1989.

Neither the names of the 91 Governors nor the 644 squares of the Watchtowers are correct in this work. However, Appendix C, by Robert Cousins, offers a complete analysis of the 91 locations of Earth controlled by the 91 Governors. I have modified this order in light of my own research in this direction.

Schueler, Gerald J. *An Advanced Guide to Enochian Magick*. St. Paul: Llewellyn Publications, 1987.

Includes both an overview of different number values ascribed to the Enochian alphabet and a complete analysis of the 91 + 1 Governors and their connection to the Watchtowers. The Watchtowers, however, are not corrected in light of these correspondences.

Wang, Robert. *The Secret Temple*. New York: Samuel Weiser, Inc., 1980.

Wang offers both colored plates of the Enochian Watchtowers and instructions for making and coloring them. The letters upon the Watchtowers, however, are not correct, nor are any other printed versions except the Watchtowers appearing in the Eleventh Key of *The Key of it All*.

Yates, Frances A. *The Rosicrucian Enlightenment*. London: Routledge & Kegan Paul, 1972.

Connects, in a scholarly fashion, John Dee to the formation of the Rosicrucian movement, the same premise Mathers arrived at through his own occult researches in the British Museum.

XII. KEY TWELVE

TAROT

Cartwright, Fairfax. *The Mystic Rose From the Garden of the King*. London: Watkins Publishing House, 1976.

Idries Shah premises in an appendix to *The Way of the Sufis* that the correct order of the Tarot is an initiated Sufi secret. This text gives this esoteric order of the Tarot, based on a tower composed of 21 cells, each a Tarot card of the Major Arcana, through which the 22nd card, The Fool, wanders to obtain his initiation.

Case, Paul Foster. *An Introduction to the Study of the Tarot*. New York: Azoth Publishing Co., 1920.

Derived from Case's articles contributed to the magazine *Azoth*, this book unlocks the symbolism of Waite's Tarot in light of the *Sepher Yetzirah*. In a revealing footnote found on page 14, Case admits using Crowley's *Liber 777* to corroborate the correct planetary attributes for the seven Hebrew double letters.

—————. *The Tarot: A Key to the Wisdom of the Ages*. Richmond: Macoy Publishing Company, 1947.

The definitive text on the Qabalistic meaning of the Tarot according to the Golden Dawn esoteric Tarot.

Cavendish, Richard. *The Tarot*. New York: Harper & Row, 1975.

A good overview of the Tarot, without the working knowledge of the Golden Dawn Tarot system.

Christian, Paul. *The History and Practice of Magic*. 1879. Reprint. New York: The Citadel Press, 1969.

The third chapter details the 19th-century French Qabalistic interpretation of the Tarot. Influenced Blavatksy's view on the Tarot.

Crowley, Aleister. *The Book of Thoth*. Berkeley: Shambhala Publications Ltd., 1969.

Crowley's best work on the Tarot in light of the Qabalistic symbolism found in *The Book of the Law*. Possibly the most esoteric Tarot deck yet executed.

—————. "A Description of the Cards of the Tarot." *The Equinox* 1.8, 1912. Reprint. New York: Samuel Weiser, Inc., 1978.

A direct copy of S.L. MacGregor Mathers' *Book T*, the cornerstone of modern Qabalistic Tarot symbolism.

Gettings, Fred. *The Book of Tarot.* London: Triune Books, 1973.

An analysis of the Major Arcana based upon the geometrical arrangement of the symbols in the Marseilles Tarot deck. Highly recommended.

Kaplan, Stuart R. *The Encyclopedia of Tarot.* Vols. I and II. New York: U.S. Games Systems, Inc., 1978 and 1986.

The best possible collection of Tarot decks. Fully illustrated with commentary. Proves beyond a shadow of a doubt that Waite's picture images for the Minor Arcana, or pip cards, were original to Waite's deck as well as being an overriding influence on all subsequent decks, even Salvador Dali's surrealistic version of the Tarot.

Mathers, S.L. MacGregor. *The Tarot: Its Occult Signification, Use in Fortune-Telling, and Method of Play.* New York: Samuel Weiser, Inc., 1971.

Though this book represents a blind of the true attributes found in *Book T,* Mathers gives his real view in this brief essay as follows: "The Sepher Yetzirah . . .certainly gives, in my opinion, the Qabalistic key of the Tarot."

—————. "Book 'T'—The Tarot." In *The Golden Dawn: An Encyclopedia of Practical Occultism* by Israel Regardie, vol.4. St. Paul: Llewellyn Publications, 1970.

The complete Golden Dawn Qabalistic Tarot system as originally deciphered by Mathers. Regardie's later version found in *The Complete Golden Dawn System of Magic* should be avoided, because the attributes for the King and Knight are confused.

Papus. *The Tarot of the Bohemians.* North Hollywood: Wilshire Book Company, 1975.

Represents the esoteric, or French, order for the Major Arcana of the Tarot where the Hebrew letter Aleph is correlated to "The Magician" rather than to "The Fool."

Waite, Arthur Edward. *The Pictorial Key to the Tarot.* 1910. Reprint. New York: University Books, 1959.

The Tarot deck described in this one book, which is based on Mathers *Book T,* has influenced all subsequent books on the subject by (1) hinting that The Fool should be placed at the beginning of the deck as Key 0, (2) interchanging Justice with Strength to correspond to their Hebrew esoteric order: Justice = Key XI = Lamed = Libra; Strength = Key VIII = Teth = Leo, (3) giving Mathers' esoteric meaning for the 40 cards of the Minor Arcana in picture format, and (4) hinting at the correct Zodiacal attributes of the 16 Court Cards, in accordance with Mathers' secret astrological attributes; i.e., the bull in the throne of the King of Pentacles conceals the correct attribute of Taurus.

Wang, Robert. *An Introduction to the Golden Dawn Tarot*. New York: Samuel Weiser, Inc., 1978.

Possibly the source for the contemporary confusion concerning the Court Card attributions of the Golden Dawn Tarot system. Here the old Knight equals the new Prince, whereas the correct attribution is that the old *King* equals the new Prince.

——————. *The Qabalistic Tarot*. York Beach, ME: Samuel Weiser, Inc., 1983.

This book repeats the error found in Wang's previous work. Here again the Knight should be interchanged with the King in the Court Card order.

Wirth, Oswald. *The Tarot of the Magicians*. 1927. Reprint. York Beach, ME: Samuel Weiser, Inc., 1985.

A wonderful book containing the French Qabalistic order. In the appendix of this work can be found the Alchemical cube which Case used as the sigil for his order, the Builders of the Adytum.

XIII. KEY THIRTEEN

ENGLISH

Ahmad, Mabel L. *Sound and Number*. David McKay Company, 1924.

A fair representation of the esoteric attributes of the English alphabet, based on their Hebraic models and applied to modern numerology.

Crowley, Aleister. "The Book of the Trigrams of the Mutation of the Tao with the Yin and Yang. Liber XXVII." In *Magical and Philosophical Commentaries on The Book of the Law,* by Aleister Crowley. Montreal: 93 Publishing, 1974.

The esoteric order of the English alphabet as perceived by Crowley in light of *The Book of the Law.*

Hoffstein, Robert M. *The English Alphabet*. New York: Kaedmon Publishing, 1975.

An insightful work describing the esoteric meaning concealed in the 26 letters of the English alphabet. Contains the formulae $A+I/2 = E$ and $I+U/2 = O$.

Kuhn, Alvin Boyd. *Esoteric Structure of the Alphabet*. Mokelumne Hill, CA: Health Research, 1976.

A study on the esoteric meaning of the English alphabet in light of Sanskrit and Hebrew symbolism.

Skinner, Hubert M. *The Story of the Letters and Figures*. Chicago: Orville Brewer Publishing, 1905.

A scholarly attempt at showing the evolution of the English alphabet out of a Phoenician prototype.

MAGICK SQUARE OF AZOTH

A	Z	O	T	H
Z	ह	A	Z	T
O	अ	☿	A	O
T	ᒣ	א	Ω	Z
H	T	O	Z	A

INDEX

ASTROLOGY

MAGICK

☾ LLEWELLYN ORDERING INFORMATION

Order Online:
Visit our website at www.llewellyn.com, select your books, and order them on our secure server.

Order by Phone:
- Call toll-free within the U.S. at 1-877-NEW-WRLD (1-877-639-9753). Call toll-free within Canada at 1-866-NEW-WRLD (1-866-639-9753)
- We accept VISA, MasterCard, and American Express

Order by Mail:
Send the full price of your order (MN residents add 7% sales tax) in U.S. funds, plus postage & handling to:

Llewellyn Worldwide
P.O. Box 64383, Dept. 0-7387-0294-3
St. Paul, MN 55164-0383, U.S.A.

Postage & Handling:

Standard (U.S., Mexico, & Canada). If your order is:
Up to $25.00, add $3.50
$25.01 - $48.99, add $4.00
$49.00 and over, FREE STANDARD SHIPPING
(Continental U.S. orders ship UPS. AK, HI, PR, & P.O. Boxes ship USPS 1st class. Mex. & Can. ship PMB.)

International Orders:
Surface Mail: For orders of $20.00 or less, add $5 plus $1 per item ordered. For orders of $20.01 and over, add $6 plus $1 per item ordered.

Air Mail:
Books: Postage & Handling is equal to the total retail price of all books in the order.
Non-book items: Add $5 for each item.

Orders are processed within 2 business days. Please allow for normal shipping time.
Postage and handling rates subject to change.

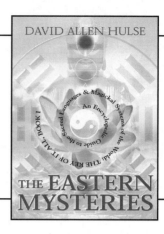

THE EASTERN MYSTERIES
The Key of It All–Book One
David Allen Hulse

The Eastern and Western Mysteries series clarifies and extends the knowledge established by all previous books on occult magick. Book One catalogs and distills, in hundreds of tables of secret symbolism, the true alphabet magick of every ancient Eastern magickal tradition. Unlike the current rash of publications which do no more than recapitulate Regardie or Crowley, *The Eastern Mysteries* establishes a new level of competence in all fields of magick both East and West.

Cuneiform—the oldest tradition ascribing number to word; the symbolism of base 60 used in Babylonian and Sumerian Cuneiform; the first God and Goddess names associated to number.

Hebrew—a complete exposition of the rules governing the Hebrew Qabalah; the evolution of the Tree of Life; an analysis of the Book of Formation, the oldest key to the symbolic meaning of the Hebrew alphabet.

Arabic—the similarity between the Hebrew and Arabic Qabalahs; the secret Quranic symbolism for the Arabic alphabet; the Persian alphabet code; the philosophical numbering system of G. I. Gurdjieff.

Sanskrit—the secret Vedic number codes for Sanskrit; the digital word-numbers; the symbolism of the seven chakras and their numerical key.

Also included—sections on Tibetan and Chinese mysteries.

1-56718-428-6, 656 pp., 7 x 10, tables, charts, softcover   **$39.95**

To order, call 1-877-NEW-WRLD
Prices subject to change without notice

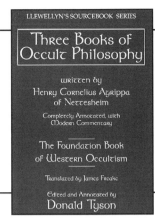

LLEWELLYN'S SOURCEBOOK SERIES

Three Books of Occult Philosophy

written by
Henry Cornelius Agrippa
of Nettesheim

Completely Annotated, with
Modern Commentary

The Foundation Book
of Western Occultism

Translated by James Freake

Edited and Annotated by
Donald Tyson

THE THREE BOOKS OF OCCULT PHILOSOPHY
The Foundation Book of Western Occultism
Henry Cornelius Agrippa, edited and annotated by Donald Tyson

Agrippa's *Three Books of Occult Philosophy* is the single most important text in the history of Western occultism. Occultists have drawn upon it for five centuries, although they rarely give it credit. First published in Latin in 1531 and translated into English in 1651, it has never been reprinted in its entirety since. Photocopies are hard to find and very expensive. Now, for the first time in 500 years, *Three Books of Occult Philosophy* will be presented as Agrippa intended. There were many errors in the original translation, but occult author Donald Tyson has made the corrections and has clarified the more obscure material with copious notes.

This is a necessary reference tool not only for all magicians, but also for scholars of the Renaissance, Neoplatonism, the Western Kabbalah, the history of ideas and sciences, and the occult tradition. It is as practical today as it was 500 years ago.

0–87542–832–0, 1,024 pp., 7 x 10, softcover $39.95

To order, call 1-877-NEW-WRLD
Prices subject to change without notice

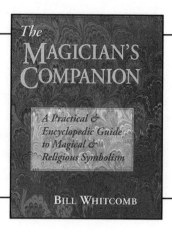

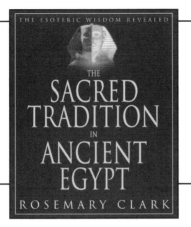

**THE SACRED TRADITION IN
ANCIENT EGYPT**
The Esoteric Wisdom Revealed
Rosemary Clark

Our modern quest for the wisdom of ancient Egypt centers on the true meaning of the symbolism, temples, tombs, and pyramids of this enigmatic motherland.

Egyptologist Rosemary Clark, who reads Egyptian hieroglyphics firsthand, examines the esoteric tradition of Egypt in remarkable detail. She explores dimensions of the language, cosmology, and temple life to show that a sacred mandate—the transformation of the human condition into its original cosmic substance—formed the foundation of Egypt's endeavors and still has great relevance today.

In addition, *The Sacred Tradition in Ancient Egypt* outlines the technology that utilized cyclic resonance, ritual, and sacred architecture to effect this ultimate stage in human evolution.

1-56718-56718-129-5, 576 pp., 7½ x 9⅛, illus.   **$24.95**

MODERN MAGICK
Eleven Lessons in the High Magickal Arts
Donald Michael Kraig

Modern Magick is the most comprehensive step-by-step introduction to the art of ceremonial magic ever offered. The eleven lessons in this book will guide you from the easiest of rituals and the construction of your magickal tools through the highest forms of magick: designing your own rituals and doing pathworking. Along the way you will learn the secrets of the Kabbalah in a clear and easy-to-understand manner. You will discover the true secrets of invocation (channeling) and evocation, and the missing information that will finally make the ancient grimoires, such as the "Keys of Solomon," not only comprehensible, but usable. This book also contains one of the most in-depth chapters on sex magick ever written. *Modern Magick* is designed so anyone can use it, and it is the perfect guidebook for students and classes. It will also help to round out the knowledge of long-time practitioners of the magickal arts.

0–87542–324–8, 592 pp., 6 x 9, illus., index, softcover   **$17.95**

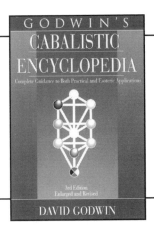

GODWIN'S CABALISTIC ENCYCLOPEDIA
Complete Guidance to Both Practical and Esoteric Applications
David Godwin

One of the most valuable books on the Cabala is back, with a new and more usable format. This book is a complete guide to cabalistic magick and gematria in which every demon, angel, power, and name of God ... every Sephirah, Path, and Plane of the Tree of Life ... and each attribute and association is fully described and cross-indexed by the Hebrew, English, and numerical forms.

All entries, which had been scattered throughout the appendices, are now incorporated into one comprehensive dictionary. There are hundreds of new entries and illustrations, making this book even more valuable for Cabalistic pathworking and meditation. It now has many new Hebrew words and names, as well as the terms of Freemasonry, the entities of the Cthulhu mythos, and the Aurum Solis spellings for the names of the demons of the Goetia. It contains authentic Hebrew spellings, and a new introduction that explains the uses of the book for meditation on God names.

The Cabalistic schema is native to the human psyche, and *Godwin's Cabalistic Encyclopedia* will be a valuable reference tool for all Cabalists, magicians, scholars, and scientists of all disciplines.

1–56718–324–7, 832 pp., 6 x 9, softcover   **$34.95**

THE SACRED MAGIC OF ANCIENT EGYPT
The Spiritual Practice Restored
Rosemary Clark

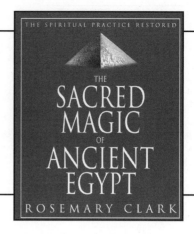

Rosemary Clark restores the ancient Egyptian temple tradition for modern practice. For those who seek a deeper realization of Egypt's legacy, here is a guide to living the history of a culture that believed its sacred tradition was a timeless conduit to divine knowledge.

With an elaborate canon of religious and philosophical wisdom that is conveyed through hymns, litanies, spells, and ceremonies, *The Sacred Magic of Ancient Egypt* offers the serious practitioner an authentic blueprint for creating a modern temple and entering an exclusive dimension of the ancient mysteries.

1-56718-130-9, 448 pp., 7½ x 9⅛, illus.   **$24.95**